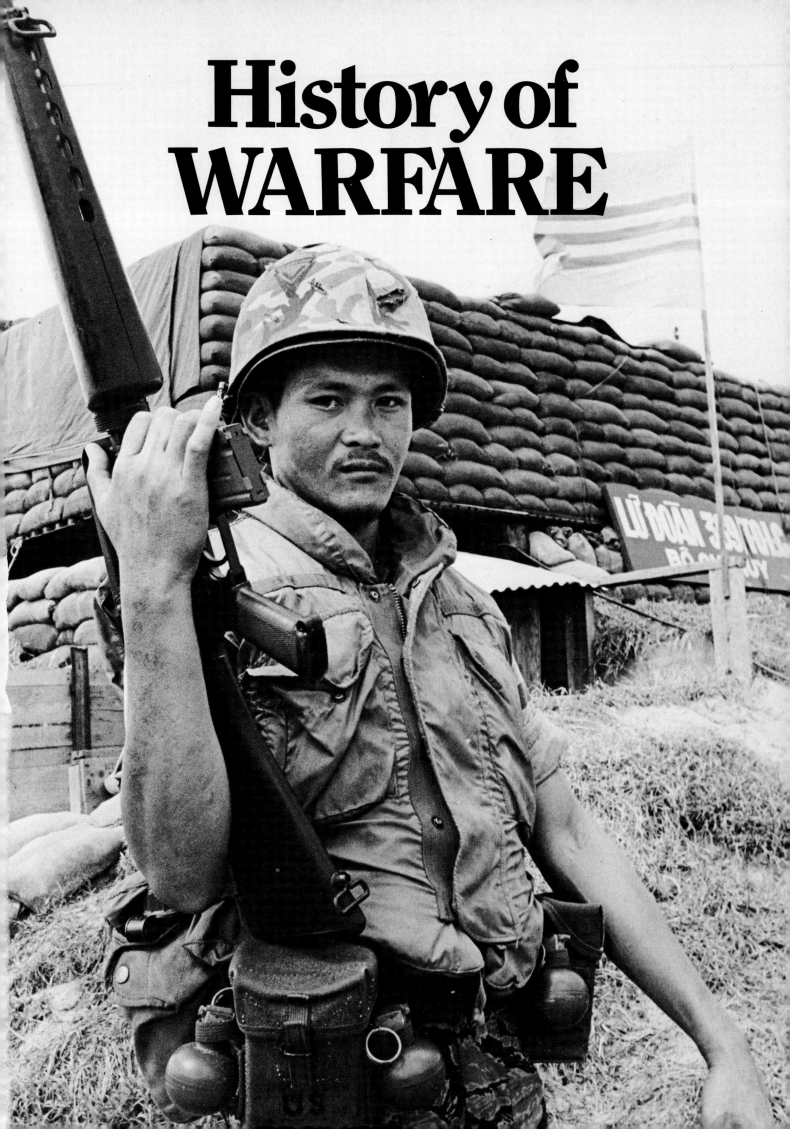

History of
WARFARE

History of WARFARE

H W KOCH

GREENWICH EDITIONS

This edition published 1998 by
PRC Publishing Ltd,
Kiln House, 210 New Kings Road
London SW6 4NZ

Produced for Greenwich Editions
10 Blenheim Court, Brewery Road
London N7 9NT

ISBN 0 86288 129 3

Printed in Hong Kong

Page 1: A South Vietnamese Marine on guard at
an outpost near Quang Tri in 1972.
Pages 2-3: The Battle of Bunker's Hill by
John Trumbull.
This page: The British crew of an American-
made Stuart tank await a German advance,
Egypt, September 1942.

Parts of this book were previously published as
Medieval Warfare, Rise of Modern Warfare, and *Age
of Total Warfare.*

CONTENTS

INTRODUCTION

Organized violence has had all too large a role in the shaping of society from the earliest times to the present day. In the world today almost every nation, no matter how small, has an army and the enormous military budgets of the superpowers are well known to readers of this book. It is equally clear to anyone living in the modern world that these massive military arsenals, including many thousands of nuclear warheads, must be managed and controlled with the utmost care. Military force has played and continues to play a central part in the development of the world. It is, therefore, essential to understand how warfare has contributed to the evolution of politics, government, economic and social affairs, and how military techniques themselves have developed, for without such an understanding the terrifying possibility of a nuclear holocaust becomes all the more likely.

It hardly needs saying that superiority in the waging of war has been the foundation of individual, national and imperial power through the ages but this has had more far-reaching consequences than a superficial examination might suggest. The career of Napoleon Bonaparte, for example, obviously founded on his military prowess, might seem to have come to nothing with his utter defeat in 1815 but even in an area as unmilitary as civil law, the *code Napoléon* still remains the foundation of French legal practice.

If a more general statement of the important consequences of military superiority is required, an overview of world history in the eighteenth and nineteenth centuries provides a striking illustration. By 1700 the European nations had developed and could maintain and arm military forces far more efficient and powerful than those existing in any other region of the globe. By 1900 this lead in military affairs had, of course, been greatly extended, and in the intervening period the countries of Europe, along with the USA, a former European colony, had used this domination, directly and indirectly, to rule or control almost every area of the world. The military aspects of this process are often overshadowed by the industrial, technical and financial developments normally described in the general term Industrial Revolution but the military developments supplied a vital and often a directing part in the more general process. Making guns for army and navy was the inspiration and cornerstone of many an ironmaster's business. The result can be summed up in the well-known comment of a Victorian satirist on one of the

Above: A British howitzer battery during the Battle of the Somme.
Left: A facsimile from the 15th century *Das Mittelalteriche Hausbuch* showing a wagon castle or defensive laager.
Right: A present-day British soldier with 7.62mm machine gun.
Page 6-7: The Battle of Isandhlwana, 1879, a notable British defeat at the hands of South Africa's Zulus.

British army's colonial campaigns in the late-nineteenth century,

> Whatever happens we have got
> The Maxim gun, and they have not.

Military superiority, the 'Maxim Gun', clearly depended on a complex combination of scientific and industrial skills to build the device, financial skills to pay for it and the professional soldier who operated it, as well as the more directly military skills involved in employing it. The result, the creation of a European dominated world, was, as the writer noted, never in doubt.

Superficially the world today may seem to be very different, with over 160 independent nations rather than a handful of great empires, but the competing ideologies of capitalism and Marxism that dominate much of the relationship between these nations are themselves of clear European origin. Perhaps, too, leaders of starving Third World countries criticized for their large arms expenditures are in fact demonstrating a clearer understanding than their critics allow of how the world got to be the way it is.

Even if the consequences of military affairs were not so extensive, wars and soldiering have involved so much human activity that studying them would be worthwhile in itself. That warfare has tended to evolve toward a more unrestrained form of total war can only heighten the importance of such a study. The seemingly limitless destructive potential of modern weapons can only confirm this importance.

Barbarian warriors of Europe and their weapons.

THE ROMAN EMPIRE AND THE RISE OF THE BARBARIANS

The principal forces with which the Romans had to contend were the Germanic tribes to the north, tribes which on the surface were vastly inferior in their political, social, economic and military organization. The Germans did not comprise a single political and social unit at the beginning of the year 1 A.D. but were divided into various tribes, each settling within an area of one hundred square miles. Because of the danger of hostile invasions, the marches of these territories were left uninhabited, the population concentrating itself in the interior. Some twenty Germanic peoples lived between the rivers Rhine and Elbe as well as the Main to the south in an area covered predominantly by woods and·swamps. The approximate density of the population, living from subsistence agriculture, amounted to 25 per square mile. The size of the individual tribes varied from 25,000 to 40,000, which would mean that each of them could muster 6000 to 10,000 warriors.

Their social structure also explains their early vulnerability to attacks by the Roman legions. Each people divided itself arbitrarily into large family units, *geschlechter* (kinships). (Towns and cities to which family members could have migrated and intermingled did not exist at this time.) These family units were also called *hundreds*, because they either comprised a hundred families or a hundred warriors. The hundred which included family members ranged in numbers from 400 to 1000 and lived on a territory of a few square miles in a village which was situated according to the suitability of the immediate environment. Women and men unfit as warriors carried on what little agriculture there was.

In times of war the members of the hundred formed one troop of warriors. The German word *dorf* (or *thorpe* in the Nordic countries) connotes such a warrior community. The thorpe was also a form of assembly; troop is its direct derivative.

Hence, the Germanic tribal community consisted of villages or settlements, the territory it covered was called a *gau* and its basic military unit was the hundred. Each community had its elected head, the *ealdorman* or *hunno*.

The *hunno*'s official function was twofold; he was the head of the village community and the leader in war. Although the post was not hereditary, evidence exists showing that the custom of electing the sons of *hunnos* in succession was widespread. Since the leader in war also had the privilege of getting a larger share of the booty than the other members, the riches accumulated by the leaders allowed them to have servants and to rally the bravest around them who would defend their lord unto death. From these families the popular assembly of the people, the *thing*, would elect its leader, the *first*, a term which in German became the *fürst*, or the prince, whose functions also included holding courts throughout the *gau* to administer justice.

What stands out from all this is that the Germanic peoples were rather few in number; yet all the chroniclers from Tacitus onwards tell us about the fierce bravery of the Germans and their military effectiveness. Considering their small numbers individual bravery would have amounted to little if there had not been an efficiently functioning military structure. Unlike the Romans, the Germans·knew nothing of military discipline. Among the Germanic tribes the cement which held them together was provided by the organic ties within a village, a hundred, or for that matter within an entire tribe.

Of course the effort and the bravery of the individual were essential but of value only when exercised within a coherent tactical body, and that body was the hundred composed of men related to one another by ties of blood. There is no evidence to show that the hundreds ever carried out military exercises. They displayed none of the drill of the Roman legions, but their inner

Left. *The Teutoburger Battles.*

Below. *Captured Germanic woman: detail from Trajan's Column.*

cohesion, based upon the certainty of being able to rely fully on those around you, was superior to that shown by the Romans. A Roman force when defeated usually scattered. A Germanic force in similar straits usually remained intact because it was an organic body. The *hunno* had the advantage of commanding a 'natural' force rather than the artificial one of his Roman counterpart. By the military standards of Rome, the Germans were a rabble, and from a Roman perspective rightly so, but as the Romans were to experience time and time again, this 'rabble' was efficient. The Romans eventually came to realize that the Germans confronted them with a different type of military organization explicable only against the background of their social and political construction.

Tacitus provided us with a description of the way in which the Germans fought on foot. He portrayed them as tactical bodies which were as deep as they were wide—in other words front and rear and both flanks are equally strong: 400 men, 20 deep and 20 wide, or 10,000 men, 100 deep and 100 wide. Naturally the most exposed positions of such a formation would be the warriors at the flanks of the first line, because they were threatened by their opponent from the front as well as from the side. This square was the basic tactical formation of the Germans, in the same way as the phalanx was the original tactical formation of the Romans. In an attack the phalanx had the advantage of bringing more weapons to bear than the square and had greater maneuverability for its wings. The weakness of the Roman phalanx was the vulnerability of its flanks especially when attacked by cavalry, and cavalry was one of the strengths of the Germans. To show equal strength in all directions the Germans preferred deep formations.

These two different tactical approaches have their origins in technological development. The Germans possessed relatively little protective armor and few metal weapons. Consequently the Germans placed their best armed men in the front ranks to protect those less well armed in the center of the square. Another advantage which the Germanic square had over the phalanx was that it was tactically more mobile and it could more easily adjust to its geographical surroundings than the linear formation, much in the same way as the Napoleonic divisional column proved superior to the linear tactics of the eighteenth century.

Tacitus described the arms of the Germans as follows: 'Only few possess a sword or a spear with a metal head. As a rule they carry spears capped with a short and narrow metal point; the weapon is so handy that it can be used to spike as well as to throw. Cavalry carries only shield and spear. Those on foot also carry missiles (stones or stone balls catapulted by a hand sling.) The Germans enter battle bare chested or, at the most are clad with a light cover which hinders them little in their movement. Far removed from them is any idea to shine in the splendor of their weapons. Only their shields are painted in glaring colors. Only very few possess armor, hardly anyone a metal or leather helmet.

Their horses are distinguished neither by their beauty nor by their speed. Nor are they in contrast to us, trained to carry out maneuvers of many kinds. The Germanic cavalry rides either straight forward or with one movement to the right—a circular movement so that no one remains behind.

The main strength of the Germans are their foot troops; for that reason they fight in mixed formations in which the foot troops, because of their physical dexterity, are required to adjust to the movements of the horsemen. For that purpose the quickest young men are selected and put at the point where the cavalry has its place.

To leave one's place as long as one pushes forward again is not interpreted as a sign of fear but one of clever calculation. They salvage their wounded and dead even under the most unfavorable of battle conditions. The loss of one's shield is considered as a particularly great disgrace; he who does is not allowed to participate in a religious

celebration or in the *thing*. Therefore many a one who has come back from war in good health, has taken the rope to put an end to his disgrace . . .'

The shield was made of wood or wickerwork covered with leather. Such headgear as there was, was made of leather or fur. The long spear had to be used with both hands, which of course did not allow its bearer to carry a shield. This in turn led to the gradual adoption of armor taken either directly from the Romans on the battlefield or made from leather. In addition it was the task of those carrying smaller weapons like hand axes to protect the spear-carrying warrior with their shield. Something that has hitherto found no adequate explanation is why the Germans who had used the bow and arrow in the Bronze Age did not continue to use that weapon. The bow and arrow did not reappear until the third century.

After the Romans had captured Gaul, their main motive for trying to make inroads into the heartland of Germany seems to have been to secure their provinces from the attacks of the Barbarians. It was not the kind of countryside which looked particularly inviting, nor did it prove suitable for Roman-style battles. A rough climate, seemingly endless forests, dangerous swampy regions were hardly worthy of conquest.

Securing Gaul by subduing nearby Germanic tribes posed the major problem of securing supplies. Caesar could afford his campaign in Gaul, for supplies were plentiful there. However, supplying large armies in the German interior was another matter, lacking as it did any network of communications other than its rivers. Drusus's first attempt was abortive; he had to give up and return to base. In his next attempt he decided to

Above. *Mounted Germanic warrior carrying a simple round shield: detail from Trajan's Column.*

Left: *German envoys before Emperor Trajan 113A.D: detail from Trajan's Column.*

Tenth-century portrayal of the Hunnish invasions.

utilize the existing waterways. He built a canal from the Rhine to the Yssel which gave him access to the North Sea coast via the Zuider Zee. He also used the river Lippe which in the spring is navigable right up to its source. He moved along the Lippe upwards into Westphalia, and at the point where the river was no longer navigable he built a Castle at Aliso which was to be a supply rather than a fortified base from which the interior of Germany was to be subjected to Roman rule. Roman expeditions ventured into the interior where they were relatively well-received by the German tribal chiefs. To some the Romans appeared as welcome allies in their own tribal conflicts, particularly against the ambitions of the chief of the Markomani, Marbod, who had established his rule in Bohemia and was now extending it to the lower Elbe. However, the moment when the Roman commander in the region, Quintilius Varus, attempted to establish Roman supremacy, the Germans annihilated his three legions and their auxiliary forces in a three-day battle in the Teutoburger Forest in 9 A.D.

Neither precise date nor location of the battle is totally verified by historical evidence. The traditional version of the Germans luring the Roman Legions into the forest is no more than a fable. What is certain is that the legions of Varus marched during the autumn, accompanied by their entire train. This indicates that Roman forces had been operating in the German interior during the summer months and were now returning to their winter quarters on the Rhine or at Aliso. Had Varus set out to quell a rising by the Germans he would hardly have set out with all his baggage. The unsuspecting Varus believed himself to be among friends. After all, the leader of the Germanic tribe

of the Cheruscans, Arminius, had himself been in Rome as a hostage; he received part of his education there, and had been made a Roman knight. However, resenting attempts to establish Roman overlordship Arminius headed a conspiracy against the Romans and ambushed them.

The Roman force consisted of three legions, six cohorts of auxiliaries, and three troops of cavalry; estimates of their total strength vary between 12,000 and 18,000 combatants plus 12,000 more making up the train. As soon as the first battle cries of the Germans could be heard at the head of the column which extended about 2·5 miles, the vanguard halted near present day Herford. A suitable place was chosen, hastily fortified and surrounded by a stockade and moat. As the column arrived it assembled inside the stockade. The thought must have occurred to Varus to return to his original summer camp which was well-fortified, offering better protection than this makeshift fortification. But he was bound to have been short of food supplies, and the way back was unlikely to be less dangerous than the way ahead. Apart from that there was every likelihood that the castle was in German hands already. Varus was forced to jettison all his surplus luggage as well as his wagons. On the next day, in a better formation than before he marched out with the aim of reaching Aliso at least. Although the territory was an open field, the harassing attacks by the Germans seemed weak, with little cavalry to support them. But Arminius held his horsemen back, not wishing to expose them to the Romans. On that day the Romans covered ground slowly, and progress was slowed down even further when towards the end of the day they again entered the forests. As they approached the dark Doerren Gorge they found that the Germans had blocked its exit and occupied its heights. To get out of the canyon they had to attack up-hill. Outflanking movements were impossible and even the weak attacks by the Germans had been sufficient to cause serious losses. The Romans were forced to camp, exposed to the incessant attacks which the Germans maintained throughout the night. All this was made worse by the onset of violent fall storms and rains which transformed the soil into a quagmire in which it was even more difficult to fight on the next day, let alone make headway. Roman attacks against the Germans repeatedly came to a halt, while the lightly equipped Germans could attack and withdraw at will. Failing to storm the pass the Romans were now firmly locked in the Doerren Gorge without any hope of escape; morale disintegrated. Varus and a number of his officers committed suicide and the bearer of the Roman eagle jumped into a swamp to ensure that Rome's insignia

Frankish warrior grave from the period of the Great Migrations. Warriors were usually buried with all their military equipment.

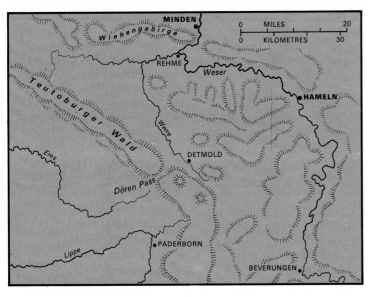

Battle of Teutoburger Forest.

would not fall into German hands. The remainder surrendered except for a few, primarily cavalry, who managed to escape and make their way to Aliso where they were besieged. Successful strategy rendered them able to break out and get back to Roman lines along the Rhine. The Germans, now fearing that a strong Roman force would come to avenge their comrades, withdrew back into the interior.

In fact the Romans were in no position to mete out retribution. Tiberius hurried to the Rhine to ensure the security of the frontier of Gaul and to restore the badly mauled army. The contested succession to Emperor Augustus in Rome made Tiberius's presence there more important than launching a major military venture in Germany.

Once established on the Roman throne his adopted son, Germanicus, undertook two major campaigns. Whether in fact he achieved two victories over the Germans is subject to speculation. Some authorities relegate it into the realm of deliberate myth-making on Germanicus's part for his own political ends.

Be that as it may, Arminius evaded an open battle, since he realized that the Roman forces were superior to his own. Instead he fought a war of attrition, for which the land was ideally suited, while the Romans faced the ever-present danger of having their lines of supply to the Rhine cut. Nevertheless it was quite within the military capacity of the Romans to subject Germany. Purely defensive war can lead to negotiations but never to victory. Among the Germanic tribes opinions began to divide sharply. Arminius's father-in-law, Segestes, led the Roman party which planned and carried out the murder of Arminius. Nor was Tiberius in an enviable position. The concentration of Roman legions in Germany under Germanicus could bring about the same situation as that of Caesar and his legions in Gaul.

What the Battle of Teutoburger Forest clearly indicated was that the conquest of Germany would be slow, bloody and expensive, and could be carried out only by an extremely able general furnished with extensive powers. These very powers could become a threat to the Emperor in Rome. Nor was it advisable for the Emperor to leave Rome for an extensive campaign lasting for years. The Battle of Teutoburger Forest and its following skirmishes under Tiberius and Germanicus were 'little more than an apology for a final retreat to the Rhine, which henceforth was to remain the northeastern frontier of Latin civilization.' Or as Sir Edward Creasy put it, 'Had Arminius been supine or unsuccessful . . .

this island would never have borne the name of England.'

During the halcyon years of the Roman Empire, which came to an end with the death of Marcus Aurelius in 180 A.D., the flow of Germanic peoples into the border territories of the Empire was steady and therefore controlable. Each successive tribe which asked for permission to live within the confines of the Empire was required not merely to obey the dictates of the Emperor but to be prepared to defend the Rhine-Danube boundary in case of a border incursion on the part of fellow Germans living across the frontier. This system not only worked well from a military point of view. It had the effect of 'civilizing' resident as well as non-resident Germanic tribes, transforming a nomadic and warrior race into a pastoral one.

The period between 232 and 552 A.D. marks the transition from Roman to Medieval forms of war. The struggle between the Germanic tribes and the Roman Empire was drawing to a close. So was the Roman Empire.

In military terms battles now showed the supremacy of the cavalry over the infantry. One of the causes of Rome's final collapse was the sudden invasion of eastern Europe by the Huns, a new race of horsemen, formidable in number, rapid in their movements, and masters of the bow and arrow. They encountered the Goths, a Nordic Germanic tribe which by the beginning of the third century had left Sweden and spread from Pomerania to the Carpathians and from there to the Black Sea. (This movement was part of the Great Migrations in the course of which Franks, Allemani and Burgundians moved into the lands between the Harz mountains and Danube and when the Allemani began to move further westwards, they posed an

Sixth-century Allemanic helmet but of southeast European origin which probably came to the Allemani by means of the battlefield.

The Fury of the Goths (Painting by Paul Ivanovitz).

immediate threat to Gaul. In August 357 A.D. Emperor Julian met them in battle near Strasbourg and defeated them.)

The people most immediately affected by the pressure of the Huns were the Goths. It is not possible to tell why they obtained the names Ostrogoths and Visigoths respectively. Probably the terms originated only after the Goths had settled near the Black Sea where their settlements spread from the River Don to the mouth of the Danube and the southwestern hills of the Carpathians. The Romans were quick to recognize both the danger as well as the potential usefulness. Under Emperor Severus Alexander (222–235) the Goths were paid handsome subsidies to defend the frontier and otherwise maintain peace. This relationship was only of short duration. With ever-increasing frequency the Goths, in particular the Ostrogoths, raided eastern and southeastern border provinces of the Roman Empire. However, these raids turned into a major invasion, not because the Goths had realized the endemic weakness of the Roman Empire, but because they were badly pressed by the Huns who defeated them at the Dnieper in 374 A.D. forcing them to seek refuge south of the Danube. Here they built up an extensive Empire from a center in the Hungarian plain. Eventually, the Hunnish threat reached such proportions that the Roman Empire lost control of its western provinces. Menaced by the Huns, both Roman armies and the Germanic tribes added the bow to the weapons of the foot soldier and placed a renewed emphasis on the rapid mobility of their cavalry. Fear of the Hun caused the Ostrogoths, the Franks and the Romans to become allies. In 450 A.D. together they faced the Huns on the plain of Châlons and victory was won over the Huns, not by superior tactics but by Theodoric's heavy horsemen who simply rode them down.

The Huns had been stopped and turned back, and the self-confidence of the Germanic tribes, especially that of the Ostrogoths, had been immensely strengthened. More than ever before, they now posed a threat to the collapsing Roman Empire.

For more than three centuries Romans had drawn German auxiliaries into their armies and thereby initiated a process which inducted Germans and other tribes into the Roman army. One could hardly speak of a *Roman* army any more. The Roman army of the fifth century was not the same as it had been under Tiberius and Germanicus. The German mercenaries, paid in money and in kind had increased their demands over the centuries. The land grants they received at the frontier for their own agricultural pursuits were in themselves not dangerous as long as the Empire was strong enough to keep these frontier forces at its most exposed and vulnerable spots. In that role the mercenaries played a part vital to the security of the Empire. But when the Barbarians, recognizing the weakness at the center, demanded the ownership of land not just its use, the danger became imminent that the Empire would be barbarized.

In Italy a rising of Germanic mercenaries under Odoaker had successfully taken place. Emperor Zeno, of East Rome, anxious to regain West Rome and to remove the Ostrogoths from his immediate vicinity, presented the Ostrogoth king, Theodoric, with Italy, a present which had to be conquered first. Theodoric's task was to vanquish Odoaker and to settle the Ostrogoths in Italy. Whether or not Theodoric or Odoaker won was immaterial, either way Byzantium was bound to gain by losing at least one enemy or a potential one. Theodoric, accompanied by his host of warriors and their families, won.

It must be noted that the Great Migrations had transformed some of the tribal institutions profoundly. Five centuries before, most of them lived in settlements, each family community in its village under its *hunno* or *ealderman*, a collection of family units held together by tribal ties. The *fürst* and his institutional apparatus was simple and served its purpose. Migrations of the scale that took place in the first few centuries A.D., and the campaigns associated with them, required power to be more centralized. Furthermore to preserve continuity and its resulting tribal security, the holding of supreme power became hereditary. Out of this situation grew the concept of kingship. Whenever an entire Germanic people entered the service of the Emperor in Rome or Byzantium, a Germanic prince was simultaneously made a Roman general and became the link between his people and the Emperor. Gaiseric, King of the Vandals, ruled North Africa, on behalf of the Emperor but he soon rejected Roman overlordship, and felt strong enough to claim sovereignty for himself.

On the other hand the Frankish Empire, in contrast to the Vandals and the Goths who were conquering *peoples*, was created by a conquering *king*. The family of the Merovingians under Clovis managed by sheer ability to gather numerous Germanic peoples, and with them conquer large parts of Gaul and thus establish Frankish rule. The elective principle could not operate with such vast numbers. The crown became hereditary, though never uncontested. But in spite of several civil wars, the institution of the centralizing office of the crown remained.

Inevitably the same causes that lay at the root of Germanic kingship led to a transformation of the military structure of the Germanic tribes. Military hosts of a size between 10,000 and 30,000 men require a more sophisticated structure than the hundred of old. It was not possible for the prince or the king to issue his orders to a hundred or more *hunni*. Additional ranks of

Hilt of a Frankish sword.

command had to be created, institutions of command that functioned efficiently. Furthermore, in the past while still settled, a primitive form of agrarian communism served the needs of the hundred and the families. During the Great Migrations this was no longer possible. Thus the Great Migrations were also vast campaigns of plunder. When the Germans stormed Gaul they pillaged and plundered the towns. In consequence the spacious Roman urban planning gave way to reconstructed towns, whose buildings and streets were narrow to provide better defense, whose outskirts were surrounded by thick walls and watch-towers: they were the first of the medieval cities.

But looting and pillaging did not resolve the problem of supplies for armies and their dependants on the move. No people could afford to live hand to mouth. Storage places had to be established to hold supplies for future needs, and these had to

Conquest of the Cantabrian by the Visigoth King Leovigildo. (Panel from the ivory reliquary of San Millan de la Cogolla, eleventh century).

Statue of Charlemagne (742–814) King of the Franks and Roman Emperor.

be administered. Thus the *hunni* needed subalterns who would collect, distribute and store the gains.

Nor could the king alone govern at the top without an intermediary between him and the *hunni*. He delegated his authority to his counts, who on his behalf administered strictly defined territories.

Evidence for the new structure of the military hierarchy has come down to us from the Visigoths, but it can safely be assumed to have applied with some variations to the other German tribes of the time as well. The military structure began with a leader of a maximum of 10,000 men; the next unit was 500 strong and so on down to the hundred, which was divided into groups of ten. The vital core within this structure, however, was still represented by the hundred which, from an organizational point of view, was just large enough to cope with supply problems.

Having stressed the origin of the Germanic monarchy and the hereditary principle, it would be a mistake to assume that once established it remained unchanged. For instance when Theodoric died without issue, he *appointed* the young son of his sister as his heir. She was to act as regent until the boy had grown up to assume his responsibilities. But her son Athalaric died while still an adolescent. His mother Amalsuntha was unequal to the task that confronted her when Byzantium decided to reconquer Italy from the Goths, so the Ostrogoths reverted to the *elective* principle. The heroic Vittigis, Totila (who in his personality represented the rare synthesis between Gothic simplicity and courage and Latin culture) and the depressive Teia were all elected by the Ostrogoths.

The bulk of the Ostrogoths were warriors, but among the Franks the warrior represented only one part of a rather more numerous people. Even among them, once the Carolingian Empire had disintegrated, the elective principle returned, though in a different form. The German kings of the Middle Ages were formally elected by the most important of their magnates, the electors.

During the Great Migrations kingship was still too narrowly based to create a dynasty that could rest upon its ancestors. The kings emerged from the strongest families, renowned for their fame in battle. Fame in practical terms was reflected by the material gains they had made. At a lower level the same applied to the *hunni*, who in the process of evolution became the Germanic warrior nobility.

The strongest concept of kingship existed among the Vandals. Originally located between the rivers Elbe and Vistula they gradually moved south. Pressed by bad harvests and consequent starvation they moved on, ultimately invading Spain in 409. In 429 they crossed the Straits of Gibralut into North Africa, the

granary of the Roman Empire, which was divided into six Imperial provinces which the Vandals conquered one by one. In 442 the Romans and the Vandals under King Gaiseric made peace. Though of short duration—the Vandals invaded Italy and sacked Rome—West Rome was no longer in a position which would have allowed it even to consider the reconquest of the lost provinces. Under the Emperors Leo and Zeno of Byzantium major campaigns were launched against them led by several generals the last of whom, Belisarius, was ultimately successful in conquering the Vandals. After the death of Gaiseric the Vandals politically disintegrated and became easy victims. The last King of the Vandals, Gelimer, is known for little more than surrendering to the forces of Byzantium. The kingdom of the Vandals had experienced a meteoric rise but had disappeared with equal speed. Their hostility towards the Ostrogoths had deprived them of a vital ally. They could not match the resources of Byzantium alone.

Not all German tribes were affected by the Great Migrations. The Markomani (the ancestors of the Bavarians), the Allemani and the Franks traveled only relatively short distances or simply spilled over into neighboring regions. Frequently the newcomers established large landholdings whose native populations accepted the protection of the Germanic *hunno*. In return they rendered services on the land. The situation of the Britons when overcome by the invasions of the Anglo-Saxons was very similar. The native population was subjected and, in time, absorbed. From the *hunni* or *ealdorman* emerged the Anglo-Saxon nobility, the earls. By contrast, the Franks although establishing large estates, produced no nobility during that early period. The Merovingians ensured that they ruled by way of their counts alone. The traditional institution of the *hunno* declined in significance to that of a mere village administrator.

The fact that West Rome had fallen, does not mean that the Barbarians who had brought this about were actually aware of it. When Theodoric set out for Italy in 488, he did so as the representative of the Emperor of East Rome. In numbers the Ostrogoths were approximately 200,000 strong including their families. Odoaker and his men were first encountered on the banks of the Isonzo River, but they were thrown back and the Goths made the crossing. On 30 September 489 they conquered Verona. Odoaker then withdrew to Ravenna, in those days like Venice, a water city. From there he counterattacked recapturing Milan and Cremona and beseiging Theodoric in Pavia. Only with the aid of the Visigoths could Theodoric return to the offensive, once again beating Odoaker and pushing him back behind the walls of Ravenna. The population at large supported Theodoric, a support shown by a peninsula-wide conspiracy which with one blow removed all supporters of Odoaker in Italy. For three years, until 493, Odoaker defended himself in Ravenna. After having been promised his personal security, that of his family and the maintenance of his royal dignity, he surrendered in February 493. Soon after Theodoric's entry into Ravenna he held a banquet at the Palace Leuretum. Odoaker was guest of honor. Theodoric killed him on that occasion with his own hand, and Odoaker's followers met the same fate.

Theodoric, already King of the Goths, by virtue of his conquest, had proclaimed himself King of the Italians as well, a step which crossed the intentions of Emperor Zeno. But as yet Zeno was in no position to retaliate. The Gothic rule in Italy was characterized by the dualism between the Romans and the Italians of the provinces on the one hand and the Ostrogoths on the other. While the former retained their institutional and administrative apparatus directed as it was towards Byzantium, Theodoric, with a few exceptions, excluded the native population from his army. His reign in Italy was determined by his relationships with Byzantium in the east and the Frankish kingdom in the north. But he was unable to convince Zeno that he was not simply another Odoaker any more than he could convince the Frankish King Clovis that he was not set upon further conquest. Nor was his position improved by the re-establishment of cordial relationships between the Papacy in Rome and the Emperor. Jointly they decided to persecute the heretics within the Christian faith, believers in the Arian 'heresy' to which the Goths adhered. Before the matter came to a head Theodoric died suddenly in 526. At that time his empire included Italy, Sicily, Dalmatia, Noricum, Pannonia, Tyrol, Grisons, southern Germany as far north as Ulm, and Provence—an empire too large for the Goths to sustain.

This became clear very quickly after his death when Justinian of Byzantium took the first steps to reconquer Italy. The expedition was to be led by Belisarius, who had already distinguished himself against the Persians. As his first objective he reconquered North Africa from the Vandals, a natural launching point and supply base for an invasion of Italy. In 535 Belisarius landed in Sicily, and most cities opened their gates to his forces; the reconciliation between Church and Empire bore its fruits. In May 536 he crossed the Straits of Messina and took Naples. At that point the Goths elected Vittigis as their King. To avert any threat from the north Vittigis ceded Provence to the Franks and, trusting as he was, he left Rome to the care of Pope Silverius who promptly opened its gates to Belisarius. For three years Vittigis laid siege to Rome. It was 'the grave of the Gothic

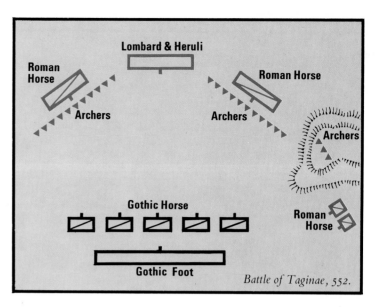

Battle of Taginae, 552.

Hippic phalange formation (Byzantine military treatise, eleventh century).

monarchy in Italy,' dug by 'the deadly dews of the Campagna.' Starvation and pestilence ravaged throughout Italy, decimating natives, Goths and Byzantine invaders alike. Only the Byzantines had no shortage of manpower. Other Germanic tribes such as the Franks who made inroads into Italy at the time did so for their own aggrandizement and not to assist the Goths in any way. Vittigis retreated to Ravenna where he was besieged by Belisarius. In order to put an end to the blood-letting Vittigis offered Belisarius the Gothic crown. He accepted, entered the city, took Vittigis prisoner and sent him and some of his associates to Constantinople. However, Justinian became suspicious that Belisarius might become another Theodoric, and recalled him to Constantinople. When he left Italy the Goths had been reduced to holding a single city, Pavia. However, in 542 Totila was elected King ('quite the noblest flower that bloomed upon the Ostrogothic stem'), and he recovered the whole of central southern Italy, except Rome and a few other fortresses in a rapid campaign. After he had taken Naples, Totila laid siege to Rome. Belisarius was sent back to Italy.

Rome was taken by Totila in December 546. The Byzantine forces were left holding only four fortresses in Italy. Belisarius returned again to Constantinople and was replaced by Justinian's Court Chamberlain, Narses, a man who conducted his generalship less with flamboyance than with the precision of a mathematician. In the meantime Totila had taken Sicily again and manned 300 ships to control the Adriatic. By the spring of 552 Narses had mobilized his forces fully, composed mainly of Barbarian contingents, Huns, Lombards, Persians and others. Finding his way south blocked by Teia and his Gothic warriors at Verona, he outflanked them by marching close to the Adriatic coast, reaching Ravenna safely. When Totila received the news in the vicinity of Rome, he took almost his entire army, crossed Tuscany, and established his base at the village of Taginae, the present day Tadino.

The two armies prepared themselves for battle. Narses's disposition show his superior generalship. He immediately recognized the tactical significance of a small hill to the left of his flank which he occupied with archers. He dismounted his Lombards and formed them across the Flaminian Way and on each of the flanks of the phalanx he placed 4000 Roman foot archers with cavalry behind them. His calculation was accurate. Totila had ranged his cavalry in front of his infantry intending to win with a single charge. He advanced directly into the trap Narses had set for him. The Gothic cavalry failed to break Narses's center and instead was rapidly depleted by the archery and the spears of Narses's warriors. Spears and bows proved decisive

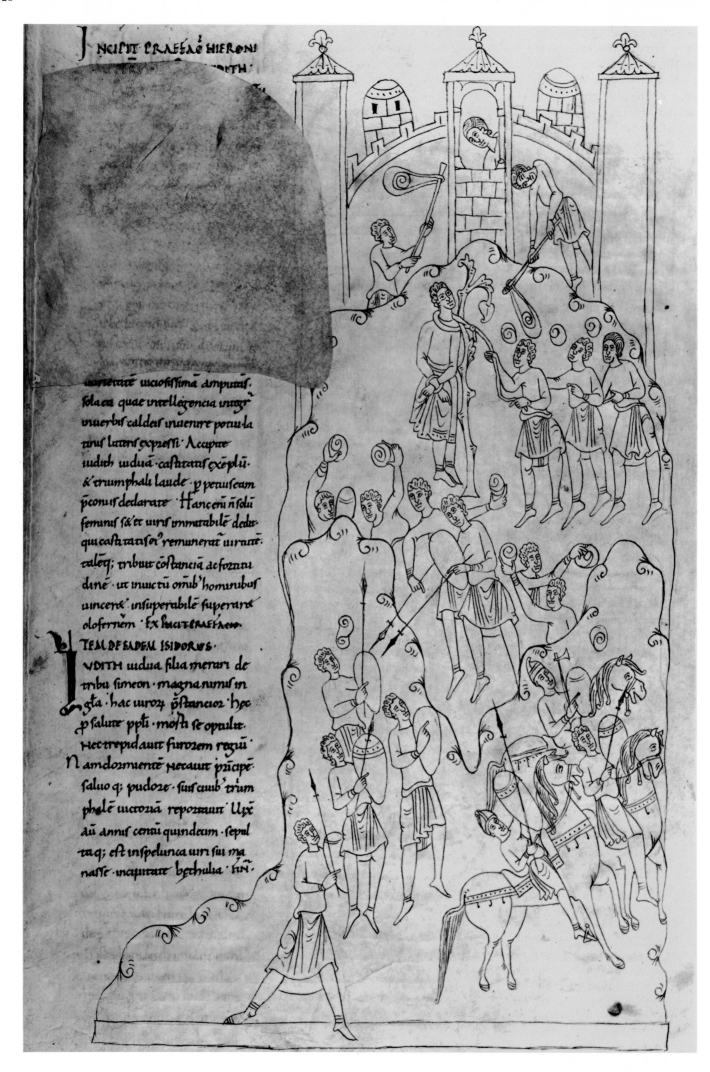

INCIPIT PRAEFA̅C HIERONI

varietate uiciosissima̅ amputans.
sola ea quae intelligencia integr̅
inuerbis caldeis inuenire potui la
tinus latens expressi· Accapite
iudith uidua̅ castitatis exe̅plu̅
& triumphali laude ꝑ petuis eam
ꝑconiis declarate· Hanc eni̅ n̅ solu̅
femnis s̅c̅et uiris imitabile dedit
qui castitatis eor̅ remunerat̅ uirtute̅·
taleq̅ tribuit co̅stancia de fortitu
dine· ut inuictu̅ omnib̅ hominibus
uincere̅· insuperabile superaret
olofernem· EX LIBRO IERETERSO

ITEM DE EADEM ISIDORVS·
IVDITH uidua filia merari de
tribu simeon· magnanimis in
gta· hac uiror̅ p̅stanciior· hec
ꝑ salute ppti· morti se optulit·
Nec trepidauit furore̅ regu̅
Nam dormiente̅ necauit p̅ncipe̅
saluo q̅ pudore· suis cu̅b̅ triu̅
phale uictoria̅ reportauit· Uix̅
au̅ annis centu̅ quindecim· sepul
taq̅ est inspelunca uiri sui ma
nasse· inciuitate bethulia· tñ·

against Totila's cavalry attack (as it was to prove, centuries later, at Crécy). Some 6000 Goths were killed, among them Totila.

After the death of Totila the Goths elected Teia as their new King. The role he played was in accord with his doom-laden character. At the foot of Vesuvius he defended himself for two months and was finally slain in battle at Mount Lettere. The moment of capitulation of the Goths had come. They were to leave Italy and settle in any Barbarian kingdom of their choice. The greatest Barbarian empire hitherto established in Europe had come to an end. The last of the warriors of the Ostrogoths, carrying the body of their dead King upon their spears, trudged down the slopes into history.

Their brothers, the Visigoths, held out for a few centuries longer, into the first decade of the eighth century. Within the course of three and a half centuries they had traveled through Sweden, east-central Europe, the eastern shores of the Black Sea, to the Balkans and Greece, then moved up the Dalmatian coast into Illyria, turned round into Italy marching south, until nearly at its tip they turned back along the Mediterranean coast until they had reached Spain by the middle of the fifth century. During the middle of the fourth century they were converted to Christianity, the work of Bishop Wulfila, who translated the Bible into Gothic. Like so many other German tribes they entered Italy not to despoil it but to ask for land grants in Venetia and Dalmatia as well as grain and subsidies, in return for which they offered their military services. Rome, already in its final agonies, refused. Alaric, the King of the Visigoths, was not in a position nor did he intend to replace the Roman Empire with one of the Visigoths for he was far too weak. Like the Vandals, the Visigoths tried to cross over to Africa. But a storm wrecked their boats in the Straits of Messina twice and they could not assemble another fleet. Still, the Romans were impressed and intimidated. Since the days of Hannibal no Barbarian tribe had penetrated their peninsula so far south. The sudden death of Alaric cut these ventures short. He perished after a fever and his warriors buried him with his weapons and personal treasures in a grave in the River Busento near Cosenza. For that purpose they temporarily diverted the river restoring it to its original path once the King had been put to rest. Then they moved along the coast to create their kingdom at Toulouse which lasted almost ninety years and from which they were expelled by the Franks. Withdrawing into Spain, they re-established themselves again at Toledo, expanding throughout the Iberian peninsula (with the exception of its northwest corner which was held by the Suebs) and reaching north beyond the Pyrenees into Aquitaine. Like the Ostrogoths they had become Arian Christians, but submitted to Catholic conversion by the end of the sixth century until they were finally pushed back by the Islamic invasions. By then Romans and Visigoths had mixed to provide the nucleus from which the knighthood of Castile arose.

The Visigoths' problem was similar to that of the Ostrogoths', they held an area too large to be effectively defended. Militarily and socially they were made up of a warrior nobility which, after the last strong king was slaughtered, did not produce another king capable of containing the centrifugal forces at work within their society.

The Visigoths like most of their contemporaries fought on horseback, carrying round shields, swords and daggers. They wore defensive armor; even the mail shirt was not unknown. The provincial levies, raised by the Visigoths much against the will of those who had to serve, carried whatever they had, usually crude weapons and represented the unarmed foot sol-

diery. One craft in which the Visigoths excelled was in the building and use of missile-throwing devices, stone-throwing machines and fire arrows.

The period of the Great Migrations and the decline of Rome saw a considerable change in military tactics. The early Germanic tribes such as the Cheruscans could hardly maintain the same tactics and style of combat in an environment so different from the Teutonic forests. Cavalry moved to the fore, as both the Battles of Strasbourg and Adrianople showed.

'Hitherto infantry normally had been the decisive arm, and when they relied upon shock weapons, they had little to fear from cavalry as long as they maintained their order. But the increasing use of missiles carried with it an unavoidable loosening and disordering of the ranks. The old shield-wall began to be replaced by a firing line, and because archers and slingers cannot easily combine shield with bow or sling, and as the range of these weapons is strictly limited, and, further still, because they are all but useless in wet weather, opportunity for the cavalry charge steadily increased. The problem was how to combine missile-power with security against cavalry . . .' (Fuller).

The Ostrogoths excelled in their use of cavalry, fighting with lance and sword but not with bow and arrow. That, among other things, proved their undoing at Taginae. Archers on foot, as individuals, could not afford to take on horsemen, but protected by their own cavalry, fortification or favorable terrain they could be highly effective.

The effectiveness of the infantry depended on their tactical order. The wild bravery of the old Germanic tribes was of little use when facing Roman forces in open field. However, the old Germanic square formation would have been worth maintaining had it been able to adjust itself to new weapons such as archery. The Byzantine foot soldiery made this adjustment. They were mainly Germanic auxiliaries, but the use of bow and arrow had to be imposed from above. Furthermore, the old Germanic square battle formation was an organic unit, a family organization. With the Great Migrations this bond was seriously weakened, if not altogether dissolved. Outside its social context the Germanic square lost the qualities which it once had possessed. The tendency moved towards the individualization of combat, the maximization of individual effort by putting the warrior on a horse, without giving up the facility to fight on foot should the occasion arise.

If warfare was changing, Europe had changed. The Roman Empire had all but disappeared. On its debris settled a series of Germanic kingdoms in Italy, Germany, Gaul, Spain and Britain. Yet the influence of Rome remained, for the Barbarians had been exposed to and affected by it over centuries. The Barbarian war-band ethos weakened and discipline as a prerequisite to any ordered and settled life made itself felt. The glory that had been Rome continued to exercise its magnetic force to the extent that its heirs had nothing better to do than to try to perpetuate it by emulating it. And beyond the fringes of the old Empire and the new rulers, new hosts of Barbarians lurked ready to seize their chance at invasion. And most important, the institutional framework of the Empire, shaky as it may have been towards its end, underwent a rejuvenating experience at the hands of the Roman Catholic Church.

Left. *Foot soldiers carrying shields, lances and slings (eleventh century).*

Right. *Weapons of a Germanic warrior (Southwest Germany, third century).*

Danish ships invading England.

THE CHALLENGE
FROM THE EAST

The Islamic Invasion

The spread of the Islam during the eighth century was a factor of profound importance for the consequences it had both upon the Roman Empire as well as for the Germanic tribes in central and western Europe. After the collapse of West Rome, the Barbarians who had shattered it were in varying degrees absorbed by its culture and traditions, ultimately claiming continuity and direct succession of their kingdoms from the Imperial past.

What erupted during this process of absorption was the Islamic expansion which came quite unexpectedly. From the depths of the Arabian Peninsula rose a tidal wave which transformed not only North Africa but Europe. It originated in an area with which the Roman Empire had had little contact. For the protection of Syria against the nomadic Bedouin tribes it had constructed a wall much in the way in which Hadrian's wall was built in Britain as protection against the raids of the Picts. But Syria is in no way comparable with the English North, the Danube and the Rhine. The Roman Empire had never considered its outermost southeastern frontier as highly vulnerable. Its legions were concentrated in the north and west. The southeast was of importance only in so far as it was a trade route over which spices and rare cloths were imported into the Empire. That changed in 613 A.D. when Mohammed, a hitherto unknown native trader of the city of Mecca, began to preach a new revelation. He claimed to have experienced divine visitations and demanded the destruction of all idols on pain of eternal damnation. Archangel Gabriel had revealed to him to submit only to one God—a demand in opposition to the polytheistic faith of his Arab contemporaries—but at first his gospel fell on deaf ears. In fact he was compelled to leave Mecca in 622. As he moved on he mixed Arab aspirations with Jewish and Christian beliefs, and ears became more receptive to his message. Though in parts not dissimilar to other Oriental religions, Mohammed's gospel suited the warlike tendencies of nomadic tribes. For their livelihood Mohammed and his followers constantly preyed on the caravans of his Meccan relations; a religious war was in the making.

Islam connotes submission and implies brotherhood among all Muslims, since differences among humans are of so significance before Allah, the one true and everlasting God. This message was driven home emphatically in the lines of the Koran. Combative religious fervor was heightened by the promise of a paradise into which all those would be accepted who died in battle against the infidel. The alternative to that paradise was scorching hell.

Three years after leaving Mecca Mohammed was ready to fight all infidels, Jews, Christians and other heathens. He did this so successfully that in 630 he re-entered Mecca as the uncontested leader of a new faith. Two years later he died and his father-in-law Abu Bakr took over the direction of the movement, calling himself the successor, the Caliph.

Little note of that was taken in Constantinople, which was much more preoccupied with the activities of the Germanic tribes than with anything else. Also the struggle with the Persians had left both East Romans and Persians in a state of exhaustion. Syria, Palestine and Egypt had been restored to Byzantium. Emperor Heraclius could now think of resuming the policy of Justinian aiming at the restoration of the position of East Rome in the west where the Longobards held vital parts of Italy while the Visigoths had deprived Rome of its last positions in Spain. East Rome was not given that chance. The simultaneous Arab invasions into Europe and Asia took place at a speed comparable only to those of Attila and, later, Genghis Khan. However, the Arab conquests were of relative permanence.

Compared with the Germanic tribes who over centuries fought at the fringes of the Empire until they penetrated it, the Arabs with one blow captured mighty positions. In 634 they conquered the Byzantine fortress of Bothra; a year later Damascus fell into their hands; in 636 the whole of Syria was theirs. Another year later Jerusalem opened its gates to them, while at the same time they conquered Mesopotamia. This was followed by an attack upon Egypt, and Alexandria was taken in 641. This was followed by the conquest of Cyrenaica and advance parties of Arabs penetrated as far as Tunisia.

Obviously the Arabs gained much by the surprise element of their attack, its sudden and unexpected impact and by the way in which they managed to sustain that impact. Quick on horses and camels, both products of an environment which could

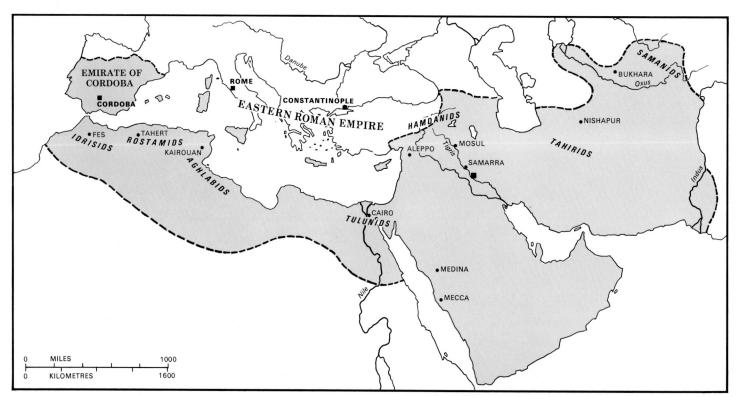

Right. *Viking warriors: detail from the Oseberg Tapestry.*

Left: *The spread of Islam.*

make do with little for a long time—a characteristic which of course applies to their riders too—armed with lance, sword, bow and arrow, they were unencumbered in their movement by the kind of baggage trains which Roman armies, or for that matter the Germanic tribes, carried with them.

The question has been put why the Arabs were, unlike the Germans, not absorbed into the fabric of Roman culture. The answer is that they were in possession of a spiritual power, the Islamic faith. Theirs was not a quest for new lands, for territorial expansion, but the submission of the world as they knew it to Allah. That submission did not necessarily mean the conversion of the conquered, but simply obedience to God and his prophet Mohammed. Religion and national faith are one and the same thing. Every Muslim is a servant of Allah. The conquered are their subjects compelled to pay taxes but stand outside the community of the faithful. The wall between faithful and infidel is almost unsurmountable. By comparison the Germans had nothing else to do than to try to put themselves in the service of the conquered and adapt their style of life to theirs. The Koran says that if it had been Allah's will he would have

made of mankind one people. Therefore there was no need to carry on missionary activities. The faith of the infidel was not attacked but simply ignored.

The Germans in the provinces of the Roman Empire were Romanized; not the Arabs. Their conquest of the Mediterranean put an end to the *mare nostrum* of the Empire. The Mediterranean world no longer represented one entity, but was divided into a Christian sphere in the north and the Muslim sphere in the south. Latin civilization was extinguished in northern Africa.

However, their main objective throughout their conquest was the citadel of the infidel empire, Constantinople. As early as 655 the first attempt took place. Besides being good horsemen the Arabs had been excellent sailors and they decisively defeated the Byzantine fleet. Only internal dissension among the Muslim leaders forced the abandonment of the conquest of Constantinople. They returned to that project thirteen years later, but not with the sense of purpose the first attempt had displayed, partly because Muslim endeavors elsewhere took priority. In the west the Atlantic coast was reached and by 711 Spain had

26

Right. *A Saxon axeman.*

been overrun, while in the east the Arabs had penetrated into the Punjab and in central Asia they reached the frontiers of China.

In 715 Caliph Suleiman set into motion again the conquest of Constantinople. His first move was to send two armies into Rumania. These operations did not yield any concrete results. On the other hand, the overall situation was dangerous enough for Emperor Leo to withdraw to Constantinople, where he immediately replenished the stores and arsenals of the capital, had the fortifications repaired and engines of war mounted on them. From land Constantinople was virtually unassailable; it could not be taken by storm. It could only be blockaded by closing the Bosporus as well as the Dardanelles. Hence sea power was crucial and Emperor Leo's fleet was inferior to that of the Muslims. Caliph Suleiman's brother Maslama decided to surround the city by advancing on land and on sea. While Maslama commanded the land forces, Suleiman was in charge of the naval operations. The precise numbers of Muslim forces involved cannot be stated with any degree of reliability. The claim that the army was 80,000 strong while the fleet contained 1800 vessels with another 80,000 men aboard is very doubtful. Nevertheless in other parts of Egypt and Africa further vessels were made ready for action. Maslama appeared before the outer walls of Constantinople on 15 August 717 and attempted a land attack at once. In the face of the skills of the Byzantine engineers

and their missile equipment, the attack had to be abandoned. Maslama prepared to blockade the city. He encamped outside the walls, fortifying it strongly, and instructed the fleet to divide into two squadrons, one to cut off supplies coming from the Aegean, the other to move through the Bosporus to cut off the city from the Black Sea. All seemed to go well until the second squadron, approaching the Bosporus, was brought into some confusion by strong currents. Emperor Leo immediately recognized his advantage, sailed out with his galleys, and poured Greek fire—a mixture of sulphur quicklime and naphtha which ignites immediately when whetted—on them destroying approximately 20 Muslim ships and capturing several others. The action proved decisive. The Muslims made no further attempts upon the Straits until the following year when an Egyptian squadron under cover of darkness closed it. In the meantime, however, the blockading Muslim land forces had undergone a severe winter which depleted their numbers seriously. Leo, in another surprise attack, scattered the Egyptian naval force, and followed it up with a successful attack upon the Muslim forces opposite the Bosporus. Meanwhile his Bulgarian ally Tervel and his army gave battle to Maslama. In the vicinity of Adrianople some 23,000 Muslims are alleged to have been killed. Maslama and his forces had to abandon their blockade. Leo's victory had stemmed the Muslim tide; the Byzantine

Empire was shored up for another seven centuries. Had Constantinople been captured, it is safe to assume that the Muslims would have taken the route into Europe as they were to do later on, and as the Muslims who had swept north up the Iberian peninsula were doing.

From Spain they entered Aquitaine in 712; in 719 they occupied Narbonne and in 721 they laid siege to Toulouse. Defeated there by Duke Eudo of Aquitaine, they returned to the region in 725 occupying Carcassonne and Nîmes, moving into Burgundy which they thoroughly ravaged and penetrating as far north as the Vosges mountains.

By that time the Frankish house of the Merovingians was in a state of decline, actual power passing into the hands of the Mayors of the Palace. In that role the Mayors were able to acquire large territorial possessions for themselves: Pipin II, the father of Charles Martel (the Hammer), had made himself lord of the territory between the Loire and the Meuse and of Aquitaine. In that position, of course, he was a threat to Eudo who, as far as his territories were concerned, feared the Franks as much as the Arabs. When Eudo, in the turmoil caused by the Islamic invasion, declared himself independent from Frankish overlordship, Charles Martel marched against him, defeated him and pacified the territory.

Eudo, to secure his southern flank, entered into alliance with a Muslim Berber chieftain, whose daughter he married. The Muslim Governor of Spain, Abd-ar-Rahman, greatly disapproved of this action, defeated the Berber chieftain and sent Eudo's wife to the Caliph's harem in Damascus. He then decided to invade Aquitaine. Crossing the Pyrenees in the northwest, he entered Gascony spreading terror throughout the territories. At Bordeaux Eudo met him in battle but was utterly defeated; Bordeaux was taken, sacked and burned. From there the Muslims marched in the direction of Tours. As one monkish chronicler put it:

'Then Abd-ar-Rahman pursued after Count Eudo, and while he strives to spoil and burn the holy shrine at Tours, he encounters the chief of the Austrasian Franks Charles (Martel), a man of war from his youth, to whom Eudo had sent warning. There for nearly seven days they strive intensively, and at last they set themselves in battle array; and the nations of the north standing firm as a wall, and impenetrable as a zone of ice, utterly slay the Arabs with the edge of the sword.'

The account is scanty, probably in part because very little is known of the Muslim's military organization, except that most of them were Moors and were mounted. Unlike in North Africa they do not seem to have used bow and arrow but depended upon their swords and lances. Armor was scarce.

About the Franks one is better informed. They relied mainly on their infantry made up of the personal troops of Charles, which had to be kept busy at all times for plunder was the only pay they got. To these came local levies, generally of ill-equipped men. It was a very primitive army compared with that of the Goths; discipline seemed to have been entirely absent, and the only thing that kept it together was the availability of food. Once food was scarce the army dissolved. Among the Franks horses seem to have been used for purposes of transportation only. But the Frankish warriors wore armor and fought with swords, daggers, spears and axes.

The Muslims had not anticipated the arrival of Charles Martel and his forces. After a few days of maneuver and countermaneuver, the Muslims decided to bring their offensive strength into play. They opened with a cavalry charge that made the earth tremble. Charles had drawn up his host in a solid phalanx which repelled charge after charge. Abd-ar-Rahman was killed, and the onset of night ended the battle. When the Franks expected a renewed attack in the morning, they noticed the Muslims had disappeared. They fled south leaving their plunder behind them. That they refrained for some time from renewing their attacks north of Pyrenees has little to do with the defeat they suffered, but rather more with substantial internal divisions among the Islamic peoples. For Charles Martel, however, this victory elevated him to a position of pre-eminence that allowed him to transform a tribal state into the Frankish Empire.

Three years later the Muslims were back again. In 735 the Arabs conquered Arles, once again invaded Aquitaine and ventured as far north as Lyons. Charles Martel returned, wrested Avignon from them, but failed to expel them from Narbonne, a city which only in 759 was captured from the Muslims by the son of Charles Martel, Pipin. The Islamic invasion resulted in developments which in their significance equaled the event which caused their origin. For centuries the center of Europe had been the Mediterranean. It was the connecting link between the countries of antiquity. Hellenic and Latin civilization gave that region its imprint. Later on even a common religion was a further force of integration. The invasion of the Germanic Barbarians certainly shook the structure of the Empire, toppled its political apex in West Rome, but did not destroy the structure of the Empire, let alone its culture. The Barbarians had nothing to put in its place. They were only too eager to adapt all that which they recognized was superior to their own culture. Nor did they possess an idea with which to counter the concept of Roman universalism. Their invasions caused serious tremors, but in time they were assimilated; there is nothing to show otherwise.

Under the sudden impact of the Islamic invasions the cultural, economic and social unity of the region was broken. The link that had connected east and west across the sea was severed. Byzantium was thrown back upon its own resources to main-

Emperor Otto I the Great (912–973).

no longer forthcoming. In the light of this development the Church was compelled to look for another power capable of filling the void left by East Rome. The alternative was found in the strongest of the successor kingdoms, that of the Franks.

The Frankish tribes which had been brought under a form of unity by Clovis were, in spite of their contact with the Roman Empire, among those considered to be the least civilized by Roman standards. By contrast with the Gothic tribes their weapons and tactics during the sixth century bore a greater resemblance to the arms with which Arminius encountered the Romans than to anything used in southern Europe.

'The arms of the Franks are very crude; they wear neither mail-shirt nor greaves and their legs are only protected by strips of linen or leather. They have hardly any horsemen, but their foot soldiery are bold and well-practiced in war. They bear swords and shields, but never use sling or bow. Their missiles are axes and barbed javelins. These last are not very long; they can be used either to cast or to stab. The iron of the head runs so far down the stave that very little of the wood remains unprotected. In battle they hurl these javelins, and if they strike an enemy the barbs are so firmly fixed in his body that it is impossible for the enemy to draw the weapon out. If it strikes a shield, it is impossible for enemy to get rid of it by cutting off its head, for the iron runs too far down the shaft. At this moment the Frank rushes in, places his foot on the butt as it trails on the ground, and so, pulling the shield downwards, cleaves his uncovered adversary through the head, or pierces his breast with a second spear.'

The throwing axe, the *francisca*, was another favorite Frankish weapon. It was a single-bladed axe with a heavy head which in shape and function was not dissimilar to the tomahawk of the North American Indian. Added to it were, of course, shield, sword and dagger. These weapons, though primitive, nevertheless show an important difference from the Germanic weapons a few centuries before. The amount of metal used in them allows two conclusions; firstly, that iron ore, or metals in general must have been more accessible then; secondly, that some degree of industrial processing must have been achieved.

Their weapons were indigenous products, they owed nothing to Roman examples. A strong conservative attitude among the Franks is betrayed by the fact that once they did adopt weapons and armory other than their own, they tended to hold on to them, even though they had become obsolete elsewhere. In their conquest of Gaul they were quick to utilize the available manpower reservoir and enrolled Gallic levies under their own banners. For the Franks this was easier because under the Merovingians, the traditional Germanic unit, the hundred, based upon blood ties, had ceased to play its function. However, among both Ostrogoths and Visigoths as well as among the Vandals it continued almost to their very end so that these tribes had been rather less able to integrate military levies from outside than the Franks. In terms of Frankish policy in Gaul this meant that the native Gauls were quickly assimilated into Frankish society until all distinctions were blurred. Even Frankish names were adopted. Again this contrasts starkly with the dualism existing in Italy between the Ostrogoths on the one hand and the Romans and native provincial population on the other.

The tactics of their foot soldiery continued for some time to adhere to the old Germanic square, often mistakenly described as a great disorderly mass of unarmored infantry fighting in dense column formations. Only during the course of the sixth century did they show any signs of Roman influence. Slowly armor made its appearance and so did horses, but as the Battle of Tours indicates horsemanship had not made any great headway by the middle of the eighth century. They were a means of transport for the King, his friends and officials, and were only very slowly adopted by the lower ranks. But innovations, even

tain her position in the east. Her claim to represent the Roman Empire as a whole could no longer be upheld, and gradually it transformed itself into a Greek state. Meanwhile the Bulgarians, Serbs and Croats spread the Slavic influence southwards on their route into the Balkans. Constantinople had its hands tied defending itself in the east without wishing to face similar burdens in the west, whether on the Italian peninsula, along the Danube or the Rhine, let alone Gaul and Spain. Byzantium had contracted to an area limited by the Illyrian coast in the west and by the upper Euphrates in the east. From now on it spent most of its energy defending itself against the onslaught from the east and south. In fact Byzantium was separated from the developments in the west.

If it can be said that Byzantium was forced back on its own resources, the same applies to the West. At first this looked like a separation from its cultural roots, from the intellectual inspiration which Europe had derived from them. Of course Muslim settlement in Spain brought the West nearer to the Orient, but intellectually the Arab world had little to offer to the West at that time. Indeed, Islam had no desire to offer anything. Western Europe was isolated from the rest of the world. The Mediterranean, that vital artery of commerce, was almost closed. Western Europe also had to rely on its own resources.

Yet there remained one institutional link: the Roman Catholic Church. Orientated as it had been at first towards Byzantium which could offer secular protection, that protection was when used at the top, could cause adverse comment. In the sixth century one bishop among the Franks was chided because when riding into battle he wore armor plate across his chest instead of the sign of the heavenly cross. By the middle of the seventh century, however, breast plates had come into general use among the Franks. Their helmets were rather different from those of the Romans and have been described as 'a morion-shaped round-topped head-piece, peaked and open in front, but rounded and falling low at the back, so as to cover the nape of the neck.' Those for the common soldiery were made of leather. Metal ones were to be found among the Frankish commanders. The shield was not made of iron but of wood, only the edges were bound with iron.

The use of cavalry was underdeveloped among the Merovingians due to their horses which, compared with those of the Muslims, were cart-horses; any battle between Arab and Frankish cavalry would have courted a major disaster for the latter. The Merovingians had discouraged the growth of a nobility within their ranks, preferring to delegate administrative and military duties in their provinces to counts or dukes directly appointed by them—probably in anticipation of that problem that was to dominate most of the kingdoms of the Middle Ages, that of the 'overmighty subject.' The King's appointee upon his command rallied the Frankish forces of his province as well as all freemen among the Gauls. To be the King's administrator as well as one of the military commanders entailed honor but relatively low material rewards. While elsewhere large estates developed, the Frankish Kings let land out only in small parcels on a possessory not a proprietary basis, another device to contain the power of what was in essence a nobility of service, not one of birth. Large landholdings became common among the Franks only when the last economic consequences of the Islamic invasions had worked themselves throughout Europe. And whenever such checks as the Merovingian Kings introduced to maintain power in their hands on occasions did not curb the ambitions of a subject and his family, they had no scruples about slaughtering the potential rival, as well as his entire family.

Since Frankish soldiers did not receive any pay, they had to live off the land in times of war, irrespective of whether or not the territory crossed was that of a friend. As the Merovingian dynasty declined, its counts were prone to take greater liberties, question the King's commands, and in the end did pretty much as they liked. Only the Arab threat forged them together again into a community of interest, and when the Merovingians were replaced by their mayors, the reins were pulled tightly together again. Out of the confusion of conflicting and rivaling competencies a firm military and administrative hierarchy was forged. This trend began under Charles Martel, his son Pipin the Short, and was finally completed by Charlemagne.

Anglo-Saxon psalter illustrating Viking ships invading the shores of Britain.

The European periphery: Vikings and Magyars

Relations, especially those of a hostile nature between the Franks and the Norsemen, date back to the sixth century when Theudebert of Ripuaria slew Hygelac the Dane in combat. Hygelac was the brother of Beowulf. This appears to be the earliest recorded encounter between Franks and Vikings. Apparently thereafter the Vikings were too busy fighting one another to have much time for the world to the south. Late Merovingian Franconia offered few attractions. But once the reputation of Charlemagne echoed through Europe, its sounds were heard in the fjords of the north. When he had conquered the Saxons the influence of the Franks also moved nearer. The leader of the Saxons, Widukind, found refuge in Jutland. If he told them his side of the story the tale must have been terrible enough. When he had finally returned to Saxony and accepted Christian baptism, the potential danger of Franks to the Scandinavian north was bound to have increased.

The term Viking does not indicate a tribe but rather an activity. An adventurer who took to the sea was said to go *i viking*. The term, like that of Norsemen, is simply one of convenience and includes not only Danes and Norwegians but also many other adventurous folk who joined them on their expeditions and became part of their society. There are no adequate explanations to the questions who they originally were or what caused them to take to their boats and pillage the British Isles and the European mainland. Overpopulation may have been one reason, overpopulation of those areas of Denmark and Norway which allowed a subsistence agrarian economy. Nordic saga has it that approximately one century before Christ a chief by the name of Odin ruled over a city in Asia:

'The Roman Emperors were going far and wide over the world, beating down all peoples in battle; because of the unrest many lords fled from their lands. When Odin looked into the future and worked

magic, he knew that his offspring would dwell and till in the northern parts of the earth.'

Odin, endowed with supernatural powers, then led his people into the lands of the north to rule over the country and the men he found there. Although a saga, considering the area from which the Norsemen are supposed to have migrated, it is probable that their wanderings across Asia into northern Europe were part of the first stirrings of the Great Migrations. Once in their new homelands they developed considerable skills in woodcraft and metal work. Soon these lands became too small for large families, because among the Norsemen polygamy was commonplace. The economic pinch probably coincided with what we now might call a technological advance in the Norsemen's ship-building in which they first ventured along their own coasts and then across the seas, to Ireland, England and the Frankish Empire.

Of course sagas may supply us with indications on the basis of which one can speculate, but they are not evidence. Moreover they were not put to paper before the twelfth century. The account of the raids of the Norsemen have been handed down to us by the chroniclers, that is to say by their victims; the Norsemen themselves left no written records. The only concrete evidence left by them is of an archeological nature, such as the fourth-century vessel discovered at Nydham in Denmark. This shows a very low-sided ship equipped only for rowing, long, light and undecked. Its overall length was 76 feet, rowed by 14 pairs of oarsmen. It is more than doubtful that with a boat of this kind the treacherous waters of the North Sea could have been braved. But when, at the beginning of the eighth century the sail was introduced, the Norsemen lengthened and deepened the hulls of their boats, strengthening their structure all around. One such authentic surviving example is the Gokstad ship found near Oslo towards the end of the last century. Although still equipped with oars, it was primarily a sailing vessel. That was the kind of boat with which the Vikings made their assault upon Europe, and in perhaps their most daring expedition under the leadership of Leif Ericson they ventured across the Atlantic and set foot upon the New World five centuries before Columbus.

In their early raids upon Ireland, England and the Frankish Empire they appeared to have been very primitively armed, no better than the Germanic tribes when they first collided with the Romans. Such helmets and mailshirts they had seem to have been obtained from their slain victims or by trade. Therefore the majority of the raiders in the late eighth century were wholly unmailed. Within a span of half a century this had changed profoundly. From their enemies they had not merely captured arms, armor and equipment superior to their own, but also the skills of making it themselves. By the middle of the ninth century all Norsemen warriors wore mailshirts, based very much on the Frankish model. Even their shields were at first copies of those of the Franks. The shape of shield such as we find on the Bayeux tapestry is a product of the late ninth or early tenth century.

Archeological discoveries show the weapons of the Norsemen to have been double-bladed short swords with a small hand-grip and devoid of a cross-guard. In the course of their struggles with the Franks they adopted longer blades. Their spears were very similar to those of the Frank; only their axes were very heavy instruments, with a long wooden shaft which required both hands for its use. The axe was of course more than a weapon; it was a tool necessary for the repair and construction of their ships, to fell trees for encampment, purposes for which the small Frankish axe was unsuitable. In their skill of using the

France during the period 451–732.

Viking-type helmet worn by the sixth warrior on the first wagon (early Icelandic ms).

KINGDOM OF THE FRANKS, 768
EXTENT OF CHARLEMAGNE'S EMPIRE

The French Kingdom in 768.

bow they were never matched by any of their adversaries, with the exception of Muslims on the southern shores of the Iberian peninsula.

When the Norsemen first appeared on their plundering expeditions, they operated on the basis of hit-and-run raids. At that time they could still be dealt with because the raids were individual ventures with very few boats involved. This changed during the ninth century when their massed fleets appeared on the shores of Ireland, England and the Frankish Empire. Then the boats were left under strong guards at their point of anchorage, while the bulk of the Norsemen made their way inland. In Ireland resistance to them was ferocious but lacking in organized leadership. England was also vulnerable because of its political divisions. In the Frankish Empire the Norsemen's impact was limited as long as Charlemagne reigned. But one monk records what is alleged to have been Charlemagne's reaction

when in the year of his coronation as Emperor of the Romans he was having a meal at the shores of the Mediterranean and Viking boats were sighted. He writes:

'When the Norsemen heard that Charles was there, they vanished in marvelously swift flight. Rising from his table, the most just and devout Charles stood looking from the window, while tears ran down and no one dared speak to him. Then he explained his tears to his nobles in these words: "I do not fear that these worthless scamps will do any harm to me. No, I am sad at heart thinking that while I live they dare intrude upon this shore, and I am torn by a great sorrow foreseeing what evil they will do to my descendants."'

If the account of this chronicler is to be believed, and there is nothing that would speak against it, Charlemagne had good reason to be anxious about the future, and his fears were more than vindicated.

After what might be called their phase of hit-and-run raids, the Norsemen turned to the next phase: full major invasions of the three major areas of their previous operations. That phase was marked by the changing character of the invasions. No longer did the Norsemen come simply to plunder; they came to settle. This is true of Ireland where they created and administered cities. It is true of England which they penetrated and, as already seen, it is true of the Frankish Empire. It was the last great migration of Nordic peoples before the sixteenth century, a migration which threatened the very survival of Europe's romanesque civilization.

Like the Franks, so the Anglo-Saxons at first were in despair of how to meet the new threat when it appeared on such a massive scale. They were prepared for any threat on land, but not one coming from the sea. When the Viking boats appeared in mass on the coast and rivers leading to London or York, each boat disembarking 40 warriors created havoc. While the Norsemen quickly rounded up all the horses they could lay their hands on and transformed themselves into mounted infantry, no defense mechanism existed to check or delay the rapidity of their movements.

The main objects of attack were monasteries and churches which were both holders of wealth as well as centers of the medieval culture that was developing on the ruins of Roman civilization. They were the repositories of the art and literature

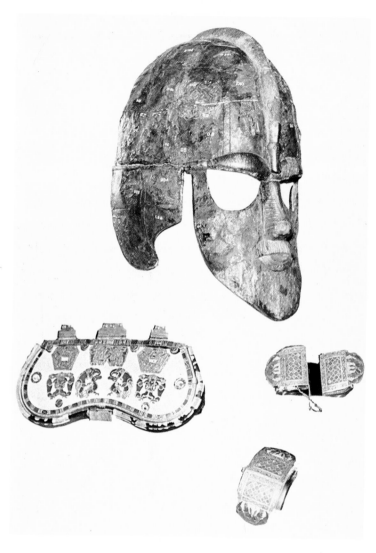

Above. *Treasures from the royal long-ship excavated at Sutton Hoo, c 650.*
Left. *The Storming of Ipswich by the Danes (Painting by Lorentz Ipplich).*

of the period. Commerce already in a state of stagnation since the Muslim invasions came to an almost complete halt when the Norsemen fell upon Europe.

They approached the lands to be despoiled from two major routes. The Norwegians chose the northern route over which quite a number of them had migrated to the Shetlands and the Orkneys and where they established their settlements. From there they made their way along the east and west coasts of Scotland as far as Lincolnshire in the east and down to the Isle of Man and to Ireland in the west. Ireland was a particularly rewarding area because it had escaped the impact of the Barbarian invasions. The climate was genial and Irish monasteries were filled with an abundance of wealth. Ireland was first attacked in 795, but from 850 onwards began a systematic campaign of conquest. As of 850 A.D. the Norsemen stayed permanently in Ulster; in 853 King Olaf founded his Dublin kingdom, and coastal colonies were established at Wexford, Waterford and Limerick. For 150 years the Norsemen exercised supremacy over Ireland and their power was not broken until the Anglo-Norman conquest in the reign of Henry II. The Isle of Man was not surrendered until 1266, the Shetlands till 1462 and the Orkneys until 1468.

The Danes preferred the southern route. Sailing directly from their own shores they were brought into immediate contact with east and southeast England, with the Low Countries and, once through the Channel, with Brittany, the Bay of Biscay and the Strait of Gibraltar from which they ravaged the coasts of the Mediterranean even capturing Sicily in a later

phase. The Swedes, on the other hand, concentrated their efforts in the Baltic, entered Russia, which was the name they had given to it and opened up a southerly route as far as Constantinople.

The Anglo-Saxon Chronicle registers the first raids upon England. In 787 it records:

'In this year King Beorthoric took to wife Eadburh, daughter of King Offa; and in his days came for the first time three ships from the Norwegians from Hoerthland: these were the first ships of the Danes to come to England.'

As far as the chronicler is concerned there is no distinction between Danes and Norwegians, but they were most probably Danes.

Again in 793 it records:

'In this year terrible portents appeared over Northumbria, and miserably frightened the inhabitants: there were exceptional flashes of lightning, and fiery dragons were seen flying in the air. A great famine soon followed these signs; and a little after that in the same year on 8 January the harrying of the heathen miserably destroyed God's church in Lindisfarne by rapine and slaughter . . .'

King Egbert of Wessex fought them successfully in a pitched battle at Hingston Down in 838, but two years later they sacked London and again pillaged Lincolnshire and Northumbria. From 850 the period of systematic conquest began. More than 350 Viking ships did not return home after they had looted Canterbury, but their warriors wintered on the Isle of Thanet. It was the beginning of their permanent settlement. Fifteen years later the so-called 'great Army' of the Norsemen landed in East Anglia, and a year later in 866 they moved on to York. Northumbria, divided by political feuds, could offer no resistance. Then in 870 the great Army turned south towards Wessex, establishing its base at Reading, from which it could control the Thames and receive its supplies and strike at the capital of Wessex, Winchester.

The King of Wessex they faced was Alfred the Great. A deeply devout man as well as a very brave one, he decided to resist. But having no military organization worthy of the name, he tried to win time by negotiating with the Danes. He agreed to pay tribute providing the Danes evacuated Wessex. With that he won five valuable years in which to reorganize his forces.

The Danes had the advantage of being professional warriors prepared to fight all the year round. Against that Alfred had the old Anglo-Saxon *fyrd*, which by the ninth century was no longer a host of tribal freeman. As in the Frankish Empire, the feudal system was making its appearance; military service became connected with land-ownership, and even prior to Alfred's succession the nucleus of the *fyrd* was a small group of experienced soldiers, which on Alfred's instruction were constituted as a mobile infantry, to meet the Danes on their own ground. The mounted men were made up of the King's own close followers, his retainers, and those of the ealdormen, as well as from the heads of the shires, the thanes. He provided them with incentives, greater landholdings and turned them into a specifically military class whose expertise was rewarded with greater privileges. In Alfred's own words his society was composed of those who prayed, those who fought, and those who worked.

In contrast to the Franks Alfred recognized the importance of sea-power and initiated the construction of a fleet of long ships which in design and performance proved superior to those of the Danes. What Alfred's sailors lacked were the skills and the experience of the Danes and that could not be obtained in the short span of time available to them.

At strategically important points in Wessex, particularly on

Right. *Unearthed at Gokstad, Norway, this ship is one of the most remarkable finds dating from the Viking period. It was originally defended by a line of 32 wooden shields along each gunwhale. Painted yellow or black alternatively, the shields were reinforced at the center by an iron boss and overlapped to form a scale-like protection for 16 oarsmen.*

Below right. *Frankish warrior of the Carolingian period portrayed in carved ebony.*

its frontiers in the south and on the Thames, he built fortified strongholds, putting the responsibility for their maintenance upon the local people who had to provide the soldiers as well as the provisions. When the five years were up Alfred refused to pay further tribute and the Danes resumed their attacks. The first came in 876 from the west. After almost two years of inconclusive engagements, the Danes under their leader Guthrum struck a surprise blow which scattered Alfred's forces; Alfred himself had to seek refuge in the Athelney fens. But within a very short time he managed to reassemble his forces once again and defeat Guthrum at Edington in 878. As a result Guthrum agreed to be baptized, and eight years later a further agreement was concluded which delimited the Scandinavian settlers' territory in East Anglia and Mercia. The success of his policy is demonstrated best when one looks at the outcome of another Danish invasion between 892–896, this time coming from France. On three occasions the Danes traversed the country into West Mercia, expecting support from their countrymen. The majority, however, remained on their settlements. The Danes left without having achieved anything.

With his victory Alfred achieved more than just the supremacy of the Wessex dynasty among the Anglo-Saxon kingdoms. It was of European significance. What would have happened to the seedlings of Europe's medieval civilization had the Norsemen established their rule in the British Isles and used them as a base for their operations against the European mainland is not very difficult to imagine.

For England their threat had been banished, for subsequent Norse enterprises remained limited in scale and effect. What remained was an enduring horror and fear of them. In 1014 Olaf of Norway with his men helped the fugitive King Ethelred to return to England and take London from its Danish captors. The chronicler tells us:

'The Viking leader took his ships under London Bridge and wound cables round the stakes which supported the bridge, and taking the cables, they rowed all the ships downstream as hard as ever they could. The stakes were dragged along the bottom until they were loosed under the bridge . . . and the bridge came crashing down, and many fell into the river. . . . Now when the citizens saw that the River Thames was won, so that they could no longer prevent the ships from pressing up inland, they were stricken with terror at the advance of the ships and gave up the city.'

And most likely they would pray as did the French who had introduced this line to the litany of the Church, 'From the fury of the Norsemen, God deliver us.'

Under the combined threat from the Norsemen and the Magyars, Europe in the ninth century underwent several important military changes. In the Frankish Empire and its successor kingdoms the traditional levies of foot soldiery were quite useless in meeting a threat such as that posed by the Norsemen. They were clumsy and slow to assemble and move, and in combat were no match for the warriors of the north. They lacked the professionalism and experience which their enemies combined. The military aspect of nascent feudalism now began to gain in importance. The system of vassalage already developing during the eighth century provided the means of creating a class of military experts. At first they were people among the retinue of the monarch, but through subinfeudation the king's personal vassals would acquire knights of their own. Frankish counts and vassals at the Court of Charlemagne were expected to appear mounted. Their own retainers were equally expected to be mounted. It was the beginning of a period of over 400 years in which the cavalry dominated the field and its quality decided the battle. True, after the death of Louis the Pious, Frankish knights, in spite of their mounted levies, did not seem to have fared particularly well against the Norsemen, but it was a military failure at the root of which was the political instability of the late Carolingian period. To what effective use cavalry could be put to use against Barbarian raiders on horseback was to be demonstrated in Germany where, with the election of the Saxon Duke Henry I as King of Germany, stability returned and grew under his son Emperor Otto I, called 'the Great.'

The rise of cavalry meant in the final analysis that the defending forces could keep up with the Vikings in speed. It was more likely to break a Viking shield wall than ill-equipped levies on foot. The feudal pyramid running from the king downwards to his vassals and counts could produce a large number of knights well-equipped in arms and in training all year round, sustained in the end by the economic basis of the feudal system, the land.

Another transformation that was further accelerated by the invasions of the Barbarians from the north and east was the fortification of the towns and larger settlements. It was not a development that had its origins during that period. As already mentioned, in the provinces of the former Roman Empire it was a direct response to the devastation caused by the tribes of the Great Migrations. Previously spaciously laid-out towns and settlements were reconstructed as narrow, walled cities that could be defended. What was new was the building of castles as a specific defense requirement. Alfred the Great's burghs fulfilled the same function as the *burg* to King Henry I, who erected a whole series of them to defend his eastern frontier. King Odo in his Edict of Pitres of 866 which recognized the all-importance of cavalry, also laid down a policy of the construction of fortifications. When the great Viking siege of Paris took place, the city was already fortified. To the surprise of the Franks the Vikings constructed siege machinery such as towers and missile-throwing machines. They were good in adapting what they had seen elsewhere. What they did not know was how to use it effectively. Hence they settled for a tribute and left. The further rise of fortification, the growing dominance of cavalry, and the decline of infantry are the features that mark military development in the ninth century.

In the eastern part of the former Frankish Empire the threat of the Slavs and Magyars was added to the threat of the Norsemen. There, the old tribal duchies of Saxony, Bavaria, Swabia, Franconia and Lorraine combined and elected one of their own, Duke Henry of Saxony, as King of Germany. His election marks the origin of the German state.

This new kingdom, however, was weaker when compared to its Carolingian predecessor, because Henry had to recognize the dukedoms as independent, autonomous political units. He or any of his successors might replace a duke, but he could not eliminate the dukedom by dividing it among others. Such a precedent would have alarmed all the other dukes. The successors of Charlemagne, although they had acquiesced to it by necessity, did not look favorably upon the development in which their vassals acquired their own vassals, and in this way, their own military force. But needing the military force badly there was nothing else they could do.

This, of course, now also happened under Henry I. But since he was the product of his vassals, it was in their common interest to maximize their military force to the fullest extent which the feudal system allowed. In a later period the problems inherent in the feudal system came to the fore when the King's policy was not shared by one or more of his major vassals. Because as German King, even though from Otto the Great's day onward every King until Charles V acquired the Imperial crown, he was no more than a *primus inter pares* among his vassals. Since the feudal system implies also the delegation of authority downwards, in terms of offices and functions, and as these were inheritable, vassals acquired a quasi-sovereignty. This applied to the military sector as it did to that of the administration, and of course military and administrative functions were more often than not combined in one person. In the military sector feudalism in Germany and France offered the opportunity of personal aggrandizement, of keeping any size of military force a duke was capable of raising and supplying.

In 919, the year of Henry's election, none of that was felt. He had his power in Saxony firmly established and then went on to strengthen the military system as he found it. In one of the first gatherings with fellow dukes and bishops, a campaign was decided upon and every prince swore solemnly that he would come with all his men, a custom lasting well into the thirteenth century. The number of knights each vassal brought was up to him. The Carolingians had tried to establish fixed numbers for each vassal and had failed. Henry did not even try. Consequently one is in the dark about the precise numbers involved in each campaign, and this holds true for most of the campaign contingents of the Middle Ages.

Henry's main pre-occupation was with the Magyars, who first made themselves heard when they came from Hungary and invaded Bavaria's eastern marches, present day Austria, in 862. From the beginning of the tenth century onwards they regularly invaded Germany coming, like the Huns, on swift ponies, interested more in booty rather than combat.

Their attacks were made by small, widely spread-out bands, and like the Vikings in their first phase, they disappeared as quickly as they had come. Rapidity of movement was their major asset. Henry upon his accession to the throne realized that he was not yet sufficiently prepared to meet them, and therefore in 924 concluded a pact with them in which he promised them the payment of an annual tribute. Then he began to consolidate his military position. First, like Alfred the Great, he built his castles along the frontier, constructed by the population of the region, of which every ninth man was to live in the castle. Cities like Merseburg, Nordhausen, Quedlinburg and Goslar owe their existence to Henry's program of castle-building. As in centuries to come when the British sent their criminals to colonies, Henry sent his convicts to build castles. Finally in 933 when the Magyars once again attacked Thuringia Henry met them with his forces at the River Unstrut. The Magyars suddenly confronted with the German might took to their heels.

The battle on the Unstrut did not end the Magyar threat. After Henry's death they resumed their attacks in 954 with a major invasion, followed by a second one in 955. Again numbers are unknown, but chroniclers report that they had never been seen in such numbers before. They crossed Bavaria and laid siege to Augsburg at the River Lech. Henry's successor, his son, Otto, moved rapidly with his forces from Saxony, an army amounting to approximately 7000 men, almost all of them mounted knights, coming from Saxony, Bavaria, Swabia, Franconia and Bohemia. When Otto and his host approached the Magyars broke camp, the main body engaging Otto, while a smaller detachment, outflanking the German forces, turned up in the rear of the Swabians and slaughtered them. The Franconians under Duke Conrad came to their relief. Otto and the Bavarians, who had contained the Magyars so far, ordered a general charge. The Magyars on horses much smaller than those of the Germans, most of them without armor, discharged a volley of arrows before they were overtaken and slain. But Otto's forces had suffered heavily as well. Duke Conrad was killed the moment he lifted his helmet to get some air.

For two days Otto's forces pursued the Magyars capturing several of their leaders whom they promptly hanged. After the Battle of the Lechfeld the Magyar danger had been banished forever.

THE EUROPEAN RESPONSE: 'FEUDALISM'

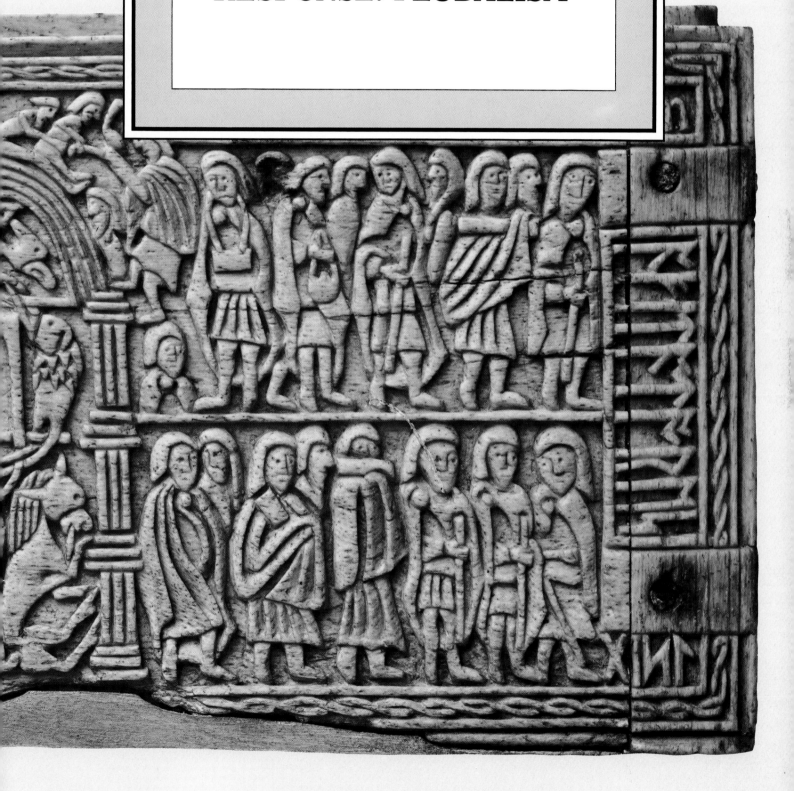

Medieval man knew nothing of 'feudalism.' He only experienced it and was part of it. As a term it was invented for the convenience of historians and sociologists describing similar arrangements made by society in Europe and elsewhere in response to a changed economic and social environment. It was a response to economic and military necessities, involving large-scale social repercussions.

The Islamic invasions had thrown Western Europe back on its own resources in more than one sense. They had disrupted the traditional network of commerce. Specie became rare. The only source of wealth was land. But it would be an over-simplification to cite the Islamic invasions as the sole factor responsible for the origin of feudal society. It is marked by three characteristics, all of which show that other factors were at work as well.

Firstly there is the particularist characteristic. The states which succeeded the Roman Empire were, generally speaking, decentralized. Each state or territory was made up of several imperfectly integrated components, a process in which the old tribal ties still played a very great part. This resulted in a division of power between the King and his counts, a division based not on functional criteria, but on those of a territorial and tribal nature. The early medieval state was not a centralized unitary state but a kind of personal union under the King, whose office was the bracket holding it together; hence the bracket was as strong or as weak as the King who represented it.

Secondly, in the absence of an institutional apparatus, personal relationships were instrumental in the exercise of power. Thus feudalism was a system of personal rule, the only means available to govern a great empire (such as the Carolingian) based on a subsistence economy, underdeveloped communications, a state lacking as yet the necessary institutions which would have made greater centralization possible. The feudal state was a patrimonial state, patrimony exercised by the King and from him downwards by his lords.

Thirdly, there is the hierarchic characteristic, a result of the close connection between Church and monarchy, a connection based on the acceptance that all power derives from and is delegated by the Lord, handed out on loan to those who exercise it at the various levels. It is very much the opposite of the idea of the sovereign prince or the sovereign people, all power deriving either from the prince or the people. During the greatest days of the Papacy this culminated in the Papal claim that the Papacy alone represented the supreme authority for all Christendom.

The Carolingian Empire (751 A.D. to 987 A.D. in France and to 911 A.D. in Germany) represented a synthesis of Roman and Germanic traditions. The Germanic tradition is reflected in the personal character of the political and military leadership; the Roman tradition is found in institutions such as the Church which operated within the administrative framework inherited from the Empire. The early counts received a written commission, but they stood directly under the King.

Even during the Merovingian period (approximately 500 A.D. to 751 A.D.) changes took place, transformations which were signposts towards that kind of feudalism which blossomed out fully in the post-Carolingian period. The old Frankish army, made up of the King's close associates and the local levies they raised, made way for a professional caste of warriors on horse. Once the stirrup came into widespread use among the Franks during the second half of the eighth century, the horse was no longer solely a means of transport. It could now be used for fighting. 'Speed could be converted into shock. Spears need no longer be thrown but could be couched as lances and rammed home.' This new caste established itself under the King by means of a private treaty, combining personal and legal aspects, namely vassalage and benefice.

Vassalage represented the fusion of Roman and Germanic concepts. The Germanic concept of military service was voluntary, a concept diluted by the Gallic custom of compulsory participation and the Roman idea of a private soldier. Since the eighth century the Franks based military service on the principle of mutual loyalty and mutual obligations. In return for service the lord guaranteed the livelihood of his vassal as a member of his household or by giving to him a piece of land in fief. The land grant was the benefice, or fief. Originally fief meant the possession of livestock. The holder of the fief had the livestock on his fief at his disposal as well as the proceeds of the land. However, in the early phase of the feudal period he did not possess it—something that was to change later on. But this socio-economic relationship capsulated another threefold re-

Receiving and weighing coin, 1130–74. The figures are probably copied from an earlier ms.

Scenes from life in Anglo-saxon Britain (Trinity College Cambridge ms, 1130–74).

lationship characteristic of the feudal age: military specialization, land tenure and mutually binding personal obligation.

In the Merovingian kingdom not only the King but some of his lords had vassals as well. In other words, in its final phase enough military specialists were held by the King's vassals to constitute private armies. Charles Martel successfully curbed this development, but dire necessity made subinfeudation indispensable to raise the military forces necessary to wage war against the invading Muslims.

Vassalage replaced the Germanic relationship between prince and subject based on the family unit. Indeed by becoming a vassal, he implicitly renounced protection by his kinsfolk. Instead he accepted it from a more powerful lord. It is significant, however, that the vassal relationship did not reduce the status of the vassal as a free man but elevate it, for it was an honor to serve with the lord.

These changes did more than merely produce a caste of professional warriors. They affected the peasant as well. The settled peasant was no longer the man who looked after mobile livestock, he also turned to the arable soil. The very nature of this occupation tied him to the soil. He could no longer perform military services without seriously affecting his agricultural function and thus his output. And, it must be remembered that next to the plague, food-shortage was the major fear of medieval society. But the peasant too was in need of protection. The village community was no longer in a position to give it. Consequently many peasants by the act of commendation voluntarily sought the protection of a lord, who in return ultimately became their master and proprietor of their land. It was the beginning of the Germanic peasant's road from the position of a freeman to that of a dependant or even a serf. The medieval military specialist, the knight, could not till the soil of his benefice, but the peasants whom he protected could and, depending on circumstances, he could enlarge his property holdings at their expense.

The King was the fountain of justice, but size of territory and the nature of the lines of communication within his kingdom made it impossible for him to administer it. Therefore another feature of the feudal system was the granting of judicial power and authority to the vassals, to secular as well as ecclesiastical princes, which further increased the vassal's social and political position. To landed property, offices were added as fiefs in Germany and France with long-term attendant consequences: excessive particularism in the former, exaggerated regionalism in the latter.

Three factors then characterize medieval feudalism. The military factor produced a highly-trained and specialized warrior caste, knights, tied to their lord by bonds of loyalty and mutual obligations. Secondly, the socio-economic factor brought forth an agrarian economy on a basis which insured the income of the warrior caste. Thirdly, the factor of lordship opened to members of that caste the possibility of exerting considerable influence in affairs of state, or for that matter, as in Germany, to turn their own lands into semi-autonomous principalities, which more often than not acted against the interests of the central power as long as that power was lacking the political and technical means to centralize.

Feudalism was a stage in the development of human society, the product of many factors, but it did not affect all segments of human society in the same way and with equal intensity. In Europe it was most prominent and reached its highest forms in the successor states of the Carolingian Empire—Germany, France and parts of Italy and Spain—states which had their origin not in the direct transition from tribal unit to state, but by having been exposed to close contact with a disintegrating empire and its culture and by having passed through an intermediary stage of assimilating and integrating those traditions. Outside that area the formation of states took place without the feudal system developing intensely, if at all. The Nordic states as well as Poland and Hungary showed little if any feudal structure, but developed from tribal associations into states. Their warrior caste was not of feudal origin. Military service was generally obligatory.

England, perhaps, is a special case. The formation of its early kingdoms took place on Romanized soil, but considering the relatively short duration of Roman occupation, and the almost complete rupture of its connections with the world of Rome after the Romans had left, Roman influence was minimal. Compared with the Frankish Empire it represented a geographically manageable unit. Until the Angevin Kings, there were no signs of wishing to expand beyond the natural frontiers of the island. The disproportion between the task and the means to master it was much narrower there than in the Frankish Empire or its successors. Of course this does not mean that feudal elements did not exist in England, but they operated within certain limits, of which geography was one. A professional warrior caste developed in England as elsewhere, the thane holding five hides of land, but it was socially more open to members from other strata of society, such as merchants. It had its countervailing power in the continuing traditional institutions of Germanic origin such as the county, shire, and the hundred, which in England survived much longer than anywhere else in Europe, the usefulness of which the Normans were quick to recognize and to adapt for their own purpose. Yet even before the arrival of the Normans a relaxation of the old ties of kinship was noticeable. For the peasant to seek the protection of a lord is one indication. Village communities, or communities of kin among the Anglo-Saxons had the right to object to the sale of their land from time immemorial. Only the King with the agreement of the *witan*, an assembly made up of the nobility of birth and of men of wealth, created to check or advise the king, could turn such land into *bokland*, that is an inheritable possession. Thus after the Norman conquest, William the Conqueror by the right of conquest was able to claim supreme ownership of all the land of the realm and carry his

principle into practice that all land was the King's to grant as and when he saw fit. Although England was to experience the aberrations of the feudal system, their destructive effects were far more limited than elsewhere.

All this was very much in its infancy at the beginning of the Carolingian Empire. What is important though, is that by the time of Charlemagne's accession to the throne (800 A.D.) the feudal system had sufficiently developed to have established a caste of professional warriors, a military body permanently in being to meet the manifold threats. Their equipment was fairly expensive, and the existing evidence showing just how expensive it was, is indicative of the absence of the cash nexus, because its cost was measured in cows:

Helmet	6 cows
Coat of mail	12 cows
Sword with scabbard	7 cows
Leg armor	6 cows
Lance with shield	2 cows
Horse	12 cows

Forty-five cows were hardly inexpensive. Furthermore for a longer campaign a knight needed to take with him spare horses and in addition to the supplies which he had to provide from his own resources, he required the cart and horse to pull them as well as the driver. Considering the sweep and extent of Charlemagne's campaigns, their cost must have been extraordinary.

Below. *The Royal body guard of King Alfonso III, El Magno of Asturias (866–c 909), with swords, lances and shields (Liber Testamentorum Regium, Oviedo Cathedral).*

Right. *An example of early armor showing mail shirts and conical helmets. The illustration depicts David fighting Goliath and the Philistines (Bible of San Isidore de Lleo, 1162).*

vade & dñs tecu
e sh mtis sius. 7 in
caput eu vestiuit
gladio ei sup ves
harmat' posset in
consuetudine. Dixiq
incedere'. qa nec
ta. ttulit baculum
i manib'. & elegit
lapides de torrete.
vale cm habebat se
7 accessit adunsum
iccedens lapping
ante eu. Cucq ispe
cto. despexit eu.
s i pulcher aspectu.
udo ego canis su
baculo? Et malechi
dixer ad do. Veni
uas uolatilib' celi &
ad filisteu. Tu uem
clipeo? ego aut
exercituu di ag
vodie. & dabit te
peucia te 7 auferã
cadauer castror
lib' celi 7 bestis tr
els misit? 7 mouer
o igladio nec i asta
bellu? 7 tradet uos i
ffilte? & uem
do. festinaurt do

Goliath

Ceciderunteq uulnerand philistim in
uia sari usq ad geth. & usq accaron.

nô. et reusi se
uut isrt cobu
rentes post ali
engenas et con
calcates castra
eorum.

Et reuertentes filii isrt postquam psecu
ti fuerunt filistros iuaser castra eor ds

But the decisive turn which was to determine most of Charlemagne's policy had already been taken by his father Pipin. During his reign the Anglo-Saxon missionaries had begun their campaign to convert the Germans east of the Rhine to Christianity; their leader and outstanding representative was St Boniface, the Englishman from Devonshire who was to become the Apostle of the Germans. Pipin lent the missionaries his full support, because, religious reasons apart, the conversion of the Frisians, Saxons, Thuringians and Bavarians, all of them neighbors of the Franks, would make them less dangerous and easier to incorporate into the Frankish kingdom. St Boniface in that way became the direct link between the Carolingians and the Papacy. The Pope and Pipin needed one another. Pipin was *de facto* King of the Franks, but in a time when the royal title was of divine origin he was in need of having it confirmed *de jure* by the supreme spiritual authority in Christendom. The Pope, on the other hand, was about to break with Byzantium, whose form of Christianity in the light of Catholic orthodoxy was developing into heresy. Furthermore the Longobards to the northeast were increasingly making inroads on papal territory. The Papacy was in need of a secular protector, and who was better suited for that role than the Franks? With the Pope's sanction Pipin was formally crowned King among his assembly of notables. This arrangement of expediency became a fateful connection, determining the course of European history for almost 700 years. When Charlemagne came to the throne the problem of the conversion of the German heathens had not been fully solved. The Saxons presented another major obstruction. Nor was the relationship between the Papacy and the Longobards an easy one. Their conquest by Charlemagne bore no relationship to any concrete interests of the Frankish kingdom. Charlemagne carried it out for the Pope. The Papacy, after its break with Byzantium, and longing for the restoration of the old Roman Imperial Crown, crowned Charlemagne Emperor of the Romans on Christmas Day 800. The Papacy had become the supreme ecclesiastical and political arbiter in Christendom.

More relevant to Frankish interests were the renewed invasions of the Muslims across the Pyrenees. From that struggle was to emerge the famous *Chanson de Roland*, one of the great epics of the Middle Ages. Equally important was Charlemagne's campaign against the heathen Saxons between 779 and 804. The annexation of the Saxon territory was a strategic necessity for the security of the Empire which pushed its frontiers eastward to the Rivers Elbe and Saale. To the east were the Slavs and south of them the Avars, a people of nomadic character who originated in Mongolia. The Saxons had been converted at the point of the sword; 10,000 of their nobles were decapitated on the banks of the River Aller near Verden, but the Avars were completely exterminated. The Slavs were relieved, for the Avars had established a reign of terror over them. The fact that Charlemagne's campaigns were extensive is unfortunately not matched by any major field battles which would give us a true picture of the fighting and the tactics deployed. In the wars against the Saxons, lasting for over 33 years, only two actual battles took place, of which only the place names have been left to posterity, such as Detmold.

Although this would suggest that the Franks were formidably armed, evidence describing the equipment of Charlemagne's forces is very scarce. One commander calling his levy together required that every horseman was to be equipped with shield, lance, dagger, bow and arrows—a rather curious assembly of weapons, since the shield and the lance were bound to get in the way of the bow and arrow in action. The Carolingian knights appear to have used both sword and lance in close combat. The knights were professional warriors, but again there is no evidence to indicate that they subjected themselves to systematic tactical exercises.

When Charlemagne died in 814 he was succeeded by his sole surviving son Louis the Pious. As Louis had three sons the question arose of how the Empire should be divided among Lothair, Louis the German and Pipin, and how in fact an empire could be divided that had one imperial crown. With whom of the three should the imperial dignity rest? Primogeniture did not exist among the Franks. This resulted even during Louis's lifetime in fraternal struggles which rent the empire asunder. The Treaty of Verdun of 843, dividing the empire into three equal shares, was a compromise solution, eliminating in practice the idea of imperial unity. The imperial crown and the center part from Frisia to Italy went to Lothair. Louis the German received Germany, and Charles the Bald, the son of Pipin, France. After Lothair's death the struggle over the inheritance broke out anew until in 911 the last of the east Frankish line of Carolingians died. During that internecine strife the last remnants of the Merovingian administrative institutions, the counties, became feudalized and fiefs were distributed between the various supporters of the contesting parties.

The Empire's weakness coincided with the onslaught of the Norsemen. From 834 onwards they systematically devastated the coast from Frisia to the Gironde, destroying such cities as Nantes, Rouen and Bordeaux. After 855 they advanced up the Elbe, the Seine and the Loire. Taking to horses they erupted into the Auvergne; Amiens, Paris and Orleans were burned. They attacked Spain and Morocco and burned Pisa. In the north they sacked London and advanced to Bedford and York. At the same time Arab corsairs based on Corsica and Sardinia, stormed the towns of Sicily and Calabria, and then ravaged Campagnia and Tuscany. Even Rome was not safe from them.

One of the reasons why these Barbarians from the periphery of Europe could operate almost unopposed—only the Irish are reputed to have put up a stiff fight against the Norsemen—is what one may call the European civil war over the succession to the Carolingian Empire and the Imperial Crown. As long as the Emperor constituted the generally recognized authority, he was in a position to rally together such forces as were needed to meet a particular threat. But once that central authority had been eclipsed and the Kings became dependent on the good will of their counts, bishops and vassals, the picture changed. Only from the vicinity of the area directly under the control of the King could forces be mustered. Nothing or little came from remoter regions unless they themselves were affected by foreign invasion.

The Norsemen, coming from Denmark and Norway, represented a movement whose causes are analogous to that of the Great Migrations. They came from areas which because of their size and climatic conditions could not feed or sustain them at the level of many of the countries in their vicinity. Their total force was considerably smaller than the other Germanic tribes which had preceded them. What made them so terrifying to a society which had moved up several rungs on the ladder of civilization was the confrontation with the original, almost primeval warrior type which many of their forefathers had been when they settled in central and western Europe.

In England the Norse threat welded the Anglo-Saxon states together. In the Frankish Empire after Louis the Pious until 911 the organized will to unite was lacking. Nor was the Frankish military organization prepared and equipped for a threat coming from the sea and up the rivers. The Empire of Charlemagne had never possessed any naval force. Attempts to build one were made but so half-heartedly that four years before Charlemagne's death the Norsemen could invade Frisia, burn and plunder it, and sail off in their boats again before a Frankish force could be assembled. Under Louis the Pious nothing at all was done to secure the seas and the shores of the Empire. The possession of a fleet and their skills in handling it gave the Norsemen advantages which a military organization built exclusively for the purposes of land warfare could not match. The initiative lay with the invader who could appear at any point on the coast or in any river mouth, and the damage was done before countermeasures could be enacted. Attempts were made to turn the peasants into militia, but the feudal system had estranged them sufficiently from the craft of war to render them useless. They were slaughtered as quickly as their livestock. It was more advisable for them to take to their heels, and most of them did.

Thus the Norsemen could make their way down the Rhine, burn Aix-la-Chapelle, make their way down to Koblenz, and then up the Moselle to Trier. The Empire was paralyzed by their appearance and by its preoccupation with the wars for succession under the later Carolingians. Yet even the temporary unification of the Carolingian Empire, under Charles III, when one might have expected a concentrated effort to meet the danger, made no difference.

Charles III was hardly a warrior, and even less a hero. He preferred negotiation, and concluded a treaty with the Norsemen in which their leader, Godfrey, accepted baptism and married a Carolingian princess. In addition, payment in gold and silver was made to them and land was allocated to him and his men in Frisia. When the Norsemen laid siege to Paris Charles appeared with his entire army on the north bank of the Seine and occupied Montmartre. The Norsemen withdrew to the south bank where they remained. Charles avoided battle, concluded a new treaty paying ransom for Paris, and allocated Burgundy to the Norsemen as winter quarters. The disgust among the Frankish nobility was so great that they dethroned Charles.

When Charles had been deposed the western Franks had chosen Odo to be the defender of Paris. As Duke of the Franks he ruled the territory between the Seine and the Loire. But rivalry among the western Franks soon erupted again, the dissenters crowning Charles the Simple. The Norsemen took due advantage. For the rest of the ninth century they devastated the countryside between the Loire and the Rhine. Charles the Simple also preferred compromise to pitched battle; in 911 Jarl Rollo was given permission to settle his warriors and their families in the Caux area. But warlike habits did not die easily. The pursuits of an agricultural life were hardly tempting when the riches of churches, abbeys and monasteries lay at the Norsemen's threshold. They continued their raids in Brittany, Artois and other areas. In the end Rollo claimed the Orne and then the Cotentin peninsula. Normandy was in the making, although the Normans had yet to be absorbed into the feudal system, something which was never fully accomplished. A century later William the Conqueror, recognizing the strengths but even more so the weaknesses of feudal society, set out on the last voyage of major conquest with men of Norse decent and imposed his own version upon England, rather more efficiently practiced there than on the European mainland.

Infantry and cavalry with swords, spears, bow and arrow, and small round shields (Mozarabic ms, tenth century).

The Battle of Stamford Bridge fought in 1066 is here depicted with armor
and heraldry of the thirteenth century. This scene is found in the Chronica
Majorca compiled in about 1250 (Cambridge University Library ms).

ENGLAND AND THE FEUDAL MILITARY SYSTEM

Had not Arlette, the daughter of the tanner of Falaise, captured the passions of Duke Robert of Normandy, there would not have been the offspring William of Normandy (1028–87) and history might have taken a different turn. William was one of the contestants for the English throne after the death of King Edward the Confessor (1004–66). Harold, one of the other two claimants, established himself on the throne first, but allegedly bound by an act of homage, through which he became the vassal of William of Normandy, he had also promised to support William in obtaining the Crown of England, a promise which by his own succession he had broken. Harold claimed the oath was invalid because he had taken it under constraint.

William now decided to reverse the decision. His political preparation included submitting his claims to the Pope for decision. After due examination by the Pope and his Cardinals William's claim was upheld, and a banner was sent to William from the Holy See, consecrated and blessed for the invasion of England. Its conquest became something like a crusade. William's army contained the chivalry of continental Europe of which the Normans considered themselves the elite. The spring and summer of 1066 was full of the sounds of busy preparation in Normandy, Picardy and Brittany. King Harold could not fail to see the threat. He was making preparations to meet it when a Norwegian invasion in the north under King Harold Hardrada landed on the Yorkshire coast, and made its way towards York routing all opposition. The entire region from the Tyne to the Humber submitted to him. Within four days Harold and his army reached Yorkshire and took the Norwegians by surprise. In the Battle of Stamford Bridge the outcome was long in the balance. The English forces were unable to break up the phalanx of the Norwegians until Harold decided upon a stratagem. His English troops pretended to flee and when the Norwegians set after them in pursuit, English formations, held in reserve, burst among them. It was more than a battle; it was a massacre in which the Norwegian King and the flower of his nobility perished.

Many of Harold's best men were lost too, but the most important consequence of the Norwegian invasion and Harold's rush to the north was that William and his host gained an unopposed landing on the Sussex coast. His army when gathered on the English shore is calculated to have amounted to 7000 knights, and 2000 foot soldiers, though it seems that many knights must have fought on foot, since it would have been impossible to arrange transport for so many horses. At first William was delayed by unfavorable winds; it was not till the approach of the equinox that the wind changed from northwest to west and gave William the opportunity to set sail for England. But the wind turned into a gale and many boats were wrecked and lost, causing another short postponement until, with a southerly breeze, the last and final attempt could be made. On 29 September 1066 they landed in Pevensey Bay, between the Castle of Pevensey and Hastings.

Harold was still at York rejoicing over his victory when news of the Norman invasion came. Decimated by battle he hastened immediately southwards to London where he put in a rest period of six days. Then he moved on to meet his foe, who was busily establishing his base. Norman chroniclers describe the preparations on his landing with graphic vigor:

'It (his ship) was called the Mora, and was the gift of his duchess, Matilda. On the head of the ship in the front, which mariners call the prow, there was a brazen child bearing an arrow with a bended bow. His face was turned towards England, and thither he looked, as though he was about to shoot. The breeze came soft and sweet, and the sea was smooth for their landing. The ships ran on dry land, and each ranged by the other's side. There you might see the good sailors, the sergeants and squires sally forth and unload the ships; cast the anchors, haul the ropes, bear out shields and saddles, and land the war-horses and palfreys. The archers came forth, and touched land first, each with his bow strung, and with his quiver full of arrows, slung at his side. All were shaven and shorn; and all clad in short garments, ready to attack, to shoot, to wheel about and skirmish; and they scoured the whole shore but found not an armed man there. After the archers had thus gone forth, the knights landed all armed, with their hauberks on, their shields slung at their necks, and their helmets laced. They formed together on the shore, each armed, and mounted on his war horse: all

Right. *Elevated castle for maritime attack (Vigevano's military treatise, fourteenth century).*

Left. *Miners: the wall has been underpinned and kindling is now being carried in.*

Et sic completa e pratica bona
q̃ ut p̃limũ p maiori ꝑte
catifitiaꝭ erit nitia
ꝺeo de ipa maria ṡicatur
ꝺiligentia. cat

Right. *1600 hours: Harold is killed and the battle is virtually over. Tradition says he is the man on the left, his eye pierced by a Norman's arrow. Modern historians challenge this and using contemporary sources, such as the William of Poitiers ms, believe it more likely that he is the man on the right hacked to death by a Norman sword.*

Below. *Battle scene: the conical helmets with their protective nasals worn by these Norman soldiers were designed for maximum deflection of blows to the head.*

had their swords girded on, and rode forward into the country with their lances raised. Then the carpenters landed, who had great axes in their hands, and planes and axes hung at their sides. They took counsel together, and sought for a good spot to place a castle on. They had brought with them in the fleet, three wooden castles from Normandy, in pieces, all ready for framing together, and they took the materials of one of these out of the ships, all shaped and pierced to receive the pins which they had brought cut and ready in large barrels; and before evening had set in, they had finished a good fort on the English ground and there they placed their stores. All then ate and drunk enough, and were right glad that they were ashore.

When Duke William himself landed, as he stepped on the shore, he slipped and fell forward upon his two hands. Forthwith all raised a loud cry of distress. "An evil sign," said they, "is here." But he cried but lustily, "See! my lords; by the splendor of God, I have taken

possession of England with both my hands. It is now mine; and what is mine is yours."

The next day they marched along the seashore to Hastings. Near that place the Duke fortified a camp and set up two other wooden castles. The foragers, and those looking out for booty, seized all the clothing and provisions they could find, lest what had been brought by the ships should fail them. And the English were to be seen fleeing before them, driving off their cattle, and quitting their houses. Many took shelter in burying places, and even there they were in grievous alarm.'

The main difference between the two armies was that the English army comprised in its majority foot soldiers while many of the Normans were mounted. This emerges clearly from documented sources and the Bayeux Tapestry. For Harold this had one important consequence, he could not afford to meet his enemy on a plain; the mounted knights would have broken them apart. King Harold therefore chose his position on a broad height, surmounted by Battle Abbey, which declined very steeply to the rear making it invulnerable to a mounted attack from behind, while allowing foot soldiery to slip down and take to the adjacent forests in case of a withdrawal or defeat. According to all accounts the Normans were superior in the use of their archery. Most of Harold's army were equipped with swords, spears, battle-axes and the like; most of them were professional warriors and not troops made out of local levies such as the *fyrd*.

After prior fruitless negotiations between William and Harold, on Saturday 14 October, the Normans moved into attack—horsemen, their squires and archers together. As they approached the heights on which Harold was encamped, Norman archers moved to the fore and let loose a hail of arrows, but they were clearly at a disadvantage against the Anglo-Saxons who were throwing their missiles from above; one point in favor of the Normans was that their bows had further range. This was followed by an attack from the mounted knights together with knights on foot, an attack which was slow as it had to be carried out uphill. It was repelled and the Normans were chased back. Partly they turned back because they failed to get through the undergrowth covering the approach quickly enough, but also perhaps because they thought that turning back might tempt the English from their lofty perch. However, their strength lay in their defensive position, but this very strength was also their weakness. No battle can be decided by fighting solely from the defensive. If this was the intention then the Normans succeeded in the same way as Harold had succeeded by his stratagem at Stamford Bridge. As the Chronicler tells us:

'The Normans saw that the English defended themselves well, and were so strong in their position that they could do little against them. So they consulted together privily, and arranged to draw off, and pretend to flee, till the English should pursue and scatter themselves over the field; for they saw that if they could once get their enemies to break their ranks, they might be attacked and discomfited much more easily. As they had said, so they did. The Normans by little and little fled, the English following them. As the one fell back, the other pressed after; and when the Frenchmen retreated, the English thought and cried out, that the men of France fled, and would never return.

Thus they were deceived by the pretended flight, and great mischief thereby befell them; for if they had not moved from their position, it is not likely that they would have conquered at all; but like fools they broke their lines and pursued.

The Normans were to be seen following up their stratagem, retreating slowly so as to draw the English further on. As they still flee, the English pursue, they push out their lances and stretch forth their hatchets; following the Normans, as they go rejoicing in their success of their scheme, and scattering themselves over the plain. And the English meantime jeered and insulted their foes with words. "Cowards," they cried, "you came hither in an evil hour, wanting our lands, and seeking to seize our property, fools that ye were to come! Normandy is too far off, and you will not easily reach it. It is of little use to run back; unless you can cross the sea at a leap, or can drink it dry, your sons and daughters are lost to you."

The Normans bore it all, but in fact they knew not what the English said; their language seemed like the baying of dogs, which they could

The cavalry sets off at a gallop covered in front by a body of archers (The Bayeaux Tapestry). The Norman army eventually won at Hastings owing to the superiority of their cavalry and bowmen.

not understand. At length they stopped and turned round, determined to recover their ranks; and the barons might be heard crien Dex Aie! for a halt. Then the Normans resumed their former position, turning their faces towards the enemy; and their men were to be seen facing round and rushing onwards to a fresh mêlée; the one party assaulting the other, this man striking, another pressing onwards. One hits, another misses; one flies, another pursues; one is aiming a stroke, while another discharges his blow. Norman strives with Englishman again, and aims his blows afresh. One flies, another pursues swiftly: the combatants are many, the plain wide and the mêlée fierce. On every hand they fight hard, the blows are heavy, and the struggle becomes fierce. The Normans were playing their part well, when an English knight came rushing up, having in his company a hundred men, furnished with various arms. He wielded a northern hatchet, with the blade a full foot long; and was well armed after his manner, being tall, bold and of noble carriage. In the front of the battle where the Normans thronged most, he came bounding on swifter than the stag, many Normans falling before him and his company. He rushed straight upon a Norman who was armed and riding on a war-horse, and tried with his hatchet of steel to cleave his helmet; but the blow miscarried, and the sharp blade glanced down before the saddle-bow, driving through the horse's neck down to the ground, so that both horse and master fell together to the earth. I do not know whether the Englishman struck another blow; but the Normans who saw the stroke were astonished, and about to abandon the assault when Roger de Montgomeri came galloping up, with his lance set, and heeding not the long-handled axe, which the Englishman wielded aloft, struck him down and left him stretched upon the ground. Then Roger cried out, "Frenchmen, strike! The day is ours!" And again a fierce mêlée was to be seen, with many a blow of lance and sword; the English still defending themselves, killing the horses and cleaving the shields.

There was a French soldier of noble mien, who sat his horse gallantly. He spied two Englishmen who were also carrying themselves boldly. They were both men of great worth, and had become companions in arms and fought together, the one protecting the other. They bore two long and broad bills (halberds), and did great mischief to the Normans, killing both horses and men. The French soldier looked at them and their bills, and was sore alarmed, for he was afraid of losing his good horse, the best that he had; and would willingly have turned to some other quarter, if it would not have looked like cowardice. He soon, however, recovered his courage, and spurring his horse gave him the bridle, and galloped swiftly forward. Fearing the two bills, he raised his shield, and struck one of the Englishmen with his lance on the breast, so that iron passed out at his back. At the moment

that he fell, the lance broke, and the Frenchman seized the mace that hung on his right side, and struck the other Englishman a blow that completely broke his skull. . . .

And now might be heard the loud clang and cry of battle, and the clashing of lances. The English stood firm in their barricades, and shivered the lances, beating them into pieces with their bills and maces. The Normans drew their swords, and hewed down the barricades, and the English in great trouble fell back upon their standard, where they collected the maimed and the wounded.

There were many knights from Chauz, who jousted and made attacks. The English knew not how to joust, or bear arms on horseback, but fought with hatchets and bills. A man, when he wanted to strike with one of their hatchets, was obliged to hold it with both hands, and could not at the same time, as it seems to me, both cover himself and strike with any freedom.

The English fell back towards the standard which was upon rising ground, and the Normans followed them across the valley, attacking them on foot and horseback. Then Hue de Mortemer, with the sires D'Auviler, D'Onebac, and St Cler, rode up and charged, overthrowing many.

Robert Fitz Erneis fixed his lance, took his shield, and, galloping towards the standard, with his keen-edged sword struck an Englishman who was in front, killed him, and then drawing back his sword, attacked many others, and pushed straight for the standard, trying to beat it down, but the English surrounded it, and killed him with their bills. He was found on the spot, when they afterwards sought him, dead, and lying at the standard's foot.

Duke William pressed close upon the English with his lance; striving hard to reach the standard with the great troop he led; and seeking earnestly for Harold, on whose account the whole war was. The Normans follow their lord, and press around him; they ply their blows upon the English; and these defend themselves stoutly, striving hard with their enemies, returning blow for blow. . . .

And now the Normans pressed on so far, that at last they reached the standard. There Harold had remained, defending himself to the utmost, but he was sorely wounded in his eye by the arrow, and suffered grievous pain from the blow. An armed man came in the throng of the battle, and struck him on the ventaille of his helmet, and beat him to the ground; and as he sought to recover himself, a knight beat him down again, striking him on the thick of his thigh, down to the bone. . . .

From 0900 hours until evening the English shield-wall withstood the Norman attack at Hastings. Then a ruse by the Norman cavalry made them break their ranks and they were eventually routed and roundly defeated (The Bayeux Tapestry).

The standard was beaten down, the golden standard was taken, and Harold and the best of his friends were slain; but there was so much eagerness, and throng of so many around, seeking to kill him, that I know not who it was that slew him.

The English were in great trouble at having lost their King, and at the duke's having conquered and beat down the standard; but they still fought on, and defended themselves long, and in fact till the day drew to a close. Then it clearly appeared to all that the standard was lost, and the news spread throughout the army that Harold for certain was dead; and all saw that there was no longer any hope so they left the field, and those fled who could. . . .'

William had conquered: Harold and his two brothers were slain. Both Normans and English had excelled themselves in valor, but the Normans, experienced warriors on horseback, were militarily the superior force. Two feudal professional armies had met and thus settled the future fate of the island. That the English Army was a professional force is beyond doubt. A military organization based on the old Germanic local levy, the *fyrd*, would hardly have given William seventeen days in which he established his base entirely undisturbed. William left the initiative to Harold while he completed his armaments. With the Anglo-Saxon army vanquished he proceeded to subject the country to his rule and on Christmas Day 1066 was crowned King. Realizing the importance of historical consciousness, legitimacy and continuity he had himself elected king by his vassals, claiming to be the rightful successor of Edward the Confessor. By accepting the past, he secured the formality of election by the witan and was consecrated by an Anglo-Saxon bishop.

William had been elected by his vassals and followers, much in the same way as Henry of Saxony had been elected by his dukes as King of Germany more than a century before. But there was one vital difference. Henry's dukes were his equals, each commanding his own territorial base of power. In 1066 William conquered England as the leader of a comparatively small group of alien adventurers whose power other than that given to them by William was negligible. One of William's first actions was to lay claim to the whole of the land of the realm. It was his conquest, and therefore his property. During his reign on basically still hostile soil, it lay in the interest of William's vassals to cooperate, they only stood to gain by it. And follow-

ing the practice already established by the last of the Anglo-Saxon Kings, he avoided handing land to his vassals in large compacts that would have allowed them to develop the power of their own house and thus become potential rivals. Of course any monarchy is as strong as the man who heads it. England was lucky enough to have a succession of strong Kings for more than half a century after the conquest. After that time the negative features of the feudal system became operative, but never as strongly and with such consequences as, for instance, in Germany.

William parceled out the land to his tenants-in-chief in return for military service; they in turn divided it up into knight's fees, each fee to be used to raise, equip and support a knight. William himself was not greatly concerned about how the knights were found, as long as they were found, properly trained and equipped. However, by the end of the eleventh century it was still common for barons to hold knights in their household. Those to abandon this custom first were abbeys and monasteries, to whom the presence of men-at-arms at their establishment was bound to be a nuisance. In place of the knights they were supposed to supply, they paid scutage, the money equivalent needed for raising them. But the process of dividing up baronial estates into knights' fees was only completed towards the end of the reign (1100–35) of Henry I when the first signs became evident that the custom was being abused. Royal vassals enfeoffed more knights than they were actually required to do. The Bishop of Lincoln in place of the 60 knights he was charged to provide, had enfeoffed 102. Henry took immediate steps to have the number reduced, as he was setting out for a prolonged visit to France and wanted to be sure of the loyalty of his Anglo-Norman knighthood.

The size of a knight's fee varied, ranging between four and eight-and-a-half hides of land. But extremes at either end of the scale were not unknown. In total the feudal army thus raised in England varied between 5000 and 7000 knights, added to which must come those knights recruited on a mercenary basis, which took place in England from the twelfth century onwards. But knighthood, the distinguishing military institution of the feudal age, was now also firmly established on English soil.

On the European mainland, much more so than in the British Isles, the instrument of the territorial organization of the vassal was his land from which he derived his power. His most profitable domains were equipped with castles and fortifications, which in turn became the centers of their military, economic and judicial organization. As we can see from the castles still in existence in Europe they were of large construction surrounded by high walls, with ample room for stores and accommodation for a garrison of mounted men. The supply of castle and garrison was the responsibility of the peasants of the region for whose protection the castles, at least in part, had been built. The power of the continental territorial landholder was considerably stronger than that of the King. Kingship was elective, a dukedom inheritable within the family. In England each successor to a deceased tenant-in-chief had to render an act of homage to the King, the sole owner of the land, whereupon he was enfeoffed with the territory of his predecessor; the proprietary right to the land was still the King's. No King in France or Germany could lay such a claim.

Originally, according to ancient Germanic custom, all free men could and should bear arms. But there were freemen and freemen, those who lived from the property they actually possessed and those, the original vassals, who lived from the land with which they were enfeoffed, land which was not inheritable except when a son was available who would be ready to take up the duties of his father. In case of the extinction of the

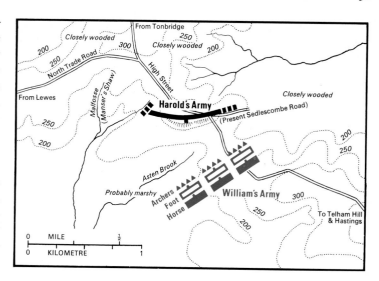

The Battle of Hastings, 1066.

male line the land reverted to the feudal lord, or at a higher level, to the King. However, by the tenth century in both Germany and France, the inheritability of a territorial fief had become customary. Service in arms meant a privileged position *vis-à-vis* those who tilled the soil. Military service became concentrated in those families who had always provided the knights in the first place, and from that originated military nobility of birth. The vassals of a King or prince who may have advised him on matters other than warfare, who may in fact have been precursors of higher civil servants, the ministeriales, also held their territorial fiefs, and began to provide knights for the King. In that way the military and the administrative nobility fused on the basis of the possession of land, and during the course of the thirteenth century possession of fiefs was restricted only to the nobility. The nobility was the army; the knight paid no taxation to his lord because his service for holding the land was his military service, a principle which in varying degrees and variations existed in European society until the French Revolution, the principle of the exemption from taxation of the nobility. Hence the fiscal burdens and other non-military services hit the peasant and the towns hardest particularly after the towns began to recover economically.

Yet it would be mistaken to imagine the life of a medieval knight as having been particularly comfortable. Their fiefs secured them only a modest living. Their equipment could hardly be called a luxury. They were frequently at war, if not in the host of the King, then much more often in that of their immediate lord, be he baron, graf, or duke to settle one of the many differences or feuds between feudal lords. Indeed it has been argued that one of the main motivations behind calling for the Crusades was the attempt by the Church to channel off the energies dissipated in the civil wars of feudal Europe into one major effort beneficial to Christendom as a whole and to the individual souls of the knights in particular.

Even knightly tournaments were not as peaceful as one might imagine. One chronicler of the twelfth century records that ten brothers of his father were killed in one tournament, giving rise to a serious feud which, before Church and prince could settle the matter, claimed many more victims. Intellectually the knight could lay no claims to distinction, nor did he desire it otherwise. Literacy and the arts were taught only at the abodes of the highest of the nobility. Nor can it be said that all the virtues associated with the age of chivalry were present in the medieval knight at the end of the eleventh century. That was an age which was yet to come.

THE SOCIAL AND MILITARY ASPECTS OF KNIGHTHOOD

The ceremony of dubbing or the accolade which formally elevated a warrior to a knight originated in old Germanic custom which used this method or a formal proclamation to announce that a young man was able to bear arms and considered suitable. Among the Goths, the Visigoths and the Franks, but probably also among most of the other tribes, the ceremony was performed at the age of twelve or fourteen. However, with the growing use of heavy horses and the increasing weight of the armor, the age moved upward to about twenty. Sometimes, of course, the accolade would be given to an auxiliary warrior of non-noble descent in reward for a particular distinction in the field of battle. The aspiring knight first had to undergo a lengthy period in which he was trained, and in which he also grew strong enough to carry heavy armor, fight in it and control his horse. From the twelfth century to the end of the Middle Ages, knighthood represented its own estate; throughout Christian Europe it was a kind of closed corporation, socially cutting across the frontiers of national descent, a characteristic shown by the European aristocracy as a whole.

The outward trappings of a knight were his knight belt and golden spurs. The belt as a symbol of the warrior class is of Germanic origin. In the early phase of knighthood, it was the privilege of every knight to elevate to knighthood by accolade any man he thought fit; accessibility to the corporation was still relatively easy. But in the twelfth century this changed; only one who was of knightly parentage could become a knight. Louis VI of France is said to have ordered that any knight not of such parentage should have his spurs hewn off on the dung heap. Frederick Barbarossa expressly prohibited the sons of priests(!) and of peasants from taking the sword-belt. The knighthood of Italy, in so far as it was Italian born, was the object of contempt and derision for centuries because the Italian cities made knights of the sons of artisans. The Order of the Templars refused the white mantle to anyone not of knightly birth—rather in contrast to the Order of the Teutonic knights later. The material consequence of being deprived of one's knighthood was the deprivation of the fief held, in other words, the destruction of the knight's economic security.

No knight could take service and a fief from his equal, since that would have made him dependent upon a person who, by being a knight, was subject to the same services. The right to enfeoff was firstly that of the Emperor or King, secondly that of the ecclesiastical princes, thirdly that of the lay princes, fourthly that of the counts, and, according to region and country, that of

Below. *Ceremony of knighthood.*

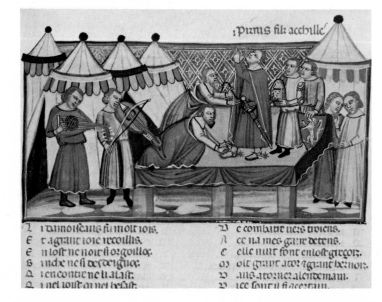

Above. *For safety and comfort while fighting on foot, knights wore doublets sewn with patches of mail beneath their armor.*

several other bodies of knightly nobility. The accolade as such would have been little more than a favor or a distinction had it not been tied to the condition to give proof of one's noble descent. In that way the accolade became an instrument of social integration and social exclusiveness, the affirmation that those who had received it belonged to the ruling class.

In England the knights were under much greater control from the monarchy than either in France or in Germany. A significant indication of that is the very term knight, derived from the German *Knecht*, connoting menial or bondman, while the German *Ritter* and the French *chevalier* literally state that they are mounted men. The knight had his shield bearer, the *knappe* or *escuyer*, the esquire who in many if not most cases was himself of knightly descent, serving his apprenticeship for knighthood in this role. In addition he had his groom, plus a lightly armed warrior for scouting purposes, and one or two foot soldiers.

This indicates that the knights were not the only warriors, but rather the upper class of the feudal army. But physical prowess, bravery and other warlike virtues can never be the exclusive property of one class, or the lack of these virtues that of another. The friction arising out of that dilemma was never fully resolved. Sons of knights who proved to be physically as well as psychically unsuited to the profession of knightly service were moved on into the priesthood or into monasteries, while the esquires supplied the fresh blood for the knighthood. Also on occasions the exclusiveness of knightly origin was broken by Emperors or Kings awarding the accolade for particularly distinguished service. There is ample evidence that such a breach of the existing rules caused protest in many quarters especially in the thirteenth century, one noble ridiculed such knights as 'scarecrows turned into knights.' On the other hand, when Frederick Barbarossa wanted to give the accolade to a particularly deserving warrior outside Tortona in 1155, the man concerned refused on the grounds that he was of low estate and should prefer to remain part of it.

Knighthood, then, is a product of many sources, some going

Above. *European sword or long dagger (fourteenth century).*

back to the tribal traditions of the Germanic tribes, but its development into a specific class has its source in the technological transformation of war. During the reign of Charlemagne, helmet, mail shirt and shield were still relatively light. But throughout the Middle Ages armor increased in weight. Whereas at first the shield was the main protection, armor increased in complexity. The helmet acquired a visor, and to the mail shirt, which originally had left the neck unprotected, armor plate was added until trunk, arms and legs were covered by armor, and finally the horse as well. Range was increased by longer and heavier lances, and the horses had to be strong, steady and sturdy to sustain the weight. The cost of all this must have been immense. Thus the economic basis, the fief, had to be sufficiently large to pay for it.

The Romans had won their campaigns employing coherent, disciplined bodies of men, tactically trained and exercised. The medieval battle was decided by the personal bravery and ability of the individual knights. They represented the main body of the army, but the heavy armor carried its own inherent limitations. When forced to fight on foot the knight could do so only in a very limited manner. Armor prevented him from charging forth afoot. Nor could he use the bow. Like modern tanks which are transported by rail or road to as near the battle zone as possible to keep down the wear and tear, so the knight's battle horse was saved for the final encounter to avoid tiring it, and it was not uncommon for a knight to have several horses in his train. Knights were incapable of carrying out the tasks of light warfare. For that purpose both foot troops and light cavalry were needed. Hence we find lightly armored cavalry forces equipped with sword and bow, and on foot, archers and men with the crossbow and swords. They were the auxiliary forces, the deployment of which was handled masterfully by William the Conqueror at Hastings. In most parts of France and Germany they re-emerged only in the course of the twelfth century as mounted bowmen, mainly as a result of the Crusades. But the soldiers on foot are in no way comparable to the

infantry of antiquity. They did not operate independently but solely fulfilled an auxiliary function. Until Courtrai the actual decision of battle lay with the knights, never with the *Fussvolk*. The knights were the army; the rest is subsidiary to it. They were a professional as well as social caste. The importance of this is born out time and again. For example, Emperor Frederick II called upon his son to send him knights, because in the knights resided the fame of the Empire and the strength of his power, or again one vassal was called upon to provide 15 esquires, 'good people, born to the shield.' The knight alone was *the warrior*. Emperors and Kings were knights; women apart, their entire court consisted of knights. The chief vassals—princes, dukes and counts—were knights, and bishops and abbots surrounded themselves with them. The only other estate represented in that society is the clergy. We do not find a single example of a knight laying down his sword belt to retire and

Above. *Mail shirt and aventail, 1340.*

Left. *Rowelspur, 1370.*

Left. *Servants gird medieval knights with swords.*

Right. *Two horsemen tilting with lances in a public exercise of their prowess* (Histoire du Graal).

Far right. *Battle scene* (Histoire du Graal).

Below right. *Mounted-man-at-arms, a scene from a North French manuscript illustrating the Apocalypse (thirteenth century).*

attend to the cultivation of the soil. However, there are many examples of knights retiring into monasteries.

At the beginning of the Carolingian period many knights were still known to reside in urban communities, in the towns that sprung up around burghs or castles, such as those founded as frontier defense posts by King Henry I of Germany. The *Burggraf* actually headed the town. In the early fourteenth century, in the Flemish cities, the lower knightly nobility were the allies of the burghers and artisans who, in an uprising equivalent almost to the Sicilian Vespers, tried to rid their towns of the Francophile upper bourgeoisie and French overlordship in general. Many former servants of knights settled in towns and cities to pursue trade and commerce, or a particular craft. But it seems that over the centuries the vast majority of the knights remained

on the land, on their fief, the basis of their economic and social power.

The Middle Ages knew hardly any example of the common military training of European knighthood. What thorough training they received was imparted individually, and a special profession developed: those who did nothing other than to train the sons of knights for their future task and position. First this training took place within the family, and then on active service with a knight, as his esquire for example.

Tournaments were the public exercises in which the up-and-coming future knights could display their ability. Over the years these became encounters which on occasion could be extremely fierce when it became customary to use sharp instead of blunted weapons. The tournament reflected in some aspects

real battle conditions. As in battle the horses did not charge at full speed; considering the weight they carried this would have been impossible. The knights rode together but not in a tactical formation, the prerequisite of which would have been joint tactical training, something the mounted knights of the Middle Ages never knew.

Nor did the knight know the discipline of a drilled formation. The feudal state knew order and subordination; it knew obedience, but *not* what was understood as military discipline in the Roman armies and in the armies of the European territorial states from the seventeenth century onward. Discipline is based upon command and carries with it, if the command is not obeyed, the power to punish. It implies the full command of the commander in chief over his army, its officers and generals. The medieval prince, by comparison, was rather weak in power. He could exert pressure on his vassal. He could deprive him of territory previously granted by him, as was the case when Frederick Barbarossa deprived Henry the Lion of his Bavarian possession because Henry refused to support the Emperor on his crusade. What Frederick Barbarossa could not do was to deprive him of his Dukedom of Saxony. Henry the Lion stayed at home, considering it more important to pursue the colonization of his eastern marches than to waste his resources on a far-off

Left. Composite armor from Schloss Churburg, Germany.

Right. Mounted man-at-arms and horse in full armor. The horse has a protective 'chauffron' over its head.

tary realities of the Middle Ages. Nor were there any articles of war governing the behavior of the knights during a campaign. During the First Crusade keeping the host of knights together was a greater problem than meeting the enemy in combat. The sack of Constantinople had nothing to do with the aims of the crusade and little to do with trying to vanquish heresy among Christendom, but much more to do with the desire for loot among the unruly knighthood.

Once their spoils declined, the moment they felt the economic pinch, declining agricultural production through bad harvests, or depopulation through disease, many a chivalrous knight of the Middle Ages saw it by no means dishonorable to waylay the merchant trains, or hold towns to ransom, to use the slightest pretext to feud with the object of hopefully making booty.

The right to call a feud lay with every freeman of country or town. It was possible, and did in fact happen, that bakers, cooks and kitchen-boys announced a feud with their regional nobility, who usually had a sense of humor and ignored it. Some general laws about the feud did exist; for example it had to be proclaimed three days before actually beginning. A feud announced applied not only to the person who had given cause for it; it applied to his kith and kin, to his servants, free and unfree, as well as to the entire community which might want to assist and protect him. If the object of the feud was a town, then it applied to all its inhabitants. In the fourteenth century it was common usage that prisoners taken in a feud could be killed, if keeping them alive would endanger one's own life, and the vanquished in a feud lost his property. At a higher level, the prisoners of an Emperor, King or prince became his servants.

The property of the loser was that of the victor, including people that were unarmed. Accounts are frequent of entire harvests having been ravaged, villages burned down, livestock driven away, the peasants either killed or carried away as serfs. Only Christian women were not allowed to be touched. They were left their clothes and other parts of their wardrobe. In the conquest of castles an even greater degree of chivalry is alleged to have prevailed. The ladies, apart from their wardrobe, were also allowed to keep their jewelry. Whether this rule was always observed is a little doubtful. The wars of medieval Europe were mostly caused by family feuds among and between related dynasties. The wars of the Plantagenets in France, the Hundred Years' War, the wars between Germany and France, the Bohemians and the Hungarians all started as family feuds. Large armies banded together, but scarcely fought more than one major battle, after which they drifted home again, both because of the lack of money to keep the army in the field, and because the vassals were anxious to get back at the earliest possible time. In the history of the Holy Roman Empire of the German Nation there is not one Emperor who succeeded in persuading all his vassals to support him on a campaign. Strongly fortified towns were difficult to conquer. In 1447 the city of Nuremberg conducted a feud with the majority of the German princes. The city then comprised 20,000 inhabitants; the struggle lasted for three years, Nuremberg surviving because the princes never thought of laying siege to it. Sometimes when a town captured its feuding opponent it dealt with him leniently because to do so was to its own advantage. In 1373 the knight Hennele von Streif proclaimed his feud against Worms, because the city had captured two waylaying robber knights whom it promptly hanged. Hennele found support among the knights of the castles in the vicinity and began to despoil the countryside around Worms. For the burghers of Worms this was rather too costly. They cut their losses by taking Hennele into their service at a price of 200 guilders annually, and Hennele subsequently

adventure. Even the Italian communes swore an oath to Frederick Barbarossa, after he had restored his position there, in which they promised to carry out every order of the Emperor which he gave *in the exercise of his rights*. In other words, they were not prepared to obey *any* order. The fief could be withdrawn by the lord, a process which was more easily done further down the feudal pyramid than near the top where the vassals were princes of territories which their ancestors had owned long before a kingdom of France or Germany existed. The Norman dynasty in England had the advantage of being able by what one might call—grossly oversimplified, of course—one vast act of expropriation to assume all land and thus make themselves into the sole source of power.

When family quarrels tore the dynasty apart, as under the successors of Charlemagne or under the Saxon Kings, both under Otto the Great and in the eleventh century under Henry IV, the weakness at the apex of the feudal pyramid was felt down to its very bottom. The centrifugal forces inherent in the feudal system began to be felt disastrously, and could only be curbed but never retarded by another strong dynasty or monarch. Exceptions to this pattern were the knightly orders, such as the Templars and later the Teutonic Knights, orders which had firm rules which had to be obeyed to the letter, rules derived from the Order of the Cistercians of St Bernard of Clairvaux the initiator of the Cluniac monastic reform movement.

Military discipline therefore was an artificial product, inapplicable to and contradicted by the political, social and mili-

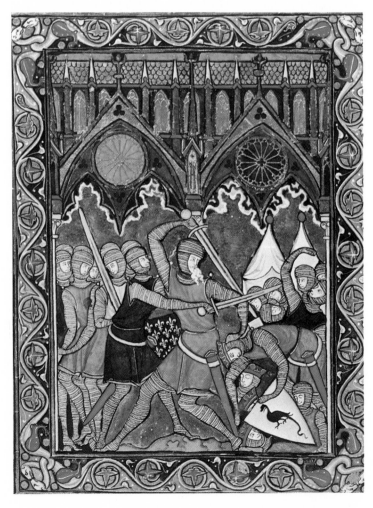

Left. *Foot soldiers in armor* (Psautier de St Louis, *1270*).

Above. *Horseback battle scene* (Histoire du Graal*)*.

Left. *Four mail-clad men-at-arms slaughter Thomas à Becket. Their attire is a good example of the armor of the period.*

proved to be a very loyal and efficient servant of the interests of the city of Worms.

While the cities took recourse to a feud only as a last resort—commercially in the long run they stood to lose more—for princes and nobility it was a source of income, and needless to say even more for the lower rungs among the knighthood. Many of the medieval feuders became infamous. Only very few remained alive in popular folklore, like Apel of Gailingen, a knight renowned for the frequency with which he sought feuds with financially rewarding victims, as well as for his waylaying activities. His major enemy was the city of Nuremberg, into which he rode one day, halting before a smithy to have his horse shoed. As the smith completed the work Apel asked him to whom the pair of boots hanging at the gate of the city wall belonged. He got the reply that these were Apel of Gailingen's boots. Apel pulled them down, thrashed the guard at the gate with them and told him to tell the magistrate that Apel had come back to fetch his boots. Freebooting stood at one of the extremes of the development of medieval knighthood.

If one looks at the military aspect of medieval knighthood one finds that the warriors of Charlemagne and Otto the Great had much in common. They bore much the same weapons and were not excessively heavily armed. They were prepared, and capable if need be, to fight on foot. This also holds true of the Normans of William the Conqueror. Foot soldiers as such, and men equipped with bows were the exception rather than the rule. From the late eleventh century however, a greater degree of differentiation can be noted between heavy cavalry, light cavalry, bowmen on foot and sword fighters on foot. Theoretically two possibilities of their deployment were possible. To group each arm, if we can call it that, separately, or simply to group them around the main body of the army, the armed knights. Hastings seems to have been an illustration of a partial application of the first possibility, but generally the application of the second dominated. Not one of the auxiliary branches would have been able to engage the mounted knights. The light cavalry, almost unarmed, was no match in combat for the heavily armed knights unless they fought with bow and arrow, which they did not. The one with the greatest chance of engaging the knight at a distance was the bowman on foot. That would have required very strong nerves, because he had to let the knight come quite close for the arrow to be lethal (the kind of nerve required in the Second World War to let a Russian T-34 tank come into a range of 40 feet and then launch the *Panzerfaust*). The greater the safe distance between knight and bowman the surer was his own survival. Therefore a body of bowmen without being covered and protected by the heavy knights, or by protection afforded by geography as in Wales and Ireland, faced no alternative other than its own destruction.

Another opportunity among those on foot lay with the warrior with a blank hand weapon. What havoc they could cause with their axes or halberds we have seen in the Norman chronicler's account of the Battle of Hastings. With strong nerve, good luck, and circumspection they could get at the horseman from the side by killing the horse and dismounting him. Should the knight not have been killed as a result of being trapped by the horse, he would still have been at a position advantageous to the footman, because of his lack of physical maneuverability constrained as he was by his armor. Also troops of foot soldiers forming up as groups with the use of spears and pikes could ward off the heavy cavalry, but once a gap was cut the infantry was lost.

In fact prior to the Hussites and the Swiss the only offensive actions by infantry against mounted hosts of knights seem to have been the Battle of Courtrai in 1302 when the Flemish cities won over the French and the Battle of Bannockburn in 1314 when the Scots defeated the forces of King Edward II. For the rest, the function of the foot soldiery was always subsidiary and auxiliary in function. Therefore they were deployed to support to the best of their ability the action of the main arm, which was the only arm expected to bring about a decision. They operated partly on the flanks and partly mixed within the main con-

Below. *European armor in the Middle Ages.*

Above. *Foot soldiers prepare for battle.*

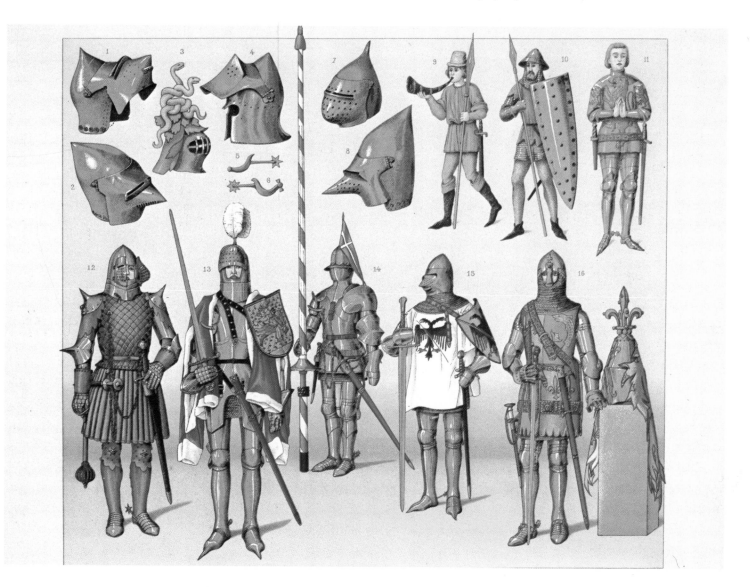

tingent. In this manner foot formations appeared in the battles of the Middle Ages.

It has been suggested that these auxiliary arms were of three-fold origin. Among them we find those of the old warrior class who did not become part of the knighthood; secondly, the burghers of the cities anxious to obtain training and experience in the profession of arms entered the medieval host as pikemen and bowmen; thirdly, of course, they were recruited from every knight's immediate entourage in the field, his esquire and other servants who until the twelfth century had remained non-combatants. For a knight, heavy and clumsy on his horse, it must have been an asset to have by his side a rather more flexible individual.

The nature of the mixed forces and their respective tasks are illustrated in a speech which Charles of Anjou is claimed to have made to his soldiers before the Battle of Benevent in 1226. He advised his men that it was more important to hit the horses than the men; deprived of their horse the enemy, almost immovable in his armor, could be easily felled by the foot fighters. Therefore every horsemen should be accompanied by one or two of his entourage, and if there were no others they should hire a mercenary, because experienced in war they would understandably kill horses as well as their toppled masters.

As the cavalry with its slow pace caused by the heavy armor rode on, it was not difficult for a footman to keep pace. The chronicler of Henry II's conquest of Ireland, Giraldus Cambrensis, renders a good account of the different systems. Although the Normans had understood perfectly how to transfer their military system to England it was quite different from that encountered in Wales and in Ireland. While the Normans sought the open plain, the Welsh and the Irish preferred mountainous territory, or simply as difficult a physical terrain as possible. The Normans preferred the field; their opponents preferred the woods. The Normans armed themselves heavily which was quite suitable for open combat, but along narrow, mountainous paths, in swamp-infested woodland, he who travels light travels easiest. The warrior on foot had the advantage over the warrior on horse. This was even more true if he were armored, for it would be difficult to dismount on a forest path, let alone fight.

A knight and his immediate entourage in combat were generally called a lance. Precisely how many there were to a lance is impossible to say, perhaps up to ten men. However, medieval chroniclers, or for that matter the commanders of the feudal host, counted the number of their army not by the total number of combatants present but solely by the number of knights, an important illustration of the military and social importance of the role of the knight.

In battle the bowmen advanced ahead of the knights and did as much damage to the enemy as possible, but still proceeded close enough to the cavalry to be able to withdraw quickly into the folds of its protection, as demonstrated in 1066 at Hastings. Pikemen, or foot soldiers with sword, adopted the role of advance guard if they had to clear away obstacles designed to delay or hold off the cavalry. At Hastings they were clearly not warriors with pikes but only with swords. Knights fought on foot only under rather exceptional circumstances, as in many engagements in Crusades when the supply of horses had become scarce.

The knights did not range themselves in any particular tactical order. They just advanced on their mounts with little attention being paid to a straight linear approach. Only the Order of the Templars had issued a rule saying that no brother was to attack on his own initiative or to ride outside the formation. They did not attack like modern cavalry, aiming at achieving maximum impact and maintaining, insofar as this was possible, the impetus of the attack. Instead they rode on slowly to engage the enemy riding equally as slowly towards them in combat. The medieval battle compared with those of later periods must almost have been a slow-motion study of individual combat, of knights encased in their armor slowly raising their heavy weapons and bringing them down on their opponents. It must have been a far cry from the speed, cut and thrust operations of the cavalry engagements of the eighteenth century.

Left. *Rustic vassals conscripted into the army as foot soldiers formed an invaluable part of any fighting force. (Latin ms 1390, eleventh century).*

Below. *Armor-clad knights armed with lances and hafted arms ride slowly to engage in individual combat with their opponents. Compared with the speed of eighteenth-century cavalry engagements, these medieval operations must have seemed like studies in slow motion.*

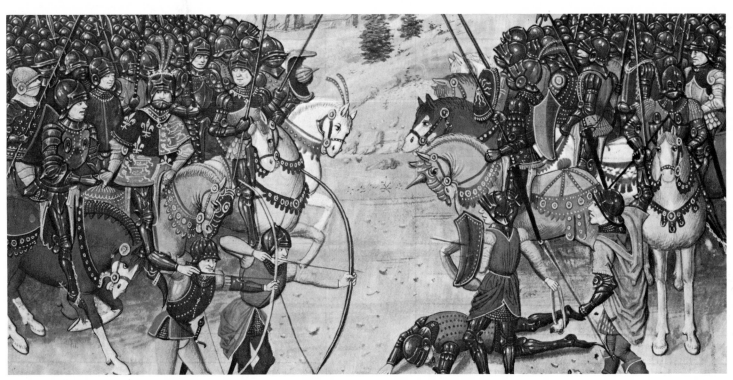

*Close-up of horseback battle scene (*Histoire du Voyage et Conquête de Jerusalem, *1337).*

THE CRUSADES

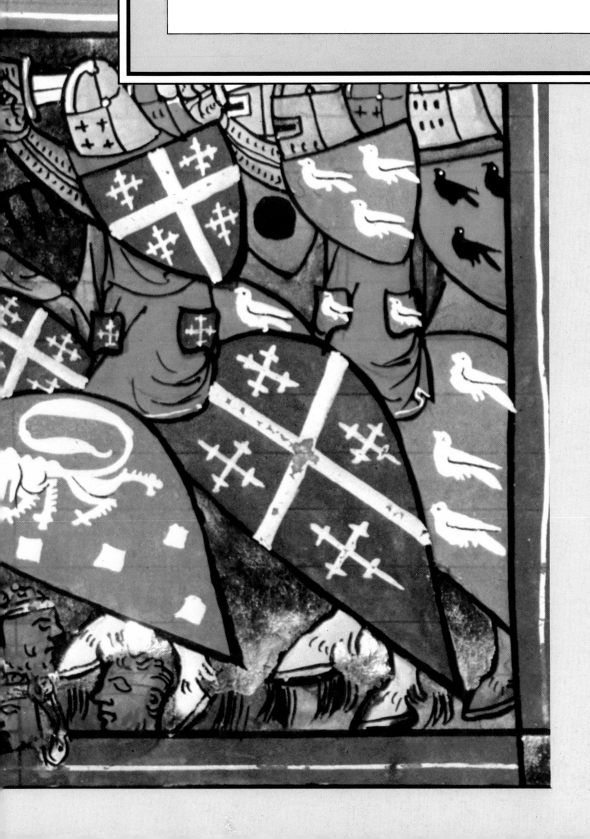

Pope Gregory VII had seen it as his life's task to unite Christendom under papal supremacy. Canossa on the one hand, his death in exile on the other, are the hallmarks of the victory as well as defeat of his policy. It was up to his second successor, Pope Urban II, to issue the call on all knights of Christendom to take up arms against the infidel who were in possession of the Holy Land and to reconquer it. But the original idea for a Crusade goes back to Gregory, when he received an appeal by Emperor Michael VII of Constantinople for assistance against Turks and Muslims. For Gregory it must have been an ideal opportunity to attain his three major aims: firstly, to subject the heretic Eastern Church to Rome; secondly, to turn the Kings and princes of Christendom into his vassals under the banner of a Crusade; and thirdly, by the Crusade itself to retrieve the land from which Christianity had sprung forth and return it to its rightful owners. His preoccupation with Emperor Henry IV in the investiture contest dominated all other activities. Added to the Papacy's own motives for a crusade came other factors such as the rapid rise of a feudal aristocracy in Europe, which tended to pervade the surrounding regions, the growth of the cities and the rise of their prosperity with a population eager for mercantile expansion.

Christianity's counterattack against Islam had already begun. Perhaps Charles Martel can be considered its first representative. But in the eleventh century the Genoese and the Pisans had driven out the Muslims from Sardina and thus achieved supremacy of the Tyrrhenian Sea. The Normans had begun to gain a foothold in southern Italy which they were quick to expand in order to conquer Sicily from there in 1060, a task not accomplished until 1091. On the Iberian peninsula the attack was well under way as well. The Ommiad Caliphate of

Right. *Crusader. (Westminster psalter, twelfth century).*

Below. *Knights before and during battle (*Histoire du Voyage et Conquête de Jerusalem, *1337).*

Above. Battle outside the walls of a town (Egyptian ms, twelfth century).

Below. Crusaders, c 1100.

Cordova, after reaching its height and splendor in the early tenth century, had broken apart, leaving behind a number of independent emirates. This had provided the opportunity for a Christian offensive. At the eastern end of the Pyrenees Charlemagne's Spanish March had become the county of Barcelona. To the west the Basques in their mountain country had managed to defend themselves successfully against Muslim and Frankish dominance alike and in the process create their own kingdoms of Aragon and Navarre. Other Christians in the mountains of Asturias had given birth to the kingdom of Leon, extending south to the Douro River. A frontier region on the east, named for the castles built to defend it, became the kingdom of Castile. Aided by Frankish knights from the north and west these kingdoms during the course of the eleventh century managed to make considerable inroads at the expense of the territorial holdings of the Muslims in Spain. In 1085 Alphonso VI of Castile conquered Toledo, the fall of which resounded throughout the world of the Islam, while two years later an expedition made up of Pisans and Genoese captured Tunis and burned the whole Muslim fleet there.

Furthermore, throughout the ages the lands of the Orient, though strange to Occidentals, had never become fully alien. Byzantium, the islands of the Aegean, and Asia Minor had always remained important stations for trade. The Venetians, the Genoese and the Pisans brought the luxuries of the east to the west in their vessels. But more important, Christianity's most holy relics attracted masses of pilgrims every year, particularly since the Cluniac reform movement of the tenth century. Pilgrims from central and western Europe upon their arrival in Byzantium were overpowered by the splendor of its architecture, its basilicas and palaces, its vast markets and the abundance of merchandise they had to offer, which contrasted so sharply with the stark simplicity of their own homelands. Byzantium's

وبحمل القفص والجمالة والقفص والزبالة انها لفغت علي بالله فاضاعت بقض من رجعها

نسد من رجعها فلما اثني وزنت بالرقبة درهما وقطعة وقلت لها ان رغبت في المشتوف المعلم

واشرت الي الدرهم فوجي بالسر المبهم وابت ان نرجي نحذي القطعة وابيرجت

ان الي استنخاض البدر بالنجم والابلج الهم وقالت دع جدك عما بد لك فاسقطه

طلع الشيخ ببلدته والسغر وبايج بردته فقالت ان الشيخ من اهل سروج وهو الذي وشي

Left. *The Sultans' Guard sound a trumpet blast to inspire the Muslim troops* (Séances d'Harari, *Arab ms*, thirteenth century).

Above. *Stragglers in First Crusade being set upon by Hungarians.*

military forces were largely mercenaries from the Germanic tribes. Descendants of the Norsemen served side by side with those of Anglo-Saxons, Franks, and Normans. Greece still had lost nothing of its intellectual reputation. But the connection which tied the Occident closest to the Orient was that of the religious faith. The Holy Land was the ultimate aim of any pilgrim. Since the days of the Great Migrations, pilgrims, after they had visited the graves of the Apostles in Rome, gathered in the harbors of the Italian coastal towns to sail to Constantinople, and from there made their way into the Holy Land. It was a venture not without serious dangers from marauders who might lie in wait for pilgrims anywhere along the long route. But the Caliphs themselves never obstructed the pilgrimages. And upon their return home they spread the news of ventures and splendors encountered far and wide, in the cities as on the land.

Hence when Pope Urban II called upon Christendom to liberate the Holy Grail from the hands of the infidel the overwhelming response came from a climate of opinion that psychologically as well as practically had been well-prepared for such a vast undertaking. From the Roman Catholic Church comprising the French, English, Spanish, Danes, Germans and Italians, the call for the Crusade originated, and for the bulk who followed it, the mystical current of this call dominated all other considerations and motivations which also played their part. This mystical current is one reason for the failure of the Crusaders to develop a rational strategy. But that really is a characteristic adhering to most of medieval warfare. Although tactical and strategic concepts never completely disappeared, the product of the feudal system, the feudal knight, was too much of an individual, too independent to accept the kind of leadership capable of applying firm tactical schemes. And without tactics there can be no strategy. When in the course of the fourteenth century the beginnings of the great transformation in warfare emerged, the picture changed entirely.

In the two years from Pope Urban's original summons, hosts

of preachers had carried it into all corners of Christendom. Urban himself spared no pain or hardship to spread the message in person, traveling from palace to palace pointing out the importance of eternal salvation which could be gained in the Crusade, but also rather more the gains to be made this side of eternal life: new lands for Kings and vassals, the profits to be made by the merchants and craftsmen in equipping this crusading host, and to the unfree of both town and countryside, the status of a freeman if he enrolled under the banner of the cross.

The nobility of Europe assembled, particularly the French. However the first shortcoming, after the Crusades had assembled at Constantinople, was that no supreme commander was appointed. There was no united crusading army but a confederation of forces. Strong rivalry existed between both the forces themselves and their leaders. Prominent knights in the ranks included Robert Rufus, son of William the Conqueror; Godfrey of Bouillon, Duke of Lorraine; Hugh, Count of Vermandois, brother of Philip I of France; Robert II of Flanders and Raymond, Count of Toulouse, leader of the largest contingent of the Crusaders.

At Constantinople the first problem was encountered in the person of Emperor Alexius who respected the motives of the Crusaders from the west as much as the Czechs appreciated the forces of the Warsaw Pact powers who had come to rescue them from the dangers of imperialist aggression in 1968. Unlike the Czechs, Alexius was still in a strong position. To safeguard his own situation he demanded that each crusading leader swear an oath of allegiance to him. Only Godfrey of Bouillon sub-

mitted to this. The others ignored it. The problems which they encountered thereafter were mostly of their own making. One major problem, however, was not: their lack of geographic knowledge. An utter lack of geographical information about the countries of the Levant and Asia Minor in general existed

The First Crusade 1097: the Christians fight against the Turks at Constantinople (Engravings after medieval sculptures).

among the Crusaders. The only ones with any knowledge at all in the west were the Genoese and the Pisans, but their knowledge was primarily restricted to sea routes. The route from Europe to the Bosporus was well-known and well-traveled since the beginning of the eleventh century, but what lay beyond that on the way to the Holy Land was *terrum incognitum*, except to the Byzantines of course, and the Crusaders had to accept their guidance or ignore it. Since they were suspicious of the Byzantines they usually ignored it. In 1101 Raymond of Toulouse marched with his contingent by an incredibly circuitous route from Abcyra to Gangra and from there to Amasia. It was a choice made by Raymond himself, in place of the route recommended by Emperor Alexius. Raymond was to repeat this mistake more than once and illustrated that most of the troubles which the Crusaders encountered once they had moved into Eastern Europe on their way to Constantinople were of their own making. Presumptuousness, selfishness, improvidence and downright carelessness marked their course, so much so that it is astonishing that they achieved anything at all.

Once in Asia Minor they were incessantly harassed by Turks and other tribes. The territory was unsuitable for the battle formation's usually made by feudal knights. Often, crusading contingents, such as that of William of Poitiers, were attacked when crossing streams surrounded by rocky highlands. Too scattered to form a line of battle, hemmed in by geographic obstacles, they were surrounded by the Turks, and those who did not manage to cut their way through into the hills and mountains were slaughtered. Those on foot stood no chance at all. The Crusaders, equipped only with the tactical knowledge of the knight, the shock tactics of heavily armed cavalry, had

Top. *Crusaders crossing the Bosphorus, 1097 (After a drawing by Weber).*

The powerful Eastern fortress of Jordan, Shaubak Castle.

treated the other arms merely as auxiliaries. Compared with them Byzantine tactics were infinitely more sophisticated, an asset which they owed mainly to what they had learned from the Turks and the Arabs. As Sir Charles Oman stated:

'They were (1) always to take a steady and sufficient body of infantry into the field; (2) to maintain an elaborate screen of vedettes and pickets round the army, so as to guard against surprises; (3) to avoid fighting in broken ground where the enemy's dispositions could not be described; (4) to keep large reserves and flank-guards; (5) to fight with the rear (and if possible the wings also) covered by natural obstacles, such as rivers, marshes, or cliffs, so as to foil the usual Turkish device of circular attacks on the wings or the camp guard; (6) always to fortify the camp; (7) never to pursue rashly and allow the infantry to get separated after a first success.'

In spite of these tactics the Byzantines had suffered severe setbacks at the hands of the Turks. The Crusaders, totally ignorant of them, too arrogant to stoop to adapt anything from

Above. *Assyrians at the siege of Jerusalem, 1099 (*Silos Apocalypse, *1109).*

Left. *The horsemen of the Four Seals armed with crossbows and swords like Saracens (*Silos Apocalypse, *1109).*

the 'Greek monkeys,' stumbled into their own disasters.

At first this did not seem to be the case. In 1097 they laid siege to Nicaea which surrendered after little more than a month. Then they moved on to Antioch and from there to Tripoli. Finally in January 1099 the crusading armies set out for Jerusalem. En route, Godfrey's younger brother Baldwin turned east with his forces on the pretext of protecting the flanks of the main army; in reality, however, he was looking for land which he could conquer for himself. As the armies advanced on Palestine, they traversed territory short of water supplies and almost barren in foodstuffs. But upon entry into Palestine the environment changed. The country was full of fruit and vegetables; the towns had plenty of wine, bread and cheese.

Three years after the beginning of the Crusades they reached Jerusalem, positioned high on its hills and surrounded by strong walls and towers. Its defenders had driven away all the livestock and poisoned the wells around the city. The siege was established along the traditional pattern. The Crusaders built siege towers, siege ladders, ram and pole, mangonels, ballista and trebuchets.

'Before we attacked, our bishops and priests preached to us and commanded that all men should go in procession in honor of God around the ramparts of Jerusalem . . . Early on Friday we made a general attack but were unable to do anything and fell back in great fear. Then at the approach of the hour at which our Lord Jesus Christ suffered for us upon the cross, our knights in one of the wooden towers made a hot attack, with Duke Godfrey and Count Eustace among them. One of our knights, named Letold, clambered up the wall. As soon as he was there, the defenders fled along the walls and down into

the city, and we followed them, slaying them and cutting them down as far as the Temple of Solomon, where there was such slaughter that our men waded in blood up to their ankles . . . The Crusaders ran about the city, seizing gold, silver, horses, mules, and pillaging the houses filled with riches. Then, happy and weeping with joy, our men went to adore the sepulcher of Our Lord, and rendered up the offering they owed. The following morning we climbed to the roof of the Temple and fell upon the Saracens who were there, men and women, beheading them with our sword.'

The chronicler who has left us this account indicates the priorities existing among the knights quite clearly: first to render unto themselves the plunder they believed to be their's and then after that accomplishment to perform their act of worship. The city had been won, but the conquest did not establish unity among the conquerors, some of whom now wished to return home. Godfrey of Bouillon was acclaimed King of Jerusalem, an honor which he enjoyed for only one year before he died of typhoid fever.

In the meantime the Crusaders consolidated their success by defeating an Egyptian army sent to reconquer Jerusalem. Generally speaking, non-Turkish Muslims proved an inferior fighting force, less ably led than the Turks, and after the Egyptian defeat at Ascalon in August 1099, the Crusaders dominated the interior of Palestine. Only Damascus, Emesa, Hama and Aleppo were still held by the Muslims. Very important was the capture of the harbor city of Jaffa, without which the Crusaders could not have been supplied. But the Muslims rallied once again and by 1144 recaptured Edessa, the fall of which reverberated throughout Europe and caused the preaching of the Second Crusade by St Bernard of Clairvaux. Godfrey of Bouillon before his death had recognized the dangers inherent in the lack of any formal organization in the Crusading army. What was needed was a tighter reign of order and discipline. He ordered as a preliminary measure that there should be 20 canons of the Holy

Sepulcher, monks whose task it was to guard and defend the tomb of Christ. They were required to swear obedience to the prior of this order. Soon these knights became known as 'the most worthy' they carried white mantles decorated with the red cross of Jerusalem. This order was soon followed by that of St John. Up to the end of the Crusades, the military orders represented the very backbone, the elite of European knighthood, of the Crusading movement.

St Bernard of Clairvaux was one of the men instrumental in founding the Order of the Templars which he described in 1125:

'They are not lacking in proper bearing at home or in the field, and obedience is not lacking in esteem. They go and come according to the order of the Master; they put on the clothes he gives to them and demand from no one else either clothing or food. They avoid opulence in both; only essentials are cared for. They live with one another happily and with modesty without wenches or children in order that they do not lack evangelical perfection, without property in one house, of one spirit, endeavoring to maintain the bond of peace and tranquility so that in all of them one heart and one soul appears to live. At no time are they idle or wander about with curiosity. When they rest from their struggles against the infidels, in order not to eat their bread for nothing, they improve and mend their clothes and arms. Chess and boardgames they despise, they do not cherish the chase nor the bird-hunt. They hate the vagabonds, the minstrels, all excessive singing and acting as excessive vanity and stupidity of the world. They do not go into battle stormily and without thought, but with due consideration and caution, peaceful like the true children of Israel. But once the battle has begun then they press into the enemy without fear, considering the enemy mere sheep. And if there are only a few of them they trust in the help of Jehovah. Therefore one of them has managed to drive a thousand before him, and two ten thousand. Also in a curious combination they are gentler than lambs and more ferocious than lions so that one has doubts whether to call them monks or knights. Yet they deserve both names, because they partake in the gentleness of monks and the bravery of the knights.'

Crusaders attacking a castle using a ballistic siege weapon: see bottom left (Histoire du Voyage et Conquête de Jerusalem, fourteenth century).

Siege of a fortress, 1438.

This was the ideal, and St Bernard's description is the vision of this ideal, which was to give new impulses to the Crusades and their preachers. Their success was considerable, Emperor Conrad III of Germany and King Louis VII of France took the cross in the spring of 1147. On their way through Asia Minor they met with various disasters which decided Conrad to take his forces by sea to the Holy Land while Louis opted for the land route. In the Holy Land they united and met up with Baldwin, the brother of Godfrey of Bouillon, who by then had become Baldwin III, King of Jerusalem. At Jerusalem Conrad,

Right. *Richard I (1157–99) and the Saracens making a treaty (Corpus Christi ms, c 1240).*

Below. *Fleet of the Crusaders before the coast of the Holy Land, 1386.*

Louis and Baldwin together with the grand masters of the Templars and the Knights of St John held council and decided to attack the city of Damascus. It was the largest army the Crusaders had so far put in the field, though precise numbers are impossible to obtain. For instance, the sources of the First Crusade speak of a 100,000 knights and some 900,000 others. Subsequent studies have shown that the highest number of knights engaged in any one battle in the Crusades cannot have been more than 1200 and, as at Ascalon, 9000 foot soldiers; after that the knightly hosts seem to have ranged between 260 and 1100, with foot soldiers numbering 2000 to 3000 at the very most.

As they laid siege to Damascus the question arose as to who was to have the city once it had been conquered. As no straightforward answer could be decided, the siege was declared a mistake, and since Turkish relief forces were on their way, the

Above. *The Saracen horsemen on the left are unencumbered by heavy suits of armor, giving them that definitive advantage over the Christians (right) which led to the Christian defeat at the Horns of Hattin.*

Right. *The siege of Antioch (*Histoire de Jerusalem *by William of Tyre, c 1250).*

Far right. *Richard the Lionheart and Philip II of France during the Third Crusade.*

Crusading army left. Conrad returned to Germany in 1148, and Louis to France in 1149. The Crusaders were pushed back by the Muslims. Among them was a sixteen-year-old boy named Saladin. Devoutly Muslim and fanatically anti-Christian, he grew up to become one of the great characters of medieval history, a man who in spite of his fervently held convictions retained, as a politician as well as a general, a cool head throughout his life. Since Mohammed, no Muslim succeeded in uniting the peoples of the Islamic world more than he. By 1169 he had established himself firmly in Egypt and was intent upon expelling the crusaders from Palestine where they occupied parts of it, supplied by sea, which was also the protection of one flank, and on the other by a chain of mighty castles. As long as these castles could hold out and as long as the lines of communications and supplies in the eastern Mediterranean could easily be maintained, their position, if not unassailable, was from the point of view of defense, a very strong one. Although relations between the Crusaders and Constantinople were difficult at the best of times, as long as Byzantium threatened the Syrians from the north, enough Muslims were diverted from the Crusaders. This changed drastically for the worse when Emperor Manuel of Byzantium decided in his turn to take the offensive against the Muslims, but he was defeated on the 17 September 1176. Without Byzantium the Crusaders could not hold Palestine in the long term. The collapse was delayed until Manuel's death in 1180 and the quarrels over the succession to the throne of Byzantium weakened it to an extent from which it never recovered.

In the meantime in 1177, Saladin had taken his forces across the Egyptian frontiers, heading for Jerusalem. But caught unaware his army was routed by the Crusaders. However, he quickly recovered and resumed campaigning the following year. The campaign proved inconclusive and since both sides were tiring over the struggle for Palestine, Baldwin and Saladin agreed to a two-year truce. It provided that Christian and Muslim merchants could cross each other's territory. The sight of so many rich caravans, full with merchandise was too strong a temptation to be resisted by Reynald of Chatillon. One day he waylaid a caravan and plundered it. As far as Saladin was concerned the truce had been broken. In September 1183 he invaded Palestine, but the knights would not do battle in the open, they stayed in their castles. Another truce was arranged, and broken again by Reynald.

Saladin was enraged and concentrated his troops on the frontier. This time the Crusaders emerged under the command of Guy à Lusignan, who after his death had succeeded Baldwin to the throne of Jerusalem. Marching towards Saladin, who was encamped near the Sea of Galilee, they had among them the Bishop of Acre, who is said to have carried the most holy of

relics, the Cross on which Christ had died. They camped on some rocky heights of a pass, called by its two peaks, the horns of Hattin. Water was scarce; plagued with thirst, exhausted by the march, the soldiers looked down upon the village of Hattin and beyond at the glimmering waters of Lake Galilee.

The Muslims took the initiative. Setting fire to the dry grass leading up to the Crusaders, they followed with a massed attack of arrows. Many knights are said to have fallen from their horses, not because they had been hit by a weapon, but from sheer exhaustion. The following day Saladin reinforced his archers with horsed archers and seventy camels carrying nothing but arrows. Parts of the Crusaders were cut off from the main body of the King's army. The Saracens cut their way into the ranks of the knights and their foot soldiery and, as one Arab chronicler said: 'Terrible encounters took place on that day; never in the history of the generations that have gone have such feats been told.' All order disappeared; charge after charge mounted by Saracens scattered their enemies, many of whom, including the King, they took prisoner. Finally they also captured the Holy Cross. Saladin had Reynald of Chatillon beheaded. The Kings and the other nobles were spared. Saladin's victory, conducted as it was literally against the Cross, was a blow from which the Crusades never recovered.

The defeat gave birth to the Third Crusade, the signal being Saladin's capture of Jerusalem where in place of the Red Cross

Above. *Saladin's troops ravage the Holy Land* (Histoire de Jerusalem *by William of Tyre, c 1250–60*).

Left. *Crusaders process round the walls of Jerusalem.*

Below. *Siege of Antioch* (Histoire de Jerusalem *by William of Tyre, c 1250–60*).

against the white background the golden banner of Saladin now fluttered. This new crusade was to be led by Emperor Frederick Barbarossa, Conrad's successor, accompanied by Philip of France and by Richard the Lionhearted who as a soldier was Barbarossa's equal. Barbarossa was considered a worthy foe, a true successor of Charlemagne and Otto the Great. But Barbarossa's role in the crusade was cut short; he never reached the Holy Land. He drowned in an unexplained accident in a little river in Cilicia. The army at first tried to come to an agreement with Saladin. It had captured Acre in 1191 but then Richard and the Duke of Burgundy beheaded 2600 captives. In the September of that year the Crusaders achieved a magnificent victory at Arsuf. It was mainly Richard's victory; he deployed his knights and foot soldiery more judiciously than any of his predecessors and contemporaries. Saladin withdrew and resumed his old policy of harassment. The fact that the Crusade did not achieve its objective has more to do with the

Defeat of the Turks before Antioch (Bibliothèque Nationale ms 5594).

self-seeking ambitions of the monarchs concerned than with anything else. Consequently in 1198 Pope Innocent proclaimed the Fourth Crusade. Its leader was the semi-blind Doge of Venice, Enrico Dandolo, at the ripe old age of eighty. His main task was to assemble the fleet to carry the Crusaders to the Holy Land. As they assembled in Venice, there was no money to pay for the vessels. This diverted them into Dalmatia and into the heart of the Byzantine Empire until they arrived at the gates of Constantinople where the Byzantine Prince Alexius Angelus, son of the dethroned Isaac II, persuaded the Crusaders to reinstate his father. On the 7 April 1203 the Crusaders stormed the city from the water side and Isaac was restored. The Crusaders now waited outside the city for payment of 200,000 marks. No money was forthcoming, and worse still another palace revolution deposed Isaac II again. Considering themselves freed from all obligations the Crusaders set about to storm the city by land and sea. The city held out a few days, but ridden by internal dissensions it no longer mustered the strength it once had. On 13 April 1204 it fell and for three days it was a scene of carnage and

Above. *Crusaders bombard Nicea with captives' heads (*Les Chroniques d'Outremer*).*

Left. *Frederick Barbarossa about to embark on his crusade (*Chroniques des Rois de Bourgogne, *c 1500).*

Below. *Richard I unhorsing Saladin, Sultan of Egypt.*

plunder. For the Crusaders Byzantium was a heretic empire, to a Christian worse than infidelity. But more attractive, the riches it offered outdid anything the Holy Land could offer. Byzantium, so far the bulwark in the East against the Turks and Asia, was destroyed. For more than two centuries it lingered on, but politically it ceased to play a serious factor in European politics.

Politically the Crusades had crushed such barriers which existed between the Muslim world and the West since the days of the Arab invasions. In spite of the petty squabbles, treachery, and deceit, they were the last grand demonstration of the Christian Universalism that was the bracket holding together the successor states of the Roman Empire. Among the French, who always considered the Crusades as a predominantly French affair—which, on occasions, it was—it kindled the spirit of

nationhood, in the same way as the *reconquista* kindled that spirit among the peoples of Spain and Portugal. The Church under Innocent III reached its zenith. The Pope was the King of Kings; his spiritual control, however, required an economic basis, supplied ultimately by indulgences and clerical tithes. Opposition to that, combined with an increased knowledge gained at Byzantium and from the Arab world, led to speculation, to doubt. The cross of Hattin had not been able to hold back the conquering hordes of Saladin. Did this not reflect upon those who claimed to be its bearers and upholders? Heresy was rife; speculation, doubts all nourished man's innate spirit of inquiry. The questions asked, more so than the answers given, were the great driving force that was to change the world—or the picture which medieval man had of it.

Left. *Richard the Lionhearted
(Tile panel from Chertsey Abbey).*

Below. *Knights of the Holy
Ghost embarking for the Crusades.
This voyage, in fact, was never
undertaken, but the knights were
told to prepare for their departure
pending a final decision concerning
their future to be taken at Rome
(After a fourteenth-century French
miniature from* The Statutes of
the Holy Ghost at Naples *now at
the Louvre, Paris).*

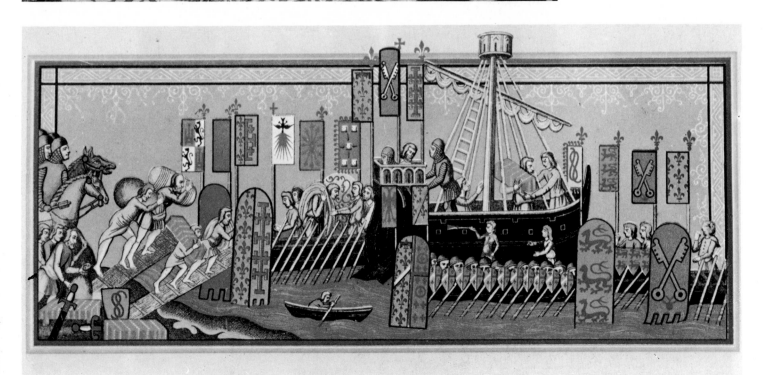

THE TEUTONIC ORDER

Defeat of the Turks at Dorylaeum 1097 by Godfrey de Bouillon during the First Crusade. The Crusades inspired the formation of the knightly orders such as the Teutonic Knights. Initially they functioned as a medical order similar to the Knights Hospitallers of St John but they eventually developed an exclusively military role (Saintes Chroniques d'Outremer).

Quite distinctive from medieval knighthood are the knightly orders which date back to St Bernard's appeal for support to mount the First Crusade. He had issued the rules of the Templars to two knights, Hugo of Payens and Godfrey of St Omer, and called for recruits in a tract which he wrote:

'The warriors are gentler than lambs and fiercer than lions, wedding the mildness of the monk with the valor of the knight, so that it is difficult to decide which to call them: men who adorn the Temple of Solomon with weapons instead of gems, with shields instead of crowns of gold, with saddles and bridles instead of candelabra; eager for victory not for fame; for battle not for pomp; who abhor wasteful speech, unnecessary action, unmeasured laughter, gossip and chatter, as they despise all vain things: who, in spite of their being many, live in one house according to one rule, with one soul and one heart.'

St Bernard's foundation did not put an end to the 'hero of the Age of Chivalry' and his courtly pursuits, but encountered the restless, vacillating secular knight errant, who flew from adventure to adventure, or sacrificed himself in the service of his lady-love, leading his individual life and entirely destructive to the firm fabric of the state, with a closed, rigidly disciplined corporation, dedicated to the service of Christ, the spiritual head of the knightly corporation. They were monks and lay brethren, actively serving a common purpose with the New Testament and the sword, men who subordinated themselves to a common master. In modern terminology they were activists of the sword and the word, recognizable by uniformity of dress, the mantle with the cross, and their uniformity in style of life.

Like the original idealistic impulse, often at the root of the origin of many human institutions, the first impetus could not be sustained indefinitely. By the end of the twelfth century

Above. *Among the European warrior nobles who considered it an honor to serve with the Teutonic Order was Henry Bolingbroke.*

Left. *Emperor Frederick II (1194–1250), the greatest of the Hohenstaufen emperors.*

spiritual knighthood seemed almost at the point of extinction. The institutions of Knights of the Templars, whose members were mainly French, and those of the Knights of St John, composed largely of English and Italian members, were on the wane and near the point of disintegration. Yet precisely at this point in time, in 1190, a new order made its appearance, one which was to be called the *Deutschritterorden*, the Teutonic Order. The initiative for it, however, did not emanate from the clergy, nor for that matter from German knights, but from German burghers, merchants from the Hanseatic cities of Bremen and Lübeck.

These merchants in the Holy Land showed compassion for their compatriots among the disease-ridden siege army encamped on Mount Turon outside Acre. They established a hospital, dedicated to the Virgin Mary, in which sick German knights were cared for by the merchants. Once Acre had been taken, they obtained a land grant there on which a church and hospital were built, and they then applied for official recognition as a spiritual corporation of the Brothers of the Hospital of St Mary of the German Nation. This was granted by Pope Coelestin III in 1196, and again confirmed by Pope Innocent III in 1199. The latter confirmation, however, insisted that the corporation become a knightly order which would take its rules from the Templars, while its hospital rules were to come from the Order of St John.

This new order of German knights never distinguished itself in the Holy Land; it fought no famous battles there, nor did it enjoy that abundant wealth which had been the cause of the corruption and decay of the older orders. It was, and remained, a purely Germanic movement, one of the most significant features of which, particularly in the context of its long-term development in the colonization of the German east, was its close association with the German burghers. As a founder of cities and towns, and as a protector of and participator in the trading ventures of northeastern Europe, it established its reputation. But once the interests of the cities and merchants on the one hand, and those of the Teutonic Knights on the other began to diverge, the order declined. Throughout its history the Teutonic Order consisted of three main branches. Firstly there was the German branch, concentrated primarily in southern and southwestern Germany, including Alsace, with possessions in Burgundy. Secondly there was the branch in Livland (Latvia) and thirdly, the Prussian branch with its center at Marienburg. After the residence of the Grand Master was transferred to this castle, it became the center of the Order as a whole.

The inner core of the order comprised clergy and laymen. Their way of life was governed by strict rules; personal property had to be renounced. Each house of the Order consisted of twelve brothers, in accordance with the number of Christ's disciples. Their head was a bailiff, called the *Komtur*. A brother of the Order was to have neither his own seal or coat of arms. His was the only white mantle with the black cross.

When a Master of the Order died, his deputy convened all the *Komturs* of Germany, Prussia and Livland, as well as of Apulia. Their function was to elect thirteen members who in turn would elect the new Master. Qualification for this office, as well as for membership in general, was not noble origin, but to be a freeman and to have been born in wedlock.

Throughout its duration the Teutonic Order was never an

Marienburg Castle, the principal fortress of the Teutonic Order.

aristocratic body, nor was it a corporation which accepted only people of knightly origin, or those who in fact had had knighthood bestowed upon them by the Grand Master. The first masters of the Order were burghers of the city of Bremen. But that Grand Master, Hermann von Salza, whose personality determined to a large extent the early fortunes of the Order, had probably risen to his high rank from that of a *ministeriale* at the court of Emperor Henry VI and his son Frederick II. Only in 1216 did Pope Honorius III insist that the Grand Master of the Order should be of knightly or of honest birth to ensure that he could be made a knight. This was to prevent illigitimate sons of princes, or those of the Grand Master himself, from turning the office into a hereditary commodity.

Nevertheless knightly ethics determined the institutions, attitudes and behavior of the Order. Its highest officer was the Grand Master. Although obliged in all important matters to take control from experienced brothers and to take into consideration the decision of the Chapter of the Order, he was, during the heyday of the Order an extremely powerful man. Only during the final stages of the Order's disintegration did the Grand Master's government degenerate into a government in which the other officers of the Order shared.

Below the Grand Master were the offices of the central administration: the *Grosskomtur*, the *Ordensmarschall* or *Grossmarschall*, the *Spittler* (hospitaller), the *Tressler* (treasurer) and the *Trapier* (quartermaster). Following the occupation of Prussia, the office of the *Grosschaeffer* gained in significance, since it acted as Ministry of Trade, administering and guiding the continually expanding commercial relations of the Teutonic Order. The territory of the Order was divided into *Komtureis*, each headed by a *Komtur*; smaller territorial subdivisions were headed by *Vogts* or caretakers. In spite of the fact that the Order

was a specifically German institution, it did accept foreigners into its ranks, particularly Poles, as well as other Slavs.

The Order's rise was closely linked with the rule of Emperor Frederick II. He was quick to recognize the potential of this relatively new and unknown Order. Unlike the other orders, this one, free from both feudal ties and the influence of temporal and spiritual lords, was still capable of being turned into an elite body for the Emperor's purposes; Frederick's greatest confidant was the first Grand Master of stature, Hermann von Salza. For over two decades Hermann was his counselor and friend on account of his personal qualities which combined unflinching loyalty with stable judgment and political good sense. These qualities enabled him to act time and again as a mediator between Frederick and the Papacy, without losing the respect and high esteem of either.

The Order's most prominent period began when Konrad of Masovia, Duke of Poland, found himself unable to repel the heathen Prussians. And so he turned to the Teutonic Knights, the *Deutschritterorden* for help, and provisionally gave a verbal undertaking that, in return for their services, he would reward them with the territories of Kulm along the River Vistula.

Hermann von Salza immediately received backing from Frederick and then from the Papacy which issued the Golden

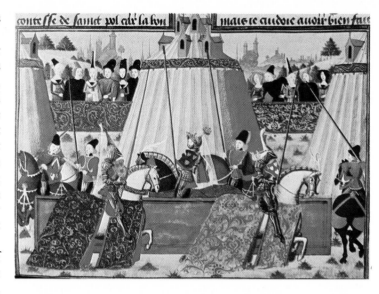

Bull of Rimini of 1226. This laid down the future task of the Teutonic Order, as well as setting out in minute detail the constitution of a future state in northeastern Europe. The privileges accorded to the order included that 'all gifts and conquests are to be the free property of the Order, which is to exercise full

Above. *Medieval tournaments provided a public arena in which knights could display their military prowess (*Chroniques de Froissart, *fourteenth century).*

Left. *A German tournament of the fifteenth century: the object of the tournament was to unhorse one's opponent and break a lance against his armor.*

Below. *Jousts were perfect occasions on which to vaunt heraldic Coats of Arms.*

Above. *In this assault on a medieval city, the lancers engage in battle in the foreground while soldiers scale the walls armed with handguns (Ghent ms, fifteenth century).*

Left. *German knight pierces the neckpiece of his opponent.*

Below. *Saladin and his Saracen horsemen (*Histoire du Voyage et Conquête de Jerusalem, *fourteenth century).*

territorial rights and be responsible to none. The Grand Master is to enjoy all the privileges that pertain to a Prince of the Empire, including all royal privileges, and in Prussia the Order shall be free from all Imperial taxes, burdens and services.' The future territory of the Teutonic Order was to be 'an integral part of the monarchy of Empire.'

Obviously the importance which the undertaking was to acquire could not have been foreseen in 1226, but the position of the Order and its future was assured by the charter. Beside the Teutonic Knights, another order was and had been active in the conversion of the heathens in the northeast, namely the Cistercian monks. These Hermann von Salza also managed to win over so that they became his allies, and the two orders together represented the main pillars of the missionary activity in the northeast.

The heathens, occupying the coastal plains of the Baltic Sea from the Vistula to the River Memel, had already been subjected to unsuccessful attempts at conversion earlier. The rivers flowing into the Baltic gave access to the interior, and on land the territory was traversed by traders making their way to Poland and as far as Novgorod. The territory around Kulm and Löbau had become Polish but, like the entire region between Vistula and Memel, was not exclusively inhabited by Prussians but by numerous other tribes as well. Even before the arrival of

the Teutonic Knights, German colonists brought in by the bishops of Kulm posed a threat to them from the west and south; furthermore Germans had settled along the Baltic coast under the protection of the Bishop of Livland. They traded mainly with the interior, protected by a knightly Order foun-

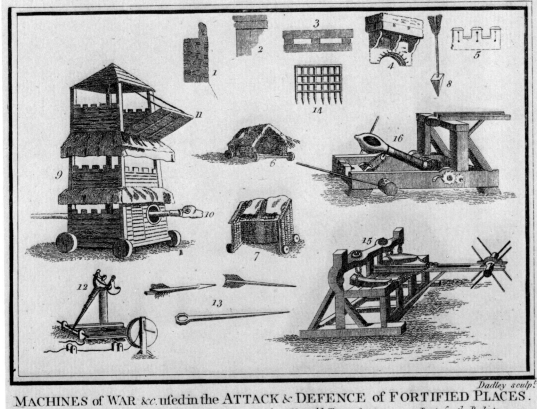

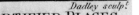

MACHINES of WAR &c. used in the ATTACK & DEFENCE of FORTIFIED PLACES.

Dadley sculp.t

1 Section of the Wall of the Ballium.	5 Crenelles & Oilets.	9 A Moveable Tower of 3 stages.	13 Darts for the Balista.
2 Section of a Machicolation.	6 The Sow.	10 A Battering Ram.	14 Herse or Portcullis.
3 A Plan of ditto.	7 The Cattus.	11 A Bridge to let down for storming.	15 The Balista.
4 A Perspective view of ditto.	8 A Dart called a Quarrel.	12 Onager or Scorpio.	16 A Catapulta for discharg.g Darts.

Above. *Heralds proclaim a tournament.*

Left. *An eighteenth-century engraving depicting medieval siege instruments.*

ded by the Bishop of Riga, which ultimately fused with the Teutonic Order. They were instrumental in spreading German rule, language and occidental culture across Courland, Latvia, and Estonia.

In fact the Teutonic Knights arrived rather late at the scene. Indeed, in the context of the thirteenth century, they can be considered almost an anachronism at a time which saw the beginning of the decline of medieval knighthood. Time and again nobles refused to support their lords. Poetry, inspired by the cult of courtly chivalry, was on the decline; no further epics were forthcoming: no *Chanson de Roland*, no *Nibelungenlied*. Louis IX of France represented the swan song of European knighthood; a new order was on the threshold of power, whether represented in France by Philip the Fair and his *Realpolitik*, or by England in the form of the House of Commons.

During that epoch the Teutonic Knights set about creating a new state of their own, thus forging the last link of the colonization that had begun with Charlemagne's subjection of the Saxons and which in the course of the next two centuries had moved across the Elbe to the Vistula. Without being aware of it, the Teutonic Knights lived on borrowed time. They set about their task speedily, the land around Kulm and Löbau was converted, and by 1230 Konrad of Masovia handed it formally over to the Order. But the creation of a German state was bound to be felt as a potential threat by the Polish nobility. The common interest of the religious cause stopped at the point where practical political conflicts of interest began to emerge.

Yet during its early years, around 1230, the Teutonic Order showed little inclination to carry out its missionary activity by force of arms, since their initial number were rather small. Also its economic base was rather weak. Only after 1230 did growth set in, through additional land grants made to the Order elsewhere, and through the increasing land taken under cultivation in Prussia. In one report, the membership of the Order in Prussia in the days of Hermann von Salza was listed as approximately 600, while in the late 1270s the membership had increased to over 2000. It was not the brothers of the Teutonic Order who alone conquered and settled the land, but the crusading folk, recruited by the brothers throughout the German Empire and beyond. Whoever participated in the crusade in Prussia would be relieved of penance for past wrong doings. In 1231 the Master Hermann Balke, sent by Hermann von Salza together with seven other brothers, headed a crusading army and crossed the Vistula. German vessels sailed up the Vistula with supplies and building materials, and the first castles of the Teutonic Order began to raise their powerful and arrogant silhouettes against the eastern skyline: Thorun, Kulm and Marienwerder, bases from which further expansion could be undertaken, and the centers upon which the attacks of the natives were concentrated.

But the Prussians and other tribes in the region were at first totally unaware of the threat facing them; they did not even obstruct the building of the castles. Doubtless in a majority *vis-à-vis* the invading Germans, politically they were too divided among themselves to rally together for effective action to eliminate the new threat. When they did take the first steps in this direction, they had to give way to a German minority far more effectively organized in military terms. Then the Germans drove them relentlessly into the wilderness, secured the Vistula by building a fortress at Elbing, destroying the heathen shrines, subduing and converting the natives at the point of the sword. In 1239, when Hermann von Salza died, the Order controlled more than a hundred miles of the Baltic coast; less than two decades later in 1255 Ottokar, the King of Bohemia, joined the crusade in Prussia, and there in Samland, in his honor, a new fortress was built by the name of Königsberg.

It would, however, be a serious error to equate the crusades in the Holy Land with those in northeastern Europe. In the former the territories conquered were exploited; the majority of the Crusaders returned home after a year or more service in the Holy Land. It was essentially a knightly venture. In Prussia the ties between knights and burghers were inseparable, and the newly founded settlements were established with a view to permanency. The settlers came from all parts of Germany as well as from the Netherlands. Once again this Flemish song enjoyed popularity:

> *Naer Oostland wille wij rijden,*
> *Daer isser en betere stee.*
>
> (To the East we will ride,
> There is a better home.)

The initially low number of the brothers of the Order and crusading folk determined, of course, the kind of warfare, as well as the relationship between the Order and the natives. With few in number it was hardly advisable to provoke a surrounding majority into active hostility. But with the increasing number of crusaders, together with the increasing number of castles and their steady eastward advance, ultimate intentions could no longer be hidden. In addition there emerged the inner contradiction arising from the religious motivation of the crusade and the political realities. The Germans subjecting the Prussians were in the minority but were determined to maintain their dominance. Consequently they considered it politically unwise to convert the Prussians in excessive numbers, for that would have given them rights almost equal to the Germans, and consequently would have threatened the political position of the Germans. Until 1241, however, the progress of the Teutonic Order remained relatively unimpeded, but then, for eleven years, unco-ordinated uprisings against the foreign invader took place. The Germans maintained the upper hand and by 1260 it seemed that the Order's hold on Prussia had been secured.

Yet the picture was deceptive. Hardly any of the Order, lay or clergy, troubled to acquire any knowledge of the language of the natives. The priests arrogantly destroyed ancient shrines, imposing the symbols of the new religion by force rather than persuasion. A people of peasants and shepherds was forced to bear the heavy burdens placed on them by the Order, to build castles and carry out other services. Mutual suspicion was rife, so much so that no Prussian might offer a German a mug of mead unless he had himself taken the first sip.

Moreover, what happened in Germany almost at the beginning of our time scale when Arminius the Cheruskan, educated and trained in Rome, vanquished the Roman legions, was very nearly repeated in 1261, when Prussian noblemen, educated in German monasteries, were ready to beat their masters with their own weapons. The imminent danger was recognized by one German knight who invited them to his castle and then burned it down over their heads. But the flames of the Castle of Lenzenberg became a signal for a general uprising against the Germans, lasting ten dreadful years in which German rule in Prussia was almost at the point of disappearing. Only under the Land Marshal Konrad von Thierberg did the tide turn again in favor of the Teutonic Knights in 1271. But another decade had to pass before German rule was once again established and firmly consolidated.

The uprising marked a turning point in the attitude of the Teutonic Knights toward the natives. Whereas so far, in spite of their arrogance and occasional excesses, they had been prepared to deal with the individual tribes, conclude treaties and end feuds by elaborate peace agreements, they now demanded complete and utter submission. Large numbers of the Prussian nobility were reduced to serfs, while potentially dangerous communities were deported from their native villages and re-settled in regions where they might be less harmful. Feudal obligations were imposed on them in their full severity. The system of centralized administration, introduced in Europe first by Emperor Frederick II, was adapted by the Teutonic Knights and put into operation throughout Prussia. To the natives only possessory rights were granted but not those of a proprietor. These were reserved for the influx of colonists.

In the long run this policy led to complications with Prussia's most powerful neighbor Poland, especially after the Order had established its dominance over Danzig. The first Grand Master to reside in the Marienburg at Elbing, Siegfried von Feucht-wangen decided in 1309 to place great emphasis upon the further consolidation of the territories of the Order: in his view the limits of expansion had been reached. But the threat of Prussia to the Poles was too serious to be ignored. They attacked the knights in typical medieval battle style and were defeated. After that the Order resumed the policy of aggressive expansion. During this period, between 1329 and 1382, a period in which the order reached the zenith of its secular power, it was a particular point of pride to serve as a knight in Prussia not only for Germans but for many members of Europe's warrior nobility, such as Henry Bolingbroke or Jean Bousicaut.

Warlike activities and the spread of the Gospel were not the Order's only business. Rising corn prices made the region's crop highly attractive, thus providing a powerful incentive for increased cultivation of the land and further territorial expansion. This is the time when the office of the *Tressler* and *Grosschaeffer* gained great influence. The Order introduced a principle hitherto unknown in the financial practice of the European states, namely the separation of the budget of the state from that of the Order. The *Ordensstaat* prospered at a time when the knights of Imperial Germany took to making the land routes of commerce unsafe. With the growing importance of the cash nexus the Order was quite prepared to have feudal services commuted into money payments.

The intellectual development of the Order during the fourteenth century is hardly worth discussing. There were Grand Masters who could neither read nor write. A law school at Marienburg soon withered away into obscurity. The suggestion of founding a university at Kulm was never acted upon. Indeed,

Crow and battering ram.

CROW.

monks belonging to orders of intellectual distinction such as the Benedictines were not tolerated on the territory of the Order at all. The Cistercian monks were tolerated only on account of the part they had played in the past. On the whole the Order preferred monks from the mendicant orders. The single lasting impression of the arts was the Order's architecture, which included its castles, and in particular the Marienburg, completed under one of the Grand Masters, Winrich von Kniprode. This vast Gothic brick structure is symbolic of the entire architecture of the Order. Its stylistic severity exudes the spirit of a military state, Gothic architecture devoid of the more sophisticated refinements which this style achieved in France and England. If

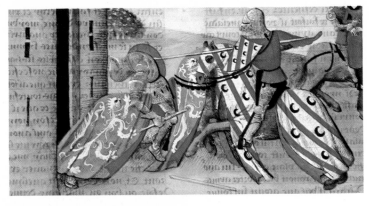

Above. *Two combatant knights (*Tristan et Yseult *by Maître Lucès, fifteenth century).*

Left. *Tournament armor for man and horse.*

Below. *Helmets and visors for tournaments (*Traité de la Forme et Devis comme on fait les Tournois *by René d'Anjou, fifteenth century).*

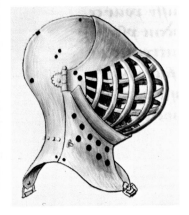

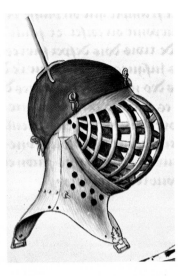

Knights engaged in a tilting match.

anything characterized it then, it was the spirit of the functional. If constrasts in attitude are expressed in architectural styles, then one need only look at the Hermannsburg on the west bank of the Narva and opposite it, the Ivangorod, at Novgorod on the east bank: the one challenging, aggressive and symbolic of the advance of Occidental Christian culture; the other of low structure, essentially defensive in appearance, nestling into the countryside rather than dominating it.

The Teutonic Order had conquered, but it also began to rest upon its laurels. It no longer cultivated the interests that had once existed between the Order and the immigrants who had settled and cultivated the country. The Order consisting of celibate monks had institutional but not personal roots in the land. Its members became estranged from their own people, in particular those living in the cities. Even members of the landed gentry who were not members of the Order believed themselves to be living under a hard, strictly centralized regime. Peasants saw their way of economic development blocked by what were taken to be the Order's restrictive policies. Gradually they began to turn for support to those who had formerly threatened them, the Poles and the Lithuanians. Pomerania too, fearing the dominance of the Order, looked toward Poland. The territory of the Order was about to be cut off from its hinterland, and thus with its lines of communication with the Reich.

Not that the Reich was much concerned with the problems facing the Order. Prussia was far away; there were problems enough without it. But after Poles and Lithuanians had concluded an alliance, the Grand Master, Ulrich von Jungingen, staked all on one card. With an army of almost 50,000 men, one-third of which was on horseback, supported by artillery which in the final analysis rendered the basic function of knighthood obsolete, he confronted the Poles and Lithuanians on the 15 July 1410. The Grand Master left the initiative to the enemy, deciding to fight a defensive-offensive battle. Once the Teutonic Knights had formed their order of battle within sight of the Poles, they stayed put and waited. The Germans were strong in crossbows and in their artillery which was positioned in front of the cavalry. When the Poles attacked, the German infantry armed with crossbow and archers immediately achieved success against

the left wing of the Lithuanians who quickly retreated. But at the very center where the main force met, the Germans fared disastrously. A sudden and prolonged rain shower reduced the effect of the artillery pieces to insignificance as the gunpowder failed to ignite. In addition the Teutonic Knights adhered to traditional obsolete tactics, while the Poles concentrated their attack at one point of the German front, broke through and then with their numerical superiority of 3:1 engulfed the army of the Teutonic Order and defeated it. Among the dead was the Grand Master.

Tannenberg was not the end of the Prussian state of the Teutonic Order, but its beginning. Several more engagements followed, until the combined pressure exerted by military defeat, internal dissension within the Order and the German settlers of Prussia in town and country compelled the Order to submit. By the Peace of Thorun in 1466, Prussia became a vassal state of Poland.

Military disaster had its parallel in the economic field. The agrarian crisis which in Germany occurred during the middle of the fourteenth century and lasted for more than a hundred years, caused a serious decline in the price of wheat, while at the same time wages and prices of manufactured goods increased. Most seriously affected by this crisis were the lower ranks of the nobility, insofar as this group derived its income from the rents of tenant farmers. A strong inflationary tendency made it, on the one hand, easy for the peasants to pay their dues, and on the other hand more difficult for the nobility to live on fixed rents. The Teutonic Order as a whole was seriously affected by this, and in Prussia, whose economic base lay on the export of wheat, impoverishment set in. For the same reason the other branches of the Order were unable to inject financial aid into their Prussian branch.

Eastward expansion of German and European knighthood had come to an end. They were the last of the truly medieval knights. A century later, during the Reformation when the last Grand Master decided to secularize the land of the Order, the *Deutschritterorden* in Prussia also came to an end. What remained was the state of Prussia.

TRANSFORMATION OF WARFARE

*The Battle of Crécy, 1346: flying their banners aloft, the French and English engage in battle (*Chroniques de Froissart, *fourteenth century).*

Largely because of the Crusades profound military changes were taking place. They precipitated a boom in castle building in central and western Europe, until in the fourteenth century the feudal castle dominated every region. They had also fully opened up the Mediterranean again and restored the flow of commerce. This was reflected in the growing wealth of the towns, which helped them to gain greater political consciousness. In part, their loans had financed the Crusades and they began to recruit their own militias. How effectively they could be used against the feudal host the Battle of the Golden Spurs amply demonstrated. Yet the increasing wealth of both town and country, through the revival of commerce and the price rises during the fourteenth century, had rather adverse effects upon the feudal system, based as it was economically on static feudal duties and services in money or kind. The rising need for hard cash by the nobility caused them to commute many of the duties and services into money payment. But even commutation was a static feudal fee which with increasing prosperity the peasant found easier to pay while King, vassals and knights found it increasingly difficult to make ends meet with a static income in a world of rising prices. Hence the monarchies of Europe had two alternatives open to them. First, the extra sums needed for their expenditure could be raised from additional taxation and from loans raised from cities and merchant corporations or from private bankers. Such loans had their price, not only in money but in political terms. The lenders could and did put forward their own demands. In that way the German Hanseatic League in England obtained considerable privileges from Edward III who needed all the cash he could raise for the conquest of France. But even more important it weighted power more in favor of the House of Commons than it had done in the fourteenth century. In France it brought greater power to the parliaments until the advent of Francis I. Second, the monarchs could raise increased revenue by greater

Above. *Edward III (1312–77). From his effigy in Westminster Abbey, London.*
Left. *Edward III met at Amiens by Philip VI the other contender to the French throne (Cotton Nero ms).*

centralization in all spheres of government. In Germany it was not so much the *Reichstag* which gained by this process but those territorial princes who within their principalities could through various reforms adjust to the changed environment by a greater degree of administrative and economic centralization. The Teutonic Knights had given a splendid example of this. But while the first alternative largely took away powers from the crown with little sign that this erosion of royal power would cease, the second alternative implied the rise of the modern state, the product of the conflict of the princes with two primary forces.

The princes had to acquire unrestricted access to financial resources. In the final analysis they could not afford to rely on the resources in the possession of private financial monopoly. Those monopoly holders, families like the Fuggers and the Welsers in whose hands economic power was concentrated by the end of the fifteenth and early sixteenth centuries, could bridge the endemic gap between the declining feudal revenues of the prince and his actual requirements if it lay in their interest. Jakob Fugger had no qualms in writing blandly to Emperor Charles V: 'Without my aid Your Imperial Majesty would hardly have obtained the Roman Crown.' In the long run the majority of Europe's princes were not prepared to commit themselves into that state of dependence, either on monopoly holders or representative assemblies and instead entered the path towards centralization which led to the princely absolutist state.

The second force which they had to confront and over which they needed to obtain control was the power of the traditional estates of the realm, the political and social structure of the Middle Ages: the nobility, the church and the towns. In many cases the estates had succeeded in twisting medieval feudal tradition into something akin to democracy, insisting that public power resided in the hands of those strata of society which in fact formed the primary components of the state. What the prince had to achieve was the transfer of all power into his own

Below. *England and the English Possessions in France, 1154.*
Right. *Battle of Sluys, 1340: Edward III won a brilliant naval victory.*

hands, by turning public power into personal private property, property which had previously been run more or less together, or against one another by the estates of the realm, the holders of financial monopoly and the princes.

This successful transfer of power required changes in several directions, only one of which affects the discussion here, the change in the field of warfare, meaning the 'nationalization' of armies. However, this was a process stretching over several centuries, but at each point it marked a further decline of the feudal system. The need for mercenaries was one of the early signs, mercenaries hired not simply because one wanted to increase the feudal host, but simply because the traditional feudal host no longer met the necessities of prolonged warfare;

Incident from the Battle of Crécy, 1346 (Cotton Nero ms).

Above. *The Black Prince (1330–76) being invested with the Duchy of Aquitane, 1363 (Cotton Nero ms).*

Right. *The Tree of Battles: the Hundred Years' War.*

Far right. *The coronation of Henry IV, 1399.*

Below. *The funeral of Richard II, 1400, son of the Black Prince who was deposed by Henry IV (1367–1413).*

for example, the Hundred Years' War between France and England.

In France the Capetian line had become extinct. King Edward III as the nephew of the last King put forward his claims to the French Crown against Philip of Valois. It was foreseeable that the campaign would be a formidable venture requiring capital resources not obtainable within the realm of England. He concluded numerous treaties with German princes including the Emperor, Ludwig the Bavarian. In addition to the sums obtained from Parliament and the loan from the Hanse, he granted export licenses to many of the German Rhenish princes to ship wool to England in lieu of payment. The abbeys were compelled to make their contributions. Yet the army with

Below. *The siege of Calais, 1347.*
Right. *Guy de Greville taken prisoner at* Château d'Evreux.

Above. *Funeral attire of the Black Prince (d 1376) in Canterbury Cathedral.*

recruited serving on 'indentures,' under professional officers, English and foreign. Among the mercenaries could also be found specialists for whom there was no place within the feudal hosts such as sappers, miners and those who constructed and worked the siege engines. The mercenaries equipped themselves, an important factor in the fourteenth century which saw the full development of armor plate, an enormously costly item. And mercenaries could remain indefinitely in the field, as compared to the forty days, extended on many occasions to three months, of the feudal host.

When in 1340 Edward achieved a naval victory over the French fleet giving him naval supremacy, he could land wherever he desired. He chose Normandy in 1346. Meanwhile the French had turned towards Edward's possessions in France such as Gascony. Almost without hindrance he could capture Norman towns and plunder them. When the French forces turned towards him, Edward decided to move towards Flanders which was allied with him. He crossed the Seine with a degree of urgency, because the captains of the naval vessels had decided to return home, which cut Edward off from his English base and made it therefore all the more necessary to reach Flanders and with it the support of his ally. At Crécy he met the French army under Philip IV.

Again, figures of the size of the English army are a matter of dispute, estimates ranging between 14,000 and 20,000. What is certain is that the French army, coming in rapid marches from Gascony, was numerically inferior. Rather more important as far as the outcome of the battle is concerned is that a very large contingent of Edward's forces were longbow foot soldiers.

The history of the longbow is shrouded in obscurity. The

which he invaded France in 1339 was not a very impressive one, and that year brought no decision. The Anglo-German army quickly broke up and Edward was compelled to return to England. To muster again an almost exclusively feudal army no longer seemed possible. Apart from his own native feudal nucleus he had to turn to the recruitment of mercenary troops, who in the absence of ready cash were given the right to plunder in conquered territory. Bands of veteran mercenaries were

Right. *John of Gaunt (1340–99), fourth son of Edward III, returning from one of his numerous missions to France, 1373.*

Below. *Pikeman's helmet.*

Above and left.
*The siege of Orleans,
1428 (*Vigiles de Charles VII,
fifteenth century).

Right. *Battle of Agincourt, 1415:*
with archers to the fore and the
cavalry massed behind
(Chroniques d'Enguerrand de
Monstrelet, *early fifteenth*
century).

Below. *Joan of Arc (c 1412–1431)*
directing the attack on Compiègne,
1430 during which she was taken
prisoner. She was subsequently
burned on charges of witchcraft
(Vigiles de Charles VII, *fifteenth*
century).

Below right. *The Hundred Years'*
War: Battle of Patay, 1429
(Chroniques de Charles VII,
fifteenth century).

bow as such has been in use for centuries. As a weapon we have met it on many occasions before. But that it was not held in very high esteem in England is shown by the fact that it is not listed in the Assize of Arms of 1181. Perhaps it was not the weapon of a 'gentleman.' The crossbow derived directly from the short-bow was a weapon which Richard the Lionhearted very much admired and he went to considerable expense to hire mercenaries skilled in its use. This seems to suggest that he possessed no previous familiarity with it. The longbow appears to have been used first by the Welsh; the difference between the short and longbow is that the former is drawn to the breast and the latter is drawn to the ear and has both a greater range and a higher velocity. The crossbow was more difficult to load and therefore required more time; that problem did not exist with the longbow. During the Welsh wars of Edward I the long-bow established itself firmly in the English army.

At Crécy there was no reason why the traditional knight's battle should not have been fought, except that Edward III decided to deploy his weapons in a way which the Middle Ages had not seen before. Previously infantry soldiers armed with bows, pikes and swords had fulfilled a purpose subordinate and auxiliary to that of the feudal host. Edward decided upon a change. To insure that his firing line of longbowmen remained in combat continuously right to the last moment, he ordered his knights to dismount and to take their place between the long-bowmen, the pikemen and the other infantry. He wanted to give his infantry the kind of moral backbone which the medieval infantry had so far been lacking, and that backbone was best supplied if the knight himself would fight on foot, important when one bears in mind the eternal grudge of the infantry, that they were butchered while the lords on horse could ride away.

Philip unwittingly aided Edward's scheme by having his knights attack in individual contingents and not *en masse.* Edward's forces, positioned on a minor height, could see them come while the short uphill stretch slowed down the attacking French. Many of them were killed or unhorsed by the long-

Above. *Pike transformed into halberd – typical of the period. The knightly host on the left and the artillery on the left.*

Left. *Expedition of the Duke of Bourbon (*Chroniques de Froissart, *fourteenth century).*

Right. *Fourteenth-century armor.*

bow before reaching the actual battle-line and those who did were quickly dealt with by the knights on foot and the pikes. A crisis occurred only once on the English right wing, commanded by Edward's son, the Black Prince, then sixteen years of age. Reinforcements dispatched by his father from the center restored the situation. When Philip had his own horse shot from under him, he realized that he could not conquer and left the battlefield. Among those killed were numerous famous noblemen and over 1200 knights.

It was one of the very rare instances when a victory had been achieved purely from a defensive position. It was not the longbow which had brought victory but the manner in which Edward III had decided to fight the battle, to dismount his feudal host against all canons of tradition and conduct the battle as a combined operation. The French did not lack bravery, but they lacked what was new in battle, the discipline of a closely organized and centrally directed body.

Almost seventy years later Crécy was to be repeated, but with a difference. Henry V had landed in Normandy in 1415 and was making his way towards Flanders. But unlike Edward III he could not cross the Somme. The French prevented this by marching for five days parallel to the English army, then overtaking it and positioning themselves across his path, compelling Henry to attack. In other words, in comparison with Crécy, the position was reversed. Tactically the environment favored the English in a space of about 500 yards near Agincourt. Both sides of the battlefield were heavily wooded. Originally it had not been Henry's plan to attack; the objective was Calais, which by then had become his property. It was the French who forced him into an offensive battle. Approximately 9000 Englishmen faced the French, estimated to have numbered between 4000 and 6000. The French dismounted some of their knights and,

Left. *Henry V (1387–1422) of England.*

Below. *Battle of Crécy, 1346.*

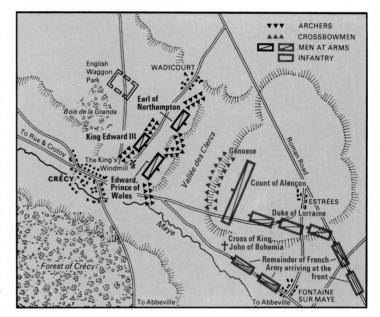

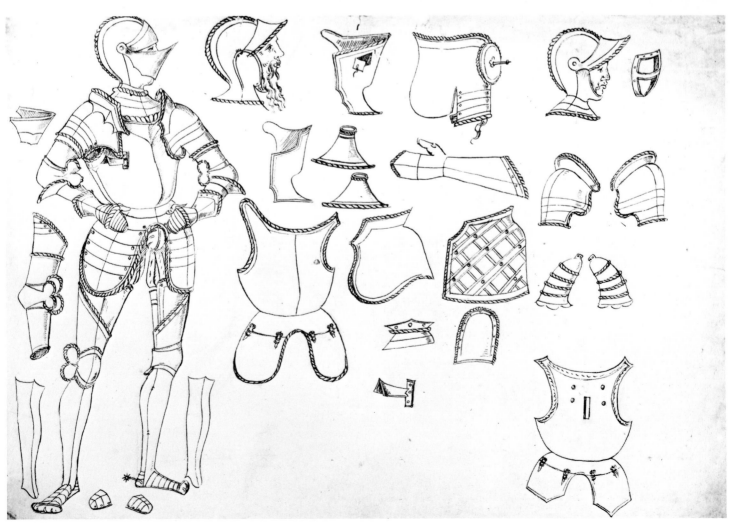

Above. *With lances couched at the ready, the Baron of Normandy and his troops attack. (*Vigiles de Charles VII, *fifteenth century).*

Right. *Hundred Years' War: Henry V storms the walled city of Rouen with cannons during the siege of 1419 (*Vigiles de Charles VII, *fifteenth century).*

like the English at Crécy, put them with the infantry and crossbowmen. Two contingents of knights remained mounted on each wing.

The largest portion of Henry's army consisted of long-bowmen to whom he added his knights, dismounted as at Crécy, but deploying them for the offensive. The French were sadly deficient in bowmen and their crossbows could never match the speed with which the English longbowmen discharged their missiles. Keeping knights and infantry in a tight body Henry's army advanced to a point at which the long-bowmen rammed spiked poles into the ground before them, surprising in view of the fact that the French cavalry could have attacked at any moment, and that the poles could have become a hindrance to the English themselves in their advance. Be that as it may, the French left the time unused and the poles can be assumed to have been placed not across the entire front but at the wings, precisely the points opposite which the French mounted knights were positioned. Once that was done the English advanced on foot, using a hail of arrows to provoke the French cavalry into attacking them. The attackers were bloodily repulsed, or run up against the obstacles erected, behind which the longbowmen dispatched them with careful aim. Then English infantry and knights, swords ready, attacked and overwhelmed them. Hindered by their heavy armor the French knights on foot were no match for the lightly armored English on foot.

At Agincourt the principle first deployed by Edward III at Crécy had been applied to the offensive. It would, however, be a

Above. *Scaling the walls of a city during an attack* (Chroniques de Charles VII, *fifteenth century*).
Below. *Besieging a fortress with longbows and cavalry.*

gross exaggeration to see in this the transformation of warfare in the fourteenth and fifteenth centuries. Important though they were, they were nevertheless merely stages of a transformation taking place at the end of the sixteenth century. They were the birth-pangs of modern infantry as was the Battle of Courtrai. The old order did not give way all that quickly. There were battles in which knights refused to dismount to do combat and had to be forced to do so under penalty of death. English

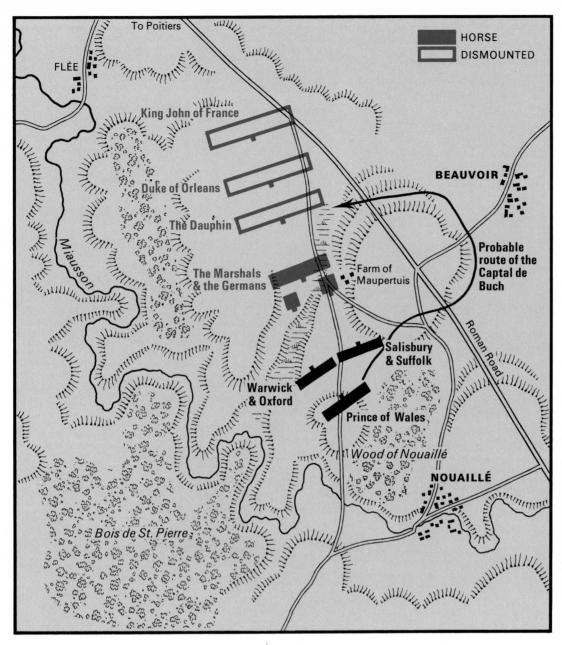

Left. *Battle of Poitiers, 1356.*

Map labels:
To Poitiers
HORSE
DISMOUNTED
FLÉE
King John of France
Duke of Orleans
The Dauphin
BEAUVOIR
Miausson
The Marshals & the Germans
Farm of Maupertuis
Probable route of the Capital de Buch
Roman Road
Salisbury & Suffolk
Warwick & Oxford
Prince of Wales
Wood of Nouaillé
NOUAILLÉ
Bois de St. Pierre

Below. *Sir Robert Knollys (c 1317–1407) with his free company.*

knighthood during the Hundred Years' War proved superior to its opponents because it was more disciplined in the military sense of the term. Though considering itself still a feudal army, it had to break with principles held sacrosanct by medieval knighthood to achieve what it did achieve. The precedent, once established, was on its way to becoming the rule. It even became fashionable for a knight to display his chivalry; to dismount and fight on foot and lead his men—a fashion which perhaps can be considered the root of the modern officer corps.

At a time when the Holy Roman Empire was showing all the signs of rapid decline, matched only in speed by that of the Papacy, out of the Hundred Years' War emerged the national consciousness of two European states, symbolized in France by Joan of Arc and the siege of Orleans and in England by Crécy and Agincourt, which signaled to Europe England's arrival as a military nation. The battles against the Welsh and Scots had taken place on Europe's periphery, and little notice was taken in Europe. But what happened in France could not be overlooked. And for England, at long last, Anglo-Saxon and Norman had fused.

Transformation of warfare had, at its roots, many influences and causes. Cities soon developed to the point where they required their own defenses both in terms of architecture and personnel. Mercenaries came to dominate the entire European military scene until the seventeenth century. In Italy the mercen-

aries formed close corporations who elected their own leaders or *condottieri*. In other parts they formed marauding bands for hire to the highest bidder. Eventually soldiery became more highly organized and professional (as exemplified by the *Landsknechte* in Germany) but this was not for many years to come.

Piece by piece the old feudal order was breaking apart, and in its place stepped new forms of military organization which corresponded more closely to the political and economic environment of the time. The German Empire tried to adjust to

Siege scene depicting incendiary missiles (Detail from the Firework Book, c 1450).

Right. *The Knight and the Devil
(Painting by Albrecht Dürer
1471–1528.)*

Below. *Helmet, sword, shield and
saddle of Henry V. The helmet on the
right is Henry VII's.*

this development by recruiting forces consisting of urban mercenaries. But they lacked the cement which had held the Swiss together; they lacked the Swiss fighting morale. Furthermore, they lacked experience as well as the ability to make independent·tactical decisions within the context of large armed formation. Towards the end of the fifteenth century greater emphasis was placed on copying the Swiss model rather than adapting what had already become obsolete.

The military system of the feudal age had become obsolete, a fact which was underlined by a bang which came from the first piece of artillery fired with gunpowder. No one knows who invented gunpowder nor precisely when. Whoever the inventor, whatever the date, it was a long time before the first gun made its appearance. The first document dates from February 1326 and authorized the Priors, Gonfalonier and twelve others to appoint persons to superintend the manufacture of a brass cannon and iron balls for the defense of the city of Florence. But

cannons were known or had been heard of in England in 1327, and a chronicler of the siege of Metz in 1324 records that cannons were used. But once known, like the printing press, the cannon made rapid progress. Even the Scots used it at the siege of Stirling in 1339. The Germans were using it in 1331 at the siege of Cividale in Friaul, and in 1342 King Alfonso of Castile made use of artillery at the siege of Algeciras. Guns are known to have been used by Edward III in the Hundred Years' War, but precise information about their use is lacking. They were not evident at Crécy nor seventy years later at Agincourt. Although guns could have fulfilled many functions at this time, they seem to have been predominantly used for sieges, not very effectively at first as at Rouen and Meaux. The one successful siege of the Hundred Years' War in which artillery was used was that of Harfleur by Henry V. But it is only from the middle of the fifteenth century that the new weapon began its triumphal march.

*Battle scene (*Chroniques de Froissart, *fourteenth century).*

THE CONDOTTIERI
AND MERCENARY CORPS

Medieval armies had been based on feudal vassalage, on popular levies and on the growing use of mercenaries. By the end of the fifteenth century feudal vassalage as far as its military aspect was concerned had ceased to function. So had popular levies which although they did not become extinct became militarily ineffective; what remained were the hosts of mercenaries who were to dominate the military scene until the seventeenth century. The English Crown had employed them during the Hundred Years' War. As that war grew in dimension so did the number of mercenaries.

In Italy, however, they had been on the increase since the thirteenth century. The Lombard League and the Papacy had finally succeeded in defeating the Hohenstaufen Emperors who had tried to subject Italy. But once the Hohenstaufen had been vanquished and their threat eliminated the city states of Italy began to fall out among themselves. Two centuries of internal strife between Venice, Genoa and Milan followed and ended only when a foreign power reasserted its control over the Italian peninsula under Emperor Charles V and the Spanish line of the Hapsburgs. At first these Italian civil wars were conducted using the forces raised by each city from among its own population, but eventually the perpetual warfare exhausted the citizens so that the cities were forced to hire mercenaries. Cities were not only at war with each other, they were at war within themselves for with the passing of the Hohenstaufens, the supporters of the imperial cause in the cities, the Ghibelline party, found themselves at odds with their opponents, the Guelphs over control of the cities, and when the old cause dropped into the background, rivalry between prominent families stepped to the fore; particularism and family feuds ran amok. Reliance on mercenary forces took on such proportions that the mercenary groups began to emancipate themselves from the political powers which had called them in the first place. Unlike the mercenaries so far encountered north of the Alps in Italy, they began to form closed corporations, who elected their own leaders, or they followed their captain, the condottiere, and operated as an

FRANCISCVS SFORTIA VICECOMES,
DVX MEDIOLANENSIS.

Hic FRANCISCVS erat, qui primus SFORTIA genti
Dux ampla Insubrium Subdidit arua suæ.

Left. *Francesco Sforza (1401–1466); who fought for or against many masters including the pope, Milan, Venice and Florence.*

Right. *English jack, 1580.*

Far right. *Detail from a religious painting showing contemporary weapons.*

independent power. During the fourteenth century one finds many names of condottieri of famous families and some new ones who were about to establish their name: the Visconti in Milan, the Mastino della Scala at Verona, the Medici in Florence or Ludovico Gonzaga at Mantua, or foreign military adventurers like Francesco Sforza at Milan or the Swabian knight, Werner von Urslingen (who called himself a Duke because he claimed his ancestors had, under the Staufen Emperors, been Dukes of Spoleto). Werner von Urslingen had been taken into service by the city of Pisa when at war with Florence. When peace was concluded between the two cities the patricians of Pisa thought it unwise and dangerous to dismiss Werner's forces abruptly. Instead they paid them a considerable sum as compensation and instructed them to move on to the territory of the former enemy to live off his land. The mercenaries must have found some attraction in this proposal because they accepted it. They decided to remain together as an army, to organize themselves properly with constables and corporals as commanders under Werner von Urslingen's supreme command. In September 1342 they gave themselves the name *la gran Compagna*, and for six months marched from province to province, exacting money and supplies in each and if these were not forthcoming, ransacking and plundering the country. Local inhabitants were taken prisoner and subjected to torture to divulge where they had hidden their treasures. Any appeal to Werner was in vain; he called himself 'the enemy of the Lord, of compassion and of

Left. *Swiss troops besiege a castle. (Diebold Schilling Amtliche Chronik, mid-fifteenth century).*

Right. *Medal of Francesco Sforza by Vittore Pisano (c 1395–1455).*

mercy.' The booty made had to be handed in to the commander and was then distributed among the men according to fixed ratios. When this gruesome *Compagna* finally dissolved, each of its members had acquired substantial riches.

The employment of condottieri, or the reason for a member of a famous family putting himself at their head, was of course to maintain the rule of a particular family over a city. In most cases this meant upholding the dictatorship. The Viscontis and the Scalas hired whole armies of mercenaries who were reliable as long as fortune favored the family. But each city was crossed and crisscrossed with plot and counterplot, which centuries later Friedrich von Schiller dramatically sketched in his *Fiesko*: loyalty was a commodity that carried very little weight. Frequently the condottieri were among the conspirators them-

selves. Men like Sir John Hawkwood or Bartolommeo Col-
leone who were noted for their loyalty to their employers were
very rare indeed. But, when discharged or when their contract
had run out and was not renewed, they could not see any reason
why they should not join their former enemies. After all, it was
loyal military service over a stipulated period of time which
they offered and sold, and not 'loyalty' itself.

The armies of the condottieri in Italy had one major advantage over their mercenary companions in central Europe.
They remained a force-in-being; they did not disperse in all
directions once a contract had ended and therefore as a military
formation acquired a professionalism which other mercenary

forces did not possess. Obviously, they were also superior to the
levies which the towns and cities of Italy exacted from their own
population, a practice never formally abolished, but one that
simply decayed. For a city state set upon territorial expansion a
large army was required, larger than a city like Venice or Genoa
could muster from its population by civic levy. Such numbers
were simply not available and the population did not possess the
proper military training. Venice and Genoa had been old enemies, rivaling each other on the trading routes of the Mediterranean, so that in its early stages the conflict had been a maritime
one. The Venetians achieved maritime dominance but were not
content with that and began a policy of territorial expansion

reaching out into their neighbors' territory: the march of Treviso, the Patriarchate of Aquileia, and those of Padua, Verona and Milan. Experienced in naval warfare they were, but in warfare on land they were not, so Venice hired condottieri armies and achieved the improbable: the conquest and maintenance of a land empire by foreign armies commanded by foreign generals. However, many occasions did occur in which one or the other of the condottieri tried to develop his own political initiative to the detriment of his employer. But the Venetians had quick and drastic means of cutting short such attempts. Having their own spies close to the condottieri they were usually well informed and when Francesco Carmagnola, one of the greatest condottieri of his time, was suspected of treason he was lured back to Venice under some pretext and upon arrival in the city was promptly executed in 1432. The Venetians enjoyed a reputation of dealing with their own members equally as

effectively; they did not balk at cutting off the head of a *Doge*.

Venice's greatest antagonists on land were the Viscontis and the Sforzas of Milan both of whom employed and led armies of mercenaries and were as able as the Venetians themselves. They blocked Venice's bid for Lombardy. Only the invasion of Italy by Charles VIII of France in 1494 put an end to this internal strife. The Papal States having forced an alliance between Venice and Milan and supported by Ferdinand and Isabella of Spain, together fought the French intruder.

However, the condottieri had already undergone an important transformation. No longer choosing to work for an employer they began to work for themselves. The first progenitor of this new development was the renegade Templar knight, Roger de Flor, one of the captains whom Frederick of Aragon discharged after the end of his conflict with Charles II over the Crown of Sicily in 1302. Eighteen thousand Germans,

Above. *Italian condottieri: these mercenary soldiers hired themselves out to whoever required their services.*

Left. *A knight aims a lethal blow at his opponent with his sword. As revealed by skeletons exhumed from medieval graves, such a blow could split a man from shoulder to thigh.* (Histoire de Roland, *thirteenth century*).

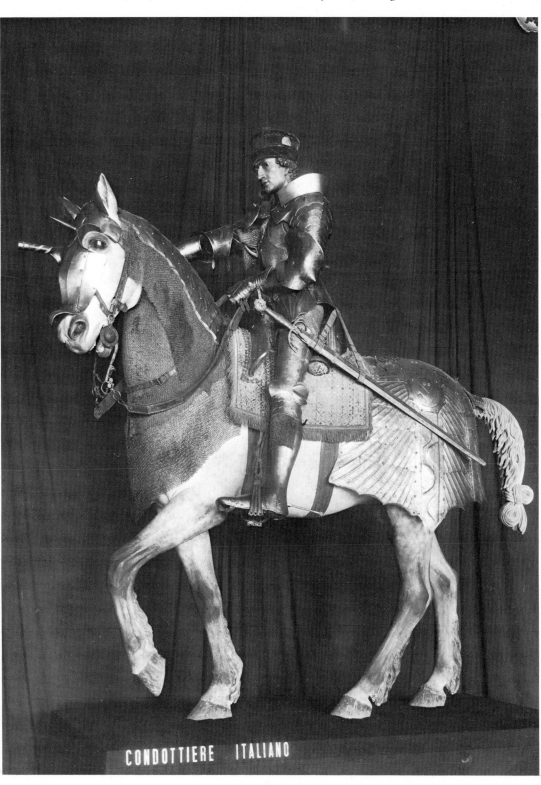

CONDOTTIERE ITALIANO

Right. *Mounted Italian condottieri clad in fifteenth-century armor.*

French, Italian and Catalan mercenaries who were temporarily unemployed were persuaded by Roger to stay together and embark upon an expedition into the Levant to drive the Turks from the gates of Constantinople. That was the objective which was never attained; instead the expedition degenerated into wild plundering of the Christian states of the Near East. Roger himself fell victim to an assassin and the men under his command seized the Frankish duchy of Athens and established a Duke of their own. This may well have been the example Werner von Urslingen tried to emulate with apparent success. When he returned to his Swabian home, he lived peacefully and in great prosperity until his death in 1354.

Werner' successor, *Fra Moriale* as the Italians called him (but properly Walter of Montreal), an expelled knight of the order of St John, was the archetype of the free-wheeling, freelance soldier who gave his support to whoever best suited him, broke agreements according to his own counsel and refused to be bound by any terms of contract. Building on the foundations Werner von Urslingen had laid, he developed a command and

Right. *Soldiers loading cannon. The more sophisticated firearms and cannon eventually transformed medieval warfare.*

greatest number of unemployed soldiers which Europe had yet seen were let loose. Many of them remained in compact units, dispersing to the south of France making, for instance, the region around Avignon unsafe, and from there to Spain or across the Alps to Italy. This additional surplus of soldiers enveloped Italy, but also changed her military tactics. The lessons of Crécy which these men had learned they now applied in southern Europe.

Fra Moriale's army consisted of 6000 horsemen and 2000 footmen armed with crossbows. His tactics were still those of medieval warfare in which the foot soldiers played only a subordinate role in the cavalry. This was to change within a matter of a few years. Instrumental in bringing about this change was the Englishman Sir John Hawkwood who arrived in Italy in 1361 and served in and finally commanded the 'White Company' made up largely of disbanded English mercenaries. It comprised 2500 horsemen and 2000 archers, and the proportion in favor of foot soldiery continued to change. By 1387 Hawkwood as condottiere was in the employ of the Lord of Padua, Francesco de Carrara who at that time was fighting the Veronese and the Venetians. Hawkwood had been blockading the access routes to Verona for two months, but finding himself short of food supplies as well as having his communications with Padua cut he was forced to lift the blockade. While trying to make his way to Castelbaldo where provisions were stored, he was closely followed by the Veronese and before reaching his supply base was forced to give battle near Castagnaro, not far from his objective. Fortunately he was in a tactically favorable position, his flanks protected by a canal on the one side and by marshes on the other. His battle-line consisted of dismounted knights at the center, with the archers placed along the bank of the canal. Behind the battle-line he kept a mounted reserve. Both sides possessed some primitive artillery pieces but they were not deployed, probably because the damp ground of the marshes would not carry the heavy machines. Hawkwood left the attack to the Veronese who for reasons unknown had difficulties in forming their own lines and were not ready to attack until noon. The first sally was directed against Hawkwood's flank protected by the canal and his archers. The attack was repelled; so were several others which had mounted in strength so that Hawkwood's forces had to yield some ground. By that time the full force of the Veronese was engaged

Above. *Soldiers in combat* (Histoire des Nobles Princes de Hainault, *fifteenth century*).

Right. *The rival armies of two Swiss cities met at Freienbach in 1443.*

administrative structure which for its time and in the mercenary context, was rather sophisticated. He commanded the army advised by a council (of which, of course, he was the head), ordered by secretaries and accountants, and judged by a judiciary apparatus in the form of camp judges, a provost marshal and a gallows. In 1353 he carried out a circular tour of central Italy in the course of which he extorted 50,000 florins from Rimini, 16,000 from the Sienese, 25,000 from Florence and 16,000 from Pisa. With these funds he could well afford to keep an army of 8000 men all regularly paid. A year after his 'grand tour' he hired himself out to the city league of Padua, Ferrara and Mantua against Milan. That he must have been a man of some wealth is shown by the money he lent to the Roman Senator Cola di Rienzo. En route with his forces to Lombardy he made a personal detour to Rome to collect this money and he received his due reward: Rienzo had him arrested and beheaded.

A new influx of mercenary troops invaded Italy after the Treaty of Bretigny between Edward III and John of France; the

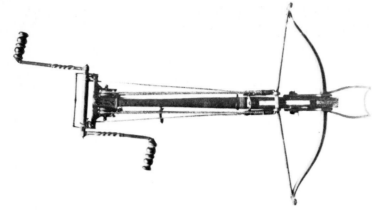

while Hawkwood still had his reserve which he now used. His horse-mounted archers crossed and recrossed the canal and attacked the Veronese on their open flank. The Veronese wavered but when Hawkwood's attack was supplemented by a frontal attack from his forces already engaged in the center, the Veronese were routed. It was a victory for Hawkwood, tactically significant because in combat all his men had dismounted.

It cannot be said that among the condottieri in Italy this change from mounted men-at-arms towards infantry was a lasting one. For infantry to be effective it must operate in large numbers. The condottieri and their troops were, however, as far as their tactics were concerned, still the product of the military tradition of the feudal age. Furthermore the condottieri themselves changed; that is to say, their country of origin changed. In the fourteenth century they were predominantly of German, or of English origin. In the fifteenth century, however, condottieri and their mercenaries were largely French. And although the lessons of Crécy and later those of Agincourt were not entirely lost, as far as the French were concerned the lessons applied to a conflict with the English and not in any other theater of war. They thought too little of their own foot soldiery to be tempted to abandon their feudal military traditions. Since the Italians themselves had no proper infantry, what, from the French point of view, was the point of dismounting? Geographical and topographical factors were ignored. Lombardy and southern Venetia, marshy and water-logged were hardly a suitable terrain for cavalry. Also, as outlined in the previous chapter, warfare became more expensive; the good condottiere had to husband his manpower carefully and avoid serious losses, as there was a limit to what the cities could pay them. The strategy pursued became one of attrition; maneuver and countermaneuver were preferable to head-on clashes. The mercenary

Swiss infantry armed with pikes and other hafted arms attack the oncoming cavalry (Diebold Schilling Amtliche Chronik, fifteenth century).

was interested in staying in the field as long as possible, to be paid as long as possible; therefore his own pecuniary interest dictated the prolongation of a campaign as long as possible. Unlike the Swiss, he had no home to go back to and to sustain.

The campaigns of the condottieri developed into an intricate sophisticated tactical game which could only become unstuck when an unexpected novelty appeared on the field. For example, in 1439, the Bolognese put a body of hand-gun men in the field against Venetian knights and their pellets penetrated plate and mail killing a number of them. When the Venetians eventually won, they killed all the Bolognese prisoners because of their use of such a cowardly weapon. Viewed in much the same way was the use of the submarine by the 'Big Navy' advocates in the First World War. It was simply an illustration that, in Italy too, medieval warfare was coming to an end. The condottieri of the fourteenth and fifteenth centuries represented not the swansong of medieval tactics and knighthood but their death rattle.

However this does not apply to the mercenary as such. He was to occupy the battlefield for much longer. During the Hundred Years' War, France was the area most plagued with them. There they robbed, burnt and pillaged entire cities and provinces at will. After the Treaty of Bretigny serious thought was given to the problem of how France could rid itself of that cancerous growth. Pope Urban V, while still in exile in Avignon, which itself was threatened by the marauding bands of mercenaries, proposed in all seriousness to rally all the mercenaries for the purpose of another Crusade into the Holy Land to protect the faithful from the infidel. No chronicler has re-

Above left. *Fifteenth-century crossbow.*

Right. *The siege of Montagu Castle, 1487.*

Below. *Sir John Hawkwood (d 1394) an honorable man with a great sense of loyalty, he ranks as one of the greatest of the mercenary captains.*

Above. *Besieging a fortified town with cannon.*

Below. *Foot soldiers in close combat* (Chroniques de Froissart, *fourteenth century*).

corded the reaction of the mercenaries, but it it is not difficult to imagine.

Attempts were made to divert them from provinces of the German Empire, such as Alsace and Lorraine, into Switzerland and Spain. There were signs indicating the slow but steady decline of these roving gangs, when the renewed conflict between England and France gave them a new temporary lease on life and a corresponding aftermath when it had ended resulting in some devastating raids into Germany's western provinces.

The first really practical suggestion of how to overcome this problem came from King Charles VII who, after his successes against the English, called an assembly of the estates in Orleans in 1439 and proposed the creation of a standing army. The assembly granted him the funds for a standing army of fifteen companies, each numbering about 600 men and 9000 mounted men. A close confidant of the king, the wealthy and patriotic Jacques Coeur, advanced the first sums. At the same time the assembly decided to prohibit feudal lords from keeping their own troops. All that was allowed was a small garrison for their castles. Only the king was allowed to have troops, appoint officers and levy taxes for their maintenance. The captains of the

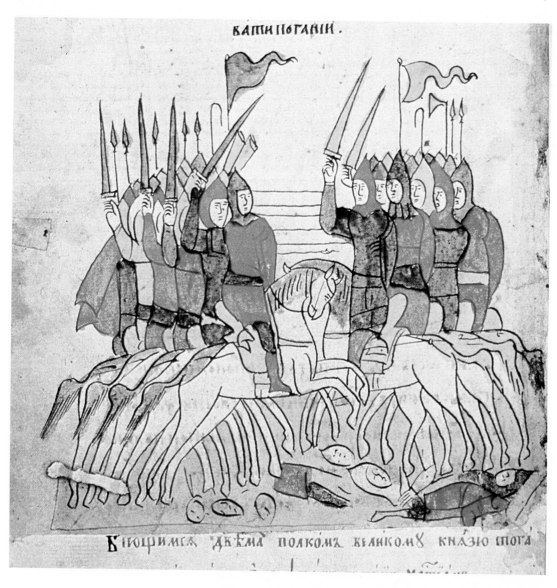

Right. *Mid-sixteenth century ms illustrating a stylized encounter between the Christians and the Tartars (Yates–Thomson ms 5).*

ВАТИ ПОГАНІИ .

БПОЧРИМСА ДКЕМА ПОЛКОМЪ КЕЛНКОМУ КНАЗЮ ІПОГА

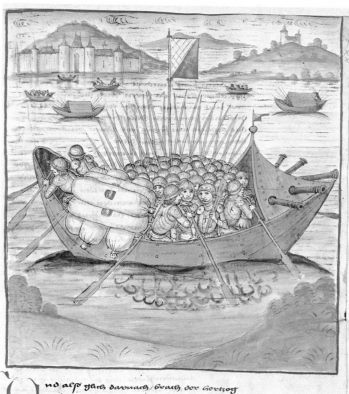

Below right. *Zurich soldiers embark on an engagement (Diebold Schilling Amtliche Chronik, mid-fifteenth century).*

forces were made fully responsible for the conduct of their men. Armed men or gangs should be pursued, caught and handed over to the courts.

These decisions met with immediate opposition from the feudal lords, who feared the erosion of their own positions as power became concentrated in the hands of the king. The provincial estates, however, after the impact of the Orleans decisions had taken the initiative and recruited the most reliable mercenary troops, to expel the other mercenaries and force the feudal lords to abandon their opposition. Some of the mercenaries were not ready to give up very easily. Charles VII found it necessary to mount a special campaign against them. In this he was successful; several mercenary captains were executed while their men were granted amnesty on the condition that they would return to their place of origin and pursue a civilian occupation.

The first ordinance concerning this standing army dates back to 1445, six years after the assembly at Orleans. It introduces provisions for the first permanent system of taxation, a distinctive novelty since permanent taxation was unknown during the Middle Ages. Taxation was limited to the attainment of specific aims or requirements; once achieved the particular tax levied for them ended.

Of course all medieval kings had tried to circumvent these limitations by means of scutage and commutation and thus raise forces of their own, but these resources were rather more limited than the income derived from a regular tax revenue. The formation of the French 'Ordinance' companies resting on the firm foundations of enacted tax legislation was a major progressive step in the history of military forces. It ensured regular pay and more important for the future, it supplied a basis that allowed further development.

The nucleus of an administrative apparatus existed in the days of Louis IX in the thirteenth century. To administer his mercenary troops he had appointed as his deputy responsible for affairs of war, a constable, under whom there were marshals, a grand master for the footmen, and a paymaster-general. In the organization of his army, Charles VII adapted the structure of the mercenary armies. The feudal military host had been divided up into banners; contained under the banner of each lord and his men were all the arms then in use. Their size varied according to the interest and ability of the lord to finance his banner. Once the mercenary armies appeared, the lord of the banner gave way to the captain of the mercenaries. The mercenaries of Edward I, grouped in hundreds, had their hundred leaders. And when in place of a unit of hundred, the unit of a thousand men developed, its leader in the thirteenth century was called the Millenarius.

The shape and structure of the companies of Charles VII developed slowly. One stipulation of the early phase is significant: it was desirable that the captain of each company be a man of some financial substance. Firstly, of course, he was responsible for the conduct of his men and if he possessed means of his own a heavy fine was considered a punishment of greater impact than a reprimand. Secondly, in the long term, this unintentionally ensured that captaincies and later all commissions in an officer corps (as yet undeveloped) would go to the higher social strata. No reliable figures exist about the actual size of each company. As elsewhere, it is likely to have depended on the circumstances. More important than the size was the existence of a standing military force, directly subordinated to its captain and through him to the king, a permanent force which

would train and go to war together and ultimately represent an aggregate of military experience not only of the individual but of the unit and thus of the army as a whole.

However, one would be mistaken to assume that with this innovation all problems were solved. The army was far too small to meet the needs of the French Crown who therefore still had to rely on its vassals to supply men. But in that case they were divided into companies and received regular pay as did the king's professionals. However, further alterations were to follow. Already King Charles V, in the fourteenth century, had tried to order that the entire male population of his kingdom should train itself with the bow or the crossbow. But his nobility, fearing an armed and trained peasantry, successfully, insisted that he rescind the order. Charles VII in his turn decreed that every fiftieth household should train an able-bodied man with the bow. The men thus trained were to meet on every feast day in common exercise and to swear an oath to obey the call of the King when they were needed. Like the King's forces they were divided into companies. In times of war they were regularly paid and for their exercises in peace times they received certain tax exemptions.

In principle it was a sound measure, in practice it proved a failure, because however useful training with the bow might have been it did not give the men the experience and stamina required in battle. Charles VII's son, Louis XI, therefore had these companies dissolved. It was reputed that the only things they could kill were chickens. What remained were the new companies supplemented by the feudal levy but this levy too was adapted to the new structure. However, popular levies or civic levies in France proved as unreliable, unpunctual and deficient in real military training

Charles VIII of France (1470–98) entering Naples.

changes going on in the world. As we have seen, the condottieri relapsed into medieval tactics and methods, in a terrain where it would have been greatly to their advantage to take to the new methods which many of them had already experienced first hand.

Nevertheless, Charles VII's introduction of a policy of separating his forces according to arms was a precedent which remained with us. It was picked up and used by an entirely new force that had come into being, the *Landsknecht*.

Infantry troops lay siege to a town with cannon.

Bill (fourteenth century).

as did their counterparts in England, Germany and Italy.

Naturally levies, whether feudal or civic, between the ninth and the thirteenth centuries displayed many of these adverse features, but they were part of a political, social and economic system which at that time could not be changed and within which all concerned had to operate. But once the socio-economic environment of the late Middle Ages had been transformed, and the cash-nexus replaced the value of land, the old military system could also be replaced by one which corresponded with the new socio-economic realities. Paid military service based on general taxation replaced service based on the fief held by the vassal.

Other innovations of Charles VII stated that each company have its own banner, while its sub-units would carry pennants, and that each banner should be a different color so that it was easily distinguishable in the field, while the pennants carried numbers in the colors of the company banner. Furthermore, in place of the mixed fighting customary of medieval hosts, Charles divided his army into branches according to the weapons carried, and for this purpose issued regulations aimed at the combined operation of all branches in battle. These regulations sound very modern, and are doubtless the product of a highly fertile military brain, but in essence they were visionary rather than practical. One cannot transport man from one age into the next within a matter of weeks, months or years, let alone with the stroke of a pen. Centuries of ingrained habits and mental attitudes took a long time to accept and adapt themselves to the

PROFESSIONALISM

Battle of Cadore (Copy of painting by Titian, Uffizi, Florence).

The outgoing fourteenth century provided a new addition to the field of warfare: the first national army, or the first people's army, the Swiss. It was composed of the free peasants and the burghers of the towns. All Swiss males physically fit were subject to conscription and possessed the privilege to carry arms. In practice, though, only volunteers were called and the number of soldiers for each canton was determined according to the number of its inhabitants. In addition, particularly strong and able-bodied young men were conscripted for pikemen, since not everyone could handle the pike. It was also possible to provide a substitute for one's own person, though this custom does not seem to have become widespread before the middle of the fifteenth century.

The principle of general conscription in a country with a population that lived almost exclusively on a subsistence agricultural basis, numbering hardly more than 500,000, was bound to have consequences affecting both strategy and tactics. Even to keep four or five percent of the male population under arms represented a burden which a country like Switzerland could hardly carry over a prolonged period of time. The soil had to be tilled, the livestock had to be taken care of. Therefore the men could serve only for relatively short periods. Consequently Swiss armies could never apply a strategy of attrition but had no other choice than that of annihilation. Their tactical body was the old Germanic square based on kinship and community, and when it entered battle the policy of defeating and dispersing the enemy was insufficient for the military requirements determined by the economic and social structure of the Swiss. An enemy, simply defeated, could fight again. To prevent him from so doing was the strategic objective of the Swiss levies. Taking of prisoners was strictly forbidden. A dead enemy was the only good enemy for he could no longer attack. Whoever fell into the hands of the Swiss was butchered in cold-blood. Although they were keenly interested in taking plunder, they had to swear an oath not to plunder the bodies of the fallen until the battle had been successfully concluded. To take prisoners and to plunder delayed the battle and whoever made himself guilty of such a delay was court-martialed, the most lenient sentence being to lose an arm by the sword. Hanging or de-

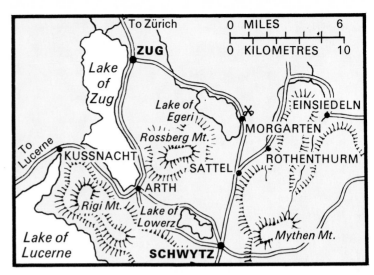

capitation for that offense was not uncommon. When, in the Burgundian War, a town offered only slight resistance to the Swiss, its population, men, women and children, were killed without mercy. The garrison of one castle were thrown alive from the castle tower. Those who had managed to hide were tied up in bundles and thrown into a nearby lake.

The core of the Swiss square consisted of lightly armed men equipped with long and short axes and short swords. They were surrounded by pikes several lines deep, whose task it was to break up the mounted attackers. Crossbows and later on firearms played only a minor role, because the Swiss aimed at engaging the enemy at close quarters as quickly as possible, where those equipped with swords, pikes and axes enjoyed a clear advantage. The excellent co-ordination of their close combat weapons gave to the Swiss foot troops on the battlefield, the strength and steadfastness which had been lacking in preceding centuries, when their role within the feudal army had never been considered a decisive one. Mounted attacks on a Swiss square came to a halt in front of the pikes, obstructing the

Below. *Note the square formations of the* Landsknechte *with the frontline apparently cut down.*

Left: *Battle of Mortgarten,
15 November, 1315. One of the
early Swiss battles.*

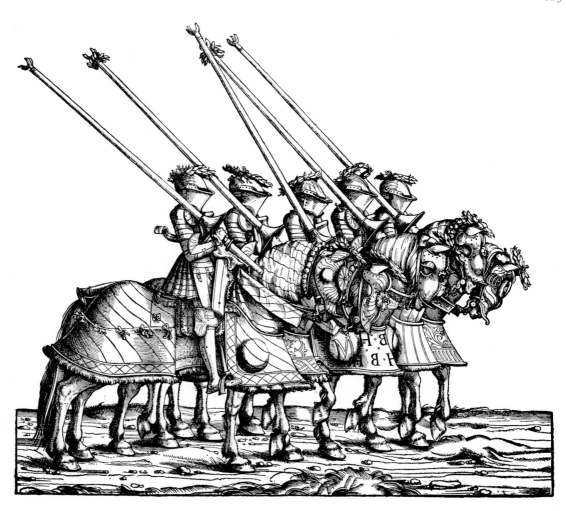

Right. *German engraving in the
style of a woodcut by Hans
Burgkmair 1577: Maximilian's
knights in triumphal procession
after a successful joust. These series
of woodcuts known as the*
Triumphs of Maximilian *form
one of the most accurate and
valuable sources of information
regarding the armor of the period.*

advance of those following behind, providing, of course, that the pikes held their position. With the Swiss those who in the early Middle Ages had been named the *fanti*, the 'boys,' as the foot soldiers were contemptuously called by the knights, became the full-fledged infantry, which from then on was as decisive as any other branch of the armed forces on the battlefields of Europe.

And more important for the Swiss themselves, they established their own independence. In 1231 and 1240 Emperor Frederick exempted the cantons of Uri and Schwytz from all feudal duties other than those owed to the Imperial Crown directly. They were joined by Unterwalden and in 1291 signed the 'Eternal Alliance,' which bound them to support each other. After the end of the Hohenstaufen dynasty, followed by the disorder of the Interregnum, Rudolf von Hapsburg was elected German King and crowned Holy Roman Emperor. With the rise of the House of Hapsburg a formidable threat began to face the Swiss. Pursuing a policy of securing his own family domain first, he endeavored to expand the Hapsburg crown lands as widely as possible, and since he held possessions close to the Swiss, they were naturally anxious that the Swiss cantons not round off his possessions in the southwest. To stave off the Hapsburgs was the cardinal point of Swiss policy. In 1315 Duke Leopold of Hapsburg was ambushed by the Swiss at Mortgarten near the Lake of Egeri not very far from Lake Lucerne. Caught with his feudal host on a narrow road dominated on either side by rock faces, the Swiss unleashed avalanches of rocks upon the Hapsburg forces. Leopold had been careless enough not to send a vanguard ahead and rode firmly into the trap. Once the stone avalanches had taken their toll the Swiss descended from the heights and slew whoever was left. Mortgarten was a successful ambush, although not a full-fledged field battle, but it was sufficient for Zürich, Zug, Glatus and Bern to join the Swiss cause. Systematically they set about

expelling the Hapsburgs from their positions in Switzerland.

Another Leopold, the nephew of the one defeated at Mortgarten, took it upon himself to bring about a reversal. With an army of about 4000 men he took the offensive against the Swiss forces numbering approximately 6000 men. Instead of moving as had been expected against Zürich or Lucerne he turned towards the town of Sempach two miles north of Lucerne, which had once been in the possession of his family but like Lucerne had joined the Swiss Confederation. He gathered his forces near the Sursee, at the southeastern corner of which is Sempach. After laying siege to the town he turned east to meet the Swiss, who had gathered by a bridge crossing the River Reuss at Gislikon. Neither the Austrians nor the Swiss were quite sure about each other's whereabouts. But less than halfway to the Reuss the Austrians met the Swiss. The ground steeply rising in the east was held by the Swiss, and the knights dismounted when they arrived and tried to storm the heights on foot. Their crossbowmen gave the Swiss considerable trouble. Duke Leopold himself took part in the fighting at that point, believing he had engaged the main force, but it was only the Swiss vanguard. Unexpectedly for the Austrians the Swiss formations appeared from the north, their squares cutting like red-hot knives into the flanks of Leopold's forces. The attack was so powerful that the knights fighting on foot were simply swept away. Leopold and a great many of his knights were clubbed to death on the field of battle. What Courtrai had signaled, Sempach completed. The Swiss had demonstrated that they could vanquish feudal chivalry by ambush at Mortgarten, that their squares could defeat the mounted knights at Laupen and that on the open field they could take offensive action against the knights. The days of the medieval knight were running out. A new age was dawning, but few seemed to have realized it.

The Swiss now took the offensive against Swabia, showing time and again that their infantry was seemingly invincible.

Below.Landsknechte *council of war outside a besieged town.*

Right. *Georg von Frundsberg (1475–1523). The most prominent leader of the* Landsknechte *(Painting by Amberger).*

This was the turning point in military history of the Middle Ages. Considering their reputation, it is not surprising that it did not take very long before offers reached the Swiss to make their troops available to other warlords. The first conscription that took place in Switzerland in response to an outside request came from Florence in 1424, which was prepared to pay the Swiss 8000 Rhenish guilders for 10,000 men to serve for three months. By the end of that century such offers increased so greatly that it became a very profitable business for the Swiss cantons, and transformed the Swiss people's army into a mercenary force. However, the difference was that Swiss contingents were not made up of soldiers of fortune. They came from their own cantons and from their local communities. The long-term consequence of this was that the loss of blood was too severe for the Swiss to sustain for an extended period.

However, the Swiss had retained their supremacy on the battlefields of northern Italy and Burgundy for over a century. From the moment that the cantons began hiring their troops to foreign magnates the seeds of decay in the Swiss military system had been sown. Jealousies and rivalries weakened the cantons and destroyed the reputation of their levies. They ignored new developments in weapons and methods of fighting, for example, the advent of light cavalry, improved musketry and the increasing mobility of field artillery went almost unnoticed by the Swiss. With 10–15,000 pikemen the Swiss were prepared to take on any number of horsemen and were successful until they met their match in the *Landsknechte*, who had synthesized Swiss techniques with the latest developments which the Swiss had ignored. The *Landsknechte* did not object to the strategy of attrition practiced by their commanders. In the struggles be-

tween Emperor Charles V and Francis I of France over the possession of Lombardy, the Swiss contingent had simply left the battlefield because they were tired of the continuous marching maneuvers; according to their tradition, they expected a decisive engagement and were anxious to finish it.

In 1522 when the French commander Marshal Lautrec recruited another 16,000 Swiss, the Swiss demanded that the enemy be defeated by a massed attack with pikes and swords. The army of Charles V was commanded by the Italian Field Captain Prosper Colonna. It consisted of 19,000 men made up of Spanish infantry commanded by Pescara and German *Landsknechte* under Georg von Frundsberg. In April the imperial forces had established their position at a small hunting *château*, Bicocca, northeast of Milan. Colonna had built an intricate network of field fortifications, interconnecting trenches and earthwalls and an assault, though not impossible, was a risky undertaking. Lautrec had no intention of doing so. He was superior in numbers, with 32,000 men and intended to maneuver Colonna out of his position. This caused open mutiny among the Swiss: if the command was not given to attack, they would return home. Warned by his experience of the preceding year Lautrec gave in. He had another cause for concern, the rivalry between the leaders of the Swiss: Albrecht von Stein and Arnold von Winkelried. They had never liked each other, and they transferred the rivalries of the cantons they came from, between Bern and the original three cantons, to the battlefield. Winkelried had an international reputation and was instrumental in the Swiss attempt to overthrow the duchy of Milan in order to annex that territory to the Swiss confederation. At the battle of Marignano in which the Swiss were defeated Winkelried had blamed Stein for leaving the battle prematurely thus causing the Swiss defeat. He could not prove it and had to withdraw the charge. At Bicocca the two Swiss captains gave an appearance of unity, although Stein was the driving force behind the attempt to have the attack carried out. Lautrec drew up his plan of battle accordingly; 16,000 Swiss were to attack frontally, the other half, the Venetians and French, were to take Colonna's forces in the flanks. The two flank movements were to begin first, and once the enemy was engaged on his flank the Swiss were to make their frontal attack. The Swiss foiled this plan. They had been for weeks in a mutinous condition anyway and fearful that victory would be attributed to the forces who engaged the enemy first , they did not wait for the order to attack but stormed onto the battlefield on their own initiative. Suffering heavy losses they took the first trench and stormed part of the earth wall but then met a forest of the German *Landsknechte*'s pikes while Spanish musketeers took them under fire. The Swiss fought bravely, Winkelried on top of the wall challenged Frundsberg to come and fight it out with him. Frundsberg, sure of his success, ignored the challenge. Winkelried lunged into the phalanx of pikes and was killed outright. A terrible slaughter ensued in which the Swiss were thrown back leaving 3000 men killed including Stein. After the battle the ascendency of the Swiss confederation forces was over and, that of the German *Landsknecht* was about to begin.

The Hussite wars and the humiliating defeats which the Imperial German forces had sustained in them had made a reform of the existing military system absolutely necessary, all

Emperor Maximilian's (1459–1519) armory at Innsbruck.

the more so since the reforms in France did not escape notice. The turning point was the Battle of Guingate on the 7 August 1479 in which a Burgundian army consisting of Flemish foot soldiers defeated the French. The Burgundian army was led by Archduke Maximilian of Hapsburg, son-in-law of the Duke of Burgundy who had been killed in battle at Nancy two years before. Maximilian, the future Emperor Maximilian I, under the impact of that event recruited Flemings and trained them in the tactics of the Swiss and thus, two years later, achieved victory. He had placed great emphasis in his recruitment campaign on the fact that the recruits came from the same districts, another adaptation of the Swiss system which ensured common social origin, thus social homogeneity and community feeling. The victory at Guingate had neither strategic nor political consequences because Maximilian could not pursue the enemy

Right. *German mercenary helmet, 1550–1560.*

Below. *Halberd, 1488.*

Artillery of Maximilian I.

to impose his conditions. Moreover he was short of cash—the troops he had hired left for home. So he moved to other territories to recruit men and their contemporaries and called them *Landsknechte*.

There is no English equivalent for this term. To apply the term mercenary to them is misleading because they differed in their original composition and constitution in several important respects. As Maximilian's original instructions made quite clear, the troops hired were to originate from the same region. They were soldiers from a common region, serving as a unit, though not always under the same masters. They can be traced back to the popular levies of the Merovingian period, which since Charlemagne and the rise of the feudal system had been pushed into the background by the feudal host and had decayed. There are occasions when one sees this levy recurring, foot soldiers from the same region ready for action under a common leader to whom they had sworn obedience, or under a leader whom they had elected themselves. They had their own courts and were all freemen. A forerunner of the *Landsknecht* unit fought in 1276 for Rudolf von Hapsburg. After the battle the knights decapitated prisoners the unit had made without asking its permission, and its members refused further service. A hundred years later the city of Ulm and the League of the Swabian cities recruited a unit of free *Knechte*, who called themselves the Federation of Liberty. Since then these troops had played an important part in most feuds in Germany, under different names and with varying successes. In Holstein they were known as the Black Guards, and were the 'marine infantry' of the vassals of the Hanse. By that time of course their composition was very mixed, as can be expected, and included the dregs of society including murderers, but according to their code of discipline, marauders found harsh justice from their fellows, punishment ranging from being suspended by the limbs on chains to being burnt.

Battle of Laupen, 21 June, 1339.

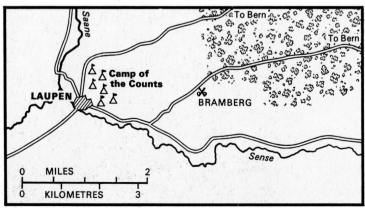

On those rare occasions when a city of the Reich did send its contingents to the emperor they were clothed in colorful garments, for purposes of recognition as well as demonstrating the city's status. *Landsknecht* was a convenient term for Maximilian to use. The estates of the empire were as anxious to rid themselves of the plague of mercenaries, as were those of France and other countries. Maximilian's recruiting drive immediately provoked suspicion; after all it was peace, whereupon Maximilian retorted that they were servants of the land, the proper meaning of *Landsknecht*, and this was shown by the method of recruitment, their origins and the rigid discipline imposed on them.

Between 1482 and 1486 he recruited them in the Rhineland and in the regions of the lower Rhine and trained them in the same way, or according to the Swiss model as he had done with Flemish troops. By 1486 *Landsknecht* had become a generally accepted term. Needless to say it required time to bring them up to the standard of the Swiss, but once this was achieved the Swiss contingents and *Landsknechte* viewed one another with deep hostility. The Swiss, conscious of their superiority, jeered at them, while the *Landsknechte* leaders would tell their men that they were every bit as good. Under Duke Sigismund of Tyrol, led by their captain Friedrich Kappler they defeated the Venetian condottieri in the Battle of Calliano in 1487. A year later, as part of the army of the Empire on their way to the Netherlands, they took quarters in Cologne. When Swiss troops also appeared at the gates of the city the Archbishop of Cologne refused them entry to avoid clashes between them and the *Landsknechte*. In 1490 when Maximilian campaigned against the Hungarians, the *Landsknechte* stormed Stuhlweissenburg, and their European reputation as equals to the Swiss was established. By that time Maximilian had two regiments of *Landsknechte*, each comprising 3000 to 4000 men.

They were devoted to Maximilian which was precisely what he had sorely lacked. He made sure that those contingents coming from the cities were conscious of representing a military elite. Nevertheless, from the start they proved to be a peculiar political institution, difficult to handle. They were a professional fraternity and war was their life's profession, often defiant and obstinate, but in battle unsurpassable in their bravery, and able to suffer hardship.

Maximilian recognized that the feudal military system, especially its economic aspects, needed replacing. The recruitment of a *Landsknecht* was organized on a completely new basis. A colonel, usually a warrior of some repute, was given an imperial patent to recruit men and for that purpose received a lump sum in advance. Often however, he kept a considerable part of the money for himself, relying instead on promises of the large booty. Many *Landsknechte* had to finance themselves, as far as their equipment was concerned. The colonel was in fact a military entrepreneur. Unlike Charles VII of France who managed to raise his small standing army by means of taxation granted by his estates, Maximilian and his successors could never persuade the Reichstag to do likewise. Hence to empower a colonel to raise the force was an expedient of a rather fragile nature. Cash was always short, and the only chance *Landsknechte* had of getting their money was from the booty they made on each campaign. Moreover, the Reichstag also put geographic limitations on the Emperor's power to conduct his recruitment campaigns. The Reichstag or the diet at Worms of 1495 granted him the right to recruit throughout the empire but only for the imminent campaign in Italy. Otherwise he was restricted to his own crown lands.

There is ample evidence that in their early recruitment campaigns, the recruiting officers accepted only men of good character and once they had taken their *Handgeld* they were recruited. The weapons had to be supplied by the recruit himself. Dishonesty among the recruiters was frequent and developed into a large-scale enterprise. Money was demanded for more *Landsknechte* than had actually been recruited. Weapons of those who received double pay, usually men of considerable experience who fought in the front echelons, were given to simple *Landsknechte* who received only the normal pay, and the recruiters kept the extra pay. On the regimental roll, however, the individual was listed as receiving double pay. In that way both the Emperor and the recruits were cheated.

The colonel upon receiving his patent appointed his captains who in turn appointed their lieutenants, ensigns, sergeants, supply masters and corporals. The latter post was also elective. The banner was to the medieval host what the *Fähnlein* was to the *Landsknechte*. About 400 men served under their flag and between ten to 18 *Fähnleins* made up a regiment, but both regiment and *Fähnlein* were administrative and not tactical units. The tactical unit was, as among the Swiss, the square, also called the battalion.

The major strength of the *Landsknechte* was their inner structure and the order that reigned within it. The *Landsknecht*, like any other profession, formed their corporation, similar to the guilds of the crafts and trades. Prior to battle the captain of each unit had to consult with the unit's council, called the 'ring' and inform it of his plans and listen to its opinion. Each unit elected its own representative who was to act as its spokesman before the captain. Jurisdictional and disciplinary powers lay with the supreme field captain, who exercised power with the aid of a magistrate and his assistants. The assistants came from the *Fähnlein* and were thus *Landsknechte* themselves, but in special cases the *Landsknechte* had the right to judge and carry out punishment over one of their members themselves. The accused was arraigned before the 'ring' first and had to answer for his action and defend himself as well as he could. If found guilty the *Landsknechte* immediately carried out the sentence, running the gauntlet of the pikes. All this was designed to give the *Landsknechte* the inner cohesion with which the Swiss had excelled themselves. They had their own constitution, the *Artikelbrief*, the letter of articles, upon which each recruit had to swear. In themselves these were not new, similar devices had been used by Emperor Frederick Barbarossa and by the Swiss, but the Germans had adapted them to their own needs. Georg von Frunds-

The Emperor Maximilian I (Painting by P Rubens, 1577–1640)

berg, renowned as the 'Father of the *Landsknechte*' advised the swearing in to take place in small groups, because 'when they come together in one great assembly not sworn in, they will not swear on the letter of articles and instead will put forth their own demands according to their liking, to which you will have to accede and thereafter you are no longer safe. One cannot force warring people all the time, therefore one has to have the law upon which they have sworn to show them.'

The content and form of these articles varied greatly, but the basic ingredient was the same; a contractual obligation between the *Landsknecht* and whoever pays him. They swore to undertake their duties, and the Emperor, to meet his side of the bargain, had to pay them as agreed, as a faithful lord to his men.

Square formations of militiamen engage in battle (Drawing by Albrecht Dürer, 1471–1528).

They swore to be obedient to all orders received; the principle of obedience was unequivocal and it was explicitly stated that it applied to all, irrespective of rank. In the sixteenth century the monthly pay of a *Landsknecht* amounted to four guilders. Often, however, arguments arose over this and the *Landsknechte* demanded that the month should begin or end with every battle or storming of a town. King Francis I of France once had to agree to keep the *Landsknechte* in his service for ten months and on the day before that battle to give them a month's extra pay. Phillip of Hesse, the German prince who became famous because his bigamy was sanctioned both by Melanchthon and Luther, advised his sons to conduct only defensive wars because otherwise the demands of the *Landsknechte* could not be met.

Right. *Battle of Sempach, 9 July 1386.*

Bottom. *Note the prominence of the infantry militiamen in the Battle of Pavia, 1525, in which Francis I of France is captured by Charles V. This marks the eclipse of the House of Hapsburg and its dominance in Europe.*

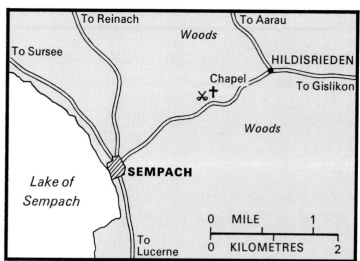

Furthermore the *Landsknechte* had to refrain from forming their own 'trade unions.' Complaints could be taken up by their own representative, or in other cases a *Landsknecht* in double pay, whom they would elect to bring the complaint before the captain. The feudal age did not end abruptly, and traces of it are to be found in the Letter of Articles. Horsemen were not recruited individually but in small units, the knight with his mounted aides, and they enjoyed special privileges as did other specialists such as artillerymen, engineers and sappers.

Every man was ordered to look after his own weapons, clothes and, wherever it applied, his own horse, which all had to be bought from quartermasters. They had also to buy their own food sold by the sutler-women which each *Fähnlein* had in its train. Since they could hardly carry the supplies needed for such a large army, inevitably the *Landsknechte* supplied themselves from the land, and in that respect were as much a plague as the mercenaries they replaced. In some Letters of Articles specific

Below. *Swiss forces confronting the Hapsburg feudal host in 1499.*

reference was made that fodder for horses, bread, vegetables and other foodstuffs were the only commodities allowed to be taken in friendly or neutral lands, while the taking of livestock and household goods and the breaking into of cupboards and chests was strictly forbidden. Some letters limit the demand of complete obedience only to the captain of the *Landsknechte*'s *Fähnlein*, others extend it to all captains.

Once a town or a city had been captured the orders of the colonel had to be obeyed strictly by all *Landsknechte*, even if pay was still outstanding. The occupying force was compelled to carry out fortification work, a stipulation which on many occasions caused difficulties, because the *Landsknechte* declared it was beneath their dignity to carry out manual labor. In case of fighting among the *Landsknechte* themselves it was expressly forbidden to call upon the 'nation' because if the fellow countrymen, in most cases men from the same province, came to help a full-scale battle would develop. Such fights were not infrequent, especially over women, supplies and booty. Duelling was not forbidden, but had to be fought with blunt weapons far from the main camp. Whatever booty the *Landsknecht* could make was his; only gunpowder and artillery pieces had to be handed over to the field captain.

The Letters of Articles were therefore a constitution as well as a rudimentary code of discipline with which to operate mass armies—at least by the yardstick of the late Middle Ages. They supplied part of the cohesion within which the effort of weaker individuals was maximized within the framework of the large unit. And large it had to be, for whoever led the greatest contingent into battle won. No state in the Middle Ages was economically strong enough to operate such mass armies, but this changed with the emergence of the French national state,

Above. *Battle of Novara, 6 June 1513. Victorious Swiss pit their forces against a French-Coalition Army.*

Below. *Battle of Pavia, 1525. Frundsberg defends the forces of Francis I.*

*Emperor Maximilian visits a gun
workshop.*

the consolidation of the English Crown under the Tudors, the emergence of Spain, and the territorial aggrandizement of the Hapsburg dynasty. It changed not in the sense that the funds which had previously been lacking were now suddenly available, they were more accessible, but never in sufficient quantity to carry out the campaigns conducted in the fifteenth and sixteenth century. Therefore, as far as the *Landsknechte* were concerned the financial problem was an endemic one. Maximilian had tried to create an elite troop loyal to him, but how could he and his successors maintain that loyalty if they could not meet their own part of the contract? In Central Europe the answer to this fundamental problem was supplied only in the seventeenth century by Wallenstein.

Shortage of pay was made up by booty, and to obtain it excesses were unavoidable. The songs of the *Landsknechte* at the time tell in drastic terms of the woe they brought to the territories in which they fought. However excessive cruelty was not a characteristic peculiar to the *Landsknechte* or to the mercenaries (the so-called Age of Chivalry abounds with examples); the difference is one of proportion. Much larger numbers were now involved, and when a city was stormed by masses of *Landsknechte*, a few thousand of them raped and pillaged and not a few hundred knights as before. Often after a city had capitulated, having been promised that life and property would not be violated, the gates would open and the looting would start

immediately. A field captain or a colonel might have been able to deal with individual offenders, but how could he put his entire force on trial? And if he tried to punish selected individuals to set an example, the individual concerned would count on the support of his comrades. The provost coming to arrest one of them would find himself confronted by the entire unit. Quite apart from that, the *Landsknechte* knew very well that their superiors were as interested as they were in taking booty, that they were making their profits at the expense of their men, and to a large extent were compelled to do so by their ultimate employer's shortage of funds.

In their campaigns the *Landsknechte* carried with them an extensive train. Each of them wanted to have his women with him, or at least a boy servant. Women of course were indispensable to care for the sick and wounded. But that was not their only purpose. In 1567 when the Duke of Alba marched from Italy to Flanders, his army was accompanied by 400 courtesans. Such luxuries encumbered the movement of the troops. Among the German *Landsknechte* women were used to carry the men's baggage and other belongings; the average weight carried by any woman in the train has been estimated to have been about 50 to 60 pounds. One has to consider the dead weight which such a train represents when looking at their tactics.

Their main weapon was the pike. Upon receiving the order to form a snake, the command was given to level the pikes. The

II

snake was the ordered movement by which a marching column forms into an attacking square. This movement required considerable exercise to carry it out successfully and it seems to have been achieved with greater exactitude in the late fifteenth century than later, when the *Landsknechte* were burdened with their entire train. They functioned well in set battles, but when the *Landsknechte* came upon the enemy unexpectedly it was rather more difficult.

Nor was the handling of the pike easy. As one contemporary writes:

'The most unpleasant feature was the vibration of the shaft. I have myself experienced when fighting with the long pike that it is almost impossible to hit the target, because the point vibrates so much,

particularly in a hefty thrust, but mostly when the full length is used with the right arm fully stretched. It requires a sure slow thrust, carried out with thought and waiting for the right opportunity, to hit in combat an armored *Doppelsöldner* at the most favored points at the neck or abdomen and catch precisely the joints of his armor.'

Superior masses beat inferior masses, but often the forces were equally matched. To solve the problem posed by equal masses one had to cut a breach in the other. Before the advent of musketry and artillery, this task fell to a very select group. Firstly they had to be particularly strong because they had to wield a double-edged sword larger than themselves with both hands. This sword was so heavy that it allowed only one stroke which had to hit its target on the first attempt; if that failed its

Francis I taken prisoner at Pavia. Note the elaborate armor protecting the horses and particularly the 'crinet' which runs down the back of its neck.

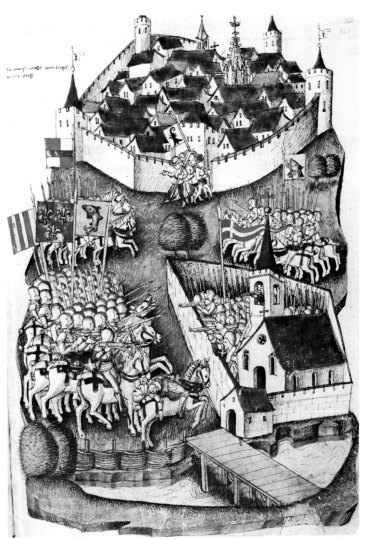

Landsknechte *maneuvers. The cavalry armed with pikes and crossbows prepares to attack the occupiers of the city.*

carrier would be pierced by the pikes of the enemy. In such engagements shortly before the armies met, this select group would step out of the second row, slightly ahead of the first; this constituted its surprise element. Because of the risk involved, strength alone was not sufficient. Even special monetary incentives were not enough so therefore more often than not, men who stood under sentence of death were given a chance to redeem themselves. These men of the greatest courage or deepest despair were those belonging to that group which

the *Landsknechte* called the *Verlorener Haufe*, the lost company. They had to hack their way into a square a hundred wide, a hundred deep.

They were no longer needed once musketry was widely used by the *Landsknechte*. The crossbow had already been abandoned by Emperor Maximilian in 1507. The Swiss and German examples found their imitations throughout the European mainland but with varying results. In France Louis XI after his defeat at Guingate, tried to form his infantry along the same principles but never managed to equal it except in 1507 outside Genoa. Francis I tried, equally unsuccessfully. His infantry was renowned for deserting in masses, as in 1543 when French infantry, meant to defend Luxemburg deserted, leaving the fortress to the Germans. In Spain it is claimed that King Ferdinand of Aragon called in a Swiss force to use as a model for his own infantry. Whether this is true or not, the Spanish infantry when it emerged and began to fight in Italy did so in exactly the same way and with the same tactics as the Swiss and the *Landsknechte*. At the Battle of Ravenna in 1512 the Spanish infantry acquired a high reputation which it was to maintain for a century and a half. What is unique about the Spanish is that they displayed and maintained their own national character from the start. The time had not yet come when the Spanish empire had the resources of the New World behind it. Castile and Aragon were too poor to hire mercenaries; necessity obliged them to draw on their own people for military resources. They and the *Landsknechte* remained the dominant fighting force on the battlefields of Europe until the middle of the seventeenth century.

A royal tapestry of Spain depicting Spanish galleys off Tunis.

ueue et Emperador desde Rada ala Gole ta. y alli manda affentar el exercito enia parte don de
del Emperador y sus successores enel Reyno de España. Manda el Emperador fortificar la B
el exercito Casi mediado el mes de Agosto. Bueluese el infante don Luys conla armada de Portug
con las galeras de España, Los Alemanes e Italianos enotras naues se boluieron a sus tierras. El R
que lleuan los soldados viejos Spañoles se parte con determinacion de combatir la ciudad de Afric

VT REPETIT CAESAR GOLETTAM ET PRISTINA CASTE
HANC MVNIRE IVBENS CVSTODI TRADIT IBERO
INQVE FIDEM RECIPIT PERCVSSO FOEDERE POENVM
REGIBVS HISPANIS QVID VECTIGALIS IN ANNOS

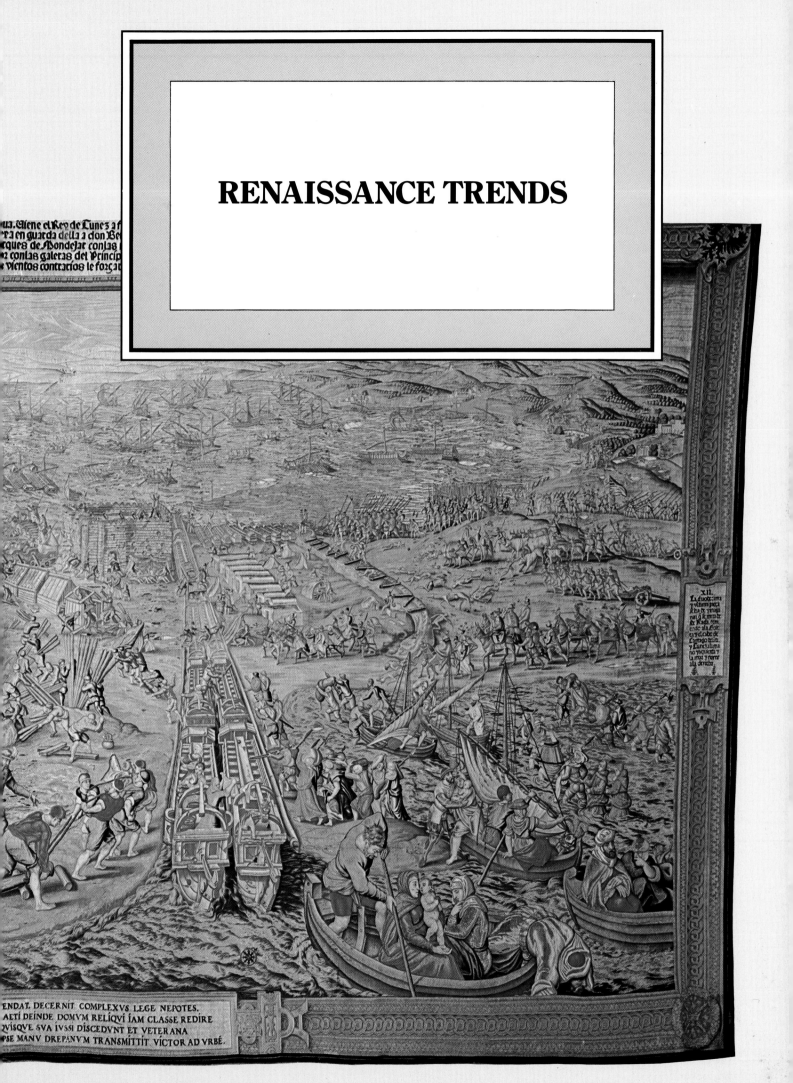

RENAISSANCE TRENDS

After Constantinople fell into the hands of the Turks in 1453, the Byzantine Empire, which had lasted for a thousand years, disintegrated. In a short siege 250,000 Turks with a formidable artillery force had overcome the seemingly impregnable walls of the city and its 9000 defenders. The second Rome had collapsed. On its debris arose the Ottoman Empire, significant for Central and Western Europe because of its expansionist policy, which in the span of two centuries would lead it to the gates of Vienna. As a power factor it began to play a serious role in the struggle between Emperor Charles V and Louis XII and his son Francis I of France. Francis created a precedent which was to become a cardinal point in French foreign policy for centuries to come, of trying to keep Central Europe in check by alliance with the strongest powers on its eastern frontier.

The fall of Constantinople caused an exodus of artists, scientists and artisans, from which both the West as well as the East benefited. In Russia Ivan III initiated the consolidation and the expansion of Muscovy. Byzantine architects made important contributions to the building of the ducal palace in the Kremlin, symbolizing the Muscovites' claim that the Kremlin was the rightful successor of Constantinople, the Third Rome.

In the struggles between Charles V and Francis I, the Emperor remained supreme, but his victory was as hollow as was his claim to the continuance of the universalism of the Holy Roman Empire. His was the last rearguard action of the Medieval Empire. It was beyond his strength to rule an empire over which the sun never set, from the newly discovered Americas to the Balkans, from the shores of the North Sea and the Baltic to those of the Mediterranean. He admitted this by the resignation of his crowns to his son and brother. Retiring to the abbey of St Juste he died after having caught a cold while rehearsing his own funeral. He had been carried in an open coffin by the monks through the abbey and exposed to draft.

In his wake stepped forth the national and territorial states of modern Europe. National states consolidated themselves quickly in the West, from Spain and Portugal to France and England. The center of Europe, however, was the crater of the explosion called the Reformation. The scattered fragments which this event, the German Revolution, left behind developed either new life of their own, growing into strong territorial states, or became mere pawns in the power game

Mid-sixteenth century Muscovy warriors.

Philip II of Spain (1527–98) and Mary I. His marriage to the ill-fated Mary Tudor took place in 1554. (Engraving by Joseph Brown).

of states stronger and more consolidated than themselves.

By the end of the fifteenth century, the medieval mounted host ceased to play its role. The infantry and the tactics of the Swiss, the *Landsknechte* and the Spaniards had replaced it, and throughout the sixteenth century fire weapons developed and increased at such a pace that within the span of 150 years they reduced the pike to a merely decorative weapon. The invention of gunpowder had not immediately been followed by that of the fire weapons. The transformation of explosion into powers of penetration was yet to take place. To bring about an explosion was easy. Gunpowder was often encased and used when mining a fortification under siege, but it was another matter to convert the energy thus released into a concentrated direct propellant for a missile, to transform the explosive force operating in all directions into a force operating in one direction only.

Who invented the first fire weapon transforming explosives into power to penetrate is not known. Whoever hit upon the ideas of using a tubular instrument, of providing it with a hole for ignition, of cleaning the saltpeter, and of loading such an instrument, remains equally unknown. Reports of such early artillery pieces being employed came first from Italy, then from France and England, Spain and Germany, all during the first half of the fourteenth century. The first report of such fire weapons being actually deployed in fighting comes from two German knights in 1331. What evidence there is seems to indicate that during their early use they were loaded only once, because the crew consisted of one man to two artillery pieces.

Gunpowder itself was still in need of considerable refinement because ordinary saltpeter ignited only with difficulty. Therefore the problem was to find the right mixture of saltpeter, sulphur and carbon substance, a problem which preoccupied the military chemists until well into the nineteenth century. In any event, the first literary evidence refers to the 'infernal' noise these machines of war were making. When Luther condemned weapons of war he explicitly listed the fire weapon. The example of what the Venetians did with their Bolognese prisoners who had used firearms has already been cited. In 1467 when the condottieri fought against Florence using fire weapons, the Florentines ordered that no quarter should be given to them if captured. Thirty years later the condottiere Paolo Vitelli ordered that all musketeers among his prisoners should have their hands hacked off, because it was undignified that noble knights should meet their end in that way at the hands of common foot soldiers. He said this in spite of the fact that he used fire weapons himself. Among the risks a gunner took, apart from the fact that his infernal machine might blow up in his face, was that upon capture he would be put into the barrel of his artillery piece and shot out himself.

The time and method of warfare which this new weapon was about to replace had its lamentors:

'Hardly a man and bravery in matters of war are of use any longer because guile, betrayal, treachery together with the gruesome artillery pieces have taken over so much that fencing, fighting, hitting and armor, weapons, physical strength or courage are not of much use any more. Because it happens often and frequently that a virile brave hero is killed by some foresaken knave with the gun . . .'

The oldest guns appear to have been relatively small. Large pieces used specifically for siege operations, however, were in evidence from the latter part of the fourteenth century. The city of Nuremberg had one such piece, christened 'Chriemhilde'; the barrel weighed 275 kilos and was pulled by 12 horses. Its wooden base, or cradle, in which it was put for operation needed 16 horses. This was followed by four wagons carrying 11 stone balls each for ammunition and another five wagons

Pedro of Castille (1334–69).

with the rest of the equipment. The greatest artillery piece still in existence in Vienna is over eight feet long. The stone ball it fired weighed 600 kilos.

The earliest specimens were made of wood held together by metal rings, then out of iron and fourteenth-century gun barrels were cast from bronze, but technology in that respect did not advance very quickly. Even by the end of the fifteenth century exact cylindrical barrels were a very rare achievement, and

Right. *Conquest of Granada, 1481–1492.*

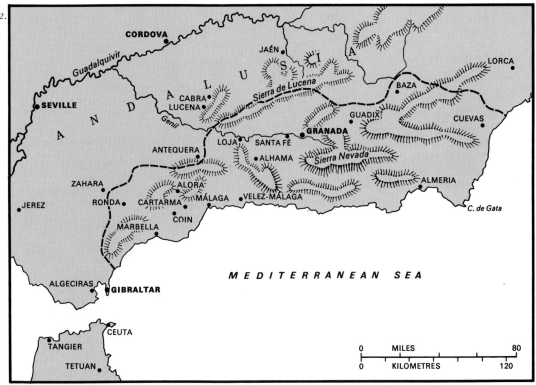

The siege of Constantinople, 1453.

required two men to service it, one man to aim and the other to ignite the gunpowder with a slow match. As on the artillery piece the hole for ignition was on top of the barrel. Once that hole had been drilled in the side and a small pan holding the powder had been attached it was possible for a musket to be fired by one man, aiming and firing it at the same time. From that primitive base began the technical development culminating in the wheel lock. Cartridges too were soon in evidence contained in uniform, small wooden cases. The early musketeer carried about a dozen of these with him as well as his powder horn. The gun sight came up in the early fifteenth century. The recoil of the gun provided difficulty until it was overcome by various devices culminating in the wooden shaft and butt.

The early musket or arquebus, as it was immediately called, demonstrated its advantages over the crossbow with an effective range of approximately 250 feet compared with the crossbow's maximum of 130 feet. The musket came into use during the first two decades of the sixteenth century. It was less clumsy and therefore easier to handle. The barrel rested on a fork to insure steadiness of aim. Light enough to be carried, its bullet had a velocity strong enough to penetrate even the heaviest armor and mail, something which could not be achieved by the muskets' early forerunners. Nevertheless the handfire weapons were still crude and not always easy to operate.

Inevitably handfire weapons became the subject of public

proper lafettes did not exist until the late seventeenth century, at least one that was adequate for the size of gun carried and quickly movable. When during the fifteenth century metallurgical technology had advanced to make iron casting possible, the stone ball was replaced by the metal ball, and they were able to reduce the walls of fortifications into rubble very quickly. The first to have used them appear to have been the French in northern Italy in 1494.

With the appearance of the gun, gunsmithery became a recognized profession of considerable repute. Almost like the chemists gunsmiths treasured their knowledge dearly, keeping its secrets to themselves and handing it on only to their pupils. One such gunsmith wrote a treatise concerning the entire technology of gun and gunpowder manufacture as well as on loading, aiming and firing a gun. Written originally in 1420 it circulated only in very close circles and was not seen in its printed version until 1529. How effective the early siege guns were is difficult to assess. But the fact they must have rated highly is shown by the numerous examples of requests by those who lacked such instruments. Nuremberg lent its Chriemhilde to various borrowers. Frederick of Brandenburg in 1414 asked the Teutonic Knights to loan him their gun to bring his unruly Brandenburg nobility, entrenched in their castles, to heel. In open battle the effect of the big guns was at first minimal. How to aim was an art in itself which had to be acquired first. Often the first salvo was too high, and since loading was not easy, the opposing infantry had enough time to advance to an area within its range. It seems that initially the affect their noise had on morale was greater than the result achieved by the projectile.

Handfire weapons made their first appearance almost simultaneously with that of the artillery piece. The earliest specimen

Right. *Maneuvers (Military treatise by Wolf von Senftenberg, 1570).*

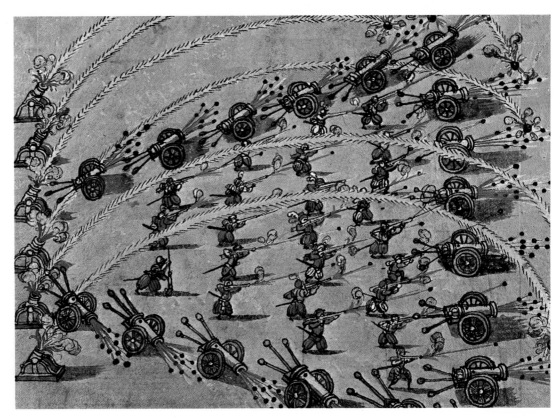

Below. *Battle of Lepanto, 1571.*

142

controversy. A French writer recommended the re-introduction of the crossbow, since they were not so vulnerable to rain as was the powder of the musket. This controversy was also carried on in England where one writer praised all the advantages of the longbow, pointing out that in wet weather the musket would be useless, whereupon the reply was made that wetness equally affected the bow. Furthermore expert longbow shooters were rare, and the musket was a weapon on which everyone could be trained fairly easily. Still, as late as 1627 at the siege of La Rochelle, the English longbowman was very much in evidence.

The French armies in Upper Italy carried handfire weapons in 1495. The Swiss used them in 1499, and the use of them by the *Landsknechte* of Frundsberg is recorded in 1526. But the first major encounter in which both sides used handfire weapons extensively was in 1503 between the French and Spaniards in southern Italy. The French, led by the Duke of Nemours, tried to dislodge the Spaniards from their fortified position in Barletta. When the French did not succeed and withdrew, the Spaniards, under the leadership of Gonsalvos of Cordova, made a sally from their position with light cavalry and two detachments of arquebusiers. French detachments turned to attack the Spanish cavalry which, pretending to flee, led them in front of the muzzles of their fire weapons which brought the French

Top. *King Louis XI of France, a descendant of the Viscontis of Milan reinstates his claim to the Duchy of Milan and captures Ludovico Moros, Duke of Milan, in 1500.*

Above. *The reconquista of Spain: entry of Ferdinand and Isabella into Granada 1492.*

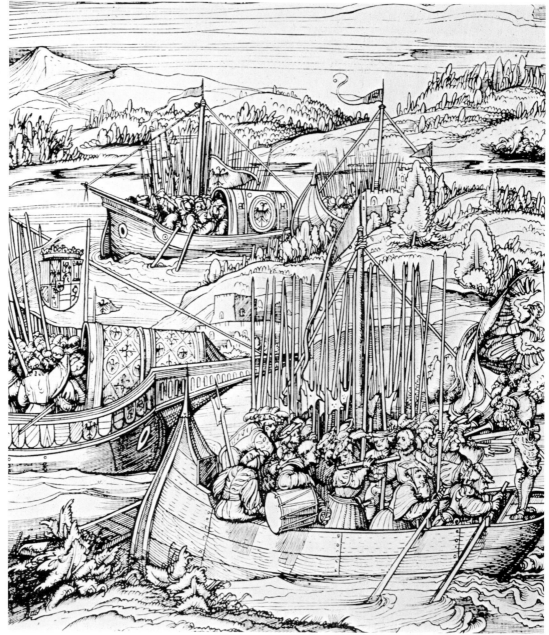

Right. Landsknechte *transported by boat down the Upper Rhine.*

Below. *Philip IV the Fair of Castille who married Joanna daughter of Ferdinand and Isabella.*

Right. *Renaissance statue of Theodoric the Great.*

attack to a halt while the Spanish cavalry regrouped, renewing its attack which the French were no longer able to resist. This encounter was repeated on a much larger scale in the same year at Cerignola where, as Fabricio Colonna said, it was no longer the valor of the general and his troops which decided the issue but the wall and the trench occupied by Spanish musketry, who beating off the French massed attack counterattacked with muskets and cavalry and decided the battle in favor of the Spaniards.

Spain had once again entered the military scene and was assuming the part of a major European power. In 1479 Ferdinand of Aragon and Isabella of Castile assumed their joint rule of the two kingdoms. Spain was not unified, but a beginning had been made. The issues which cemented the ties between them firmly were religion and external threat. With the onset of the age of heresy and the Council of Constance, Pope Sixtus IV established the Inquisition in 1478. The fall of Constantinople had re-awakened the fear of another major Muslim invasion on the Iberian peninsula. Muslims still ruled in southern Spain. These factors together produced the last phase of the Spanish *reconquista*. A local incident, the capture by a Spanish nobleman of Alhama southwest of Granada, inspired Ferdinand and Isabella to support him and extend this to a crusade against the entire Moorish community in Spain. The Muslims under Abu Hassan tried to recapture Alhama, but in their hurry they had forgotten their siege train in Granada. He had to return to fetch it, but by then news was received that Ferdinand was advancing with an army of 4000 horsemen and 12,000 foot soldiers. Abu Hassan laid a highly successful ambush which might have ended Ferdinand's venture had not Hassan been dethroned by his son Boabdil through an intrigue in his own camp. Hassan could not pursue his success and sought refuge at the court of his brother Abdullah at Malaga. A year later, in 1483, the victor of Alhama, the Marquis of Cadiz, set out to raid the Malaga region but was completely routed by the Muslims under Abdullah. Boabdil, anxious not to leave all the glory in the hands of his uncle, decided to capture the town of Lucana, but instead was captured by the Count of Cabra.

Boabdil was a rare catch and Ferdinand decided to release him

on submitting to conditions which would bind him and Granada to the Spanish Crown. Boabdil accepted a two-year truce and the condition that Spanish troops could cross his kingdom to the territories of his father and uncle. Pope Sixtus IV was elated by the Spanish success, in view of the fears entertained after the Muslims under Mohammed II had captured Ortranto in 1482. He sent a standard and a silver cross to the Spanish King and Queen for the crusade against the Muslims on their own soil. This crusade now became the great common denominator for the Spanish nobility (eliminating their customary factiousness) and for the soldiers who were to be part in the struggle of the Cross against that of the Crescent.

As in the rest of Europe, feudal levies in Spain were no longer a force to be relied upon. Therefore Isabella, resourceful as she was, used the recently created constabulary, which in Spain was the seed bed of its national army. In addition Swiss mercenaries, German *Landsknechte* and many other volunteers from France and England were recruited. With that army she hoped to capture the Arab castles. But for that artillery was required. Gun founders and gunsmiths were invited from Germany, France and Italy, forges were built and guns were cast. A supply train of 80,000 mules kept the siege forces supplied. Distinct novelties in the Spanish forces were the creation of a corps of field messengers to keep the flow of communications, information and orders moving throughout the theater of war, and a field medical service for the wounded, the first recorded case of a modern field hospital.

The Spanish army assembled at Cordova numbered 80,000 troops, 10,000 horses, and over 35,000 infantry. The rest were specialists such as gunners, engineers and miners. Nor was the element of sea power ignored in a country surrounded on three sides by the sea. The Castilian fleet was to cut the lines of communication between the Muslims in Spain and their brethren in Africa. In this they succeeded, while on land a series of sieges reduced the Muslim castles systematically. Towns and castles which surrendered were treated leniently; those which

Battle of Ravenna, 2 April 1512: the victorious French against the papal – Spanish army.

Arquebus from a fifteenth-century German ms.

resisted were reduced to rubble, and in one case where a town had been taken, but whose garrison subsequently revolted, over a hundred of its inhabitants were hanged on the walls. In 1487 Malaga was captured, and by 1489 the whole of Granada was Ferdinand's. All he had to do was to occupy it. The last center of resistance was the city of Granada itself. It held out until 1492 while Ferdinand devastated its immediate environs. When it finally surrendered on 2 January 1492, the last Muslim stronghold in Europe had ceased to exist.

Spain, with the exception of Navarre, had been united; situated between the Atlantic on the one side and the Mediterranean on the other, protected in the north by the Pyrenees, Spain was in an impressively strong position since the New World had been discovered and Spain began to exercise its mastery over it. What the Hundred Years' War had achieved in France and in England, the *reconquista* achieved in Spain. A tide of Spanish nationalism surged forward which would not tolerate the alien elements within it any longer. Jews had the choice between baptism and expulsion, but the Moors were systemati-

cally decimated. In the same year as the surrender of Granada Spain formally became a united country.

Militarily its infantry had shown its strength and steadfastness which were increasingly to be displayed all over Europe during the next century and a half. Now the Spanish forces marched for the Spanish Empire, an Empire which for a short time was to include most of civilized Europe. In 1520 Charles, the grandson of Ferdinand, was elected Emperor of the Holy Roman Empire of the German nation.

The battle for supremacy between the Empire and France, fought out in northern Italy, dominated the first quarter of the sixteenth century. It ended with Charles' forces victorious but incapable of securing a worldwide empire. On the other hand, while the kings of Christendom quarreled, the Turks advanced in the Mediterranean and into the Balkan countries, and met almost no resistance until in 1529 they were stopped at the gates of Vienna. (Towards the end of the next century that spectacle was to be repeated.)

However, the most important war for the future political development of Europe occurred in the second half of the sixteenth century and arose from the rebellion of the Netherlands against Spain. Charles had inherited them and added them to his Spanish possessions. Under his son Philip this over-lordship came to be violently resented in the northern provinces of the Netherlands for religious and economic reasons. The prosperous Flemish cities had been early converts to the cause of the Reformation, and when Philip II ascended to the Spanish throne in 1556, envisaging himself as the counter-reformer *par excellence* and insisting upon the principle of religious uni-formity, according to the principle *cuius regio eio religio*, war was inevitable. The first signs of trouble appeared in 1559 when Philip's regent, Margaret of Parma, introduced reforms de-signed to end the privileges of the Flemish patricians such as patronage and preferment and to curb their powers generally. The nobility of the Netherlands bound itself together by a document called the 'Compromise.'

Riches hitherto unknown streamed into Spain from the New World, without doing Spain much good, for the bullion re-ceived was spent mainly on war, and went into the hands of the bankers of Genoa, Antwerp and Augsburg. The Spanish Netherlands had developed into Europe's most prosperous region. The vessels of the Dutch merchants reigned supreme on the trade routes between Europe, America and Southeast Asia. Economic power was available to sustain a rebellion against the Spanish. The Dutch Protestants under the influence of Cal-vinism, whose principles corresponded more with their own economic realities and future aims, saw in that rebellion not only a means of repelling the onslaught of the Counter Refor-mation, but at the same time the opportunity through which they could wrest maritime supremacy from Spain and transfer it to their own cities. In a struggle lasting many years the battle-hardened Spaniards failed to subdue the Dutch. Philip's axis which ran from Flanders to Milan was beginning to disin-tegrate. In essence it was a conflict between the powers of commerce and the powers of an almost purely military state. The Dutch had developed their native industries, their wool mills at Leiden, their bleaching processes at Haarlem, their shipbuilding industry and those indirectly associated with it,

Above right. The rulers of Europe: Emperor Frederick III, Maximilian, as Roman King, Ferdinand II, King of Spain, Henry VII King of England, Philip the Fair as representative of Burgundy, and Charles VII King of France.

Bottom right. Fifteenth-century German armor-smith. During that period the city of Augsburg was particularly renowned in Europe for the quality of its armor.

Below. Walnut pistol with engraved inlay.

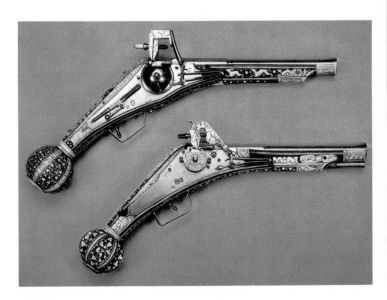

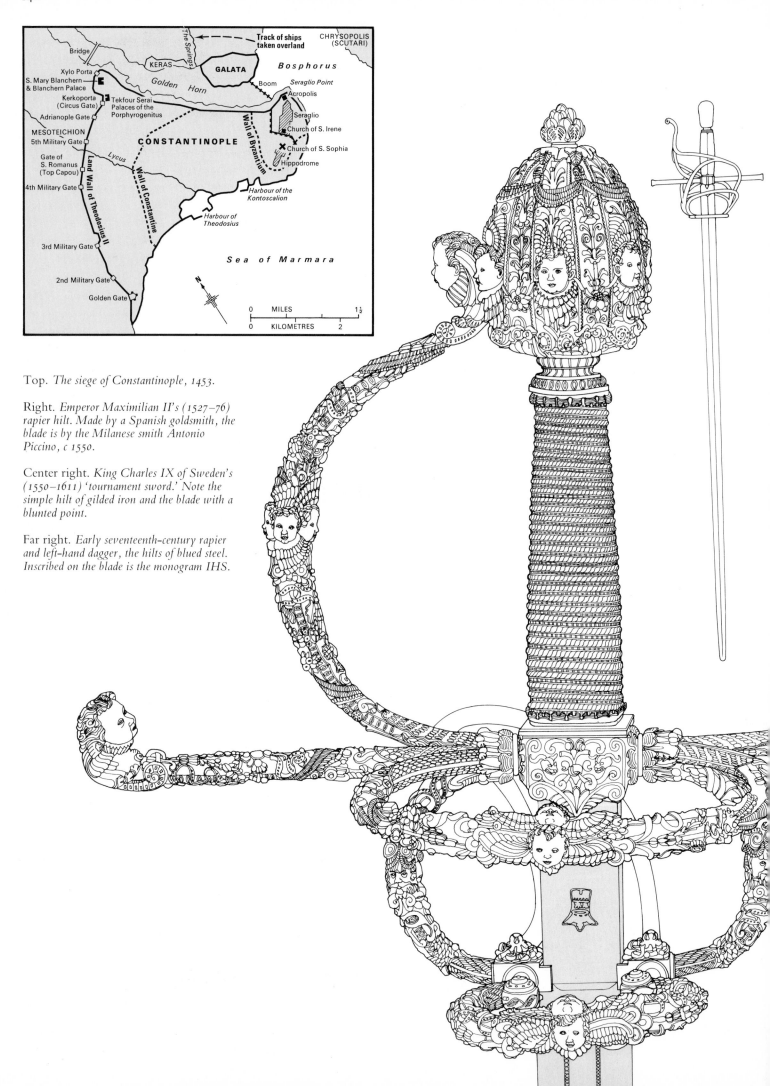

Top. *The siege of Constantinople, 1453.*

Right. *Emperor Maximilian II's (1527–76) rapier hilt. Made by a Spanish goldsmith, the blade is by the Milanese smith Antonio Piccino, c 1550.*

Center right. *King Charles IX of Sweden's (1550–1611) 'tournament sword.' Note the simple hilt of gilded iron and the blade with a blunted point.*

Far right. *Early seventeenth-century rapier and left-hand dagger, the hilts of blued steel. Inscribed on the blade is the monogram IHS.*

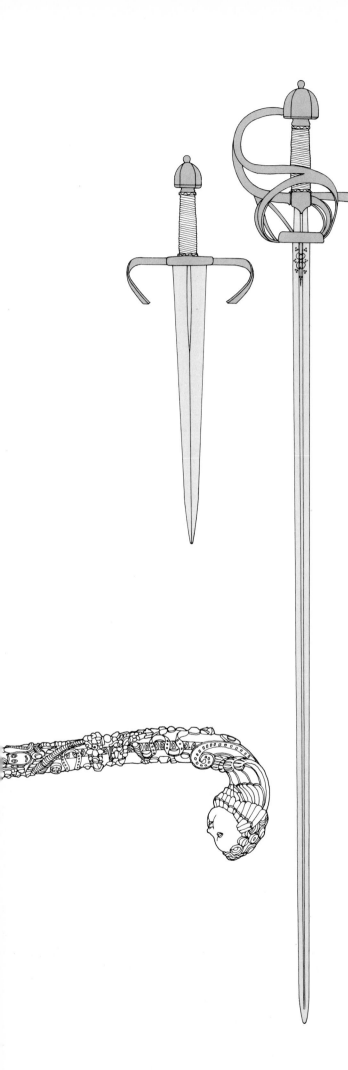

Armor of King Ferdinand of Portugal.

and the processing of imports which came from overseas, sugar, tobacco and diamonds. It was a Jesuit who coined the phrase that heresy furthers the spirit of commerce.

In 1567 the Duke of Alba, entered the Netherlands at the head of a Spanish army made up mainly of Spanish contingents but also Walloon, Italian and German mercenaries. He was opposed by a force that did not have a united core such as the Spaniards did. The German, English, Scottish and French mercenaries, lacked that bond which united Philip's army, the hatred of heretics. However, they did have an efficient army. Their first weapon of defense derived from their geography; by opening the sluices of their dykes, they put up a defensive barrier which was difficult to overcome.

But it cannot be said that the Dutch won that conflict because of their superior patriotism, let alone because their forces were militarily superior to those of the Spanish. Indeed, on occasions resistance in the Netherlands was often impeded by merchants who were inclined towards peace. Rich cities like Amsterdam delayed their break with Spain for many years. Military supremacy undoubtedly lay on the side of the Spanish, and this did not change when Elizabeth I of England aided the Netherlands, first surreptitiously and then openly. Nor did the defeat of the Armada in the English Channel affect the issue so profoundly as to tip the scales against the Spanish in the Netherlands. What made all the difference was that the Estates General could pay its mercenary forces regularly, while the Spanish were short of cash even to pay their own men, let alone their mercenaries. Without the economic means to conduct war, corruption among the Spanish captains became rife; mutinies of increasing

Left. *Advancing infantry squares.*

Right. *Besieging a fortified city (Swiss ms, mid-fifteenth century).*

Far right. *Siege of the fortress in Fillech in Upper Hungary illustrating the direct bombardment of interior of the fortress. Notice the main siege base on the far upper left.*

Below. *Attack on the Spanish Armada by fireship, 1588.*

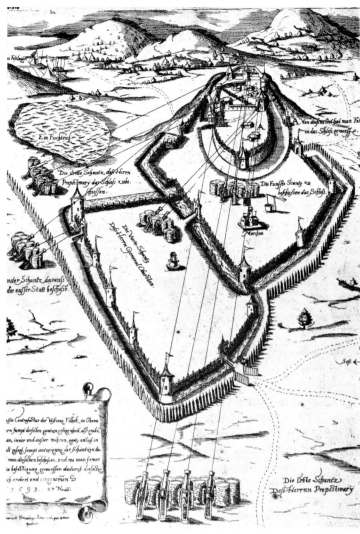

frequency destroyed the military effectiveness of the Spanish army. On 4 November 1576 when the mercenaries could not be paid, the town hall of Antwerp and several hundred houses were ravaged by the *furia espagnola*, and 10,000 of its inhabitants were killed.

The army of the Estates General faced considerable difficulties. Their commanders were the Princes of Orange of the House of Nassau, but they were under the permanent and minute scrutiny of the merchants. Members of the Estates General participated in the decision-making process at military headquarters. Moreover each commander had only those troops for which his province paid. The merchants were at the beginning unwilling to part with the sums required to keep an army in the field. But in their own interests they had to pay punctually, and that punctuality kept their army in being, while the superior power of their opponents was eroded because the enemy lacked economic substance. Great emphasis was placed on the training of men and officers, and since the Dutch contingents were small and numerous which increased their tactical mobility, the demands on men and officers were correspondingly higher. The Dutch could keep the Spaniards at bay on land; they could not conquer them. Where the Spanish Empire could be conquered by the Dutch was on the High Seas, which was really the least of their offensive operations. When in the end the Spanish gave the Dutch their independence, it was because they had been successfully repelled on land for 80 years; on the High Seas they had to yield completely to the Dutch. In the course of the struggle between the Netherlands and Spain a new military theory was developed which broke the remnants of military practice of the Middle Ages which had been left.

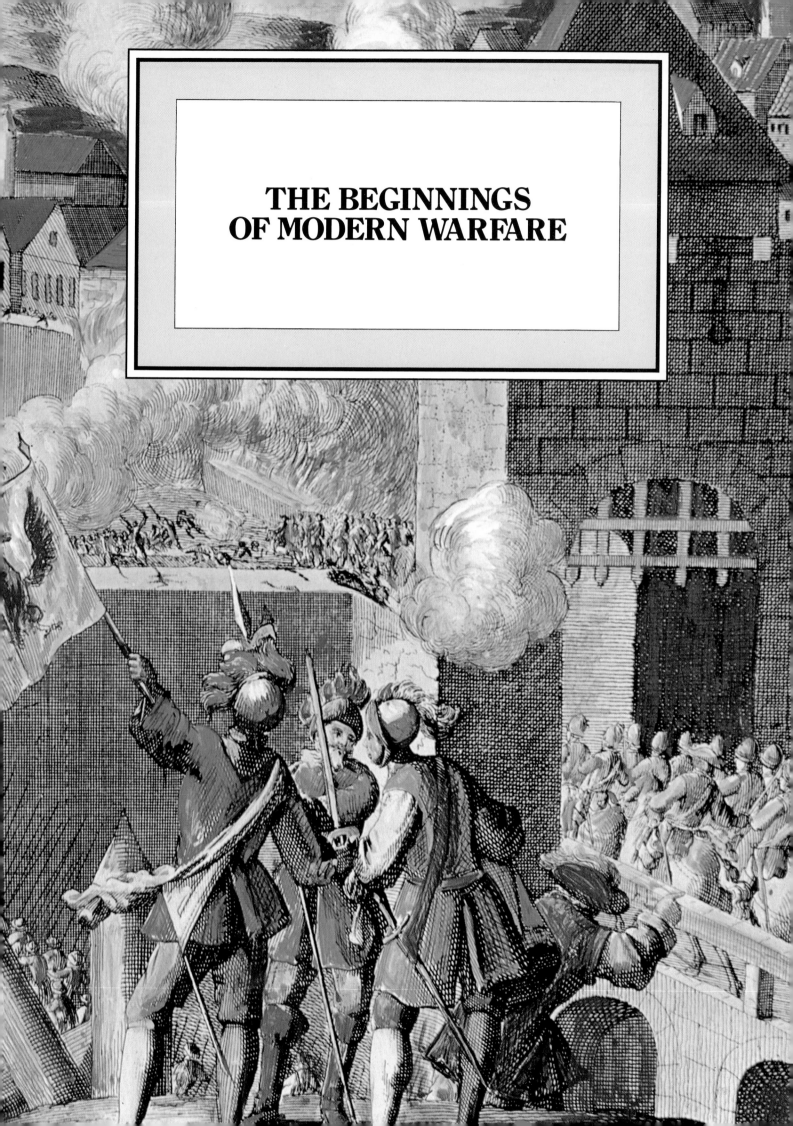

THE BEGINNINGS
OF MODERN WARFARE

During the sixteenth century the Reformation swept across central Europe like a tidal wave. Almost the whole of Germany, including the Austrian crown-lands, became Protestant or members of the rapidly developing Protestant sectarianism. It rent the German body politic asunder, the German princes deciding their religious affiliation not so much by religious criteria but political ones – namely what advantages would be gained by joining one side or the other. In vain Emperor Charles V tried to mediate, but all he managed to achieve was a compromise in the Peace of Augsburg of 1555, which established the principle of *cuius regio eius religio*: whoever ruled the state determined the religion of his subjects.

The defenestration of the imperial officials from the *Hradcany* in Prague in 1618 was not the cause of the Thirty Years' War, only the trigger. In fact, although the three officials had been thrown from a height of over 50 feet by enraged Protestant nobles, all three of them escaped injury. The Bohemians renounced the Habsburg overlordship and in its place chose Elector Frederick of the Palatinate, a son-in-law of James I of England, as their rightful king. The issue was sealed with the defeat of the Protestants at the Battle of the White Mountain on 8 November 1620. On 20 March of the same year Archduke Ferdinand had succeeded to the throne as King and Emperor of the Holy Roman Empire of the German peoples. Ferdinand II's aim was two-fold, though first and foremost, as he was a product of Jesuit education, came the restitution of Roman Catholicism throughout the Empire as the one and only faith, and with it of course the restitution of all the lands of which the secular powers had deprived the Church for the past century. He had already carried out a Counter Reformation in his own territories. Secondly, hand in hand with achieving the victory

Previous spread. *Imperial troops sack the Protestant city of Magdeburg on 20 May 1631. Some 25,000 of the city's inhabitants perished.*

Above. *The execution of 45 Bohemian noblemen in Prague, 1621. Such scenes followed Catholic victory at the Battle of the White Mountain in 1620.*

Below. *The Defenestration of Prague, 23 May 1618. Rebel nobles hurl the Emperor's advisers through the windows of Hradcany Castle.*

Below right. *Maximilian of Bavaria, 1573–1651.*

of the Counter Reformation, following others of his time, he endeavored to concentrate power in his own hands. His opponents in this respect, however, were not simply the estates, but above all the princes of the Reich, or Empire, who, Catholic or Protestant, had managed to enrich themselves considerably in the wake of the Reformation, in terms of territory as well as effective power, with which they were loath to part. Although single-minded on the issue of the dominance of Roman Catholicism, Ferdinand II was less so in the pursuit of his second aim until the right kind of adviser stood by his side.

The defeat of the Protestants in 1620 brought the Danes and King Christian IV into play on the Protestant side. As Duke of Holstein, the King was also a prince of the Empire. In the war against the Danes and the German Protestant princes there emerged a nobleman from Bohemia, Albrecht von Wallenstein, Duke of Friedland and of Mecklenburg, a man who among the established nobility in Germany was a mere upstart. Yet he was the man who, from the first, realized the endemic weakness of the Holy Roman Empire, namely the excessive play given to the centrifugal forces inherent within it. A modern state needed centralization, and such centralization could be achieved only at the expense of the established privileges of the German princes. To bring them to heel the Habsburg dynasty required an army of superior striking power, an army permanently in being. But from where should the Emperor take such an army? The princes of the Reich, even the Catholic Maximilian I, Elector of Bavaria, were averse to the accumulation of any further power in the hands of the Emperor. And then came Wallenstein, who upset their calculations.

Wallenstein, having sound economic sense, maximized the output of his estates to such an extent as to enable him to raise,

on the Emperor's behalf, an army which was quite independent of those meager forces which the Imperial Diet of the princes at Regensburg was willing to grant. It was largely with that army that Wallenstein expelled the Danes from German territory and vanquished their German allies, concluding, in 1629 with King Christian, a peace of such moderation as to keep him out of the war until long after Wallenstein's assassination. He also frightened off the French who, under Richelieu, intervened on behalf of the Protestants. True, Wallenstein did not make Ferdinand II a present of his army; ultimately the Emperor was to pay him back. Even Wallenstein's resources were limited, however, and he introduced a war levy throughout the Austrian crownlands and the territories of the German princes of the Catholic League. The princes complained of extortion and that their lands were being bled dry, complaints which were entirely unjustified. Wallenstein, in fact, took only as much as he needed, leaving behind ample funds to maintain agricultural production – thus being able to collect the same contribution year after year. The inherent consequence of these contributions was that it made Ferdinand II increasingly independent of his liege lords. The war seemed almost at an end when, on 6 March 1629, Ferdinand II proclaimed the Edict of Restitution, according to which all previously secularized Church lands throughout the Empire would have to be returned to the Church. It was the most unfortunate document of the Thirty Years' War, for once again it consolidated the Protestant princes and also brought into play two external forces: Gustavus Adolphus in the north, from Sweden, and Cardinal Richelieu in the west, from France. To Richelieu the religious issue in central Europe was irrelevant, but the growing consolidation of Habsburg power in the Reich was a danger. Gustavus Adolphus elevated himself to the defender of Protestantism in Germany, aided financially and militarily by Roman Catholic France. Before that happened, however, the Catholic princes scored one success against Ferdinand. Since, to all intents and purposes, the war had ended, they pressed him successfully to dismiss Wallenstein, which he did on 13 August 1630.

Less than a month before Wallenstein's dismissal, Gustavus Adolphus had made a landing at Peenemunde at the head of 13,000 men on 6 July 1630. His aim was to bring the entire Baltic provinces under Swedish control – an aim all the more important since Wallenstein had previously succeeded in bringing almost all German Baltic and North Sea harbors under Imperial control with the aim of fortifying them and then, with the aid of the Hanseatic League, to cut off the Swedes in the Baltic and deprive the Dutch of their lucrative trade there, and transfer this trade into Imperial hands.

If Gustavus Adolphus did nothing to stop this development, the German Empire would soon be in a position to build its own ships in its own shipyards and the Emperor would no longer be dependent on the good will of the Hanseatic League, Poland and Spain. However, without allies Sweden was not in a position to move against such a formidable enemy as the Habsburgs. Gustavus Adolphus' closest adviser, his chancellor Axel Oxenstierna, cautioned him against any kind of invasion, but in Sweden there was still Richelieu's special envoy Charnacé promising French subsidies, agreeing even to the exorbitant sums which Gustavus demanded. He also insisted that France and Sweden enter the war simultaneously. This Richelieu refused since he hoped that he could still draw the princes of the Catholic League, especially Maximilian of Bavaria, onto the French side. Gustavus Adolphus then turned to Denmark but King Christian roundly refused. It was at this point that Ferdinand's Edict of Restitution was proclaimed. Now Gustavus Adolphus had his pretext as the savior of the Reformation

in Germany and found as his first allies many of the German princes of the Protestant Union.

The Swedish army's arrival, military aspects apart, had disastrous effects upon Germany. For 18 years they marched through Pomerania, Mecklenburg, Saxony, Brandenburg, Thuringia, Franconia and Bavaria. They were in Munich, along the Rhine, on the Elbe, in Bohemia and Moravia, virtually before the gates of Vienna. The fame of their leaders, from Gustavus Adolphus to Gustav Horn, John Banér, Lennart Torstensson, Wrangel and Hans Christopher von Königsmarck, was as legendary as was the brutality and cruelty of the army, and for decades after the cry 'The Swedes are coming' was enough to silence unruly children. Hans Jakob von Grimmelhausen in his *Simplicius Simplicissimus*, published 1668, provides a very graphic picture of their actions. Gustavus Adolphus introduced the principle in this war that any country occupied by the Swedes had to be relentlessly plundered in order to deprive the enemy of any sources of supplies. He and his successors made little distinction as to whether the country occupied was Protestant or Catholic.

During the last decade of the war the population of central Europe could escape death chiefly in two ways. One was to take up residence within the walls of a heavily defended city because the Swedes were not prepared to engage in protracted sieges, the other was to disperse into the forests and moorlands and live from whatever they could find there. As the chronicler reports: 'In many parts no horse, no goat, no cat and dog has been left.' Mice, rats, cats and dogs acquired the reputation of delicacies, and instances of cannibalism were apparently common. For that reason, within the cities, guards were posted at cemeteries and at the gallows. The Swedes' conduct deteriorated particularly after the death of Gustavus Adolphus. Marshal Banér readily admitted that there was no way of stopping his troops from their excesses.

In 1630 Gustavus Adolphus was in no particular hurry. By the time of Wallenstein's dismissal he had raised his army to 40,000 men and, on 23 January 1631, an agreement with France was concluded which gave Gustavus a French subsidy of 500,000 livres and for every following year double the amount. He had to respect the neutrality of the princes of the Catholic League, which the Swedish king was ready to do providing none of them offered any resistance. By the spring of 1631 his army was fully prepared.

Gustavus Adolphus was an ardent disciple of Prince Maurice of Orange. In many respects he completed his military reforms and used them as the foundation of his own strategy. Gustavus' experience of war began when he was 17, and he was determined to learn from experience. Accepting Maurice's maxim that mobility is based on thorough drill and discipline, and discipline upon a sound administration, he insisted on high levels of efficiency during his time as a military commander. Drunkenness and coarse language were severely punished, though in an army that was to increase to 70,000 during his time, successful enforcement of discipline, such as Cromwell was to impose upon the New Model Army, must have been difficult, if not impossible.

With the exception of Wallenstein, the areas in which he exceeded all his contemporaries 'were tactics, organization and arms.' The Scotsman Munro, who fought under Gustavus at Breitenfeld and Lützen, recorded: 'A regiment such as this acts like an organism, it has one body, one movement, all ears hear the same command, eyes turn simultaneously, hands move as though they were one hand. The highest tactical unit was the brigade, arranged in linear pattern six deep, alternating with musketeer and pike units. The musketeers, to cover themselves against a cavalry charge, moved behind the pikes and reloaded their muskets while the reserve pike units would fill gaps in the line left by them.' Apart from perfecting infantry as well as cavalry tactics, Gustavus Adolphus added his own unique contribution by putting to full use the inherent potential of the artillery. He was the first great field gunner, who, in order to increase the mobility of his forces, reduced the vast range of artillery types and calibers and designed lighter types of gun carriages, and standardized his artillery into three main types. First there were siege guns weighing 60, 30 and 15 hundredweight, second the field pieces of 24, 12 and 6 pounders, and third, regimental pieces, two to a regiment, which were light 4 pounders. Gunnery drill, especially for regimental gunners, was stepped up to a pace which enabled them to fire eight rounds to every musketeer's six shots. In contrast to the Spanish system, Gustavus reduced his trains to an absolute minimum which meant that his army had to live largely off the land, although this was also supplemented by the setting up of supply depots along the army's line of advance.

During the first few months after his arrival on German soil, while Gustavus was still in the process of assembling his forces,

the German Protestant princes were still reluctant to join him; only Hesse-Kassel and the dukes of Saxony-Weimar openly did so, but gradually, through a mixture of persuasion and outright pressure, he brought the rest over on to his side.

At first the Swedes occupied Pomerania and Mecklenburg, and in April 1631 Frankfurt-an-der-Oder was stormed. In the meantime the Imperial forces, under the command of Marshal Tilly, besieged the strongly fortified Protestant city of Magdeburg. Count Johann Tilly wanted to conquer the obstinate bishopric, which the Protestants described as 'our Lord's chancellery,' for the son of the Emperor. From December 1630 Magdeburg was under fire by the siege guns of the Imperial forces; the people of Magdeburg appealed to Gustavus Adolphus for help, but the Swedish king did not react. On 20 May 1631 Tilly's cavalry, under the command of General Gottfried Heinrich Graf zu Pappenheim, went into the attack and stormed the city by way of two breaches which the siege artillery had made. As the soldiers followed, fires started to break out in all parts of the city; who laid the fires has remained a matter of conjecture to this day. For three days and nights the city was

Above left. *The Swedish King Gustavus Adolphus landing at Rugen in 1630, at the start of his invasion of northern Germany.*

Below left. *The Emperor Ferdinand II, who reigned from 1619–37.*

Above. *King Gustavus Adolphus of Sweden, 1594–1632.*

Right. *Seventeenth-century German soldiers.*

Below. *Spanish cup-hilt rapier, made in Toledo, circa 1670.*

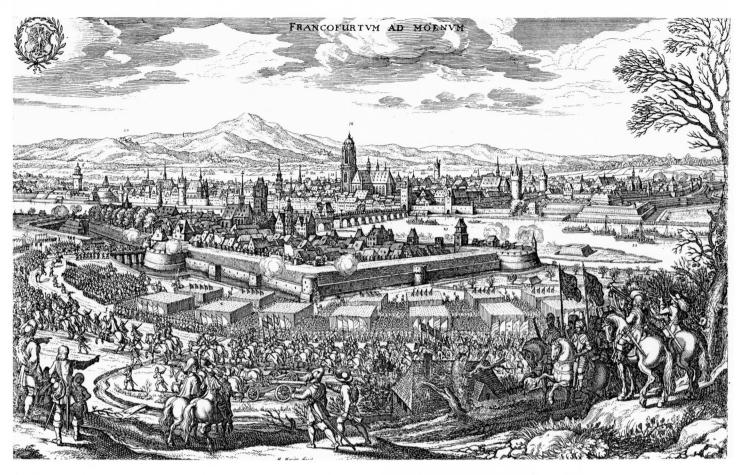

FRANCOFVRTVM AD MOENVM

sacked and all that remained of what had been one of the most flourishing and richest German cities was the cathedral and some fishermen's huts along the River Elbe. Of 30,000 inhabitants, 25,000 were killed. Magdeburg was the Hiroshima of the Thirty Years' War.

Early in June of that year Gustavus Adolphus virtually forced his brother-in-law, the Elector of Brandenburg, into alliance with Sweden. Saxony followed his example.

On 17 September 1631 the first decisive battle was fought between the Imperial forces and those of Gustavus Adolphus. The Swedish-Saxon army amounted to about 39,000 men, the forces of the Catholic League, about 36,000. The Swedes were superior in cavalry by 2000 men, but, much more important, they enjoyed a great superiority in their artillery – 75 pieces against Tilly's 26. All that Tilly had to rely on was what he assumed to be the superior quality of his troops.

Tilly, coming from the direction of Leipzig, assembled his forces in 17 squares to the right of the village of Breitenfeld on top of a low ridge in front of which, at a distance of about a mile and a half, flows the rivulet Loderbach parallel with the ridge. It would be an obstacle during the attack, not a very great one, but an obstacle nevertheless. His flanks were exposed on both sides, which did not seem to matter very much considering the depth of the Spanish squares.

Gustavus Adolphus' forces approached on a wide front across the plain with the sun on their backs. At first Gustavus attempted an attack against Tilly's right wing, but had to abandon it because the crossing of the Loderbach resulted in unexpected difficulties. Gustavus' forces extended beyond Tilly's left wing and on this broad front they now crossed the Loderbach, an opportunity ideal for attack by Tilly, a man 'short in stature . . . meager and terrible in aspect; his cheeks were sunken, his nose long and pointed, his eyes fierce and dark.' Although, apart from Wallenstein, the most able Imperial general and a master of Spanish tactics, he allowed this opportunity to slip by. Fearing his exposed left wing could be outflanked and circumvented by the

Above. *The entry of Gustavus Adolphus into Frankfurt-am-Main, 1631 (contemporary engraving).*

Left. *Johan Baner, 1596–1641, the most capable of Gustavus Adolphus' generals. He commanded the right wing of Swedish horse at Breitenfeld, and distinguished himself at the passage of the Lech. The defeat of the Elector John George of Saxony at Wittstock in 1636 was his most brilliant success.*

Below right. *Gustavus Adolphus leads a cavalry charge at the Battle of Dirschau, 1626 (oil painting by Jan Marsin de Jonge, 1634).*

Below. *A contemporary view of Irish mercenaries in the service of Gustavus Adolphus, wearing plaid-like garments probably made from an early form of tartan.*

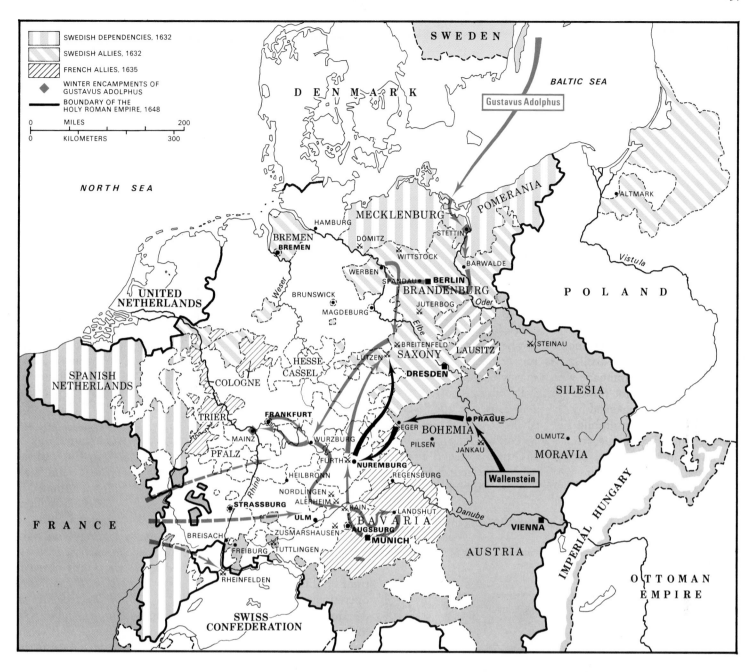

SWEDISH DEPENDENCIES, 1632
SWEDISH ALLIES, 1632
FRENCH ALLIES, 1635
WINTER ENCAMPMENTS OF GUSTAVUS ADOLPHUS
BOUNDARY OF THE HOLY ROMAN EMPIRE, 1648

MILES 0 — 200
KILOMETERS 0 — 300

SWEDEN

BALTIC SEA

Gustavus Adolphus

DENMARK

NORTH SEA

POMERANIA

ALTMARK

MECKLENBURG

STETTIN

BARWALDE

Vistula

HAMBURG

DOMITZ

WITTSTOCK

POLAND

BREMEN

WERBEN

SPANDAU

BERLIN

BRANDENBURG

Oder

UNITED NETHERLANDS

Weser

BRUNSWICK

MAGDEBURG

JUTERBOG

Elbe

STEINAU

SILESIA

SPANISH NETHERLANDS

HESSE CASSEL

COLOGNE

BREITENFELD

LUTZEN

SAXONY

LAUSITZ

DRESDEN

TRIER

FRANKFURT

MAINZ

WURZBURG

PFALZ

FURTH

HEILBRONN

NUREMBURG

NORDLINGEN

ALERHEIM

REGENSBURG

EGER

BOHEMIA

PILSEN

PRAGUE

JANKAU

OLMUTZ

MORAVIA

Wallenstein

STRASSBURG

ULM

RAIN

LANDSHUT

BREISACH

ZUSMARSHAUSEN

BAVARIA

AUGSBURG

MUNICH

Danube

IMPERIAL HUNGARY

VIENNA

FRANCE

FREIBURG

TUTTLINGEN

AUSTRIA

RHEINFELDEN

OTTOMAN EMPIRE

SWISS CONFEDERATION

Rhine

Swedes, however, he sent his ablest cavalry commander, Pappenheim, to the left to secure the position there. Immediately Pappenheim and the Swedes were fiercely embroiled in battle and Tilly was now forced to act, especially as the Swedish artillery came into action with devastating effect. Tilly therefore took four of his squares from the right wing and, with cavalry support, attacked and brought havoc among Gustavus' Saxon cavalry, who were novices in the art of war by comparison. Both these actions on the left and right wings caused a deep cleavage, which meant that the bulk of the Swedish army had no enemy in front of it. The Swedes exploited this opportunity, moved into the center and, from there, to the rear of Tilly's forces. Moreover, the Swedes had repelled Pappenheim's attacks. The Swedish cavalry and their tactical interaction with the musketeers proved superior to anything Tilly could offer. They faced the attacking Imperial cavalry with a mighty salvo by the musketeers, who then withdrew, and the momentary confusion was immediately exploited by the Swedish cavalry, who counterattacked.

The point of decision lay on the Swedes' left wing, where the Imperial square had made short work of the Saxon cavalry. Gustavus Adolphus re-formed his cavalry, and, as a prelude, exploited his superior artillery firepower of three to one and followed up this cannonade with a massive cavalry attack. The Imperial squares, not drilled effectively enough to retire systematically and weakened by the havoc caused by the Swedish artillery in their immobile squares, disintegrated and stampeded. The whole battle, from the Swedish point of view, was predominantly a cavalry action. Of Gustavus' seven infantry brigades, only three were involved in the actual fighting. Pappenheim's cavalry failed to match the combined tactics of the Swedish cavalry and infantry. His forces were so demoralized that Pappenheim could not rally them again for a new

Below. *A German soldier of the early seventeenth century in the act of loading his match lock musket.*

assault. Tilly had been wounded several times in the fracas and decided to withdraw toward Halle. His infantry, captured by the Swedes, joined Gustavus Adolphus *en masse*. Tilly had lost 11,000 men, the Saxons 3000, the Swedes 1500. With that victory, the command of the whole of northern Germany fell into the hands of Gustavus Adolphus; there were no longer any obstacles leading to western and southern Germany.

Gustavus moved to the south, entered the city of Nuremberg in the spring of 1632, and defeated Tilly again at the River Lech shortly afterward. In this battle Tilly was heavily wounded; his right leg was smashed, gangrene set in and he died a few weeks later in Altötting in Bavaria, the Black Madonna of Altötting being a traditional focus for pilgrimage. Bavaria was completely defenseless. The Elector Maximilian walled himself up in the fortress of Regensburg while Gustavus conquered Ingolstadt, Augsburg, Landshut and finally Munich. The campaign had little to do with warfare, opposition being virtually nonexistent; the Swedes could advance as they pleased and plunder along the way.

Ferdinand II found himself in a dilemma. Having dismissed Wallenstein, there was no one to replace him. Since the autumn of 1631 Ferdinand had endeavored to get Wallenstein to return, in spite of the implicit humiliation which this step meant for the Emperor. For every Imperial general it implied a personal shortcoming because none of them had so far been able to stop Gustavus Adolphus. Wallenstein rejected Ferdinand's first approach, but Ferdinand did not give up – he even implored him to become his Supreme Field Commander. Only through the intervention of personal friends of both the Emperor and Wallenstein did the latter give in to the request. This culminated in the Göllersdorfer agreements of 12 April 1632. In these Wallenstein promised to put up a new army within a few months, to increase it to a strength of over 100,000 men, and to take over the command. In return he demanded that he exercise absolute command, in other words remain unimpeded by the obstructionist politics of the court in Vienna, and that, as far as military operations were concerned, he possessed complete freedom of decision. Ferdinand agreed and transferred absolute powers to him.

Wallenstein was the only statesman in the Imperial camp; he was also the only one who represented the cause of the Reich and not necessarily that of the dynasty. He was the only one equal in stature to Richelieu and to the Swedish Chancellor Oxenstierna. Wallenstein's basic premise was his unshakeable conviction that within the Reich there was no room for foreign powers, whether Spanish allies, the French or the Swedes. In a nutshell, he pursued a policy of purely German national interest, one which Ferdinand had unswervingly adhered to and which would not only have strengthened the Habsburg dynasty but changed the course of Germany's entire history for centuries to come.

Wallenstein began his recruitment drive and, in weeks rather than months, he had again under his banner the nucleus of his old army. He had reserved for himself the prerogative of appointing his own officers down to company level; in that way no officer's position could be bought, but was awarded according to ability. Gustavus Adolphus had not reckoned on Wallenstein's speed: hardly had the Swedish king left Munich

Above right. *Johann Tserclaes, Graf von Tilly, 1559–1632.*

Above, far right. *The sack of Magdeburg, May 1631.*

Right. *The siege of Magdeburg, 1631. This contemporary engraving shows the majestic skyline of a city soon to be ravaged by Imperial troops.*

Ill.^{mus} atque Excell.^{mus} D.D. Ioannes à Tserclaes S.R.I. Comes,
Baro de Tilly et Marbais ; Sacræ Cæs: Maif:^{is} nec non
Ser.^{mi} Electoris ac Bauariæ Ducis, locum tenens Generalis,
Consiliarius & respectiue Camerarius. &c.

Lucas Kilian. Aug: Sculpsit A.º 1629.

MAGDEBURGVM.

Above. *The death of Gustavus Adolphus at the Battle of Lützen, 1632. His body, stripped by looters, was later found under a pile of the dead.*

when Wallenstein announced that his preparations were complete and that the new Imperial army under his command could take to the field. Expecting Wallenstein to turn to Saxony, Gustavus pulled his army out of Bavaria and southern Germany and marched north. But Wallenstein, instead of marching into Saxony, wanted to unite with the remaining forces of the Catholic League under Maximilian of Bavaria, cut off the Swedes and prevent them joining the Saxons. By the end of June the Bavarian and Imperial troops had joined forces. It came as a shock to Gustavus. He tried to move his forces out of Bavaria rapidly, force-marched them via Augsburg and Schwabach only to realize that Wallenstein had succeeded in cutting

Below. *The armies of Gustavus and Wallenstein meet at Lützen, 16 November 1632 (contemporary engraving).*

him off from the Saxons. There was nothing left for him but to march to Nuremberg and encamp himself behind its strong fortifications. Wallenstein moved north and established his positions southwest of Fürth between Zirndorf and the Alten Veste.

For six weeks the armies confronted one another, with Gustavus trying time and again to tempt Wallenstein to attack him at Nuremberg. Wallenstein had not the slightest intention of exposing his troops to the concentrated fire of the 500 pieces of artillery waiting to receive the Imperial troops. It was a turning point in the history of warfare. Wallenstein provided the first classic example of the strategy of attrition which was to dominate European warfare for the next century and a half.

It did not bother him that the Swedish king received reinforcements from the Rhine, Swabia and Thuringia to the extent that it trebled Gustavus' forces. Wallenstein had taken account of this in his calculations because the more troops the Swedes gathered, the more difficult would become their mobility; be-

cause of the size of the trains involved, the more difficult would also become the problem of feeding and supplying an army of that size in a static position. He had maneuvered the Swedish King into a position which presented only two alternatives: to attack Wallenstein or to withdraw. His calculations proved right. At the height of his military career, surrounded by a reputation of invincibility, Gustavus attacked the Imperial positions on 1 September 1632. Wallenstein had planned his fortifications in an entirely novel way: he had not built up a continuous line, but instead established a chain of individual fortifications in an almost zigzag formation, where every corner not occupied by troops could be reached by his artillery. There were no blind spots where a breach could be made.

For four days the Swedes mounted attack after attack without achieving the slightest success. During the night of 4 September, Gustavus decided to break off the engagement. He had lost 7000 men, three time as many as the Imperial forces. According to the rules of war valid at that time, there was no victor and no vanquished, but contemporaries quickly realized that, because Gustavus had failed to conquer, because he had failed to overwhelm Wallenstein, he had also lost the battle. Wallenstein was not only a superb general and statesman, for his time he was also a sound economist. Realizing that soldiers were expensive, especially since he had put his own funds at the disposal of their upkeep, they had to be used sparingly. Under such conditions attrition paid greater dividends than the wasteful procedure of laying siege to a city or entering into an open

field battle. It was a lesson quickly learned by his successors and fellow generals throughout Europe.

On 16 November 1632 the two generals met again on the plain of Lützen, again near Leipzig. Gustavus intended to head Wallenstein off his supply base at Leipzig. The battle began during the late morning after the fog had lifted. It was the most ferocious and tough battle of the Thirty Years' War. It raged the whole day under the continuous fire of the artillery of both sides. It was fought with 'such fury, as no one has ever seen before,' as Wallenstein noted the following day. By the evening the elementary rules for open field battles had gone overboard; the battle was one mighty scene of butchery, an orgy of merciless killing. It raged on into the night and nothing was heard except the firing of guns and muskets, and the shrieks of the attackers and the attacked. Only as the night wore on did the battle gradually come to an end. Again there was no victor and no vanquished; both armies were completely exhausted. But the most important outcome of it was that the Lion of Midnight, as Gustavus Adolphus was popularly called, had been killed in battle. The war now took on a new direction.

Wallenstein's successes in 1632 were not rewarded with gratitude any more than had those before 1630. His name lay at the root of the growing power of the House of Habsburg in Germany and Europe. The German princes fully realized that

Below. Another view of Lützen. Gustavus at the head of the Swedish right wing, prepares to attack Wallenstein's weak left (contemporary engraving).

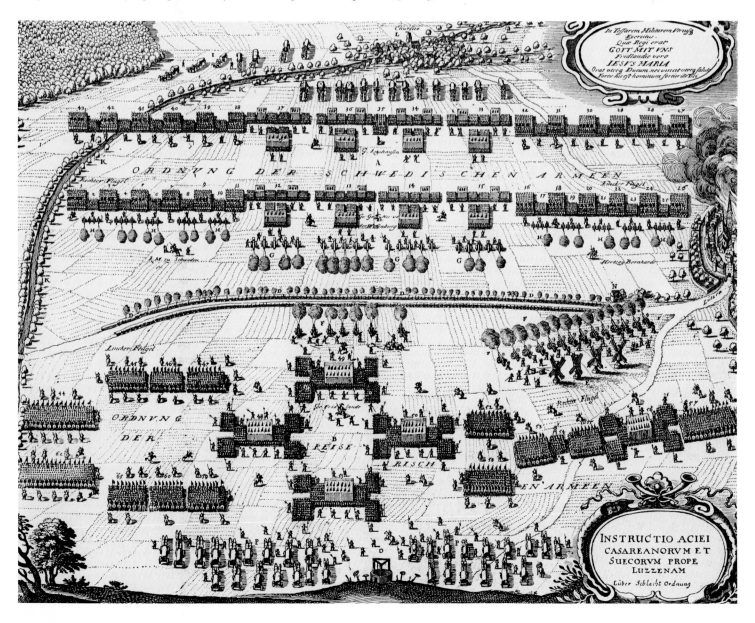

any further consolidation of the Emperor's position and any additional power he acquired was bound to have consequences detrimental to their own positions. Ferdinand's confidence in Wallenstein lasted as long as the Imperial army was and remained an indispensable instrument of Habsburg policy. The princes of the Reich, led by the Elector of Bavaria, Maximilian, sent petition after petition to Vienna directed against Wallenstein in particular and the Imperial policy in general. Wallenstein's successes threatened their own privileges, and their intractability caused Wallenstein, in a moment of anger, to remark that 'there will be no peace and quiet in the Reich until the moment when one of their heads is put before their feet. One will have to teach the Electors some manners. They must depend on the emperor and not the emperor on them.'

The crisis of confidence between Ferdinand and Wallenstein began in December 1633, when the latter explicitly ignored Ferdinand's orders and left his army in winter quarters. Philip IV of Spain suggested the setting up of an independent Spanish army in Alsace and along the Rhine with the task of protecting not only Alsace and the Rhenish territories, but the whole of southern Germany including Franconia. Since the number of the Spanish troops was insufficient for this task, Wallenstein's army was to reinforce them and his position would be subordinate to the Duke of Feria. Wallenstein immediately recognized that the Spanish project would completely undermine the Emperor's position in Germany among Catholics and Protestants alike, since no forces were more hated than the Spaniards. Ferdinand's position would become dependent on Madrid. Wallenstein succeeded in making this point but, in addition to the German electors, he now had the Spaniards as his enemies at the court of Vienna. He also argued that the time was favorable for concluding peace and any additional Spanish intervention would prolong the war indefinitely.

Throughout 1633 Wallenstein tried to win over Brandenburg and Saxony to the Imperial side. What he managed to achieve was a declaration of their neutrality. He tried to negotiate with Oxenstierna, but since Sweden insisted upon gaining territory in Germany all contacts were broken off. Wallenstein acted fully within the competencies granted to him by Ferdinand in the Göllersdorfer agreements. When suddenly rumors began to spread about Wallenstein conducting treasonable negotiations, rumors emanating from the German princes, Wallenstein reminded Ferdinand of that agreement. He defended his refusal to give up the army's winter quarters by claiming that the soldiers would otherwise perish or despair.

Wallenstein's decision, combined with his political negotiations, fed doubts in Ferdinand's mind which were strongly supported by the protests of the Electors. By the end of December 1633 Ferdinand decided not simply to dismiss him but to remove him by force. Blind to his own real interests and with a ready ear for the conspirators against Wallenstein around him, he pronounced a formal ban on Wallenstein on 24 January 1634. With that public ban, valid throughout the Reich, almost all Wallenstein's commanding officers left him. A month later, on 25 February 1634, the last Saturday of the carnival season, six dragoons led by the French captain Devereux broke into Wallenstein's residence at Eger and murdered him. The Habsburgs' bloody carnival had reached its climax. Habsburg's only statesman, a man acting for the interests of the dynasty as well as for Germany, left the scene; gone was the opportunity for the establishment of an absolutist monarchy of the House of Habsburg over a truly united Germany. In its place stepped a multitude of sovereign absolutist German princes. Had Wallenstein succeeded, there would never have been any need for a Bismarck; Cardinal Richelieu could be relieved.

The war dragged on for another 14 years, bringing more devastation over central Europe. To assess the damage of the Thirty Years' War statistically is virtually impossible as there are too many gaps in the evidence. What is relatively certain is that the German population residing in the countryside declined by 40 percent, while in the cities every third person became a victim of the war. In Bohemia the population declined from three million to 780,000. In 1618 there were 35,000 villages; at the end of the war in 1648 only one in six was inhabited, the rest having been burned down. Foreign troops brought the pestilence to Munich, and within four months 10,000 burghers had died. In Württemberg the population had already declined from 400,000 to 48,000 by 1641. In the Palatinate in the same year there was only one-fiftieth of the original population left. Magdeburg lost 90 percent of its inhabitants, Chemnitz 80

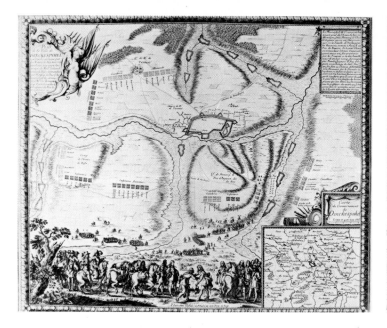

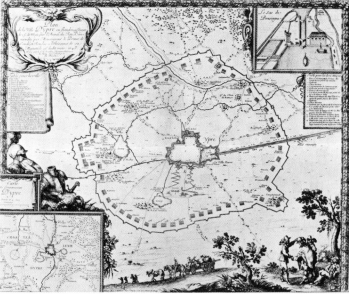

percent, Berlin and Colmar each 50 percent. The account of the Swedish army alone is debited with the complete destruction of 1500 cities, 18,000 villages and 200 castles.

The Westphalian peace confirmed Germany's fragmentation. The Habsburgs had failed in their bid to reimpose Catholicism in Germany. They were still emperors of the Holy Roman Empire, but every territorial prince now possessed the right to conduct his own foreign policy irrespective of how this policy affected the Reich as a whole. The real victor was France; although Sweden was also on the victorious side she did not possess the resources to maintain her positions in Germany longer than six decades. France gained the bishoprics of Metz, Toul and Verdun, Breisach, the entire Alsace, 10 cities and 40 villages in the Reich, and the right to traverse Germany with its troops and supplies.

What remained for the Habsburgs was precious little; the only substantial gain was the nucleus of Wallenstein's army, which became the nucleus of the standing army of the Habsburg dynasty. But it still possessed enough strength to maintain itself as a great power.

The remnants of Wallenstein's army – nine infantry and ten cavalry regiments – were the core of an army which a few decades later would repel the Turkish onslaught on Vienna, finally drive them back and storm Belgrade during the War of the Spanish Succession. Led by the genius of Prince Eugene, they played a principal part in checking once and for all the territorial ambitions of Louis XIV. This army, in fact the first standing army in Germany, was based on voluntary recruitment. The Vienna *Hofkriegsrat*, Court War Council, a kind of central organ combining general staff, military cabinet and the ministry of war, issued a directive that only Germans could be recruited to serve in German regiments, because, so the directive said, 'foreigners do not easily become accustomed to the comradeship of our people.' By 1705 the Austrian army comprised 100,000 men, and on the eve of the Seven Years' War 165,000. Ultimately it contained 12 different nationalities, all formed in their own regiments but with German as the language of command.

The work of expanding the foundations which Wallenstein had left behind was in the main that of Count Raimondo

Left. *The ambitious Czech adventurer Albrecht von Wallenstein, a freebooting Imperial general, murdered by a group of disaffected officers at Eger in February 1634.*

Far right. *Wallenstein's soothsayer surveys the body of his murdered master (nineteenth-century painting).*

Right. *A German swept-hilt rapier, circa 1660.*

Above. *French and Hessian troops under the Duc d'Enghien (soon to be Prince de Condé), besieging the Swabian town of Dinkelsbühl in 1645.*

Above right. *A contemporary engraving from the same series shows Condé's forces besieging the town of Ypres in Flanders. Ypres, whose strategic location made it the scene of numerous battles, was besieged on 13 May 1648 and fell on the 29th.*

Montecuccoli (1609–81), a man who was immediately impressive for his wide-ranging, almost universal education. He was one of many in the seventeenth century who were aware of the spiritual and intellectual problems of modern life and who tried to analyze them scientifically. This general not only produced great feats on the battlefield against the Turks and the French, but was also the author of one of the major works on military theory which, more than a century later, served Scharnhorst, the Prussian reformer, very well. Thus on strategy he wrote: 'He who believes that progress can be achieved in the field without engaging in battle contradicts himself, or at least voices such a peculiar opinion as to bring ridicule upon himself. . . . Once the troops notice this, how much greater would become their fear of the bravery of the enemy! Of course one should never engage in battle without careful thought, and even less should one allow the enemy to force one into battle; all that one has to do is to recognize the right moment for battle. After all, in the final analysis it is necessary to be ready to fight and to gain control of the battlefield; whoever wins the battle wins not only the campaign but also a sizable piece of territory. Therefore, even if someone appears to be well prepared for battle, the mistakes which he may have made in maneuvering earlier on may be supportable, but however well he may have performed in other respects, if he has previously failed to grasp the lessons taught by battle he is unlikely to conclude the war with honors.' In other words, commence battle only when you possess an obvious advantage; without it, whether the battle is won or lost the long-term result is likely to be inconclusive.

In 1683 church bells rang throughout the Habsburg Empire: the Turks had launched an invasion, reaching the gates of Vienna by July 1683. The imperial court left the city in great haste for Passau. What remained behind was a defending force of 22,000 men commanded by Ernst Rüdiger Count Starhemberg. The army of the Reich rallied more quickly to the relief of Vienna than one would have expected, though some of the forces, like those of the Elector of Bavaria, Max II Emanuel, were so badly equipped and supplied that more of his soldiers died or fell sick on the march than were killed in the actual battle. For two months the Turks attacked incessantly, but, assisted by the Viennese burghers, the Reich army beat back every attack. Vienna had become the shield of Germany; the Turks were determined to take the city before reinforcements could arrive.

By 7 September 1683 reinforcements had arrived; they came along the right bank of the Danube and positioned themselves at the Kahlemberg, the bald mountain outside Vienna from which, on a clear day, one can see as far as Bratislava and into the Hungarian plain, while to the south and southwest the summits of Styria and Carinthia are clearly visible. On 12 September battle commenced. Down from the heights of the Kahlemberg marched the Habsburg and Reich regiments led by the Bavarian Elector, and, supported by a surprise attack which Starhemberg mounted from the city, victory was complete. Kara Mustafa the Vizier, commanding the Turks, received the silken cord from the Sultan: a general who lost a battle of this kind had also lost his right to live. The Grand Vizier committed suicide, his head was cut off and sent on a silver platter to the Sultan. The battle also enabled another man to make his first major mark: Eugene, Prince of Savoy (1663–1736). He was the younger son of a side branch of the House of Savoy and had first tried his luck at the court of Louis XIV. He was small of stature and quite ugly; fortune was not on his side. Therefore he turned to the Habsburgs, where his career was rapid. At the battle of the Kahlemberg he commanded the dragoon Kufstein regiment.

The victory of the Battle of the Kahlemberg was not followed up – the soldiers were too busy plundering the oriental treasures of the Turks and, above all, their wine. The campaign gathered only slowly in pace again, but two years later the Hungarian capital Ofen was captured, and a little later Max Emanuel, at the head of his Bavarians, stormed Belgrade. For the first time in 300 years the Magyar nobility bowed to the Habsburgs and accepted their overlordship, and Emperor Leopold had his son Joseph, then only nine years old, crowned King of Hungary. The Habsburg Empire's policy gained new direction, away from the Reich and into southeastern Europe and the Balkans.

The Turkish invasion had been the product of an alliance between France and the Ottoman Empire. It was repelled with the fervor of a crusade. The German princes had never been so united since the Reformation and, after the defeat of the Turks, were never to be so again until the iron hand of Bismarck forced them into unity. French policy, insofar as it included the Turks, had failed, and Louis XIV decided on a campaign of rape and pillage along the Rhine. He annexed the Reich city of Strasbourg and then moved down the Rhine conquering Speyer, Mainz and Trier. But the emperor, aided by England and the Netherlands, reacted promptly and expelled the French from the Palatinate. The French withdrawal was accompanied by a scorched earth policy to ensure that no supplies were left behind; Cologne and Bingen were burnt to the ground by the forces commanded by General Ezéchiel de Mélac; he also had the Schloss of Heidelberg burnt down, the ruins of which are a reminder of the warfare of absolutism under the auspices of Louis XIV to this day. The war over the Palatinate ended only in 1697 with the Peace of Ryswick; France held onto the Alsace and Strasbourg.

A la fin ces Voleurs infames et perdus, Comme fruits malheureux a cet arbre pendus, Monstrent bien que le crime (horrible et noire engeance) Est luy mesme instrument de honte et de vengeance, Et que c'est le Destin des hommes vicieux Desprouver tost ou tard la iustice des Cieux. 11

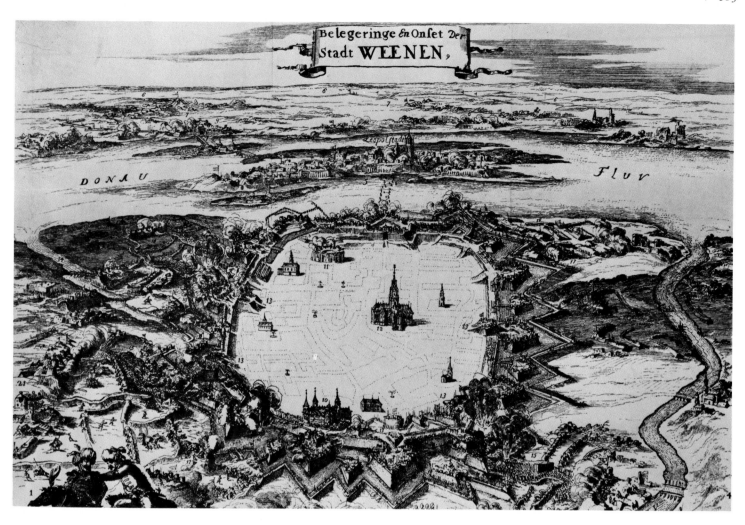

Belegeringe En Onset Der Stadt WEENEN,

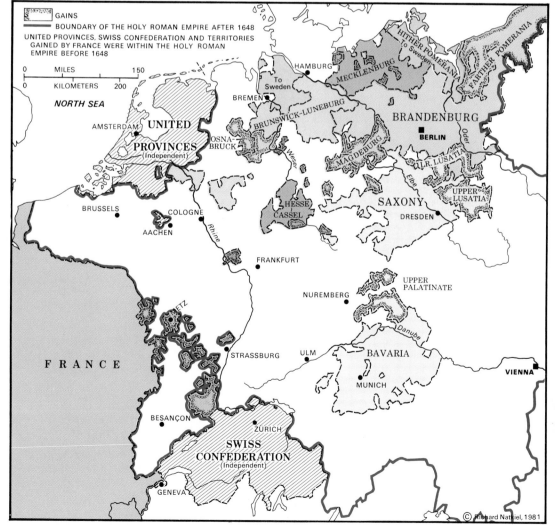

Above. *C Decker's contemporary engraving shows the Turks battering at the walls of Vienna. St Stephen's cathedral can be seen in the center of the town, with a broken bridge across the Danube behind it.*

Below. *The Austrian Count Starhemberg, defender of Vienna against the Turks in 1683.*

Above. *Graf Leopold Joseph von Daun, 1705–66. An able Austrian general, Daun was the first to defeat Frederick the Great's army, at Kolin in 1757. Though defeated at Leuthen the same year, he again defeated Frederick in 1758. Daun was a skillful strategist, who specialized in schemes which forced the Prussians to attack him in strong positions.*

In 1714 the Turks renewed their attack, and again the German princes rallied to Habsburg's side, but mostly to learn military craft from Prince Eugene. Delays ensued and only in 1716 did an actual major battle occur; Eugene defeated the Turks and then, moving toward the east, conquered within two months the entire Banat and its capital Temesvár. The Sultan had lost his last bastion in Hungary. However, Eugene wanted to achieve a durable peace as well as a military victory. Upon his initiative the Habsburgs agreed a settlement policy calling German peasants, particularly from Bavaria, Swabia and the Palatinate, to settle and cultivate the Banat, which had now been completely depopulated by the Turks. It was the last chapter of German colonization to the east.

In the spring of 1717, after thorough planning, Eugene moved down the Danube toward Belgrade, which had fallen again into Turkish hands. He crossed the River Save and established his fortification south of the city flanked by the Drave and the Danube. By the middle of July the siege began with a continuous artillery bombardment. For three weeks the Imperial forces tried to wear down the Turks: sappers laid their mines and breaches were made in the outer walls, but not enough was achieved to tempt Eugene to mount a direct assault. Moreover, Turkish relief forces were approaching from Adrianople led by the Sultan himself. After their arrival the relief army took up position behind strong earthworks and soon Eugene's forces were exposed to heavy fire. In Vienna the position was already considered hopeless for Eugene. Devoid of any illusions he decided in favor of a major surprise stroke. In the early hours of the dawn of 16 August, at three o'clock in the morning, he attacked the Sultan's forces. In spite of their tenacious defense, they were beaten and the Grand Vizier ordered withdrawal southward. Eugene refrained from pursuit, for it was sufficient to have thrown out the Turks and caused their withdrawal. On the following day Belgrade surrendered and the capitulation document was signed on 18 August.

Finally, on 21 July 1718, the Peace of Passarowitz put an end to the almost century-old struggle between the Ottoman Empire and the Habsburgs and this, but for a short episode between 1737 and 1739, stabilized the position of the great powers in the Balkans until well into the nineteenth century.

Prince Eugene was appointed President of the *Hofkriegsrat*, a position which gave him both military and political power. Like Wallenstein he engaged in high diplomacy, not for the sake of personal aggrandizement but to expand and stabilize the power of the Habsburg dynasty. Unlike Wallenstein, however, he considered the German Reich and its consolidation as largely irrelevant. He preferred, on the basis of a firm system of alliances, to establish a balance of power within Europe, as was also borne out by his policy toward France, and thus to contribute to a general peace.

His personality, his military genius, his sound political judgment, combined with his deep interest in philosophy and the creative arts, was ideal for the leadership of what in essence was the new Austrian army, transforming former mercenaries into God-fearing regular soldiers. He paid particular attention to the training of his officer corps, every member having to exhibit qualities of bravery and chivalry; as he put it: 'Gentlemen, you have only one justification for your life if you continuously, even in moments of the greatest danger, provide an example . . . so that no one can blemish you.'

More so than the rank and file, the Austrian officer corps represented an international body. Little wonder that the military nobility from all corners of Europe came to serve in the Imperial army. Of course, the dynastic ties with Spain and Italy provided easy access, and the fame of the great field marshal exercised its magnetic powers. As a result of the wars with France and the Ottoman Empire, national sentiments re-emerged in Germany, and the Austrian officer corps was attractive to many German officers of the Reich, among them many members of the ruling German dynasties. Last but not least, German burghers joined in numbers.

When Empress Maria Theresa succeeded to the throne in 1740, she found after the death of Prince Eugene that neglect had set in, partly due to financial mismanagement, and therefore one of her first endeavors was to put through all-embracing reforms. Obviously she faced greater difficulties than her young Prussian contemporary who succeeded to the throne in the same year; the latter's father had left behind a sound financial base. Moreover she was a woman who, by the very nature of her sex, could not enjoy such immediate rapport with her officer corps as young Frederick. However, she tried to open the officer corps to all talents, irrespective of social origins. It was always 'a sign of her particular sympathy and grace.' Soldiers who were not of noble origin and who, in the course of 10 years, performed distinguished service, were ennobled and thus taken into the officer corps. She founded the Maria Theresa Medal, which was awarded for extraordinary bravery as well as the moral courage to take independent action that deviated from actual orders given, provided the action was successful. In 1752 she also founded the Theresian Military Academy, which was a modern training institution for the officer corps as well as for future officers. The teaching program excluded anything that would turn the young man into a courtier and cavalier. Instead, they were expected to become efficient soldiers and leaders of men. Much to her regret, Austria's higher nobility was loath to send its offspring to the academy since they felt that the sixteenth- and seventeenth-century ideals of the courtly chevalier were more worthwhile than military drill combined with mathematics and the natural sciences. Thus the early products of the Military Academy, situated outside Vienna in Wiener-Neustadt, were the sons of impoverished families who had served the Habsburgs faithfully. Also, it was difficult to gain general acceptance for this new aristocracy of the sword as equals of the established nobility. They therefore served side by side with officers who had purchased their commissions. Venality in the Austrian officer corps did not disappear until after 1867.

The rank and file was subject to the same severe discipline as was customary in all armies in Europe of the time. Corporal punishment was a general rule, as was running the gauntlet for desertion. Excesses of punishment in the Austrian army took on such dimensions that Maria Theresa found herself compelled to intervene and limit the instances or the number of offenses for which corporal punishment could be decreed. That she did not entirely succeed is shown by the fact that the number of desertions in the Austrian army was considerably higher than in the Prussian army, although it can hardly be said that Prussian discipline was less severe.

Nevertheless, on the battlefield the Austrian army always gave a good, even excellent account of itself, though lack of discipline in occupied territories was always a pronounced feature. For instance, when Austrian and Reich troops, including Prussian formations, occupied Bavaria in 1704 during the War of the Spanish Succession, Austrian behavior was such as to result in a large-scale peasant rebellion throughout Franconia and Lower and Upper Bavaria, a rising which, for a moment, threatened the entire position of the Imperial forces there. In a report on this event to Emperor Joseph I in Vienna, great attention was paid to the difference in behavior found between the Austrian and Prussian troops stationed in the area; whereas the latter were always rigidly disciplined, the former became notorious for their excesses against peasants and their tendency to plunder whenever the opportunity existed.

However, it was not until 1748 that the Austrian army introduced a general training manual, compulsory for all the Austrian forces. Its author was Field Marshal Daun, who actually did little else than copy that used by the Prussian army for several decades. But Daun also insisted on thorough tactical training, a training which every year culminated in field maneuvers, again imitating practices followed in Potsdam since the days of Frederick William I. That Daun's reforms yielded results was shown by the improved performance of the Austrian army during the Seven Years' War. He also placed great emphasis on the instruction that no differences be made between the nationality groups.

Of course, considering the difference in the social structures between Austria and Prussia, the former being subject to the political influence of the estates and the civil service, the latter being a military state pure and simple, it was inevitable that efforts at reform took a much longer time to be implemented. To that end Austria possessed neither the inner unity nor the charismatic personality of an ubiquitous soldier king at the center whose every wish was an immediate command. In spite of the endeavors of Maria Theresa and others, it was never possible to overcome the particularism of the estates and provinces, especially when raising arms. Therefore Austria could conduct a major war only in close alliance with other great powers. On the basis of her own resources Austria would never have been capable of fighting the Seven Years' War against Prussia.

Above. *The Empress Maria Theresa of Austria, 1717–80.*

A significant role in Austria's military history at this time was the expansion and consolidation of the *Militärgrenze*, the military border which separated her from the Ottoman Empire. The early beginnings of this military border go back well into the sixteenth century, when, for the first time, François I of France entered into an alliance with the Ottoman Empire in his struggle against Emperor Charles V. The inroads made by the Turks in the seventeenth century demonstrated that the provisional measures taken then were no longer sufficient. To halt the Turkish advance and to defend the newly recruited settlers required a firm system of defense, which ultimately consisted of a protective wall intersected with strong fortification stations; garrisons secured the entire southern Slav area of the Habsburg territory over a length of 1500 km.

The border troops were partly regular soldiers complemented by special formations of militia troops recruited from the German settlers within the area. Maria Theresa aimed at a total of 47,000 troops for this purpose, though the estates were willing to grant her finance only for a third of that amount. In addition they had to be relieved annually. Nevertheless the *Militärgrenze* was more than just a fortification. By-products were the opening up of the land by a network of roads, new villages, and the irrigation of a barren plain to form an agriculturally prosperous region. Prince Eugene considered the area important and upon his initiative schools were built and compulsory elementary schooling was introduced. It was a frontier zone of military, economic and political importance. The frontiersmen were farmers and soldiers alike and, most important from the point of view of the settlers, they were all free peasants, free from any feudal or similar obligations. They enjoyed proprietary as well as possessory rights. The *Militärgrenze* fulfilled its functions for 350 years until it was swept away by the havoc of twentieth-century warfare.

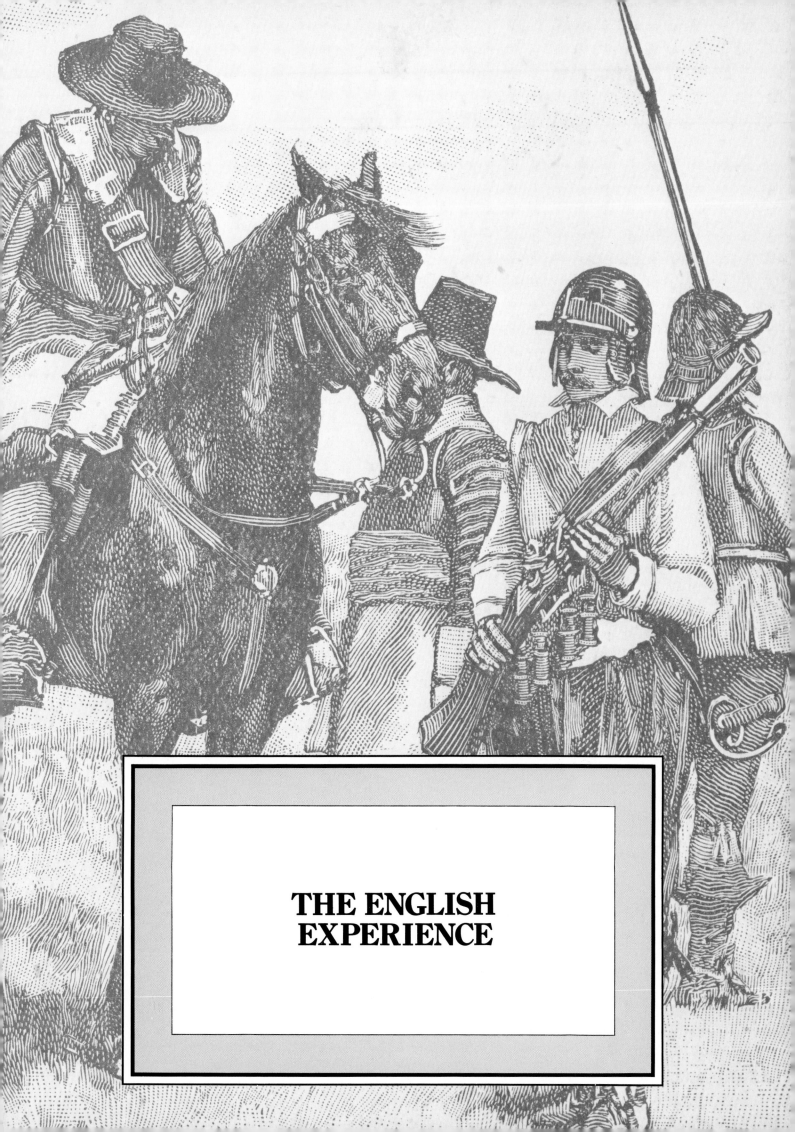

THE ENGLISH
EXPERIENCE

From a constitutional point of view the history of medieval England is largely the history of the evolution of a legal code and of an efficient administrative framework of local government, both making for an improved centralized government. This process of centralization went on continuously, though at varying pace, dominated as it was by the medieval concept of kingship, which throughout the centuries had – in spite of Magna Carta – remained unchanged. Consequently it was inevitable that the monarchy should gain more and more power, though not always uncontestedly. After there had been a breakdown in the direct exercise of power by the monarchy, as during the Wars of the Roses, it seems hardly surprising that, with the advent of the Tudor monarchy, there should not only be the reassertion of monarchical power but also a development of its ideological foundations and its propaganda. The alleged divine right of kings may well be considered an implicit foundation of Tudor rule.

Simultaneously, with the exultation of royal position, a social revolution had begun under the reign of Henry VIII which did not necessarily create but did accelerate the development of a new social class with new economic power; this development went hand in hand with what one might call – with qualifications – growth in the power of Parliament, whose sanction and support Henry VIII found necessary to obtain in his break with Rome and legal formation of the Church of England. In addition, the reigns of Henry VIII and Elizabeth I saw the rise of a propertied gentry, which had acquired considerable riches from the spoils derived from the dissolution of the monasteries and seizure of other church property. These developments, among the gentry and Parliament, represented a potential time-bomb should the king ignore this shift of economic power that had taken place in favor of an increasingly vocal and politically articulate section of the population. In a way it may be said – even at the risk of greatly oversimplifying complex issues – that the 'Reformation Parliament' and the dissolution of the monasteries, all shrewdly managed by Thomas Cromwell, were the first steps to the scaffold upon which Charles I was to expire.

By the time Charles I assumed the crown of England in 1625, the currents that had once forced crown and parliament into alliance had ceased to operate. On the contrary, parliament, in part representing a new class and in part reflecting reformed religious beliefs, soon began to feel the exercise of royal power as an encroachment on its political privileges. These privileges were derived in part also from a mythical source, namely the myth of the Magna Carta.

In fairness to Charles Stuart, it must be said that, from a purely economic point of view, his position was not dissimilar to that of John Lackland: dependent on static tax revenues, he had to make ends meet in an economically inflationary environment. Moreover, while in comparison with Elizabeth I his policy and handling of parliament may be considered inept and unwise, one may also justifiably ask whether one can judge him from a purely English frame of reference. He ought to be viewed within the context of his age – as a representative of the absolutist tendencies which gained the upper hand throughout the mainland of Europe. It can be argued that, while he represented the forces of modernity, Parliament represented the forces of reaction. Can one, for instance, really accuse him of breaking promises, or of breaking an unwritten constitution? The contractual bond of a promise assumes a level of equality between the contracting partners. Against the background of the age of absolutism it is unlikely that Charles I ever accepted any level of equality with parliamentary negotiators; instead he felt that he was acting under duress. Can one accuse him of

Below left: King Henry VIII of England, 1491–1547.

Top right: The Parliamentarians besiege Pontefract Castle, 1648.

Right: The Battle of Naseby, 14 June 1645, a Royalist defeat.

Below: Cromwell at the Battle of Marston Moor.

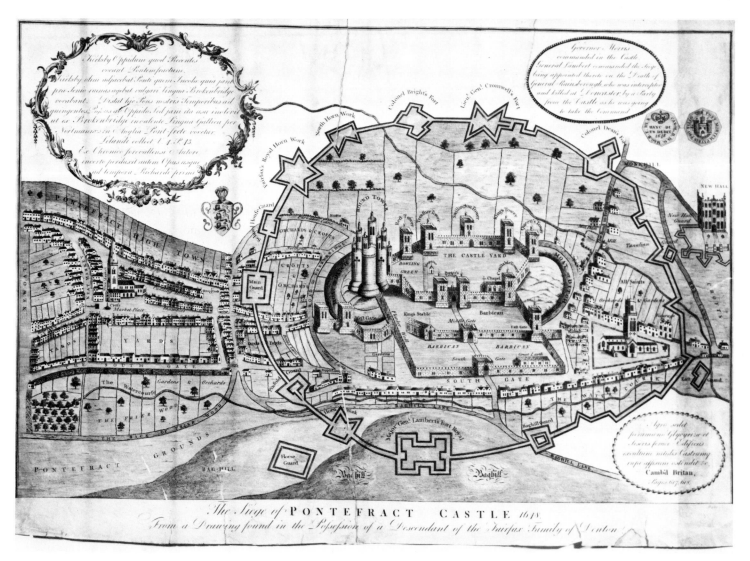

The Siege of PONTEFRACT CASTLE 1648.
From a Drawing found in the Possession of a Descendant of the Fairfax Family of Denton.

Left. *The Parliamentarian leader John Hampden, who played a leading part in the events leading up to the Civil War and was mortally wounded in a skirmish at Chalgrove Field in June 1643.*

Above. *The Battle of Edgehill (engraving, nineteenth century).*

Right. *Thomas Wentworth, Earl of Strafford, 1593–1641. Initially a firm supporter of Parliament, Strafford later sided with the King and was appointed Lord Deputy of Ireland in 1633. Accused of plotting to overthrow Parliament with an Irish army, Strafford was attainted by Parliament and executed in May 1641.*

breaking the constitution, which at that stage was still in its infancy, creating precedent rather than following it? In retrospect, many of Charles's actions may be judged as politically unwise and insensitive to recent change, but many of the actions of Parliament were perhaps presumptuous.

Of that large part of Parliament which opposed Charles it is often maintained that the motivation of its actions was determined by economic interests, masked by political and religious pretexts. Some recent historians have proposed that economic considerations were important motive forces, but it is equally vital to establish what people then *felt* to be important. Taking the religious issue as one example, even superficial scrutiny of contemporary sources demonstrates that, in spite of doctrinal changes, religious sentiment still permeated the fabric of English society. Society in England and Europe was not yet secularized.

Consequently, given this circumstance together with the Protestant doctrine of free individual examination of conscience, the liberty of conscience, it was unlikely that such a principle would remain restricted to the narrow confines of theological discussion. Instead, it was immediately applied to political issues. For the Puritans – who, it ought to be emphasized, represented only one segment of the Protestant movement in England, though politically one of its most powerful and articulate segments – metaphysical freedom carried the corollary of political liberty. If God had created man to enjoy liberty, then it would be against His laws to deny him that liberty

in the exercise of his day-to-day affairs. In short, the Puritan concept of society acknowledged the existence of the all-permeating and everlasting presence of God in all spheres of life, but for the same reason rejected the assumption that the divine right of monarchs could place any restrictions on their subjects in the exercise of their full liberties. For the King and his critics the ideological factor was not a suddenly and conveniently discovered tool, but one which had been part and parcel of the fabric of British society for centuries.

It was this environment of which Oliver Cromwell was a product when he vigorously supported the 'root and branch' petition which sought to abolish episcopacy. He pushed himself into prominence with his spirited defense of John Lilburne, the radical Puritan writer, when Charles I and Archbishop Laud were set upon pursuing a policy similar to that of Emperor Ferdinand II with his Edict of Restitution. Against this background one should first investigate the developments which took place during the period 1640–60 and the career of Oliver Cromwell, particularly its military aspects.

If we compare 1660 with 1640 it can be observed firstly that the royal endeavors toward absolute monarchy had been strongly defeated and that the financial independence of the king was at an end. The struggle over this matter which had lasted from the reign of Edward I to Charles I was at long last over. The so-called 'Glorious Revolution' of 1688 was neither a revolution nor glorious but simply underlined what had been achieved between 1640 and 1660. Secondly, by 1660 the predominant influence of the House of Commons in the government of the nation was permanently established. Thirdly, in the sphere of religion the complete and definite rejection of the doctrine of the Roman Catholic Church was assured, while, on the other hand, the position of the Church of England after the Restoration was no longer quite the same as before. Fourthly, and of more immediate impact, was the permanent disappearance of the prerogative courts, and with them all danger from royal prerogative. Although an attempt was made to revive it, this attempt brought to an end the rule of the Stuart dynasty in England. Lastly, and perhaps surprisingly in view of the internal crises, in the realm of foreign policy, England's name and power was respected and feared in Europe as never before.

These developments seem vast, but to give the major share of credit for them to Oliver Cromwell is to ignore the specific nature of the Puritan revolution. The irony is that the term 'Puritan' is really a mirage of a common denominator which, as such, had no existence in reality. On the contrary, the very absence of such a common denominator on the one hand, and the monopoly of effective power in the hands of Cromwell's army on the other, successfully prevented a really revolutionary settlement from the very outset. What this settlement, if such it can be called, did was to confirm the economic and political relationship that had already existed and been recognized before the outbreak of the Civil War. In that respect one may wonder whether the Civil War was not only an act of folly, but one of futility as well.

If, for argument's sake, we now allow the description 'Puritan' to be applied to the House of Commons at a time when its endeavors and policies were fairly unanimously supported by its members, then the Puritan revolution began in 1640 and ended in 1642. Within that time span, absolute monarchy had disappeared for ever. But that, of course, was not so apparent then as it is now. At that time, the struggle with absolute monarchy was by no means over and its revival still seemed a real threat.

It could be said that legislation of 1641, approved and signed by a desperate king, was as responsible for the demise of abso-lutist royal hopes as the Civil War itself. The first act the Long Parliament passed secured its regular meeting; this was a profound development as previously it was the king's prerogative to call and dismiss parliaments at his will. A little later Parliament went a step farther in the same direction by a still more revolutionary enactment – that the existing Parliament should not be dissolved or prorogued except by its own consent. This was asking Charles to surrender even more power than the previous Bill had required, and deprived him of all his usual weapons against Parliament; however, in the excitement caused by the execution of the King's closest confidant beside Archbishop Laud, Thomas Wentworth (Earl of Strafford,) the King seems to have signed it without much consideration. The collection of such taxes as 'tonnage and poundage' or customs duties was made illegal. Also ship money, one of the most hotly disputed issues of the day, was abolished although, contrary to Whig mythology, it had been levied only on harbor towns, and was in fact used for the construction of naval craft; building the foundation of British sea power under Cromwell when commanded by Admiral Blake. Compulsory knighthood, the abuse of royal forests, and impressment for the army by royal prerogative were ended, and the royal right of purveyance limited.

Returning to parliamentary legislation between 1640 and 1642, important changes limiting arbitrary government were effected by Parliament with reference to the prerogative jurisdiction of the royal council and the special court which had grown out of it. The extraordinary jurisdiction of the king in his council, above the ordinary common law, was brought to an end; it had existed since the establishment of the Norman monarchy and, in the twelfth century, had originated the beginnings of modern common law. With it disappeared the Councils of the North and Wales and the ordinary jurisdiction of the Privy Council. Hence, from a constitutional point of view, it

Below. *The first major battle of the Civil War, fought at Edgehill on 23 October 1642. The eighteenth-century artist has shown the participants wearing the costume of his own day rather than the military dress of the seventeenth century.*

The BATTLE of EDGE-HILL.

session of the Long Parliament opinion in the House was fairly unanimous over the legislative program of reform. The revolutionary changes proposed by Cromwell and his friends 'split the house asunder' and formed the parties for the Civil War. All that was required now was an understandable but nevertheless ill-considered action by Charles I to light the fuse to a very formidable powder keg.

Such then was the first act of the revolution, an act instigated and promoted by slightly more than half the membership of the House of Commons. It was the beginning of a radical revolution, no longer specifically Puritan because for a large part Puritan sentiment had found itself accommodated by the results of the first session of the Long Parliament; radicals like Cromwell and Pym precipitated the split in the Commons and helped to make the ensuing conflagration inevitable.

Cromwell's role as a politician was resoundingly negative, yet his role as an outstanding military commander seems beyond dispute. Indeed, his military ability may well explain his failure as a politician, since it is very rare to combine brilliance in the profession of arms with an ability to manipulate politics.

Before the wars, Cromwell was a gentleman farmer, descended from a nephew of Thomas Cromwell, the minister of Henry VIII. Few men realized the potential of the somewhat notorious Member for Cambridge in the Short Parliament, known as much for his political and religious radicalism as for his slovenly appearance. But it was John Hampden who remarked 'that though sloven, if we should ever come to break with the King (which God forbid), in such a case he will be one of the greatest men of England.'

Though devoid of any previous training and experience, at the outbreak of the Civil War Cromwell was commissioned as a captain in the cavalry of the Parliamentary army, commanding over 60 horsemen and noncommissioned officers. Even at this early stage Cromwell displayed a possession of those rare qualities of command and resolution which no training can impart. However, of more immediate and practical advantage was that he could gather around him a military clan such as his son plus Henry Ireton his future son-in-law, Valentine Walton his brother-in-law, John Hampden and Edward Whalley, his cousins, and Viscount Mandeville, later Earl of Manchester.

At the time of his appointment Cromwell was 43 and had a great conviction of righteousness and belief in divine sanction for his decisions, convictions which inclined him toward sectarian independency and determined his political and military career.

It seems certain that, out of the family clan under Cromwell's

may well be said that in the years 1640–41 much more was achieved than in the period of the Civil Wars and Cromwell's Protectorate, something that seems to have been overlooked entirely by Macaulay.

In devising and advocating this new legislation there exists no evidence that Cromwell played any conspicuous part. It bears out one of his main characteristics, his essential indifference to political institutions and systems, while his religious commitment is shown by the importance he attached to radical religious settlement in his advocacy of the 'root and branch' petition. He seemed to have had little success with it in a house as yet not divided against itself, though critical of the king's policies and the incompetence which had brought about the Scottish wars. The House was not inclined toward radical policies in the ecclesiastical sphere which, in the first session of the Long Parliament, were of purely secondary importance anyway.

It was in the course of the second session that Cromwell attained real prominence when he, Pym and others helped to draw up the 'Grand Remonstrance,' which detailed their grievances and suggested reforms. This document was fathered by deep suspicion after the Irish massacres which the monarch could not be trusted to suppress. In Pym's view, taking into account the absolutist inclinations of Charles I, he could not be trusted with an army in the first place. In that remonstrance Parliament asked, among other things, that the royal ministers should be 'such as Parliament may have cause to confide in.' If we speak of Parliament here, we must bear in mind a body with a majority of 11 with 148 voting against it, while in the first

Above left. *The Battle of Edgehill: another eighteenth-century view of the action.*

Right. *Charles I addressing his army while on the march from Stafford to Wellington in September 1642. He assured his supporters that they would meet 'no enemies but traitors,' and went on state his intention of governing according to the laws of the land and maintaining the Church of England.*

Left. *Robert Devereux, Earl of Essex, commanded the Parliamentarian forces at Edgehill.*

direct influence, emerged the idea of a military association, and that because of this Parliament, on 22 October 1642 – the day before the Battle of Edgehill – approved the formation of county defense unions. From these in turn emerged the Eastern Association of Norfolk, Suffolk, Huntingdon and Lincolnshire centered on Cambridge, Oliver Cromwell's constituency. This rendered the eastern counties the most powerful bulwark of the Parliamentary army.

These counties provided England's first standing army. At the beginning of the Civil War no standing army existed except in Ireland; armies were raised when the occasion arose, as for instance against the Scots. In the Middle Ages, as a result of its strongly centralized monarchy, England had had a highly effective military establishment which virtually annihilated itself in the Wars of the Roses. By contrast, the Tudor monarchy was not based on a strong military organization but on a rather refined local policing and administrative system, seeing the growth of the Justices of the Peace.

Attempts at reviving a voluntarily recruited army were made from time to time, mainly to keep down the Irish, but Parliament's distrust of its misuse put an end to them. Indeed, the fear of a standing army such as Thomas Wentworth was developing in Ireland was one of the main issues which led him to the executioner's block. It would have seemed reasonable for England to support the Protestant cause in Germany, considering that the Elector of the Palatinate was Charles I's brother-in-law, but in Germany and the Netherlands all that was forthcoming from England were a few contingents of auxiliary troops.

What existed for the defense of the realm and the maintenance of order originated from the Middle Ages, namely that each county had to provide forces and officers proportional in size to that of the county. In other words it was a militia. Arms were stored in local arsenals and military exercises were carried out; every summer they met for a one-day exercise. They were called the Trained Bands, but it is said that they preferred to spend the day in more leisurely pursuits than organized training. Needless to say, their military value was low. Nor could they be used outside the realm. These deficiencies made themselves felt immediately when Civil War broke out.

There were English officers and auxiliary troops who had participated in the Thirty Years' War on the European mainland in the Dutch, French, Spanish and German Imperial armies. Thus, despite the absence of a standing army, on the eve of the Civil War there were numerous individuals experienced in the methods of continental warfare – particularly among the cavalry, the most important arm on the battlefield. Prince Rupert, nephew of Charles I and known as the 'Mad Cavalier,' instilled his own experience into the Cavaliers. He taught his men to charge home at the gallop, sword in hand, and only to use firearms once the enemy had been broken. Cromwell was very quick to learn from his opponent and curtailed the undisciplined charge so characteristic of the early Parliamentary cavalry.

Cromwell realized instinctively the importance of morale. While the Cavaliers fought for the 'King's Cause,' to ask men simply to fight for Parliament and against absolutist despotism

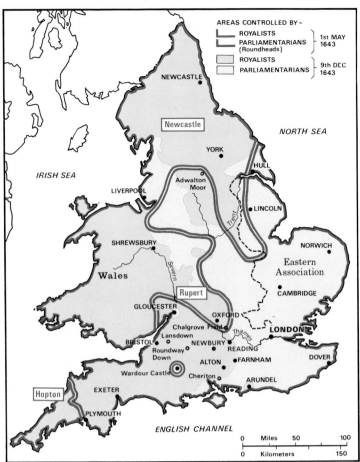

was too abstract and uninspiring. Cromwell's greatest achievement was to inspire the men under his own command with his own religious convictions and to select men of his own religious persuasion for the command of his troops. Soon the latter enjoyed a reputation for avoiding, as Baxter put it, 'those disorders, mutinous plunderings and grievances of the country which debauched men in armies are commonly guilty of.' The religious cause, the call for 'liberty of conscience,' created troops as brave, as serviceable and as eager for victory as their opponents.

This, of course, did not manifest itself in the early engagements such as Edgehill. The Earl of Essex's defeat by the Royalists put Parliament on the defensive and pointed to the need for a thorough reform of the Parliamentary army. Although Cromwell's own role at Edgehill remains obscure, its lesson was not lost upon him. The growing prominence of the Eastern Association was a direct consequence, as was the type of officer and men in it. 'You must get men of spirit,' said Cromwell to Parliament according to his own testimony to Hampden. In his Eastern Association he set out to create just that type of body. In the words of an anonymous writer of a newsletter in circulation in May 1643, 'As for Colonel (which by then he had become) Cromwell, he hath 2000 brave men, well-disciplined; no man swears but pays his twelve pence; if he is drunk, he is set in stocks, or worse; if one calls another roundhead he is cashiered: insomuch that the counties where they come leap for joy of them, and come in and join with them. How happy were it if all forces were thus disciplined.'

Though evidence of this kind must not be believed too readily, Cromwell in a series of letters during the same year pointed out, 'I beseech you to be careful what captains of horse you choose, what men be mounted: a few honest men are better than numbers. . . . I (would) rather have a plain, russet-coated captain of horse that knows what he fights for and loves what he knows, than that which you call a gentleman, and is nothing

else. . . . I have a lovely company; you would respect them. They are no Anabaptists, they are honest, sober Christians: they expect to be used as Men!'

The first really decisive battle was fought on 2 July 1644 at Marston Moor. It was brought to a successful conclusion for Parliament primarily because of Cromwell's skillful handling of his cavalry, the men of his Eastern Association whom he had trained the previous autumn and winter. It was also a battle which raised his name to national preeminence on both sides alike. Before the battle he was relatively unknown; after it Prince Rupert commented that Cromwell 'could himself evoke a more fierce and enduring spirit from the people than even that which he here magnifies. His 'Ironsides' (a name which Rupert gave to Cromwell and which was applied to his own regiment and was applied later to Cromwell's entire army) are the most fearless and successful body of troops on record, even in our annals: these fellows may have been, and I believe were, for the most part fanatics. Hypocrites never fought as they fought.' And Sir Philip Warwick added that 'they chose rather to die than fly, and custom removed fear of danger.'

But Marston Moor also demonstrated that the reforms initiated after Edgehill were still far from complete; the entire army needed the discipline and spirit of Cromwell's 'Ironsides.' This reorganization of the army between 1644 and 1645 was primarily Cromwell's work, a task completed with outstanding success. He was convinced that peace and stability could be obtained only through a crushing defeat of the enemy. The iron discipline of Swedish officers, hired especially for the purpose, molded raw levies into steady soldiers; since Parliament lacked experts in engineering and artillery, Cromwell did not hesitate to also use the services of French and German officers – though in time it proved advisable to keep them apart to prevent Franco-German feuds. What finally emerged was the 'New Model Army,' a standing force and a highly professional army – but an army in which Cromwell and his 'Ironsides' dominated.

Far left. *Prince Rupert of the Rhine, 1619–82. King Charles I's nephew Rupert served with distinction in the Dutch army before joining his uncle on the outbreak of the Civil War. He was one of the most able Royalist commanders, and was not merely the dashing cavalry leader of popular legend (engraving after van Dyck).*

Right. *A Royalist receipt of January 1644 for various armorers' tools.*

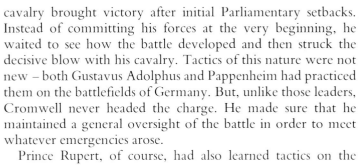

Below. *Sir Thomas Fairfax, 1612–71, besieging the Royalist capital of Oxford, 1646.*

This also meant the domination of the Independents' religious sectarianism over the Presbyterianism of Parliament – rejecting Presbyterianism as a compromise with evil.

The reputation Cromwell had established for himself is shown by the impact upon the Parliamentary army of his arrival near Naseby on 13 June 1645. Cromwell then served nominally as Lieutenant General under Thomas Fairfax. The news spread like wildfire among the army that '"Ironside" is come to head us!' The battle was fought on the following day. Though Fairfax was in overall command of the army, Cromwell's cavalry brought victory after initial Parliamentary setbacks. Instead of committing his forces at the very beginning, he waited to see how the battle developed and then struck the decisive blow with his cavalry. Tactics of this nature were not new – both Gustavus Adolphus and Pappenheim had practiced them on the battlefields of Germany. But, unlike those leaders, Cromwell never headed the charge. He made sure that he maintained a general oversight of the battle in order to meet whatever emergencies arose.

Prince Rupert, of course, had also learned tactics on the continent but, whereas his forces scattered in the pursuit of the enemy after a successful attack (and usually allowed themselves to be diverted by plundering his baggage train,) the discipline instilled into Cromwell's soldiers allowed their commander to rally the forces again immediately, to follow up an attack or to deploy them at other vital points. At Naseby, after the initial success, Cromwell ordered three regiments to pursue the enemy horse and then used the rest of his troops to attack the enemy's exposed left flank. Having beaten them, he penetrated farther and fell upon the Royalist center, which soon collapsed. Charles I had been decisively defeated, a defeat inflicted upon him mainly through the exertions and bravery of the New Model Army. Composed as it was mainly of Independents, this meant not only the triumph of Parliament but the ascendancy of the Independents over Parliament, finally culminating in the Protectorate under Cromwell.

Naseby finally established Cromwell's military reputation among friends and foes alike. The Earl of Clarendon, a hostile witness, had to admit that 'he was one of those men whom his very enemies could not concern . . . for he could never have done half that mischief without great parts of courage, industry and judgment. He must have had a wonderful understanding in the natures and humors of men, and as great a dexterity in applying them . . . he attempted those things which no good man durst have ventured on; and achieved those in which none but a valiant and great man could have succeeded . . . yet wickedness as great as his could never have succeeded nor accomplished those designs, without the assistance of a great spirit, and admirable circumspection and sagacity, and a most magnanimous resolution.'

At Naseby the New Model Army was only one of several armies which Parliament put into the field. In the first Civil War there were no fewer than 21,000 Scots under Leslie. But after Naseby – apart from the Scots – the various separate armies, such as those of Nottinghamshire under Major General Poyntz or Wiltshire and the four western counties under Major General Massey, were absorbed into the New Model Army or disappeared altogether. Within a few years Cromwell had created one highly professional standing English army, an army in which promotion frequently depended on merit, although the principle of seniority did not disappear altogether.

Cromwell's own religious attitudes and, later, his constitutional position were not without influence upon appointments and promotions. A contemporary of Cromwell asserted that he weeded out 'godly and upright-hearted men' to consolidate his own position and replaced them with 'pitiful sottish beasts of his own alliance.' This was hardly an unprejudiced view but, when commanding his own Eastern Association, Cromwell did dismiss Presbyterian officers and later on he also dismissed officers who were opposed to his Protectorate because of their republican inclinations.

The execution of the King crowned the revolution. In six years Cromwell had become a famous and invincible cavalry commander and the creator and molder of the New Model Army. His importance as a factor in the political life of the

General FAIRFAX with his FORCES before the City of OXFORD

Above. *Edward Hyde, Earl of Clarendon, 1609–74. One of Charles I's leading advisers, Clarendon also enjoyed the confidence of Charles II and played a leading part in bringing about the Restoration (portrait by Sir Peter Lely).*

Left. *Thomas, Baron Fairfax. Sir Thomas Fairfax for most of his career, this brave and honorable Yorkshireman was the first captain general of the New Model Army.*

Right. *King Charles I of England, 1600–49.*

country had risen correspondingly. However, regarding the execution of Charles I, it is open to question whether to attribute any preconceived designs to Cromwell; on the contrary, it seems that he was loath to encourage any such fundamental uprooting of society as would be produced by an act of regicide. The decision to take such drastic and radical action was probably a product of circumstances rather than the result of a long-term plan.

With Charles held prisoner, divisions appeared among the forces opposing him. On the one hand there was the Presbyterian Parliament, no longer radical but anxious about the potential political, social and economic consequences of its previous actions, and which was now ready to restore Charles on condition that he inaugurated Presbyterian forms of worship. On the other hand there were the Independents who controlled a large part of the army, and one feels that to a degree Oliver Cromwell himself desired a religious settlement which would include toleration of the various different forms of Protestant Puritan worship. Issues were further complicated by the fact that the Independents themselves represented a far from homogeneous body, containing a wide spectrum of attitudes ranging from the middle-class toleration of Cromwell to the religious, social and political radicalism of the Levellers. One cannot observe without a sense of irony how the revolution rebounded on Cromwell – the radical of the Long Parliament became the moderator, conciliator and appeaser of his own radicals. By his social and economic background one might have taken him for a Presbyterian, by religious inclination an Independent; in practice the former controlled the latter. Many of Cromwell's subsequent actions are perfectly explicable when one recognizes this fact, and when one also realizes that he was

not a Robespierre and Napoleon rolled into one; he was a commander who very often found himself sitting on the points of his pikes rather than commanding them. Certainly at the political level, he was a man who acted under the constant threat that, unless he represented the army's interests, 'they would go their own way without him.'

Such a situation inevitably placed Charles in a position where he believed he could play one faction against the other to his own advantage. In the ensuing negotiations between Parliament and Charles, Charles and Cromwell and Cromwell and Parliament, mutual suspicions were rife. The three bodies distrusted not only each other, but the New Model Army even distrusted Cromwell. Under these circumstances Cromwell's objective had to be to maintain the unity of the army; he was playing for time he could ill afford – a solution to the problem posed by the presence of the captive King was imperative. Charles's escape and the invasion of England by a Scottish army by agreement with the King precipitated a conclusion. The second Civil War was soon over, and Preston decided not only the Scottish issue but also that of Parliament, and by implication that of the King.

The idea of ending the farce with Charles by bringing him to trial had definitely taken root in the army, and was fostered by the Levellers throughout the country. No doubt, a noticeable shift of public sentiment in favor of the King aggravated the situation and made a solution even more pressing. The burden of the standing army rested heavily on the country and had already manifested itself in various ways. In 1648 the citizens of London, for instance, commemorated the king's accession to the throne 16 years earlier by lighting a bonfire, drinking to his health and clamoring for his return.

It is a matter for conjecture how far the months of September to December 1648 were, for Cromwell, months of inner wrestling, or whether they were months in which the army built up pressure which ultimately forced Cromwell on to the course of regicide. But the stage for the trial was set without Cromwell's initiative and direct knowledge by Colonel Pride's purge of Parliament. The dominating impression the observer gains of these months is really of a man trying to control the course of national events, trying to ride on top of a tidal wave and anxious to prevent the execution of the King so far and as long as he could, without compromising his own position with the army, but ready, if necessary, to bring him to rough justice and exact the supreme penalty. In the final analysis the security of the state was at issue and Cromwell considered himself a lawful power ordained by God 'to oppose one name of authority, for those ends, as well as another.' The decision, however, rested with Charles who, having refused Cromwell's last offer, let events take their course, believing that graves are the precondition for

A. Seine Kön: Maÿ: an dem Block. B. Doctor Juxon. C. Colonell Tomlinson. D. Colonell Hacker. E. F. die 2. Executorn. C R V·N 1649

Far left. *Pikeman's armor of the type issued to the New Model Army.*

Center left. *Cavalry trooper's lobster-tailed helmet, breast and back plates.*

Left. *English pikeman's armor circa 1620. Although armor of this type was used during the Civil War, this suit is too elaborate for wartime manufacture.*

Right. *Steel gauntlet, circa 1650. Gauntlets of this type were worn to protect the bridle arm against sword cuts.*

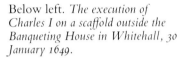

Below left. *The execution of Charles I on a scaffold outside the Banqueting House in Whitehall, 30 January 1649.*

resurrection. The end came one frosty January morning in 1649 on the block outside Westminster Hall. The radical revolution ground along its path cumbersomely and inexorably, with Cromwell, the one-time radical and moderate, being as much its victim as was the aspiring absolutist King Charles I.

Nevertheless, Cromwell's political shortcomings cannot detract from his achievement of creating an army as disciplined and armed as it was effective. The pike, a prominent weapon in 1643, had been virtually replaced by 1650. When the Civil War began pikes and muskets operated together but in a rather disorderly fashion and without the tactical organization deployed on the continent. Pikes served as defense against cavalry attacks but there is also evidence that units equipped with pikes fought one another. Gradually, however, the musket won the upper hand, particularly when it could be used as a club in close combat. Another factor in favor of the musket was the greater mobility and speed of the musketeers, who wore no armor whatsoever. In the first years of the Civil War the distance infantry could cover on foot was 10 to 12 miles a day. With the discarding of armor and the introduction by Cromwell of uniforms – red coats – the average marching distance increased to 15 to 16 miles a day. The closing campaign of the first Civil War, the second Civil War and the subjugation of Ireland and Scotland bore witness to growing professionalism.

After Cromwell had taken over command from Fairfax, he was assisted by a council of officers, whose opinion, however, was also sought in matters of politics. When, in 1647, the army became increasingly dissatisfied with Parliament, the Levellers elected their councils from the rank and file to represent their grievances. Cromwell put down this potentially very dangerous development firmly and ruthlessly.

The Irish campaign in particular demonstrates Cromwell's art of generalship at its best. Politically he divided the Royalist Protestants from Ireland's Roman Catholic leaders, and he achieved an almost perfect cooperation between the army and the fleet and thus mastered his logistics problems. He deployed his troops effectively there, although the terrain was quite different from that in England.

In the subjugation of both Ireland and Scotland a series of systematically conducted sieges contrasted strongly with early campaigns. Cromwell laid great stress on the role of artillery, which increased progressively in firepower. The sieges of Pembroke Castle, Pontefract and, later, Drogheda showed the devastating effect of Cromwell's siege trains. Both Wexford and Ross began to negotiate for surrender after the first day's cannonade.

The massive deployment of artillery and the concentration of large forces on a narrow front illustrate Cromwell's philosophy of warfare – that in order to force a decision, a decisive victory must be attained. He was not a man of slow maneuver and countermaneuver. General MacArthur's maxim in World War II might well have been Cromwell's: 'There is no substitute for victory.' A war of lengthy maneuvers was bound to deplete troops and stores; long-drawn-out sieges could involve sickness and epidemics among the siege forces. The determination to defeat the enemy completely and speedily so as to restore peace quickly largely explains the ferocity of Cromwell's attacks. He was no sentimentalist about war. Chivalry had no place in a religious conflict fought with the fervor of a crusade: it merely prolonged it. In Cromwell's eyes, war was a bloody and dirty business which must be concluded as quickly as possible by all available means. The cost in human lives of a short but decisive assault would in the long run be lower than that involved in a long, protracted siege. It would also be more economical, argued Cromwell in a letter to Parliament in 1650: 'Those towns that are to be reduced, especially one or two of them, if we should proceed by the rules of other states, would cost you more money than this army hath had since we came over. I hope, through the blessing of God, they will come cheaper to you.' However, there were exceptions. At Clonmel Cromwell's forces were bloodily repulsed and suffered about 1000 casualties.

Cromwell's power of direct command over the entire military forces increased together with the increasing professionalism of the army. During the early campaigns, councils of war had played an important part; their resolutions were not simply arrived at by a general's order, but 'after much dispute.' Councils were still held before the battles of Preston and Dunbar. However, after Fairfax had been replaced by Cromwell as Commander in Chief, the latter made sure that his influence was not only felt but that it also prevailed. He did this by first discussing the issues directly with the most important of his subordinates such as Lambert and Monk, reaching a conclusion, and then, at a full council meeting of the officers, having Lambert explain why and how a battle would have to be fought.

The eve of Dunbar saw Cromwell and Major General John Lambert 'coming to the Earl of Roxburgh's house and observing' (the enemy's) 'posture. I' (Cromwell) 'told him that it did us an opportunity and advantage to attempt upon the enemy, to which he immediately replied, that he had thought to have said the same thing to me. So that it pleased the Lord to set this apprehension upon both our hearts at the same instant. We called for Colonel Monk and showed him the thing: and coming to our quarters at night, and demonstrating our apprehensions to some of the colonels, they also cheerfully concurred.' What Cromwell does not make clear is that it was Lambert who did the 'demonstrating' and explaining to the colonels.

Of course, Cromwell, compared with his contemporaries, fought a war with limited objectives within a territory surrounded by water. That in itself ensured that he did not have to fear invasions from any side; moreover he fought with, strictly speaking, a national army imbued with the same religious and political ethos. The number of mercenaries or foreigners within

Left. *Sir George Wharton, painted by van Dyck, circa 1645. His dress, with its thick leather buff coat and back and breast plates is typical of that of mounted officers on both sides.*

Right. *Major General John Lambert, 1619–83. One of the ablest Parliamentarian generals, Lambert died in prison after the Restoration.*

Below. *Cromwell at Dunbar, 3 September 1650. Cromwell delivered the decisive blow in this brilliant victory at the head of his own regiment of cavalry.*

Le General Major Lambert, 1.er Conseiller du Con.l de My-lord Protecteur d'Angleterre &c.   *B. Moncornet.*

his troops was small and limited to certain arms like artillery and the engineers. In addition, he fought civil wars, even when these extended to Scotland and Ireland. Civil war is the only form of war in which one knows exactly whom one kills, and this knowledge imparts a brutality and cruelty which completely excludes the slightest element of chivalry. The opponent is not only the enemy but an antagonistic principle which has to be exterminated. This very much applied to Cromwell's wars and their ferociousness, brutality and cruelty were unparalleled in British history up to that time.

In his New Model Army Cromwell had established a rough proportion of one horseman to every two footmen. Among the cavalry the horseman with spear and the heavily armed cuirassier gradually disappeared, making way for the harquebusier armed with carbine, pistol and saber. The dragoons, of which the New Model Army contained one regiment, were simply mounted infantry, whose name derived from the name of the short-barrelled musket they carried. Originating in France and

Germany during the Thirty Years' War, they fulfilled the task of vanguards and reconnaissance units in Cromwell's army. Unlike the rest of the New Model cavalry, dragoons did not wear buff coats but red ones like the infantry, and hats instead of helmets. Tactics of infantry and cavalry alike were not new but adapted from those of the continental armies.

While Cromwell's relationship with his army was excellent at all times, that with Parliament was anything but good. By 1660, 'the predominant influence of the House of Commons in the government of the nation was permanently established.' This had little to do with Cromwell personally. Although Parliament had appointed him Lord General, he sometimes appeared to have been as great an enemy of that institution as had been Charles I and Archbishop Laud: the Long Parliament was first purged by his army, and then violently expelled by him; his own Parliament, the 'Parliament of Saints,' nominated largely under the influence of the army, was carried away in hysteria and in the end committed suicide; and of the Parliaments of the Protectorate, elected on the basis of a new franchise and operating within limits determined by Cromwell, the first was purged within a week and then dissolved, with the second lasting just a week longer than its predecessor. Such a record would hardly suggest a striving toward 'the permanent establishment of the House of Commons in the government of the nation.'

To conclude, however, that Cromwell was an uncompromising enemy of parliamentary institutions would be to distort the actual record – he was indifferent toward any form of government, indifferent to a degree of ignorance. All that mattered to him was that parliament fulfilled that function which he considered of overriding importance: to guarantee the security and liberty of conscience, Papists excluded of course. Unfortunately Cromwell's concern for religious liberty was not matched by one for effective practical politics, leading in the end

Above. *A contemporary broadsheet pays tribute to the achievements of Cromwell in Ireland.*

Below. *The Battle of the Boyne, 1 July 1690. William of Orange secures his grip on the English throne by defeating the deposed James II.*

to a parliament incapable of any positive action. This incapacity was not due to its composition but because of Cromwell's utter inability, shared by his predecessors Charles I and James I, to control parliament by the methods which had been employed by Elizabeth I. James's failure to follow her example had led to the winning of the initiative by the Commons, while the failure of Charles involved him in a predicament that ultimately proved fatal. With Cromwell it put him in a position which almost inevitably branded him as an enemy.

The methods by which Elizabeth so effectively controlled her parliaments were electoral maneuvering, patronage and the development of a nucleus of experienced privy councillors and royally controlled Speaker of the House, in Parliament itself. In the last years of her reign these methods were challenged both by the development of a Puritan parliamentary machine independent of the Privy Council and also by the Earl of Essex's plan to pack the House but, fortunately for Elizabeth, both challenges were weathered by the political acumen of the two Cecils. The indifference of James I to any shrewd approach in handling the Commons allowed them to turn tables upon him and his son. John Pym, a successor of the Cecils but working against Charles I, controlled patronage, the Speaker and the front bench. With his death in 1643 such control ceased and Parliament dissolved into fragmented interest groups, finally purged by Colonel Pride.

Whatever there may be said against the Rump Parliament, it nevertheless provided the most systematic government of the interregnum; 'it governed efficiently, preserved the revolution, made and financed victorious wars and carried out a policy of aggressive mercantile imperialism,' the basis of Britain's future world power. Its managers were a small group of determined and single-minded men such as Sir Arthur Hesselridge and Thomas Scott, stout republicans all. In their eyes, republics alone were the political systems capable of producing a commercial empire. On the other hand, their policy of mercantile aggression, as exemplified in the Navigation Acts, was diametrically opposed to the sentiments of the Independents whom Cromwell represented; it was the policy of an 'oligarchy' and therefore detested by that body which had really made the revolution – the army.

In the absence of a firm extension of the hand of the executive in the Commons, it was inevitable that policymaking would be surrendered to that group which was sufficiently organized to wield political power. For the Independents the only alternative was either to organize themselves equally as well, or to remove their rivals by force. Their sentiment being largely that of the army, the result was expedient, swift and clear-cut – the Rump was ejected by force.

What followed was the Barebones Parliament, dominated not by an oligarchy but nominated on the basis of lists drawn up by the Independent sects; the oligarchy was replaced by an equally well-organized small body of radicals which stood in place of the broken Levellers: Anabaptists and Fifth Monarchy men, supported and controlled by Cromwell's alter ego, Major General Harrison. It does nothing to recommend the political acumen of Cromwell as a parliamentarian that, in contrast to

Above. *General George Monck, Duke of Albemarle, 1608–70. Captured while in the King's service, Monck joined the Parliamentarian army and fought in Ireland during the Second Civil War. A leading architect of the Restoration, Monck served on Charles II's council and earned popular acclaim by remaining in London during the Plague of 1665.*

Left. *This vigorous contemporary engraving shows William's troops fighting their way across the Boyne.*

the extreme wing of his own army, he himself had failed to recognize the root of the trouble of the Rump's failure and therefore took no action, despite the fact that the Parliament was one of his own choosing. Having urged them to make good laws, he withdrew, refused to sit on committees to which he had been elected, and expected Parliament to manage itself. Hence Harrison and his men took control to the extent that, within six months, the moderate sections within it 'surrendered back to the Lord General the powers which, through lack of direction, they had proved incapable of wielding.'

In response, Cromwell, far from having a plan of his own, four days after the dissolution, accepted a new constitution devised by Major General Lambert and his party of more moderate senior army officers, another piece of evidence of the total absence of any grand design on Cromwell's part.

This constitution invested Cromwell as the Lord Protector and altered the franchise, not by changing the social base of representation, but by cutting down borough representation and greatly increasing county representation. This really meant a shift from the boroughs, where patrons and parliamentary managers had built up their forces in Parliament, to the county gentry. The latter were seemingly independent of patronage and, being freely elected from within the fold of the Puritan Independents, they would naturally agree with aims and methods of Cromwell's rule. Individual patronage would be replaced by government patronage. But, having taken the first step, Cromwell failed to take the second: no direct and effective management of the House was attempted, with the result that into the power vacuum created stepped Hesselridge, Scott, Bradshaw and others who had managed to get themselves elected into the House from which they had been purged in 1653. Needless to say, in the end they were ejected, as they had been before. What followed was a policy of political makeshift and improvisation – the second Protectorate, but no consistent policy.

Paradoxically Cromwell and his army were one another's greatest liability. For Cromwell the army was the base of his power and, in the absence of a political counterforce, his military force was the only pillar of support and reliance. Consequently he was not always his own free agent when making political decision. With the army Cromwell stood – without it he would fall.

Cromwell's singular failure to put any tangible institution with clearly defined powers and limitations in place of the monarchy, which he had helped to depose, made him a liability to the army because, in essence, he also failed to devise an acceptable constitutional framework within which a standing army would have its proper place. This placed the army in a position outside what had hitherto been considered as constitutional in England. Consequently, by 1658, and even more so two years later, the majority of Englishmen who desired nothing more than a return to constitutional legality regarded Cromwell's army as a glaring extra-constitutional institution to be done away with. Cromwell's failure as a politician ensured the unpopularity of any standing army in Britain for the next 150 or so years.

Cromwell was brilliant as a military leader of men and brilliant in his generalship – but it was a brilliance which relied on the successful adaptation of techniques and tactics already in practice elsewhere. As his campaigns in Ireland and Scotland showed, he was also as bold a strategist as he was a tactician. Yet to evaluate his position in relation to his European military contemporaries is virtually impossible, since he never had to face men of the caliber of Gustavus Adolphus, Wallenstein, or Tilly – the master generals of the Thirty Years' War.

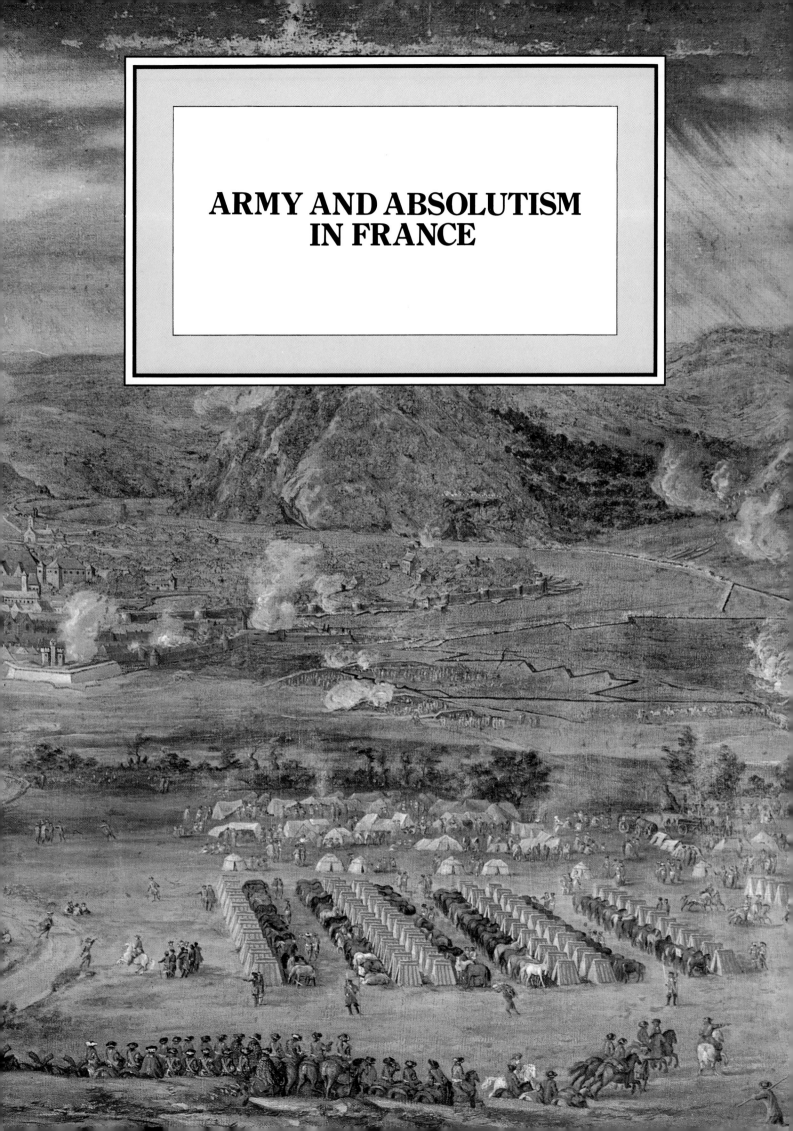

ARMY AND ABSOLUTISM
IN FRANCE

Under the guiding hands of Cardinals Richelieu and Mazarin, during the second half of the seventeenth century, the French monarchy had established its reign firmly throughout France. The religious wars had come to an end, the nobility had been subordinated to the crown and the opposing estates had been reduced to a state of political impotency. France was a unitary state and had an absolute monarchy epitomized and personified in Louis XIV, who, after the death of Mazarin, exclaimed: 'Now gentlemen it is time that I shall rule. You shall support me with your advice if I ask you for it.'

Louis XIV ruled with absolute authority. Believing that the King possessed this authority by divine right, it was taken for granted that his training and insight was therefore superior to that possessed by any other man. He concentrated all power in his own hands, refusing to share any part of it with anyone, even with members of his own family; even his private life was used to enhance the public display of his majestic divinity, representing the personification of the French state.

The French people accepted this absolutism; its right to dominate the life of millions was not doubted. After the extensive period of internal civil strife in the sixteenth century, the desire for peace, order and effective authority was paramount. One not only kissed the hand of the king, one respected him almost like a deity. For a long time no objection was raised, even though Louis XIV's personal regime meant the continuation of the unequal distribution of social burdens and privileges. It was accepted that it did not exclude acts of personal arbitrary action; that the subject was virtually nothing other than the tool of the whim of the monarch; that Louis' policy involved France in a whole chain of wars of aggression which sapped the life-blood of France, as well as straining France financially and economically beyond its resources. On the contrary, it may be suggested that the French basked in the glory of the Sun King.

Under his rule France experienced the strongest concentration of power she had so far possessed, power which attracted the whole of Europe but also limited him in the field of foreign policy. The hegemonic ambitions of Louis XIV, in spite of great territorial gains, could not be realized simply because Britain and the Habsburgs blocked any further French expansion. All the more intensive, however, was France's intellectual and artistic predominance. Since 1648 France was considered the motherland of civilization. The influence of the French language, philosophy, literature, poetry and theater was tantamount to a world conquest. The culture of the Versailles court and its luxurious lifestyle found admiration and imitation throughout Europe. The machinery of state, built and refined by Richelieu and Mazarin, was so efficient that it continued to work successfully for a long time, even after Louis XIV's reign.

France was the richest and most populated country in Europe. It would have remained the wealthiest if its policy of war, its expensive buildings and the squandering lifestyle of the Age of the Baroque had not overtaxed the physical and economic resources of the nation. The political purpose of its economic strength was not based on any idea of individual happiness but on the intention to serve the glory of the state, to enrich its fame and power. While its power shone in its fullest glory, however, the seeds of decay and downfall were already present.

This strong, secure state was the result of a highly centralized administration and the exercise of strict discipline in all spheres of life. The king ruled with the assistance of a cabinet comprising only three able ministers for finance, military affairs and foreign policy. Because they were experts in their respective fields, they could influence royal decisions, but the final decision was made and the last word spoken by the king. The bureaucracy was divided into various *ressorts* representing the executive

branches of the state administration. The decisions of the cabinet were handed on for execution to *intendants* who, with full executive powers, ruled the provinces and cities, responsible only to the king. They could be dismissed and replaced at any time. The higher nobility was deliberately drawn into the court at Versailles; their tasks were limited to local administration and the carrying out of the lower judicial functions. Ancient privileges and special regional rights were, with a few exceptions, removed. The *parlements*, the local courts of appeal in Paris and other cities, were completely deprived of their powers. An army of royal civil servants ran the bureaucracy and ensured the execution of royal edicts.

This development was paralleled by a thorough change in the military forces, which the sovereign now required in the form of a standing army. This in turn required a considerable amount of money derived from general taxation. To obtain the necessary revenue required a strict centralization of the financial administration. The power of the estates to dictate the granting of money supplies had been broken. The old concept that general welfare was guaranteed only when the requirements of the sovereign did not reduce the property and welfare of the individual was abandoned. The subjects had to carry the burden if the state was to maintain its stability. Direct and indirect taxation increased significantly, and, as long as general prosperity existed, the state's revenue increased correspondingly. The Minister of Finance, Jean-Baptiste Colbert, directed the nation's finances with great care and circumspection. He was anxious to exhaust all possible sources of revenue, but was reluctant to increase taxation. However, as time went on, he found it difficult, if not impossible, to balance the budget of the state with the expenditure required for the hegemonic policies of Louis XIV. His aim was to establish economic self-sufficiency with a favorable balance of trade; this was to be achieved by ventures in foreign policy which, at the expense of other countries, would increase the power of France. He was the inventor of mercantilism, according to which national wealth rested on the monetary resources of the state, resources achieved by the export of goods and services. The unitary state was also a common market, which did away with local and regional tolls but expanded the network of roads and waterways, supported trade and commerce as well as overseas trade. Manufacturing industries were subsidized. To ensure that surplus production was exported abroad in order to increase the royal revenue, Colbert protected infant French industry by tariffs and prohibited the export of raw materials. The attempt to expand France's economic power through overseas expansion, however, aroused the enmity of Holland and Britain.

The social structure, at first glance, remained the same as in the Middle Ages. Nobility, clergy, burghers and peasants seemingly appeared as a body of subjects subordinated to the crown, though living side by side in great social inequality. The king held all the power, the feudal estates all the rights.

The clergy formed the First Estate. The nobility, the Second Estate, was deprived of most of its political functions but still possessed exemption from taxation, and enjoyed the exercise of patrimonial jurisdiction, pensions and sinecures. By these

Previous Spread. *The second siege of Besançon, May 1674.*

Left. *Louis de Bourbon, Prince de Condé, 1621–86.*

Right. *Cardinal Mazarin, 1602–61.*

Below. *French warships repulse the Duke of Buckingham's ships in their attempt to relieve the Huguenot stronghold of La Rochelle, 1627.*

privileges Louis XIV tied the nobility to his crown. He particularly favored it by granting it commissions in the army. To the privileged nobility also belonged the upper ranks of the clergy.

The Third Estate was formed by the *haute bourgeoisie*, some members of which Louis elevated to the nobility of service. Since the deficit in the royal household continuously got larger, Colbert vastly increased the number of purchasable offices and thus introduced venality in office holding; this resulted in a spread of the privileges and the monopolization of many sources of income, be they in trade or commerce, in the hands of a few families. Merchants, bankers and manufacturers thus began to form independent circles in the cultural life of France.

The peasantry and the poorer people of the towns formed the Fourth Estate. Deprived of any political rights, they carried the full burden of taxation and also owed feudal services on the estates of the nobility. The peasants were in a parti-

culary depressed state since agriculture was held back in favor of emerging industry by prohibitions of exports and the holding down of prices for agricultural produce, to allow cheap bread for urban workers in lieu of raising their wages. On the day of the storming of the Bastille, 80,000 workers were in Paris; an urban proletariat was emerging.

The social structure of the absolutist state also influenced the structure of the army, the central pillar of French absolutism. Upon it rested the prestige of France. Although the country had possessed a powerful army under Cardinal Richelieu during the first half of the seventeenth century, it was not a unified institution or the backbone of absolutism; it was the private property of the colonels and captains who, empowered by the king, recruited their soldiers.

To achieve his political aims, however, Louis XIV required a strictly disciplined, well-trained and reliable army. This was all the more necessary after such victorious generals as Condé and Turenne joined the nobility's uprising known as the Fronde, in the middle of the war against Spain. The army had therefore to be dedicated solely to the king. By 1640 the French army amounted to 100,000 men. Changes were made when Louis XIV began to control things himself; under his Minister of War, Le Tellier (1603–85) and his successor, his son the Marquis de Louvois (1641–91), a thorough reform was carried out and the army more fully integrated into the state. The external form was maintained, such as the division into regiments and companies as military, economic and administrative units; so was the structure of command. The internal structure, however, needed changing. The most important measure introduced was the transfer of supreme command to the king. The mercenary elements were eliminated – every soldier was now the soldier of the king, a factor underlined by the swearing of a personal oath of allegiance. Some of the former colonels retained their posts, but their troops became the property of the sovereign; the colonels were now servants of the state. Gradually their rights of jurisdiction over their troops were eliminated as was their right to appoint their own officers. The granting of a commission was now the right of the king, as was any promotion. Auditors were introduced who, in the name of the king, exercised jurisdiction and monitored the behavior of each unit. Strict military discipline was introduced, although corporal punishment was not applied.

As in any other army of the time, the main problem was to pay soldiers promptly and punctually. This function was taken over by the state as well. Increased revenue had to be raised, and one consequence, among others, was the emergence of a modern bureaucracy which dominated administration. The *intendants*, subject to the Minister for War, had full powers of military administration, including the responsibility for supplies when the army was on the march. It was up to them to pay the soldiers punctually and to prevent any misappropriation of funds. This implicit distrust of the officers was fully justified – there were numerous instances when officers had to be reprimanded or threatened with severe penalties for financial irresponsibility. The soldier was supplied with everything he needed. Throughout the country arsenals and depots were established for the supply of equipment, and a medical corps was formed.

The standing army maintained the principle of voluntary recruitment. However, since the Crown did not want to deplete the number of peasants and workers, as many foreigners as possible were recruited. Swiss, Italian, German, Hungarian, Scots and Irish soldiers formed their own regiments. In times of peace the army was not dissolved but the nucleus of each

Above left. During Richelieu's siege of La Rochelle a fortified mole was constructed to seal the city off from the sea.

Below left. Geometrical fortifications developed by Vauban.

Right. King Frederick William I of Prussia, 1688–1740.

Below. King Louis XIV of France watches the progress of a siege.

Far left. *Vicomte de Turenne, 1611–75.*

Left. *Claude Louis Hector, Duc de Villars, 1653–1734.*

Below left. *The family of Jean-Baptiste Colbert, Louis XIV's financial expert.*

Right. *John Churchill, Duke of Marlborough, 1650–1722.*

Far right. *Prince Eugene of Savoy, 1663–1736.*

regiment, the cadre, was maintained to facilitate quick recruitment for the next campaign. It also maintained the intrinsic combat value of each regiment.

Louis' expansionist aims, however, were out of proportion to the numbers of voluntary recruits he could obtain and, very much against his original intention, forcible recruitment had to be resorted to in rural districts, sometimes by drawing lots. Also, in November 1688, the Minister for War reintroduced militia regiments, which had had their origin in medieval France and had since almost disappeared. They were to serve in garrisons and fortresses. By 1670 France's standing army amounted to 138,000 men, a century later 290,000, and, by the beginning of the French revolution in 1789, 173,000.

An entirely new innovation was the building of a line of fortresses reaching from Dunkirk to the Pyrenees to protect the country against foreign invasion. Even during the Thirty Years' War, Spanish troops had managed to penetrate as far as Paris. This new work was essentially the product of Sébastien le Prestre de Vauban (1633–1707), 'the King's Engineer.' He built 90 fortresses, all based on precise mathematical calculations, containing depots and arsenals. Their purpose was not primarily to provide an unbroken line of defense, but rather a secure base for any offensive operation.

The French art of building fortifications at the end of the eighteenth century developed with the rising age of technology. The trained engineer and mathematician replaced the traditional artisan architect. The universal soldier of the time, the most educated individual in the army, was the engineer, who not only built fortresses but specialized in improving and inventing new arms.

Before military garrisons were built, the bulk of the soldiers were still quartered with civilians, whose relations with one another were strictly laid down in a special manual devised for this purpose. New uniforms, unified leadership, common training and common arms and equipment were the foundations of the army's discipline, with the primary purpose of maximum efficiency.

In time the old colonels had been replaced and the officer corps had become the domain of the nobility; it was another way of subordinating a potentially rebellious nobility to the state. The French nobility soon considered the commission as its exclusive privilege and closed itself off from other social strata. The extent of Louis' warfare, however, severely decimated it; three sons and one grandson of Colbert were killed in action in the years between 1688 and 1702. There were no longer enough noblemen to make the number of officers required. This in turn introduced venality in the holding of commissions – the sale of officer patents. The positions of supreme command from the colonels upward remained a preserve of the nobility, however, while the sons of the second estate became the subalterns. Soldiers of the king's bodyguard who had particularly distinguished themselves were promoted to *officiers du fortune*, but the highest rank they could obtain was that of captain.

For a long time the army of Louis XIV was regarded as the best when considering performance and organization. Marshal Turenne gained the French a reputation as invincible which held until the victories of Marlborough in the Wars of the Spanish Succession. At the beginning of these wars, the French army was allied with the Elector of Bavaria, Max Emanuel, a general of great ability, and it was intended to unite the armies operating in Italy and Germany and then to make a thrust toward Vienna. Max Emanuel was not only a good general, he was also very ambitious and the refusal of the Emperor to elevate him from an elector to a king, as he had done in the case of the Elector of Brandenburg in 1701, led him to seek his royal fortune in alliance with the French king.

In 1704, however, the Imperial forces gained the upper hand when the Duke of Marlborough marched southward toward the Danube against the will of the government in London. In the true tradition of the strategy of attrition, engagements were avoided at first, and maneuver was met by countermaneuver. But when the allied forces defeated a Bavarian contingent and they were able to cross the Danube, the possibility of a decisive battle was envisaged. The supreme command was divided, however, one part of the allies being commanded by Marlborough and Prince Ludwig von Baden, the other by Prince Eugene. French and Bavarian troops then managed to gain a seemingly unassailable position. Max Emanuel played for time, hoping that the longer he held out the stronger the

possibility became that Marlborough would have to withdraw and return home on orders from London. However, Eugene and Marlborough decided to attack the Bavarians at Blindheim (Blenheim) near Augsburg on 13 August 1704. The allies enjoyed a slight numerical superiority, but it was not that which secured their victory but their superior generalship. Although the allied French and Bavarian troops were taken by surprise, Eugene's attack on the enemy's left flank was temporarily halted by the French. But while they held one another in check, Marlborough succeeded in breaking through the middle between Blindheim and Ober-Glauheim, scattering the center of the enemy's forces and then attacking the flanks and the rear. The French and Bavarians at Blindheim had to capitulate. The myth of French invincibility had been broken, Louis XIV's territorial ambitions had been checked once and for all, and his hegemonic policy had been broken. Nevertheless his army organization served as a model for many of his contemporaries.

In fact, his rule had inaugurated a military revolution. For the first time a new type of soldier, the professional soldier in the service of a dynasty, the *miles perpetuus*, made his appearance, replacing the mercenary and the *Landsknecht*. True, the beginnings of this development were already visible in Wallenstein's

Left. The Duke of Marlborough discusses plans for the siege of Bouchain with his chief engineer, Colonel Armstrong.

Below. The Battle of Blenheim, 13 August 1704.

Right. This tapestry, completed in 1715, is one of a series commemorating Marlborough's victories in the War of Spanish Succession.

INSULÆ

Top and above. *Silver medal commemorating the victories of Marlborough and Eugene.*

Left. *A holster cover used by Marlborough.*

Below left. *Another part of the Duke's holster covers.*

army, but their full results were cut short by his assassination. He had left a nucleus with which the Habsburgs could continue, but Louis XIV's army subsequently became the model to be followed.

In contrast to his historical predecessor, the soldier was now dependent upon the existence of the state for which he served. Also, in contrast to the former mercenary, he was subjected to the severest discipline and acquired an extensive and thorough basic training before being thrown into combat. He was a small cog within a highly complicated war machine, the product of new tactics and arms technology. He was part of a firmly disciplined body of men, not of a band of warriors who strolled toward the enemy, the battle dissolving quickly into individual engagements. A strictly disciplined body of men also had to apply its weapons systematically. Therefore every part had to react promptly to a central command and with great precision to maintain the order of battle. Within the framework of this structure every soldier fulfilled a precise function. And in order to fulfill the purpose of combat he had to transform the orders of his commanders into immediate action. The professional ethos also produced solidarity between comrades and superiors and led to a community of a unique sociological type.

The mercenaries had deteriorated into brutal bands, a pest to friend and foe alike. Only with the greatest of effort could they be kept within the bounds of discipline. Originating with the rise of the cash nexus, they were always dependent on the solvency of their masters; they were military entrepreneurs. But, despite their articles of war, there was never any real possibility of the establishment of a military tradition, let alone the tradition of a particular military group. They were not tied

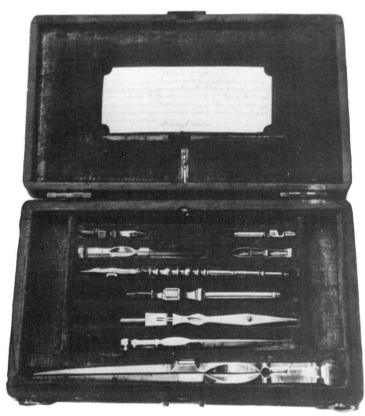

Above. *A case of mathematical instruments used by Marlborough.*

Below. *Plan of the Battle of Blenheim. The most remarkable of Marlborough's victories was this defeat of the French forces of Marshal Tallard in 1704.*

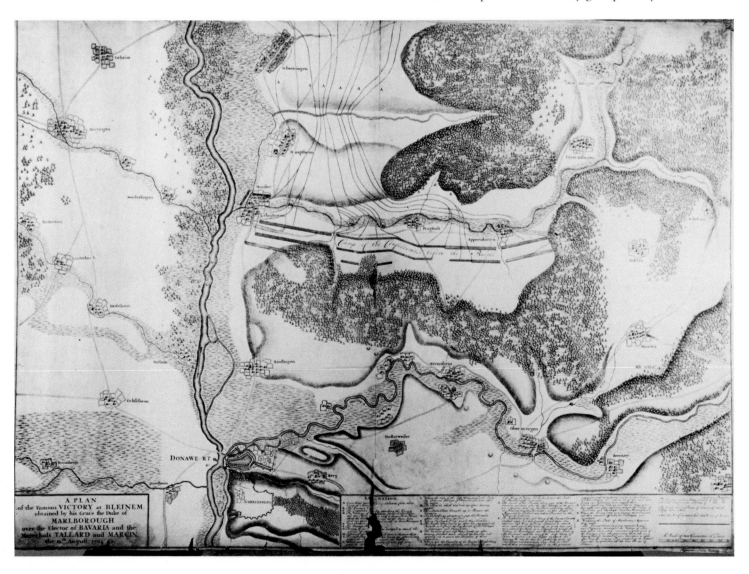

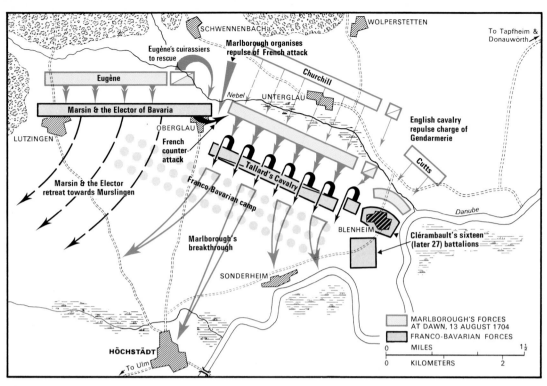

Above. *A grenadier lighting his grenade.*

Below. *The Battle of Ramillies, 23 May 1706, a telling defeat for the French under Marshal Villeroy at the hands of Marlborough.*

to any state, their officers rarely shared a common social background and, more often than not, they degenerated into an undisciplined band. They were dependent on their own supplies, and were therefore accompanied by an immense train which was even more difficult to keep in proper order than the mercenaries themselves. The lack of any medical corps often caused a substantial depletion of their numbers through illness and disease. Even the strictest of mercenary captains regretted condemning many of the men they sent to the gallows simply because they were the ones who had had the bad luck to be caught plundering. The new infantry tactics and the introduction of firearms had furthered their existence because what counted was the number of mercenaries one could put in the field. Therefore every prince hiring them was intent upon putting the largest possible number in the field, irrespective of whether or not he could pay for it. Consequently, pay remained in arrears and, since every man has to live, they plundered wherever they could; they also mutinied, with all the associated consequences. The original intention of selecting mercenaries carefully according to character and ability could never be put into practice. These were the shortcomings which made any reforms such as Emperor Maximilian I attempted abortive.

It was the achievement of the absolutist monarchy as exemplified by Louis XIV which put an end to these basic evils step by step. With the integration of all the military forces into his absolutist unitary state, he transformed the disadvantages of keeping a standing military force into an asset of the highest military efficiency. According to his example, other sovereigns throughout Europe created military legislation which promoted military discipline from its very foundations. This legislation, often called 'Articles of War,' had little in common with similar articles existing among the mercenaries. It provided an absolute yardstick for soldierly ethos and behavior, and contained, next to a catalog of soldierly duties, judicial and disciplinary measures which secured internal order. In great detail it told the soldier what and what not to do while in garrison or on a campaign, and informed him of the punishment to expect for any contravention. The articles of war also determined the relationship between subordinates and superiors. At the beginning of this list of duties was a paragraph stressing that an obedient, brave and decent soldier was also a true Christian, who would therefore regularly attend church services. The heaviest penalties were meted out to rebels, mutineers, deserters, thieves, plunderers, marauders and rapists as well as excessive drinkers. Considering the recent historical background there was every reason to list every conceivable offense. Once the recruit had thoroughly familiarized himself with these articles, he was taken under oath, and thereafter they were read to him time and again to ensure that they were never forgotten.

Like the mercenary armies before it, the new standing army divided itself into three main groups: infantry, cavalry and artillery. The branch which at first provided the greatest difficulties for Louis XIV was the cavalry, because the French nobility was loath to part with its medieval traditions – it was reluctant not to fight with heavy armor and, although light cavalry had come to the fore, they preferred German mercenaries to fulfill this function. But in time they, too, came to accept it. The basic formation was the regiment: it was the largest closed body of troops and consisted of infantry companies and cavalry squadrons respectively. This form of organization was the most suitable for administrative reasons. Each regiment had its own contingent of troops responsible for recruitment and supplies. But, while the regiment was primarily an administrative unit, the battalion was the primary tactical unit in combat. On the battlefield several battalions could be combined into a brigade under one commander. Larger formations did not yet exist, as the principle of mixed arms was still unknown. Therefore in peacetime one served only in the regiment and the company.

In the course of the eighteenth century the artillery gained its own importance and recognition as a separate branch, equal in status with infantry and cavalry. It took some time to overcome the traditional prejudices of the infantry and cavalry against this purely *technical* weapon, and for a long time it was reserved for the lower orders of society. In peacetime, like the other two branches, it was divided into regiments and companies; in time of war it was formed into batteries.

The mercenaries and the *Landsknecht* already had their own engineering units. With the development of modern fortress war, these technical auxiliaries were now required even more and from them ultimately emerged the modern engineer, another separate branch of the army.

The structure of the army in peacetime actually meant that generals had no practical work to do since, above the regiment, there were no positions of command. They were therefore entrusted with other posts such as that of governor or other offices of state. During the war they led army contingents of varying size, either within the existing order of battle or as

Guerard inue

GRENADIERS.

Chaque Regiment d'infanterie a une compagnie de Grenadiers qui n'ont ni pique ni dra:
péau ils sont armé de fusil depeé et bayonnette, et d'une grenadiere pendant en bandou=
liere, le Roy Crea en ... une compagnie de 100. Grenadiers à cheval, tous gens choisis et
en fit M.r de Riotot Capitaine, ils marchent à la tete de la maison du Roy sans y être
compris, la recruë s'en fait des troupes de l'armée, et celle des Grenadiers a pied de leurs Reg.

N. Gu

Les Cavaliers sont appellé n
ils sont armé de mousqueto
cela sappelle vedette. Les
de rang dans l'armée marche
pour armes le fusil le sabr

Left. *British and French cavalry collide at the Battle of Malplaquet, where Marlborough won a costly victory over Villars.*

independently operating formations. The military supreme command was in the hands of a field marshal with a wide spectrum of duties. For the duration of a campaign he was surrounded by a body of military advisers, a very select group to which the term general staff was applied, but it was not the general staff within the modern meaning of the term.

The standing army also required continuous drill in peacetime, and training manuals were written and issued with which all training had to conform. Less than a century before, training was left in the hands of the individual bodies of mercenaries.

Army uniforms were rather colorful and corresponded, insofar as a military uniform allowed, with the fashion of the day. But first and foremost they fulfilled a military function. The first basic uniform was introduced in the armies of Gustavus Adolphus, followed by Cromwell's red coats and those of the French army designed in Paris. At first French uniforms were rather elaborate but, within a relatively short time, functional needs predominated. The French army wore white coats with facings of different colors. The Bavarian Elector Max Emanuel dressed his troops in light blue, the Russians used dark green and the Austrians, white. Prussian troops wore dark blue, since Frederick William I was determined to use as much as he could of Prussia's own resources; Prussia produced its own cloth and the only dye which they could manufacture and which would stand all weathers was dark blue. Indeed, during the reign of Frederick William I and his son Frederick, Prussian military fashions pushed French influences into the background.

Of course, colorful uniforms also served as a demonstration of power by the individual princes, particularly on the parade ground. But they served also a more practical purpose: in battle vision was often obscured by dust and smoke and the color of the uniform allowed the commander to estimate the number of troops confronting him.

Departments of the military bureaucracy directed the entire economic administration of the army. Their staffs, too, had to be well trained and efficient because on them in turn depended the efficiency of the entire army. Regimental and company chiefs were no longer military entrepreneurs in the old sense, but nevertheless one of their major tasks was to dedicate themselves to the adequate supply of their troops. This applied particularly at the company level. The prince, the chief and owner of the army, had delegated responsibility for this to company commanders, who received money and supplies for their troops, plus additional funds for the recruitment of new soldiers. The recruitment fund was a particular source of complaint since it helped the company commander to increase his own income. Wherever he could impress or recruit soldiers cheaply the surplus went into his own pocket; the same applied to supplies. In addition certain weapons, and other equipment such as horses, were often the personal property of the company commander, particularly in the French army; to take over a company required personal wealth and property.

Every general and colonel had his own lifeguard, which was usually the first company of the regiment. He was their 'chief.' But, as already indicated, in peacetime generals and colonels did very little practical military work – they left the task of working with the troops to a deputy or lieutenant colonel; the lifeguard, life company or *Leibkompanie*, if not commanded by the chief

Far left. *French horse and foot grenadiers, circa 1710.*

Left. *French cavalrymen and dragoons of the early eighteenth century. At this period dragoons were trained to fight on horse or foot.*

himself, was commanded by lieutenant captains or staff captains, while all other companies were commanded by premier lieutenants, which is roughly equivalent to today's first lieutenant.

In France the influence of the Estates had been removed, so they no longer put any obstacles in the way of the standing army. Things were not as easy elsewhere, however, as the Great Elector of Prussia was to experience. But wherever there was a struggle between a ruler and his estates about maintaining a standing army, it was usually decided in favor of the former.

The French army, like any other at this time, was a state army, but it was not yet in the true sense of the word a national army. It was largely made up from more or less voluntary recruits and contained more foreigners than natives; they were sometimes supplemented by citizens but only in cases of dire emergency. The duty for every subject to perform military service, however, did not exist, and for very good reasons: society and state or monarch did not represent an entity, they existed side by side, the people were excluded from political life and enjoyed no political rights worth speaking of, and their interests were not necessarily, in reality, identical with those of the state. Populations, in the cabinet politics of the Age of the Baroque, were traded like chattels and they consequently may have had little interest in the defense of their country. Armies of that age were not defensive forces but primarily used for conquest, highly qualified and well equipped; this required thorough training in logistics, tactics and control of weapons, and took time to achieve. For this purpose the popular levy was virtually useless.

Nevertheless the medieval laws concerning popular levies were never revoked. Machiavelli was one of the first modern theoreticians of war who advised the prince to base his power not on doubtful mercenaries but upon a patriotic citizens' army according to the Roman example. The implications of this demand, however, were not fully recognized by him insofar as they concerned military discipline and the rigors of military training. There were occasions when princes took recourse to the medieval levy, and attempted to transform it into a kind of national service; Brandenburg-Prussia and Bavaria are outstanding examples. Elector Max Emanuel of Bavaria tried to do this but, his ambitions being far in excess of the country's resources, he failed. Others, like Count Wilhelm von Schaumburg-Lippe, attempted to raise an army exclusively from their own subjects. Considering the small size of his state he became the object of ridicule by his contemporaries and his army always suffered heavily in battle. In the sovereign absolutist state where the subjects were pressed into military service, it was on orders of the sovereign and the idea of national service could consequently strike no deep roots.

Ideological principle was involved in the question of national service. But the profession of arms served specific needs and functions, and it was in the interests of a civilized state strictly to separate the military and civilian populations. Mercantilist principles set natural boundaries to the size of armies. In practice this meant that the productive sectors of the nation, who also did so much for raising its material and cultural riches, had to be exempted from any kind of military service; this applied to all burghers of the towns. Only the lowest layer of society, the daily-wage laborer for instance, could be made available. The net result was that every soldier recruited abroad deprived the enemy of a soldier and retained for the state a working individual. Those exempted had their military service transmuted into money payments in the form of taxation – thereby increasing the royal chest and its military striking power.

The operation of recruitment lay in the hands of the regi-

Right. *A French bronze cannon, circa 1670.*

Below. *Uniforms of French infantry of the sixteenth, seventeenth and eighteenth centuries.*

ments and companies. Recruitment was carried out within one's own boundaries as well as elsewhere. The French army found a rich recruitment ground in the devastated regions to the east of its frontiers; German cities were also profitable areas. Prohibitions and limitations on recruitment existed only in the Habsburg crownlands and in Silesia; permission was given on the basis of contracts, ensuring that the recruitment commander paid a certain sum to the sovereign or the city fathers.

What has been said so far about standing armies does not

mean that they eliminated all the evils of the mercenary armies. The profession of arms had been considerably improved, though problems still remained. The main difficulty was no longer the financial support of the forces, but raising and replacing them. Armies throughout Europe were getting bigger all the time. The numerical factor played an increasingly important role in existing infantry tactics, which were steadily advancing along with the improvement in firearms.

The large size of an army which had to be paid at all times,

during peace or war, resulted in a reduction of pay for the individual soldier. He was paid roughly three talers per month as compared to the 10–18 guilders in the Thirty Years' War. The times had passed when one joined the army simply because of the profit motive. Nor did the soldier possess the automatic right to gain booty at will: plundering, requisitioning and marauding were offenses which were strictly punished. As a result recruits were less forthcoming.

Furthermore, continuous drill in barren garrisons was

unattractive to many. Nor was there much opportunity for promotion, in contrast to the armies of the mercenaries and *Landsknecht* in which every member had the marshal's, or rather the colonel's, baton in his knapsack. The highest a soldier could rise was to non-commissioned officer. With a few exceptions, in reality the officer corps of the absolutist army remained a closed community.

Stricter discipline did not encourage recruits. Offenses against military discipline were severely punished, and this process was now subject to proper military jurisdiction. Every punishment was meant to constitute an example to the rest. To be beaten by the corporal's stick was still the mildest form of punishment, yet it was considered to be deeply dishonoring. A more severe punishment was riding on a wooden horse or donkey, or being tied to a pole with the feet standing on sharpened poles. Equally severe was being tied hand to feet for several days. Fortification work, particularly pulling a heavily loaded cart to which one was tied with iron rings, was as feared as was running the gauntlet, a punishment introduced particularly for deserters. Because desertion was so frequent it was uneconomic to punish it by death; the deserter was therefore subjected to a kind of punishment which would incapacitate him for only a few days. According to the seriousness of the offense, he had to run the gauntlet several times, the maximum being 36. In a case such as this, however, the punishment was spread over several days, as a soldier could not be expected to run the gauntlet more than 10 times on any one occasion; nevertheless, fatalities did occur. Mutiny was punished by death through shooting, and other forms of capital offenses were punished by the standard punishments also in use for certain breaches of civil law, like death on the gallows, the sword or the wheel.

As volunteers were increasingly hard to come by, recruiting teams took recourse to guile and force, even though the impressed soldier, rebelling at first against his fate, was all the more likely to bring upon himself the wide range of punishment. Forcible recruitment resulted in increased desertion, resulting in even more forcible recruitment; a vicious circle. Desertion proved to be an insoluble problem in the armies of the absolutist age.

Nor did the treatment meted out to the common soldier do much to elevate the standing of the professional army in the eyes of the burghers. They despised it as an institution, while the soldier himself felt like a prisoner in an establishment from which escape was difficult and associated with serious risks. Soldiers could no longer maltreat civilians, at least not in their own country – they maltreated themselves. For this reason the emerging Enlightenment considered the standing army as the greatest evil of the age.

In the higher echelons changes had different implications. It is

true that Prince Maurice of Orange had established a socially homogeneous officer corps; but with the integration of the nobility in the absolute state, however, commissions gradually became their exclusive preserve. They became even more of a caste, ranging above the bourgeoisie. United by the same social origin and a personal oath to the king, and with claims to special privileges, the officer's code of honor developed; the officer corps lived a life characterized very often, particularly in France, by rather unmilitary and cavalier habits, aggravated by the venality of office holding. In action, however, they led at the front and not from behind; in the middle of battle they had to be an example to their men. Within the officer corps, the artillery officers were an exception insofar as they lived a separate existence. Technicians and mathematicians, in most cases, they did not share the same social origins and were consequently not considered equals by the rest. This changed only with the changing role of artillery toward the end of the eighteenth century.

On the whole, however, the officer corps of Europe formed an international caste of warriors; on every battlefield where European armies encountered one another, it also became a rendezvous for the European nobility. In 1745 at Fontenoy, the officers first complimented one another and then each asked the other to fire the first volley. Their exclusiveness, however, often degenerated into sheer arrogance, particularly toward civilians. To ensure perpetual social homogeneity, Louis XIV established cadet institutes in which the male offspring of the military nobility were educated, ultimately to become officers, a practice begun by the Great Elector in 1653, when he established a Knight's Academy, and expanded systematically by his grandson Frederick William I, who established regular cadet institutes.

All this was accompanied by a revolution in tactics. Medieval knighthood did not primarily owe its decline to the invention of firearms, but to the superiority of effective bodies of infantry. In the days of the mercenary and the *Landsknecht*, the main emphasis lay in the superior numbers and mobility of their infantry squares. As already indicated, the rediscovery of the military writers of antiquity supplied Maurice of Orange with new tactical theories. The main organizational unit was the regiment, subdivided into 10 companies, each company about 150 men strong. Its arms consisted of pikes and muskets on support forks, the pikes being about eight yards long. Each company comprised 75 pikemen and 75 soldiers armed with firearms – harquebusiers and muskets. At first the pikemen formed the center of the battle order, flanked on both sides by firearms. It was a broad front divided into three parts, but it was not identical with the company structure, containing between 600 and 750 men and called a half-regiment. Though still large

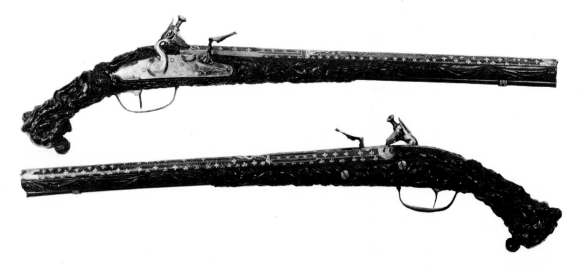

French flint-lock pistols, presented to Louis XIV by the city of Lille. The stocks, of dark walnut, are carved with Hercules skinning a lion.

formations, they were more maneuverable than the large Spanish squares. A Dutch half-regiment covered a front of about 80 yards. To ensure that any breakthrough by the enemy could be held up within a distance of about 150 yards, a formation of the same strength was arranged in the same order, 10 men deep. It was a return to the Roman example. Initially, artillery was used very sparingly: about 10 guns to 10,000 infantry.

The cavalry was subdivided into companies of 100 men arranged to protect the rear and flanks. Gustavus Adolphus developed the reforms of Maurice of Orange, closing up even further the ranks of his infantry which he called brigades, numerically as strong as the half-regiment but integrated with cavalry and artillery. The infantry brigade was now only six men deep, and the introduction of lighter muskets, which did away with the cumbersome forks and used paper cartridges which improved the speed of loading, allowed the infantry to advance six deep, fire and retire behind the pikemen for reloading. Gustavus' main arm was his cavalry, organized in squadrons of 200 to 300 horsemen; its impact had to be so overpowering as to throw the enemy. He placed equal emphasis on his artillery. Toward the end of the seventeenth century, the new French infantry line, the *ordre mince*, made its appearance; it was the first appearance of linear tactics in modern warfare – a result of greater troop maneuverability and progress in arms technology.

The firepower of the infantry increased after the demise of the old wheel-lock and arquebus. After the Thirty Years' War they were replaced by flintlock muskets of English origin. The combination of paper cartridges, bullet and gunpowder facilitated the loading process. The new musket however, was still vulnerable to the weather and was to remain so until the middle of the nineteenth century. Whereas with the old musket the rate of fire was one round in three minutes, this now increased to five rounds in two minutes. The loading process took about 24 seconds. The new musket weighed nine pounds, about three pounds less than the old one, but its extreme range was not much beyond 250 yards; the most effective range was anything less than 50 yards. Since these muskets were muzzle loaders, it was practically useless to fire in a prone position; to reload, however, the infantryman now required less room and could thus operate closer to his neighbors, which helped to tighten up the formation. The formation could now fire also in a kneeling position while the second line fired above it, the third line being engaged in reloading. Vauban's invention of the bayonet with socket and short horizontal arm was also of decisive importance. The rifle now fulfilled the dual function of firearm and pike; the pikemen had become obsolescent and by the end of the seventeenth century, had disappeared altogether, though the theory was perpetuated – until his defeat at Kolin, Frederick the Great believed that a massed bayonet attack was to be preferred to an aimed volley of muskets.

Nonetheless, it was believed that victory could be achieved only by superior firepower. The introduction of the iron ramrod by Prince Leopold of Anhalt-Dessau, *der alte Dessauer*, improved reloading speed. By thinning out the linear formation to three lines, one hoped to avoid providing the artillery with an all too easy target; moreover, by extending the order of battle in width, there was the possibility of outflanking the enemy.

The thin line was the characteristic of the new infantry tactics, stretching miles across the battlefield. On the whole it was a very fragile formation which had always to avoid losing touch with neighboring companies. To ensure that, the formation had to march at an equal pace, at equal step; running into the attack was impossible. Changes of direction, turning off to the left or the right, were virtually impossible since they would have disorganized the entire line. All maneuvers were carried out as one. Natural obstacles, such as villages and woods, were whenever possible avoided.

The tactical basic unit was now the battalion, while the regiment remained intact for organizational purposes, such as administration and logistics. Every battalion was one formation within the line of battle. It comprised approximately 700 men. Attached to each battalion were two light pieces of artillery to strengthen the resistance against the enemy's cavalry attack. The object was to decimate the enemy through continuous fire before the assault was attempted. The battalion was subdivided into divisions and these in turn into platoons. The most effective arrangement consisted in dividing the battalion into four divisions and eight platoons. Each battalion comprised five companies but, in the application of linear tactics, the lines of division very often cut through a platoon. In the center of the battalion was the flag group. Surrounded by NCOs and a platoon of musketeers, the flag group, like the banners of the knights of the Middle Ages, served as a point of orientation during the confusion of battle. Beside the infantryman the grenadier made his appearance, originating in France in 1625, equipped with musket and grenade. In the course of the eighteenth century they became the elite formations. Behind the first battalion came the second within a distance of 200 to 300 yards; they not only supported the front line but had to repel attacks on the flanks. If the numbers permitted, a third battalion followed the second, the entire formation being an elongated square.

The purpose of the cavalry was to protect the flanks until the battle had developed to a stage where they could be used in attack. Heavy cavalry were employed mainly in battle while light horse did scouting duties. Dragoons were infantry on horse. Cavalry fought in squadrons formed in two deep lines. The regiment consisted of five squadrons, each squadron having 150 horses and men. Light cavalry was actually a Hungarian invention, first adopted by the Austrian hussars and subsequently becoming an integral part of all European armies. A feature of cavalry attacks was that they were not mounted with the firing of pistols, but with the saber; only in close combat was recourse taken to firearms.

The artillery included light artillery – three and six pounders – used with the battalion front. Their range was about 1000 yards, but they were really effective only at half that distance. Ammunition consisted of cannon balls or bullets and rusty fragments in a linen sack or tin container. Grapeshot was very effective against cavalry, providing the gun crew was well drilled and disciplined. The heavy artillery consisted of 12 and 24 pounders, seven- and eight-pounder howitzers and 10- to 50-pounder mortars. The range of the 12 pounder was about 1200 yards.

Their tactical deployment was related to the position of the line. Reference has already been made to how the light artillery was arranged. Heavy artillery was at first posted in front of the line, but had mainly a defensive rather than an offensive function, except in the case of sieges.

The battle picture was roughly as follows: both lines advanced toward one another at about 15 yards per minute, the cavalry accompanying the infantry at the same pace. Once in firing range, infantry fire began until one side or the other decided that the opportunity to attack with cavalry had come; close combat then followed until one side was thrown back and retreated. One of the drawbacks of linear tactics was the great care that had to be taken to avoid one formation losing touch with another; this weakness was solved, partially, by Frederick the Great.

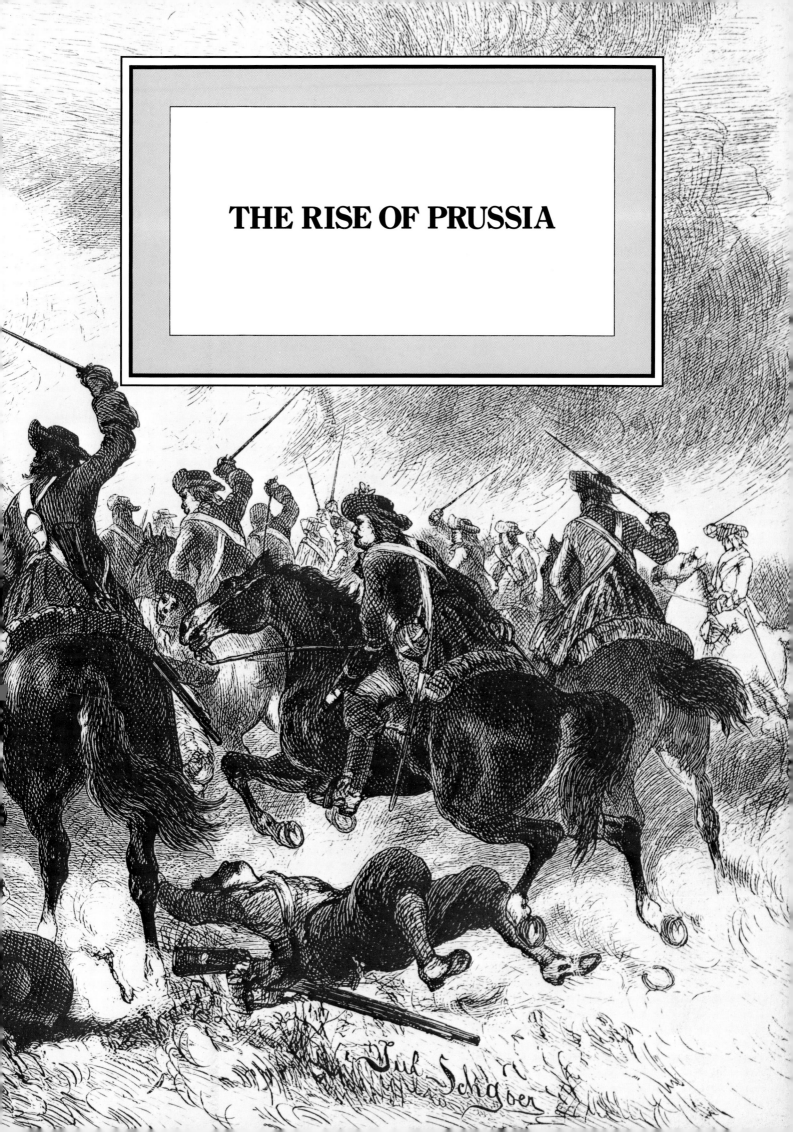

THE RISE OF PRUSSIA

The defeat of the Teutonic Order by the forces of Poland and Lithuania on 15 July 1410 was not the end, but the beginning, of the Prussian state. Several more engagements followed until the combined pressure exerted by military defeat, internal dissension and the German settlers in Prussia compelled the Order to submit. By the Peace of Thorun in 1466, Prussia became a vassal state of Poland; eastward expansion of Germany and Europe had come to an end. A century later during the Reformation, when the last Grand Master decided to secularize the land of the Order, the *Deutschritterorden* in Prussia also came to an end. What remained was the name of the country and the one-headed, black imperial eagle which Emperor Frederick II had given to Hermann von Salza and the black cross upon a white background. The most important remnant, however, was the nucleus of a future Prussian state.

When Frederick William, later known as the Great Elector, of Brandenburg, came to the throne in 1640 he was 20 years old. Some of his territories were still held by the Swedes, such as West and East Pomerania with most of the harbors on the River Oder. His inheritance consisted of five very different and separate territories: Brandenburg – 'the Holy Roman Empire's sandbox,' the Duchy of Cleves, the counties of Mark and Ravensburg, and Prussia. As Duke of Prussia Frederick William was the vassal of the King of Poland. In other words, his possessions were strewn across the north of Germany, touching the northwestern and northeastern extremities of the Reich.

Brandenburg was totally ravaged, and had a population of only a million and a half. Fewer than 10 farmers were found in some villages between the River Spree and the Oder, and they lived hand to mouth. This German territorial state had either to grow strong again or else perish.

With the appearance of Frederick William, the military element stepped to the fore for the first time in the history of Brandenburg. On his mother's side he was descended from the House of Orange and he had spent part of his youth in the Dutch Netherlands, where he paid great attention to the organization of the standing army; this knowledge was transferred to Brandenburg together with French modern arms technology. He was also, however, deeply influenced by Dutch Calvinist thought, which differed from German Lutheranism in that it promoted all state activities for the purpose of its expansion and prosperity.

The Calvinist striving for success in all spheres of life had been one of the driving forces of the Dutch Protestants in their struggle for liberation from the Spaniards. Experience of such a religiously motivated policy of state was vital for Frederick William, as well as its corollary of being personally accountable to God. In accordance with Calvinist creed, he saw himself as a chosen tool of the Lord whose task it was to consolidate his political position, to expand it and thus help his people who were on the verge of starvation.

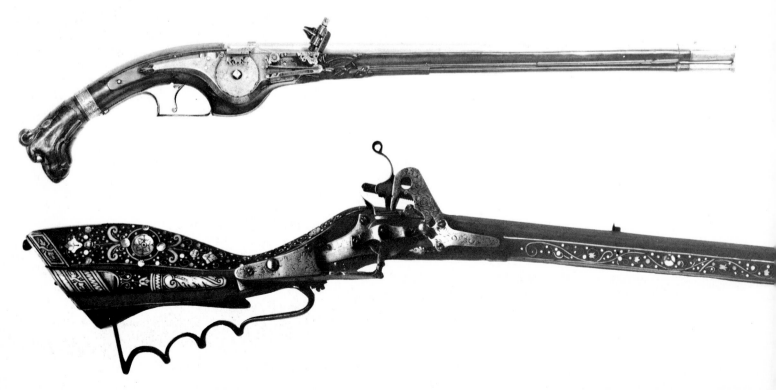

It was not enough to have inherited territory. What the Hohenzollern prince lacked was the effective strength to maintain it – his territorial possessions existed only at the mercy of his stronger neighbors. This in turn had allowed the Estates in each territory to assert their own power and pursue their own interests without considering the impact on the Hohenzollern territories as a whole. His greatest territorial asset was Prussia, which had been spared most of the ravages of war; here the Estates used their position to play off the Hohenzollerns against the Poles. Yet, from an economic point of view, Prussia was more important to Frederick William than was Brandenburg. As Duke of Prussia he possessed immense domains with considerable economic resources and a great number of subjects. This was a direct consequence of the settlement policy of the Teutonic Order, which had concentrated the largest part of the land in its own hands, a large percentage of the population having been reduced to the state of serfdom in the course of the preceding century. The primary economic importance of this population was that it could be taxed without first having to ask the representative assembly of the Estates, and this made Prussia the Hohenzollern's most important single source of revenue.

Another important source of revenue was Königsberg. It exported not only Prussian but also Lithuanian produce, major commodities being wheat, hemp and furs. The Teutonic Order had already attempted to acquire a share of the resulting revenue by introducing an export toll. Then, during the course of the Thirty Years' War, the Swedes occupied Pillau at the exit of the *Frisches Haff* until 1635, although, after that date, the toll revenues reverted back to the Duke of Prussia. Since the Duke of Prussia was still a vassal of the King of Poland at the time, however, the latter demanded his share as well. This his predecessor had to concede, and Frederick William was compelled to accept the situation upon his accession. The revenue of that part of Jülich-Cleves held by the Hohenzollerns was also in Dutch hands.

The political position of the Hohenzollerns in Brandenburg was, relatively speaking, still stable. After all, they represented the resident ruling house. Brandenburg relied on extensive sheep farming and wool production, although this had seriously declined because of the war. Other major sources of revenue were the river tolls levied on the Oder and the Elbe; as the

mouths of these rivers were in the possession of other states, however, control of trade lay outside the power of the Hohenzollerns. Stettin, for example, always managed to maintain its predominance over Frankfurt-an-der-Oder.

Thus the legacy left to Frederick William was not an enviable one. In the early years of his rule he relied heavily on the advice of his mother. Upon her initiative several memoranda were drawn up to analyze Brandenburg's problems, but they failed to supply practical solutions. They emphasized the impossibility of continuing the war against the Swedes, but at the same time stressed the need for loyalty toward the Habsburgs and the Holy Roman Empire. How these two policies could be reconciled remained unanswered. But one point was made to which Frederick William paid great attention: the need for an effective standing army, without which the House of Hohenzollern would not be in a position to pursue active politics at all but would simply remain the political objective of others. A policy of general appeasement toward the Estates was recommended.

At first Frederick William tried to pursue a course of establishing cordial relationships with the Estates. He attempted to involve them in discussions about the relationship of Brandenburg with the Holy Roman Emperor, the problem of Pomerania

Above left. The Great Elector, Frederick William of Prussia, 1620–88.

Left. A German wheel-lock pistol, made in Nuremberg, circa 1630.

Below. A German wheel-lock rifle of about 1600.

Right. The Swedish King, Charles X, 1622–60 overlord of Frederick William and Brandenburg – Prussia until the treaty of Labrau in 1656.

CAROLVS   GVSTAVVS

King of Swethens, Goths, & Vandalls, greate prince of Finlne, Duke of Esthonia, & Carelia Lord of Ingria, & Crowned An.º Dom: 1654.   P.S excudit

Above. Prussian dragoons of the Great Elector's army formed up for a formal parade.

and the question of disarmament. From his experience in the Dutch Netherlands and his observations of the politics of the Estates-General, he expected constructive assistance. But he was to be disappointed. The Estates showed little interest in questions of grand politics; all that mattered to them was the preservation and extension of their own material privileges. This was a lesson Frederick William remembered when formulating his future policy. During the process of joint consultation, it was agreed to investigate the complaints raised about the Brandenburg troops and to reduce the army.

The combat value of the existing army was highly doubtful. Most of the officers and men represented the dregs of society, swept to the surface by the Thirty Years' War. A precondition of forming a new army was the dissolution of the old one. On the other hand, it was imperative to come to an arrangement with the Swedes as soon as possible, and negotiations without the backing of an army would be futile. His endeavors met with limited success, and in 1641 a two-year armistice was agreed between Brandenburg and Sweden. While it relieved Brandenburg from making war, the armistice left the Swedes in the positions which they held in Brandenburg. In other words, the armistice highlighted Brandenburg's political and military impotence. Sweden sacrificed nothing at all, which may have been the reason why Frederick William never exchanged the document of ratification, managing time and again to raise another point in need of further clarification until the general settlement of the Peace of Westphalia in 1648.

As for his predecessors, Frederick William's relationship with Poland was of primary importance. The Stuhmdorf armistice with the Swedes had given the Poles cause for alarm, for they feared that they would now be exposed to military pressure from the Swedes. Frederick William assured the Poles that he would not put Prussia's harbors at the disposal of the Swedes. In

general, however, he tried to keep King Vladislav IV of Poland in the dark about his arrangements with the Swedes, so that he could use them as a lever with which to obtain a formal investiture of the ducal crown or the *de facto* assumption of power in Prussia through his deputy. But Vladislav, contrary to Frederick William's plan, insisted that he also appear at the investiture, which finally took place on 7 October 1641. Little less than a month later, on 1 November, Frederick William entered Königsberg and attended the Prussian Diet. The Diet granted him, among other things, the introduction of an excise tax which was to become one of the most important forms of taxation throughout Brandenburg-Prussia. It represented a form of indirect taxation by taxing consumption. As the administration of taxation in Prussia lay in the hands of the nobility, however, this ensured that they did not suffer too much.

The nobility has generally become known as the 'junkers,' yet it is a misleading term because its present-day connotation does not go back farther than the revolution of 1848, when among liberals it became a term of abuse directed against the Prussian nobility. In fact a *Junker* was originally the son of a noble house; in the Middle Ages he often served his military apprenticeship as the esquire to a knight. In more modern armies there was also the *Fahnenjunker*, or ensign, the rank held prior to receiving a full commission.

Moreover, the term as generally used tends to obscure the fact that in Prussia, as elsewhere, the nobility consisted of what, for the sake of convenience, one might describe as the higher and lower nobility. In East Prussia there were the *Grafenfamilien*, the families of the earls and counts, the knights bound to them by

IOANNES CASIMIRVS.

ULADISLAI frater: In Gallijs, dum in Hispanias proficiscitur, velut proditor in custodia detinetur; at patrocinante innocentia non sine honore dimittitur. Redux in Italiam ad inclytam IESV societatem transit, è qua paulo post Purpuratorū adscribitur senatui; inde Fratri defuncto in Regno successit An. 1648. ducta etiam uxore fratris, indulto Pontificio, sed absque prole. Arridet principio fortuna; deuictis Cosachis, Tartarorum quoque triginta millibus deletis: sed vertitur in luctum sors infida: irruunt cateruatim hostes, Moschus, Brandeburgicus, perduelles Cosachi, Transiluanus, et Carolus Suecorum Rex à discessu, Magnæ Cristinæ Regnum adeptus. Actum erat, nisi Leopoldi Imperatoris exercitus rebus desperatis opportunè affuisset. Tunc animis aucti Poloni hostem eyciunt, urbes, arcesque recuperant. Rex tandem fessus portui quærit, abdicatoque solio in amicam se recipit Galliam, post tot titulos S. Germani Abbas, ubi priuatam per quadrienniū vitam religiosissimè coronauit. An. 1672. Regni 20. Ætatis 63.

feudal obligations, and in the sixteenth and seventeenth centuries that class from which the higher nobility drew country administrators such as the *Landräte*. The greater number of lower nobility during the same period, however, ensured that they ultimately dominated the provincial Diet and to all intents and purposes entered into a lasting alliance with the higher nobility. With the development and extension of demesne farming and the decline of the manorial system came also a substantial increase in the economic power of the Prussian nobility east of the River Elbe. It acquired and usurped privileges which were, in view of Frederick William's need for the assistance of the nobility, confirmed by him in 1653 and remained fundamentally unchanged until the Prussian Reform Movement of the early nineteenth century.

The build-up of the army dates from the spring of 1644, after Frederick William had achieved a degree of internal as well as external stability. The strength of the army varied according to need and circumstance, and only after 1660 was it possible to transform it into a regular standing army. Nevertheless Frederick William and his councillors were clear in their minds about the need for a small, efficient army in Brandenburg-Prussia. Only two objections were raised: the money an army would cost, and the suspicion it would arouse among the Swedes.

Against those objections, however, stood the considerations

Above left. King John Casimir, who succeeded his brother Vladislav on the throne of Poland.

Below left. King Vladislav IV of Poland, 1595–1648.

Below. A more martial portrait of Vladislav.

Vladislaus vi. Polonia et Suecia Rex Serenissimus et Potentissimus

in favor of an army, succinctly put in a memorandum submitted in 1644 by Curt Bertram von Phul, a member of the Brandenburg nobility who had served in the Swedish army. Phul argued in favor of an army because its existence would increase the diplomatic prestige of Brandenburg-Prussia; he also made the point that a disciplined standing army would be of considerable economic benefit, as it had proved in the United Netherlands and in Sweden, where the army was one of the driving forces of the infant manufacturing industries and also, by its very needs, stimulated commerce. Though basically sound, the expectations inherent in these ideas were not realized until the eighteenth century.

Frederick William proceeded cautiously with his recruitment program, entrusting it to a close confidant, Johann von Norprath. It was to be conducted in the region of the lower Rhine, in other words away from the close proximity of the Swedes who might become suspicious. The garrison fortresses in Brandenburg and Prussia were also slowly increased. But the core of the new army was built up in Cleves, where, because of the war between Spain and the Netherlands, the Estates-General decided to pull out their forces, thus leaving it to Frederick William. By 1646 approximately 3000 men were garrisoned on the lower Rhine, recruited mainly from Dutchmen and Prussians.

One major problem remained, the endemic problem for most armies at the time, namely how to pay the army. The main contribution came from the Duchy of Prussia, though, because of the Swedes, payments were made secretively and the Estates were circumvented. Councillors and members of the Prussian Diet, as well as representatives of town and countryside, were approached individually and persuaded to give their support. But there was still a substantial gap between Prussia's contributions and the amount needed. Loans were raised in the cities, but we still do not know all the sources from which the army was financed in its early years.

Major difficulties were encountered in Cleves, for the Estates there were vehement in their opposition to army recruitment and the consequential levying of contributions. The need for an army, its purpose and function in the general context of the policy of Brandenburg-Prussia were explained to them in great detail. It was to no avail – they were willing to grant supplies only if Frederick William would pull the troops out of Cleves. Although Frederick William was willing to concede the point and transfer the troops to the county of Mark, he could only do so once the respective garrisons there had been evacuated by the Imperial troops. Therefore, because of the unreasonableness of the Cleves Estates, Frederick William had little choice other than to raise taxation without consent. This was possible in the countryside but met strong opposition in the cities, where, because of their refusal to cooperate, no administration existed to assess and collect the taxes. Frederick William also encountered the opposition of Austria and the Dutch, who opposed this kind of taxation on political principle. For the time being Frederick William and the Estates could reach no common ground; both sides got themselves involved in an extensive pamphleteering war about the rights and wrongs of taxation without consultation – arguments which, across the North Sea

in England, John Pym and John Hampden, among others, had put forward a short time before.

Meanwhile Sweden was turning its attention away from Germany and toward Denmark. Frederick William tried to mediate, but his attempt was ignored. However, the changing military situation compelled the Swedes to give up their occupation of the fortresses of Frankfurt-an-der-Oder and Crossen, which they could have defended only with great difficulty against Imperial troops; Brandenburg-Prussia had to promise that it would not allow these fortresses to be occupied by the Austrians. Obviously this was an embarrassing demand because it was by no means certain that Brandenburg-Prussia had the necessary strength to prevent them, nor whether such forces were strong enough to obstruct the transit of Imperial troops. Apart from that, Brandenburg-Prussia was still, at least formally, the ally of the Habsburgs. After lengthy and protracted negotiations, in which, by force of necessity, the representatives of Brandenburg-Prussia were not always the most honest of men, a treaty was agreed upon and the fortresses evacuated by the Swedes in July 1644. The first soldiers of the new army of Brandenburg-Prussia entered virtually upon the heels of the Swedes.

The Swedes also seemed ready to discuss the question of Pomerania, which Frederick William wanted returned, but, because of his connections with the Empire, Brandenburg-Prussia could not overindulge in such negotiations. The impotence of the state when faced by a major power, however, was demonstrated during the course of the same year when, in order to support the Danes, Imperial troops traversed Brandenburg with impunity, leaving Frederick William in a position he could do very little about.

It was that impotence which caused Frederick William to look for support from any major power ready to give it. During the discussions leading to the Peace of Westphalia feelers were stretched out in all directions. France seemed sympathetic but was not yet ready. Yet, the rise of Brandenburg-Prussia during the seventeenth and eighteenth centuries was facilitated by the Peace of Westphalia in 1648, which brought it important territorial acquisitions. Although, for the time being, Sweden exercised control at the mouths of the Oder and Elbe, Brandenburg-Prussia's position along these rivers ensured it an important role, since they carried by far the greatest part of German exports. In addition, her territorial holdings along the River Weser and the lower Rhine placed her in a key position between Germany's north and south, between the northwest, particularly Hamburg, and the territories southeast of Brandenburg, those of the upper Oder and their neighboring territories. A policy of opening up and expanding the existing network of communications, roads and canals, which continued for over a century, consolidated that position. It allowed the export of Prussian grain into the densely populated regions of northwestern Europe, and this trade contributed to Brandenburg-Prussia recovering relatively quickly from the

Cannon of the fifteenth, sixteenth and seventeenth centuries. This plate depicts an assortment of weapons, including some early breech loaders (left center), and multibarrelled weapons for use at close range.

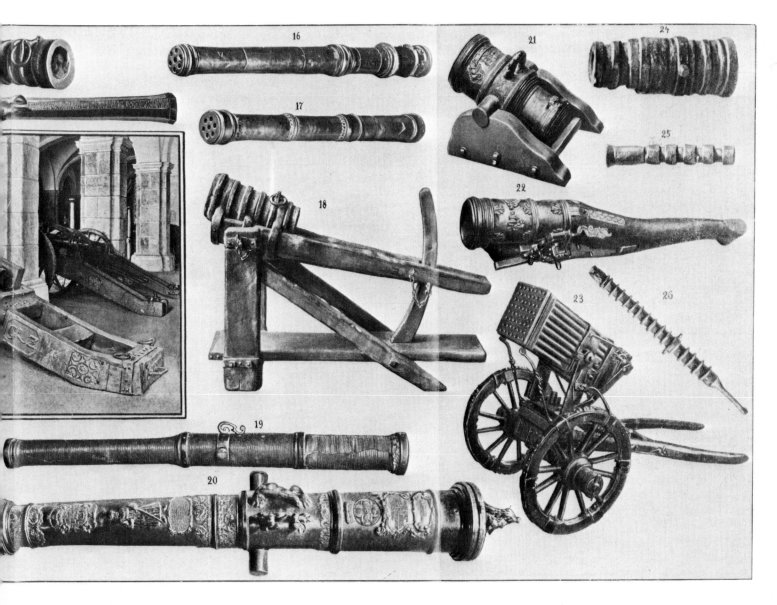

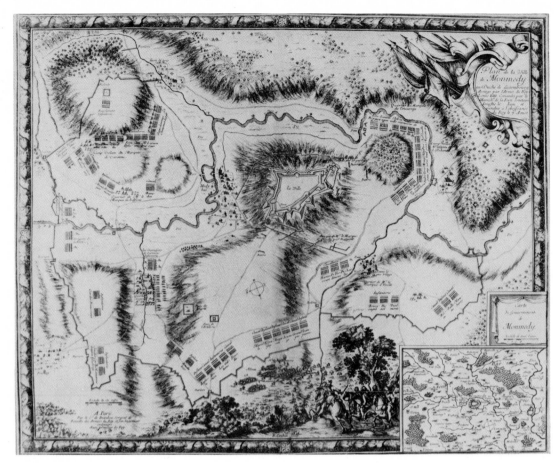

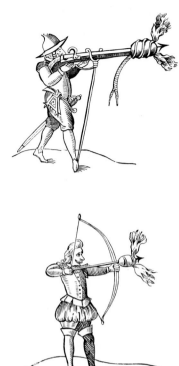

devastation of the Thirty Years' War. The territories of Cleves, Mark and Ravensberg provided additional economic resources; while Ravensberg produced cotton, Mark possessed a sizable iron-and-steel industry and Cleves, cloth and silk manufacture.

In 1655 war broke out between Sweden and Poland, which posed a serious problem for Frederick William as the vassal of the Polish crown. He had to rally to the support of King John Casimir but, by that time, Poland was already showing serious internal weaknesses of the kind that, little more than a century later, led to its destruction. The Swedes advanced victoriously, casting an eager eye upon Prussia, which would have been useful to them as an important operational base against Poland. Frederick William endeavored to mediate but was met by outright rejection from the Swedes. Confronted by the choice of supporting Poland or eventually being destroyed himself, he abandoned his liege lord. The victorious Swedes chased John Casimir out of his country, from where he sought refuge in Upper Silesia, and Frederick William was forced to accept Swedish overlordship. On 17 January 1656 the Treaty of Königsberg was concluded, in which he accepted Prussia from the hand of Sweden's Charles X. He also opened the Prussian harbors of Memel and Pillau to the Swedes and shared with them the revenue from the harbor dues. Apart from that, he had to promise to support the Swedes with 1500 men of his own army.

Hardly had the treaty been concluded when the fortunes of war turned against the Swedes. At the head of a popular movement, John Casimir returned to Poland and expelled the Swedes. This, of course, further increased Brandenburg-Prussia's value as Sweden's ally and, on 25 June 1656 by the Treaty of Marienburg, the former was promised part of the Polish spoils, should Poland be defeated. The alliance culminated in the three-day Battle of Warsaw in which the army of Brandenburg-Prussia received its baptism of fire. For the first time it proved highly superior to its opponents. It was hardly in Frederick William's interest, however, to have a Swedish overlord. When Austria

and Russia seemed to rally to the side of the Poles, the Swedes were even more on the defensive. Now the moment seemed opportune for Frederick William: he was in a strong enough position to demand that Charles X agree to the revocation of the bonds of vassalage and recognize Frederick William as Duke and sovereign of Prussia in his own right. This was agreed upon at the Treaty of Labiau on 20 November 1656. Negotiating in all directions, Frederick William would have been quite prepared to support John Casimir, only the Polish monarch overestimated the strength of his own position and rejected demands identical to those accepted by Charles X. However, the court of Vienna indicated to Frederick William that he would receive its fullest support if he refrained from helping the Swedes. The Swedes, now also under attack from the Danes, were in a dangerous position and demanded that Frederick William take on the Poles by himself.

At this point an election proved decisive. Emperor Ferdinand III had died on 2 April 1657, and it therefore proved important to win over the Elector of Brandenburg-Prussia to the Habsburg side for the ensuing election. The Elector's main condition was the recognition by Poland of his sovereignty over Prussia, a condition to which John Casimir agreed only under the severest of pressure from the court of Vienna. By the Treaty of Wehlau of 19 September 1657, Prussia once again became sovereign; the former territory of the Teutonic Order became a German state again.

The Swedes, quite rightly, felt betrayed, but Frederick William could not, in view of the general vulnerability of his territories, afford to pursue a policy other than one that actively furthered the interests of his state. Adherence to rigid loyalties would have been praised by none of the surrounding major powers; his situation demanded flexibility, involving changes in alliances according to the needs of Brandenburg-Prussia. The Elector of Brandenburg-Prussia's vote decided the election in favor of the Habsburg Leopold I against the other candidate, who was none other than Louis XIV of France.

Far left. *The siege of Montmédy in Luxembourg. The citadel capitulated to the French on 7 August 1657.*

Left. *Early seventeenth-century incendiary devices.*

Above. *The Emperor Ferdinand III, whose death in 1657 led to Prussian independence from Poland.*

Right. *The army of Louis XIV in Spain, 1645.*

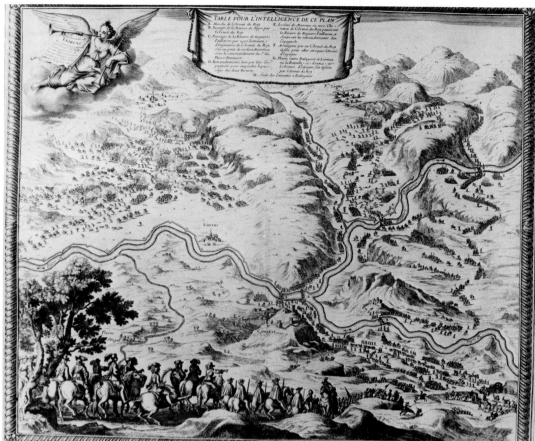

In August 1658 the Swedes renewed the war, this time against Denmark. Frederick William's army had now increased to 30,000 men and precisely at this moment he decided to attack the Swedes, expelling them from Schleswig and Holstein. Sweden's major ally France had her hands tied in the war with Spain and could give no support. Only after the Peace of the Pyrenees had been concluded in 1659 was Mazarin in a position to be of assistance. He objected to Prussia holding Eastern Pomerania and assembled an army 40,000 strong, enough of a threat to persuade the Poles and the Empire to cease supporting Frederick William. Poland had liberated its territory. The new emperor, in spite of Frederick William's decisive vote, was not interested in continuing the war since Spain had made its peace with France. Brandenburg-Prussia was on its own.

France now acted as mediator, but a settlement was arrived at only after the death of Charles X. At the Peace of Oliva, near Danzig, on 3 May 1660, Frederick William was in an isolated position and had once again to cede Eastern Pomerania to the Swedes. The only major concession he obtained was the confirmation of Prussia's sovereignty. He was a disappointed man whose ambitions seemed to have come to little.

For almost 20 years now he had governed by listening to his closest advisers. Oliva represents a watershed in his style of government, because, from then on, he accepted no counsel other than his own and became one of the main representatives of princely absolutism in Europe. His position was strengthened by a sense of mission to establish Brandenburg-Prussia as a major power within the Holy Roman Empire, a sense of mission strengthened by his stern Calvinism. As the Elector, elected by divinity, he took it upon himself to turn his state into a formidable power, come what may, and if necessary against the will of his Estates. In 1653 the Brandenburg Diet had met for the last time. The Prussian Diet proved recalcitrant, trying to play off the Poles against the Elector. Open conflict broke out until, in 1662, Frederick William landed with 2000 men in Königsberg. The Prussian Diet was brought to heel. When one of his

Prussian noblemen conspired with the Poles and escaped to Poland, he had him abducted and Colonel Christian Ludwig von Kalckstein was decapitated in the city of Memel. In 1673 and 1674 Prussia paid the first taxes not granted by the Estates, and, without its consent, troops were garrisoned in Königsberg. Brandenburg submitted in the end, but, as in Prussia, at the price of confirming the privileges of the nobility, notably exemption from taxation.

The Rhenish provinces proved more difficult. After the Peace of Oliva, however, Frederick William largely stripped them of their privileges and brought them into conformity with the rest of his territories. His major instrument of enforcing centralization was the establishment of a uniform financial administration, closely connected with the administration of the army. The army of Brandenburg-Prussia developed along similar lines to the French army, and the policies of Louvois were closely emulated by the Elector.

An army that in peacetime was kept in its garrisons, with apparently little purpose other than drill, was something which most of the Elector's subjects could not understand. At best it was a useless luxury which heavily increased taxation. For every cow, pig or sheep slaughtered, a fee had to be paid which went into the army coffers. After many previous abortive attempts to explain his reasons to the Estates, the Elector did not see any need to try again.

One innovation finding general approval was the introduction of severe discipline in the army. Parsons and chaplains in their pulpits and officers before their men had to announce that any act of plundering would be punished by hanging. Any officer who physically attacked a civilian would be stripped of his rank for a year and would have to carry a musket as a common soldier. Every unit had its own Bible and a religious service was to be held every morning and evening.

Some of the new measures did not survive the Elector's reign. For instance, he proscribed the beating of soldiers by their officers and NCOs and abolished the system of running the

gauntlet. Even deserters did not automatically go to the gallows. Every court martial sentence had to be confirmed by the Elector personally. All recruitment had be carried out in the name of the Elector himself. Artisans and peasants were exempt from recruitment. In other words, he tried to professionalize the army and give it the same degree of respectability which other professions and trades enjoyed.

Frederick William created the regiments and appointed colonels, though throughout his reign the general practice continued that the regimental officers were appointed by their colonels and not by the Elector. He recognized that there was a need for reform and equally recognized that an officer corps of some homogeneity could not be created overnight but would be the product of decades of growth. As a result, he was quick to see the advantages of Louis XIV's creation of a cadet corps for the training of officers. Such officers were therefore essentially products of a common mold shaped by the French absolutist monarchy. The Elector adapted this idea by creating the *Ritterakademie*, which his grandson was to transform into regular cadet institutes. The officers of Brandenburg-Prussia were no longer to be soldiers of fortune who came and went as they pleased, but a group of military leaders whose fate was closely associated with the fate of the country which they served.

This, in the long run, made the army an ideal instrument for integrating the nobility into the Hohenzollern state, but, in the short run, it was precisely this nobility who provided some of the main opposition to the standing army. Reasonably enough, Frederick William did not trust his officers drawn from the nobility to the same extent as did his successors. In the composition of his officer corps the attempt is clearly discernible to balance officers of native Brandenburg-Prussian origin with those of perhaps doubtful social origins. His most redoubtable general, Field Marshal von Derfflinger, was an Austrian, the son of a peasant according to one source, of a tailor according to another. He had made his fortune as a *condottiere* in the Thirty Years' War before he joined the service of Brandenburg-Prussia. The Elector made a point of keeping counsel with his senior officers when on campaign; these meetings were forerunners of the consultations of a general staff.

It took time to infuse the officers with a sense of personal loyalty toward the dynasty, an *esprit de corps*, and it equally took time to organize them into men capable of operating within a centralized framework of command. Problems of insubordination were endemic. The bulk of the army came from recruitment on the 'open market' and the size of the army was dependent on whether there was war or peace. The Elector did

Above. *Field Marshal von Derfflinger, 1606–95, who rose from humble origins to eminence in the Great Elector's army.*

Left. *The Great Elector crossing the ice of the* Kurisches Haff.

the Netherlands, England and Sweden. But Frederick William went a step farther – in return for an annual subsidy of 40,000 thalers, he promised Louis his active support after the death of the king of Spain. It would have amounted to a secret alliance against the Netherlands, against whom, in spite of admiring them in principle, he had serious practical grievances. Because of debts he owed them, they still occupied parts of his Rhenish territories, and they took sides, so he believed, with the unruly Estates there. There was another side to this question: which would be preferable, an uncomfortable and occasionally un-couth Dutch Netherlands as a neighbor, or a strong France whose ambition to acquire the left bank of the Rhine was clear to everyone?

The issue was debated by the Elector's family, by his councillors and by his generals. It divided all, but gradually a majority in favor of an alliance with the Netherlands emerged. It was concluded on 6 May 1672, the Netherlands bearing half the cost of the recruitment of an army of 20,000 and their pay. The talks subsequently turned on Frederick William, however, when England and France opened hostilities against the Netherlands, but the Netherlands remained isolated save for their alliance with Brandenburg-Prussia. Also, the Netherlands did not pay the subsidies they had promised.

The Emperor refrained from interfering and, although Frederick William had not yet declared war upon France, this did not stop the armies of Louis XIV from occupying his Rhenish possessions. The quick collapse of the Netherlands enabled Frederick William to extricate himself from the affair with as little damage as possible. He undertook to give no further aid to the Dutch while the French returned most of the territories which they had occupied; all were to be returned after the conclusion of peace with the Dutch. Louis XIV also undertook that, in the course of a negotiated settlement with the Dutch, he would press them to pay the arrears of subsidies due to Brandenburg-Prussia. At the same time he granted a subsidy of his own. In the wake of this settlement, France embarked upon a series of annexations of territories of the Holy Roman Empire, for example the Reich cities in Alsace, which mobilized public opinion in Germany against France. In the pamphlet literature of the time, Francophobia, caused by a fear of French predominance, was closely allied with the ridicule of Brandenburg-Prussia, and the Elector in particular because of his inconsistency and untrustworthiness.

Vienna now attempted to form a Great Coalition against Louis XIV. Austria allied with Spain, Denmark and the Netherlands, an alliance joined ultimately by Brandenburg-Prussia; Spain and the Netherlands paid his subsidies. The campaign brought no laurels for his troops, however; they suffered serious reverses and outright defeat at the hands of Turenne. The Imperial commanders and Brandenburg-Prussian generals blamed each other for the adverse outcome. While the mutual recriminations reverberated through Central Europe and the Elector's forces were moving into their winter quarters in Franconia, alarming news arrived: on Christmas Day 1674, the Swedes had invaded Brandenburg and were ravaging the territory. Sweden had joined France. Frederick William was now standing on his own again – no Imperial troops rallied to his support and the problem that faced him was to cross the whole of central Germany in the spring of 1675 as rapidly as possible to meet the Swedes. His army was not simply an army on the march, but a migration – apart from supply and baggage trains, there were the dependants of the soldiers as well. For every 7000 soldiers there were approximately 2000 to 3000 dependants.

The achievement of getting the army to Brandenburg in time was mainly that of Derfflinger. In order to give greater

once entertain the idea of introducing, at least in Prussia, conscription or some kind of national service, but quickly abandoned this idea because, as yet, he did not trust his subjects enough, least of all those in the duchy of Prussia. In peacetime the army averaged approximately 7000 men, in time of war about 15,000 up to a maximum of 30,000.

In spite of his introduction of a uniform system of taxation and its efficient collection, the revenue was not enough to keep a force of that strength under arms. This made the Elector dependent on subsidies paid by the great powers – the Dutch Netherlands, Austria, Spain and France – subsidies which necessitated a considerable degree of dependence on the foreign policy of others and frequently changing sides, always according to the advantages offered by one side or the other.

When, in 1667, Louis XIV attempted to bring the Spanish Netherlands under his control, Frederick William's reaction was determined by another problem. In Poland John Casimir had abdicated and the French advocated the Prince de Condé as his successor, which was hardly promising for the security of Prussia. Louis XIV was prepared to drop the candidacy of Condé, however, providing Prussia maintained neutrality in the war over the Spanish Netherlands. Frederick William agreed, and Brandenburg refused to join the alliance between mobility, he divided it into small contingents spread over a distance of 130 kilometers, maintaining continuous contact between them by the use of cavalry units. Within two weeks the army was back in Brandenburg. Derfflinger, by that time already 70 years old, surprised the Swedes at Rathenow and they pulled their troops out of the fortress there; the Swedes were far superior in numbers, but simply did not know it. Derfflinger ordered their pursuit while the rest of the army caught up with them at Fehrbellin. In the early morning of 28 June 1675, the Elector issued his last orders and Derfflinger attacked the Swedish encampment with his dragoons and infantry. He was very weak in artillery; only 13 pieces were available to him, while the Swedes had 38 guns of which, fortunately for Brandenburg-Prussia, only seven managed to fire. The battle was a great victory for Brandenburg-Prussia; it cost the Swedes 2000 men, while Derfflinger's casualties totalled 500 killed and wounded. Fehrbellin, taken by itself, was a minor battle, but it established the fame and reputation of the Prussian army.

To ensure that the Swedes would be chased out of Brandenburg entirely, Derfflinger took a selected force of soldiers and cavalry, covered over 300 miles in 10 days on horseback – one has to bear in mind that the cavalry horses of the Prussian army of that period had all the graces and characteristics of carthorses! – and inflicted another defeat at Tilsit. Frederick William realized immediately that, if he could maintain his success against the Swedes, it would cost them the whole of Pomerania. He allied himself with Denmark, and both the Danes and the Dutch fleet exerted pressure upon the Swedes. The campaign now became drawn out, both main antagonists reverting to the strategy of attrition to save men and resources. But it was systematically and thoroughly conducted, lasting through 1675 and 1676 and into 1677. Frederick William's main objective was the capture of Stettin in order to control the mouth of the River Oder. From July to December 1677 it was besieged and bombarded from sea and from land. Toward the end of December, the walls of the city were breached and the final assault was about to be launched when it capitulated. The garrison was

offered honorable conditions which it accepted, and the city's privileges were fully confirmed by the Elector, who since Fehrbellin was referred to as the 'Great Elector'; on 6 January he entered the city and was paid homage. With Stettin, Greifswald and Stralsund were also captured – Pomerania was in Prussian hands.

If Frederick William believed that the other powers would agree to his conquests, he was seriously mistaken. The Netherlands and Spain had already made their separate peace with France, and in Vienna it was said that it would not be in the interest of the Emperor to allow the emergence of a new *Vandalking* on the shores of the Baltic. In the meantime, the French had encouraged their Swedish allies to undertake a new diversion against Brandenburg-Prussia, culminating in the winter campaign of 1678–79, which was far more demanding than the battle of Fehrbellin. It was a campaign of attrition in which the Swedes sustained heavy losses both of men and equipment. The culmination was Frederick William's crossing the ice of the *Kurisches Haff* with horses and sledges and successfuly expelling the Swedes once and for all, or so he believed. It was an immense personal effort on his part – almost 60 years of age, his body was ravaged by pain and gout. But the gains which he had expected were not forthcoming. At the Peace of Nymwegen on 5 February 1679 the Emperor made peace with France and Sweden. The Great Elector had only one ally left: Denmark. He no longer possessed the strength to maintain his position in the north and northeast as well as in the west. Peace with France and Sweden became imperative. In the Peace of St Germain of 29 June 1679 he had to return Pomerania to the Swedes; all he gained were minor frontier corrections. The territorial *status quo ante* had been reestablished.

Frederick William believed himself betrayed by Emperor and Reich, conveniently forgetting the vacillations of his own alliance politics. His policy and attitude were also influenced by the Silesian question, or rather the Emperor's attitude toward it. In 1675 the last of the Silesian Piasts, Duke George William of Liegnitz, died. By a treaty dating back to 1537, parts of Silesia

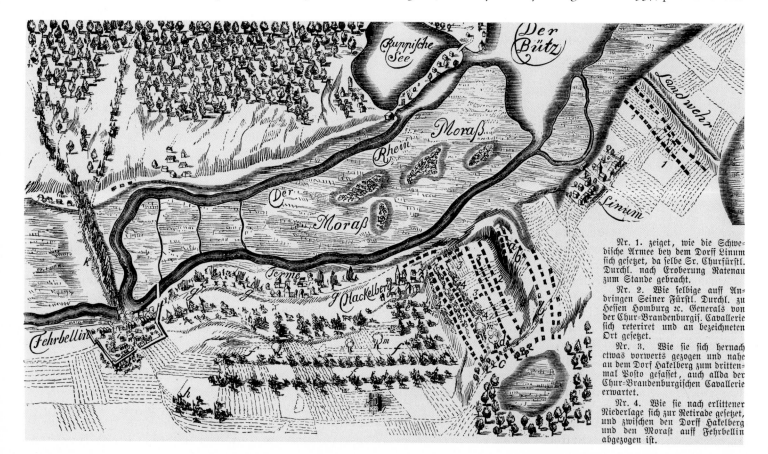

Nr. 1. zeiget, wie die Schwedische Armee bey dem Dorff Linum sich gesetzet, da selbe Sr. Churfürstl. Durchl. nach Eroberung Ratenau zum Stande gebracht.

Nr. 2. Wie selbige auff Andringen Seiner Fürstl. Durchl. zu Hessen Homburg 2c. Generals von der Chur-Brandenburgis. Cavallerie sich reteriret und an bezeichneten Ort gesetzet.

Nr. 3. Wie sie sich hernach etwas vorwerts gezogen und nahe an dem Dorf Hakelberg zum drittenmal Posto gefasset, auch allda der Chur-Brandenburgischen Cavallerie erwartet.

Nr. 4. Wie sie nach erlittener Niederlage sich zur Retirade gesetzet, und zwischen den Dorff Hakelberg und den Morast auff Fehrbellin abgezogen ist.

Right. *The Great Elector presides over the destruction of the Swedish army at Fehrbellin in June 1675. Although scarcely a major battle, Fehrbellin established the Prussian army as a force to be reckoned with.*

Below left. *A plan of the Battle of Fehrbellin, clearly showing the marsh which hampered the Swedish retreat.*

were to become Hohenzollern possessions, but Vienna would not hear of it and simply annexed it as part of the crown lands of Bohemia. Even the demand for compensation was rejected. As a result of the Emperor's treatment, Frederick William again turned toward France. Having been deprived of Pomerania by France's power, he now accepted the inevitability of the country's rise and, by joining it, hoped to regain what he had lost.

Complex secret negotiations ensued. At the same time Louis XIV continued to be engaged in a policy of annexation toward German territories which he chose to call *réunions*. But Louis and Frederick William wanted an alliance with one another for different purposes: Louis in order to back his policy of *réunions*, Frederick William, who also wanted to draw Denmark into the alliance, in order to direct it against the Swedes. The alliance was concluded, but without Denmark, and ultimately benefited France and not Brandenburg-Prussia. Louis XIV's 'Rape of Strasbourg' in 1681 tarred Frederick William with the same brush, probably even worse, for his support of France was taken as a betrayal of the Reich. Still, Frederick William continued to entertain hopes that France would support him against the Swedes. Only in 1683, when Sweden, instead of renewing its treaties with France, accepted subsidies from the Emperor and the Netherlands, was France interested in keeping Sweden in check with the aid of Brandenburg-Prussia and Denmark. On 30 April 1683 two alliance treaties were concluded, one between France and Brandenburg, the other between France, Brandenburg and Denmark. Sweden was to be expelled completely from Germany. In point of fact the treaties were not fully fledged alliances at all, but preliminary provisional agreements; Frederick William made the mistake of not realizing this. The treaties were never ratified. Furthermore, additional aid for France arrived on the political scene of Europe which was less expensive, while being a much greater threat to the Emperor: the Turks. Realizing how low his value had sunk *vis-à-vis* France, Frederick William now offered his aid to Vienna in return for subsidies and territorial compensation. Thoroughly disillusioned and distrustful of Frederick William by now, the Emperor rejected the offer, insisting that, as a Prince of the Empire, it was the Elector's duty to come to the assistance of the Reich now that it was threatened by the armed might of the heathens. The relief of Vienna from Turkish siege took place with the help of the king of Poland – John Sobieski – and the Elector Max Emanuel of Bavaria; except for a very small contingent, Brandenburg-Prussian troops had no part in it.

In the meantime the Emperor was once again deeply involved in negotiations aimed at a settlement with France, or at least an armistice. Louis was prepared to conclude it, providing he could hold the gains he had made by his policy of *réunions*; in this he was successful. His alliance with Brandenburg-Prussia had served its purpose, but it was not a Brandenburg, let alone a German, one.

At the time of his death in 1688, the Great Elector had succeeded in transforming his state into a formidable power, but not yet, as he had hoped, into a major one. All his foreign policy objectives had been frustrated. Even belatedly turning his back on France did not change anything. Nor was he able to transform Brandenburg-Prussia into a commercial power of any significance. His ambitions still lacked the solid base of power, political and economic, with which to sustain and expand them. Hence it is not because of his achievements that he is to be remembered as an impressive monarch of the Baroque, but because of his vision and because he laid the foundations upon which others could build and transform at least part of his ambitions into concrete reality. What he left behind were the beginnings of the Prussian state, the Prussian army, its bureaucracy and, perhaps among its subjects, an emerging awareness of Prussian statehood.

When the Great Elector died he left an army 30,000 strong. Taxation and subsidies from other powers alone were no longer sufficient to maintain this army; the need to finance the army was one factor responsible for his expanding trade and commerce. One of the main aspects of his domestic policy had been to attract immigrants to Prussia and in this context, during the last years of his life, the revocation of the Edict of Nantes in 1685 had played into his hands because it attracted some 20,000 French and Walloon Huguenot immigrants. Possessing more highly developed commercial and industrial skills than the majority of the native population, and having also a rather better education, the Huguenot immigrants represented an asset. Their contribution to the commercial, industrial and intellectual development of Brandenburg-Prussia can never be overestimated.

In terms of institutions, he left behind the General War Commissary, the Secret Court Chamber and the Secret Council that represented the nucleus of the bureaucratic machinery which was to develop over the next century and imposed a centralized administration. Naturally, even this nucleus changed in course of time. The Secret Council declined into insignificance while the Secret Court Chamber, assuming the administration and control of all electoral domains, gained immensely until, in 1713, it was transformed into the General Finance Directory.

Of the three aims of the Great Elector's foreign policy – the achievement of sovereignty in Prussia, the acquisition of *Vorpommern* and a general rounding off of his territories to give his state greater coherence – only the first had been achieved. Of this he was very much aware, indeed after the Peace of St Germain he had a memorial medal struck bearing a line of Virgil: *Exoriare aliquis nostris ex ossibus ultor* (May from my bones an avenger arise.) He did.

The political subordination of the Estates established the Prussian absolutist regime, a regime which, in spite of the concessions that had been made to the nobility and in the light of the political and economic circumstances, could hardly afford to degenerate into a dictatorship of the nobility, let alone the dictatorship of one prince in the interest of one group. The very fragility of Brandenburg-Prussia demanded the integration of more than just one interest group into the state. Brandenburg-Prussia was in the process of emerging as a European power, but its fundamental vulnerability remained, resulting from its geographical position, scattered dynastic possessions and poverty of natural resources. Within the confines of the Germanic body politic, this emergence of the new state was of revolutionary long-term significance. But it was also revolutionary at its very source. In terms of colonial territory of the Holy Roman Empire of the German Nation, Prussia represented the northeastern marches. As Britain's American colonies were later to demonstrate, colonial existence tends toward benevolent neglect on behalf of the central power, and it tends to weaken the ties of tradition and encourage creative independence.

Like England, the Prussian state rested upon a single radical act of secularization of land, carried out in Brandenburg-Prussia by its adoption of Protestantism. With a single stroke Duke

Above. *The Great Elector's son Frederick I, styled King in Prussia rather than King of Prussia.*

Above right. *The international jurist Samuel Pufendorf, 1632 – 94, whose* Life and Deeds of Frederick William *was a major advance in the writing of contemporary history.*

Left. *The Treaty of Nymwegan, 1678, ended Louis' Dutch war on terms which gave the French room for subsequent expansion.*

Right. *An enthusiastic if confusing view of Prince Eugene's victory over the French at Luzzara in northern Italy, August 1702.*

Albrecht had cut the ties with the past, and his excommunication inevitably elevated Protestantism into a constituent principle of state. The subsequent influence of Calvinist thought simply underlined this fact.

A further revolutionary feature which can be attributed exclusively to the Great Elector was its character as a military state, extending its territory and maintaining its presence on the battlefields of Europe for almost two centuries.

Prussia as a state was a work of art, a Renaissance state in the true sense of Jakob Burckhardt's term: 'With immense effort Brandenburg-Prussia raised herself from the debris of Germany.' Prussia would hardly have survived in the interest of only one group exclusively or predominantly. During the reign of the Great Elector a major constituent principle of this new state became visible, namely a kind of *étatisme*, an ideology of the state community which subjected dynasty, aristocracy and subjects alike, and which represented a revolutionary break away from the still-prevalent feudal dynastic conceptions of, for example, the Habsburgs.

Given that condition of natural weakness, compensated for only by highly artificial devices, it had to be the object of the dynasty, of the state, to regulate society in such a manner which, on the one hand, would prevent periodic discontent from becoming a source of internal unrest and revolution, while, on the other, making it unnecessary to maintain law and order by force. It was an essential point of policy to prevent dissatisfaction from arising in the first place and to absorb political, social and economic conflicts within the existing institutional framework. This was the distinguishing feature which characterized absolutist monarchy in Brandenburg-Prussia, in contrast to France and other absolutist countries. Again, the first signs of this policy are discernible during the reign of the Great Elector,

as are the beginnings of an institutional framework capable of initiating and carrying out reform from above and thus preventing revolution from below. Prussia's governmental apparatus was to be the very embodiment of the ideology of the state community.

By 1688, when the Great Elector died, the general European situation had changed in a way that favored the rise of the Hohenzollern state rather more than had been the case during his lifetime. Sweden, whose external ambitions were in inverse proportion to its actual resources, lost its predominance over the Baltic, while Russia emerged as a great power. This did not immediately lead to Brandenburg-Prussia acquiring the position she desired in the Baltic region, but Sweden's decline nevertheless removed a major threat. Poland, in the throes of dissolution under its future Saxon rulers, removed for the time being another threat from the frontiers of the Hohenzollern state.

Most important was the Anglo-French conflict, global in character but focused in Europe, over the question of the Spanish succession, in which Britain supported the House of Habsburg in the interest of a balance of power and thus effectively contained the French interests in the hegemony of Europe. The Peace of Utrecht reestablished a balance of power in Europe between Britain, France and Austria with the additional power of Brandenburg-Prussia.

The Great Elector's successor, Elector Frederick III, was born of a very different mold from his father – he loved the splendor of the Baroque and introduced it into his court and country irrespective of the expense, with the result that his country ran seriously into debt. But, nevertheless, by supporting the Habsburg cause in the War of the Spanish Succession with an army, which under Prince Leopold von Anhalt-Dessau was constantly improved, he gained the Habsburg's agreement to royal dignity. He became Frederick I, King *in* Prussia. Prussian troops had proved decisive at Blenheim in 1704, their contribution had been vital at Turin in 1708, and they earned themselves the reputation of being the most steadfast soldiers on the battlefields of Europe during the last great battle of the War of the Spanish Succession, at Malplaquet. Prussia's Crown Prince Frederick William, a participant, was horrified by the slaughter. The total casualties amounted to 42,000 men. Upon his return to Berlin, and assisted by the *Alte Dessauer*, he initiated further improvements in Prussia's army. While the king squandered the country's resources, his son drilled his troops. When King Frederick I died in 1713, the influence of Versailles upon the royal court in Berlin disappeared abruptly; the influence of Sparta was to come.

Right. *The Battle of Ramillies, 23 May 1706. Allied troops engaged in the congenial tasks of pursuit and plunder.*

Below left. *Marlborough and Eugene enter the French position at the costly victory of Malplaquet.*

Below. *A letter written in French by Marlborough announcing his victory at the Battle of Oudenarde in 1708.*

12 July 1708

Duke of Marlborough
his own letter after Battle of Oudenarde

Monseigneur.

Comme Monsieur le Comte de Hompesch a l'honneur de faire part à Vostre Altesse Electorale de l'heureux succès que le Bon Dieu Nous a donné hier sur les Ennemis, j'ay esté bien aise de me servir de la même occasion pour Luy en faire mes tres humbles felicitations, espirant qu'avant que la Campagne finisse, il s'en rencontrera quelque

THE NEW SPARTA

The body of King Frederick I of Prussia lay in state in February 1713 in full Baroque splendor, surrounded by the trappings of an age he had loved, admired and done so much to emulate in his barren kingdom. The chief event of his reign had been his elevation to the title of King in 1701. At his feet, deep in thought, stood the new king, Frederick William I. Rather abruptly he straightened himself, turned on his heel and walked out of the room, leaving behind not only the body of his father, the guard of honor and the dim light of the candles, but also another age. The threshold which he crossed led into an era that he meant to be vastly different from that of his father.

Macaulay has described him as being a man whose 'character was disfigured by odious vices, and whose eccentricities were such as had never before been out of a madhouse . . . the mind of Frederick William was so ill regulated, that all his inclinations became passions, and all his passions partook the character of moral and intellectual disease.' A true reflection of nineteenth-century Whig sentiment, but a nicely turned phrase alone does not make good history, though Macaulay is not the only one to have fallen victim to this superficial impression; after all, it was one shared by many of Frederick William's contemporaries. With utter incomprehension they observed the unfolding of a spectacle that seemed to contradict the very essence of the spirit of the age, the beginnings of the European Enlightenment. The generous and careless rule of the first Hohenzollern king was to be followed by the rule of a man who carefully appreciated the resources of his territories, or the lack of them, a man who reversed the principle of the Baroque Age that revenue had to be adequate to meet expenditure by stating that expenditure should on no account exceed available revenue.

His succession to the crown was tantamount to a revolution against the hitherto prevailing form of princely absolutism. While the art of the Baroque appealed to the senses and dominated not only the Habsburg Empire, Spain and France but also the Protestant courts, Frederick William's Calvinist heritage quickly asserted itself by drastically reducing the pomp and splendor, making way in his kingdom for a functionalism in style and appearance of government hitherto unheard of. No wonder contemporaries viewed him as the 'Barbarian from the North.'

Within hours of his father's death, he assembled his first council and ordered that all valuables such as precious stones, silver and rare furniture in the various royal residences be listed and the latter then sealed. The following day the army swore their loyalty to the new king. For the next eight days his father's

ministers were forbidden to approach him about government matters. After that period had elapsed, he confirmed everyone's position and emphasized to them that, while his father had found his pleasure in architectural ostentation and great amounts of jewels, he himself would gain satisfaction by building an army of good troops. Only Rüdiger von Ilgen, who had looked after Brandenburg-Prussia's external affairs up to this time, had two new officials attached to him; together they formed the Cabinet Council, whose members were later to be known as cabinet ministers.

Five weeks later came drastic economy measures. They began with horse fodder: ministers and other notables, who until then received fodder for 20 or even 30 horses, were to receive fodder sufficient for only six. Lesser mortals, such as the court chaplains, received none at all. The royal stables were reduced from 600 to 120 horses. 'My father gave everyone horse fodder so that they would follow him across the country, but I cut it down so that everyone stays in Berlin,' said Frederick William.

This measure was followed by a military reorganization which he had even planned in great detail, when still Crown Prince. The costly and resplendent force of guards, who gave great pleasure to the eye but were of little fighting value, were transformed into regiments of the line; the Swiss guards, introduced by his father, were dissolved completely. All that remained of the guards was one battalion, the king's very own tall grenadiers, which he had commanded as Crown Prince and which he paid and equipped from his own personal income. The cavalry was reorganized into 55 squadrons, each numbering 150 horses, while the infantry was ordered into 50 battalions, or 25 regiments; the artillery, for the time being, was to number two battalions. These economy measures enabled Frederick William to save enough money to increase the total number of his army from 39,000 to 45,000 men. His father's death, from that point of view, had come at a convenient moment; on the eve of the Peace of Utrecht, 1713–15, the Prussian forces, until then tied down in the west to support the Habsburg cause, became free and Frederick William was able to maintain them with his own resources rather than being dependent on foreign subsidies.

The court next underwent royal economies. Its members, that is to say officials, had their salaries cut, in many cases down to 25 percent of what they had received under Frederick I, and in one particular case even down to 10 percent. These were the lucky ones, for the majority of personnel were made redundant and transferred either into the administration or the army 'according to their inclinations to the sword or the pen.' The office of Master of Ceremonies was one that was abolished, making a short-lived appearance only in the form of a practical joke by Frederick William when he appointed his court jester, Gundling, a disreputable historian addicted to drink, to the post. Even as renowned an architect as Andreas Schlüter, the sculptor and architect to whom Berlin owed the Schloss and the masks of dying warriors at the *Zeughaus* (the royal arsenal just beyond *Unter den Linden*, now the Museum for German History in East Berlin), could no longer expect any royal commissions and therefore went to St Petersburg, where he died shortly afterwards.

However, to explain the King's economy measures exclusively in terms of economic motives would show only one side of the coin. Calvin's teaching of divine predestination had played an important part in the King's education. His teacher, Philippe Rebeur, himself a French Huguenot refugee, asked him whether he belonged to the Lord's chosen few, to the elect, and whether he could thus be sure that the House of Hohenzollern

Below left. *Frederick William I, who established the distinctively militaristic character of the Prussian state. He created the best army in Europe, bequeathing a formidable military instrument to his son Frederick.*

Below. *The Academy of Sciences in Berlin was founded in 1715.*

Verkleinertes Titelblatt des Gründungsberichts der Akademie der Wissenschaften in Berlin, mit einer Abbildung des Observatoriums.

would be blessed with fortune, the sign of the Lord's divine benevolence. This question was to preoccupy Frederick William throughout his life, causing hours of brooding and searching torment, so much so that, in the education of his own children, he explicitly prohibited the teaching of Calvinist predestination. Upon Frederick William himself it had left its indelible mark. Indeed, one of the vital motivating forces behind Frederick William I was religion, his own brand of reformed Lutheranism. One of the reasons, perhaps, why his personal rule never degenerated into absolute tyranny was his deeply rooted conviction that one day he would have to account for his deeds to his Maker. Of considerable importance in this context is the Pietist movement and its influence upon Prussia.

Though the importance of the personal connection between Frederick William I and August Hermann Francke, the Pietist reformer at Halle, can be overstressed, the Pietist influence as an integrating force within Prussian society in the eighteenth and nineteenth centuries seems to have been frequently underestimated, if not altogether ignored. Basically Pietism was the German 'Puritan' reaction to the Thirty Years' War, with its questioning of the Lutheran faith. The Pietists opposed the Lutheran acceptance of the world as it is and the submission of the individual to it; they accepted Luther's hope for the day of judgment, but they criticized man's social environment. To Luther's call for reform merely of the church, they added the call for the reform of the world and its social institutions. Pietism as a religious and social force was highly complex, and worldwide in its aspirations.

As far as Prussia was concerned, the Pietists aimed to produce responsible subjects: members of society who, irrespective of their station in life, would turn their social conscience toward the common good. Their schools were by far the most advanced in the kingdom and thus, through what at first was a

personal connection between Frederick William I and Francke, the avenue was opened for products of the Pietist schools and academies to enter the Prussian civil service, the army and its officer corps. Pietism produced a social and religious ethos which characterized the Prussia of the eighteenth and early nineteenth centuries. It was a religion suited to civil servants and officers as much as Puritanism was, according to R H Tawney, a religion suited to entrepreneurs. It was a religion sober and hard, drawing into its circle all the Estates of the kingdom. In conjunction with the transformation of the feudal estates of the *Junkers* into private holdings in return for financing and officering the army, Pietism played a major role in the defeudalization of the Prussian aristocracy. In the army Pietists obtained chaplaincies, and the army and the administration therefore became the major channels through which Pietist thought percolated to the lower levels of Prussian society.

Theoretically at least, 1717 saw the beginnings of compulsory elementary education in Prussia, and, among the new schools that were founded, those of the Pietists were the most numerous. The ideal product of their education was not the aristocratic cavalier of the Age of the Baroque, but the businesslike, pragmatic state functionary. This, perhaps, supplies one expla-

Left. A formal portrait of Frederick William.

Right. Frederick William inspecting his giant grenadiers.

Below. Frederick William and his cronies at the Tabak-kollegium, *or Smoking Session.*

nation as to why Germans outside Prussia rarely considered the highly placed Prussian civil servants or Prussian officers worth emulating, but looked rather to the French *grand seigneur* and the English gentleman.

Class lists from 1700 onward supply ample evidence of the great number of Prussian officers and higher civil servants who were graduates of Pietist schools, schools which selected talent from all social classes. Even Prussia's commercial policy was influenced by the Pietist movement, which believed that commerce must be for the benefit of the state and, through the state, for the benefit of all rather than for the enrichment of the individual. There is certainly a case for arguing that, whereas in Britain the rise of Puritanism coincided with the emergence of a modern capitalist economy, the Pietist strain of the Puritan movement in Prussia lay at the foundations of an emerging state socialism – a feature of particular long-term significance when one examines the emergence of liberal institutions in Britain and their absence in Germany a century later.

Actively supported by the dynasty, Pietism permeated all levels of society with an ethos in which all efforts were directed toward maintaining and securing the whole, even if this operated at times at the expense of the individual. The demand of unconditional, unflinching fulfillment of one's duty by all – nobility, burghers and peasants alike – led to situations of which it can well be said that Frederick William I and his son Frederick the Great treated their subjects worse than dogs; it must be added, however, that they treated themselves no better. Duty and the common good were principles enforced at a time when elsewhere their harshness was giving way in favor of comfortable, humane and liberal ideas, in an age inclined more toward Epicurus than Seneca, and when insistence upon the fulfillment of human duties receded and was replaced by the demand for human rights; Prussia meant to catch up, thus causing considerable discomfort all round. The moral implications of Seneca's *vivere est militare* had validity only in Prussia by the end of the eighteenth century.

Frederick William I continued the policy initiated by his father of supporting the Pietists and their institutions, a policy which he realized was yielding immense dividends for the Prussian state. Yet he never became a Pietist himself and, in spite of his reformed Lutheranism, the stern Calvinist streak in him never disappeared. He saw himself and his every action as accountable to God. The prosperity of the state was a sign of divine approval; given Prussia's fragility, positioned in the midst of great powers, the task of the monarch was that his every action be an example to his subjects lest divine approval be withdrawn. It is against this background that one must examine the conflict with his son in later years; it makes the excesses of the king more explicable than through transposing nineteenth-century liberal value judgments.

Frederick William acted in this spirit from the day he succeeded to the throne. It determined his attitude toward his own family as much as it did toward the nobility and his other subjects. His reign also marked the final phase of the struggle between the Hohenzollerns and the Brandenburg and East Prussian nobility over the former's policy of centralization. However, in Frederick William's reign this struggle no longer took the form of personal confrontation, but rather obstruction of the administrative reforms of the king, reforms which whittled away what powers the nobility still possessed in relation to the monarchy. As he put it himself: 'I shall ruin the authority of the *Junkers*; I shall achieve my purpose and stabilize the sovereignty like a rock of bronze.' The provincial Diets, the last strongholds of the *Junkers*, were allowed no other function than that of implementing the king's ordinances. To ensure that even at that level, no obstacles would be placed in his way, however, he deprived the Diets of their administrative effectiveness by appointing his own officials at all administrative and executive levels of the kingdom. It was that step that really laid the foundations of the Prussian civil service.

In such a predominantly agrarian society, the successful functioning of the bureaucracy required specialized knowledge an increasing measure of expertise and thus a division of labor. Even an absolute monarchy cannot concentrate all knowledge and expertise in one man or a small group of men. Hence intrinsic in the growth of any bureaucracy is the tendency toward its independence, toward emancipation from an absolutist monarchy. Frederick William I was well aware of this danger, as also was his son, and what he therefore built up was a very dependent, purely technically functioning apparatus which was intended to do little more than to carry out the will of its princely managing director.

Even this was not enough, however; if among other things the bureaucracy was to check the nobility, the danger of the bureaucracy becoming too independent could, according to Frederick William, only be met by recruiting the bureaucracy from the aristocracy as well as from the educated middle class. This would foster rivalry between the two social classes, now side by side within one institution, and prevent an alliance between them against the monarchy. Besides, the religious ethos which permeated Prussian society of the eighteenth century in general, and the army and bureaucracy in particular, was itself a major check against conflicts of interest ever taking on such proportions as to endanger the fabric of the state.

In fact the effective replacement of the remnants of medieval institutions by a centralized monarchic state, run efficiently by a civil service, constitutes the major achievement of Frederick William I. The army and the civil service became the main pillars of the kingdom of Prussia, a kingdom made up of highly diverse components artificially held together by the two institutions which represented most prominently the state community.

A major step toward the consolidation of the Prussian state was taken by Frederick William's ordinance of 13 August 1713, which declared all royal domains and property as indivisible and inalienable. His father had already abolished the ancient rule allowing a nobleman to do as he liked on the new lands or territories he had acquired. Frederick William's measure constituted a further move toward the transformation of the territories into a unified state. Since for more than a century and a half the nobility of Brandenburg-Prussia had encroached upon the royal domain as well as upon the property of the free peasants, substantial land transfers had taken place without ever having been officially registered. In East Prussia, for instance, this process was not really noticed until Frederick William replaced the multitude of dues and taxes by one general land tax, a tax determined by the size of the holding and the quality of the soil; this in turn required a survey of the lands of the province. In the course of this survey it was revealed that one-third of the land holdings of the Prussian nobility in East Prussia had been illegally acquired from either the royal domain or the peasants.

Upon Frederick William's accession to the throne, the Prussian administration consisted essentially of two main bodies: the General Finance Directory responsible for the administration of the royal domains, and the General War Commissary responsible for the administration of the army and the revenue. Both bodies possessed far-reaching judicial powers in administrative affairs, and each had branches in every province of the kingdom. However, until the reign of Frederick William, these provincial branches had been subject to considerable control by the local notables. From the beginning of his reign, the influence of the Estates in the provincial branches of the central administration was eliminated: most notably they lost any control over the determination of taxation. In other words, what to all intents and purposes had been provincial tax offices became

commissariats, which were staffed and controlled from the center.

The provincial commissaries, now organs of the central administration, extended their influence considerably. Originally part of the military and financial administration, they now acquired many important functions: policing powers over their districts, economic administration, particularly in the towns and cities, supervision of the guilds, and promotion of the manufacturing industries and their protection against foreign competition.

Yet, in spite of this centralized administration, competition between the two major instruments of government and their respective subordinate organs was keen. Ultimately Frederick William could find no other solution to end the feud than to unite the Finance Directory and War Commissary into what became the General Directory. In instructions devised by the king and written in his own hand, he laid down the powers of this new office. It was now responsible for the entire financial and internal administration, including military finance and army supplies. It was composed of four provincial departments, each department headed by a minister under whom were three or four councillors. The first department encompassed East Prussia, Pomerania and Neumark, the second the Kurmark, Magdeburg and Halberstadt, the third the Rhenish provinces, and the fourth the Westphalian provinces of the kingdom. To ensure that the horizon of each department was not limited to

Above. *A trooper of the Prussian Leib Dragoon Regiment, 1740.*

Far left. *Prussian military punishments included hanging, shooting, 'riding the wooden horse' and running the gauntlet between two rows of soldiers armed with sticks.*

Left. *Austrian infantry of the period 1704–10. On the left a grenadier extracts a grenade from his pouch.*

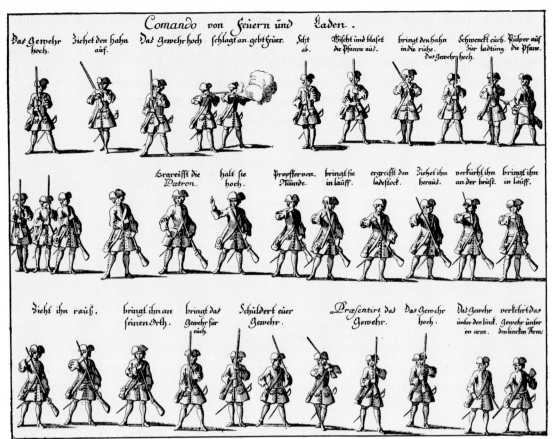

Comando von Feüern ünd Laden.

Left. *Infantry drill of 1720.*

Below right. *A Prussian military manual of 1735 shows infantry loading their muskets.*

Far right. *Soldiers of the Anhalt-Zerbst Infantry Regiment.*

Below. *Soldiers of the German state of Württemburg. A general is on the right, a grenadier on the left and a cuirassier in the background.*

the geographical area under its control, the king delegated to each department specific tasks which affected the whole of the kingdom. Thus the first department was responsible for questions affecting the frontiers of the kingdom and for turning forests into arable land; the second for the maintenance of the main roads, the marching routes of the army, and for military finance; the third for postal affairs and the mint; and the fourth looked after the general accounts.

This fusion also took place at provincial level, the new offices, called War and Domains Chambers, being responsible for the towns and general taxation as well as for the countryside and for revenue derived from the royal domains. As in the central authority, the decision-making process was a collective one, each councillor being head of a particular department or area consisting of towns, country and domains, and decisions being taken after joint discussion.

In order to facilitate their smooth functioning, the chief administrators of each province, the *Landräte*, posts previously filled by nominees of the Estates, now became the king's civil service which the king, without consulting any other body, filled with his own men. Of course changes of this sort were not brought about without resistance; resistance from the nobility and very often from the officeholders themselves. The latter had previously been recruited from the province in which they took up their office; Frederick William insisted that his civil servants should not work in the area of their origin. Two officials who, because of this ruling, were to be transferred from Königsberg to Tilsit and who opposed the move were told by the king: 'One has to serve one's lord with one's life and possessions, with honor and good conscience, with everything except one's salvation. This is for our Lord, but everything else must be mine. They shall dance to my tune or the devil will fetch me!' Note that the emphasis is upon the devil fetching him rather than them!

In a wider European sense, the seventeenth and eighteenth centuries saw the transformation of the state and society based on the power and economic resources of the Estates – their

origins rooted in medieval Europe – into an absolutist state. In Brandenburg-Prussia this period covered the time between the Great Elector and Frederick the Great. Yet not one absolutist monarchy ever had truly absolute power because of the historical accretion of interdependent relationships which no ruler could sever entirely, and which represented checks to any monarch's freedom of action.

In economic terms this change was paralleled by the rise of the mercantilist system, which found its first expression in France under Louis XIV. Economic power was subordinated to the purposes of state. The beginnings of this process in Brandenburg-Prussia can be seen in the construction of an administration serviceable to the whole state. But these were only tentative beginnings which were not developed under Prussia's first king, who had neither the inclination and ability for administration nor the vision to realize the importance of an efficient administration. The accession of Frederick William I brought a resumption of the policies of his grandfather.

One would misunderstand not only the essence of his work but also the character of the man if Frederick William's domestic policies were considered as an imitation of the French example. On the contrary, France, that is to say the French monarchy, had accumulated a serious national debt; Frederick William ended his reign with a surplus. In France the maxim was that revenue had to be created to meet the demands of the monarchy; in Prussia the financial expenditure of the state, including the monarchy, was adjusted to the available revenue. The Age of the Baroque, whether in France, Austria or Spain, was built on credit, credit obtained through banks and increasing taxation. Baroque splendors, whether at Versailles, in Salzburg or the residence of the Bishop of Würzburg, the court of Dresden, were built on the backs of the people – chiefly the peasants. With their sweat and toil, 'culture' was created.

Frederick William's determination to reverse this trend meant that there was no longer any place in Berlin for architectural ostentation. For the first time in Prussian history, an annual budget was established based on the revenue that could be expected, and from that the expenditure for the individual departments or areas was determined.

The pronouncement of the eternal indivisibility of all royal domains and other landed possessions amounted to a proclamation of the indivisibility of the entire territory of the state, thus removing the ruler's privilege of doing what he liked with his territories and subjects. It was the first step toward transforming Prussia from a royal state into a state community.

In his encouragement of trade and manufacture, Frederick William gave considerable support to two young merchants, David Splitgerber and Gottfried Adolph Daum, who in 1712 had set up a small store in Berlin. Since they were not citizens of Berlin but originated from Pomerania and Saxony respectively, the Berlin guild prohibited them from trading in actual goods. They concentrated their activities on buying and selling wholesale and on commission. In so doing they developed connections with Leipzig, Hamburg and Danzig, and even as far as London, Amsterdam, Bordeaux, Venice and Lisbon. The king took due notice of this and soon became a customer. They supplied him with ammunition and rare metals, and soon other members of the royal court and Berlin's society were among the clientele. They expanded Prussian trade into Russia by founding the highly successful Russian Trading Company. They went on to buy arms factories, and established new arms factories in Potsdam. They also purchased ironworks and sugar refineries.

Frederick William's policy toward the textile industry was determined by the requirements of the army. Upon his ac-

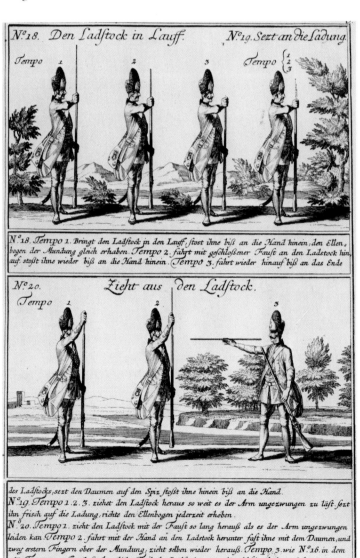

The evolution of Prussian dragoon uniform between 1688 and 1845.

cession to the throne he had his close confidant Johann Andreas Kraut, later to be a minister, found a warehouse and a textile factory in Berlin; it produced the cloth for all the uniforms of the Prussian army. In 1723 it was turned into a state enterprise subject to the General Directory. Toward the end of his reign, almost 18 percent of the Prussian labor force employed in manufacturing trades was concentrated in the textile industry, supplying the home market and feeding an extensive export trade to Prussia's eastern neighbors. The industry was centered in Berlin, Prussia's western provinces – Brandenburg, and, after the Seven Years' War, Silesia.

Neither the Great Elector nor King Frederick I had been in a position to conduct wars, or for that matter even to keep an army of the size they possessed, without subsidies from abroad. At the death of Frederick I the Prussian army had reached a total of 39,000 men. During the reign of Frederick William I that figure was doubled and paid for out of Prussia's own resources. To turn the army into the kind of instrument which displayed such versatility under his son at Mollwitz, or such resilience at Kunersdorf (see Chapter 17), required first of all widespread reforms. First to be affected was the officer corps, which under his predecessors still consisted in part of noble, or allegedly noble, adventurers from all over Europe. Frederick William dismissed all doubtful elements and on principle refused to recruit new members from countries other than German ones. Then, to ensure a supply of officers as well as to tie the bonds between the Prussian nobility and the monarchy closer, he virtually compelled the native nobility to serve as officers. The nobility was also discouraged from serving in armies abroad and although, after granting allodial, or proprietary, rights to their land holdings, there was no longer the medieval feudal tie based on land between the monarchy and nobility, Frederick William I nevertheless insisted on vassalage expressed in terms of service to the crown and state. In that way the Prussian army proved the major institution through which, in due course, the aristocracy was integrated into the state.

Nevertheless, Frederick William's granting of allodial rights

did cause some protest at first, for the higher nobility was deprived of services rendered by the lower nobility; he wanted these services to be commuted into money payments. It caused legal wrangles before the Imperial Court Council which were never resolved. In the meantime, Frederick William proceeded on the basis of the decrees he had issued.

His policy was basically revolutionary in changing existing social relationships, but it was carried out within a very conservative context. This combination of innovation and conservatism was facilitated by Brandenburg-Prussia's social structure. Until well into the nineteenth century Prussia's economic power base was its agrarian economy; the ratio of rural to urban population toward the end of the eighteenth century had been calculated as seven to two. The increase in royal revenue between 1713 and 1786 was not due to increased taxation, specifically land tax or the excise affecting the towns, but was the result of the cultivation of additional land and the maximization of agricultural output. The Prussian provinces supplied by far the larger part of the revenue and the role of the towns, cities and their manufacturing industries at this time has frequently been overestimated, as the result of remarks made by Frederick the Great. Equally, of course, it was neither city nor town which formed the recruiting ground for the army but the land, and it was precisely this relationship between Prussia's military system and its agrarian economy that determined the kingdom's social structure.

The standing army of the Great Elector, a remnant in parts of the private armies of the Thirty Years' War, was an establishment of princely absolutism, 'nationalized' by being turned from a private into a state instrument. The initial heterogeneity of its officer corps was of considerable advantage as the landed nobility was still powerful enough to obstruct the ruler's policies, and particularly because the Prussian *Junker* aristocracy took time to be integrated into the new state. Yet, after the reforms of Frederick William I, the army became the major institution through which the nobility could be absorbed into the state.

Until 1730 the army was recruited at random, and frequently by force, from among the German and east European population, substantially from among the peasants of Brandenburg-Prussia. As a result, Prussia's western provinces suffered a great depletion of their population as the peasants simply fled into neighboring German territory – a trend almost as pronounced in Prussia's eastern provinces. Therefore, a decline in agricultural output was inevitable, and with it a decline in state revenue. That prospect was sufficient to compel Frederick William I to seek a compromise between the demands of his military policy and the requirements of Prussia's agrarian economy.

·First he endeavored to deal with the situation by prohibiting the forcible recruitment of peasants in Prussia and the escape of his subjects to other territories; neither of these measures proved satisfactory. On the contrary, the regiments had to extend their recruitment then to areas outside Prussia, and expenditure was increased and so, by implication, was the drain of gold away from Prussia. The problem was finally resolved by two expedients. First Frederick William realized that, with its increasing influx into the officer corps, the roles of the Prussian nobility were now military as well as economic – regimental and company commanders alike were also agricultural entrepreneurs, and in order to reduce their recruitment expenditure they tended to look for recruits among the peasants of their own estates. This in turn was bound to affect agricultural production adversely unless the peasant serving in the army was given leave to tend the land during certain periods of the year. Allowing for such leave not only ensured agricultural output, but also meant that the officer/landowner saved the pay he would have given his peasants. This pay could then be used for recruitment outside Prussia. The other measure was that individual regiments enrolled all the young males living in the district in which the regiment was garrisoned. Once enrolled their recruitment by other regiments was forbidden, thus curbing recruitment by more than one regiment in any regimental area.

Frederick William's policy was a combination of these two expedients. He divided the country into clearly defined regimental and recruitment districts, called regimental cantons, and made the enrollment of the youth of each canton compulsory, stipulating at the same time that, after the initial basic training, every soldier would be subject to three months' military service per year. For the rest of the year he would be 'on leave.' Thus a balance was established between the needs of the agrarian economy and the requirements of the army. In addition to the regular soldiers there were now the serving peasants, soldiers who, nine months out of 12, would also be peasants on their masters' estates.

The result of the *Cantonal Règlement* of 1730 was a rapid acceleration in the growth of the Prussian army between 1731 and 1733; not only that, there was a transformation and militarization of Prussia's social structure. The peasant now played an important threefold role, which Frederick the Great clearly recognized when he said that the peasants formed the class 'which deserves the greatest respect of all, because their fiscal burdens are the heaviest, they supply the entire state with essential foodstuffs and, at the same time, the largest number of recruits for the army and also a steady addition to the number of burghers.' A state whose economic strength depended on the maximization of existing agricultural resources and on increasing the amount of land under cultivation could not afford depopulation, and had to 'maintain that species of peasant which is most admirable.' The state of the peasantry was consequently of fundamental importance to Prussia, for 'it represents its foundation and carries its burden, it has the work, the others the fame.'

More than any other action of Frederick William I, this piece of legislation integrated aristocracy and peasantry into the state. The burghers in the towns, as yet too insignificant to matter very much in terms of military potential, were exempt from military service, but they too had to play their part by quartering the troops and, more importantly, by supplying the members of the lower echelons of the growing bureaucracy.

As yet there were hardly any garrisons for the army. Soldiers

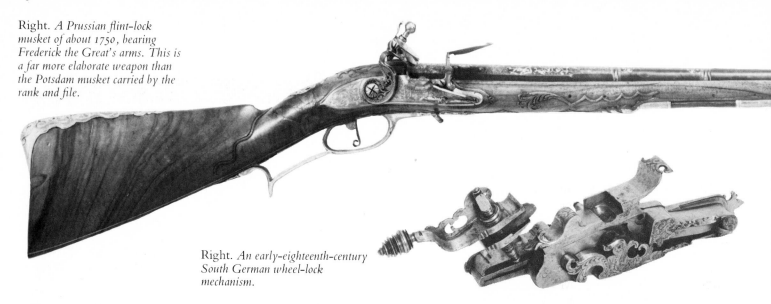

Right. *A Prussian flint-lock musket of about 1750, bearing Frederick the Great's arms. This is a far more elaborate weapon than the Potsdam musket carried by the rank and file.*

Right. *An early-eighteenth-century South German wheel-lock mechanism.*

were quartered in the towns and had to buy and cook their own food; many of them were married and in their spare time pursued a trade. In order to look after children orphaned by war or those who were neglected by their parents, Frederick William founded the *Potsdamer Militärwaisenhaus*, the Potsdam Military Orphanage.

Of the soldier's equipment, only uniform and weapons were supplied; many smaller articles of clothing had to be bought by the soldier himself and paid for through deductions from his wages. This ensured that the army was also an economic driving force within the urban economy. Given the fact that the excise tax was levied on the towns only and that the presence of troops in the towns inevitably increased consumption, then it is understandable that Frederick William once remarked: 'When the army is on the march, then the excise loses one-third.' This primarily economic motivation explains Frederick William's reluctance to deploy his forces in any warlike action; it also goes some way toward explaining his foreign policy.

Frederick William was not simply the commander of his army, he was also its royal drill sergeant, inspired and influenced by his friend Prince Leopold of Anhalt-Dessau, *der alte Dessauer*. The latter's introduction of the iron ramrod, mentioned previously, increased the firepower of the Prussian infantry to a degree unmatched by any other European army at the time. But since an attack was based on linear tactics, that is to say bringing three lines of infantry against the enemy, the bayonet attack remained particularly important, and tall grenadiers were considered the most suitable. For this reason, it has been said, correctly, that Frederick William I, when still Crown Prince, acquired his passion for the tall grenadiers whom he later formed into his own personal bodyguard. This was the one passion on which he was prepared to spend considerable sums quite recklessly. (The source of income which financed this hobby came not from the normal state revenue but from two other sources: the king's own private income derived from his estates, and a specially established recruitment fund to which voluntary contributions could be made. This fund was the chief avenue by which venality in officeholding entered the Prussian bureaucracy.)

In his foreign policy, Frederick William's objective was to consolidate and maintain what had so far been achieved by his ancestors and by himself. In his testament of 1722 he implored his successor: 'I beg you not to begin an unjust war, because God has forbidden unjust wars. You must give account for every man killed in an unjust war. Look at history and you will see that nothing good has come from unjust wars. This, my dear successor, demonstrates the hand of God . . .'

Repetitious though this passage is, it makes clear the intensity of the religious conviction of Frederick William's character. His preoccupation with the state's economy also finds expression when he writes: 'The welfare of a regent is based upon the fact that the land is well populated: population is the real treasure of your land. When your army is on the march outside Prussia, the gate taxes will not be one-third of their usual level when the army is in the country . . . the administration of the domain will be unable to pay rents and that is tantamount to total ruin.' Prussia's army did not only consume two-thirds of her revenue, it also provided a large market for Prussia's young domestic industries and was part of the domestic market that Frederick William so actively fostered.

Upon his accession, Prussia had regained her freedom of action in foreign policy with the conclusion of the Peace of Utrecht on 11 April 1713. But, cautious by nature, Frederick William was loath to involve himself immediately in the confused pattern of the Second Great Northern War. When Peter the Great visited Berlin in 1713 he tried to draw Prussia into an alliance with Russia. For the Prussian king, however, the domestic situation in the kingdom had priority. He said it would take at least a year to get the country's finances in order; after that he would make his decision. Nevertheless, not only did he immediately commence financial reforms, he also simultaneously increased the army by seven regiments.

His major objective was, like that of his father and grandfather, to obtain Stettin and thus have direct access to a major harbor in the Baltic and control of the River Oder. Since Charles XII of Sweden was most likely to die without leaving an heir, the question of the succession to the Swedish throne was uppermost in the minds of the European cabinets. One very likely contestant was the Duke of Holstein-Gottorp, a brother-in-law of Charles XII. Frederick William I promised to support the duke's claims, in return for which he received the promise of Vorpommern up to the River Peene. Nothing came of it; in fact Stettin was conquered by a combined force of Russians, Poles and Danes. This incident was enough for Frederick William to decide whose support he really needed in order to further his aims – Russia's. On 6 October 1713 he concluded a treaty at Schwedt with Prince Menshikov, according to which Prussia was to receive in trust Stettin and Vorpommern up to the River Peene until the conclusion of the hostilities; for the duration of the war Prussia was to undertake the occupation of this territory. To give this arrangement greater permanency, he supplemented it with a secret treaty with the Russians on 12 June 1714 which was to guarantee Prussia the occupied region, while Russia would acquire other Swedish Baltic provinces. Shortly after, in November 1714, Denmark joined this alliance, and also George, the Elector of Hanover.

The sudden return of Charles XII from exile in Turkey introduced further alarm and confusion. Frederick William adopted a reserved attitude, hoping that, by way of negotiations, Sweden would grant the same concessions. These bore no results, however, and on 1 May 1715 Prussia declared war on Sweden. The latter, in a very unfavorable military situation, under strength and no longer enjoying the support of France, had to yield to its opponents. Charles' legendary forced ride across Europe had been in vain. In 1715 he had to capitulate and, three years later, while laying siege to the fortress of Fredriksten, he was killed by a shot through the head. For Frederick William I the net gain was the desired territory of Vorpommern and the city of Stettin, and thus control of the Oder.

Frederick William's close relationship with Peter the Great was not viewed with favor in Vienna, where it was felt that they could no longer rely upon him as unquestioningly as they had been able to rely upon his father. Partly to alleviate this impression and to appease the Habsburgs, he entered into a fully fledged alliance with the latter in 1728, while two years before he had ratified the Pragmatic Sanction which confirmed the indivisibility of the Habsburg crown lands and admitted a female successor to the throne.

Despite his involvement in the web of alliances so typical of

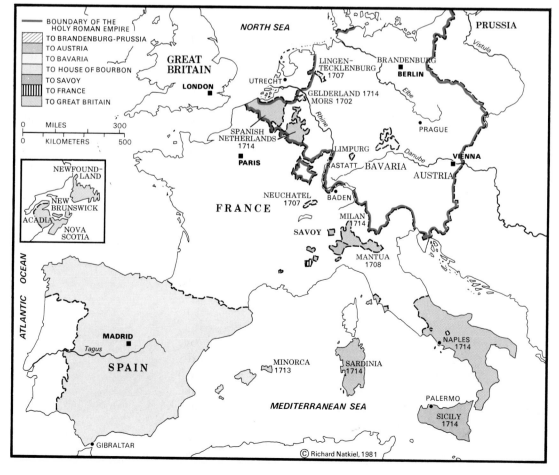

Above. *Field Marshal Prince Leopold of Anhalt-Dessau. The 'Old Dessauer' was a close friend of Frederick William I and had immense influence on the organization of Prussian infantry. Although he never enjoyed quite the same relationship with Frederick, he remained a leading figure until his death in 1747. Three of his sons were soldiers, with varying degrees of success, in the Prussian army.*

the eighteenth century, Frederick William, with the exception of the episode which brought him Vorpommern and Stettin, carefully avoided any aggressive foreign policy. He loved his soldiers too dearly to see them slaughtered on the battlefield. Despite the size of his army, he was one of the most pacific kings of his age. It was a policy which paid handsome dividends.

As the state of the Teutonic Order accomplished in its time, the Prussian kingdom under Frederick William succeeded in an epoch-making achievement, significant not only in the history of Germany but also in that of Europe. With a total population of 2,500,000, it maintained from its own resources an army of 60,000, whose annual budget amounted to about 5,000,000 thalers out of a total state budget of about 7,000,000 thalers. By 1740, the year of Frederick William's death, he had accumulated reserves of about 8,000,000 thalers. In terms of its population Prussia was the twelfth among the European powers, in terms of the peacetime condition of its army the fourth, and in terms of its military effectiveness the first.

By the end of his reign Frederick William could look back on the solid achievement of the consolidation of a state based upon an institutional framework, within which the endeavors of all the elements were directed toward maintaining this artificial structure. The militarization of the agrarian society and the Pietist ethos were well on the way toward combining into a specifically 'Prussian' way of life, which was bound to retard liberalization of Prussia's political, social and economic order. The accent was on stability and conservation, which inhibited the free flow of social forces. By 1740 the God which Hegel was to adulate was already in existence: the God by the name of *der Staat*.

Above. *The young Frederick greets the gouty Frederick William I.*

Right. *Frederick the Great as Crown Prince, wearing the uniform of an infantry officer and the Order of the Black Eagle.*

Left. *Queen Sophia Dorothea, Frederick William's wife and Frederick the Great's mother. Sophia Dorothea showed Frederick affection as a child, and did something to soften the impact of his overbearing father. When she died, in July 1757, Frederick, campaigning near Prague, took to his bed for two days.*

The Battle of Leuthen, 5 December 1757. The bitter fighting around the walled churchyard of Leuthen, held by the Franconian regiment of Roth Würzburg and assailed by the 3rd Battalion of the Prussian Guard.

THE CLIMAX OF ABSOLUTIST WARFARE

C. RÖCHLING
1898

It was rather remarkable that the state founded by Frederick William I was completed by his successor. The fundamentally different personalities and inclinations of father and son gave good cause to expect radical changes of policy.

When he was Crown Prince, and eight years before he wrote his *Anti Machiavelli*, Frederick II, the Great, recognized the geopolitical factors underlying his conception of Prussia's future foreign policy. In his view, a territorially fragmented kingdom stretching across the northern part of central Europe had only two alternatives: the first was to live in harmony with all its neighbors, which would be equivalent to a permanent state of fearful impotence and would lead to a hopeless defensive position in case of conflict; the second was to acquire such territories as would consolidate and secure the kingdom, without too much regard for existing dynasties.

Internally he built on the foundations laid by his father; in his external policy, however, he abandoned the caution and timidity which had characterized the policy of both his father and grandfather, and instead pursued power politics – a little recklessly at first. He made his 'rendezvous with Fame,' a policy which was to take the state to the brink of disaster on several occasions, but from which it managed to emerge victorious. On the battlefields of Silesia the alliance between crown and aristocracy was finally forged which was thereafter to characterize the Prussian state until 1918. In contrast to the Habsburgs, domestic and foreign policy ceased to be subject purely to dynastic considerations, and became instead subject solely to *raison d'état* as Frederick understood it.

The primary focus of his attention was Prussia's position as a significant power and his ambition to turn it into a great power. Although in 1740, immediately after coming to the throne, he dissolved his father's Guard of Giants, he increased the army by seven infantry regiments, which meant that by 1741 Prussia possessed an army of more than 100,000 men.

At the time of Frederick's accession, tension was mounting between France and Britain as a result of a war that had broken out between Britain and Spain in 1739. This situation tempted Frederick to renew the old Prussian claims on the Duchy of Jülich and Berg. By negotiating with France or Britain, both of whom were anxious to secure Prussia's military aid, he hoped to gain decisive support.

While negotiations were still in progress, Emperor Charles VI died quite unexpectedly on 20 October 1740. This had great bearing on the limits of Frederick's ambitions. In Russia the czarina had died, and her death and the ensuing confusion ensured Russia's inactivity for the time being. Habsburg territory, in particular the economically prosperous province of Silesia, would also provide Prussia with an advantageous springboard *vis-à-vis* Poland (if, as it seemed likely, it disintegrated in the near future), and at the same time threaten Saxony. Two days later he called a meeting with Minister Podewils and Field Marshal Schwerin and informed them of his decision to obtain the richest province of the House of Habsburg; he wanted to hear their views as to how he could achieve this, not whether he should attempt it.

Of course claims existed dating back to the sixteenth century, to the time of Elector Joachim II and the treaty of 1537, according to which three Silesian duchies (Liegnitz, Brieg and Wohlau) were to come to Brandenburg after the death of the last of the Piast princes. That line had in fact become extinct in 1675, but the Habsburgs had simply pocketed these provinces without regard to existing treaties. Frederick would now make use of

Right. Frederick the Great watching the construction of his palace of Sans-Souci.

Below left. Frederick the Great as crown prince.

Below. Elizabeth Christina of Brunswick-Bevern, who married Frederick in 1733. The marriage was not a success, and she saw little of her husband.

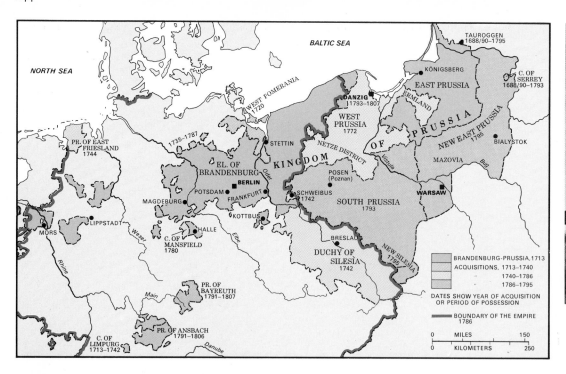

these treaties as a pretext to prise the jewel of Silesia out of the Habsburg crown.

Podewils suggested settling the matter by negotiation. Frederick, however, decided to confront Europe with a *fait accompli*: march before the winter, negotiate during the winter, was his motto.

Frederick's generalship was to develop to unexpected heights during the next 23 years, but that does not mean that, on the eve of the First Silesian War, he was a relative novice in the craft of war. For one thing, he possessed the military training every Prussian officer received, for another he was also an avid student of the military writers of the period.

The Prussian army which Frederick commanded may well have been the first of its type in Europe, but as an army it was still inexperienced. The true importance of light cavalry had not yet been recognized, and the infantry had yet to withstand the test of fire. On the whole, there existed general agreement among the tacticians of the period that, with linear tactics of attack and defense, concentrated fire was preferable to general fire, or, as Scharnhorst was to put it later, individual firing was to be avoided, while only entire salvoes would yield any result. Ten men killed or wounded simultaneously would more likely result in the enemy battalion's withdrawal than 50 killed by a salvo over the entire front of the battalion. Individual fire would lead to wastage of ammunition and excessive wear of the arms, and the officers would lose control over their men.

The ideal way of firing was thought to be to divide each battalion, which in battle would be lined up three deep, into eight platoons; they would fire rapidly one after another, thus maintaining continuous fire and preventing the enemy's cavalry from breaking into the infantry formations. Frederick considered these the ideal firing tactics as well, but was aware that, in practice, they might not be carried out so successfully. What tended to happen was that the first salvo was discharged according to plan, and even three or four platoons might fire in sequence, but, despite the strictest discipline, it would then degenerate into general firing and the officers could do little more than wait until they could advance or withdraw.

It was generally accepted that the attack was to be carried out by the entire line of infantry, which would advance while firing, and would culminate in a bayonet charge. The actual use of the bayonet, however, was relatively rare and it was more of a psychological threat than a real one; in practice, ramming a bayonet into the enemy was one thing, extracting it was another, and quite often could be achieved only with considerable effort, wasting far too much time in the heat of close combat. Once the attacking line met the defense face to face, the latter tended to give way. These tactics corresponded very closely with the composition of the armies at the time. The soldier had no function other than to obey orders, advance in equal step, with an officer at the flank of each formation and one behind. The speed with which the salvoes were fired was a maximum of four per minute, the average being two or three per minute. Salvoes were fired according to command until one had advanced to the enemy's lines, where no real combat was expected. These tactics placed a premium on collective obedience and stifled individual initiative, but were ideal for armies with large numbers of soldiers fighting only for the pay they received, with little personal allegiance to the state or dynasty to which the army belonged.

The most difficult problem was that of firing while moving and, theoretically, an advancing platoon should halt and then fire. Again it was an exercise that could be nicely demonstrated on the parade ground but was hardly feasible in battle. The development that took place during the wars of Frederick's reign was to let the infantry storm forward without firing, using fire only in pursuit and defense; preparatory fire was carried out by artillery. Yet it was a development not uniformly followed in the Prussian army, and throughout the three Silesian wars it varied from battle to battle. More often than not the Prussian army attacked accompanied by rapid musket fire; this resulted in heavy enemy losses which, however, were matched by the losses inflicted by the defenders. In the end, all that was gained by these tactics was the maintenance of what Delbrück calls 'the stability of the tactical body.'

One of the problems of linear tactics was that a line of infantry three deep could be broken through all too easily. The tacticians of antiquity had already realized this weakness; they tried to meet it by introducing a second line whose function it was to strengthen the weak points of the first and ward off attacks from the flanks and the rear. Particularly because of the vulnerability of the flanks, battalions were positioned facing outward to repel an attack from the sides. The aim of most generals was to place their troops on as wide a front as possible so that, as a result of the length of one's own line, it was possible to

Left. *Frederick, wearing his familiar snuff-stained blue uniform, arrives to inspect the progress of a building project.*

carry out a flanking movement, enveloping one of the enemy's wings and causing him to falter from the side rather than being defeated by means of a frontal attack. The disadvantage of this was that the longer the line, the thinner it was, and therefore the forces attempting the maneuver lacked that superiority of numbers necessary to bring it to a successful conclusion. Topographical factors introduced immense difficulties, particularly when the battlefield was hilly or undulating.

In effect this maneuver was hardly ever successfully deployed, but the problem which gave birth to it seriously occupied Frederick and resulted in the 'oblique' order of battle. That is not to say that Frederick was its inventor, however; the significance of the flanks had been recognized for centuries, and Frundsberg, for instance, the 'father of the *Landsknecht*,' always barricaded his flanks. During the Battle of the White Mountain, 1620, in the Thirty Years' War, similar precautions were taken by the Imperial and Protestant forces. In the Wars of the Spanish Succession attacks were already no longer carried out with equal intensity over the entire front, but tended to be weaker on one wing in order to strengthen that one which was to envelop one of the enemy's wings. Blenheim, Ramillies and Turin are appropriate examples. The origin of the oblique battle order was found in the classics, in the writings of Vegetius, while the first modern military theoretician to take up the problem was Habsburg's Montecuccoli, with whose writings Frederick was very familiar; he advised that the best troops should be positioned on the flanks. The initiative in the battle should then originate from that wing which qualitatively and quantitatively was the stronger.

The French writer Folard, from whose works Frederick ordered extensive extracts to be made, paid considerable attention to the importance of the oblique order of battle, while from the writings of another French military theoretician,

Right. The consecration of Maria Theresa as Archduchess of Austria, November 1740.

Below left. Marshal de Puységur, whose military theories had an important influence on Frederick the Great.

Below right. The title page of de Puységur's influential book on the art of war.

Below. Raimundo Montecuccoli, 1609–80. An Italian nobleman who fought for the Imperial Army in the Thirty Years' War and subsequently had a distinguished career fighting the Turks and the French.

Feuquières, whose views were identical with those of Folard, Frederick adopted entire passages to include in his instructions. In short, the concept of the oblique order of battle had existed among military theoreticians and generals for some time. Frederick was quite familiar with it; his contribution is that, after several attempts which involved at least one complete defeat, he applied it successfully.

Actually, to strengthen one wing more than another was fairly simple, but as soon as the enemy recognized this he did the same thing, strengthening his wing that was opposite the weaker one. In theory the result could well have been a battle in which one wing chased the other, the opposing armies revolving like a cartwheel. For the oblique order of battle to become fully effective, one would have had to envelop the enemy flank with one's attacking flank. Since no enemy was fool enough, however, to expose his flanks deliberately, he therefore positioned himself at right angles to the direction of the expected attack, and the attacking force was faced with the major task of wheeling around. This was a movement of considerable complexity because the traditional linear tactics had made little allowance for that degree of mobility. Marshal Puységur, another formative influence on Frederick's military thinking, suggested breaking up the linear formation into battalions. However, this carried the intrinsic risk of multiplying the number of flanks, each battalion now having its own flanks instead of being part of a continuous line. Consequently, it was of the utmost importance to keep the intervals between the battalions as narrow as possible, yet large enough to allow for greater mobility. It was one of the tasks of the cavalry to protect these spaces, in addition to the protection of the flanks.

Furthermore, the oblique order of battle was only an

ART
DE LA GUERRE,
PAR PRINCIPES ET PAR RÈGLES.
OUVRAGE DE M. LE MARÉCHAL
DE PUYSEGUR.
Mis au jour par M. LE MARQUIS DE PUYSEGUR son Fils,
Maréchal des Camps & Armées du Roy.
DÉDIÉ AU ROY.
TOME PREMIER.

A PARIS, QUAI DES AUGUSTINS,
Chez CHARLES-ANTOINE JOMBERT, Libraire du Roy pour l'Artillerie
& le Génie, à l'Image Notre-Dame.
M. DCC. XLIX.
AVEC APPROBATION ET PRIVILEGE DU ROY.

advantage when the attacking wing was stronger, while the rest of the line tied down the maximum number of enemy troops; speed was of the essence to prevent the enemy from taking countermeasures. In other words, the attack had to come as a surprise, and success would be achieved the moment the enemy's front had been enveloped on one of his wings.

The oblique order of battle is therefore what the German historian Delbrück quite rightly called 'a tactical work of art,' which Frederick developed not at one stroke but over the years, putting into practice at least eight different variations of it. Just because it won Frederick some spectacular victories does not mean that, by itself, it was a guarantee of success; it could very well happen, as it did at Kunersdorf, that, if not thrown at the first attempt, the enemy would hold his position; this would ultimately lead to both lines meeting head on and thus to a battle with all the available forces deployed, with none in reserve. That such an order of battle could be defeated by other tactics

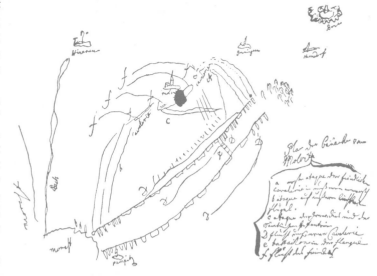

Above. *Field Marshal von Schwerin, 1685–1757, was an educated and humane man, whose feud with the Old Dessauer divided the Prussian officer corps for the first years of Frederick's reign. A brave and capable commander, he was killed at Prague in May 1757 while striving to rally his own regiment.*

Left. *The Empress Maria Theresa of Austria, who reigned from 1740–80, improved the administration of widespread accumulation of lands and tried to better the lot of her subjects.*

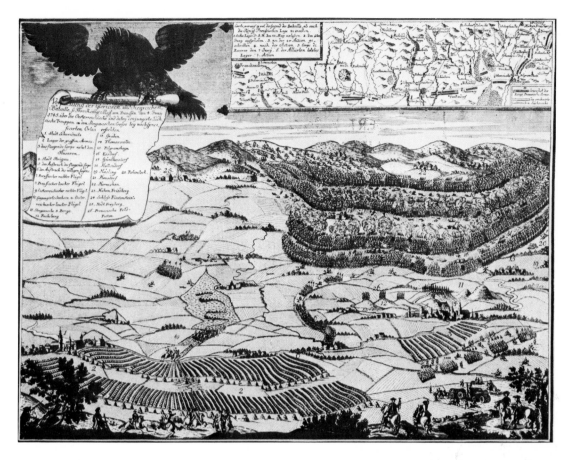

Left. *Frederick's own sketch of the Battle of Mollwitz, 10 April 1741. Things initially went so badly for the Prussians that Frederick was advised to leave the field. His solid infantry saved the day, and Frederick reappeared the following evening.*

Right. *Frederick the Great's victory over the Austrians and Saxons at Hohenfriedberg, 5 June 1745.*

was amply demonstrated when it was carried out by the Prussian army against Napoleon's forces in 1806.

The best definition of the oblique order of battle is that supplied by Delbrück, who describes it as 'that form of battle in which the entire line of battle represents a little interrupted or uninterrupted front. It is a characteristic of the wing battle that one wing is advanced while the other is withheld, and that the attacking wing is strengthened to catch the enemy in the flank or even in the rear. . . . The oblique battle order is a subform of the wing battle which was adapted to the elementary tactics of the epoch. The reinforcement of the attacking wing can consist of infantry in the form of preliminary attacks preceding the main attack, or adding reserves during the battle as well as cavalry or artillery.' This approximately represents the body of ideas on military tactics which Frederick the Great possessed on the eve of the outbreak of the First Silesian War.

Without knowing or foreseeing the ultimate consequences of his action, Frederick was determined to annex Silesia. 'Who would have thought that destiny had chosen a poet to topple the political system of Europe and to turn upside down the political combination of its rulers!' he wrote to his friend Jordan. 'My youthfulness, the burning embers of passion, my thirst for fame, yes, even curiosity admittedly, a secret instinct, have torn me from the joys of tranquillity. The satisfaction of seeing my name in the gazettes and later in history has seduced me,' he admitted on another occasion.

The First Silesian War was undoubtedly a *Blitzkrieg*; the army was in a state of complete preparedness, utter secrecy was maintained and all stratagems of diplomacy were exploited. Frederick was still making diplomatic proposals to Maria Theresa when his troops entered Breslau. He rallied France to his side, while the Habsburgs were supported by Britain and the Netherlands; even Russia seemed to range herself against him.

Just at that point Frederick gained an impressive and temporarily decisive victory at Mollwitz on 10 April 1741. In order to occupy Silesia, Prussian troops had been scattered widely over the province. Meanwhile Austria's forces, some 14,000

strong under Field Marshal Count Neipperg, managed to cross the Sudenten passes from Bohemia into Silesia and were about to cut the Prussian army into two, forcing Frederick to accept battle. At Mollwitz the Prussian army, under Field Marshal Schwerin, gained its first major victory. It was not Frederick's personal victory, though he had drawn up the plan of battle, which envisaged a tentative application of the oblique order of battle. Although superior to the Austrians in infantry and artillery, the Prussian cavalry was inferior in quality as well as in quantity and the Austrian cavalry virtually swept them from the battlefield. Defeat stared the Prussians in the face. On Schwerin's urging, the king left the battlefield for his own safety. Schwerin, grabbing hold of the colors of the First Battalion of Guards, then rallied the Prussian infantry and artillery again and, in one massive effort, attacking as though he was on the Potsdam parade ground, threw the Austrians. The Austrian attempt to separate the Prussian forces had miscarried. Parts of Silesia remained in Austrian hands, however, with only the small part of Brieg going to Prussia.

The result was an alliance with France and the support of Elector Charles of Bavaria for the Imperial throne instead of Maria Theresa's husband. In 1742 he was duly elected in Frankfurt as Charles VII.

In the meantime Frederick had learned the lesson of Mollwitz and reorganized his cavalry. Cuirassiers, who had been the dominant part of the cavalry on heavy horses, were retrained on lighter horses that were quicker and less clumsy to maneuver; the hussars under General von Zieten were expanded, as were the dragoons. The Prussian cavalry earned its first laurels at the Battle of Chotusitz on 17 May 1742 in which the Austrian army was again defeated, a defeat of sufficient impact to persuade Maria Theresa to make peace with Prussia at Breslau on 28 July 1742. Silesia in its entirety was now in Prussian hands.

The peace was not of a very long duration; Maria Theresa was determined to regain Silesia. Austrian forces had expelled the French beyond the Rhine and a new coalition, this time between Austria and Russia against Prussia, seemed to be in the making. In the light of this prospect, Frederick decided to take the initiative in the form of a preemptive strike and in August 1744 broke the Peace of Breslau: the Second Silesian War began.

Frederick's armies moved into Bohemia and captured Prague, compelling the Austrians to leave Alsace. They returned from the Rhine by forced marches and threatened to cut Frederick's lines of communications; this compelled him to withdraw from Bohemia into Silesia. Now the Saxons, supported by British subsidies, joined the Austrians and added another 20,000 men to Frederick's enemies. A war of attrition followed; at no stage was Frederick able to force his enemy into battle, and time and again he was outmaneuvered. Doubts about his ability as a military leader began to be voiced within the Prussian officer corps, the example of Mollwitz being invoked. Even more drastic consequences could be seen among the rank and file of his army, of which 17,000 deserted either to the enemy or simply just out of the army. Maria Theresa, seeing herself on the threshold of the liberation of Silesia, proclaimed that the citizens of the province no longer owed any allegiance to the king of Prussia.

A quality now began to show in Frederick which was the basis of the claim to greatness that his contemporaries and posterity made on his behalf. This claim does not rest on the brilliance of his victories, for they are matched by the severity of the defeats he suffered. It rests in part on his capacity, when threatened and when near to the point of defeat, to generate unexpected resources and, despite great odds, to force fortune in his direction.

Since the middle of March 1745, the king had been with his army, relentlessly training and drilling his troops. Instead of guarding and defending the mountain passes that led from Bohemia into Silesia, Frederick decided to meet the Austrians on Silesian ground. All avenues into Silesia were kept under close observation during the spring of 1745, and every move of the Austrian forces was reported to Frederick in his headquarters in Schweidnitz. On the evening of 3 June 1745, reports were conclusive. Seventy thousand Austrians and Saxons formed into eight columns moved from the Sudeten passes into Silesia between Hohenfriedberg and Pilgramshain. The commander of the Austrian army, Prince Charles of Lorraine, finding the mountain passes unoccupied, had no doubts about the outcome of any battle: 'There would be no God in heaven if we should not win this battle.' Apparently there was not.

Contrary to Austrian expectations, Frederick attacked their left wing. First the Saxons, then the Austrians were thrown. For the first time the Prussian cavalry proved vastly superior to Austria's. The dragoons of the Ansbach-Bayreuth regiment rode into attack sweeping everything before them, their 10 squadrons destroying six battle-hardened Austrian infantry regiments and capturing 66 flags. The enemy lost 10,000 men killed and wounded. In military terms it was a splendid victory for Prussia's soldiers, the air of triumph still captured in the stirring tunes of the *Hohenfriedberger Marsch*, the composition of which has been attributed to Frederick himself, and probably rightly so. This result reestablished confidence in his leadership; it was his first personal military victory. Mollwitz had been that of Schwerin, Chotusitz was argued by the Austrians not to have been a victory at all, but there was no doubt as to who had been the victor at Hohenfriedberg. Frederick had triumphed with a concept that ran contrary to established military thinking; instead of taking the initiative himself he had left it to the enemy, thus tempting Austria into Silesia. Once there he had attacked and inflicted a resounding defeat. Frederick pursued the enemy for another three days. Then the fronts came to a halt again, for the Austrian army in Bohemia still represented a formidable

force and, in the light of the experience of the previous winter, Frederick did not venture beyond Königgrätz.

If Frederick could have had his way now, he would have made peace, provided that he could have retained Silesia. But his great opponent Maria Theresa was still prepared to fight; George II in Britain, behind the backs of his ministers, also advised Austria against making peace. In the meantime Emperor Charles VII had died and Maria Theresa's husband was crowned Emperor Francis I, with the Elector of Brandenburg and the Palatinate dissenting.

In the early autumn of 1745 Frederick was preparing to withdraw from Bohemia to take up winter quarters in Silesia. Mistakes had led to numerous mishaps; Frederick's cabinet secretary Eichel, the man entrusted with all of Frederick's political secrets, had been captured by the Austrians, as had his baggage. The threat of the Saxons diverted a substantial part of the army, the main part of which was now 22,000 strong in Silesia. Prince Charles of Lorraine now attempted to impose Hohenfriedberg in reverse on Frederick. Frederick's army was encamped at Soor, which Charles intended to attack by surprise with a numerically much superior force of 39,000 men. On 30 September 1745 at five in the morning, Frederick received the first news while already convening with his generals. Frederick was trapped, withdrawal or evasion being made impossible by geographical factors. He decided that the only salvation lay in attack. This unconditional readiness to accept battle and attack with a fervor decided the battle, as though all the odds were in favor of the Prussians. Again the Prussian cavalry made the ultimate and decisive contribution. Frederick's military contribution was again significant, but still no sign was discernible that peace could be obtained. He therefore turned against the weakest link of his enemy, the Saxons.

To prevent the Austrian and Saxon armies from uniting, Frederick attacked the Saxon forces at Kesseldorf near Dresden on 15 December 1745. The Prussian Army was commanded by the very man who had given it its decisive shape, the close friend of Frederick's father, Prince Leopold of Anhalt-Dessau, *der alte Dessauer*. While his battalions lined up in battle formation, Prince Leopold, on horseback in front of his troops, took off his hat, drew his sword, raised it to the sky and loudly prayed: 'Oh Lord if today you should not bless us with victory, please make sure that the scoundrels on the other side will not get it either!'

The Prussian infantry advanced as they had done on the parade ground, salvo following salvo accompanied by the concentrated fire of the artillery. Even before the Prussians encountered the Saxons in close combat, the latter took to their heels. It was a battle conducted almost to the letter of the instruction manual for infantry tactics. The battle was won, the Saxons were beaten, and were prevented from uniting with the Austrian army. The immediate consequence of this victory was that Frederick entered Dresden, the Saxon capital, and this was the point at which Maria Theresa decided to terminate a venture which had brought her armies serious reverses, while raising Prussia's military glory to hitherto unknown heights.

On Christmas Day 1745, Austria and Prussia concluded peace in Dresden; Prussia retained Silesia. Frederick returned to Berlin, and for the first time the title 'the Great' made its appearance in the popular vocabulary. Believing, if only for a short time, that his career as a general had come to an end, he decided to devote himself to more peaceful pursuits. The consequences of his actions at the beginning of his reign, however, had not yet run their full course.

Nevertheless he did not neglect his army. The tasks of civilian administration were even closer coupled with the requirements of the army than had been the case under Frederick William I.

Right. *A mounted trooper of the Hesse-Darmstadt Lifeguard, with a dragoon and drummer of the Dragoons of the Guard, 1750.*

Bottom left. *A Prussian grenadier presents arms to an officer of the Foot Guard.*

Bottom right. *Hungarian hussar and infantryman in Austrian service.*

Below. *Officer and hussar, Hesse-Darmstadt, 1763.*

Hessen-Darmstadt.

Reiter
der Leibgarde zu Pferde.

Dragoner und Trommler
der Garde des Dragons.

Um 1750.

Offizier des Gardebataillons.

Grenadier.

(Preußen

fter Bogen.
III. Jahrhunderts.

Supply depots were established throughout the kingdom, and the system of mobilizing supplies was improved to the extent that, whereas each regiment had previously required 12 days to be fully mobilized, it now took only six days. Civilian and army administration was transformed into a precision machine to meet any eventuality. The *Landräte* were now to a very large extent also responsible for supplies and quarters being available at any time for troops on the march, each quarter having at its door a shield on which the number of soldiers to be billeted was listed. In contrast to his father, Frederick also took recourse to recruiting foreigners to the extent that they could make up to two-thirds of each company; however, this measure was not fully implemented until in the later stages of the Seven Years' War. In the border territories, fortresses were improved and extended.

All the Prussian army maneuvers during the 10-year period between 1746 and 1756 were conducted with the aim of perfecting the oblique order of battle. Frederick has often been de-

scribed as a representative of the battle of annihilation, a kind of precursor of Napoleon. This was hardly the case, for he was in principle wedded to the system of his time, the strategy of attrition. He was never able to annihilate his enemies – his forces were too small. All he could do was to weaken them to the point at which they were prepared to enter into a negotiated peace settlement.

He acted carefully and cautiously most of the time, and gave battle to serve as a deterrent effect upon his enemies. During the Seven Years' War, pressed on many fronts, he hoped to shake off his enemies through decisive battles, and he could afford to risk battle because his army possessed superior tactical mobility, which gave it a good chance in the attack. But the dependence on his supplies always necessitated protecting vital provinces so that he could never appear on the battlefield with his entire army. While his victories on the whole did not help him very much, defeat never brought him to his knees. Many of his battles were sudden reactions or responses to the enemy's

Right. *The Austrian statesman Wenzel Anton, Prince von Kaunitz, 1711–94. Kaunitz, the most agile diplomat of his age, helped bring about the Diplomatic Revolution of 1756.*

Below. *The Battle of Lobositz, 1 October 1756. Lobositz was something of an accidental battle, won by the dogged determination of the Prussian infantry.*

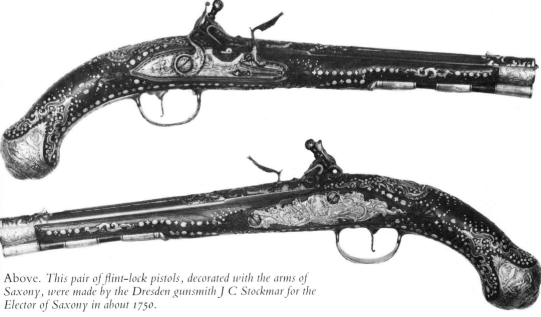

Above. *This pair of flint-lock pistols, decorated with the arms of Saxony, were made by the Dresden gunsmith J C Stockmar for the Elector of Saxony in about 1750.*

Above. *The able Austrian commander Leopold Joseph von Daun, 1705–66, Frederick's adversary on many battlefields.*

Left. *Frederick launches his army against the overextended French at Rossbach, 5 November 1757.*

Right. *The Battle of Prague, 6 May 1757.*

Below. *General Frederick William von Seydlitz, Frederick's hard-living, hard-riding cavalry commander who led the decisive charge at Rossbach.*

initiative, the consequences of which he averted by giving battle almost immediately. Frederick fully realized his limitations: 'With such troops one could conquer the world, if the victories were not as disastrous to the army as they are to the enemy.' The decision to give battle he described as a 'means to vomit which one gives to a sick man if no other course of salvation exists.'

By 1755 dark clouds were assembling on Prussia's horizons. Since 1746 an Austro-Russian defensive alliance had existed, potentially directed against Prussia. Britain, increasingly engaged in war with France over colonial predominance in North America, concluded in September 1755 a treaty with Russia according to which the latter was to protect Hanover. The specter of encirclement stared Frederick in the face, so in January 1756 he concluded the Convention of Westminster with George II, guaranteeing the neutrality of Germany in the imminent Anglo-French conflict. Meanwhile, France was busily negotiating with its former archenemies, the Habsburgs. The Convention of Westminster gave Frederick the hope of having neutralized the Russians, whom he feared most, and he was consequently highly alarmed by news of extensive Russian military preparations. His suspicion of being encircled was further confirmed when, in May 1756, Maria Theresa's chancellor, Count Kaunitz, brought about the 'Diplomatic Revolution' by inducing the French to reverse their alliances. In April 1756 the existing Franco-Prussian alliance expired, but it was primarily the Convention of Westminster which caused France to join the Habsburg camp.

Frederick believed, to the end of his days, that the initiative for his encirclement came from Vienna. Yet in fact it came from the Russians, who pressed the Austrians to take action, and threatened that they would act on their own if necessary. A plan

'to wipe out Prussia' did exist and it was drawn up in Russia. British alarm at Russia's military preparations was allayed with assurances that these were being made in order to keep her treaty with Britain. Frederick assumed that the British could keep the Russians under control, but what he did not realize was that Russia was rather more anxious to make war on Prussia than Austria. 'From the start it set out to produce a plan for the reduction of the power of Prussia, and it continued in existence almost to the end of the Seven Years' War, dealing with all aspects of that conflict, diplomatic, military, financial and administrative. It was a council especially intended for the direction of what we call the Seven Years' War – only it began that work in March 1756, five months before Frederick attacked Saxony.' (Sir Herbert Butterfield).

Russia was the driving force; it offered 80,000 men to Maria Theresa and both Russia and Austria were making political preparations 'to goad Prussia into making the attack.' Frederick was only partially, if at all, aware of all this. He believed the center of the conspiracy to be in Vienna, and now decided to arm himself with all speed and as much noise as possible to show his neighbors that he was not to be caught unawares. He inquired in Vienna several times about the purpose of Austria's military preparations, but, receiving evasive answers, he put himself at the head of his army on 28 August 1756 and occupied Saxony.

His main army consisted of 61,600 men and, with the occupation of Saxony and the capitulation of the Saxon army in the fortress of Pirma on 16 October 1756, Frederick had gained a secure base for the further conduct of his operations; with the onset of winter, however, the attack on Bohemia had to be abandoned. Frederick took the Saxon troops which had capitu-

lated into his army, a serious error because, at decisive moments, they were to desert *en masse*.

On 18 April 1757, after abandoning his winter quarters, he assembled his army in four groups near Chemnitz, Dresden, Zittau and Landeshut, a total force of 116,000 men, while 30,000 Prussian troops covered East Prussia. He operated on external lines, meaning his army was widely spread out, and entered Bohemia. The Austrians, equally strong, were to the southeast of him. The aim of the operation was to penetrate to Leitmeritz with two army groups to get at the rear of Prague, while the other two groups were to march upon Prague directly. The plan succeeded, but now came the siege of Prague, which could be achieved only by starving out the garrison of 50,000 troops. At the same time he had to ward off the Austrian relief army under Field Marshal Daun. Time was pressing, and so were supply problems. The French, Russians, Swedes and the army of the Reich were also about to attack. Daun's forces gave cause for concern since there was no defensive position Frederick could take, whilst Daun, in his position west of Kolin, cut off the Prussian lines of supply. Frederick attempted first to storm Prague; he applied his oblique battle order but lacked the strength to envelop the enemy's flanks. Signs of rout were evident among the Prussian army when Schwerin, as at Mollwitz, took hold of the regimental colors and at the head of his battalion stormed the Austrian positions. Under murderous Austrian defensive fire, the aged field marshal was killed, his body entwined with the colors. The infantry attack was decisively supported by the Prussian cavalry under General von Zieten. It was the bloodiest battle so far in the history of warfare, and the Austrians lost over 15,000 men. However, though a breach was made, Prague was not taken and the bulk of the

Above. *Von Schwerin surveys the ground.*

Left. *Frederick rides forward across the snow-covered ground at Leuthen.*

Below left. *Menzel's unfinished painting shows Frederick addressing his generals before Leuthen, telling them of his intention to attack a numerically superior and strongly positioned enemy.*

Austrian army withdrew into the fortress; Frederick held it under siege, expecting in vain that it would shortly fall.

Frederick now had to turn to Daun. Lacking the element of surprise, Daun expected Frederick at Kolin, with his army of 54,000 pitched against Frederick's 33,000. Daun's men waited for the Prussian attack; Frederick again decided in favor of the oblique order of battle, but the premature action of one of his generals, who initiated a cavalry attack, turned it into a battle over the entire front. Time and again the Prussian infantry lines advanced against the volleys of the Austrian army, and time and again they were thrown back. When the Saxon cavalry regiments from Poland rode a devastating attack against the weakest link in the Prussian line of battle, the Prussian troops would no longer go forward. Frederick in person had gathered 40 men of the Anhalt regiment to attack when an Englishman, Major Grant, called to him: 'But Sire, do you intend to conquer the batteries on your own?'

The battle was lost for the Prussians, and it could have been a disastrous defeat had Daun pursued them. But being cautious, the idea did not appeal to him. The defeat at Kolin on 18 June 1757 gave Frederick's plan of campaign an entirely different face. He now had to give up Bohemia altogether, and the siege of Prague was raised. Within his family, doubts were voiced about Frederick's generalship: his brother, Prince Henry, wrote a letter on the evening of the battle to his sister Amalie: 'Phaëthon has fallen, we do not know what will become of us.'

Moreover, problems emerged elsewhere. The French had beaten the Hanoverian forces of the Duke of Cumberland; Frederick dealt with that problem at once by returning to the tactic of the strategic defensive but combining it with the tactical offensive. A French army under Prince Soubise, sup-ported by troops of the Empire, moved toward the River Saale intending to attack Frederick in Saxony. Frederick anticipated this with a force of 20,000 against the enemy's 50,000. On 5 November 1757 at Rossbach, the Prussian army attacked the enemy while it was still on the march. The attack demonstrated the high degree of mobility achieved by the Prussian army, which, while marching parallel to the French columns, formed itself into attacking echelons without the slightest difficulty. The Prussian attack threw the French into a state of utter confusion, confusion which was turned into a rout by the Prussian cavalry under General von Seydlitz, which scattered the enemy in all directions. Thereafter the French army ceased to play a significant part in the Seven Years' War in central Europe.

'That battle,' said Napoleon, 'was a masterpiece. Of itself it is sufficient to entitle Frederick to a first place in the rank among generals.' The French guns, their colors, baggage and mistresses had fallen into the hands of the Prussian army. The victory of Rossbach had an immense psychological impact upon Germany: 'Never since the dissolution of the empire of Charlemagne had the Teutonic race won such a field against the French. The tidings called forth a general burst of delight and pride from the whole of the great family which spoke the various dialects of the ancient language of Arminius. The fame of Frederick began to supply, in some degree, the place of a common government and a common capital. It became the rallying point for all true Germans, a subject of mutual congratulation to the Bavarian and the Westphalian, to the citizen of Nuremberg. Then first was it manifest that the Germans were truly a nation . . .' (Macaulay).

Rossbach also symbolized the beginning of Germany's literary and cultural emancipation from the French – in spite of a Prussian king who culturally was rather more a product of France than of Germany. Rossbach was the Agincourt of the German people.

But it was not only in Germany that the effect was felt. In Macaulay's words: 'Yet even the enthusiasm of Germany in favour of Frederick hardly equalled the enthusiasm of England.

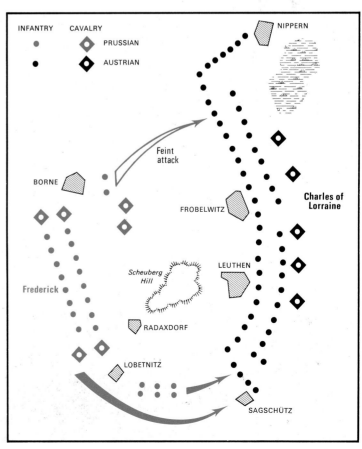

The birthday of our ally was celebrated with as much enthusiasm as that of our own sovereign; and at night the streets of London were in a blaze of illuminations. Portraits of the hero of Rossbach, with his cocked hat and long pigtail, were in every house. An attentive observer will, at this day (April 1842), find in the parlours of old-fashioned inns, and in the portfolios of printsellers, twenty portraits of Frederick for one of George II. The sign-painters were everywhere employed in touching up Admiral Vernon into the King of Prussia. This enthusiasm was strong among religious people, and especially among the Methodists, who knew that the French and Austrians were Papists, and supposed Frederick to be Joshua or Gideon of the Reformed Faith.'

Frederick had no time to enjoy his victory, however – Rossbach had given back to him his operational freedom. After having invaded East Prussia the Russians had been thrown back again. Prince Charles of Lorraine, though, had deeply penetrated into Silesia with his main army; the Duke of Bevern had not been able to resist this advance and encamped himself in a defensive position awaiting Frederick to retrieve the situation. Frederick's aim was to reconquer the whole of Silesia before the winter put an end to campaigning. He required the province to resupply his army and to give it a rest, as well as an operational base against Bohemia and Moravia. If he could not beat the Austrians decisively, there was little chance for a peace settlement.

On 13 November 1757 the king set out with 18 battalions and 29 cavalry squadrons, roughly 14,000 men. He had to cover well over 200 miles in the shortest possible time, and abandoned the route along which his supply depots were established. The troops lived off the land. *En route* one piece of bad news chased the other. The Austrians had conquered the fortress of Schweidnitz, then inflicted a defeat on a Prussian contingent near Breslau and occupied the city. Zieten was sent out to stabilize the situation, in which he partially succeeded; by 2 December he returned to the main army with 20,000 men, while Frederick had been encamped since 28 November at Parchwitz. There, in the camp, almost miraculous changes were brought about: the

discouraged and exhausted Prussian troops transformed themselves again into a military force seldom seen in the eighteenth century. Virtually free from deserters, it was again the old core of the Prussian peasant infantry. Frederick did all he could to encourage his soldiers. Then, on the evening of 3 December, he assembled his officers, generals and commanding officers and addressed them:

'Gentlemen! . . . I have prepared a plan of battle that I shall, and must, wage tomorrow. I shall, against all the rules of the art, attack an enemy which is nearly twice as strong as ourselves and entrenched on high ground. I must do it, for if I do not, all is lost. We must defeat the enemy, or let their batteries dig our graves. This is what I think and how I propose to act. But if there is anyone among you who thinks otherwise, let him ask leave here to depart. I will grant it him, without the slightest reproach. . . . I thought that none of you would leave me; so now I count entirely on your loyal help, and on certain victory. . . . Now go to the camp and tell your regiments what I have said to you here, and assure them that I shall watch each of them closely. The cavalry regiment that does not charge the enemy at once, on the word of command, I shall have unhorsed immediately after battle and turned into a garrison regiment. The infantry regiment which begins to falter for a moment, for whatever reason, will lose its colors and its swords, and will have the braid cut off its uniforms. Now gentlemen farewell; by this hour tomorrow we shall have defeated the enemy, or we shall not see one another again.'

The Austrians were spread out over a front stretching a mile and a half, in a defensive position, while Frederick's forces occupied a considerably shorter front, at the village of Leuthen. The Prussians succeeded in concentrating their main effort against the left wing of the Austrians, who, instead of attacking the Prussians while they were still in the process of forming up, were content to wait and let them come. They also failed to recognize until it was too late where Frederick would place the main emphasis of his attack. At first it seemed to the Austrians that the main force of the Prussian attack would be directed against their center; then, before they realized what was hap-

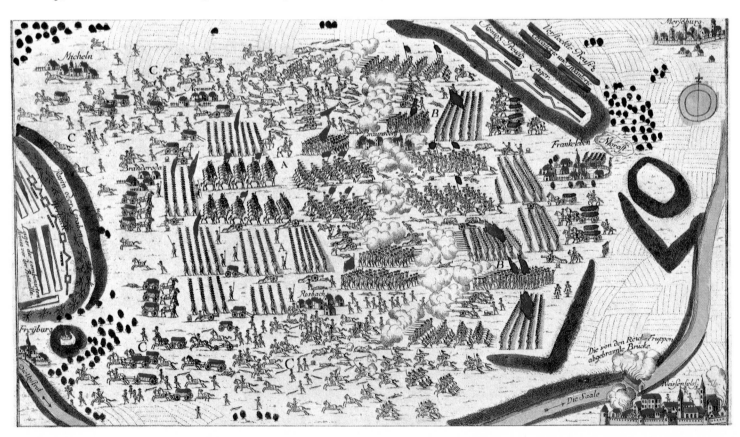

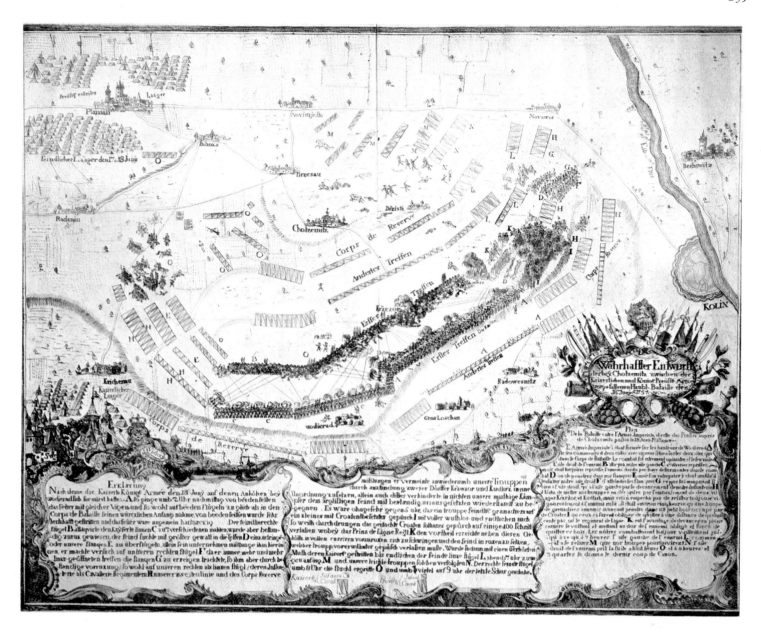

Left. *A contemporary artist's view of Rossbach.*

Above. *The Battle of Kolin, 18 June 1757. Frederick's attempt at a flanking attack went badly wrong, and the ensuing battle cost his army 15,000 casualties (contemporary Austrian plan).*

Right. *The German artist Knotel's view of Frederick addressing his generals before Leuthen.*

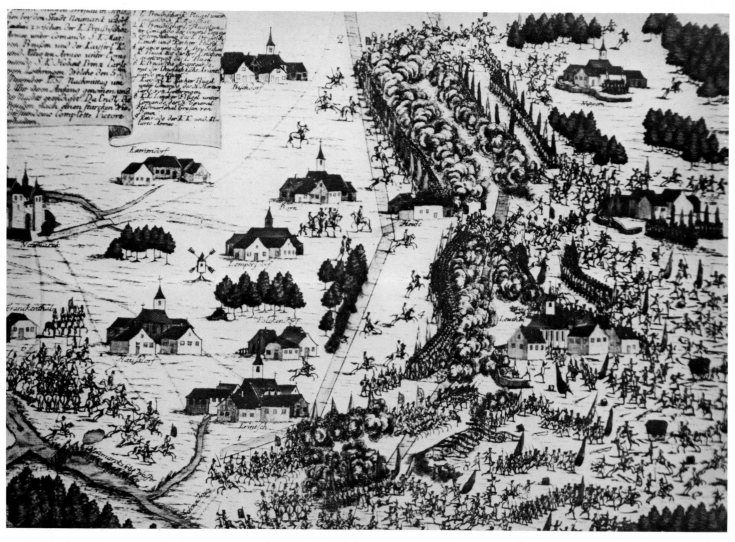

Left. *Another contemporary view of Leuthen.*

Below left. *A panoramic view of Leuthen, looking along the length of the Austrian position. The Austrian left flank (bottom) is already in trouble, and a fierce fight is developing for the village of Leuthen itself.*

Below. *On 30 June 1758 the Austrians ambushed a large ammunition convoy bound for Frederick's siege lines before Olmütz. The raid was so successful that it led to Frederick's abandonment of the siege.*

pening, the Prussian troops re-formed and attacked the Austrian left flank. The oblique order of battle proved a complete success and Leuthen became a resounding defeat for the Austrians. In a state of disorganization and chaos they left Silesia and withdrew into Bohemia. True, they had fought bravely, the village churchyard had been defended by them like lions. But still they were overcome by the Prussians; Frederick had once again secured his prize. On the evening of that day on the snow-covered, bloodstained ground of Leuthen, dimly lit by camp fires, a voice began to sing among the groaning of the dying and wounded and within seconds the entire Prussian army took up the hymn: 'Now Thank We All Our God' – *der Choral von Leuthen*. Even Frederick, the religious sceptic, was deeply moved.

Rossbach and Leuthen also paid dividends in the realm of foreign policy. In April 1758 an agreement was signed between Prussia and Britain in which both powers promised not to enter into a separate peace and Prussia was given an annual subsidy of £670,000. For Frederick things seemed to look up again; he could return to his original plan of attack against Austrian territory. In 1758, however, he chose Moravia rather than Bohemia as his area of operations. He hoped to force Maria Theresa to make peace by conquering the fortress of Olmütz, but it was not to be taken and this compelled him once again to abandon the strategic offensive. The Russians had returned to East Prussia, conquered Königsberg and compelled the city to pay homage to the czarina. There was little that Frederick could do about East Prussia, but when the Russians advanced into Neumark, bombarding Küstrin with their artillery, their objective became clear, namely to link up with the Austrian forces. This he had to prevent at all costs. On 25 August 1758 at Zorndorf, the main Prussian and Russian armies encountered

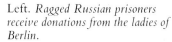

Left. *Ragged Russian prisoners receive donations from the ladies of Berlin.*

Right. *As night fell across the battlefield of Leuthen a Prussian grenadier began to sing the old hymn* Nun danket alle Gott. *Soon more than 25,000 men were singing it in gratitude for survival and victory.*

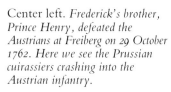

Center left. *Frederick's brother, Prince Henry, defeated the Austrians at Freiberg on 29 October 1762. Here we see the Prussian cuirassiers crashing into the Austrian infantry.*

Below right. *An English engraving shows the Prussian lines rolling forward at Leuthen.*

Below left. *Austrian cavalry cut up retreating Prussian infantry at Kunersdorf, 12 August 1759.*

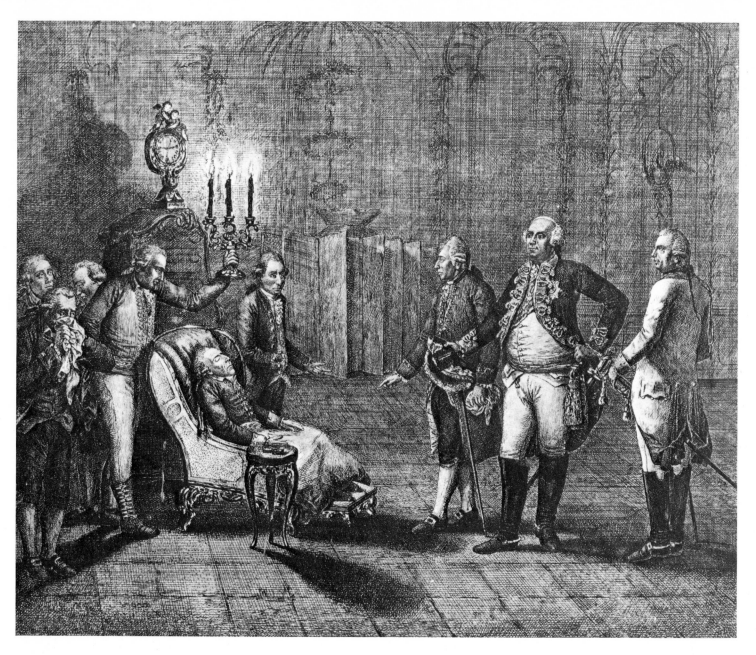

each other for the first time in major battle. It lasted all day. The Russian infantry fought with steadfastness and bravery, and with a defiance of death that made even Frederick shudder. The Prussian battalions showed signs of exhaustion and at one point Frederick personally led his men into attack. The Prussian cavalry under General von Seydlitz, riding attack after attack, once again stabilized the situation in favor of the Prussian army. The battle ended not because the Russians had been defeated, but because night intervened. Short of ammunition, the Prussian army looked forward rather apprehensively to the renewal of the struggle on the following day, but next morning they were relieved to find that the Russians had withdrawn, leaving behind 20,000 casualties, half of the original strength. Frederick had secured his objective of preventing the Russians from linking up with the Austrians. When the British envoy, Sir Andrew Mitchell, congratulated Frederick on the battlefield for his victory, Frederick pointed toward Seydlitz and said: 'Without him we would have fared badly.'

Using the advantage of interior lines of communication, Frederick now turned toward the River Lausitz, where Daun seriously threatened the Prussian army commanded by the king's brother, Prince Henry. The Austrian surprise attack upon Frederick's unfortified camp at Hochkirch during the night of 13 October put an end to his underestimation of Daun. The Austrians captured more than 100 pieces of Prussian artillery.

Hochkirch also, however, provided a demonstration of the discipline of the Prussian army. As Field Chaplain Küster records in his memoirs: 'Here in the complete darkness, in which the watching eye of the officers could not supervise his men and command them to form up into their ranks, nor call back those that had been separated from their units, here the bulk of the musketeers demonstrated that they knew their duty even without the command of an officer.' In this battle Frederick's soldiers performed the impossible, a withdrawal in exemplary order, and Daun did not venture to pursue the Prussians. Daun's failure to exploit his success allowed Frederick to grasp the initiative again, and in the end maintain control of both Silesia and Saxony.

By the beginning of 1759 Frederick came to accept that, because of limited resources of men and materials, he could fight only a defensive war to maintain Silesia and Saxony. A shortage of manpower slowly made itself felt, and a number of the best generals had been killed; in the Seven Years' War more than 1500 officers were killed, including 33 generals in the years between 1756 and 1759. In his personal life Frederick had also suffered tragedy; his favorite sister had died of gout, the family disease of the Hohenzollerns. He himself was suffering from it, and it was taking its toll of his own personal stamina. In the spring of 1759 the Russians renewed their attack, beating the Prussian forces under General Wedel in the Neumark, and

Left. *The death of Frederick, early in the morning of 17 August 1786.*

Right. *The Empress Maria Theresa.*

Below. *The Seven Years War in northwestern Germany: In July 1761 Ferdinand of Brunswick defeated the Duc de Broglie at Vellinghausen.*

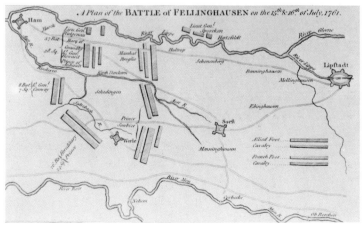

approached Frankfurt-an-der-Oder. Frederick decided to attack them at Kunersdorf near Frankfurt. On 12 August 1759 he had 53,000 men under his command; the combined force of Russians and Austrians numbered 70,000. The Prussian army concentrated its attack on the Russians, who were in well-entrenched positions with their artillery positioned on the commanding heights to the northeast. Frederick again took recourse to the oblique order of battle, but the resourceful Russian commander, General Shaltikov, made a riposte. By fortifying his forces at the center heavily, he made them virtually invulnerable to attack, and made them available for use as reinforcements in either the left or the right wing. Frederick attacked the Russian left wing across extremely difficult ground, and the attack soon got bogged down in the Russian defensive fire. Attack succeeded attack, each suffering the same fate, and the intervention of the Prussian cavalry was cut short when Seydlitz was wounded. Two horses were killed under the king. Then the Austrian cavalry commanded by Marshal Laudon, an officer whom Frederick had once rejected for service in the Prussian army, attacked and routed the Prussian forces. As at Zorndorf, Frederick took up the colors of Prince Henry's regiment and, shouting to his soldiers, 'Lads, do you want to live eternally?', took them into attack. When that failed he tried to form a defensive line, but the Prussian army was in disarray, fleeing back toward the River Oder in the west; the king himself was nearly captured by Cossacks.

The Prussian army was beaten, and soundly at that. For the next 24 hours Frederick thought that his end, and the end of his state, had come.

While the king was in a state of despair, however, Prussian discipline reasserted itself. His adjutants collected what remained of the army. It had lost 25,000 men, the Russian army

19,000. Instead of the Austrians and Russians venturing upon a common pursuit of the Prussian army, however, they followed their different aims. Shaltikov had overestimated the Prussian resources and, after the losses he had sustained, was not prepared to sacrifice much more for Austria's benefit, while Daun was more interested in reconquering Silesia than in marching into Berlin; Russians and Austrians moved off in different directions. Frederick had also lost Dresden, and Saxony now became the theater of operations again. But Prussia's prospects seemed gloomy; shortages of every kind increased his wish for peace. Jointly with England he proposed peace negotiations in November 1759, but Austria, encouraged by her successes, rejected the proposal. Frederick failed to achieve his campaign objective for 1760, namely to recapture Dresden, and consequently had to give up Saxony and withdraw into Silesia, while Prince Henry kept the Russians in check in the northeast. At Liegnitz Frederick achieved his first major success against Laudon since Kunersdorf. Confidence resurged among the Prussians. Frederick

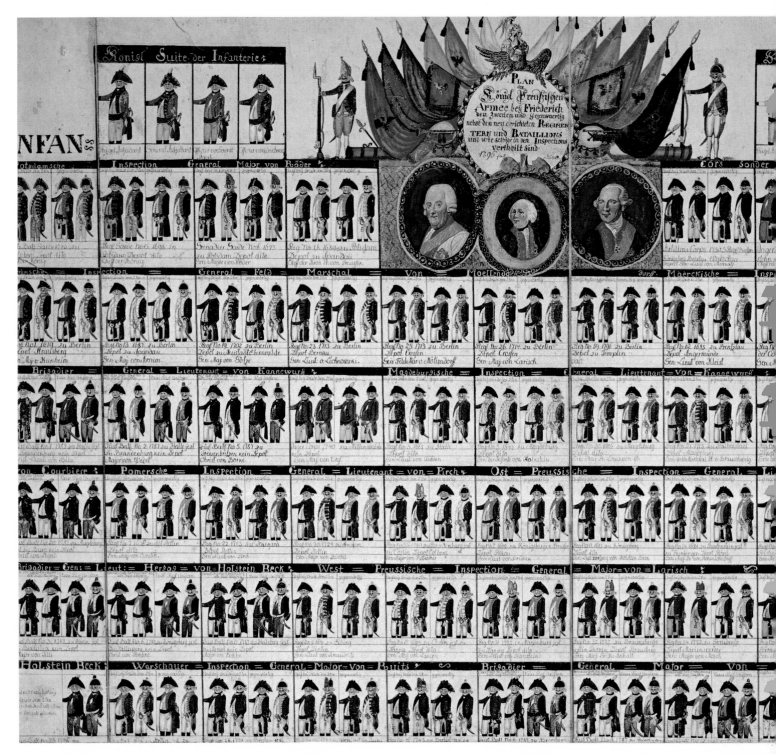

thought he could now force fate and attempt one more bid for Saxony. On 3 November 1760 he fought and won the Battle of Torgau, but the weakness of his forces did not permit him to follow up this victory and achieve his actual objective, the capture of Dresden.

Since the death of George II in 1760, Pitt, Prussia's most faithful ally, had been hard pressed in the Lords and Commons by a faction demanding peace, in the light of Britain's recently acquired supremacy in Canada. That desire for peace was shared by France, Russia and Austria, who now agreed to Frederick's earlier suggestion of convening a peace congress at Augsburg. However, because Frederick made Prussia's participation conditional on the acceptance of his demand that Prussia should not lose any of its territory, the congress was never convened. Britain's ally now became the most serious obstacle to peace.

Frederick's lack of manpower was approaching dangerous proportions. Volunteer regiments were set up, while in the regular army two-thirds of the men were foreigners; even

cadets from the age of 14 were called into active service. With such devices he increased his army again to 100,000 men. Encamped at Bunzelwitz in Lower Silesia, he awaited the enemy attack, an attack which could well have been the *coup de grâce* for his forces had not Daun overestimated the Prussian strength and refrained from attacking. On 5 October 1761 Pitt resigned, and Britain virtually abandoned Prussia.

Then on 5 January 1762 a miracle happened that Frederick had not expected: Czarina Elizabeth died and her nephew, the Duke of Holstein-Gottorp, Peter III, became her successor. An ardent admirer of Frederick the Great, he declared Russia's disinterest in all conquests and recommended to the allies a speedy end to hostilities. Peace between Russia and Prussia was signed on 22 May 1762, and the Russian forces received orders to return home. Thus most of the campaign of 1762, with the exception of the Battle of Freiberg on 29 October when the Austrians were defeated again, had followed the traditional eighteenth-century pattern of warfare, the strategy of attrition.

Austria, facing financial ruin, felt that the war was exacting sacrifices hardly justified by the reconquest of one province. Dire economic necessity compelled Austria and Prussia to agree on an armistice for the winter of 1762–63. Britain concluded its separate peace with France at Fontainebleau on 3 November 1762; it precipitated the initiation of discussions between Prussia and Austria. Frederick gave assurances that he would return to Saxony whatever he held, without indemnities. Ultimately, these negotiations led to the conclusion of the Peace of Hubertusberg in 1763 by which Frederick retained what he had had in 1740 – namely Silesia. His rendezvous with fame had led him along avenues which he had hardly expected in 1740; indeed, on several occasions during the Seven Years' War he expressed regret over this youthful folly. Frederick the Great, the Prussian army and Prussia as a whole were totally exhausted, but Prussia had been established as a major power in Germany as well as in Europe.

Left. *An invaluable source of uniform detail, this colored drawing by von Muhlen shows the uniforms worn by Frederick the Great's infantry.*

Right. *Frederick the Great: the warrior king in old age.*

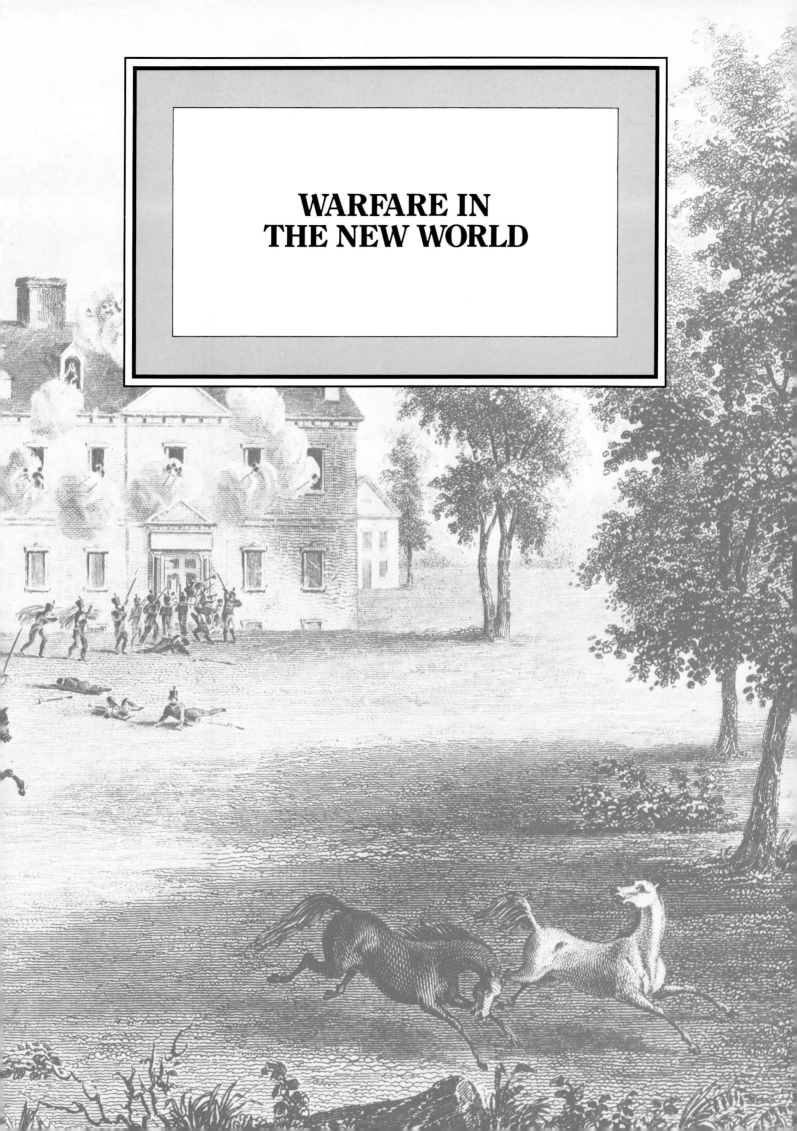

WARFARE IN THE NEW WORLD

Since the late sixteenth century North America had been the object of European colonization, primarily by the British, Dutch and French. The Dutch colonial empire in North America was the most short-lived. Ever since the days of Cromwell and the rise of his navy, Britain and Holland had eyed one another distrustfully, envious of each other's commerce. This state of affairs did not change after the Restoration in 1660. Conflict usually began among the trading companies overseas, after which the respective mother countries then intervened. Hostilities between Britain and Holland began in this way in West Africa in 1664. After subduing the Dutch there, an English squadron set out for North America and seized the Dutch settlement of New Amsterdam, changing the name to New York. All this took place before any formal declaration of war between the two countries was issued – in fact war was not declared until February 1665. Such action was highly popular in England; Cromwell's former confidant, General Monk, said, 'What matters this or that reason? What we want is more of the trade which the Dutch now have.'

France had been established in Canada since 1603, moving into the interior and then southward along the Mississippi where, in 1682, she established the territory of Louisiana. France's colonial policy was not dissimilar to that which had been pursued by Spain in South America. Its emphasis lay mainly on commercial exploitation, the search for minerals and the beaver trade, all with the intention of producing additional revenue for the empty coffers of Louis XIV's treasury. These ventures were also accompanied by intense missionary activities by the Jesuits among the Indian tribes. Virginia had been in British hands since 1584, Massachusetts since 1620, Maryland since 1632 and the former Dutch colonies of New York, New Jersey and Delaware since 1664. In 1683 William Penn founded the Quaker colony of Pennsylvania and in 1713 Britain also gained Newfoundland and Nova Scotia, which brought them, of course, into sharp conflict with the French.

British settlements were established with the intention of territorial expansion and were therefore much more densely populated than those of the French; this was particularly the case in New England, where the influx of immigrants came in two major phases, before 1640 and after 1660 – in other words, at times when life for the Puritan sects was rather uncomfortable, during the reign of Charles I and after the restoration of Charles II. The French Huguenots emigrated to Canada for similar reasons, but Louis XIV was not prepared to tolerate what he considered heretical settlements in Canada. Therefore they had to find another place of refuge much farther to the south in the Carolinas, where they made a permanent residence – incidentally, side-by-side with the Roman Catholic communities which had already established themselves there. By the time the Treaty of Utrecht was signed in 1713, there were 158,000 British colonists in New England and 20,000 French colonists in Canada. By 1748 the French had increased their number to 80,000, but the British colonies outstripped them by well over a million.

By the Treaty of Utrecht the French lost Newfoundland and Nova Scotia to the British. To compensate for this the French established the fortress of Louisburg on Cape Breton Island controlling the entrance to the St Lawrence River, and tensions increased anew between British and French settlers. In 1745, when France and Britain were at war, New England settlers under the command of William Shirley, Governor of Massachusetts, assisted by five British men-of-war under Admiral Warren, laid siege to Louisburg and, after five weeks, captured it. However, it was only a temporary gain. By the Treaty of Aachen in 1748, Louisburg was returned to the French.

Previous spread. *On 4 October 1777 Washington made a surprise attack on British headquarters in the village of Germantown. The attack was foiled by a fog which threw the assaulting columns into confusion.*

Right. *A French view of the defeat.*

Far right. *King George II 1683– 1760, succeeded to the throne 1727.*

Right. *Forces from the New England colonies forced Louisburg to capitulate in 1745. The subsequent peace treaty returned the town to France. This contemporary British print emphasizes the role played by British forces, which was in fact relatively minor.*

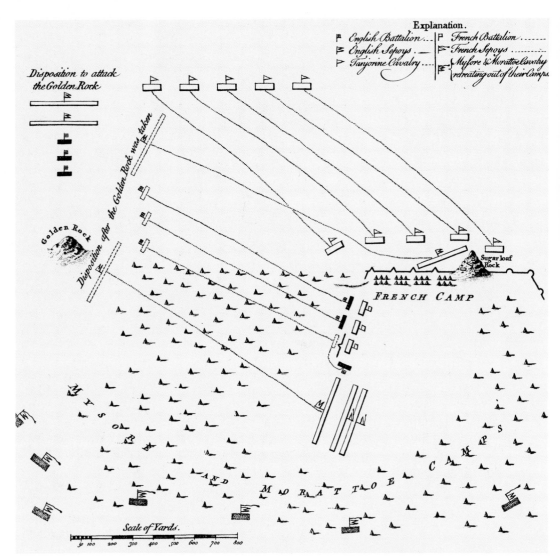

Disposition to attack
the Golden Rock

Golden Rock

Disposition after the Golden Rock was taken

Explanation.

English Battalion....   French Battalion........
English Sepoys___   French Sepoys..........
Tanjorine Cavalry....   Mysore & Morattoe Cavalry
retreating out of their Camps.

Sugar loaf
Rock

FRENCH CAMP

MYSORE

AND MORATTOE CAMPS

Scale of Yards.

50 100   200   300   400   500   600   700   800

Above. *William Pitt the younger,
1757–1806, denounced Britain's
struggle with her North American
colonists.*

Left. *British troops were active on
the plains of India as well as in the
backwoods of North America. A
contemporary plan of Major
Stringer Lawrence's attack on the
camp of the French and their
Indian allies, September 1754.*

Below right. *The mortally
wounded Major General Edward
Braddock retreating with the
remnants of his force.*

Below. *Braddock was ambushed
by the French and Indians near
Fort Duquesne on 9 July 1755.*

Hardly had the treaty been concluded than the French Governor of Canada, de la Gallisonière, initiated a scheme which attempted to cut off the British settlements from the rear. He sent out an expedition into the Ohio region and claimed it in the name of Louis XV. The objective was to link Canada and Louisiana by a chain of forts and contain the British to the eastern seaboard; the British colonists, however, had already begun their westward expansion. In small groups they penetrated the Appalachians, some of them settling in the fertile valleys, others making their way to the southwest into Tennessee or to the northwest into the bluegrass region of Ohio. In 1753 the British Governor of Virginia, Robert Dinwiddie, sent out a young man by the name of George Washington, supported by a small number of soldiers, to establish a fort at the point where the Allegheny and Monongahela rivers joined. In 1754 Washington was sent out again, this time supported by 400 soldiers and Indians; a series of minor skirmishes ensued between the French and the British, but the French, far superior in numbers, compelled Washington to surrender.

So far Anglo-French relations in North America were characterized by 'mutual pestering,' but Washington's surrender changed all that. In the spring of 1755 two regiments were sent to North America from Britain. From Alexandria in Virginia they were sent out under the command of General James Braddock, accompanied by Washington, who had since been released by the French, with the objective of capturing Fort Duquesne, which had been built on a site which Washington, in fact, had selected as suitable for a fort a couple of years earlier. The military expedition consisted of 1400 British regulars and 600 members of the Virginia militia. The regulars advanced as though they were on a European marching route; Braddock ignored all advice given to him to the effect that North America was not a theater of war to be compared with Europe, and that traditional forms of advance and tactics did not apply. He marched on in a column of three rows, drums rolling and fifes blaring, with the result that, in the forests along the Monongahela River, he was ambushed by the Indians, mainly Iroquois, supporting the French, 863 soldiers being killed including Braddock. James Fenimore Cooper, in his *Leatherstocking Tales*, has left us a very graphic account of this ambush. However, hardly one of the Virginia militia was killed, for they knew how to exploit the geographical advantages the country offered and were not prepared to act as foolhardily as Braddock and his troops. But then, from the point of view of the British regulars, the colonial militias were hardly considered to be soldiers: at best they were good support forces, at worse a disobedient rabble who cared little for taking orders from regular officers.

When the French and Indian War officially broke out in 1756, the French sent out the Marquis de Montcalm to Quebec to take over command of the French forces in Canada, which were under the governorship of the Marquis de Vaudreul.

Actually Montcalm's arrival had been preceded by that of Lord Loudon and General James Abercromby, the former to take over as commander-in-chief of the British forces. 'I do not augur very well of the ensuing summer; a detachment is going to America under a commander whom a child might outwit or terrify with a popgun,' was Sir Horace Walpole's comment on the commander and his expedition. In fact, Loudon and Abercromby both lacked drive and initiative. Decisive action was not their *forte* – first they procrastinated the entire summer in taking Fort Ticonderoga, an objective which they abandoned when they thought that the capture of Louisburg would prove less arduous. Arriving near the fortress, they found out that the French fleet was superior to their own, so they abandoned the project altogether. Montcalm, meanwhile, was given time to assemble his 8000 French Canadians and Indian tribes at Ticonderoga undisturbed and then march upon Fort William Henry, which they quickly forced to surrender.

Only a change at home had any effect on circumstances in North America. When William Pitt joined the Newcastle administration he virtually ran the country. Relying on Prussia to deal with France in Europe, he concentrated all British efforts to defeat and expel the French army from Canada. With a shrewd eye for talent, political and military, he selected the best soldiers and sailors and replaced Loudon by Abercromby. Then he recalled General Amherst from Germany and sent him out to North America. Pitt's instructions were to capture the three pillars of French power in Canada in 1758: Fort Duquesne, Ticonderoga and Louisburg.

Louisburg was the first objective because it controlled the St Lawrence River. Since 1748 it had been further fortified and contained a garrison of 3000 soldiers under the command of the Chevalier de Drocour; they were also supported by 12 warships. Pitt in turn raised 22 warships of the line, 15 frigates and 120 transports; they were to carry and support 14 battalions of infantry as well as artillery and engineers, all under the command of Amherst.

He set sail for Halifax accompanied by Brigadier General Lawrence and Brigadier General James Wolfe. Sailing from Portsmouth on 19 February 1758, they arrived at Halifax on 28 May. They found all necessary preparations had been made and put to sea again, anchoring in Gabarus Bay on 2 June. The British immediately destroyed the major French batteries and Wolfe, advancing round the harbor, captured Lighthouse Point. Having got that far, the siege of Louisburg could now be pressed home. On 26 July Drocour surrendered to the British and the St Lawrence River was now open. Amherst tried to persuade Admiral Boscawen, in charge of the naval forces, to

sail up the river to Quebec, but he considered the obstacles too serious and the project was abandoned.

The capture of Fort Duquesne, which was the gateway to the west, was entrusted by Pitt to Brigadier General John Forbes. With a backbone of 1500 Highlanders supported by 4800 men of the colonial militias, including Washington, he set out early in July. Forbes made a number of errors, similar to Braddock's, but he managed to patch them up. The French had already realized that they were in an untenable position, so they evacuated the fort and burned it down; all that Forbes found were the smoldering remnants. The site is now part of Pittsburgh.

The capture of Ticonderoga was important because it opened the land route for the British to advance upon Montreal and Quebec. The operation was initially commanded by Abercromby but, being unsure of himself as usual, he handed over command to his deputy, Lord Howe. Howe was one of the few British officers who was prepared to forget all he had learned about traditional tactics – indeed, he had been trained by the American ranger Robert Rogers. He assembled the largest British force yet seen in North America: 6350 regulars and 9000 militiamen. At the end of June 1758 he broke camp at Albany and advanced to the ruins of Fort William Henry. There, on 5 July, his army began to cross Lake George in over 1000 vessels. On the next day he landed to head a reconnaissance party, but was almost immediately killed by a rifle shot. This put command back into the hands of Abercromby, who had little will and courage left.

Three days later the army encountered the first French obstacles which Montcalm had erected. Abercromby ordered a frontal assault without waiting for his artillery to come up. The

Left. *Lieutenant General Sir William Pepperell at the siege of Louisburg.*

Right. *Jeffrey, 1st Lord Amherst, 1717–97. This formal portrait, after Sir Joshua Reynolds, shows Amherst overlooking the heights of Abraham in 1759. Armor was by now out of date, and was depicted only as a convention in such portraits. This is particularly ironic in Amherst's case, for he was an enterprising, forward-looking officer who had little use for the stiff formality which had contributed to Braddock's defeat.*

Below. *Raising the British flag at Fort Duquesne, 1758. George Washington, seen in the center of this nineteenth-century print, took part in the expedition as an officer of colonial militia.*

British mounted seven assaults but were mowed down by the defending French infantry. The British troops retreated in disorder, making their way back as best they could to the landing place. Ticonderoga held firmly under Montcalm, though overall the balance sheet for the British in 1758 was not bad: they had captured Louisburg and Fort Duquesne. Also, in a brilliant sortie carried out by Colonel Broadstreet, British forces crossed Lake Ontario and burned down Fort Frontenac. The main gates into Canada were open.

Pitt decided that in 1759 the attack should be mounted on a broader front from the mouth of the St Lawrence River to Lake Erie. In the meantime, Amherst had also succeeded where Abercromby had failed – he drove the French from Fort Ticonderoga. Amherst's orders were now to move on to Montreal and Wolfe, supported by the Royal Navy, was to take Quebec. A third army under General Prideaux was to advance up the Mohawk River, clear Lake Ontario, occupy Niagara and so clear the trade route to Lake Erie.

Wolfe had already had a distinguished career: he had fought in Germany in the 1740s and had been present at Culloden. He disdained the colonial militia, however, and believed that the Red Indians were fit only to be exterminated. But he took immense care about every detail, and had learned from Braddock's disaster: 'The regiment will march by files from the left, and is to be formed two deep; if the front is attacked, that company that leads is immediately to form to ye front two deep and advance upon the enemy; the next is to do the same. Inclining to ye right of the enemy, the next to ye left if the ground will permit of it, and so on to ye right and left, until an extensive front is form'd, by which the enemy may be surrounded. And as an attack may be sudden and time lost in sending orders, these movements are to be made in such a case by the several officers without waiting for any. If the column is attack'd on ye left, the whole are to face to ye left and attack ye enemy, on ye right ye same; if in ye rear, the rear is to act as the front was order'd, the whole going to the right about; if on the right and left, the two ranks are to face outwards, if in ye front and rear, ye first and last companies front both ways.'

Pitt, aware that the first problem was not land but sea power, selected Admiral Saunders, Admiral Holmes and Admiral Durrell. The first two were to cooperate with Wolfe's army and the third was to carry an expedition to block the St Lawrence River against any French attempts to bring supplies to their troops.

Wolfe was given *carte blanche* to appoint his own subordinates; they were mainly under 30 years old. 'It was a boy's campaign,' as one cynical contemporary observed. Wolfe made his preparations while Montcalm, who had no idea where the major blow would fall, tried to resist Amherst at Lake Champlain and Fort Niagara. His position was not an enviable one: Canada had a population of only 82,000 to the American colonies' 1,300,000. He was also insufficiently supported from France, where the funds for royal consumption at Versailles were considered more important than those needed for the defense of Canada against the British onslaught. Inevitably, corruption flourished within the Canadian administration, leading to economic stagnation and decline: 'Agriculture and trade were paralyzed, loyalty shaken, while diminished resources, and discontented people, hastened the inevitable catastrophe of British triumph.' Yet a stroke of luck did come Montcalm's way – the British Admiral, Durrell, because he feared the tide of the St Lawrence, did not enter it, allowing 18 French vessels to pass up the river to Quebec. The French had also intercepted a letter from General Amherst which contained details of the British plan. Montcalm had rushed to Quebec and made all necessary preparations, nearly foiling Wolfe's plans.

Quebec as a fortress was considered impregnable, and had been modelled on Vauban's pattern of fortifications. Moreover, standing on a rocky hillside between the St Lawrence and St Charles rivers, there was access by land only on one side. At first Montcalm played for time, hoping that the storms and fog of the autumn would drive the British naval forces away. The British navy, however, withstood the weather and in the spring of 1759 Wolfe could make his advance. On 9 June the fleet entered the Gulf of St Lawrence, had come upstream by the 26th, and the Isle of Orleans was occupied. Having now seen Quebec for the first time, Wolfe had to devise a plan; in the meantime, however, both Wolfe and Montcalm played a game of wits. Montcalm was now running short of supplies, and Wolfe intended to force him out of Quebec and give battle. Wolfe ferried his army on flat-bottomed boats and landed near a little-known path which led the British troops up to the heights of the Plains of Abraham; this was a serious threat to Montcalm's lines of supply. The Plains of Abraham consisted of a plateau of grassland about a mile wide.

Montcalm was forced to accept battle. His total strength amounted to approximately 5000 men, Wolfe's actual battle

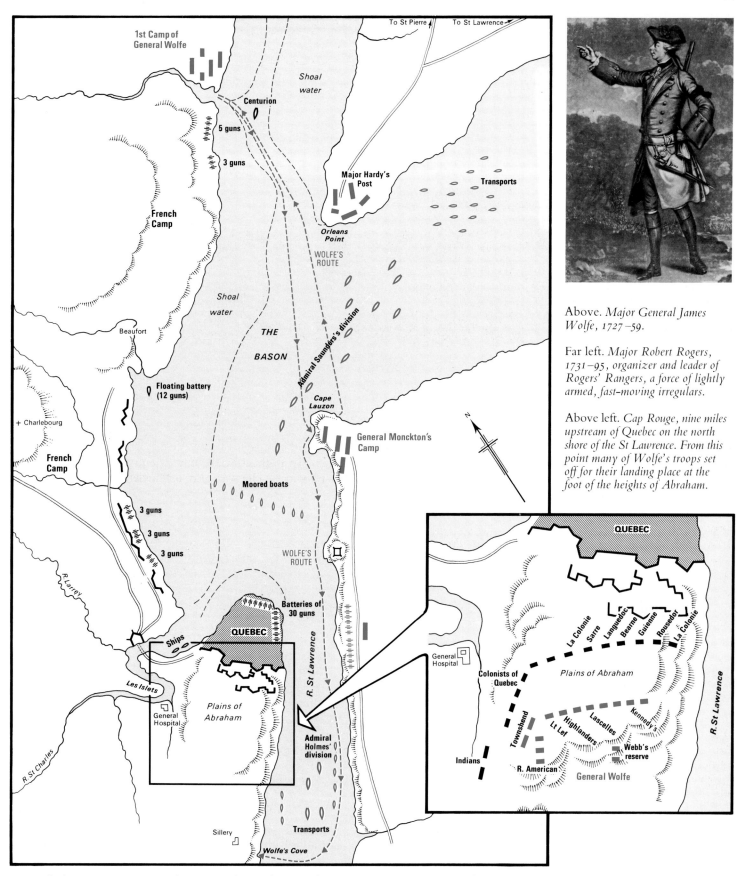

1st Camp of General Wolfe

To St Pierre · To St Lawrence

Shoal water

Centurion

5 guns

3 guns

Major Hardy's Post

Transports

French Camp

Orleans Point

WOLFE'S ROUTE

Shoal water

Beaufort

THE BASON

Admiral Saunders's division

+ Charlebourg

Floating battery (12 guns)

Cape Lauzon

French Camp

General Monckton's Camp

Moored boats

3 guns

3 guns

3 guns

R. Larrey

Batteries of 30 guns

WOLFE'S ROUTE

QUEBEC

Ships

R. St Lawrence

Les Islets

Plains of Abraham

General Hospital

R. St Charles

Admiral Holmes' division

Sillery

Transports

Wolfe's Cove

QUEBEC

La Colonie · Sarre · Languedoc · Bearne · Guienne · Rousedor · La Colonie

General Hospital

Colonists of Quebec

Plains of Abraham

R. St Lawrence

Townshend · Lt Lef · Highlanders · Lascelles · Kennedy's

Indians

R. American

Webb's reserve

General Wolfe

Above. *Major General James Wolfe, 1727–59.*

Far left. *Major Robert Rogers, 1731–95, organizer and leader of Rogers' Rangers, a force of lightly armed, fast-moving irregulars.*

Above left. *Cap Rouge, nine miles upstream of Quebec on the north shore of the St Lawrence. From this point many of Wolfe's troops set off for their landing place at the foot of the heights of Abraham.*

strength just over 3000. Both armies formed up and, at one o'clock on 13 September 1759, the battle began with the French advancing. Wolfe, his line two deep, issued 'express orders not to fire till they [the French] came within 20 yards of us . . . the General formed the line of battle, he ordered the regiments to load with an additional ball.'

The French advanced 'briskly in three columns, with loud shouts and recovered arms, two of them inclining to the left of our army, and the third towards out right firing obliquely at the two extremities of our line, from the distance of one hundred and thirty – until they came within forty yards; which our troops withstood with the greatest intrepidity and firmness, still reserving their fire, and paying the strictest obedience to their officers.'

When the lines were 100 yards apart, Wolfe's men marched forward until only 40 yards separated them from the French lines. They then fired their volley: 'With one deafening crash the most perfect volley ever fired on battlefields burst forth as if from a single monstrous weapon, from end to end of the British line.' Under the cover of the smoke the British advanced again and again, each time firing their volley. As the smoke began to clear 'we observed the main body of the Enemy

retreating in great confusion towards the Town, and the rest towards the River St Charles.' The battle had lasted little more than a quarter of an hour; the British pursued the enemy and entered Quebec.

As in every battle, a great price had to be paid; on the Plains of Abraham it was the death of Wolfe and Montcalm. The struggle for supremacy in North America, however, had been decided in favor of the British. The following year Montreal capitulated and Britain's aims had been achieved, duly recognized three years later when, on 10 February 1763, France ceded the whole of Canada to Britain. The Anglo-French struggle for supremacy had also been conducted in India, and here France was left with only five towns. That Britain could place its major effort overseas was in no small measure due to Frederick the Great's campaigns in central Europe, and there is more than an ounce of truth in the assertion that North America, the West Indies and India were conquered on the plains and hills of Europe.

However, Britain's problems were not over yet. Its treasure was depleted – the cost of warfare had been immense since Britain also paid heavy subsidies to Prussia. Consequently, it faced financial problems which had to be solved by means of taxation, taxation to be applied not only to the motherland but also to the colonies overseas. In 1760, when the French and Indian War was closed in America, the British colonists were fairly satisfied with the existing compromise between home rule and imperial control exercised by Britain. They were happy for Parliament to control Imperial commerce so long as it allowed the North American colonies to prosper, and they had no quarrels with British foreign policy which had yielded such splendid results.

There was considerable dissatisfaction in Britain, however.

Among the politically articulate sections of the population, the opinion was voiced that financially the colonies had not carried their proper share in the war. The colonists disagreed. Britain's possessions in North America had virtually doubled in size, but this also meant that the territory had to be secured and British troops stationed there, a garrison of about 10,000 men. The colonists were to be taxed for the upkeep of this protective force. Various taxation laws were introduced and, at the same time, the mercantile system was tightened by strengthening the Acts of Trade and Navigation.

So far the colonists had not objected to the mercantile system since it left plenty of loopholes; some Acts had, in fact, never been enforced. Yet the Revenue Act, the first of these new measures – and novel chiefly in its rigorous enforcement – created trouble among the colonial lawyers, who feared that a

Above. *The death of Wolfe, 13 September 1759.*

Above left. *British troops land at Montmorency, July 1759, covered by the fire of HMS Centurion (after a drawing by Captain Henry Smith).*

Left. *The death of Wolfe's gallant adversary, the Marquis de Montcalm. The French artist has been too imaginative: Montcalm did not die on the battlefield, and there are no palm trees in Canada.*

Right. *The British struck at the French nearer home: here British troops land on Belle Isle in the Bay of Biscay, 1761.*

precedent had been created, to the detriment of the American colonies. They pointed to the preamble of the Act because it proclaimed that the new duties were levied for revenue purposes. This was the thin end of the wedge and, as in Britain 120 years before, the cry was raised: 'no taxation without representation.' While colonial opinion was mobilized, Parliament passed the Stamp Act on 22 March 1765, which extended to the colonies, as it laid a tax on all legal documents, newspapers, pamphlets, etc. Considering the number of land transactions that were always taking place in the course of territorial expansion, the stamp duty on a contract selling land, for instance, was bound to be a considerable irritant. From the colonists' point of view, the Stamp Act was even more annoying than the Revenue Act: it was direct taxation and had nothing to do with the regulation of commerce. Virginia led the opposition with

Henry's speech; the Stamp Act Congress followed in New York, the first intercolonial meeting summoned by local initiative. The Congress questioned the constitutionality of the Act, pointing to the fact that the colonies were not represented in Parliament at Westminster. Whether direct representation would solve the problem was left as an open question.

The Stamp Act united colonial opinion as nothing before had done, and Britain repealed it. However, the repeal was coupled with the assertion that 'King and Parliament have full power and authority to make laws and statutes of sufficient force and validity to bind the colonies.' Tranquillity seemed to return to the colonies. In 1767, however, the Townshend Acts were introduced, a return to the policy of raising revenue through customs duties. The administration in the colonies was reorganized to ensure their enforcement, and the additional taxes

thus raised were not only to support the garrison but were also funds for the creation of a colonial civil list; this meant that royal governors and judges were made independent from the colonial assemblies. The public outcry was less severe than over the Stamp Act but still strong enough for these measures to be repealed in 1770. Tempers calmed again – except in Boston, the seat of the British administration.

However, taxation was not the only problem – there were also problems related to the Indians, the fur trade, public land and politics. The Indian problem was whether Indian hunting grounds were to be reserved for the Indians in the interest of humanity, thus stopping westward expansion. The problem of the fur trade was a question of control: who should exercise it, imperial, federal or local officials? Regarding public land, the issue was how land acquired from Indians should be disposed of and by what authority. Finally, the political difficulties arose concerning the degree of self-government to be allowed to new settlements and their relationship to the older colonies.

The urgency of these problems was highlighted by Pontiac's uprising, which showed that the colonists had, as usual, mismanaged their Indian affairs, and that British regulars were required to protect the colonists.

To find a temporary solution to the problem, the Royal Proclamation of 7 October 1763 announced a provisional western policy; this aimed to placate the Indians and prevent over-

expansion and a consequent further drain of Britain's treasury. The Appalachians formed the western frontier and the boundaries of Canada and the Floridas were settled. It was not meant as a permanent barrier to westward expansion, though a subsequent British administration declared it a permanent frontier.

Constitutional calm had followed the agitation of 1767 to 1770. Only in Massachusetts, where Governor Hutchinson took a very high hand with his assembly, did agitation continue to ferment. Samuel Adams argued that the people were 'paying the unrighteous tribute.' To mobilize Massachusetts' public opinion, he made clever use of the Boston Town meeting and had a Committee of Correspondence appointed which drafted a statement of 'rights to the colonists' with a 'list of infringements.' Over 75 towns replied and appointed in turn their Committees of Correspondence – the forerunners of a similar institution in the French Revolution and culminating in the Council movement in central Europe in 1918–19 and, of course, the Russian 'soviet.' The Committees of Correspondence were a political machine to be of service when a real issue arose. Such an issue appeared in the form of the Boston Tea Party and the consequences led to the invitation by the Virginia House of Burgesses to the other 12 colonies – or rather Committees of Correspondence – to meet in Philadelphia in September 1774. From then on the way led directly to the American Revolution, or the War of American Independence.

But what sort of army did the colonists have? It consisted of the militia, the forerunner of the United States Army. Originally the militia organization was based on the English Muster Law of 1572, when the English Parliament, in the face of the Spanish threat, wanted to ensure that all counties had an immediate military reserve at hand just in case a Spanish invasion should occur. The colonists in North America continued with it, necessary as it was in view of the Indian threat. In the course of time the law was adapted to the various changing requirements to mobilize forces at any point of the 13 colonies. It was also supposed to enable the various colonies to concentrate within the shortest possible time militia regiments at any given point in cases of emergency. From the militia originated the 'Snow Shoe Men' in 1702 and the 'Picket Guards' in 1755, whose function was to act as vanguard to the regular troops, and ultimately the 'Minutemen' in 1774, troops consisting of militiamen who could be ready for combat within a minute. In addition to these elite units, which had proved their value in the French and Indian War, there was the militia itself, consisting of the able-bodied men of each community or settlement. They were divided into companies, whose strength, however, was rarely greater than 30 men. The companies were part of regi-

Above left. Two Mohawk Indian chiefs, circa 1744.

Below right. The first engagement of the war took place when British troops set off from Boston to destroy an arms dump at Concord. The march turned into a running battle against armed colonists.

Below. British officers, in their quarters at New York, discuss the forthcoming campaign.

Die Generals und Officiers der Königlich Englischen Armee und derer Hülffs Truppen zu Neu Yorck. | Les Royalistes ou les Officiers du premier Rang de l'Armée Ensloise et des Trouppes auxiliaires à Novelle York.

Printed for Carington Bowles in St Pauls Church yard London

ments, but each regiment varied in strength depending on the number of people available in each county. The militia elected its own officers and non-commissioned officers after those loyal to the crown and appointed by the colonial governors had been removed in more or less free elections. The newly elected leaders were, of course, supporters of the cause of independence.

Military exercises, or rather drill, were carried out three times a week on the village common. The men were familiar with the tactics of fighting in the wilderness, but now they had to train themselves in the close battle order of the British troops whom they ultimately would have to confront. British officers were rather amused by these attempts, which were bound to look rather clumsy at first. In fact, when the British were encountered in open battle by the 'Continental Army,' the latter at first proved inferior. They were much better fighting the way they knew, which provided the first example of new infantry tactics before the age of absolutist warfare came to an end.

Battle commenced on 19 April 1775, when British units were ordered by Governor Gage of Massachusetts to destroy a secret arms dump which the colonists had established at Concord near Boston. As the British troops approached Lexington, about 70 riflemen barred their way. They were quickly driven off, but their numbers were increased by armed inhabitants from nearby settlements. Instead of meeting the British as on a European battlefield, they conducted a running battle against both flanks of the British troops, the colonists being well protected by the trees, bushes and general topography of the countryside. The British were forced to withdraw and, although well trained to carry out this maneuver in an orderly fashion, they were con-

tinuously harassed by the colonists and had great difficulty in making their way back; the colonists fired from all sides and evaded any direct engagement with the bulk of the British troops. Losses among the British were severe and they returned to Boston in a state of exhaustion. Neither their weapons nor discipline had had any effects upon the colonists – they just could not be driven back like an army fighting according to the conventional pattern.

The colonists could hardly have been aware that, by the use of their tactics, they were actually ushering in a new type of warfare, and a new phase in military history; even after Lexington, they tried to emulate the British in their exercises. Apart from the militia, the colonies did not have a regular military force, nor did they possess arms manufacturers or an administrative apparatus to supervise logistics and ensure supplies. When, on 15 June 1775, George Washington was appointed by the Confederate Congress as supreme commander of the military forces, his initial task was one of vast improvisation. Of course he had the militia, but the militia had its own inherent limitations. As the American Revolution was to show time and again, militiamen were loath to fight outside their state. There was as yet no awareness of a common identity – people were Virginians, New Englanders, Pennsylvanians, etc, first and foremost. The militia consisted mainly of volunteers or local levies, capable of fighting in the wilderness, but without the discipline of the regular soldier. They initially rejected notions of subordination as incompatible with the rights of a free man. Their advantage consisted in knowing their territory and in fighting individually in loose formations as *tirailleurs*, not as a closed

body of well-drilled soldiers. In open battle their numerical superiority over the British, who never had more than 40,000 men in the colonies, did not confer any advantage. At first, wherever American and British contingents met in open battle, the Americans were beaten back, frequently with disastrous consequences, namely that the militiamen simply made off home.

As individual fighters, however, they were superior to the British; they also had greater experience of war – after all, they had been fighting the Indians virtually since their arrival and the French since the late seventeenth century. They were good guerrilla fighters. Man for man the militiaman was superior to the British regular, but unit for unit inferior.

They also enjoyed another advantage, and that was in the area of supplies. Because of the militia system, arms, mainly muskets and ammunition, were stored in adequate quantities in all towns, villages and frontier outposts. It was the task of the leaders of the local militia and the Minutemen, and was accomplished successfully. Also, since, like any army, the militia marched on its stomach, the question of food supplies was imperative, and here, too, adequate stores were kept. By comparison, British troops encountered immediate hostility when they went to requisition supplies and the British army had to rely very largely on supplies from the mother country, where the naval lines were continuously threatened and interrupted by the French navy, after the conclusion of the Franco-American alliance.

The main weapon of the militia, as well of the British army, was the Brown Bess flintlock musket. One British officer described it as follows: 'A soldier will hit his man at a range of about 80 yards, perhaps even 100 yards. But a soldier must really have bad luck if at a distance of 150 yards he is even wounded. Firing at a range of 200 yards is like shooting at the moon, hoping to hit it.' It had a corn, but not a notch, for aiming. The recoil was light but the emission of gunpowder smoke was rather strong. Still, it was a usable musket, a weapon supplemented later among the colonists by the long musket known as the Kentucky rifle, which was far superior to the existing musketry. The militia also possessed artillery, but quantitatively and qualitatively inferior to that of the British. The same applied to the artillery crews. Neither the Americans nor the British had much cavalry; it was not really suited to the battlefields of North America, as had already been demonstrated.

If the Americans were to have success against the British, then it could hardly be achieved by the skirmish and combat actions of individual militia units, but by their combined force. The Continental Congress established a Committee of Safety, which appointed the individual commanders and the supreme commander George Washington. It was due to his toughness and strength of character that the American Revolution would be brought to a successful conclusion. He was fully aware that he could never beat the British in a war of annihilation, but only by expelling them from the territory of the new republic. Washington managed to hold on until the fate of the former colonies changed through French intervention. This was despite great disadvantages: the worst of defeats inflicted by the British; the opposition of many of his fellow commanders; a lack of any significant funds; and less than unanimous support from a political leadership which was more often divided than united. The Continental Congress entrusted him with the setting up of an army as a core of troops for open field battle, but, distrustful of any standing army, limited its number to 22,000 men. This army was made up of the militia troops.

Washington's task was to transform these troops into something like a regular army. The Continental Army had to be brought in line with the organizational and tactical conditions of troops of the line, inspired by a common desire to further the democratic common good. Looking for officers with great military experience, he met the man who assisted him in accomplishing this task: Friedrich Wilhelm von Steuben (1730–94). It is often maintained that Steuben was not a 'baron,' implying that he was not of noble origin. This is only partially true, however. Steuben was not a baron because this title was not used among the Prussian nobility; its equivalent was *Freiherr* and that is what Steuben was. As an officer in the Prussian army he had a highly distinguished service record in the Seven Years' War; he was the wing adjutant of Frederick the Great's General Quartermaster and left the Prussian army almost immediately after the Peace of Hubertusburg. He then served on the court of the Duke of Hohenzollern-Hechingen – the Roman Catholic line of the Hohenzollern family – and then as a colonel in the forces of the Margrave of Baden. Upon French recommendation he came to America via Paris and arrived in Washington's camp at Valley Forge in March 1778. There he was received with open arms and appointed Inspector General.

Above right. *At Lexington, on their way to Concord, the British drove off some local militia. This spirited painting gives an excellent impression of the action from the American side.*

Left. *This view of the Battle of Concord shows the British column under heavy fire from the flanks,*

Right. *A contemporary print shows the Battle of Bunker Hill and the burning of Charlestown.*

He immediately set about the task of forming an efficient army from one which had been depleted and demoralized by several defeats. In contrast to the Marquis de Lafayette, who had joined the American cause out of youthful enthusiasm and in order to serve France at the same time, Steuben completely broke with his past. He had decided to become a free American and fight for the liberty of his newly adopted country.

During the severe winter of 1778–79, he wrote his famous *Regulations for the Order and Discipline of the Troops of the United States*. Comprising 25 chapters, the manual contained the rules for exercises, field service order, general service and administrative regulations. He wrote it virtually off the top of his head, for books and other sources were hardly available at Valley Forge. In essence the product was based on his memory of the Prussian Infantry Field Manual, whose author had been Frederick the Great. The Potsdam example, though not the spirit, was the foundation of the subsequent field exercises of the American army. Of course, the manual first required approval by the Continental Congress, which it gave to the 'Blue Book,' as it was called, on 29 March 1779. For the duration of the war, next to the Bible it was the most important book for the American soldier. Thus, in a very curious way the ideas of Frederick William I, Prince Leopold of Anhalt-Dessau and Frederick the Great had made their way to the New World. To this day, if one

wants still to see truly Prussian infantry drill, one has only to visit either East Germany or West Point.

The British, overestimating their own position, left the Americans sufficient time to reorganize themselves. Steuben created a training establishment, which drilled and trained militia soldiers at considerable speed but with great thoroughness, though complaints by the men, who were quite unaccustomed to Steuben's often draconian measures, were frequent. He first established a teaching and training company, which represented the cadre force. When they drilled in public, spectators came from far and wide to see, for it was a new and strange phenomenon to see American soldiers perform exercises and maneuvers just as the Prussian army had conducted them during the Seven Years' War. The impressions left on the observers were mixed: the majority saw in them the means by which, ultimately, the British would be defeated; others voiced their concern over whether a military establishment of this kind could not become a danger to the freedom of the new republic. However, since the new republic had to deal with its external enemies first, they dismissed those doubts, for the time being at least.

Before the beginning of each exercise, Steuben inspected his men with great care, being fairly liberal with admonishments and reprimands, but also praise where praise was due. The

TEUCRO DUCE NIL DESPERANDOM.

First Battalion of PENNSYLVANIA LOYALISTS,
commanded by His Excellency Sir WILLIAM
HOWE, K. B.

ALL INTREPID ABLE-BODIED

HEROES.

WHO are willing to ferve His MAJESTY KING
GEORGE the Third, in Defence of their
Country, Laws and Conftitution, againft the arbitrary
Ufurpations of a tyrannical Congrefs, have now not
only an Opportunity of manifefting their Spirit, by
affifting in reducing to Obedience their too-long de-
luded Countrymen, but alfo of acquiring the polite
Accomplifhments of a Soldier, by ferving only two
Years, or during the prefent Rebellion in America.

Such fpirited Fellows, who are willing to engage,
will be rewarded at the End of the War, befides their
Laurels, with 50 Acres of Land, where every gallant
Hero may retire, and enjoy his Bottle and Lafs.

Each Volunteer will receive as a Bounty, FIVE
DOLLARS, befides Arms, Cloathing and Accoutre-
ments, and every other Requifite proper to accommodate a Gentleman Soldier, by applying to Lieutenant
Colonel ALLEN, or at Captain KEARNY's Rendezvous, at PATRICK TONRY'S, three Doors above
Market-ftreet, in Second-ftreet.

Far left. *A poster seeking recruits for the newly formed United States Army.*

Left. *This recruiting poster sought recruits for a loyalist unit.*

Above. *A bronze medal depicting Washington's abortive attack on the British headquarters at Germantown.*

Below. *Washington and some of his senior officers at Valley Forge.*

officers were his most willing and dedicated pupils, as were the noncommissioned officers, whom he always questioned in great detail when on parade about the condition of their men. Also he found enough time to keep in close touch even with the common soldier, who in Steuben always found an ear willing to listen to his difficulties and complaints; he was always ready to help and intervene on behalf of the individual soldier wherever this was possible. This cadre force, once brought into proper shape, then provided the model for the rest of the forces. In that way Steuben speedily supplied Washington with the kind of army he really needed.

But of course, one of the problems which even Steuben could not overcome was that the Americans possessed no military tradition in the European sense of the term. In a letter to a friend he wrote: 'But, my dearest General, you must not believe that in our army the Prussian elementary school, war training, tactics and discipline have been introduced by me. If I had tried to do that I would have been stoned to death; it is something which under the prevailing conditions I simply could not have accomplished. . . . In the first instance much is lacking in this people which is remotely comparable with the warlike spirit of the Prussians, Austrians and French. To your own soldiers you simply order do this and he does it. To my soldiers I have first to explain: this and that are the reasons why you should this and that, only then will they do it. Your army has already existed for over a century; mine for a day. My officers and noncommissioned officers were as good recruits as were my soldiers. My army renewed itself after every campaign . . . in short I had to train everything, I had to supply everything, together with my aides and deputies. All of them were first shaped by my

Far left. *Jean Baptiste Donatien de Vimeur, Comte de Rochambeau was sent, by the French government with 6000 men to support the American cause. This aid proved to be most effective at Yorktown in 1781.*

Below left. *Despite their primitive uniforms, these American soldiers have already been transformed into an efficient fighting force by the efforts of Steuben.*

Right. *American troops enter one of Cornwallis' redoubts at Yorktown, October 1781.*

Below right. *American soldiers of 1781. On the right a lieutenant wears the buff facings of troops from New York and New Jersey. An artillery private stands to his left.*

very own hand. . . . Now judge for yourself whether it was possible for me to occupy myself excessively with formal rifle drill and military parades. Against my original intention and against my better judgment I was forced to start much from the end rather than from the beginning. After all that you will surely admit that my task has not been an easy one. . .'

In spite of the underestimation of his troops expressed in his letter, Steuben's success was nevertheless surprising considering the innate dislike of the American soldier for arms drill. Another specifically Prussian element which Steuben introduced was the relative silence with which every maneuver and action, from loading the rifle to advancing, was carried out. Generals and staff officers were admonished not to shout, or to occupy themselves with minor details which could be delegated to subordinates. He instilled inner discipline into the army, and gradually it began to function like a smoothly oiled piece of machinery. It could carry out all forms of combat in closed formation, became a master in the closely coordinated salvo, as well as in dissolving from a closed formation into small individual units which, protected by what cover the country-side afforded, could hold off the enemy and, upon order, immediately reassemble into the original formation. And they learned how to attack *en masse* with bayonets fixed and levelled.

Obviously, the perfection which Steuben aimed for could never be achieved in the short time available to him. Next to the regular battalions fought the untrained musketeers as *tirailleurs*, but they could fall back on the former for protection if necessary. Indeed, the combination of closed combat with *tirailleur* tactics was one of the factors that resulted in victory over the British troops. Steuben therefore placed great emphasis on training the light infantry and expanding its numbers. He recognized that Prussian regulations and drill could not be transferred lock, stock and barrel to the American continent – not only was the geographical environment different but, as already

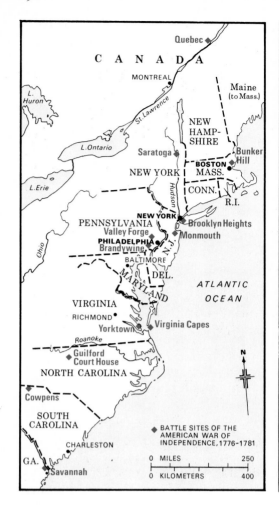

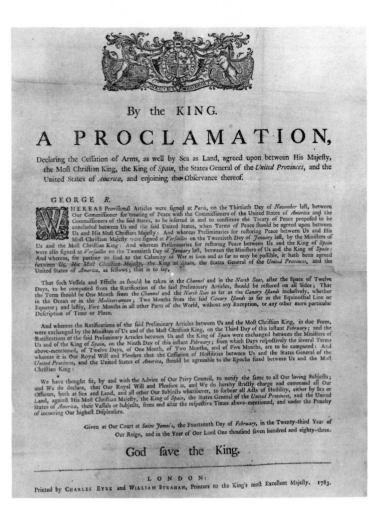

By the KING.

A PROCLAMATION,

Declaring the Cessation of Arms, as well by Sea as Land, agreed upon between His Majesty, the Most Christian King, the King of Spain, the States General of the *United Provinces*, and the United States of *America*, and enjoining the Observance thereof.

GEORGE R.

WHEREAS Provisional Articles were signed at *Paris*, on the Thirtieth Day of *November* last, between Our Commissioner for treating of Peace with the Commissioners of the United States of *America* and the Commissioners of the said States, to be inserted in and to constitute the Treaty of Peace proposed to be concluded between Us and the said United States, when Terms of Peace should be agreed upon between Us and His Most Christian Majesty; And whereas Preliminaries for restoring Peace between Us and His Most Christian Majesty were signed at *Versailles* on the Twentieth Day of *January* last, by the Ministers of Us and the Most Christian King: And whereas Preliminaries for restoring Peace between Us and the King of *Spain* were also signed at *Versailles* on the Twentieth Day of *January* last, between the Ministers of Us and the King of *Spain*: And whereas, for putting an End to the Calamity of War as soon and as far as may be possible, it hath been agreed between Us, His Most Christian Majesty, the King of *Spain*, the States General of the *United Provinces*, and the United States of *America*, as follows; that is to say,

That such Vessels and Effects as should be taken in the *Channel* and in the *North Seas*, after the Space of Twelve Days, to be computed from the Ratification of the said Preliminary Articles, should be restored on all Sides; That the Term should be One Month from the *Channel* and the *North Seas* as far as the *Canary Islands* inclusively, whether in the Ocean or in the *Mediterranean*; Two Months from the said *Canary Islands* as far as the Equinoctial Line or Equator; and lastly, Five Months in all other Parts of the World, without any Exception, or any other more particular Description of Time or Place.

And whereas the Ratifications of the said Preliminary Articles between Us and the Most Christian King, in due Form, were exchanged by the Ministers of Us and of the Most Christian King, on the Third Day of this instant *February*; and the Ratifications of the said Preliminary Articles between Us and the King of *Spain* were exchanged between the Ministers of Us and of the King of *Spain*, on the Ninth Day of this instant *February*; from which Days respectively the several Terms above-mentioned, of Twelve Days, of One Month, of Two Months, and of Five Months, are to be computed: And whereas it is Our Royal Will and Pleasure that the Cessation of Hostilities between Us and the States General of the *United Provinces*, and the United States of *America*, should be agreeable to the Epocha fixed between Us and the Most Christian King:

We have thought fit, by and with the Advice of Our Privy Council, to notify the same to all Our loving Subjects; and We do declare, that Our Royal Will and Pleasure is, and We do hereby strictly charge and command all Our Officers, both at Sea and Land, and all other Our Subjects whatsoever, to forbear all Acts of Hostility, either by Sea or Land, against His Most Christian Majesty, the King of *Spain*, the States General of the *United Provinces*, and the United States of *America*, their Vassals or Subjects, from and after the respective Times above-mentioned, and under the Penalty of incurring Our highest Displeasure.

Given at Our Court at *Saint James's*, the Fourteenth Day of *February*, in the Twenty-third Year of Our Reign, and in the Year of Our Lord One thousand seven hundred and eighty-three.

God save the King.

LONDON:

Printed by CHARLES EYRE and WILLIAM STRAHAN, Printers to the King's most Excellent Majesty. 1783.

Above. *A proclamation announcing the end of the war.*

Above far left. *General Tadeusz Kosciuszko, 1746–1817, a Polish soldier of fortune whose knowledge of fortification and military engineering was of great value to Washington.*

Left. *The surrender of Cornwallis at Yorktown, October 1781 (contemporary French print).*

mentioned, so were the attitudes of the American soldiers. A well-trained light infantry could exploit all the advantages which a bush war had to offer, while the linear tactics of the regular army could be employed wherever territory and other conditions allowed it. The light infantry did not fight statically, it conducted a war of continuous movement and its rules were adapted to the prevailing conditions. Increasingly Steuben transferred the best of his soldiers to the light infantry battalions. The wide American spaces favored operations conducted by independently acting formations. They were given a specific task; how to accomplish it was up to them. From Steuben's point of view, this represented a clear break with his own military background. He simply adapted himself to the new environment. Long before the armies of the French Revolution introduced such tactics, Washington's army already practiced them. Steuben combined two infantry brigades, each comprising two regiments, with a light battalion, two squadrons of cavalry and two companies of artillery, into a division. As the principle of total war made its appearance in the American Civil War, so the new kind of warfare which displaced that of the *ancien régime* was first practiced, not in Europe, but in North America.

It can hardly be said that Steuben's personality and innovations were received with undivided approval. As far as his personality was concerned, he was too much a Prussian and too impulsive to be easily accepted, and he found resistance, particularly among members of the Continental Congress, far removed from the firing line. Also he did not want to function forever as the educator and trainer of the army. He aimed at a command in the field, and succeeded in becoming Washington's chief of staff. His operational plans provide ample evidence that he estimated correctly the strategic difficulties of conducting a war against the superior British forces. Although he had forged an efficient army, its actual strength was by no means sufficient to accomplish bold, decisive strokes. In the autumn of 1781 he received the much-desired independent field command at Yorktown, where Lord Cornwallis was besieged with the bulk of the British main army. As the only officer with experience in dealing with fortifications, Steuben, now a divisional commander, directed the practical and engineering aspects of the siege with such success that, on 19 October 1781, Cornwallis and his troops capitulated.

The fall of Yorktown broke London's determination to continue the war; less than two years later, in September 1783, Britain recognized the independence of its former 13 colonies with the Treaty of Versailles.

That the Americans could in the end achieve decisive military successes was also due partly to the support of the French navy and a French expeditionary corps under General Rochambeau. However, in any overall assessment of the reasons for the defeat of the British army – which largely consisted of Hessian mercenaries (of which one-third were killed, one-third were taken prisoners, and one-third deserted to the Americans and settled in the United States) – one fact is certain. The British army remained bound by the static forms of linear tactics; this applied particularly to the hired German formations. By contrast, Washington's soldiers adapted Prussian military rules to their specific environment. The most important factor, however, was that the war was not between two professional armies but that, as far as the Americans were concerned, it could be described as a 'people's war.' This, combined with other factors such as the geography of the country, was to ensure ultimate victory. From the point of view of military history, the American Revolution inaugurated the beginning of the end of the tactics and warfare of the *ancien régime*.

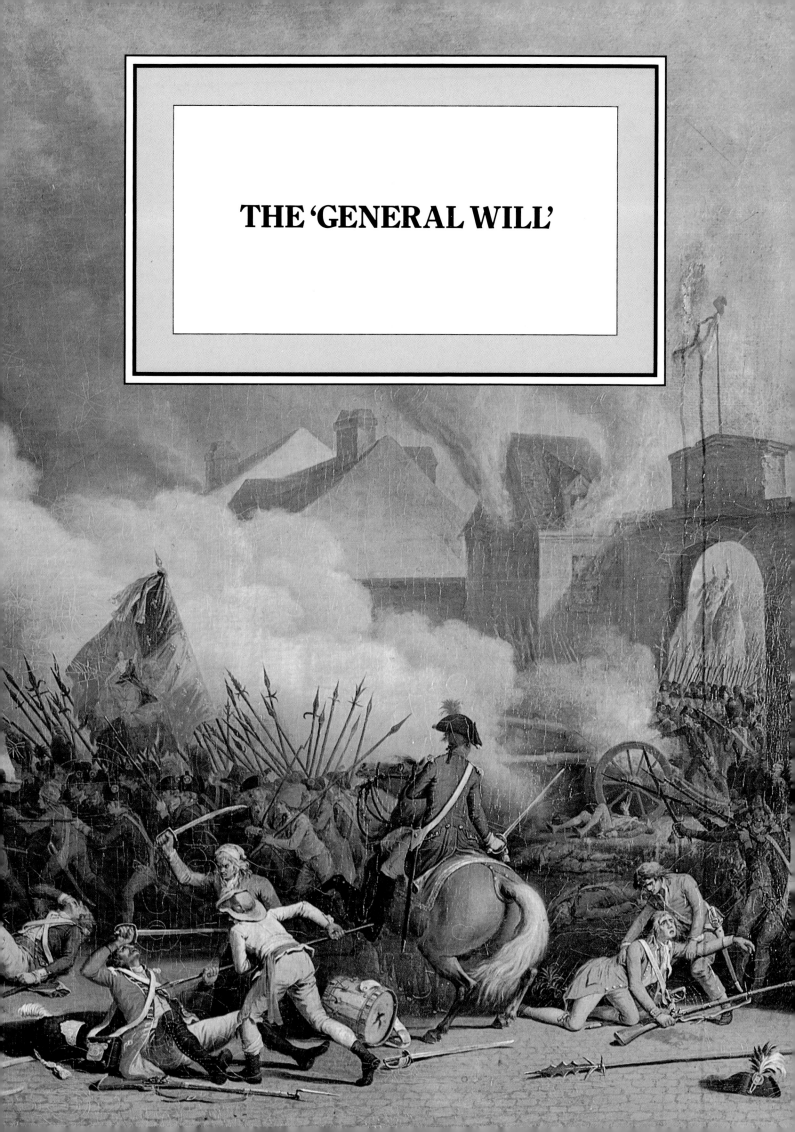

THE 'GENERAL WILL'

The Reformation had pulled God down from His high pedestal and turned Him into a subject of public discussion and controversy. It was almost inevitable that eventually those secular powers who claimed their office by divine right, especially the monarchy, should become subject to similar scrutiny. In other words, if there was no God, what point was there in having a king? John Locke with his two *Treatises on Government* did not initiate this process of debate, but he was perhaps the most widely influential advocate of it. He laid great emphasis upon the theory of contract; Locke really secularized Puritan theology – his ideas were not particularly original. According to him, the individual came and comes before society, and human dignity is innate and independent of society. Hence human dignity must not be injured or infringed – on the contrary, it must always be respected. Before forming himself into a community, man was in his natural condition, a condition in which he enjoyed complete freedom, and in which the ground he tilled was his very own. The family he founded was his domain. He owed obedience to only one law: Natural Law. That later on men formed themselves into societies does not do away with this Natural Law, he claimed, nor with those individual rights which man exercised from time immemorial. Men have formed themselves into societies out of their own free will, and they must therefore strictly control the government of that society, control it so strictly as to make any infringement of man's natural rights impossible. If a government should infringe these rights and duties, then it is on the way to becoming a tyranny. Resistance against tyranny is thus not only a right, it constitutes a major duty.

These ideas were part of the intellectual foundation of the American Revolution, and, together with the body of ideas which the Enlightenment had produced in Europe, they were also at the root of the French Revolution. This revolution was more than just a change in the form of state, it demolished royal absolutism and put into its place a bourgeois republic. The French Revolution was a consequence of economic changes which had brought material wealth and cultural influence to the upper bourgeoisie of the urban centers, resulting in greater political rights. It was fomented by a financial crisis into which France had been sinking steadily deeper for a long time, but was also the immediate consequence of widespread hunger. Shortages of bread caused deep unrest at the bottom of the social scale, while the immense national debt gave the people the opportunity to demand political concessions.

The decisive mistake made by the French monarchy was not to reform the state with the assistance of a bourgeoisie equipped with equal political rights, the Third Estate or *tiers état*. Thus the *ancien régime*, the absolutist feudal state with its barriers between the Estates, each of which had separate privileges, collapsed under the assault of its subjects. The monarchy became a constitutional one. With the Declaration of the Rights of Man on 26 August 1789, principles were proclaimed which drew the conclusion that the state was the responsibility of its citizens; the bourgeoisie would no longer be a mere tool for other purposes. In reality, however, the revolutionary state was, for the time being, the domain of the upper bourgeoisie, which alone possessed the vote. During the course of the Revolution, elements of inter-class struggle emerged, and the lower orders of society demanded equal rights. This period provides what is often seen as a classic example of the structure of revolutionary forces: their social composition, their motives, their ideology, psychology and organization. It is an example of the escalation of force: of how a radical minority, carried by widespread dissatisfaction, could bring about a political explosion.

Aware of the need for mass support, the leaders placed great emphasis upon creating a favorable public opinion. Samuel Adams' example of the Committees of Correspondence were

Previous spread. *The mob fights its way into the château of Versailles, 10 August 1792, overcoming the Swiss Guard.*

Above. *This 24-pounder is mounted on a special carriage to permit it to fire downwards.*

Left. *The opening of the Estates-General in 1789.*

Right. *A plate from an eighteenth-century English military manual showing cannon and their accessories.*

GUNNERY. PLATE CCXLIX.

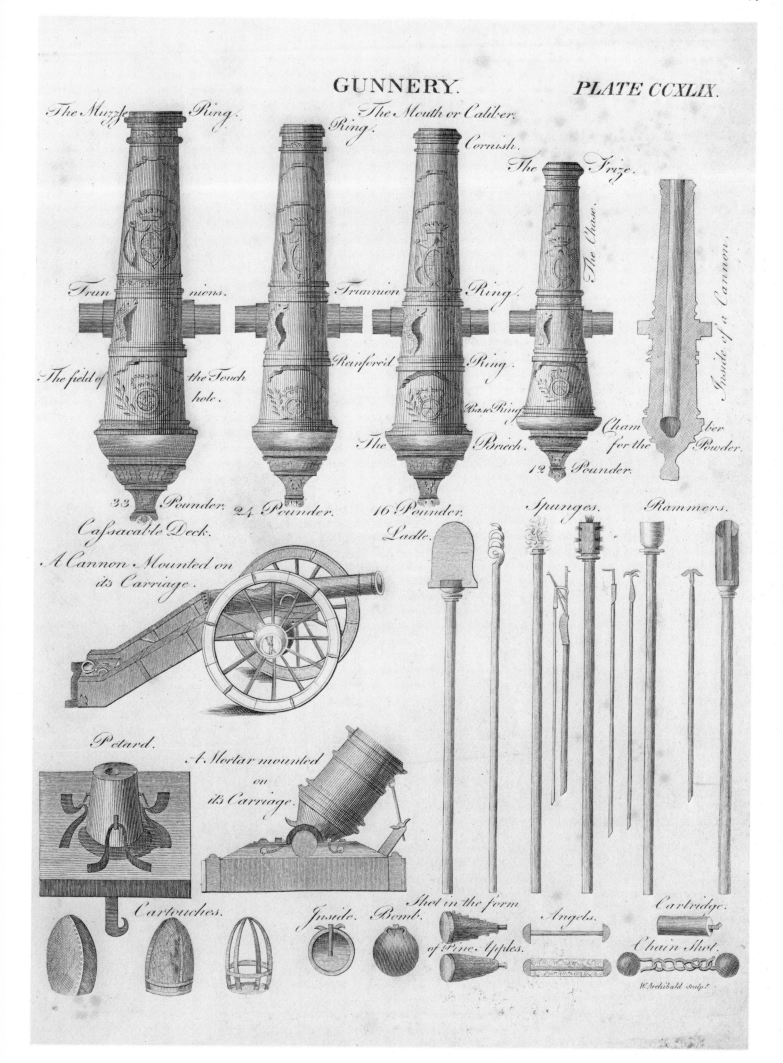

The Muzzle Ring. The Mouth or Caliber. Ring.

Cornish.

The Frize.

The Chase.

Trunnions. Trunnion Ring.

Reinforcd Ring.

Inside of a Cannon.

The field of the Touch hole.

Base Ring

The Breech.

Cham ber for the Powder.

33 Pounder. 24 Pounder. 16 Pounder. 12 Pounder.

Cassacable Deck. Ladle. Spunges. Rammers.

A Cannon Mounted on its Carriage.

Petard.

A Mortar mounted on its Carriage.

Cartouches. Inside. Bomb. Shot in the form of Pine Apples. Angels. Cartridge.

Chain Shot.

W. Archibald Sculp.

emulated, committees which emphasized aims of almost utopian proportions. In contrast to America, however, these committees gave rise to party factions. After the fall of the Bastille, the intellectuals of the Revolution created 'The Society of the Friends of the Constitution,' which covered the whole of France with its network of branches. Its core was the wealthy bourgeoisie, though its doors were opened to artisans, small merchants and traders. Under the leadership of Robespierre, Danton and Marat, the Jacobin Club became the driving force of republican agitation, promoting an 'educational' democracy, an imposed 'democracy' and the inevitable terror. The entire French population was politicized and, when in course of the Revolution France became involved in war, the military consequences were equally far-reaching; the national emergency produced a national mass army, a new type of soldier – the citizen in arms – and a new officer caste.

This first European mass army brought fundamental alterations to the methods of warfare and the principles of leadership, as well as the whole supply structure of armies. While the absolute monarchy had used its standing army in military conflicts to extend its power, the leaders of the French Revolution used force to impose its ideas and ideals upon others. Subsequently ideas, missionary zeal and propaganda determined the course of war as much as new weapons and column tactics or the system of requisition and the strategic principle of annihilation. Operations expanded over wide areas, using structured armies. The strict discipline characteristic of the Age of Absolutism made way for the excesses of a revolutionary *élan*, with all that this implied in terms of psychological incitement of the fanatical potential of the masses. The partisan, or guerrilla fighter, emerged to become one of the key figures in military history.

As we have had cause to observe before, nationalism was a key force. The Revolutionaries imbued their nation with the faith that its principles and its civilization would serve as models

Far left. *Maximilien Robespierre, 1758–94.*

Above. *Fighting in the streets of Paris in April 1789.*

Below. *A revolutionary poster proclaims Liberty, Equality and Fraternity.*

for the whole of mankind. The idealistic universalism of the intellectual currents of the French Revolution were thus transformed into an egotistical nationalism. Once the Republic had been achieved in France, territorial conquest was pursued in order to expand the ideological base of the revolution.

The development of the French Revolution can be described in terms of a geometric curve, at the start of which stood the Bourbon dynasty and at the end of which lay the Napoleonic Empire. The zenith of the curve marked Robespierre's dictatorship. Its beginning was the irreversible victory, the victory of the people over the monarchy and feudal rule. A bourgeois constitution was written whose supporters at first still shared their power with supporters of the *ancien régime*, and which at that stage did not grant equal rights to all citizens. Under the impact of the continuing economic crisis, the starving, the suffering and generally underprivileged rose against what they considered counterrevolutionary machinations. The Revolution reached its height in the form of mass hysteria directed against the church and the monarchy. The monarchy could hold the little ground left to it for a very short time. When conflict followed with the Habsburg and Hohenzollern dynas-

ties, who had combined against the Revolution, the democratic Left in France gained the upper hand and, with the majority support of the National Assembly, called for a crusade against the monarchs of Europe. The first alarming news of the defeats sustained by the Revolutionary armies precipitated the second revolution, which destroyed not only the monarchy but also the initiators of the first revolution; they became the victims of a totalitarian democracy.

In January 1793 after the king and queen were executed, the hour of the Jacobins had arrived. They united the nation by force in order to withstand the threat from outside and did so successfully. Internally, they proclaimed a new constitution of 1793, which was submitted for ratification to the people. Of 7,000,000 entitled to vote, however, only 2,000,000 chose to do so, and less than a third in Paris. Nevertheless, the executive power residing in Paris' Committee for Public Welfare, though nominally responsible to the National Convent or Assembly, pursued the cause, which meant action against its internal and external opponents. Internally those were the days of the guillotine: 'The guillotine should remain in action in France in permanency. Five million inhabitants in France are quite enough,'

Left. *The Marquis de Lafayette, 1757–1834, a liberal aristocrat who had served with distinction in the American War of Independence, was appointed commander of the Paris National Guard (contemporary French engraving).*

Below. *The philosopher Jean-Jacques Rousseau, 1712–78, whose* Social Contract *spoke of a 'general will' invested in the people.*

proclaimed Guffroy, the editor of one of the Jacobin gazettes. From that moment onward, the French Revolution lost the widespread sympathies which it had so far enjoyed abroad. The total number of victims of this phase of the Revolution is difficult to assess – at a conservative estimate, in 1792 there was a total of 1700 suicides, over 5000 'counterrevolutionaries' were drowned in the Loire River at Nantes, 2000 Royalists were butchered at Lyons and 900 in Toulon, and almost 14,000 were guillotined in Paris and other cities, having 'to sneeze into the sack.' These figures do not include tens of thousands butchered in the civil war. The Revolution ate its own children. Extremists began to express concern at the wave of murder.

In the spring of 1794 the Revolution entered the phase of 'total democracy,' upheld for the best part of three months by the personality of Robespierre. The shedding of blood was directed into more 'orderly channels.' Terror was now subjected to law in the service of public virtue. There is little doubt about Robespierre's personal integrity, and there can be no doubt that he was an absolutely committed fanatic. He was determined to establish the rule of 'reason' and Rousseau's 'General Will' and *Social Contract* by force; the revolutionary tribunals were everywhere, denunciation prospered and suspicion was cause enough to lose one's head.

Soon the Terror was being used in the interests of a total social revolution. Ideas which we would now describe as Communist made their appearance in the legislative consultations. The confiscation of church property had raised enough cash to finance the war. Peasants had gained proprietary rights over their soil, but the demand arose to bless the poor of land with the property of the enemies of the republic. This required the full support of the people and raised the alarm among the bourgeoisie. Once the foreign armies had been repelled, Robespierre stumbled over his own policies. On 28 July 1794 he too ended under the guillotine.

The forces of reaction gained ground again. Although for the time being government remained in the hands of the Revolutionary committees, the reservoir of fanatical tyrants seems to have been exhausted. When royalist reaction, however, began to set in no less brutally than the red terror of the Jacobins, the republican spirit re-established itself from 1798 in the form of the Directory. They set out to prevent any further misuse of democracy and stabilize internal conditions in France.

But the revolution had not yet run its full course. Royalists as well as members of the radical left planned their coups. The government vacillated between left- and right-wing options and opinions were divided, as they were in the National Assembly. Corruption prospered. When the threat from abroad was renewed, it seemed as though the fanatical energy of the Revolutionary army was on the decline. France was growing tired of upheaval; we may suppose that it longed for the strong man who would finally establish order.

Napoleon Bonaparte was that man and, with his *coup d'état* of 9 November 1799, he brought the chaos under control with a compromise between the old nobility and the new nobility (which he was yet to establish) and the *haute bourgeoisie*. Under his hands a strongly centralized government was established. That the First Consul became the Emperor bothered the French little; law and order had returned. The spirit of 1789, however, had not died.

For the military historian the question of particular interest is how the victory of the Revolution was brought about and how it was possible for such chaos to ensue. The old army failed almost totally, not simply because the majority of its numbers abandoned the king, but because its structure dissolved and discipline disappeared completely. Even during the pre-Revolutionary period, the French army was no longer the reliable instrument it once had been. The officer corps, however, was still the domain of the nobility, and venality in the purchase of commissions was not only widespread but almost customary – the crown needed the money. In fact, it needed the money so much that it appointed more officers than it actually required. Compared with the numerically stronger Prussian army of Frederick the Great with 80 generals, or the Austrian army with 350 generals, the French army had 1171 generals on the eve of the Revolution. The lower nobility was barred because it did not have the necessary funds for the purchase of a commission; it was represented in the army only as the lower charges, which led these ranks to oppose the monarchy.

In contrast, the noncommissioned officer corps consisted of able and experienced soldiers; many of them had participated in the American Revolution. Upon them rested the burden of the daily military duties, though they had no prospects of ever being rewarded. The bad example provided by the officer corps caused the NCOs to assume, and probably rightly so, that qualitatively they were its equal, if not even superior. Their influence upon the ranks was infinitely greater than that of the officers.

The common soldier, of course, was worst off – his pay was negligible and, to add to his grievances, the Minister of War, the Comte St Germain, introduced corporal punishment. Given the dissatisfaction among both NCOs and the rank and file, it is not surprising that they were highly receptive to revolutionary suggestions. Discontent was aggravated by divisions between the French generals and the decay of the principle of subordination. Colonels no longer always obeyed generals – hardly something that would encourage discipline in the lower ranks. The result, however, was that, at the outbreak of the Revolution, the French army was no longer an instrument upon which the king could rely unconditionally. The attitude of the army in the main was one of indifference or outright support for the insurgents. They joined the newly formed citizens' guard in large numbers; in Paris alone 6000 soldiers joined the ranks of the Revolutionaries.

The old French army largely dissolved with the Revolution. Many of its noble officers took to their heels after the storming of the Bastille, seeking refuge abroad, from where they conducted their counterrevolutionary agitation and propaganda. Therefore, only the National Assembly could reorganize the army. At first reform of the old army was attempted, but before 1792 the purpose of maintaining an army was held in doubt; it was considered more important to concentrate on the National Guards, who were founded by the National Assembly. The purchase of officers' patents was abolished – access was opened to all with talent – and the rate of pay for NCOs and guards was to be increased. All this, however, could not prevent the complete politicization of the military forces. In all regiments, radicals of various colors continued their agitation and created their Revolutionary committees. The members of the committees considered the orders the military formations received, debated them and decided whether they should be carried out or not; officers trying to enforce their orders risked their lives. National Guards and the remaining members of the regiments of the line fused. In the summer of 1790 mutinies broke out in several garrisons; the report about them submitted to the National Assembly culminated in the observation: that 'there was now no longer any power of the state which would be respected . . . the evil grows from day to day, it is not limited to certain individual formations who debate and decide what is in their interest, in Strasbourg seven regiments have formed a military

congress, each represented by three deputies. Representatives of France, hurry in order to counteract the torrent of military insurrection with your entire strength, do not wait till new storms make it even more powerful breaking the strongest of dams.' The military committee tried to introduce counter-measures but they were too weak to bring about a consolidation of the army. On the contrary, at Nancy, where three regiments of the old army were still stationed, they ill-treated their officers and plundered the regimental funds; they immediately frater-nized with the National Guards who had been dispatched to establish order. The leader of the mutiny, however, was ar-rested, tried and sentenced to serve as a galley slave. This caused such an outcry from the radicals that the sentence had to be reversed; the man was released and, upon his arrival in Paris on 9 April 1792, the city provided him with a triumphal entry.

Louis XVI's attempt to escape demonstrated dramatically that there were no more troops in any number loyal to the king; it also cost him his head the following year. Given the reaction of the foreign powers, France confronted them with what re-mained of a military force. It was under the command of gen-erals who could never be sure of their support in the National Assembly; any military misfortune might cost them their lives.

At the outbreak of Revolution few thought of war – indeed, the National Assembly publicly promised never to use a French army against the liberty of another nation. It decreed the setting up of a regular army consisting of volunteers, if necessary reinforced by the militia, for the protection of *la patrie*. The political interest in forming a new army concentrated on the National Guard, as a democratically organized force. It repre-

Above. *In 1798 a French army led by General Humbert unsuccessfully invaded Ireland.*
Above left. *Queen Marie Antoinette, 1755–93, executed during the Reign of Terror.*

Left. *The Tennis Court Oath, 20 June 1789. When the chamber of the Third Estate was closed by Louis XVI, its members met in an indoor tennis court and declared that they formed a National Assembly, and would not disband until they had framed a constitution.*

sented the early constitutional phase of the Revolution, and the role it played exemplifies and reflects the political organization of the new France. It was divided in 83 regional *départements*, all roughly equal in size and population, with 574 subdistricts and 4730 cantons. Their representatives were elected by those entitled to a vote, in other words by the bourgeoisie. They were also to provide the National Guard. This limited recruitment of the National Guard from members of the bourgeoisie added fuel to an already explosive situation, since it emphasized the class divisions between those who owned property and those who did not. The more the Revolution turned to the left, the more strongly the radicals fought the National Guards, demanding a universal franchise and the general armament of the people as the safest means to take over power.

It would be too much to expect military efficiency from the National Guard, and members of the National Assembly expressed their concern about France's military safety. As a consequence 100,000 National Guard members were formed into volunteer battalions and integrated with the remnants of the old army. Volunteers, however, were hard to come by and the old soldiers resented the privileges which the National Guard enjoyed. In this highly confused situation, France declared war on Austria on 20 April 1792. The patriots believed that this would regenerate the Revolutionary *élan* and divert attention from internal difficulties. When Prussia joined Austria, France was totally unprepared for war. There were to be three French armies, but actually only 100,000 men could be mobilized. The *Marseillaise* had a catchy tune, but it could not make up for a trained army.

Lafayette was given an army command and General Rochambeau ordered to carry the main strike into Belgium toward a line between Brussels and Namur, where they confronted 40,000 Austrians and were beaten badly. Panic broke out among the Revolutionary forces, who made their way back to Lille. Officers who tried to control and rally them were

Volontaire partant pour les frontières, en Septembre 1792.

Allons Enfans de la Patrie,
Le jour de gloire est arrivé;
Contre nous de la Tyrannie
L'étendard sanglant est levé; &c...

killed. A number of hussar squadrons, including their commanders, also deserted and joined the enemy, among whom were small contingents of troops made up of French emigrants. Austria and Prussia now planned a march directly upon Paris.

The second revolutionary phase began in Paris under this threat. The Jacobins held the existing government responsible for the disaster; they executed the king and proclaimed the Republic. They were not impressed by the proclamation of Field Marshal the Duke of Brunswick that, should any harm come to the French king and queen, Paris would be subjected to severe punishment. Lafayette tried to save the king but most of his soldiers would not follow him. With a few supporters, however, he saved himself by crossing over to the allies. It was an action which broke the last barrier between Robespierre and the establishment of a regime of terror.

The military side of the second phase of the Revolution, however, was a different picture, one that demonstrated that Frenchmen were still able to expel the enemy from French soil. Volunteers then came forward, increasing the army by late September to 60,000 men, reinforced by many old and experienced former soldiers. On 19 September 1792 about 35,000 Prussian troops penetrated to the rear of the French forces who, with 50,000 men, held a well-secured position between the River Aisne and the marshland southwest of St Ménéhould facing west. When, on the morning of the 20th, Prussian vanguards had reached the foot of the Valmy Ridge in heavy rain, the Duke of Brunswick left them there totally inactive. He wanted to take no risks until the bulk of his army had arrived. The French General Kellerman exploited this delay to the full. His battalions, representing the left wing of the French forces, occupied the ridge near the village of Valmy and he positioned his artillery there. However, even after both French and Prussians had completed their battle formation by one o'clock, no real fighting had taken place. The battle was limited to artillery fire. The cannonade of Valmy achieved very little because of the wet ground. The French expected the Prussian attack and General Kellerman rode up and down his formations shouting '*Vive la nation!*' The soldiers responded by singing the *Marseillaise*.

The Duke, however, considering that the wet conditions would make an advance extremely difficult, decided that any attack would involve heavy losses and did nothing. Both sides shot about 20,000 rounds of artillery ammunition at each other. The Prussians lost 173 men, the French 300. When darkness fell, Kellerman withdrew from the ridge unhindered. The affair caused deep depression among the Prussians – the army of Rossbach had refrained from attacking the French revolutionary army! Among the French, who considered Valmy their victory, a feeling of elation and superiority prevailed.

In the spring of 1793 the war with Prussia and Austria was formally transformed into a war of the Empire against France. The Duke of Brunswick, who after Valmy had withdrawn, once again took the offensive and recaptured parts of the left bank of the Rhine, but, through lack of coordination in the planning of their operations, every one of the allied armies acted as it thought fit without consultation with the others. By the end of the year the French were again on the offensive. In 1794 the Duke of Brunswick was replaced by Field Marshal von Möllendorf, one of the veterans of Frederick the Great's army. However, the second Polish partition, a rising of the Poles in Prussia's Polish provinces in 1794, established different priorities for Prussia, and the Peace of Basle ended Prussia's participation in the war against the French at the time.

After Valmy the French Revolutionary army went on the

Left. *The Paris mob storms the Bastille, 14 July 1789.*

Far left. *This French print of 1792 shows a volunteer on his way to the frontier.*

Right. *Marshal François-Christophe Kellerman, Duke of Valmy, 1735–1820. The oldest of Napoleon's marshals, he made his military reputation at the Battle of Valmy in 1792, before Napoleon came to power.*

offensive, capturing Landau, Speyer, Mainz and Frankfurt-am-Main. In Belgium General Dumouriez defeated an Austrian corps on 6 November 1792, the first genuine battle which the Revolutionary army won. At that point the national and basically cosmopolitan spirit of the Revolution began to take on the characteristics of imperialist expansion, and occupied territories were annexed.

This policy alarmed Britain, which tried to raise a major coalition against France. In 1793 the allied armies were more successful in their operations, Belgium being reconquered, as were the cities along the Rhine. General Dumouriez suffered a severe defeat at the hands of the Austrians, his army left him and, like Lafayette, he had to find refuge among the enemy with 800 men.

The murderous battle at Fleurus, near Charleroi, decided the revolutionary war for France. The Austrians withdrew, the French followed on their heels and, by the end of 1794, they occupied the whole of the left bank of the Rhine again; they conquered Holland and defeated at the other end the Spaniards at San Sebastian. Only Britain and Austria were interested in continuing the war. After Prussia had made its peace with France, Austria followed in 1797 with the Treaty of Campo Formio. The counterrevolutionary war of the coalition had come to an end.

One can now step back and examine the changes the Revolution brought to the armed forces. The *levée en masse* was a notable innovation. Shortage of troops was still a general problem and on 20 February 1793 Robespierre decided to introduce mass compulsory service carried out by lot; the *levée en masse* was born. All able males between the ages of 18 and 40 were liable for military service, 200,000 men being required for the volunteer battalions, 100,000 for the regiments of the line.

The immediate impact was shattering. It gave the signal to a counterrevolutionary rising among the peasants of the western provinces – a republic which forced them into military service, more readily than the old monarchy had done, was to be fought to the death. The entire Vendée was in uproar, as was Brittany and the swamplands of Poitou. Lyons, Marseilles, Bordeaux, Toulouse, Nîmes, Grenoble, Limoges and Toulon rebelled against Paris. Civil war raged and the Jacobin dictatorship, supported by the *Sans-Culottes*, formed Revolutionary praetorian guards who moved into the rebellious areas, but it took a considerable period of time and even greater bloodletting before the rising was quelled.

Even in other parts of France where rebellion did not rear its head, eligible men left the villages and took to the woods. Of the 300,000 men required, 180,000 were recruited, the major proportion from France's eastern provinces.

The *levée en masse* was a slogan that, at the time, did not become reality; instead of being a decree ensuring national service for every able-bodied man, it became a means of raising urgent replacements for the army. It was not accompanied by patriotic fervor, and had to be enforced using the threat of the guillotine. Ultimately, by 1794, 1,200,000 men were raised, including the work forces for the armaments factories. A mass army such as this was to become a dangerous instrument in the hands of a man capable of using it. It also took society a further step toward the radicalization of warfare.

In France the *levée en masse* was modified after the death of Robespierre, and in 1798 it was decreed that every Frenchman from the age of 20 to 25 was compelled to do military service, with younger men having precedence over older ones. A precondition was a state of war, and Consul Bonaparte modified it in March 1800 with the introduction of the principle of replacements. Every conscript who did not wish to join the army had

Above far left. *Fighting in Flanders in 1795.*

Above. *This engraving, produced in 1818 when Waterloo was a recent memory, shows a heroic episode from the fighting in Flanders in 1792: a French hussar trooper captures a color single-handed.*

Left. *The Duke of York defeats a French force at Landrecies in 1793.*

to pay 2400 francs and provide a substitute who would serve on his behalf.

Thus the French Revolutionary army was composed of highly diverse forces. Firstly, there were about 100,000 men of the former Royal Army, soldiers and officers who drifted back into the army from about 1792 onward, then there were the volunteers of 1791 and 1792 and the conscripts from 1793 onward. The troops which repelled the first invasion belonged mainly to the first category. The core consisted of the artillery with its mainly bourgeois officers; they were wedded to the ideals of the Revolution and, together with the cavalry units created in 1792, formed the elite of the army. From the spring of 1793 they fought in five different operational theaters: on the Belgian frontier, in the Ardennes, along the Moselle and the Rhine, in the Alps, where they fought mainly Austrians and Sardinians, and in the western and eastern Pyrenees. The entire force comprised 11 armies of varying sizes, totalling about 800,000 men, of which 600,000 were used in actual combat. Another 150,000 men must be added to this, being the men the forces used to crush the rebels in the Vendée.

Initially the internal conditions of the army were deplorable. The volunteers of 1791 were full of enthusiasm. This soon wore off, however, and their usefulness became increasingly variable. In their place came men motivated rather less by idealism and more by the prospect of booty; confronted by the enemy, a few volleys were enough to scatter them in all directions. Yet they received more pay than the old soldiers, a source of widespread friction. Service in the volunteers was limited to 12 months, and there were battalions with 120 men and companies with only nine. France therefore owed its salvation in 1793 not to her army, but to the indecisiveness and disunity of her enemies. The provision of personal equipment was poor, many soldiers dressed in rags, and many had no shoes, let alone overcoats: '. . . whole battalions were without trousers, just covered with a cloak held together by pins; when the 7th Paris Battalion marched past Danton in this condition, he remarked, "Now those are real *Sans-culottes!*" . . .' complained one female member at the National Convention.

The new Minister of War, Bouchotte, a radical, insisted that the traditional military hierarchy must never be established again. His suspicions were directed against the officers, and he fanned the embers of growing suspicion between men and officers into full flame. The bourgeoisie was not to be transformed into soldiers, but all soldiers into militant *Sans-Culottes*. The Convention appointed commisars to serve with the officers and keep an eye on them. More often than not, when a commander had ordered punishment for an offense against military discipline, the commissar annulled it under pressure from the men. Officers considered unreliable were arrested upon the merest suspicion. Commissar Billaud, during his mission to the northern army, arrested six generals on one day, and Commissar Ronsin four generals and 17 staff officers. Most of them came under the guillotine. Hardly anyone was prepared to assume command for fear of suffering the fate of his predecessor.

At the top level of command, conditions were equally desperate. The appointment of a general was a political matter, and a captain of the dragoons became Commander of the Rhine army. The goldsmith journeyman Rossignol became Divisional Commander after he had denounced his predecessor General Biron and sent him to the guillotine. The pamphleteer Ronsin climbed the ladder from captain to general in four days – he was a friend of Bouchotte. On the other hand, the young major of the artillery, Bonaparte, who was chiefly responsible for the conquest of Toulon, was made a brigadier general. The customs officer Hanriot, commander of the National Guard of Paris in 1793, was a renowned drunkard. In 1794 he ended his career in a drunken stupor by being thrown from his horse and landing on a garbage heap. Hardly had a man joined the army than he demanded promotion; it seemed that everyone wanted to order, none to obey. The Convention noted with dismay that the army had in excess of 20,000 officers. The army had been thoroughly democratized.

In 1791 foreigners who had served in the old French army and who did not wish to return home were all naturalized; they too developed into a willful instrument of terror and formed bands of thieves and robbers. Ordered to collect taxes, they often collected but pocketed the money themselves.

Right. *Karl Wilhelm Ferdinand, Duke of Brunswick, 1735–1806.*

Below. *The heights of Valmy, 20 September 1792.*

With the end of the Terror in France in late July 1794 after the fall of Robespierre, conditions began to stabilize again in the army. The revolutionary rabble developed into a professional army again, who fought not for the dynasty, but first for the defense and then for the expansion of France. The idea of liberty, equality and fraternity released immense emotional powers. 'It is a pleasure to see, how seriously the soldiers perform their duties. . . . We have a new disciplinary manual which we have sworn to obey point by point. It is strict, but the men know that as long as they stay on the path of honor they have nothing to fear,' wrote one volunteer.

But it was a will to order affairs that saved France, and the country owed much to the enormous efforts of one man, the former engineer Captain Lazare Carnot (1753–1823). Called to head the department of defense within the Committee of Public Welfare, he immediately established a central office for army administration, supervised troop recruitment, and gave the *levée en masse* a practical shape. He was not concerned about the political opinions of his subordinates as long as they followed his instructions. He was also incorruptible, and after every journey of inspection he handed back any surplus funds to the treasury. He had immense courage and publicly opposed Robespierre. The radicals would have preferred to see him under the guillotine had they had someone else to provide the organization for a war. Carnot supported the Terror as long as it served the principle of victory against the external enemy. The citizen in arms was his aim, the effective fusion of the old regiments of the line with the volunteers in order 'to turn every Frenchman into a soldier.'

The army's structure was in need of reform. He began work

Left. *A French* tirailleur *of 1805.*

Below. *This contemporary French engraving shows the recapture of Toulon by the Revolutionary forces in December 1793.*

Above. *Lazare Carnot, 1753–1823, a regular engineer officer who cobbled together the Revolutionary armies in 1793–34.*

A new military school, the *École de Mars*, was established in which 1800 sons of *Sans-Culottes* received their training as future officers. It was closed, however, with the demise of the Jacobins. When Robespierre was executed, Carnot remained and, in 1794, founded the *École Polytechnique* for the training of artillery and engineer officers. Nine years later followed the *École Spéciale Militaire*, the future St Cyr. In time Carnot sorted out the wheat from the chaff, and Europe would soon be familiar with the names of Marceau, Kléber, Moreau, Bernadotte and Ney, to name but a few of the future eminent commanders.

Carnot completely reorganized France's arms manufacture and had it working at full capacity. Tailors and shoemakers worked day and night to provide uniforms and footwear for the army. Within months he accomplished a task which normally would have taken years. However, on the whole, technical advances were few. The Chappe brothers had invented optical telegraphy in 1792 with the aid of large mirrors, and by August 1794 the first line of optical telegraphs had been built between Paris and Lille consisting of 22 stations, relaying 60 signals per minute. In the following years the network was extended all over France, but it came fully into its own only during Napoleon's campaigns. The hot-air balloon, fixed to the ground by ropes, did valuable service at Maubeuge and Charleroi, but, with the advent of Napoleonic warfare and its rapid movement, subsequently fell into disuse.

In 1797 Carnot opposed a *coup d'état* from the left and had to escape abroad, but was called back later by Napoleon, who needed an able minister of war. But he was not prepared to come until after the disastrous Battle of Leipzig in 1813, when he realized that the country needed him again. One important

in late 1793. He dissolved the most recently recruited troops, and then reorganized them through his personal selection of their officers and NCOs, to establish first a reliable core. Appointments were to be made according to talent as well as on length of service, and the election of officers and NCOs was abolished. '*Carrière ouverte aux talents*' (Career open to talent) was his motto. He appointed many new army commanders, and Napoleon had him to thank for his command over the army operating in Italy. The right of volunteers to terminate their service after 12 months was abolished, and desertion was punished by death. Officers had to share tents with their men and received the same food supplies.

Below. *On 3 March 1795 an Austrian force under the Prince of Saxe-Coburg routed a French army at Aix-la-Chapelle.*

consequence of the military revolution was general reorganization. The vast army created by conscription necessitated a new type of structure and organization, enabling simpler and more mobile forms of combat. The old army had been tied to linear tactics – was a fairly rigid body. Now it was a matter of structuring the army into individual formations, each consisting of infantry, cavalry and artillery, capable of operating independently from one another as well as jointly. Greater mobility and cooperation between the three main branches was the objective. The idea was not new, as it harked back to the Romans. Prince Moritz of Saxony had experimented with it, and other writers had put forward the idea of dividing the army into divisions in order to increase mobility. However, it was only during the course of the French revolutionary wars that the ideas were put into practice.

The half-brigades had been the first step, though Napoleon

Left. *A trooper of the Lambeth Cavalry, one of the many volunteer units raised to combat the menace of French invasion (engraving by Thomas Rowlandson).*

Above right. *A British long 6-pounder field gun crossing a ditch (plate from William Congreve's notebook).*

Left. *The young Bonaparte at the Battle of Arcola, November 1796.*

Right. *George III and the Prince of Wales at a review, 1799.*

changed them back into regiments. The half-brigade was the work of Carnot in 1793 – it was formed from one battalion of the line and two battalions of volunteers. Early in 1794 the Revolutionary army consisted of 250 half-brigades, of which 40 were light infantry deployed as *tirailleurs*. The infantry was armed as it had been throughout most of the eighteenth century, and its rate of fire was two rounds per minute. The cavalry maintained its old formations – 29 regiments of heavy cavalry, 20 regiments of dragoons, 23 regiments of chausseurs and 11 regiments of hussars – all in all about 500 squadrons of 140 men each. The artillery was divided into companies and attached to the infantry, while heavy artillery was maintained as a separate unit.

Carnot established the division, consisting of four half-brigades. Each brigade was commanded by a general and, according to need, each half-brigade or brigade could operate

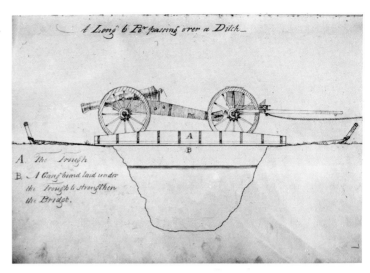

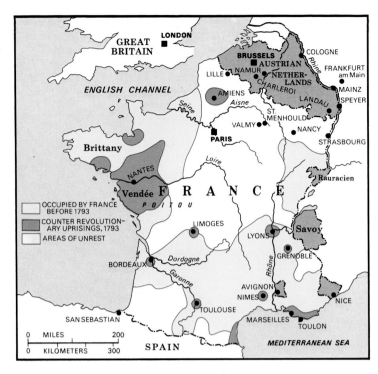

OCCUPIED BY FRANCE BEFORE 1793

COUNTER REVOLUTIONARY UPRISINGS, 1793

AREAS OF UNREST

into specific departments. One of its main functions was to conduct the operation of the army, organizing billets on the march, security and so on. It was also to obtain military intelligence and to evaluate it, organize transportation and the supply of arms and materials, as well as food, and organize the engineering branch for sieges and fortress operations. Each branch coordinated its results and submitted them to the army commander, who, with the aid of the Chief of Staff, then drafted a basic concept for the operations to be conducted. Napoleon's staff in Italy in 1796–97 comprised five personal adjutants, 26 general staff officers, including their aides, three military administrators and a commissioner responsible for civil affairs. Corps staffs amounted to between 10 and 18 officers.

New tactics also appeared on the scene. Reference has already been made to the *tirailleur* tactics, but they could never be decisive except in conjunction with larger formations. Linear tactics always involved the risk of the line, three or four deep, being broken through. The Chevalier de Folard, whose influence on Frederick the Great has already been mentioned, was one of the first to question whether a column on the march, instead of being formed up into a line of battle, could not become an offensive formation itself. If the *colonne d'attaque* of 760 men attacked in a formation 32 men deep, it was bound to break through any linear formation and then roll up its flanks. In the French Revolutionary army, however, the column tactic developed more out of necessity than design. Masses of citizen soldiers could not be trained quickly enough to master linear tactics, so they attacked in bulk, or in what was to become the column. These new tactics were applied for the first time at the Battle of Jemappes, when General Dumouriez stormed the Austrian entrenchments, though it was more a horde of infantry than a disciplined column. Improvements, however, were already noticeable in 1793 in the Netherlands, Flanders and among the Moselle and Rhine armies. The terrain was more favorable to the column tactics of the French, who were surprised by their speed and penetration. *Tirailleurs* were used to initiate the battle, testing the enemy's nerve, until the column went in to attack, massively supported by artillery fire and the cavalry.

The column was essentially a formation of infantry units one behind another, each 50 yards wide and 12 deep and divided from the next unit by a gap of 50 yards. Naturally, there were numerous variations to this basic plan, depending on the topographical conditions, and the traditional battleground, the plain, became less significant. The column was quicker and more mobile than previous infantry formations and could be changed and adapted to the situation. The old fear of gaps between the formations disappeared, as they could be covered by the faculty of greater maneuverability and by *tirailleurs* or cavalry. Moreover, upon command they could immediately change

separately. It took some time for this transformation into divisions to be achieved; once established, each division contained infantry, cavalry and artillery. Napoleon let his divisions operate separately until the moment had come to regroup them and bring about a decisive battle. He also combined divisions into independently operating army corps. Again this took time, and was achieved while Napoleon prepared for the invasion of England, during which he carried out operations with army corps until the system worked. To each army corps belonged three to four cavalry regiments, each of four squadrons. Beside the light artillery, army corps were also equipped with two heavy batteries of eight guns each, engineers, sappers and a train battalion.

That part of the cavalry which had not been detached to the brigades and divisions maintained its own organization. It was still an arm of great tactical significance as an instrument of reconnaissance and pursuit, and for rapid penetration in battle. Dragoons and cuirassiers were combined into subdivisions supported by four pieces of light artillery. The strength of a subdivision consisted of 2500 horsemen.

The headquarters of the army of the *levée en masse* was at first in a state of confusion into which only Carnot had managed to bring order. This also applied to the command structure of the individual armies. In such a large army a commander could not concern himself with each and every detail as could be done in a small army, the size of Frederick the Great's; he had to delegate tasks to other officers trained in specific military skills. What emerged was a general staff strictly rationalized and subdivided

Left. On 6 November 1792 Dumouriez drove the Archduke Albrecht's Austrians from a strong position on the heights above Jemappes.

Right. General Jean-Victor Moreau, 1763–1813. A talented general who lacked political acumen.

Far right. Marshal Jean-Baptiste-Jules Bernadotte, 1763–1844, Prince of Pontecorvo, left Napoleon's service to reign as Charles XIV of Sweden.

Above. *The bravest of the brave: Marshal Ney, Duke of Elchingen and Prince of the Moscowa, 1769–1815.*

Above. *General Jean-Baptiste Kléber, 1753–1800. A brilliant general, he was assassinated in Egypt in 1800.*

Left. *One of Rowlandson's prints from a series showing infantry drill.*

Below left. *A Gilray cartoon pokes fun at privilege and influence in the army.*

Above. *A recruiting sergeant of the 33rd Regiment.*

Right. *Bonaparte, a former artillery officer, laying a gun with his own hand at the Battle of Lodi, 10 May 1796.*

Top right. *A humorous print shows the antics of volunteer units.*

Below. *Another print from Rowlandson's infantry series shows a private of the Lambeth Volunteers.*

direction, something which previously could be achieved only by taking recourse to the oblique order of battle.

In actual battle the first column would attack, spread out if necessary and subsequently re-form, while the second column would remain behind in column formation until it was called into action. When facing an enemy attack, the column remained in a closed formation as a tactical body or square to repel it by concentrated fire.

From an auxiliary weapon, the artillery developed into a fully fledged and highly respected arm. The guns had been much improved: cannons and howitzers were made lighter and more mobile, the barrels were shortened, iron axles introduced, and the charge reduced to a third of the weight of the missile. The bulk were eight and 12 pounders and the siege guns 16 and 24 pounders. Ammunition consisted of solid shot and canister. The engineers, who in the French Army had at first served together with the artillery, were established as a separate corps, divided into mining companies and sappers. Despite genuine improvements ballistic efficiency still had its limitations. As column tactics developed, the divisional artillery was divided

and detached to the infantry wings of the second column, which were within range of the enemy. As the attack advanced so did the artillery, always trying to get close enough to subject the enemy to intensive canister fire. The artillery fired simultaneously to maximize surprise and impact.

The new infantry and artillery tactics were bound to affect the cavalry as well; if they did not take care they could come into the firing line of their own *tirailleurs*, and a well-ordered and entrenched enemy position provided few opportunities for a cavalry attack. Success could only be achieved by surrounding the enemy while at the same time subjecting him to intense artillery fire. Individual attacks by small formations were pointless; only the massive use of cavalry could achieve success. During the age of linear tactics, the cavalry was an integral part of the battle order, securing the vulnerable flanks of the infantry; now, column tactics combined with operations taking place over much wider areas provided new opportunities for the cavalry. It gained greater flexibility and could easily adjust to the changing tactical situation. It could directly support the infantry columns as well as operate independently.

Left. *A romantic print shows an officer taking leave of his wife and child before going overseas.*

Right. *A sharp fight between a Franco-Dutch and a Russo-British force in Holland in September 1799.*

Below. *British and Russian troops are evacuated from Holland, November 1799.*

THE NEW AGE: NAPOLEON

Napoleon was the master of the column tactic and he handled it with virtuosity, although some of his generals did not always fully understand it, especially when it concerned its application in large formations. He abolished the half-brigades and reintroduced the regiment, which now, in contrast to the eighteenth century, was an operational and not an administrative unit. Until his reforms of 1808, his infantry regiments moved into the field with two battalions, while the third remained behind as a depot for recruits. The normal formation of a brigade ready for attack consisted of the first two battalions of the first and second regiments positioned to the left and right of the flanks of the divisional column. The divisions of Soult and Bernadotte marched into the Battle of Austerlitz in Moravia in this order on 2 December 1805, defeating the Austrian Army.

When a fifth regiment was available, it initiated the attack by fighting as *tirailleurs*, but, as the attack of the main army progressed, it withdrew to the rear as reserve. Behind it stood divisions in battalion columns divided into three column formations. At the Battle of Borodino on 7 September 1812, the army corps under Marshal Ney attacked in the following basic form: two battalions in the center deployed with a battalion column on each wing, followed by four battalions in column formation as reserve. From 1808 the regiments comprised only four field battalions, each battalion having four infantry companies. These companies had double the strength to those of the Revolutionary army of 1791 and did not change column tactics.

In the Battle of Wagram on 5–6 July 1809, Napoleon preceded his attack with a cannonade from 100 pieces of artillery and then, for the first time, combined 20 battalions into one mass column, eight following one another and six on each flank, a grand total of 20,000 men. It was a size, however, which transcended the possibilities inherent in column tactics; the sheer mass impeded mobility and increased the losses sustained by the defensive fire of the Austrians. Because of that relative immobility, Napoleon protected his flanks with cavalry, but his attacking infantry was decimated before the stage of close combat had been reached. This measure had, however, been taken as a result of particular circumstances. The great successes of column tactics had been based on its ability to change direction and re-form quickly, for which purpose a great number of highly experienced officers, NCOs and soldiers were needed. By 1809, however, after a series of campaigns lasting over 10 years, most of his experienced officers and subalterns were already in the grave. What Napoleon tried to do was to compensate quality with quantity. He used his columns like a medieval ramming block to increase their destructive effect. At Waterloo he used very much the same tactic, though without success.

Napoleon established a way of integrating *tirailleurs* with columns; from 1804 he attached to every light regiment, and to every line regiment from 1805, a *voltigeur* company to act as *tirailleurs*, while the fusiliers formed the battle columns. These companies formed an elite and were also called *flanqueneurs*. While on the march, they were at the rear. If the battalion led the attack, they rapidly advanced to the left and right, overtook it and engaged the enemy. As soon as the battalion itself was involved in the attack, the *flanqueneurs* moved to secure the flanks. In the case of the second column behind, the *flanqueneurs* accompanied the attacks so that they were always in touch with one another as well as with the main column, always ready to secure the flanks at critical moments. When the battle developed so that the column was firing in line, both *flanqueneur* companies, each divided into two sections, took up position about 20 yards behind their column's wings, ready to act as quick reinforcements. What previously had been a wildly improvised form of combat had been transformed into clearly ordered tactics, the movements of the *tirailleurs* being fully integrated with those of the column.

All this would have been impossible if the armies had been burdened by excessive trains. The efficiency of a mass army depends on its supplies. The Revolutionary army lived off the land when operating abroad. Every infantry battalion had only two

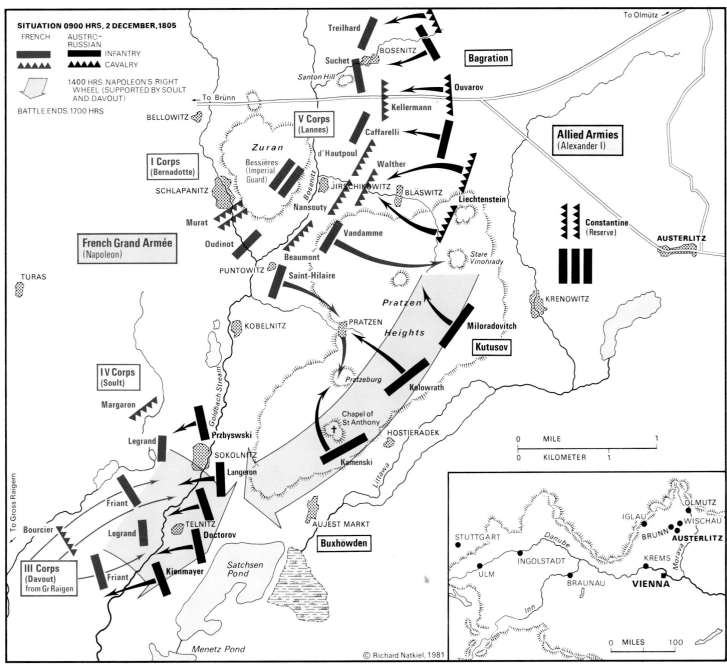

SITUATION 0900 HRS, 2 DECEMBER, 1805

FRENCH | AUSTRO-RUSSIAN | INFANTRY

CAVALRY

1400 HRS. NAPOLEON'S RIGHT WHEEL (SUPPORTED BY SOULT AND DAVOUT)

BATTLE ENDS, 1700 HRS

To Olmütz

Treilhard
BOSENITZ
Suchet
Santon Hill
To Brünn
BELLOWITZ
V Corps (Lannes)
Zuran
Bessières (Imperial Guard)
I Corps (Bernadotte)
SCHLAPANITZ
Murat
Oudinot
French Grand Armée (Napoleon)
TURAS
PUNTOWITZ
Nansouty
Beaumont
Saint-Hilaire
KOBELNITZ
IV Corps (Soult)
Margaron
Legrand
Przbyswski
SOKOLNITZ
Langeron
Goldbach Stream
Friant
Legrand
Bourcier
TELNITZ
Doctorov
III Corps (Davout) from Gr Raigen
Friant
Kienmayer
Satchsen Pond
Menetz Pond
AUJEST MARKT
Buxhöwden

Bagration
Ouvarov
Kellermann
Caffarelli
d'Hautpoul
Walther
JIRSCHIKOWITZ
BLASWITZ
Liechtenstein
Vandamme
Stare Vinohrady
PRATZEN
Pratzen Heights
Pratzeburg
Chapel of St Anthony
Kamenski
Kolowrath
HOSTIERADEK
Littawa
Miloradovitch
Kutusov

Allied Armies (Alexander I)
Constantine (Reserve)
AUSTERLITZ
KRENOWITZ

0 MILE 1
0 KILOMETER 1

STUTTGART
ULM
Danube
INGOLSTADT
BRAUNAU
Inn
IGLAU
BRUNN
OLMUTZ
WISCHAU
AUSTERLITZ
KREMS
Morava
VIENNA
0 MILES 100

© Richard Natkiel, 1981

Previous spread. *Catastrophe in the snow – the French army on the retreat from Moscow, 1812.*

Above left. *Napoleon and the Emperor Francis I of Austria meet after the Battle of Austerlitz.*

Far left. *Marshal Nicholas Soult, Duke of Dalmatia, 1769–1851. Appointed marshal in 1804, Soult delivered the decisive blow against the Austrians and Russians at Austerlitz in December 1805.*

Right. *A vivid contemporary engraving of the Battle of Austerlitz. Although the artist has exaggerated the height of the hills, he gives a good idea of the massive scale of 'The Battle of the Three Emperors.'*

Above left. *An allegorical print shows George III championing peace.*

Below left. *The Battle of Marengo, 14 June 1800. A hard-fought battle, won for the French by the timely arrival of General Desaix.*

Above. *Jacques Louis David's magnificent painting of the coronation of Napoleon.*

Right. *Napoleon's sister-in-law, Queen Hortense of Holland.*

Below. *Napoleon crossing the Great St Bernard Pass, 1801. (Jacques Louis David).*

324

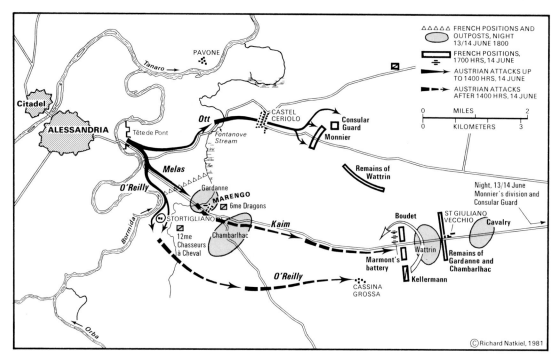

Above. An English cartoon of 1807 shows French conscripts being taken to the army roped together to prevent escape.

Below. The French army crosses the Danube on 5 July 1809, the day before the Battle of Wagram.

Below right. A French sapper (left) chats to a gunner of foot artillery.

Below far right. The mailed fist whose impact decided many battles: a French cuirassier in full dress, 1805.

transport wagons carrying food supplies, representing two full days' rations or four days on half rations. In addition, one wagon carried the tools necessary for entrenchment and field works. The supply of ammunition had absolute priority and provided no problem, and the officers carried the same baggage as their men. A wagon was also stocked with tents but, as they deteriorated, no new supplies were delivered and the soldiers had to bivouac under the open sky. Mobility was increased by living off the land, and the more ruthlessly it was exploited the greater distance could be covered. Certainly, the generals Pichegru and Jourdan would hardly have been able to win their victories in Belgium and Holland so decisively in 1794 had their movements been impeded by the magazine or depot system.

It was relatively easy to live off the land in central Europe, where the agricultural output was high. It was a different matter, however, in Spain and Russia; supply depots were established, but dependence on them would have limited speed and depth of penetration. For this reason alone, the armies had to live off the produce of the countries they invaded. To provide a graphic picture of the requirements of an army of about 250,000 men and 100,000 horses, the figures for the daily needs of such an army will suffice: 225 tons of bread, 550 tons of oats, 550 tons of hay, 450 tons of straw and 2800 tons of fresh fodder. To supply these quantities, 4100 vehicles or carts were required. The policy of requisitioning in enemy territory, therefore, reduced one's own train and gave greater mobility to the forces. No one knew how to live off the land as expertly as Napoleon did. The campaign and speedy conquest of Italy showed that, in well-populated areas, requisitioning could be carried out independently without actually reducing the numbers of troops in the field.

Napoleon did not only requisition food – he also filled the treasury in Paris with valuable war booty. This naturally contradicted the principle of preserving as much as possible when campaigning, as was widely practiced in the eighteenth century by the standing armies of the absolute monarchs. The full exploitation of all the available resources in enemy country was part and parcel of this new way of conducting hostilities. It did raise the question, however, of how far one could go. Every misuse, every excess, ultimately operated against the aggressor's military interests if requisitions reached a point at which the inhabitants took up their own arms to defend themselves or even drive out the invader. Napoleon paid the price for five long years in Spain; he paid it in 1809 in the Tyrol and in Germany in 1813.

Napoleon did not exploit resources according to any plan, and how food supplies were obtained was a matter of indifference to him as long as the quick pace of his operations was not impeded, and success on the battlefield was ensured, thus providing him with additional supplies. With that principle in mind, he had his armies march across Europe generally without establishing supply depots.

In the autumn campaign against Austria in 1805, the lack of any supply trains proved a great advantage; the troops simply requisitioned what they needed, and more, from the territories through which they marched. There had been a good harvest and, besides wheat, ample stocks of potatoes existed throughout southern Germany. The army could afford to live hand to mouth. Although the areas of requisition were divided between the army corps, almost chaotic conditions ensued as no firm rules of priority were established. Even requisitioning for an army required a carefully-thought-out system. Discipline was affected, and the old habits of plundering and marauding emerged as soon as shortages occurred. The absence of any system also led to wastage. If Napoleon's brilliant tactical victories, culminating in Austerlitz, had not been achieved with such unexpected speed, his army could well have become the victim of a major supply catastrophe. Napoleon realized this and immediately ordered the establishment of a great supply depot for biscuits, flour, oats and spirits.

The French army conducted the unexpected war against Prussia in 1806 again without supply depots at hand. It carried a supply of bread for 10 days. As before, operations developed with unforeseen speed and, after the victories at Jena and Auerstädt, the army moved in good agricultural country and therefore had no problem in feeding itself. Matters changed, however, when the army crossed the Vistula and the weather changed; winter was upon them and the supply system collapsed completely. There was not enough food to requisition, disease ravaged the army and supply trains got bogged down on the bad roads east of the Oder. Marshal Lannes reported to Napoleon on 11 November 1806 that, within a radius of 10 miles, there was no longer any bread for his army corps. Hunger became the constant companion of Napoleon's armies.

By the beginning of 1807, the main theater of war had shifted to East Prussia, where Napoleon had a force of approximately 600,000 men. Upon encountering the first Russian forces, who were fighting in alliance with Prussia, he forced them back to the Lithuanian border districts. On 7 and 8 February 1807 he met them again at Preussisch-Eylau in the first major battle in East Prussia. The Russians were under the command of General Bennigsen and were supported by the Prussian Corps L'Estoq, whose chief of staff was Gerhard von Scharnhorst. It was the first battle which Napoleon did not win, mainly because, in spite of superior numbers, he fought a winter campaign with a physically weakened army and with little prospect of successful requisitioning. He therefore preferred to move into richer provinces such as Silesia and Pomerania. Napoleon himself stated that it would have been a child's game to beat the Russians, but the fate of Europe depended on the question of food supplies.

For the spring of 1807 Napoleon made more thorough preparations. He considered a supply line stretching from the Rhine to the Vistula too risky in view of the primitive transport and lines of communication of the time, and exploited Prussia instead. Quarters and food for his troops had to be supplied by the Prussian burghers, and all existing arsenals, depots, magazines and manufacturing installations were taken over; all available sources of revenue were tapped. Berlin alone had to pay two and a half million thalers. All sources of economic productivity were turned to the service of the French war effort. Prussia had to supply all the uniforms, and even the army stationed in Poland was supplied with bread and meat from Silesia. For the first time the entire system of requisitioning, financial and food supplies, was put under the central direction of the Intendant General Drau, who established a military administration whose commissioners acted according to strict rules and instructions.

France herself supplied the least – her financial burden was no greater than would have been required for the upkeep of a

Left. *British infantry charge the French during the Peninsular War.*

Right. *Marshal Ney.*

Below left. *French household troops, before the Revolution and after the Restoration.*

Below. *French engineer officers, 1732–1845.*

Below far right. *French chevaux-légers, 1690–1814.*

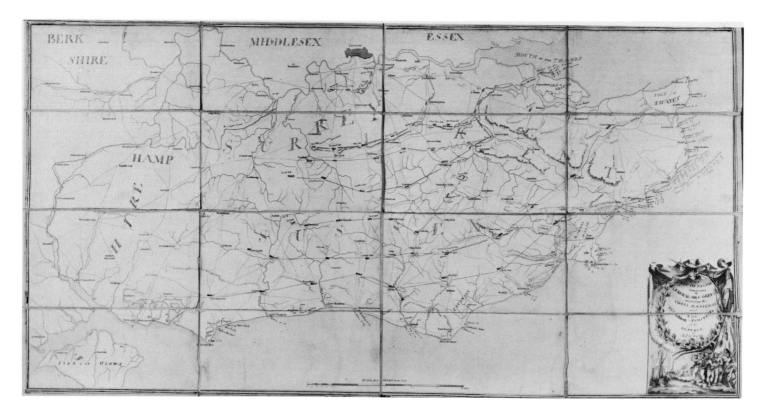

peacetime army. For France the real cost was in the number of human lives lost, especially from 1808 onward. Despite all the drawbacks of the continental blockade against Britain, in general France mobilized the entire continent's export resources which in turn had highly beneficial effects on French industry.

The near disaster with supplies in late 1806 and early 1807 led to a complete reorganization. On 26 March 1807 Napoleon ordered the establishment of eight train battalions, each divided into four companies. By 1811 the train had increased to 13 battalions, each with six companies. When he invaded Russia in 1812, a massive supply train was organized, each army corps having its own battalion. The supplies carried were intended to last 14 days.

The more the area of operation was extended, the more carefully had logistics to be considered. Taking recourse to methods already used in the previous century, Napoleon established supply stations every 10 to 20 miles along the route of advance. They ran along the Rhine from Wesel to Strasbourg and across central Germany. Each base was under the command of a general or a head commissioner. Their function was to obtain supplies, supervise local administration, carry out police functions and control all postal transport traffic, as well as to ensure that roads and bridges were maintained in good order. As long as the rear was peaceful, there was no need for large occupation forces and the bulk of the army served on the battlefield. In 1811 there were no more than 1000 gendarmes, who supervised the entire area between the Rhine and the Vistula. The widespread network of roads in central Europe aided this task. This was in direct contrast to Spain, where the line from Bayonne to Madrid could be secured only by the deployment of strong military forces against guerrilla attacks. Russia was another vital exception.

The Russian campaign provides a classic example of the interdependence between army leadership and supplies. The Emperor envisaged difficulties and had made preparations which he considered adequate. Supplies were accumulated in the area east of the Vistula sufficient for the needs of 600,000 men for one year. The only question that remained unanswered was how to defeat the enemy in the depths of Russia. If the Russians evaded battle, which they frequently did, then the pace of the

Above. A map belonging to Lieutenant General Sir Eyre Coote, showing the lines of defense around London in 1803.

Above right. A Russian painting showing French troops in Smolensk in October 1812.

Right. On 17 August 1812 the Russians put up a fierce resistance at Smolensk, and eventually withdrew having set fire to the town.

Overleaf. In September 1807 Copenhagen was captured by a British force under Lord Cathcart, after a bombardment of the forts and citadel lasting four days.

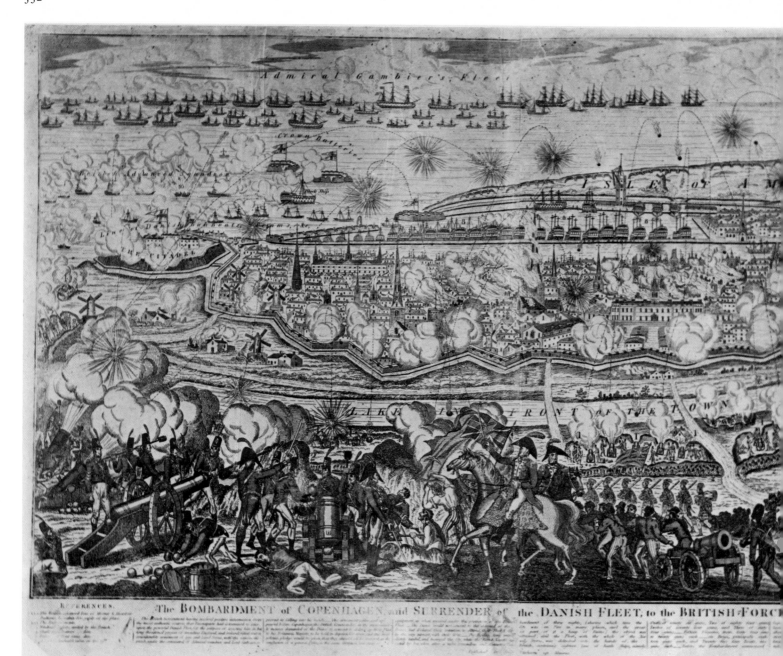

The BOMBARDMENT of COPENHAGEN, and SURRENDER of the DANISH FLEET, to the BRITISH FORCES

Left. *A popular print shows the bombardment and capture of Copenhagen.*

Below far left. *Field Marshal Augustus Wilhelm von Gneisenau, 1760–1831, a Prussian military reformer who served as Blücher's chief of staff at Waterloo.*

Below left. *General Karl Maria von Clausewitz, 1780–1831. Captured after Auerstadt in the 1806 campaign, Clausewitz decided to defect to Russia in 1812 rather than assist in the collaboration between France and Prussia. He rejoined the Prussian army in 1814, and served with distinction in the Waterloo campaign. He is best known as a philosopher of war, and his writings on strategy retain lasting importance.*

Below. *Russian helmets of the 1812 campaign.*

advance could not be increased without risking the collapse of the supplies system; to establish a line of supply from East Prussia to Moscow was impossible. Also, there was bound to be a serious shortage of horse fodder. Napoleon's intention to campaign in Russia lacked a coordinated plan. He hoped to beat the Russian army decisively near the frontier at Vilna. But the Russians evaded battle; even penetrating as far as Vitebsk brought no conclusion. Originally he had planned to leave the conquest of Moscow until 1813, but his army had reached the limits of its supply line. There were only two choices open to him: to give up and withdraw, or to march on to Moscow. Believing that supplies would be found in the agricultural regions around Smolensk and in Moscow, he opted for the latter decision.

The results were catastrophic even before Moscow had been reached. When crossing the Memel on 22 June 1812, the main army was 300,000 strong; in the course of the next few months while still on the march, hunger, exhaustion, disease and desertion had reduced it by 130,000 men, while 70,000 were combat casualties. The Russians' scorched earth policy left very little to be requisitioned, and when Napoleon reached Moscow, he conquered a burning city, not a storehouse. In the course of its retreat, the French army lost even more of its original strength. The question of supplies was not the only factor which defeated Napoleon's Russian venture, but it was a vital one.

It was virtually inevitable that the organizational, tactical and logistical changes, in conjunction with political driving forces, would revolutionize strategy. The *levée en masse* forced the entire population into arms, something which the *ancien régime* had always avoided, because a people in arms also represented a potential danger to its own rule. War was never an affair conducted according to entirely rational principles; the power of the French Revolution increased its destructive potency. Armies could be quickly organized and sent to the battlefield in great numbers. The art of maneuver, previously preferred because of the high cost of a standing army, was abandoned; the new state possessed the human resources to match even a partial defeat by quick regeneration through the supply of new troops. Human life had become cheaper. Moreover, the Jacobin army entered war with the motto of total victory. Whereas formerly operations had in the main been conducted to cut off the enemy from the rear and deprive him of his supplies, the main forces of the enemy were now the objective; the battle had become more important than the maneuver.

It is unlikely that a much shaken France would have overcome the defeats of the first two Revolutionary wars had not Napoleon come to the fore. By his superior use of the forces available to him and realizing the new requirements of the time, he became the master of the strategy of annihilation. Its practical application was the result of the restructuring of the army into divisions and army corps, of the use of troops *en masse* and the increased tactical effectiveness of the arms deployed. His forces possessed all the characteristics needed for mobile operations and his superb generalship produced the quick advance in the decisive direction. Furthermore, his ability to concentrate all available forces at the right time on the battlefield ensured victory, followed by strategic and relentless pursuit. In that way, Napoleon, in whose hands military and political leadership were united, did not only change the map of Europe but also the conduct of war. His strategy was based on the full exploitation of superior numbers, space and time. As long as the system of supplies functioned adequately, and kept pace with the swift advance of his military operations, the Napoleonic method of combined speed, mass and annihilation achieved extraordinary successes. As always, however, this new strategic concept also remained dependent on political, economic and technical factors. It presupposed a superior instrument of war, which, by 1813, no longer existed.

The war fortifications became less important. The aim of warfare was the complete annihilation of the enemy, for which all available forces were concentrated; since the cavalry had become a decisive branch, fortifications lost their operational value. Even strongly fortified cities such as Kolberg in Pomerania, which defended itself from 1806 until the Peace of Tilsit in 1807, did not seriously impede Napoleon's operations. In most cases it was quite sufficient to detach small units to keep them in check and under observation. His enemies were to learn from him: Blücher's chief of staff, Gneisenau, conducted the 1814 campaign in France in much the same manner. The more soldiers were detached for siege purposes, the fewer could be put on the battlefield. Still, Napoleon utilized the existence of strong fortresses in minor theaters of war, such as in upper Italy, for his own purposes, and in conquered territory existing fortifications were improved, such as Mantua in 1796 and Danzig in 1807. The fortifications built along the River Elbe also played an important role in 1813 as the basis for the strategic defensive line of Napoleon's forces.

Napoleon's strategy of annihilation was emulated throughout Europe. General von Clausewitz, in his work *On War*, paid great attention to it and clearly defined it. When the aim is the total annihilation of the enemy, this does not mean attacking and killing recklessly, but making the opponent defenseless, breaking his will to resist and eliminating the sources of aid and supply. The strategy of annihilation was not devoid of humanitarian principles: the horrors of war could be reduced by a quick and decisive battle which shortened the war.

Statistics show that, in its initial phase, this strategy caused fewer fatal casualties than the battles of the eighteenth century, primarily because of the increased mobility of the armies. However, the more frequently this strategy was applied, the larger were the masses on the battlefield and the greater the losses became. One of Napoleon's critics maintained that the life span of the average soldier in Napoleon's army was between 33 and 36 months. As the theater of operations of Napoleon's armies increased in size, so did the manpower requirements. Soldiers became no more than 'cannon fodder.' Napoleon's campaigns cost some 3,500,000 dead and wounded.

However, a major improvement of the time were doctors provided with horses and a military medical service, which was extended under General Larrey into a network of mobile field hospitals. At the Battle of Aboukir in Egypt in 1798, it was said that none of the 800 wounded had to wait longer than a quarter of an hour for treatment. However, with the spread of Napoleonic warfare and its immense territorial operations, the development of the field hospitals could not keep pace – hospitals could be provided but not sufficient personnel.

A vital component of Revolutionary and Napoleonic warfare was propaganda, that is to say the dissemination of the new principles of liberty, equality and fraternity, in France and then throughout Europe. In France it had sustained the Revolutionary armies and carried them forward to victory; counterrevolutionary risings, such as in the Vendée, could be mercilessly crushed, and the armies could range themselves against princely despotism beyond the frontiers of France. The *citoyen armée* believed it upheld the dignity of revolution, a dignity destined to proclaim to the world at large the principles of human rights and the recovery of allegedly inalienable natural rights of man. The Revolution had therefore not only to succeed in France, but to conquer and remove the entire *ancien régime* in Europe; it claimed to fight for the liberation of Europe from the 'world enemy.' The transformation of an ideology for domestic consumption to an expansive missionary ideal was complete. Scharnhorst says in his account of the campaign of 1794, the *Development of the General Causes for the Fortune of the French in the Revolutionary War*: 'They considered themselves enlightened, clever, free and happy and that all other nations were uneducated, akin to animals and unhappy. . . . They believed not only in their further existence and good fortune, but that they were fighting for the welfare of all mankind. Such effective motives for self-sacrifice of all kinds have not been found among any other nation.'

The French army fought with ideological weapons. Already in 1792 every allied deserter was promised naturalization and a lifelong pension, irrespective of whether he would serve France as soldier or civilian. While in combat, French guards always endeavored to come into contact with their opposite numbers to convince them of the righteousness of the French cause. Masses of leaflets proclaiming the new principles were printed in all European languages in Paris and found their way into the

Left. *The Battle of Aboukir, 25 July 1799. Napoleon completely defeated a superior Turkish force under Mustapha Pasha. Treatment of the French wounded was remarkably efficient.*

Above right. *General Gerhard Johann Scharnhorst, 1755–1813. After service in the Hanoverian army, Scharnhorst transferred to the Prussian army in 1801, and played a leading role in rebuilding it after Jena. He was mortally wounded at Lutzen in May 1813.*

Right. *King Frederick William III of Prussia, who reigned from 1797–1840.*

allied armies. They were not without effect: few Germans could be enthusiastic about fighting on behalf of obsolete feudal rule, or few British for the naval supremacy of Britain. Even Scharnhorst, while still an artillery captain in the service of Hanover, could see little purpose other than that of simply doing his duty. Confronted with the Revolutionary propaganda, the allied officers often felt rather helpless; it was a dimension of warfare they had not encountered before and for which they had not been prepared.

Nevertheless, the allied armies did not simply dissolve and the number of desertions was no higher than usual; there was also the element of historic consciousness, the memory of how France a century before had ravaged the Palatinate and of how Louis XIV had robbed ancient German territory and annexed it to France; the rape of Strasbourg had not been forgotten. These memories provided an active antidote to the revolutionary and humanistic visions of the French. Also the lack of success of French propaganda was evident when the *Sans-Culottes* confronted traditional, professional armies. The two were irreconcilable. 'One must not imagine the French Army of that time as having the appearance of its later period of glory. The *Carmagnoles*, clad in rags, without any real military spirit and countenance, who daily sent abuse and weak shots across the Rhine, hardly excited respect,' wrote one contemporary. Another, however, who had been a prisoner in France, saw it from a different perspective: 'What among us is the product of . . . exercise as well as fear, is done here upon one word naturally and without inhibition. While among the French we had acquired a free and easy way of life, now, *after return to the Austrian lines*, we were again confronted by the stiff puppet theater. I was shocked as soon as I met the first comrades on guard in their powdered wigs.'

The change from cabinet warfare to warfare accompanied by missionary, ideological propaganda only exacerbated the barbarity of warfare. The enemy was equated with the devil and the promise was to clear out hell. It resulted in a fury of national passions on all sides, which, for instance, gave the Prussian campaigns in 1813 the fervor and passion of a crusade, once they had learned their lessons from the French. Schiller summarized the French argument of liberty, equality and fraternity in the rhyme: '*Und willst Du nicht mein Bruder sein, so schlag ich Dir den Schädel ein*' – 'If you don't want to be my brother, I shall break your skull!' The National Convent ordered that no more prisoners be taken, an order largely ignored in the field.

Once Napoleon had taken over the helm of the state and army, more orderly ways were introduced in the army, but propaganda still played a major part. He raised Polish hopes of regaining their state, and his addresses to his soldiers were masterpieces of military and political rhetoric. Until the very end he managed to keep morale high, at least in France. Propaganda successes were also achieved in the fragmented German states along the Rhine and in Westphalia, where his administrative reforms did much to make him popular, but they were short-lived. As his armies flooded across Europe, living off the land and bringing oppression and disruption, the impact of his propaganda was lost – indeed it turned against him. What liberties he allowed were also strictly limited, and, master of propaganda that he was, he also feared this weapon when it was deployed against him. The entire German press was subject to French censorship, and no book could appear without being licensed first by the French. Obstinate writers landed in prison, and the Nuremberg bookseller Johann Philipp Palm was executed by firing squad at Braunau on 26 August 1806 because he had ventured to publish an anonymous pamphlet under the title *Germany in its Lowest Degradation*.

Napoleon employed an unknown number of writers and cartoonists to fill the German gazettes with whatever pleased him. The import of British newspapers and books was prohibited, which, however, did not prevent Burke's *Reflections on the French Revolution* turning up in Germany, to be duly translated by Friedrich von Gentz, later Metternich's adviser. Such censorship also extended to France and its own publications. In other words, the press became an instrument of psychological warfare as well. As Napoleon approached his military and political end, however, the truth could no longer be hidden. Even the most inspiring press appeals could not obscure the reality of being unable to pacify Spain and conquer Russia, or his failure to resist the military onslaught of Prussia, Russia and Austria, aided by those German states who were former members of the Confederation of the Rhine.

The French Revolution, at first so enthusiastically received by many Germans, later, ironically, regenerated German national consciousness in response to the Napoleonic invasions. In reacting to the Revolution, they modified the lessons taught by Napoleon and developed a type of psychological warfare which was not to be seen again in central Europe until the twentieth century. Militarily and psychologically, Napoleon was beaten with his own weapons.

By 1800 Prussia had withdrawn from the Revolutionary wars, mainly because its priorities lay to the east. Frederick William III ascended the Russian throne in 1797 and, in view of the shaky state of Prussia's finances which his predecessor Frederick William II had left, was anxious to keep out of all foreign entanglements. While Austria battled on with short interruptions until 1805, leaving Britain on her own, Prussia hoped to maintain her neutrality. When French troops violated this neutrality, however, Frederick William III mobilized his army on 6 August 1806. Napoleon demanded their withdrawal, Frederick William refused and war ensued.

The Prussian army expected to meet Napoleon west of the Thuringian forest, and, totally underestimating the rapidity with which Napoleon could move his forces, they moved into the region. However, the Prussian vanguard was defeated by the French at Saalfeld on 10 October 1806, and Prince Louis Ferdinand, a nephew of Frederick the Great, was killed. In their rapid advance the French forces bypassed the Prussians on their flank, penetrating to the rear. On 14 October the battles of Jena and Auerstädt were fought, which for Prussia were absolutely

disastrous. At Jena the Prussian army under the command of Prince Hohenlohe-Ingelfingen confronted a force three times its size, while a few miles away to the north near the village of Auerstädt stood the bulk of the army, where it enjoyed numerical superiority over the French. The army's commander, the Duke of Brunswick, was wounded early in battle; this put the king directly in charge of operations but, while not lacking in personal bravery, he lacked the gift of command, the capacity and vision necessary for quick and momentous decisions. At Auerstädt the Prussian army was beaten as soundly as at Jena. The old linear tactics proved of little use against Napoleon's columns. The fact that the Prussian troops had been bypassed and taken from the rear meant that the French fought with their backs to the River Oder, while the Prussians faced east. Their communications cut, they lacked any base to withdraw to; having been defeated, they were then also routed, the army being in complete disarray. Unit after unit capitulated, fortress after fortress surrendered.

Frederick William III immediately attempted to enter into negotiations with Napoleon, but these were rejected outright; Rossbach was to be avenged to the full. On 27 October the Corsican entered Berlin. One of his first visits was to the tomb of Frederick the Great at Potsdam; deep in thought before the sarcophagus, he turned to his attending generals and said: 'Gentlemen, if this man were still alive I would not be here.'

Frederick William and his family, together with his government, fled beyond the River Oder. Now Napoleon put forward his demands: the cession by Prussia of all its territory west of the Elbe. Frederick William tried to negotiate better terms but without success, and, against the advice of his councillors, decided to continue the war. This decision separated the wheat from the chaff among his advisers; men like Stein and Hardenberg now came to the fore to direct Prussia's fortunes. By that time Frederick William and his court had moved to Königsberg, the French close on their heels. The Battle of Preussisch Eylau and Napoleon's failure to conquer caused the latter to repeat his peace terms. Frederick William, now counselled by Hardenberg, refused in the hope that Russia's strength would soon make itself felt and change the situation in Prussia's favor. The war continued and, when Napoleon beat the Russians at the Battle of Friedland on 14 June 1807, Czar Alexander asked Napoleon for an armistice. Eleven days later, on 25 June, the two emperors met on a raft on the River Memel and concluded an agreement at the expense of Prussia. While Russia was not to sustain any losses, Prussia was to pay the bill, its continuing existence suffered by Napoleon only as a personal favor to Czar Alexander. On 9 July 1807 at the Treaty of Tilsit, Prussia lost all its territories west of the Elbe, including the city of Magdeburg, and her Polish provinces to the Duchy of Warsaw under the king of Saxony. Prussia was reduced to an area of 7311 square kilometers with a population of 4,500,000. From the western provinces which Prussia lost, the Kingdom of Westphalia was formed, on the throne of which Napoleon put his youngest brother Jerome. The Treaty of Tilsit was supplemented by the Convention of Königsberg of 12 July 1807, in which Napoleon stipulated that he would withdraw his occupying forces from Prussia only when the reparation payments demanded had been paid; no figure had then been determined.

In the course of time, however, Napoleon found himself compelled to withdraw troops from Prussia earlier than he had expected, due to a major mistake. During the same year, under dubious pretexts and to further a campaign against Portugal, Britain's oldest ally, Napoleon first subjected the northern part of Spain to his control, then forced the Bourbon King Charles IV to abdicate early in the following year and put his brother

SALAMANCA
R. Tormes
TEJARES
SANTA MARTA DE TORMES 778
CARBAJOSA DE LA SÁGRADA
Advance of Third Division and cavalry brigades
ALDEATEJADA
Light 856 841
7 Div
LAS TORRES
Cavalry 6 Div 1 Div 851 CALVARRASA DE ARIBA
841 Lt.troops
5 Div 4 Div
Lesser Arapil 861 Pt 891
ARAPILES 840
861 Lt.troops Pt 901
857 Greater Arapil
843 MIRANDA DE AZAN 901

BRITISH AND PORTUGUESE DIVISIONS
FRENCH DIVISIONS ON MARCH
FRENCH DIVISIONS IN POSITION
MILES 0 2
KILOMETERS 0 3

© Richard Natkiel, 1981

Above. *Field Marshal Gebhard Liberecht von Blücher, 1742–1819. A dashing cavalry leader, Blücher commanded the Prussian rearguard after Jena and led the Prussian army at Waterloo.*

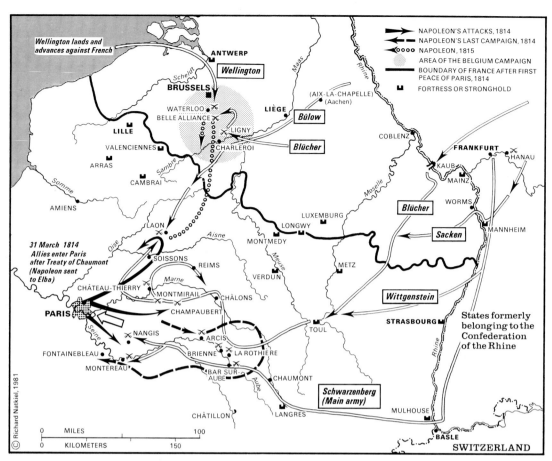

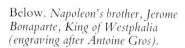

Below. *Napoleon's brother, Jerome Bonaparte, King of Westphalia (engraving after Antoine Gros).*

Joseph on the Spanish throne. Napoleon had reached the zenith of his power.

His action in Spain, however, precipitated something he had not expected – a people's war conducted by guerrilla tactics. By comparison with guerrilla conflicts in the Vendée, the irregular forces in Spain managed to resist the most powerful military might of Europe. The almost inaccessible mountainous landscape, the poor state of the roads, the extensive coastline and the relatively mild climate provided the guerrillas with sufficient advantages to match France's military power. Charged with wild fanaticism, they conducted a war of attrition accompanied by an unexpected series of insurrections in the urban centers. Guerrilla means 'little war,' but its effects in this instance were considerable. It became fully effective after 1807, when Napoleon, with forces drawn from Germany, had defeated the regular Spanish army in his campaign of 11 November to 4 December 1808. While the Duke of Wellington, as supreme commander of the Anglo-Portuguese forces in Portugal and Spain, conducted his campaigns in accordance with the old strategic rules, aiming to cut off the French from the rear and conquer Madrid, bands of small guerrilla units, each no more than 300 to 500 men strong, kept the occupying army of 300,000 soldiers continuously on its guard, and for years decisively tied it down and weakened it. The Spanish militia units supporting Wellington's army were, on the other hand, of very low combat value.

The bands of guerrillas consisted only of volunteers, mostly peasants; there were also many former regular soldiers. Sufficient weapons were available, but uniforms were not worn. Without strict central direction, each guerrilla leader operated more or less independently. The Junta-Central, however, called into being on 25 September 1808, formed a government committee 35 members strong in place of the deposed king and raised the call for the defense of Spain's sacred soil against the foreign invader. But it was no revolutionary government, and was in no way the spiritual driving force of the people's war.

The proud Spaniards, in spite of the primitive military means available to them, carried the burdens of their war with admirable patience. They fought without knowledge of organizational military principles but with guile and endurance, ignoring the cost of blood with which they had to pay. Their motives are to be found in religious and patriotic sources as well as in their allegiance to the monarchy. The social reforms which Napoleon intended and partly implemented in a very hasty fashion found little favor because the country lacked an 'enlightened' bourgeois society. On the contrary, the measures further increased the hatred of the foreigner and released passions without bounds; prisoners were hanged on the nearest tree and women butchered the wounded, in many cases taking recourse to refined methods of torture. Only those who managed to escape to monasteries or convents could be sure to remain alive, for even a short time. After the bloody suppression of the Madrid rising during the night of 3 May 1808, French court-martials had numerous citizens executed, many of whom were innocent. Goya has provided us with a horrifying pictorial record of these executions, his victims displaying impotent defiance, resignation and despair in the face of inevitable death.

This bloodbath was followed by a series of repressions. They did not cause the Spanish people to submit; as every French prisoner was hanged, so every captured insurgent was shot on the spot, both sides operating outside the existing rules of war. The Spanish guerrilla was the national resistance fighter, the underground activist; he was a partisan within the modern meaning of the term. The differences between the regular armed forces and civilians became completely blurred – they became between combatants and noncombatants. That the guerrillas also harbored criminal elements among them goes without saying, though it did little to further their cause. In cases where inhabitants were reluctant to aid the guerrillas or, worse, collaborated with the enemy, their fate was as final as was that of the invader, sometimes even worse.

The Junta attempted to organize the struggle, but without success. The partisans could not afford combat in the open; guerrilla warfare required efficient forces under a very flexible leadership. Tactical successes could have been achieved only if the bands of guerrillas, instead of fighting in independent groups, had possessed the ability to support one another. The rising had been a spontaneous one, however, lacking any military preparations whatsoever. The particularist-inclined provincial juntas were only able to rally large armed mobs, strict military discipline, in view of the prevailing chaotic conditions, being impossible. No single guerrilla leader managed to combine under his command all the other guerrilla units. They therefore had to avoid major engagements with the enemy, concentrating on ambushes and assassination wherever possible; the geography of the country favored this mode of warfare. As a result of the Anglo-Portuguese intervention, the guerrillas obtained firm support and Napoleon's troops faced hitherto unknown problems. They had to fight Wellington offensively in the first instance, but more than two-thirds of their combat troops had to be detached to secure the fortified cities. The guerrillas continuously interrupted the lines of communication, ambushed supply columns, captured couriers and successfully attacked and conquered fortified posts. No pardon was given to guerrillas, but that made no difference – for every one killed, two or three stepped in his place. Meanwhile, matters were getting more difficult for Napoleon, and he had already withdrawn 25,000 men from Spain in the spring of 1812 to strengthen his position in central Europe. It cannot be said that the Spanish guerrillas decided the issue in Spain – that decision was brought about by Wellington, who, on 21 June 1813, com-

pletely routed King Joseph's army at Vittoria. But without the aid of the guerrillas, Wellington's forces in the previous years would have had a rather more difficult stand and may not have established themselves at all in Spain.

The impact of the Spanish guerrilla movement was not limited to Spain – indeed, the Spaniards carried the torch of liberty and set aflame the emotions and passions of all those suffering under Napoleon. It strengthened the faith of those who believed that the moment was at hand to overthrow Napoleonic rule in central Europe. As elsewhere, the war in Spain was fought by means of press and pamphlet propaganda. Within a few months of its beginning, the widely distributed Spanish pamphlet literature inciting the population to resist the French had reached the German states. Here it served the same purpose, sometimes as a model, but more often in direct adaptation. The literature made its way from Spain in two directions, to London and Vienna, subsequently finding its way back into the German heartland.

The Austrian Chancellor, Count Johann Phillip von Stadion,

Above. *In April 1799 Kléber's division was assailed by a large Turkish force at Mount Tabor. The Turks failed to make any impression on Kléber's squares, and late in the afternoon, when ammunition was running low, Napoleon arrived with reinforcements and drove the Turks off with heavy loss (contemporary engraving).*

Above right. *Napoleon at the Battle of Friedland, June 1807 (painting by Horace Vernet).*

Right. *General Sir Ralph Abercromby (center) is mortally wounded as his troops defeat General Menou's French at Alexandria, 21 March 1801.*

thought that the moment had come, provided that Prussia could be rallied to Austria's side, thus restoring not only unity of action but also continuity of German history by abolishing the recent Austro-Prussian dualism. Stadion was, like von Stein, the scion of an old German family of *Reichsritter* and found in Stein a man from the same mold and of like mind. Stein, who had failed to obtain any concessions from the French by negotiation, expressed himself in favor of taking action. Frederick William III was prepared to move but only if Russia would take the same course, and of that there was no sign at the time. Spain now achieved by force what Stein had failed to obtain by negotiation: Napoleon had to move substantial forces from central Europe into the Iberian peninsula, the French occupation of Prussia was reduced to a minimum, and Frederick William III could return from Königsberg to his capital, Berlin.

Czar Alexander advocated peace; in Prussia, too, the peace party advised moderation, while Stein recommended that Prussia join Austria against Napoleon. However, a letter of his containing strong anti-Napoleonic sentiments was intercepted

by the French and Napoleon, who now realized the danger, demanded that Stein be dismissed. Stein formally resigned on 24 November 1808; he first found refuge in Vienna, then in St Petersburg.

Austria decided to make the most of the favorable circumstances that seemed to have presented themselves, hoping that, by its example, it would ultimately carry Prussia as well. The year 1809 saw the Habsburg dynasty at the head of the first attempt of the re-forming German nation to obtain its liberty by means of a national rising. The Spanish example was to be emulated in Germany. By the combined weight of popular risings along both the Danube and the Ebro, Napoleon was to be toppled. Friedrich von Gentz, Friedrich Schlegel and a host of other writers penned pamphlets and proclamations appealing to German patriots everywhere. Archduke Charles, in a public proclamation to the German people and his troops, announced: 'Your victories will free them from their chains, and your German brothers, still in the ranks of the enemy, are waiting for their liberation.' Vienna became the center for a systematic propaganda campaign – they had learned from the French! – for the rest of Germany, with branches run in Munich by Stadion's brother Friedrich Lothar von Stadion, in Dresden by the Austrian envoy Buol, and in Prussia by Adam Müller and the poet Heinrich von Kleist. The feeling of certainty that these efforts would result in a general rising of the Germans against Napoleon was the critical factor in Austria's final decision to go to war, a decision already reached in principle by the end of 1808. War began in April 1809 with an appeal written by Friedrich Lothar von Stadion and Schlegel and signed by Archduke Charles, addressed 'To the German Nation.' In Prussia Scharnhorst and Gneisenau were in favor of joining Austria, and Queen Louise said that, if Prussia's downfall were inevitable, then it would be better if it were to happen with honor.

However, the forces of Archduke Charles moved too slowly, allowing Napoleon to concentrate his army. Charles was pushed back into Bohemia and Napoleon advanced toward Vienna. At Aspern on 21 and 22 May 1809, however, Charles succeeded in inflicting the first defeat Napoleon had suffered. However, success was again not followed up and Napoleon

regained the initiative, defeating the Austrians at Wagram on 5 and 6 July. Six days later Napoleon and Emperor Francis decided to conclude an armistice, culminating in the Peace of Schönbrunn on 14 October 1809. Austria was reduced to a second-rate power, it had to participate in the continental blockade against Britain and reduce its armed forces to 150,000 men. Count Metternich, who had negotiated the treaty, now replaced Stadion as Austria's leading minister.

The battles between the regular forces of the Austrian and French armies were, however, only one aspect of the war; the other was a mass popular rising of the Tyrolean peasants. After her defeat by the French in 1805, Austria was compelled to cede the Tyrol to Bavaria. Immediately it was occupied by a mixed force of Bavarian and French troops, and France levied heavy contributions to finance its army, as did Bavaria. In addition the Roman Catholic Church in the Tyrol was to be secularized by Bavaria, whose government both at home and in the Tyrol claimed to pursue an 'enlightened policy.' Like the Spaniards, the Tyroleans were motivated by religious and patriotic causes and by their allegiance, in this case, to the House of Habsburg. Unlike the Spaniards, they already had previous experience in guerrilla fighting; a century before, in 1703, they had expelled the Elector of Bavaria and his forces, and between 1796 and 1797 had successfully defeated the French invasion until the conclusion of the Peace of Campo Formio. Another important difference was that the Tyroleans had possessed their own form of military organization since the late Middle Ages, put into proper shape by the so-called *Landlibell* of Emperor Maximilian I in 1511; it meant that, for every part of the Tyrol, a defensive force could be raised if the need should arise. The numbers depended on the size of the population in each area. More specific requirements were made in 1605 and also in 1703 after the Bavarian invasion. In case of attack the province had to provide 20,000 men in all, but only to defend the Tyrol. The province was poor in agriculture because of its climate and mountainous terrain, and was dependent on wheat imports. It was suitable only for dairy farming and hunting. The Tyroleans were natural hunters and, when supplied with weapons, could quickly form a ready force in an emergency.

Increased taxation, attacks against the Church and, finally, the introduction of conscription drove the Tyroleans into rebellion. The geography of the country was an advantage: with the exception of the *Ausserferner*, the region lying north of the Mieminger mountain chain containing the Lech Valley, the *Innerferner* or Tyrol consisted of the Inn Valley stretching from Kufstein on the Bavarian frontier down to Switzerland. To the south was another mountain chain, including the Zillertaler, Stubaier and Ötztaler Alps, crossed by several passes, the main one being the Brenner. South of it was the southern Tyrol with its provincial capital of Bozen, to the east of which was the Pustertal and, ultimately, eastern Tyrol with its provincial capital of Lienz near the Carinthian border. Access from Bavaria to the north was difficult because of the mountainous terrain, and the Inn Valley was therefore preferred – it could be reached from Austria via the Pustertal from the Lower Inn valley at Kufstein, and directly from the south, from Italy.

The rising in the Tyrol had been planned for some time by Archduke Johann. He appointed an intendant, General Hormeyr, a native of Innsbruck but serving at the court of Vienna. An Austrian army advanced up from Lienz through the Pustertal and, when they received this piece of news, the peasant leaders leapt into action, the most prominent among them being Andreas Hofer, trader and innkeeper in the Passeier Valley. Bonfires on the mountain summits signalled the attack, and the peasants expelled the Bavarian and French troops from

the Inn Valley. However, they failed to take the fortress of Kufstein. They avoided fighting in the open and instead attacked from the forests along the marching routes. On the mountainous heights they built stone avalanches which, upon the cutting of ropes, thundered down with deadly accuracy. Along the Inn Valley, city after city was liberated under the able leadership of Josef Speckbacher, and, by 11 April 1809, they had liberated Innsbruck. The peasants were jubilant over their success. But news of any victories by Austria's main armies against Napoleon was still outstanding. The Austrian army under Chasteller then arrived in Innsbruck and, moving down the River Inn, was defeated by newly arriving French forces commanded by General Lefebvre. The Austrian forces withdrew across the mountain passes, leaving the field to the French and Bavarians, who reoccupied Innsbruck. At that point Andreas Hofer assumed supreme command over the peasants, assisted by Speckbacher and the Capuchin monk Haspinger. Again they rallied their forces at the Isel Mountain, which overlooked

Above left. *The Tyrolean patriot Josef Speckbacher, 1767–1820.*

Above right. *Prince Klemens Metternich, 1773–1859, an Austrian statesman and diplomat whose conservative policies held sway for half a century.*

Right. *Wellington defeats the French at Vittoria, 21 June 1813.*

Innsbruck, and provoked the enemy to attack; by 29 May General Deroy's forces had been reduced to a point where they had to evacuate Innsbruck and withdraw down the Inn Valley. In the meantime the news of the Austrian victory at Aspern reached the Tyrol and liberation seemed at hand. The news of the defeat of Wagram and of the armistice concluded between Napoleon and Emperor Francis did not get through.

It seemed as though the armistice did not apply in the Tyrol. Generals Lefebvre and Beaumont led exclusively French forces from the north up the Inn Valley and from the south across the Brenner Pass upon Innsbruck and retook it. And again, under Hofer's leadership, the peasants rallied for a third time. Between 11 and 13 August 1809 the most ferocious battle raged at the Isel Mountain between the French and the Tyroleans, both fighting to the point of exhaustion. Indeed Lefebvre decided to retreat down the River Inn, burning towns and villages on the way. Innsbruck was spared because the Tyroleans immediately occupied it, for the third time. Hofer took over the government in Innsbruck, but Napoleon declared him an outlaw who had broken the armistice. As new French and Bavarian forces were in the process of returning, Haspinger and Speckbacher argued in favor of fighting it out, while Hofer thought the country was exhausted. Individual actions were still fought in all parts of the province, but the Tyrol could no longer rely on Habsburg support. By the Treaty of Schönbrunn, Tyrol was again confirmed a possession of Bavaria. The French now mounted a punitive expedition throughout the Tyrol, and memorial tablets on the churches still tell the bloody tale. At first Andreas Hofer escaped, hiding in a mountain hut near his inn; betrayed, he was taken prisoner by the French, perfunctorily tried, and then, on Napoleon's orders, put before the firing squad at Mantua in 1810.

The Tyrol episode was not without its consequences. On 28 April 1809, the 2nd Brandenburg Hussar Regiment in Berlin under the command of Ferdinand von Schill, already distinguished in the defense of Kolberg, marched out of the city, ostensibly for an exercise. Schill's plan, however, was not to return but to conduct his own campaign against the French troops; in this way he would force king and government to join in a general effort. Once he left the city he told his officers and men about his plan and gave them the opportunity to return. Only a handful did so, the vast majority of officers and men pressing to take action against the French at the earliest possible moment. Schill then marched south to Dessau, which he entered with a public proclamation announcing his plans and the city's liberation. He was enthusiastically received by the city's population, but public support did not go much further. He and his troops remained isolated and the popular uprising which Schill had imagined his action would incite did not materialize. His intention had been to march to Westphalia and join up with the forces of Colonel von Dörnberg, who had planned a similar rising against King Jerome. That rising, too, proved abortive and Dörnberg escaped to Bohemia. Schill, however, decided to move north to the Baltic in the hope that he and his men would be taken and saved by the British navy. He surprised the garrison of the city of Stralsund and occupied it, hoping either to turn it into another Saragossa (where in 1808 Spanish soldiers and civilians under the leadership of José de Palafox y Melci had given a splendid account of themselves in defending the city against the French) or at least hold it until the British navy should arrive. On 31 May 1809 Dutch and Danish auxiliary forces of the French stormed the city defended by Schill and his 500 men. Schill was killed in action and 11 officers of those captured were put before a French court-martial at Wesel and shot on 16 September. From Dörnberg's forces, 14 officers were selected by lot and shot at Brunswick. The remaining prisoners were condemned to serve as French galley slaves, and those that survived regained their liberty after the fall of Napoleon.

THE NEW AGE:
THE GERMAN REACTION

The German reaction to the defeat of Napoleon was the Prussian reform movement, and Prussia was to serve as a model for the rest of Germany. Within this chapter only the military aspects of the Prussian reform movement will be examined, and their effects in the War of Liberation between 1813 and 1815.

The movement's military function was inspired by General Gerhard Johann David von Scharnhorst. He originated from a peasant family in lower Saxony, and his father had been an NCO in the Hanoverian army. Serving first Count Wilhelm von Schaumburg-Lippe, he became an officer in the Hanoverian army and fought in the War of the First Coalition against Revolutionary France in the Netherlands, for which service he was ennobled. Like Napoleon, he belonged to the artillery. His most important colleagues were Gneisenau, Grolman and Boyen.

August von Gneisenau (1760–1831) had served as a young lieutenant in an Ansbach-Bayreuth regiment which, as a mercenary force, had served on the British side in North America during the American Revolution. He had experienced at close quarters the superiority of the American forces. He then joined the Prussian army and had led the defense of Kolberg. Karl von Grolman (1777–1834) was one of the youngest of the reformers. In 1809 he served on the Austrian side and then went to Spain, where he commanded a regiment of foreign guerrillas. In January 1813 he returned to Berlin and served as major on the general staff in the War of Liberation. From 1815–19 he was chief of the general staff. Hermann von Boyen (1771–1848) became Prussian Minister for War during the War of Liberation, but in 1819 resigned his post in protest against the policy of restoration, which tried to undo some of the reformers' work.

Scharnhorst displayed a great talent for education from the early days of his career. Besides Gneisenau, he was also one of the few German officers fully to realize the implications of the colonial militia of the North American settlers, and the important part they played in the defeat of Britain's mercenary forces. They enjoyed the advantage of knowing their country's geography and being able to exploit it. Once they were organized into a proper army, they were victorious. What had been demonstrated in North America was confirmed by the French Revolutionary armies. In other words, Scharnhorst had realized the significance of the *levée en masse* before it was put into practice in France. Before the outbreak of war between Prussia and France, he wrote his famous memorandum of 1806, in which he stated: 'We have begun to estimate the art of war higher than military virtues. This has been the downfall of people at all times. Bravery, self-sacrifice and steadfastness are the basic pillars of our independence. If our heart does no longer beat for them, then we are already lost.' He advocated the national people's war in an age which assumed that war was of no concern to the civilians. He received support in Berlin from patriotic circles, but the king wanted to know nothing of it. Even Stein, in his early phase, shrank back from what was bound to become a war of extermination, though later he became one of its supporters. Scharnhorst, however, was supported by Prince Hardenberg, Stein's successor as chief minister in 1809, when Scharnhorst entertained the plan of turning the whole of western Germany into an area of popular insurrection and combine it with similar actions in Pomerania and Silesia. However, it would have needed strong British support, which was not forthcoming, and the support of the czar, who counselled peace.

Prussia possessed the resources to conduct such a war even in 1806, but it would have required revolutionary political and social impulses which, in its *ancien régime*, were lacking. How could peasants living in a state of servitude and burghers almost devoid of political rights know what they were risking their lives for? The closer the ties between the population and state on the basis of a liberal constitution, the greater the impetus for

Left. *General Gerhard von Scharnhorst.*

Right. *Field Marshal Augustus Wilhelm von Gneisenau.*

Far right. *A contemporary German engraving shows French troops on the march.*

Below. *Prussian* landwehr *infantry, 1813. Note the distinguishing* landwehr *cross on their caps.*

sacrifice. Gneisenau wrote in 1808: 'It is self-evident and clever, at the same time, to give to the people a fatherland, if they are meant to defend it strongly . . . a free constitution which allows the burghers to elect their own superiors who are accountable to them. . . . If we begin first with a new municipal constitution, then this is more effective for the people who understand its benefits immediately before they understand the benefits of a new constitution for the state. If the state is given freer forms, then this satisfies the thinking heads, carries the enthusiasts, converts the pro-French and frightens the traitors.' Such reforms were carried out by Stein and Hardenberg, and the king, at the time, gave them his blessing. A people's army first required a people's state.

Scharnhorst recognized, along with others such as Stein, the need for thorough reform of state and army even before Jena and Auerstädt, and dedicated himself to this purpose. Time and again he called for new strategies and tactics, and, as director of the War Academy, which was founded on his initiative, he developed a new theory for the conduct of war. One of his most dedicated pupils was Karl von Clausewitz. All his calls for reform, however, were turned down time and again, till the defeats at the hands of Napoleon created a more favorable climate of opinion. Clausewitz summarized the ideas of Scharnhorst and his fellow-reformers in four requirements:

1 'A new structure, new armaments and equipment in accordance with the new methods of warfare.' Mercenaries and the hiring of foreigners were abolished. According to the French example, Scharnhorst reorganized the Prussian army into brigades, which combined all arms.

2 'Ennoblement of its constituents and general lifting of the spirit.' Since the mercenaries had been abolished, the severity of discipline could be reduced, since the number of deserters would be much lower. Corporal punishment was abandoned so that the army was no longer greatly feared by the people, and service in arms was respected. The proclamation of liberty had to precede national conscription. Running the gauntlet was also abolished. The Prussian army had to be carried by a spirit of conscious voluntary discipline.

3 'A careful selection of these officers commanding larger formations.' In principle, 'in peace they should display knowledge and education, in war bravery and vision.' These were the qualities required in the new officer corps. In fact, until the end of the War of Liberation, the privileges of the Prussian nobility in holding the upper ranks were effectively removed.

4 'New types of military exercises in accordance with the new methods of warfare.' One of the most important aspects of army reform was the abolition of linear tactics and the introduction of *tirailleur* and column tactics; this changed the entire training system. Drill on the parade ground was replaced by exercises in the field, and target practice was introduced in place of mere musket drill.

By these means the Prussian army managed to draw level with the French in the tactical field and the way was paved for the victories in the War of Liberation. 'The entire military system . . . which was introduced in Prussia was the attempt to organize a popular resistance against the enemy, insofar as this was possible within the framework of an absolute monarchy,' wrote Friedrich Engels, although, through the political reforms introduced by Stein and Hardenberg, the Prussian monarchy was much less absolute than Engels would have it; it was on the road, albeit a long one, to becoming a constitutional monarchy.

A fundamental change in the relationship between army and state resulted. So far the middle class, the burghers of the towns and cities, had been exempted from military service; now they were gradually drafted into the army, though not without protesting the infringement of their 'ancient privileges.' Scharnhorst argued in favor of opening up all the ranks of the army to members of the middle class, from which he himself had come,

Left. *Prussian generals, 1750–1850.*

Below left. *Prussian lancers, 1786–1845.*

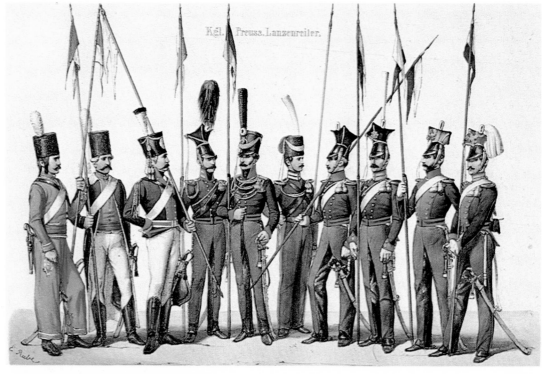

Below far left. *The Emperor Alexander I of Russia, 1777–1825.*

Below left. *Field Marshal Gebhard von Blücher.*

Below. *The liberal Prussian statesman Baron Karl von und zum Stein, 1757–1831.*

Right. *The French army withdraws from Leipzig, October 1813, under heavy pressure from the Prussians.*

and this proved a step of considerable long-term significance. Hitherto, the commissioned ranks had almost exclusively been the preserve of the nobility, while peasants constituted the rank and file. Scharnhorst's aim was to make the members of the middle class eligible for commissions, and introduced higher education as the prerequisite for advancement into the upper echelons.

The relations between army, state and society were to be reformed in such a way that the army would adopt the values and political consciousness of the middle classes. Thus the army became an institution which was to play a vital role in the process of political and social integration in the Prussian state. In July 1809, when many of the reforms had already been carried out, Scharnhorst answered objections against the entry of commoners into the Prussian officer corps in a memorandum, in which he wrote: 'If only children of noblemen possess the privilege to be employed as officers, and despite their gross ignorance and tender age, men are made subordinate to them who have knowledge and courage, then this will help the noble families, but the army will rot and never obtain the respect of the nation – it will become an object of derision for the educated.'

Education was a vital factor in Scharnhorst's reform program: 'If the education of the nation is to prosper, then the entire school system of a nation must originate from one source. . . . The same concept of the nation must predominate in all educational institutions; the same organic connections must embrace the entire education of youth and all be directed to the same goal. There is only one humanity, and every nation represents one entity within it; therefore the national educational institutions should not educate individuals or classes, but the nation as a whole, and all schools must represent one school of the nation.' Two features are fundamental to this concept: a national goal and a democratic aim, interrelated with one another. The school should not be an institution for the state, nor for the education of a particular class, nor for the preparation for a particular profession – this would only serve particularist interests and, as such, be in opposition to his views of national education. Specialization, too, at school level would breed separate interests and would not lead to the unity of all citizens in one nation. For this reason as well, all citizens had to serve in the army. 'Only by arming the whole of the people will the smaller establish a kind of equilibrium of might in a defensive war conducted against a larger who carries on a war of subjugation by aggression.'

The new army was to be based upon honor and bravery, with opportunities for anyone with ability. Wars of conquest, so Scharnhorst argued, are always dependent upon the man who has the ability and charisma to lead and inspire his army, but wars of defense depend to a much greater degree on the character of the individual soldier.

After Jena and Auerstädt, Scharnhorst was called to head a military commission. Gneisenau was also a member because of his brilliant defense of Kolberg. The commission was to enquire into the causes of the defeat and weed out those who had proved themselves incapable; it was also to submit and carry out the reforms considered necessary: 'One must give the nation the feeling of independence; one must provide the opportunities for it to become familiar with itself, so that it looks after itself, for only then will it respect itself and know how to compel others to respect it. To work toward this aim is all that we can do. To destroy the old ways, remove prejudice, lead the rebirth, watch over it and not stop its free growth, more than that we cannot effect.'

In many ways one can argue that the principle of general military service had existed in Prussia since Frederick William I's *Cantonal Règlement* of 1730, but any such view would not take account of the vast numbers of exemptions, which included all towns and cities and which necessitated the continued recruitment of mercenaries. During the Seven Years' War, especially in its later stages, forcible recruitment had been carried out; few had conceived of the 'citizen soldier,' of the duty of every citizen to carry arms for his country or to prepare for the day when he should need to use them. But then the citizen did not yet exist in Prussia, only the subject, and among the royal subjects of Frederick the Great the burghers were important chiefly commercially and were essentially unmilitary.

Stein fully supported Scharnhorst's demand for the introduction of general conscription. One of the first obstacles was financial, namely what would any army based on general conscription cost? The figure proved staggering, bearing in mind the financial obligations of Prussia toward France. It was therefore necessary to accept what already existed, namely the standing army, reform it from within and add to it an inexpensive component – the *Landwehr* or militia. Forcible recruitment was adapted and turned into a general duty of all citizens to serve in the army. In these ways the Prussian army experienced its most thoroughgoing transformation since the days of the Great Elector.

The standing army was badly in need of improvements, especially its senior officer corps. Scharnhorst's commission purged it to the extent that, of 143 generals who were still on the active list, only two remained on the eve of the War of Liberation: Blücher and Taunzien. Scharnhorst wanted to turn the army into the school of the nation, but in practical terms he

had to form a small, efficient but cheap military force for an impoverished state. The solution he envisaged was firstly to draft all who were able to carry arms. Because the Treaty of Tilsit limited the Prussian army to 42,000 men, this could not be put fully into effect until 1813. The national servicemen were to serve for a limited but uninterrupted period of time, and then were released, but remained in the reserves. The standing army and reserves were to constitute the regular army. However, to ensure that everyone served in the army, the *Landwehr* was to be called into being to act as reinforcements.

Scharnhorst devised methods of evading Napoleon's limitations on the size of the Prussian army, introducing the *Krümper* system. *Krümper* was already a popular expression in the old army for those soldiers who belonged to a particular regiment, but were on leave because of a small regimental budget; in case of war, however, they rejoined. Boyen reintroduced this 'rejoining' to obscure the real intention behind the move and, after the evacuation of Prussia by the French, the system was extended. It amounted to five men per company, later to eight, plus 15,200 Prussian prisoners of war who returned in 1809. At first they were intended to serve for one month only, immediately to be replaced by an equal number of *Krümpers*, but one month was too short a period to produce soldiers efficient in field exercises. Ultimately the period of service was extended to six months. Once released, they became part of the reserve of the line regiment, and their training continued in their home districts under the supervision of officers on half-pay. As one report put it: 'The exercises of those on leave proceed very well here. The mild treatment of the soldiers had reduced the dread non-soldiers had of military service. Young and old watch the exercises and the targets are carried by a great procession. The warlike spirit is especially kindled among the youth, whose fondest game is now playing soldiers.' At its peak the *Krümper* system produced between 60 and 80 soldiers per annum for each company.

Scharnhorst's reforms faced serious opposition, particularly from the Prussian nobility, who resented the erosion of privileges. They rejected the argument that Prussia had failed because the army had been allowed to grow weak and lazy. Scharnhorst and his fellow military reformers could see only one option open to them: thorough reform or none at all. Their opponents maintained that it could have been carried out within the established framework; they were blind to the new national currents which played so large a part in the motivation of the new military forces. They either failed to see the significance of the popular risings against Napoleon in Spain and the Tyrol, or else feared them. Nothing was more dangerous to their concept of state than an army consisting of the 'emancipated masses.' 'To arm the nation means merely to organize and facilitate opposition and dissatisfaction,' wrote Prince Wittgenstein.

Certainly the democratic trends evident in the rule that allowed the *Landwehr* to elect its own officers, and in the growing demand for the introduction of a constitutional monarchy, were ultimately the stumbling block for the Prussian reform movement after 1815. It was the middle class which was most receptive to the ideas of the French Revolution, and which most vociferously expressed the opinion that the time had come to apply its lessons to Germany.

Frederick William III did not make things easy for Scharnhorst. He could not deny that Scharnhorst was right, but he remained emotionally tied to the legacy of his granduncle, and this made him vulnerable to the arguments of those who opposed Scharnhorst. He, too, wondered what forces would ultimately be unleashed by the introduction of military conscription. He saw a need for the abolition of noble privileges in

the army and therefore approved of the introduction of formal examinations for ensigns and officers. However, he obstinately refused to close down the cadet institutes, which Scharnhorst saw merely as training schools for the nobility and unlikely to produce the necessary national elite. In the long run, however, the pressure of the growing middle class proved too strong even for the conservatives in Prussia, and the cadet institutes were opened to all suitable applicants.

It is important to note that Scharnhorst's reforms, with a few exceptions, can be discerned only in the army regulations. For instance, compulsory military service was never publicly proclaimed. *De jure* the old cantonal system of Frederick William I remained in force until March 1813, although *de facto* it had been abolished for five years. Only the tactical reforms of the army found expression in a general revision of the military manual. Of course attitudes established over a century could hardly be eliminated within nine years. After the death of Scharnhorst, and later the departure of Gneisenau and Boyen, the results of the military reforms were still visible, but the changes in attitudes that had motivated them had apparently sunk into oblivion.

Still Frederick William III was reluctant to join Austria, not only because of the czar's advice against it but because he also feared the consequences of a people's war. The reformers were disgusted: Grolman joined the Austrians and then went on to Spain, Gneisenau travelled to London and then to St Petersburg for the duration of the peace, and Scharnhorst, as a result of Napoleon's pressure, had to resign his post, although he still managed to act as an adviser. He then went on to St Petersburg and Vienna, where Metternich informed him that it was not his intention to replace French hegemony in Europe with Russian hegemony. Clausewitz went to St. Petersburg as well, where Gneisenau and Stein had set up a Committee for German Affairs.

The time for action against Napoleon would not come until Napoleon's army had been defeated in Russia. Prussia, as well as the other German states, had to provide auxiliary forces, the Prussian contingent being commanded by General von Yorck. After Napoleon's debacle, when the Prussian corps was cut off by Russian forces under General Diebitsch, the Russians refrained from attacking the Prussians and instead asked them to change sides, or at least declare their neutrality. On the Russian side, the negotiations were conducted by Clausewitz and Scharnhorst's brother-in-law, Count Dohna. The Czar dispatched a personal letter to Yorck in which he undertook not to lay down arms against the French until Prussia's former position among the powers of Europe had been fully restored. This letter was crucial; it decided Yorck to resume personal negotiations with Diebitsch. At the same time he informed Frederick William of the development, sending a Major von Seydlitz to Berlin, and hoped for definite instructions from the king. When Seydlitz returned, he had no explicit orders from the king, only evasion; by word of mouth, however, Seydlitz was to relate that negotiations with the Austrians had already begun and that Yorck should act according to the circumstances. Taking this as a blank check, Yorck met Diebitsch again on 30 December 1812 at the Poscherun mill outside Tauroggen, and they signed the Convention of Tauroggen, by which Yorck separated his forces from the French and promised to maintain neutrality.

The Russians advanced, followed by Stein, Dohna, Clausewitz, Gneisenau and Boyen. Boyen was sent to Prussia, Stein to Breslau, where Frederick William had withdrawn, while, in the meantime, Yorck's forces had already joined the Russians. By the end of February no French soldier was left east of the River Oder. On 3 February 1813 Frederick William issued an

Above. *French infantry in action in Saxony in 1813. The nearest soldier is biting off the end of a cartridge, before loading his musket.*

Above right. *The Emperor Francis I of Austria, 1767–1835.*

Right. *Wellington enters Toulouse after his defeat of Soult, April 1814.*

Below. *The Prussian Field Marshal Yorck von Wartenburg, who negotiated the Convention of Tauroggen(December 1812) which effectively swung the Prussian army away from its alliance with the French.*

in favor of attacking again but, being under Russian supreme command, he was held back. At Bautzen Napoleon forced a crossing over the River Spree.

Two battles had now been lost by the Prussians, but they were fought with such fanaticism and enthusiasm that Napoleon concluded that his opponents were rather stronger than they really were. Since he himself knew best the weaknesses of his own army, he offered an armistice which was concluded on 4 June 1813. Napoleon later described it as the greatest stupidity of his life – the French were at Prussia's frontier and the Russians were already considering withdrawing into Poland. The duration of the armistice was also well used by the allies; apart from improving both the numbers and equipment of their forces, their main effort was spent in bringing Austria into the coalition, an endeavor in which they ultimately succeeded. The armistice came to an end on 4 August 1813 and, on the 11th, Austria joined the coalition. Prior to this, Sweden had also joined and landed an army on the shores of the Baltic. The Allies now numbered 480,000 men against Napoleon's 450,000, though this superiority in numbers was in effect reduced by their disunity; only Prussia and Russia were decided upon terminating Napoleon's days as Emperor. Austria on the other hand feared that Prussia and Russia might grow too strong, and Sweden wanted to annex Norway, which at that time belonged to Denmark.

The allied autumn campaign of 1813 planned to encircle Napoleon's central position in Dresden. The main army in the south under the command of the Austrian Prince Schwarzen-

edict calling to arms all citizens from 17 to 24 years old and, on 9 February, removed all exemptions to military service which still existed, for the duration of the war. General conscription had been introduced. Under Stein's guidance the Treaty of Kalisch was signed on 27 February between Prussia and Russia. It was a risky venture for the Prussians, as it was soon apparent that the Russian forces were not as numerous as had been imagined, while the French still held considerable contingents in Germany. Austria was in favor of a new coalition but, for the time being, adopted a wait-and-see policy.

On 11 March Frederick founded the Iron Cross decoration. Five days later the Czar entered Breslau, the next day Prussia declared war on France and, on 16 March, Frederick issued his famous proclamation *An mein Volk*, which was enthusiastically received by the population. Volunteers from all over Germany, even from the Tyrol, poured into Prussia and, in the 12 months from March 1813 to March 1814, the Prussian army received more than 50,000 volunteers. For them it was a crusade against Napoleonic despotism. On the same day on which Frederick William issued his proclamation, General Yorck and his corps entered Berlin; Russian Cossacks ventured even as far as Hamburg, where they were received enthusiastically.

Napoleon had now begun to rally his forces, building a new army from the remnants that had returned from Russia supplemented by troops from the German states of the Confederation of the Rhine. Only Bavaria wavered in its support: it had lost 30,000 men in Russia and Crown Prince Ludwig advised joining Prussia. Austria was still indecisive. The first encounter between the Prussians and the French took place on 2 May 1813 at Grossgörschen. Napoleon's forces fought off the Prussian and Russian attack, but he immediately realized that this was no longer the army which he had defeated in 1806. The loss of this battle was Scharnhorst, who, though wounded, nevertheless made his way to Prague to persuade the Austrians to join Prussia. His wound developed gangrene and he died on 28 June. Blücher, whose chief of staff was now Gneisenau, was

Above left. *The Austrian Field Marshal Karl Philip, Prince Schwarzenberg, 1771–1820.*

Right. *A Meissen plate depicting the Battle of Toulouse.*

Far right. *The Allies meet at Leipzig, October 1813.*

Below. *Marshal Etienne Macdonald, Duke of Tarentum, 1765–1840.*

berg, and consisting of Austrians, Russians and Prussians, together with Blücher's Silesian army, was to force Napoleon into decisive battle. The allies achieved initial successes at Grossbeeren and Bad Hegelberg, south of Berlin, in which the *Landwehr* formations particularly distinguished themselves; the southern army, however, suffered a reverse at Napoleon's hand near Dresden. Blücher, on Gneisenau's advice, decided to escape the shackles of the high command which shunned any risk and, on 26 August 1813, attacked Macdonald's forces at the Katzbach River and inflicted a heavy defeat. As Blücher wrote to his wife: 'Today was the day for which I have wished for so long. We have completely beaten the enemy. The fighting lasted from 2 o'clock in the afternoon until the evening. Not many prisoners were taken; the troops were too embittered and killed everything. It rained the whole day and guns would not fire any longer. My infantrymen fought with the bayonet. After the battle everyone wanted to rest, but I ordered that the men and horses summon their last reserves of strength in the pursuit of the enemy.' As at Grossbeeren, Blücher's infantrymen were mainly *Landwehr* men.

Napoleon continued to concentrate his forces around Dresden, seeking to defeat his opponents one by one. The Allies' main objective was to combine their armies while Napoleon still stood between them. Bernadotte and his Swedish troops declared themselves ready to have Blücher's army move toward them and join forces; when they met they moved toward Leipzig, while Schwarzenberg's army approached from the south. Napoleon now saw the danger of being cut off in the rear

and having to fight with reversed fronts like the Prussians at Jena. To counter this danger he moved the bulk of his forces against Bernadotte and Blücher with the intention of beating them. Bernadotte was, in fact, ready to withdraw, but Gneisenau suggested that any withdrawal be achieved without crossing the River Elbe, thus not only threatening Napoleon's rear but also making it possible to combine with Schwarzenberg's forces. Napoleon's army could not find an enemy to attack. Near Merseburg the Allied armies joined and Napoleon now decided to force battle, if only because a decision in his favor would open the way to the west; he had to seek a battle in order to win an opportunity to retreat.

The Battle of Leipzig raged from 16 to 19 October 1813 and was one of the greatest battles fought in the nineteenth century. Napoleon had positioned his army around Leipzig, 190,000 men in all, against an Allied force which initially numbered 200,000, but which in the course of the battle increased to 300,000. On the 16th the Allies fought their way in to the approaches of Leipzig, on the 17th the Prussians entered the suburbs, and the battle for the city commenced the following day. Heavy street fighting raged throughout the city, the French and their allies trying to fight their way out to the west. When, however, a French corporal blew up the Elster bridge over the Elbe, a vast number of French and Confederation of the Rhine troops had their escape route cut off. Marshal Poniatowski, Polish prince and Marshal of France, tried to swim across the river and perished, as did thousands of others; the French were defeated. The Allied forces met in the market

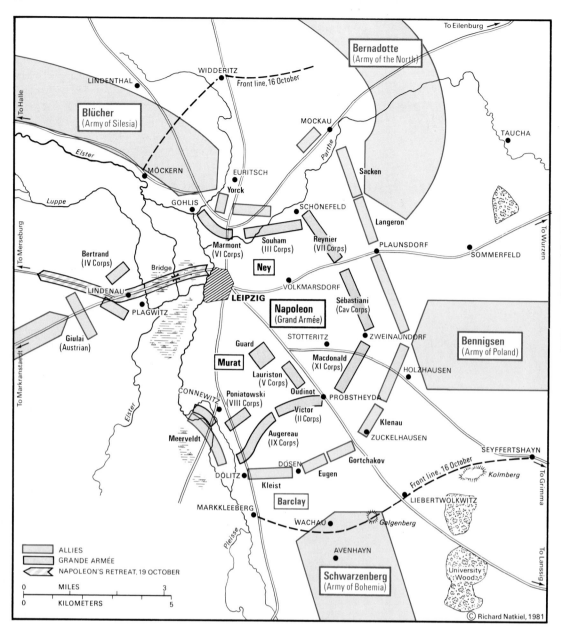

Bernadotte
(Army of the North)

To Eilenburg

Front line, 16 October

LINDENTHAL

WIDDERITZ

Blücher
(Army of Silesia)

MOCKAU

Elster

Parthe

TAUCHA

MÖCKERN

EURITSCH

Sacken

To Halle

Yorck

GOHLIS

SCHÖNEFELD

Langeron

To Wurzen

Luppe

Marmont
(VI Corps)

Souham
(III Corps)

Reynier
(VII Corps)

PLAUNSDORF

SOMMERFELD

To Merseburg

Bertrand
(IV Corps)

Bridge

Ney

VOLKMARSDORF

LINDENAU

LEIPZIG

Napoleon
(Grand Armée)

Sébastiani
(Cav Corps)

PLAGWITZ

STOTTERITZ

ZWEINAUNDORF

Bennigsen
(Army of Poland)

Giulai
(Austrian)

Murat

Guard

HOLZHAUSEN

Lauriston
(V Corps)

Macdonald
(XI Corps)

To Markranstaedt

CONNEWITZ

Poniatowski
(VIII Corps)

Oudinot

PROBSTHEYDA

Klenau

Elster

Victor
(II Corps)

ZUCKELHAUSEN

Meerveldt

Augereau
(IX Corps)

SEYFFERTSHAYN

DÖSEN

Gortchakov

Front line, 16 October

Kolmberg

To Grimma

DÖLITZ

Eugen

LIEBERTWOLKWITZ

Kleist

Barclay

To Lanssig

MARKKLEEBERG

WACHAU

Galgenberg

Plesse

AVENHAYN

University
Wood

ALLIES
GRANDE ARMÉE
NAPOLEON'S RETREAT, 19 OCTOBER

Schwarzenberg
(Army of Bohemia)

0   MILES   3
0   KILOMETERS   5

© Richard Natkiel, 1981

Above. *Bashkir soldiers, tribal horsemen in Russian service, survey the ruins of Hamburg, 1814.*

Below left. *Austrian troops, 1814.*

Below. *Off-duty Austrian infantry enjoy a game of cards among the baggage wagons.*

Below right. *An Austrian carpenter at work in camp, 1814.*

achieved, however, when news arrived that, on 1 March 1815, Napoleon had returned to France and that most of the army of the Bourbon king had joined him. The Bourbons had only just vacated Paris when Napoleon entered the city in triumph on 20 March. Among the Allies, only the Prussian and British forces were on an immediate war footing. The British army was in the Netherlands, having made its way across France from Spain, while the Prussian army under Blücher was in the Rhenish provinces. Once again Gneisenau was Blücher's chief of staff, though he had hoped for an independent command; in fact it was under Gneisenau that the office of chief of staff attained the significance it has enjoyed ever since.

At first the Prussian campaign suffered a setback near Liège: Saxon formations mutinied upon hearing that they were to be split up as a result of territorial changes which had been made to their country; they were disarmed and the ringleaders shot. Napoleon moved onto the offensive with the aim of splitting the coalition. While the center of gravity of the Prussian army was Liège, that of the British was around Ghent, their vanguards meeting in the Charleroi region. Napoleon realized that these two armies could fully join forces only if one or the other would give up its main base, and therefore believed he could beat each separately. With surprising speed he attacked Blücher at Ligny on 16 June 1815; Blücher accepted battle because Wellington had promised aid, but the Prussian and British forces were still too far apart for this assistance to come in time. Moreover, once Wellington was himself under attack by Marshal Ney at Quatre Bras, he was soon in need of all his forces himself. The Prussian lines became overextended, stretched in one direction in order to cover their rearward communications, in the other in order not to lose touch with Wellington. For hours the Battle of Ligny raged on a hot June day until, as evening approached, Napoleon used his Imperial guards to capture the town. Blücher was wounded and only the onset of darkness put an end to the battle. Retreat was now unavoidable, with Wellington likely to do the same in the direction of Antwerp.

At that moment Gneisenau issued the instruction that the

square but, although the possibility of routing the French forces existed, the Allies were exhausted. Napoleon, attacked only once during his retreat, by Bavarian forces, managed to escape beyond the Rhine.

On New Year's Day 1814 the Allied troops crossed the Rhine. Differences of opinion about the course of operations, however, delayed them again until Blücher achieved their first victory on French soil at La Rothière on 1 February, and the general advance was resumed. However, after he had suffered three quick defeats by Napoleon, Blücher rejoined the Allied armies. The Allies again wanted to withdraw but, mainly on Blücher's and Gneisenau's urging, the advance was resumed and the Allies entered Paris on 31 March 1814. A few days later Napoleon abdicated and left for Elba.

In the meantime the Congress of Vienna had assembled and, as usual, the diplomats were divided. Solidarity was quickly

354

Left. *On 30–31 October 1813 Napoleon, with the survivors of Leipzig, battered his way past a blocking position at Hanau (after Horace Vernet).*

BOUNDARY OF THE GERMAN CONFEDERATION, FOUNDED 1815

MILES 0 — 300
KILOMETERS 0 — 500

CHRISTIANIA

NORWAY   SWEDEN
             United, 1815–1905   ■ STOCKHOLM

BALTIC
SEA

DENMARK

NORTH SEA   ■ COPENHAGEN

                                                              ● DANZIG
HELIGOLAND
(Brit.)   S   I   A   RUSSIA
UNITED
KINGDOM   United Kingdom and Hanover   ● HAMBURG
           united.1815–37   Vistula
                              BREMEN   ● WARSAW
AMSTERDAM   HANOVER   ● BERLIN   U
                                                    Oder
LONDON ●   UNITED   United with Russia from 1815.
             NETHERLANDS   R   Part of Russia 1831
                      COLOGNE   SAXONY
             (Belgium independent   P   ● PRAGUE
             1830)   Rhine   ■ CRACOW
             LUX   RUSSIAN
PARIS ●   To   BAVARIA
       OLDENBURG   Bavaria   A   U   S   T   R   I   A   N
             BADEN WÜRTTEM-
                    BERG   Danube
FRANCE   VIENNA ■
                                                                BUDA ●● PEST
       SWITZ.   E   M   P   I   R   E
                                              Drava
                                                                   Danube
                              LOMBARDY-VENETIA   BELGRADE ●
              TURIN ● To Austria,1815   SERBIA
       Rhône   MILAN ●
             PIEDMONT
                    PARMA   SOFIA ●
                 MODENA
                 LUCCA   OTTOMAN
SPAIN   TUSCANY   PAPAL   EMPIRE
       SARDINIA   CORSICA   STATES
                           ● ROME   MONTENEGRO ●
                              NAPLES ●
MEDITERRANEAN   KINGDOM
                 OF THE TWO   ATHENS ■
                 SICILIES
             SEA   REPUBLIC OF THE IONIAN IS.
                                                           (British protectorate)
ALGIERS   TUNIS   ● PALERMO
                    MALTA
                    (Brit.)

Below left. *The Battle of Waterloo (contemporary English aquatint).*

Below. *Adolf von Menzel's painting of the meeting of Blücher and Wellington on the field of Waterloo. Blücher had been unhorsed and ridden over at Ligny two days before, and had dosed himself with a lethal brew of gin and rhubarb. 'I stink a bit,' he admitted when he met Wellington.*

Below right. *British wounded arrive in Brussels after Waterloo.*

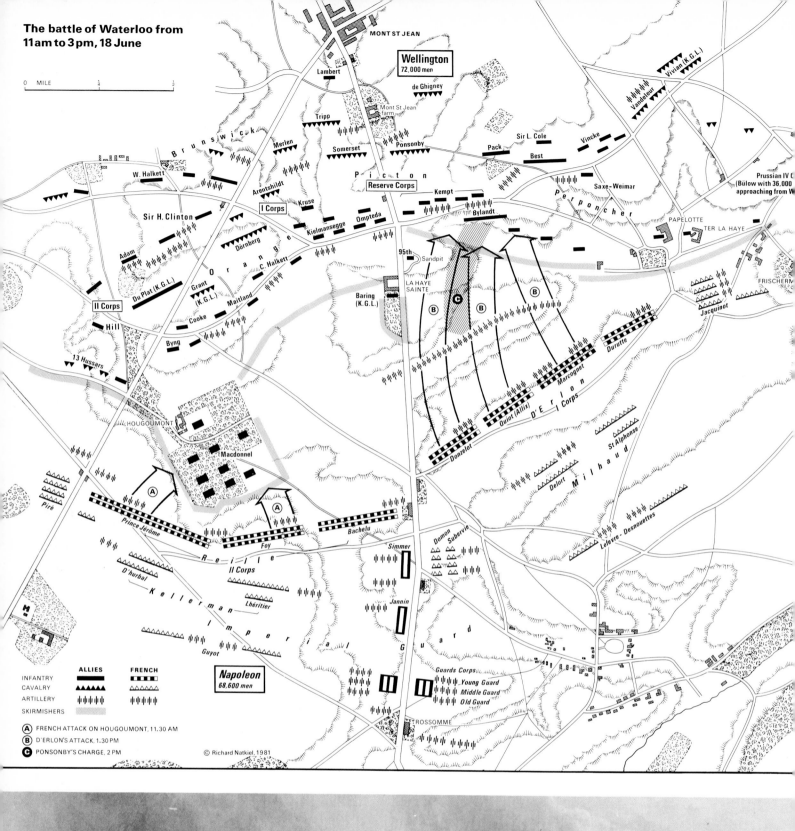

The battle of Waterloo from 11am to 3pm, 18 June

MONT ST JEAN

0   MILE   1

Wellington
72,000 men

Lambert

de Ghigney

Vivian (K.G.L.)

Vandeleur

Mont St Jean farm

Brunswick

Tripp

Somerset

Ponsonby

Pack

Sir L. Cole

Vincke

Merlen

P i c t o n

W. Halkett

Arentshildt

Reserve Corps

Kempt

Best

Saxe-Weimar

Kruse

Kielmansegge

Ompteda

Bylandt

Perponcher

I Corps

Sir H. Clinton

Dornberg

Prussian IV C
(Bülow with 36,000
approaching from W

C. Halkett

PAPELOTTE

Adam

Grant
(K.G.L.)

Maitland

95th

Sandpit

TER LA HAYE

Du Plat (K.G.L.)

O r a n g e

LA HAYE
SAINTE

Baring (K.G.L.)

II Corps

C

B

B

B

FRISCHERM

Cooke

Hill

Byng

Jacquinot

13 Hussars

Marcognet

HOUGOUMONT

Quiot (Allix)

D'Erlon I Corps

Durutte

Macdonnel

Donzelot

St Alphonse

Delort

Milhaud

A

Prince Jérôme

A

Bachelu

R e i l l e

Foy

II Corps

Domon

Subervie

Simmer

Piré

Lefèvre-Desnouettes

D'hurbal

K e l l e r m a n

Lhéritier

Jannin

Guyot

I m p e r i a l

G u a r d

Napoleon
68,600 men

Guards Corps

Young Guard
Middle Guard
Old Guard

ROSSOMME

	ALLIES	FRENCH
INFANTRY	▬▬▬	▤▤▤
CAVALRY	▲▲▲▲▲	△△△△△
ARTILLERY		
SKIRMISHERS		

Ⓐ FRENCH ATTACK ON HOUGOUMONT, 11.30 AM

Ⓑ D'ERLON'S ATTACK, 1.30 PM

Ⓒ PONSONBY'S CHARGE, 2 PM

© Richard Natkiel, 1981

Prussian retreat should not be in the direction of the Rhine but to the northeast toward the village of Waterloo, joining up with the British there. The Prussians therefore made the sacrifice of their own main base. This went against Napoleon's calculations and proved disastrous for him; he did not believe that a defeated enemy would accept a second battle immediately, and assumed that the Prussians and the British would retreat in different directions. Marshal Grouchy was dispatched with his forces toward Liège to harass the Prussians, but there were none there to be harassed. Believing that he had only one enemy to fight, Napoleon made ready to fight the British at Waterloo.

Wellington moved into defensive positions and determined to hold them: 'Our plan is simple: the Prussians or the night.' Napoleon calmly reviewed his troops in full view of the British contingents and then attacked, three major attacks being repelled by the British and their defensive fire. Nevertheless, the British position was becoming very precarious when, toward the late afternoon, the Prussian army driven on by Blücher – 'Marshal Forward' as he was called – reached the battlefield; they immediately re-formed for attack from their marching columns, taking the French from their right wing and in their rear. At first Napoleon thought that it must be Grouchy, who had about one-third of the French army with him, but soon realized his error. Blücher's attack transformed the situation completely. The defensive battle became an offensive one and the French, fearful of being taken between the British and the Prussians, tried to escape en masse. With Wellington's forces in a state of near exhaustion, the Prussians undertook the pursuit of the enemy. Gneisenau told the troops: 'We have shown the enemy how to conquer, now we shall demonstrate how to pursue.' Almost all the French artillery was captured, as well as Napoleon's carriage and personal belongings.

Blücher and Wellington met near a farm called Belle Alliance. Not much was said – both were too moved by the awareness of how close they had been to the abyss of defeat, too grateful that it had been transformed into victory. And victory was complete, for Napoleon had been toppled, his career ended. The nemesis of power had taken him to St Helena, there to end his days.

A new age of warfare had reached its zenith, but also its end. The powers of restoration, fearful of the ultimate consequences of a people's war, returned to cabinet warfare for the rest of the century, though the industrial revolution set unforeseen forces free. Metternich, and in a way his successor Bismarck, held the doors firmly closed to mass democracy and all that this implied, politically, socially and militarily, almost to the end of the nineteenth century. Ironically enough, that door was pushed open, not in Europe, but in North America, where the American Civil War provided the first indications of what Total War could mean.

Above. *Cossacks bivouacked in Paris.*

Above right. *French Cuirassiers crash into a sunken lane at Waterloo. Although there were obstacles on the battlefield, the story of the 'ravine' or 'sunken lane' was exaggerated as a convenient sop to French pride.*

Left. *The tide of battle turns at Waterloo: Wellington signals with his hat for his army to advance.*

Right. *Wellington rides through his army's drenched bivouacs on the morning of Waterloo.*

CLAUSEWITZ
AND TOTAL WAR

Karl von Clausewitz, born 1 June 1780, has for many decades been one of the most misunderstood military writers. Professor John U Nef, writing shortly after the end of World War II, counted him among the creators of a new mysticism:

'which helped to fan the flames of the world wars. Unlike Napoleon, Clausewitz was not a remarkably effective officer on the field of battle. It is reasonable to regard his doctrines concerning the philosophical meaning of war as a product mainly of the mind at work in the study.

'Clausewitz and his followers in Germany and eventually in other countries gave warfare an intellectual justification in addition to the emotional justification it derived from the spirit of resistance, of defense, bred in the heat of the French Revolution. Clausewitz's philosophy of war made use of concepts and categories directly derived from the Christian and humanist philosophies of the past, but he put them to a new purpose. For him war became a great exercise, in which the intellectual as well as moral qualities of man had unique opportunity for fulfillment. The occasion for the use of the mind was slight, of course, in the case of the private, but even for him there was a respectable place in the new warfare. The choices offered him in great battles called for tremendous grit and for some intelligence. So battles conferred upon the common man a kind of dignity which ordinary economic existence was failing to provide. As one ascended the military hierarchy from the private to the general, the intellectual opportunities increased, until for the commander in chief they exceeded those accorded men in other callings.'

In short, Clausewitz's work is denounced as the gospel of militarism.

Yet nothing could be farther from the truth. As we shall see, he clearly recognized the danger of *total war* but the criticism leveled against him would be much more appropriate to a work published a century later, in 1935, by General Erich Ludendorff, *Der Totale Krieg*, in which this German general, as renowned as he was controversial, set out to replace the 'outdated' maxims of Clausewitz with a new theory of total war. Intellectually, there is no comparison between Clausewitz and Ludendorff. The latter's work is simply one of propaganda. Ludendorff maintained that the German government during World War I had failed to mobilize the physical and mental resources of the German people which would have made them invulnerable to allied propaganda. He therefore demanded that the next war, which was to erase the blemish of the 1918 defeat, be prepared for with propaganda and that in the war itself the propaganda weapon should have a rank equal to that of the other arms. In a future war which, measured by the experience of World War I, could only be a total war, psychological warfare would be one of the decisive weapons. Therefore the psychological mobilization would be as important as that of personnel and material. In such a war Clausewitz's idea of the *primacy of politics* would be abandoned; in its place should step the *primacy of the military*, in whose hands the political and military conduct of the war would be concentrated. In total war there was no longer any place for civilian politicians.

Nothing could contradict Clausewitz's maxims more than those of Ludendorff and a host of lesser writers of the post World War I period. Therefore it is important to discuss Clausewitz the man, his work and its fullest development up to World War II, retracing our steps in the last chapter so as to proceed to an analysis of the present military position.

Clausewitz's main work, *On War*, was published posthumously between 1832 and 1834 and was well received by his contemporaries, that is, by those who possessed the same wide intellectual horizon. In the field of politics, Marx and Engels were among the first to become captivated by the work and to immerse themselves in its study. Little wonder: Clausewitz

Above: General Lord Hill, the most able of Wellington's subordinates.
Right: French cavalry officer of the Napoleonic period.
Previous page: French troops fight their way through a village during a battle of the Franco-Prussian War.
Following page: Napoleon accepts the surrender of the Austrian forces at Ulm in 1805 at the start of the Austerlitz campaign.

considered it his main aim to reconcile the theory and practice of war. What he intended was a structural analysis of the social phenomenon of war, which he took as simply one of the manifestations of social life, leaving its justification or condemnation to others. It is this motive which connects him with Karl Marx. Clausewitz did not consider reality as the testground of general maxims, but like Marx he elevated reality to a constitutive element of theory. What economics was to Marx, the history and theory of war were to Clausewitz. Both Clausewitz and Marx insisted upon the primacy of politics, a point with which even Bismarck agreed on the basis of his empirical experience, although late in life he admitted to and regretted not having read a line of Clausewitz.

The Wars of German Unification (1864, 1866, 1870–71) pushed Clausewitz's work to the fore, since it appeared that Prussia and Germany had conducted these wars fundamentally in accord with his maxims. Nowadays, since the early 1970s, there has been renewed interest world-wide in Clausewitz's work, in the United States, Europe and the Warsaw Bloc countries; indeed, in Russia, Clausewitz proved to be highly instructive to Lenin, and later to Mao Tse-tung in China and Che Guevara in Cuba as well.

Who was Karl von Clausewitz? He was born on 1 June 1780 in Burg, near Magdeburg, Prussia six years before the death of Frederick the Great. His ancestors were mainly parsons, but his father had served in the army of Frederick the Great and was retired after the Seven Years' War. Clausewitz's nobility is shrouded in mystery. There are strong indications that his father prefixed the 'von' to his name on his own initiative, without any real entitlement, and only in the later years of his son's career did King Friedrich Wilhelm III legalize this state of

he received his commission as a lieutenant, watching with great fascination the struggle between the new forces of the French Revolution and those of enlightened absolutism intent upon preserving the political and social *status quo*. Inevitably he witnessed the collapse of the 'rational art of war' and its replacement by the 'irrational warfare of the revolution.'

From 1795 until 1801 Clausewitz served as a subaltern in the garrison town of Neuruppin in Brandenburg and used his considerable leisure time there to study intensively the most recent military specialist literature. This proved a considerable asset when he was transferred in 1801 to the *Lehr-Anstalt für junge Infantrie- und Cavalerieoffiziere* – a teaching institute in the military sciences in Berlin, the forerunner of what ultimately became the Prussian War Academy.

This transfer represents the watershed in Clausewitz's career, because the head of the institute, Lieutenant Colonel Gerhard von Scharnhorst, quickly spotted the extraordinary talents of his pupil, 25 years his junior, and took him firmly under his wing, becoming not only his teacher but also his paternal friend. Scharnhorst was a military innovator born and bred. He was the first officer in Prussian service (he was originally from Hanover) to recognize that a new kind of warfare had been born in the American War of Independence, that the days were numbered in which military formations fought one another by linear tactics. His influence upon Clausewitz can be seen in Scharnhorst's paper on the military operations in Italy in May and June 1800, in which he drew particular attention to the relationship between war and politics. Scharnhorst made the point that the political and military leadership would have to agree about intentions and possibilities. If the Secret Cabinet (as it then still existed in Prussia) should act solely on military principles, it would come to grief in much the same way as if its political designs disregarded military necessities. Both elements, the political and the military, should act in concert. This was a line of reasoning which Clausewitz quickly absorbed and which was later to lead to his stipulation of the primacy of politics in warfare, the central theory in all his work.

Under Scharnhorst's guidance Clausewitz did not pursue the studies of a narrow military specialist but opened his mind to the currents of German literature and art, which were then at their strongest. Classics, literature, history, mathematics, philosophy, especially the writings of Kant and Herder, provided Clausewitz with ample stimulus.

In the campaign of 1806, when Napoleon broke Prussia's neutrality, Clausewitz fought at Auerstädt, commanding one of the modernized Prussian formations, a contingent of Prussian tirailleurs. But finally, on 28 October 1806, he became a prisoner of the French. He spent a year's captivity in fairly comfortable circumstances at Nancy. On his return to Prussia he immediately associated himself with the reform movement led by Freiherr vom und zum Stein and Scharnhorst, who had already begun the root-and-branch reform of the Prussian state and the Prussian Army. When Clausewitz was transferred to Königsberg where the Prussian government had taken temporary residence, in April 1808, he entered the inner circle of the reformers. Promoted to captain in 1809, he became adjutant to Friedrich Wilhelm III and the confidant of Scharnhorst. Also living in Königsberg was Marie Countess von Brühl who was to become his wife.

After the Prussian government had returned to Berlin – the popular risings in Spain against Napoleon had forced him to withdraw the bulk of his French forces from Prussia and evacuate Berlin – in August 1810, Clausewitz, then 30 years old and promoted to major, became instructor on the *Kriegsschule zu Berlin*, responsible for general staff courses and for Little Wars, that is, guerrilla warfare. In addition, he became the

affairs by issuing Karl von Clausewitz a patent of nobility.

Clausewitz was born into the world of enlightened absolutism and its imprint was made upon him in his early years. In Prussia, the period was marked by the centralization of all important powers including the leadership of the army in the hands of the king. It was precisely this unity which during the War of the Austrian Succession and the Seven Years' War provided Frederick the Great with a decisive advantage *vis-a-vis* his opponents in the field of political and military battle. After Frederick's death on 16 August 1786, that unity was soon lost in the hands of his weak successor Friedrich Wilhelm II, which became apparent to all when the War of the First Coalition, of Austria and Prussia against France, began in 1792.

How much the young Clausewitz observed the changes in the political and military order around him no one can say for sure. But it seems a fair assumption that he noted them in his early life and that in later years, when he was deeply engaged in the study of political and military changes, his deductions from his early experiences influenced his theoretical writings. This assumption becomes more probable when we note that at the age of nine he witnessed from afar the outbreak of the French Revolution, with its intellectual, political, social and military transformations. Seventeen years later, under the impact of the defeat at Jena, Prussia was also to be transformed.

Young Clausewitz was soon personally involved in what was to become the transformation of Europe. In 1792, at the age of 12, he entered the Prussian Infantry Regiment *Prinz Ferdinand* in whose ranks he participated between 1793 and 1794 in the First Coalition War. For Clausewitz, the high point of this war was the siege and capture of the fortress of Mainz and the expulsion of the French Revolutionary Army. At the age of 15

personal instructor of Crown Prince Friedrich Wilhelm, the future Friedrich Wilhelm IV.

Opposition to the reform movement was intense, especially from members of the traditional Prussian military aristocracy, including Yorck von Wartenburg. But nothing discouraged the reformers more than Prussia's failure to support Austria against France in 1809, and, what was worse, the alliance concluded between Prussia and France to invade Russia in 1812, in which Friedrich Wilhelm III supplied Napoleon with a Prussian contingent. Many members of the reform movement resigned from Prussian service, going to Spain, Austria and Russia. Gneisenau, a prominent reformer, wrote, 'Our fate will reach us the way we deserve it. With shame we shall go under, because we cannot deny to ourselves that the nation is as bad as its regime.' Clausewitz left the Prussian Army to serve as a Lieutenant Colonel in Russia's German Legion in the summer of 1812. King Friedrich Wilhelm III never really forgave him for this step.

In December 1812 Clausewitz played a key role as negotiator between General von Yorck commanding the Prussian forces fighting on Napoleon's side and General von Diebitsch (another German who had become a full general in the Russian Army) which culminated in the Convention of Tauroggen by which the Prussian forces declared themselves neutral. Clausewitz was the central figure in the negotiations, and it was really due to his immense efforts that the Convention was concluded in spite of much hesitation on the Prussian side. The Convention of Tauroggen was the precondition for the new alliance between Prussia and Russia and Prussia's declaration of war against France on 16 March 1813.

Nevertheless, Friedrich Wilhelm III was not ready to forgive Clausewitz's defection. Although prominent soldiers like Scharnhorst, Blücher and Gneisenau frequently intervened on Clausewitz's behalf for his reassignment to the Prussian Army,

Left: The storming of the French-occupied fortress of Badajoz in Spain by Wellington's forces in 1812.
Right: A second view of the same incident. Wellington inspects the breach in the fortress walls after the battle.
Below: A recruiting poster for a British cavalry regiment dating from 1809.
Below left: British infantry drilling during the Napoleonic period.

THE OLD SAUCY
SEVENTH,
Or Queen's Own Regt. of
Lt. Dragoons.

COMMANDED BY THAT GALLANT AND WELL KNOWN HERO,
Lieut. General
HENRY LORD PAGET.

YOUNG Fellows whose hearts beat high to tread the paths of Glory, could not have a better opportunity than now offers. Come forward then, and Enrol yourselves in a Regiment that stands unrivalled, and where the kind treatment, the Men ever experienced is well known throughout the whole Kingdom.

Each Young Hero on being approved, will receive the largest Bounty allowed by Government.

A few smart Young Lads, will be taken at Sixteen Years of Age, 5 Feet 2 Inches, but they must be active, and well limbed. Apply to SERJEANT HOOPER, at

N. B. This Regiment is mounted on Blood Horses, and being lately returned from SPAIN, and the Horses Young, the Men will not be allowed to HUNT during the next Season, more than once a week.

BOOTH AND WRIGHT, PRINTERS, NORWICH.

the King remained unwilling for the time being and declined every such request. So for the campaign of 1813, Clausewitz, still nominally a Russian officer, became chief of staff of an army corps attached to the allied Northern Army.

However enthusiastically the Wars of Liberation were greeted throughout Germany, upper-level political and military arguments about the conduct of the campaign and its aims never ceased, a fact very instructive to Clausewitz. Thus after the Battle of Leipzig (16–19 October 1813) in which the French and their allies were decisively defeated, Blücher wanted to pursue the French Army into France and end the war by a battle of

annihilation. To the Austrians, who feared a strong Russia and Prussia as much as a strong France, it was imperative that France not be completely eliminated as a military power. France's weight in a future balance of power was not to be destroyed. These differences of opinion were debated at length by the Congress of Vienna, convened in 1814 after Napoleon's first overthrow, and ended only with Napoleon's return from Elba and his journey through France to growing acclaim.

The Prusso-German forces which rallied to the aid of the hard-pressed Duke of Wellington at Waterloo in June 1815 included the III Army Corps under Lieutenant General von Thielmann, only a few months after Friedrich Wilhelm III had finally yielded to the numerous requests and taken Clausewitz back into Prussian service with the rank of colonel. Clausewitz became Thielmann's chief of staff. The relationship between the political and military conduct of war was most instructive in this case, with many of the hot-headed Prussian generals advocating a much more radical course than the politicians were willing to pursue. After the French defeat Clausewitz opposed the spreading of terror, the demand for large reparations and such extremes as blowing up the Jena bridge and the Arc de Triomphe in Paris. To his wife he wrote, 'You can imagine what kind of enemies we are making of the French and Louis XVIII, and this contrasts all the more with the English, who do not levy any contributions and do not plunder.' But then, of course, the English had not been plundered in the way that Prussia had been, nor had they ever paid the kind of tribute which the Prussians had paid to France. The main problem for Clausewitz was that the army was falling between two stools, spoiling its relationship with the French populace as well as with the French government. In the end, however, it was the politicians who won and not the generals.

After the war, Clausewitz became chief of staff to Gneisenau at the new army command at Koblenz. He also occupied this position under Gneisenau's successor, Lieutenant General von Hake. Both Gneisenau and Hake found only words of praise for Clausewitz and particularly admired his intimate knowledge of all aspects of military affairs and his wide intellectual horizon.

Early in May 1818 he was transferred and appointed Military Director of the Berlin War School. In spite of his promotion to major general in September 1818, he began to feel the onset of a policy reaction against the reform movement. His actual work

Above: Wellington's army crossing the Bidassoa River in northern Spain during the final stages of the Peninsular War.

Top right: An incident during the War of 1812 fought between Britain and the United States. This is the Battle of Queenston on 13 October 1812. An American force was defeated in attempt to cross the Niagara River into Canada.

Above right: Prussian hussars of the Napoleonic period.

Left: Hungarian infantry officers and men about 1809.

was mainly administrative, and he had direct contact with the forces only in the role of an umpire at the annual maneuvers.

However, this enforced removal from the center of power provided him with sufficient leisure to reflect upon his experiences in peace and war and to begin to put them on paper. His initial studies concerned the relationship between attack and defense, the phenomenon of the popular war as practiced in Spain and the Tyrol, the Napoleonic strategy of annihilation and the problem of effective collaboration between the statesmen and the military leadership. This was, in fact, the genesis of his work *Von Krieg*, or *On War*.

This period of reflection was interrupted by a short tour of duty as a troop commander. In August 1830 he became Inspector of the II Artillery Inspection in Breslau. When popular unrest and risings occurred in the Russian-occupied part of Poland, a Prussian Army of Observation was stationed at the German-Russian/Polish frontier under the command of Gneisenau, with Clausewitz as chief of staff. However, Gneisenau died of cholera on 23 August 1831 and Clausewitz returned to Breslau. He died of heart failure on 16 November 1831 at the age of 51. He was buried at the garrison cemetery in Breslau. In 1971 his remains were disinterred by the East German authorities and put to rest in his birthplace, Burg.

What remained was an immense legacy of writings on military-political affairs, as diverse as it was voluminous. It ranged from treatises on military history to strategic memoranda, including official and private letters as well as biographical essays and detailed treatments of aspects of the Prussian Reform period. His most significant legacy was his treatise *On War*, which in time became the foundation of the modern theory of war, a status that it retains to this day. But at the time of his death, it existed only in draft form; Clausewitz himself had considered only a small part of it as complete. The closeness between Clausewitz and his wife, Marie von Brühl, is demonstrated by the fact that she was sufficiently intimate with the workings of his mind to edit his literary legacy into a coherent volume of 849 pages. The work was published between 1832 and 1834. So far, in German alone, there have been 22 editions, not counting unnumbered editions. The first translation of the work was into Russian, but otherwise it was ignored there for most of the nineteenth century. Then came the Bolshevik Revolution and Clausewitz was rediscovered. He now has a place with the essential texts for Soviet staff training, as well as staff training throughout the Warsaw Bloc countries.

On War is divided into three parts. Part One consists of Book 1: Concerning the Nature of War; Book 2: Concerning the Theory of War; Book 3: Concerning Strategy and Book 4: Concerning Combat. Part II contains Book 5: The Military Forces and Book 6: Defense. Part III comprises Book 7: The Attack and Book 8: The Warplan. In this work, Clausewitz endeavors to produce not a military manual but something timeless on the fundamental nature of war and the theory related to it. The empirical raw materials of his study are some 139 campaigns and his own personal experience in several wars, augmented by his reflections during his postwar career.

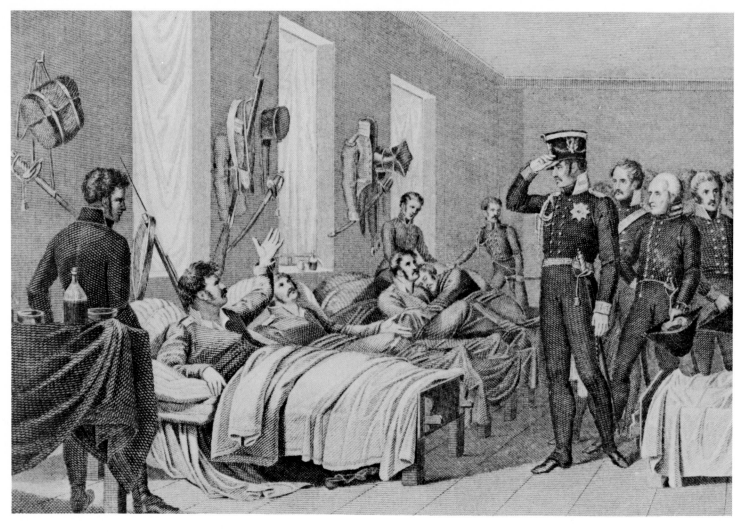

To understand Clausewitz one must understand the method with which he proceeded to examine his subject matter. He did not transform his thoughts into firm and unvarying rules. Instead he took the opportunity to treat the problems encountered dialectically, avoiding categorical statements and any tendency toward dogmatism. At every turn he viewed all sides of a given problem, examined its inner relationships critically and contrasted the advantages and disadvantages of any course of action. He rarely states his own opinions and convictions on a topic without first discussing it in detail. We find that every sentence has a counter-argument. Thus *On War* is characterized by three elements. First, it is a philosophical work, which has resulted from a dialectical method of thought and examination of the material. Second, it is a political work, since it never examines war as an isolated phenomenon, but always as an instrument of politics. Finally, it is a military-scientific work without equal, since it examines the fundamental questions of warfare. Clausewitz's thoughts on the relationship between war and politics are probably the most important and significant part of the work.

One term frequently encountered in his work is 'absolute' war. In Clausewitz's mind this represents an abstraction – a kind of war which had not yet been encountered, but to which Napoleonic warfare had come close. In other words, it means what we now call total war. If one looks for the foundations of Clausewitz's work, upon which his theory of the absolute war is grounded, one finds precise general ideas about the nature of war as such: what it can achieve and what it ought to achieve. In the first instance his ideas are deeply influenced by his outright rejection of the mechanistic theory of war prevalent in the age of absolutism and the enlightenment. Clausewitz reacted against an environment of mercenary soldiers, against armies that fought one another while the bourgeoisie went about its business in a normal peace-time fashion. Military writers like the Swiss officer and later French and Russian general Jomini developed their art of war as a geometry and algebra of action, isolated from other forms of activity. Clausewitz repudiated these notions. In his view a theory of war was not necessarily an instruction for action. The task of theory was to make the empirical evidence subject to reasonable examination and reflection. Theory, in Clausewitz's context, provided a means of organizing the empirical evidence.

In the first instance his theory appeals to experience and directs all its consideration to those combinations which the history of war has already demonstrated. In contrast to Jomini, he aimed at no more than a limited theory here. In the second instance, however, Clausewitz includes in his examination all wars from the guerrilla war – the little war as he calls it – to the absolute war. His underlying purpose was to reconcile theory and practice. Soldier that he was, he left the justification or condemnation of war to the philosophers, preferably, one might guess, to St. Augustine and Grotius. His role in the history and theory of war was analogous to that played by Karl Marx in the field of political economy. Clausewitz's concept of the absolute war was based in part on 20 years' personal experience of Napoleonic warfare, which, as already stated, had not become really absolute but had been nearer to this point than previous wars. Since Clausewitz could not foresee the immense strides of science and technology in the century to follow, the absolute war was really an abstraction to him, because war usually appears in a limited form with all sorts of frictions and constraints, much as individual battles and campaigns are subject to unexpected hindrances. These frictions and constraints prevent war from escalating to the last and ultimate consequence.

Left: King Friedrich Wilhelm III visits his wounded Prussian officers after the Battle of Bautzen, one of several 1813 battles in which Napoleon attempted but failed to crush Blücher's forces.
Above: Marshal Blücher, who wore down Napoleon's army in 1813 and thereby brought about the French defeat of that year at Leipzig.

Although absolute war does not really happen, its mere possibility, however remote, makes it a subject for consideration and reflection. Transposed into the context of our own age, Clausewitz's absolute war is total war and its ultimate and probably final manifestation, *thermo-nuclear war*. The image of absolute war always hovers in the background for Clausewitz, a war that has reached the ultimate escalation. He vehemently opposed the notion that war follows its own inner logic, that it is 'like a mine which once exploded cannot be directed or conducted, except that one has provided it at the outset with a fuse.' Passionately he rejects this idea. 'War is only half a thing since it must be considered as part of a whole, and the whole is politics.'

What does Clausewitz mean by politics? He considers it as representative of all the interests of the community. In his view, the political process stood for all human interests, it was the harmonizing of all these interests and the conflicts among them, domestically as well as in the realm of foreign policy. For a man born into the *ancien régime*, this is almost a democratic definition and brings him into close affinity with his near-contemporary, the writer Alexis de Tocqueville. In a time when the forces of reaction had asserted themselves again in much of Europe, Clausewitz's conception of politics as the representation of interests is quite modern. From that conception came his famous dictum that 'War is nothing other than the continuation of state policy by other means,' a dictum that is by no means invalidated by its inversion in our own days that politics is nothing other than the continuation of war by other means. What has changed is the technological and scientific context.

According to Clausewitz, war has to be subordinated at all times to the primacy of politics. The art of war is a policy that delivers battles instead of diplomatic notes, exchanges the pen for the sword. But war has only a different writing and language, it does not have its own logic. All political purposes belong to the government alone; in no case can the art of war become its preceptor. All that a general can ask the politicians is that they do not over- or underestimate the military means available. In consequence, Clausewitz, very much affected by his own personal experience, rejected the influence of the military upon the formulation of political policy and did not want to leave the decision for peace or war in the hands of the military. One is reminded of the Schlieffen Plan for the German mobilization in 1914, or the conduct of World War I in general when politicians on all sides abandoned control of the war to their generals until Woodrow Wilson, with his Fourteen Points, restored the primacy of politics.

It was not simply Clausewitz's conviction, but the result of his reflections based on solid empirical evidence, which led him to the conclusion that war is an instrument of politics and must be measured in those terms. In short, Clausewitz postulates the primacy of politics at all times. He contrasts a *raison du politique* against an abstract, absolute war, perhaps with too much confidence in human reason, because the question remains open whether political constraints alone – without the transformation of the economy and society to a level which would ensure peace – are a sufficiently strong barrier against absolute war. Still, there are indications in his work that he recognized the danger of a radicalization of politics that could open the floodgates to absolute war. He discerned from far the consequences of the rise of totalitarian politics.

Wars conducted with the full deployment of a nation's resources of manpower and the economy expanded the whole spectrum of politics and warfare. The far-reaching effects of the Napoleonic Wars, according to Clausewitz, 'originated in the new social conditions which the French Revolution had brought about domestically.' In other words, because war necessarily carries the character of the politics which guide it, it can become more powerful and all-embracing, as in France in the 1790s, developing dimensions in which war comes close to its abstract form. In those insights, despite all essential differences, lies a point which is very close to the concept of total war. Clausewitz saw the specter of this development very clearly, and his efforts were aimed at avoiding it.

For a time Clausewitz's fears were held at bay, ironically by nothing other than the forces of reaction after 1815. The Congress System dominated European diplomacy after the fall of Napoleon I – effectively, a coalition of states organized for the defense of commonly accepted values and agreements. This meant no unilateral change of existing treaties or of the territorial *status quo* without the consent of the other signatory powers. The basis of this system was the defense of the principle of monarchic legitimacy and the existing social order by governments which, under the impact of the French Revolution, had combined to avoid any similar upheavals in future.

Although the Congress System was short-lived because of continuing and fresh conflicts of interest among the great European powers, this did not mean that the powers abandoned a platform comprised of mutual agreements. The Congress System was replaced by the so-called Concert of the European Powers, which could be upheld as long as monarchic legitimacy and the social *status quo* were to be defended, despite the relative

Left: Mid-nineteenth century uniforms. In the top picture four Prussians are at the left (infantryman, guard cavalryman, cuirassier, and officer) and five Austro-Hungarians to the right, with two British (sharpshooter and infantry guardsman) on the extreme right. The bottom picture shows French uniforms; from left to right they are a light infantryman from the African colonial forces, a chasseur (light infantryman), an infantryman, a zouave (member of an infantry unit recruited in north Africa), a cuirassier, a lancer, and a grenadier. The British examples are taken from about 1830, the Prussian from 1845, and the Austrian from about 1840. Below: Prussian dragoon uniforms from 1688 (left) to 1845. Third and fourth from right are of the Napoleonic period. Dragoons were heavily armed cavalry, capable of also fighting on foot. Right: The victorious allies enter Paris in 1814; the red and white banner is the Prussian state flag. The allies, including Russia, occupied Paris and France for some years afterward; the Russians in particular developed friendly relations with the French population. Below right: Wellington's campaign in Spain; the British defeat the French, commanded by Joseph Bonaparte, at Vittoria in 1813.

stagnation of economic growth and physical strength in the powers concerned.

On several occasions the Concert seemed close to disintegration, as when there was an attempt to extend it to the Ottoman Empire, over the Italian question in 1859 and over the German question in 1860, 1864 and 1870. But a closer look shows that these events had been preceded by a slower but remarkable change in the relative distribution of power, which had made the political premises of 1815 obsolete insofar as they concerned Italy and Germany. The real distribution of economic power was no longer in accord with that of 1815. The significance of this lies in the fact that these changes took place within the existing framework of power and of the power structure. Consequently, in spite of change, the principles of the Concert of the European Powers survived their occasional suspensions.

Between 1871 and 1890 the territorial *status quo* was still generally accepted, but from 1890 onward until 1914 it slowly decayed, and for the first time since the *ancien régime* the powers of Europe were compelled to rely upon a balance of power among themselves and the means generally associated with this – alliances and armaments.

The reasons for the decline of the European Concert are as manifold as they are debatable. Firstly, the Concert had developed within a European framework, but it was now increasingly subject to pressures originating from areas outside Europe, pressures which the Concert simply was not strong enough to withstand. The problem of the Straits (the Dardanelles) and that of the Egyptian question are but two illustrations.

Secondly, one notices the awareness of the growth of a power vacuum outside central and western Europe, which increasingly touched upon the older traditional interests of the European powers. International stability no longer depended simply on the distribution of power in Europe, but on the distribution of power in the global sense.

Thirdly, the growth of the democratic universal franchise, the entire process of democratization, brought the emotions of the masses into the spectrum of all those factors upon whose correct assessment a stable European policy was based. The growth of democracy brought forth the age of mass politics, with its emotionally rather than rationally formulated appeals to the masses, and thus unintentionally produced a new concept of the State which included a vast range of new functions. In 1815 the respective governments had been confronted by their respective societies. Although the conflicts between society and state had not been fully resolved, in 1914 and again in 1939, temporarily at least, behind every government in western and central Europe stood the solid, phalanx of a national community. The criteria of power had shifted from the degree of political stability, maturity and geographical advantages to factors that were industrial, economic and organizational in nature.

In such a changing environment, even the primacy of politics as understood by Clausewitz was bound to mutate and change. In Germany this was particularly noticeable among the generations of generals who followed Clausewitz. Increasingly, they studied him literally; they did not interpret the sense of what he was saying, but instead turned Clausewitz's work into the very opposite of what he had intended it to be, that is, into a book of firm rules and regulations – a dogma. It was gradually emptied of its theoretical-philosophical content and interpreted as an essentially technical theory of war.

This is true, for instance, of Helmuth von Moltke, probably the best military mind the Prussian Army ever produced. As Chief of the General Staff from 1857 until 1888 he was aware of the differences there had been between the politicians and the generals during the Wars of Liberation. In a letter to his brother in 1852 he claimed that the diplomats had regularly thrown Prussia into chaos from which only the generals could save it. The Austrians, by contrast, had lost many campaigns but obtained their major gains by their cabinet policy. Moltke was at the beginning of a process which can only be called a fundamental misunderstanding of Clausewitz.

It was Moltke's belief that the primacy of politics should exist only until the outbreak of war, when it should be suspended in favor of the primacy of the military for the duration of the conflict. This amounted to the sacrifice of the essence of Clausewitz's teachings. 'Political moments,' he wrote in 1870, 'deserve consideration only insofar as they do not demand something militarily inadmissible or impossible.' On another occasion he wrote 'The military and politicians work hand in hand as far as the ends are concerned, but in its action the military is completely independent.'

'For the duration of a war military considerations have pre-eminence and predominance, the exploitation of successes or failures is a matter for the politicians,' he wrote in 1882. Moltke demanded clearly defined areas of competency, thus rupturing the ties established by Clausewitz's theory.

This is borne out by Moltke's relationship with Bismarck. Bismarck always insisted that the determination and definition of the war aims, as well as the direct personal counselling of the monarch were the province of the manager of the political process and were therefore his own personal affair. It was he, the politician, who determined the political course of the war and not Moltke. In his view it was a difficult enough task to determine the best moment to make the transition from peace to war and from war to peace, which required thorough political knowledge. Bismarck demanded and succeeded in asserting the primacy of politics against great difficulties.

The relationship between Bismarck and Moltke often reached the crisis point, particularly during the Franco-Prussian War of 1870–71, when their cooperation often seemed to be on the verge of a breakdown. The first crisis occurred at a fairly early stage with the fall of Sedan and the capitulation of the French armies there under Napoleon III. It temporarily abated and then reached a simmering point again; by January 1871 the relationship between Bismarck and Moltke was on the verge of collapse. The issues included Bismarck's complaint that Moltke and his general staff kept him completely in the dark about the military campaign, that he was completely ignored in the planning of the second phase of the campaign after Sedan and finally, that Moltke refused, at least for a time, to bombard Paris by artillery, which Bismarck considered necessary for a speedy conclusion of the hostilities. But the main theme underlying the whole controversy was the army's failure throughout the war to keep Bismarck adequately informed.

Both political and military leaders were always present in the German headquarters, so in practice it should not have been at all difficult for the military to keep the politicians informed; there was ample opportunity for cooperation. Of course it was not absolutely necessary to inform the Prussian prime minister and German chancellor about the details of any tactical measures because these were purely military affairs in the hands of military specialists. However, the matter was different when it concerned the conduct of operations which exerted a profound influence on the course of the entire war, occasions when military strategic problems were closely interlocked with problems of political strategy. This was precisely the point at which Clausewitz had considered it essential that the politician and the general cooperate closely within a common war council. In Prussian constitutional terms, this would have meant that

Above: Wellington and Blücher meet after their joint victory at Waterloo. In this portrayal by a British artist the British commander, naturally, is dominant.

Bismarck and Moltke under the chairmanship of the King or the Emperor would discuss the situation and jointly decide upon a common course of action.

Moltke later wrote that neither in the war of 1866 nor in that of 1870–71 had such a war council existed. All he had done was to inform Wilhelm I regularly about the most recent developments and submit to him suggestions for any changes. On such occasions the Chief of the Military Cabinet, Lieutenant General von Tresckow and the Minister for War, General von Roon, had been present. Bismarck, who was also always present at Headquarters, was not mentioned by Moltke at all. Moltke defined a war council differently than did Bismarck. For him it was only an institution for the discussion of problems of military leadership and the conduct of a battle or a campaign. But this kind of discussion was by no means a substitute for a conference on the military and political strategies. Moltke and his subordinates were most anxious to do all they could to keep Bismarck at arm's length whenever they discussed military affairs with the monarch. In the course of these discussions they tried to gain the maximum share of military and political decision-making and simply to exclude the political leadership. The results were ever-increasing tensions between Bismarck and Moltke and the development of a dichotomy between the military and the political leadership.

As a case in point, after the capitulation of the French Army at Sedan it would have been advisable for Bismarck and Moltke to arrive at mutual decisions about the subsequent conduct of the war, especially since on 4 September the Republic was proclaimed in Paris and a government for national defense was formed. It would have been a matter for the politicians to decide whether the German Army should be satisfied with what had been gained thus far in the interest of a quick peace, or whether it should march on Paris to encircle it and go on to occupy further French territory. None of this happened. The second phase of the campaign was initiated by Moltke's order on 3 September 1870. Bismarck was left in the cold and did not participate in the discussions leading to that decision. Wilhelm I, himself more a soldier than a politician, failed to exercise his function as the supreme coordinator.

By 19 September Paris was surrounded and Bismarck favored an immediate artillery bombardment to make the French amenable to a rapid peace. Almost two months later Moltke argued that in the question of artillery bombardment only military opinion would be operative. What lay behind Moltke's argument was the simple fact that after Paris was encircled, heavy siege artillery was not available; it took considerable time to transport it from Germany and position it outside Paris. Even when the bombardment did start, the artillery and ammunition in place were not sufficient. Bismarck, meanwhile, forever afraid of the intervention of other European powers, was anxious to negotiate peace as speedily as possible. But only by the end of December 1870 was sufficient artillery and ammunition available to undertake the siege.

Below: The British infantry, drawn up in their squares, were basic units in the tactics of the Battle of Waterloo. Squares were highly resistant to cavalry attacks, although vulnerable to artillery; but since the enemy could not easily attack simultaneously with artillery and cavalry they were very strong formations, provided the infantry's discipline was tough.
Inset: Wellington, painted in the black cloak he wore at Waterloo.

Left: En route to his final exile, Napoleon paces the deck of the British warship HMS *Bellerophon*, closely observed by the ship's officers.

Below: Wilhelm I, with Moltke and Bismarck in attendance, watches the siege of Paris.

Above: The climax of Prussian military success; King Wilhelm I stands on the parapet of a gun position as Paris surrenders. Right: Bismarck, who guided Prussian affairs from 1862 to his dismissal by the young Kaiser Wilhelm II in 1890. He is regarded as the virtual creator of the Prussian Empire and a skilful manipulator of diplomacy and military violence. But his success led to World War I.

Bismarck was furious about the lack of information from the military. In a letter to Moltke, he demanded continuous reports about the military operation, or at least copies of the telegrams which the army headquarters sent to the press, since what he read in the papers was all new to him. He saw it five days after the event. Bismarck asked Wilhelm I to mandate his presence at the council of war, since the military operations inevitably influenced or touched upon political issues. Nothing came of that request, and he complained to Wilhelm again in early January 1871 that the political leadership had not been consulted in determining the conduct of the war and had been excluded from delivering opinions on its political ramifications. He repeated his request for consultation on the grounds that newspaper reports had been his only source of information except for rumors.

This time Wilhelm I responded favorably and ordered Moltke to cooperate with Bismarck by keeping him fully informed. The Prussian General Staff took a dim view of this, but a royal order could not be disobeyed. Indeed, Moltke's immediate reaction was to submit his resignation, but on second thought he held back. He insisted, however, that the Chief of the General Staff and the Chancellor represented institutions equal in rights but independent of one another. Technically this was correct, since the King and Emperor was the Supreme Commander of

the forces. But from this moment on Bismarck managed to establish the primacy of politics.

Bismarck's success is reflected in his letter of 26 January 1871 in which the statesman and politician informed Moltke, the soldier and warlord, that he had agreed with the French to the cessation of the bombardment of Paris beginning at midnight. This was followed by a meeting between Bismarck and Moltke which paved the way for the negotiations between German and French representatives culminating in the capitulation of all Paris fortresses and the conclusion of a three week armistice. On 17 February began the peace negotiations which ended in the preliminary peace of 26 February 1871. It seemed as though Bismarck and Moltke were reconciled. However, tensions built up between them again during the final peace negotiations. While Bismarck would have been content with the annexation of Alsace, border territory of which the German Empire had been deprived by Louis XIV 200 years before, Moltke insisted on obtaining a part of Lorraine as well, including the city of Metz, in the interest of a better line of defense in any future Franco-German conflict. Under great pressure, Bismarck finally gave in. The Treaty of Frankfurt of May 1871 put an end to the war between Germany and France.

Subsequently the relationship between Bismarck and Moltke ran smoothly; as long as Bismarck was at the helm of state, military-political relationships were very much in accord with Clausewitz's ideas.

Nevertheless, the trend within the Prusso-German army led away from the teachings of Clausewitz. Pure military thinking, divorced from a political context, was on the ascendant, checked only with great difficulty by Bismarck. The work of Chief of the General Staff General Alfred von Schlieffen was twofold: to eliminate frictions in war as much as possible in a period of rapid technological and scientific change in arms and industry, and to introduce an all-embracing military preparedness for any conceivable contingency in which political decisions were again subordinated to those of the military. Schlieffen's operational plans were the product of a perfected theory of war to which the political process was subordinated. Clausewitz's theory was thus reversed, and the dogma of the battle of annihilation established.

Another important factor was the social militarization of Germany after 1860. The immense prestige accumulated by the Prusso-German army in three successive wars put the military at the apex of the social pyramid. It was an army which, apart from its budget, was outside parliamentary control. Small wonder therefore that Bethmann Hollweg (who was chancellor from 1909–17) said with resignation that it was impossible for the layman to judge military possibilities, let alone military necessities. He confirmed that the politicians had abandoned Clausewitz's charge to them to lay down firm guidelines and establish a frame of reference for military function.

Schlieffen, who was the Chief of the General Staff from 1891 until 1905, left no fundamental exposition of his views on the relationship between civil authority and the armed forces. What he did leave were numerous memoranda about a campaign against France which involved the violation of the neutrality of Belgium, Luxembourg and the Netherlands. Military considerations preoccupied him to the exclusion of political considerations. The most important document he left for his successor was the Schlieffen Plan, which envisioned the distribution of the German forces on the western frontier with a right wing seven times stronger than the left wing. The weak left wing would hold the enemy at bay and the right wing would attack north of Diedenhofen and Metz. The army would then march through Belgium, which beyond Liege was ideal flat country for an army on foot, sweep around west of Paris and defeat the French forces decisively within a matter of weeks.

In his first few drafts Schlieffen contemplated violating the neutrality of the Netherlands as well, but he abandoned this idea in the plan's final form. Although the political leaders of the Reich had been informed, first Chancellor Bülow and then his successor Bethmann Hollweg, neither raised any objections. They left military affairs to those best qualified. And Kaiser Wilhelm II was not a man capable of coordinating the political and military leadership. He rather preferred making speeches. Indeed, he went so far as to state that in wartime the politicians had to keep their mouths shut until a successful strategy allowed them freedom of speech again. Thus the primacy of the military superseded that of politics throughout the Wilhelmine period.

The Schlieffen Plan has been much criticized, especially in the context of the July Crisis of 1914 when the military timetables were a major contributory factor to the outbreak of war because of the rapid mobilization and assembly of the military forces. But this development had been foreseen a number of years before, in 1892, when the Chief of the French General Staff, Boisdeffre, and the Chief of the Russian General Staff, Obruchev, upon concluding the Franco-Russian Military Convention, agreed that henceforth the mobilization of forces would have to be carried out at a speed which would make the outbreak of actual hostilities virtually inevitable.

Every general staff devises its plans with the objective of winning a war, or at least holding back the enemy until a cessation of hostilities can be reached. From this perspective the Schlieffen Plan was no novelty, nor was the envisioned violation of neutral territory. Great Britain showed no hesitation in breaking the neutrality of Greece in World War I when this was deemed essential to the outcome of the war. It is interesting to note that even the most incisive critics of the Schlieffen Plan, like the historian Gerhard Ritter, are really at a loss to suggest an alternative to it. One of the Plan's major determinants was Germany's geographic position. It has been suggested that she was favored by her internal lines of communication. To some extent this is true, but for Germany to fight a war on an interior

line of defense would have been tantamount to fighting a war of attrition, which can only be fought by countries rich in raw materials and foodstuffs. Except for coal and a very little low-grade iron ore, Germany had no raw materials of her own to speak of; most had to be imported. To a lesser extent this also applied to foodstuffs. In contrast, countries with exterior lines of defense and communication could not only draw upon their own resources but import all else that they needed.

Therefore, from a German point of view, the war had to be quick and decisive in the west before they could enter the fray in the east, where the going was expected to be rather more difficult. But the Schlieffen Plan failed as a result of the alterations made by Schlieffen's successor, General von Moltke, a nephew of Moltke the elder. Schlieffen's basic concept had been derived from the tactics employed by Frederick the Great at Leuthen in 1757. Moltke, however, was not satisfied with one outflanking pincer; the battle he wanted to emulate was Cannae, a double pincer movement of both right and left wings taking the offensive. But a strong left wing could be achieved only at the expense of the strength of the right wing. In addition, once war had broken out, the Russians invaded East Prussia much earlier than the Germans had expected. To meet the Russian danger, the German right wing had to be further depleted for defense in the east. The result was that German manpower in France was too weak to swing around west of Paris; instead it swung around east of Paris, exposing the entire German right flank to the city that was the center of the French communications network. As a result Joffre, the French commander in chief, was able to throw his forces against the German right wing. The Miracle of the Marne meant that the Schlieffen Plan had failed, and a war of movement degenerated into a war with firm solid fronts from the Channel to the Swiss frontier. It became a war of attrition in which slowly but surely the scales began to weigh against Germany.

Inside Germany it was hoped that this development could be countered by placing even greater emphasis on the primacy of the military, culminating in the virtual dictatorship of Hindenburg and Ludendorff. It was not within their power to change the ultimate outcome.

Left: In besieged Paris, 1870, even elephant meat becomes acceptable. Right: A French artist shows an allegorical France, confronted by real Prussians, signing peace preliminaries. Below: General von Schlieffen. Bottom: General von Kluck and staff.

Clausewitz was forgotten, and after the collapse of 1918 numerous writers in Germany and other countries began to patch together a new theoretical framework. Ludendorff's *Total War* in 1935, already mentioned, was one such attempt. Such lesser lights as General Friedrich von Bernhardi, a prolific writer on military affairs before 1914, postulated that statesmanship must limit itself to preparing for and exploiting military success, according to the directions given by the military leadership. 'This will ensure accord and harmony between military and political action.'

Modern war, so it was stipulated, has a planetary character. Therefore entire states and their populations are involved in it. The differences between combatants and non-combatants had been blurred to the point of extinction. Consequently, intense propaganda must be employed to prepare the nation for the struggle and to sustain it throughout.

Not only military experts engaged in this kind of propaganda, but also writers of great distinction, such as the former shock troop commander Ernst Jünger, who in his *Total Mobilization* and *Der Arbeiter* pleaded for the primacy of the military. For Jünger, peace was only a preparation for war. The aristocracy of the trenches of World War I represented the true form of socialism. The shell crater and the trench were for him the harbingers of a new and healthier world.

Left: Joffre (left) and Foch. Joffre commanded the French army 1914–16 and has been described as 'a strategical vacuum within which buzzed his General Staff.' Foch later became supreme commander of the Allied armies on the Western Front.
Bottom: A celebrated and perhaps crucial event of 1914; motor vehicles are commandeered to take French troops to the Marne.

Such eminent constitutional lawyers and experts as Carl Schmitt and Ernst Forsthoff added to this their demand for the total state, the pre-condition of total war. 'All instinctive, progressive and in substance revolutionary forces are engaged in the attack upon the legacy of our time. The age of the bourgeoisie will be liquidated. Any resistance will have to be exterminated ruthlessly.'

'In future,' to quote Forsthoff further, 'the total German state of Adolf Hitler will be governed by a highly qualified, racially homogenous and dominating leading class.'' The anatomy of the SS state was being sketched long before it existed.

Ludendorff in his own work denied that he wished to devise a new theory of war, but the essence of that work was to turn

Top: Recently-captured French prisoners of war under German guard in France late August 1914. In contrast to May 1940, the French army did not lose its cohesion in retreat, so there were no massive surrenders of French units. Above: Leading participants of the unsuccessful rising of 1923, the Munich 'beerhall' *putsch* of Hitler's National Socialists. The German Army's predilection for meddling in politics is well exemplified here; only two of the figures (Hitler and Frick) are in civilian clothes. General Ludendorff, whose ill-deserved military reputation was a major asset for the Nazis, stands in the center.

Clausewitz upside down. Clausewitz's maxim would have to be replaced by the postulate 'that all politics had to serve war.'

We might ask whether similar writings were to be found in other countries. Certainly in the United States, Homer Lea, before World War I or in Britain, H G Wells in his *Anticipations of Mechanical and Scientific Progress upon Human Life and Thought* forecast the garrison state in which all human endeavors were subordinated to the conduct of war. In France it was Rene Quinton in his *Maximes sur la guerre* and Albert Seche in *Les guerres d'enfer*, both of which ran to several editions. G Blancon and his work *Guerre nouvelle* and the right-wing radical Leon Daudet in *La guerre totale* preached the gospel of the new militarism. Perhaps it can be said of the French that their militaristic literature was a product of a time in which France was in extreme danger.

This can hardly be said of Ludendorff in 1935 when he demanded that all the lessons of Clausewitz must be thrown on the scrap heap on the grounds that war is the highest expression of the racial will to live. Politics has to serve the conduct of war at all times. His call was a plain and simple one for the establishment of a military absolutism, preferably with himself at the helm. What made these writings attractive to a wide readership? No doubt the memory of the days of August 1914, the immense physical and psychological effort made for over four years and the effort to distill some sense and purpose for sacrifices made apparently in vain. Also, the idea of a future multi-front war made Schlieffen's concept suitable to further radicalization in the sense of conducting maximum military preparations in peacetime. Total mobilization and racial cohesion appeared to promise a solution to the problems of German society. The community of the trenches seemed an alternative to the social relationships of a capitalist society.

What influence did these writings actually have? The question is easier to pose than to answer. In the German General Staff and the bulk of the officer corps, they appear to have had very little effect. Ludendorff was considered a crank. More importantly, after 1933 it was Adolf Hitler himself who firmly subordinated the military to the primacy of politics. The Chief of the General Staff, Ludwig Beck, and in 1938 his successor, General Halder, accepted Clausewitz's demand that the military commander subordinate himself to the statesman. But Hitler's concept of politics and of the political process was not only fundamentally different from that of his predecessors, it was in fact perverted. The results of this twisted understanding of politics changed the map of Europe and of the world itself.

In 1929 General von Seekt had said that if we accept Clausewitz's dictum that war is the continuation of politics by other means, then we may as well say 'War is the bankruptcy of politics.' A nation may be able to survive such bankruptcies as Germany did after 1807, 1918 or 1945, but in our own day and age, in the face of the apocalyptical weapons of war, defeats are unlikely to be assimilated or overcome. Hence it is perhaps a salutary sign that on both sides of the Iron Curtain a Clausewitz Renaissance has begun, since both sides realize how important it has become to maintain the primacy of politics *vis-a-vis* the alleged military and industrial necessities. In 1960 President Eisenhower warned in his Farewell Speech of the monster of the military-industrial complex which was about to subjugate the political process to its own ends. Thus Clausewitz and what he wrote are as topical and relevant today as they were 150 years ago. What he anticipated with some anxiety then, sometimes in blurred and shadowy outline, had become a program a century later, and in spite of that program's leading to utter disaster, the problem of the relationship between the military leadership and the civil power has remained with us.

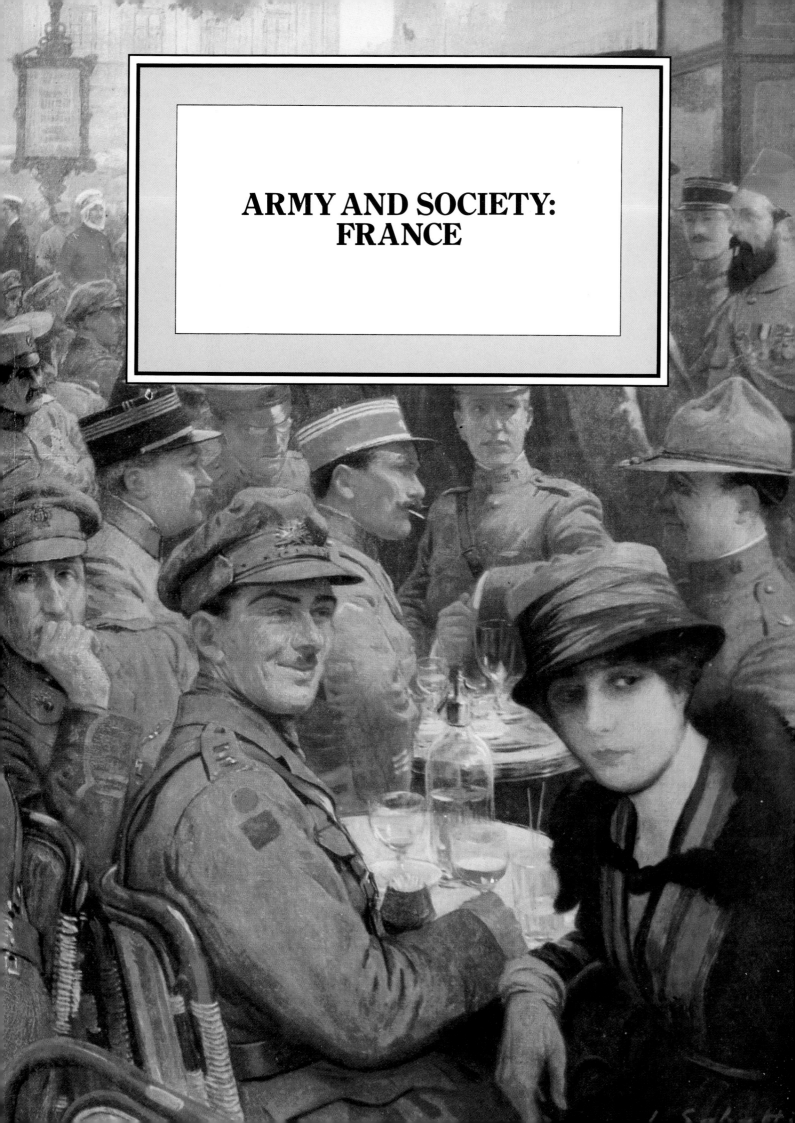

ARMY AND SOCIETY:
FRANCE

In contrast to most other European armies, the French Army during most of the 19th century was a garrison army which lived its own life, separate from the society of which it was a part. It was as much an instrument of domestic politics as it was one of foreign policy. In domestic politics it represented the means by which the various French governments suppressed revolutions.

Within French society there was for a long period a horror of the type of conscription introduced by the Revolutionary *levée en masse*. Clausewitz, during his captivity in France in 1807 when Napoleon stood at his zenith, reported many instances in which two or three policemen took thirty or forty conscripts roped together to the prefect's office. There were manhunts for deserters and missing conscripts, and their number rose by 1811 to 60,000, of whom only half could be caught. Communities, families and even entire administrative districts were held responsible for the escape of a conscript.

After the defeat of Napoleon I, his army as such was dissolved and the French officer corps was subjected to a royalist purge which introduced 14 categories of guilt. No wonder that the country was soon swamped with ex-officers who were suspected to be sources of political disquiet. A new army of volunteers was formed around the royal guard and the Swiss mercenaries, in effect no more than a police force. It was hardly an instrument to inspire popular confidence and enthusiasm. For the officer corps it was more important to display loyalty to the monarchy than to possess any valid qualifications.

Still it was an army which met the needs of France as long as the allied occupation forces were still in the country, and indeed the abolition of conscription was probably the most popular measure enacted by the restored Bourbon king. However, military service had become so unpopular that after 1815 the normal requirement of volunteers could not be met. Many of those who were recruited came from the dregs of society, attracted only by the high initial payment received upon signing up. Very often, they deserted after receiving this payment.

After the allies had left France the question arose as to what kind of an army France should have. To return to the mercenary armies of the 18th century was impossible, since most of France's neighbors had adopted the French principle of the people's army. One answer was the Army Law of 1818 drawn up by Marshal Gouvion St Cyr, which remained in force for over two generations, although the July Monarchy of 1832 and Napoleon III in 1855 made a few changes. It reflected very much the needs and fears of French society and it was bound to be, therefore, the product of compromise. It maintained the Revolutionary principle of each citizen's duty to serve in the army. However, this principle was applied to only a small portion of the male youth, not simply because of the general disinclination to do military service, but out of fear that genuine general conscription could arouse the nation as a whole to the extent that the people would become a danger to the government. The army was to comprise 244,000 men. What numbers could not be filled by volunteers were to be drafted into the army. To alleviate the draft, the choice was made by lottery, which produced 40,000 recruits in a country of 30 million. Prussia raised the same number of recruits annually from a population of only 11 million. In practice, the greatest number of recruits actually inducted in any one year in France was 34,000; in some years there were no more than 10,000 and in the 1860s the annual average was 23,000.

Those Frenchmen who pulled the right lottery ticket were exempt from military service in peace or war. Of those who had the bad luck to be conscripted, a certain proportion had automatic exemptions on the basis of physical unfitness or

family hardship, or simply because they were able to pull the right strings. Students in theological seminaries and certain universities, and those who had won prizes in the sciences and literature, were automatically deferred. In addition there was also the old system of providing a substitute. Those families who could afford to hire a substitute for an attractive monetary payment saved their sons from military service.

The period of service was first six, then eight, and from 1832 on seven years, a term during which the conscripts had to live in barracks and remain unmarried. The middle classes did not mind, since in most cases they were able to buy a substitute. But others argued that the army was bound to become alienated from the nation by this system and arch-reactionaries looked back on what they considered the good old days of the *ancien régime*. The fact that the army had failed the monarchy badly in the French Revolution was conveniently forgotten. One explanation was that this had been due to insufficient discipline, and that the long period of conscription would inevitably prevent such problems. For the bourgeoisie the army was an instrument for the protection of private property from the forces of revolution, but as the events of both 1830 and 1848 showed, despite their original loyalties the soldiers were quick to put their services at the disposal of a new regime. Nevertheless, even after 1871 Adolphe Thiers, the representative of the liberal bourgeoisie, argued on behalf of maintaining the eight-year conscription period.

What was overlooked was the fact that the increasing standards of education had made a long-serving conscript army unnecessary, as long as there was a firm nucleus of professional officers and NCOs. Also, modern warfare as it developed during the 19th century did rely less on long-serving conscripts and more on the availability of well-trained and well-led reserves, since modern war demands from the outset the mass army, which can hardly be sustained without strong reserves. The availability of seemingly inexhaustible reserves, who had trained for three years or less and could immediately be integrated into the regular army, was the source of Prusso-German superiority.

France did not lack for men who recognized the Prussian and German advantages very clearly, as well as the shortcomings of their own system, but they did not find the ears of those in power. What France lacked in 1870 were trained reserves. Despite the great achievement of Gambetta and his supporters in raising numerous armies very quickly after Sedan, not only was it too late, but the personnel were largely untrained. To emulate the Prussian system was suggested on various occasions in the French Chamber of Deputies, but those who did so found no support. For most deputies, such an army posed too great a threat to the crown and its institutions, indicating a distrust of the revolutionary undercurrents of the French population. Instead the liberals denounced the Prussian system as barbaric. As for transforming the entire country into a barrack square, it might be suitable for the territories east of the Elbe River with their subject peasants, but it was totally unsuited for such a highly cultured and civilized nation as France.

The net result for the French Army for most of the 19th century was a very low social position. Although the officer corps still represented a closed corporation of the nobility for most of the century, after the overthrow of the monarchy in 1830 and again in 1848, the space within which such a caste system could be exercised became rather limited. The French nobility did not, in fact, represent a homogenous body; it included old pre-Revolutionary officers and the new Napoleonic nobility as well as that created after the Bourbon restoration. It was a body very much rent asunder by internal quarrels exemplified by frequent duelling and lawsuits.

Suspicions of the alleged monarchist spirit of the officer corps and its support of the Roman Catholic Church were always present among the parties left of center, culminating in the great explosion represented by the Dreyfus case at the end of the century. (Captain Dreyfus, an army officer, was falsely accused of spying for Germany, and later evidence of his innocence was suppressed in a cover-up which reached to the highest levels of the army. Dreyfus was Jewish and anti-Semitic prejudice within the largely Catholic hierarchy was undoubtedly a factor in the case. He was eventually pardoned after a long and violent public debate.)

For a long time an army commission was not very attractive to the new middle classes because of the extremely low pay. The shortage of officers became so great that rapid promotions had to be made from the NCOs to fill the vacancies, another factor disturbing to the homogeneity of the French officer corps. But the officers were still in a rather more favorable position than the NCOs and the rank and file. Sons of respectable peasants, artisans and workers had to spend six to eight years with the dregs of society. The substitutes amounted to one quarter of the army and were mainly men of low reputation. But which peasant, artisan or laborer could afford 2000 francs to buy off his son? Those who were really interested in the profession of arms became regular soldiers, but they were in the minority. Soldiering on the whole was an affair of the poor and

Previous page: High noon of the *Entente Cordiale*; officers of France and her allies in a Parisian cafe. Left: Marshal Soult, one of Napoleon's best officers. Below: French troops charge a Russian Baltic fort in 1854.

Above left: The Battle of the Alma, first engagement of the Crimean War. French colonial troops attack Russian positions after scaling the Heights. Trained never to advance without artillery support, the French advance soon petered out after its brave beginning. Left: Marshal de St Arnaud, the French commander at the Alma. St Arnaud failed to pursue the defeated Russians despite British urging; he said his men could not proceed without their knapsacks, which they had left in the rear, and their artillery, which had run out of ammunition. This prevented the early capture of Sebastopol.
Above: French infantry board a British warship for the 1854 Baltic expedition. Right: French zouaves at the time of the Crimean War, equipped with percussion muskets.

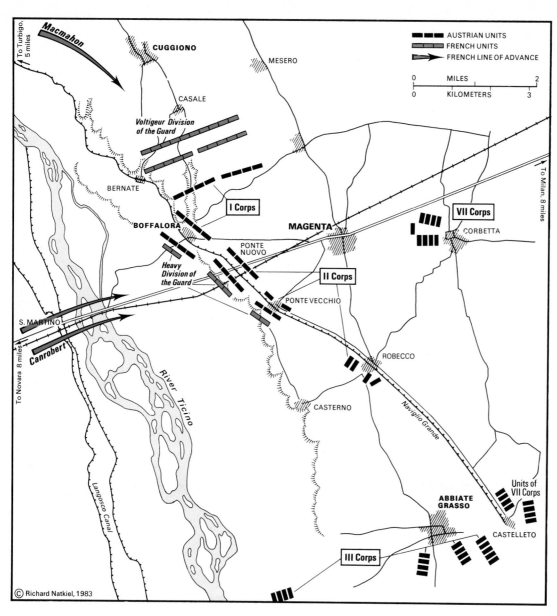

Left: Map of the Battle of Magenta. Both the French and the Austrians lost heavily in this engagement, but as the latter retreated it was adjudged a French victory. It may be regarded as the first of a series of costly battles which culminated in the loss of Austria's predominance at the Battle of Könnigratz in 1866, seven years later, at the hands of the Prussians. The French war against Austria of 1859 may therefore be regarded as opening the way for Prussia's emergence as a great military power in the 1860s. Right: On the battlefield in the evening at Magenta. The French emperor, Louis Napoleon, confers the rank of marshal on General MacMahon. Louis Napoleon, perhaps because he was a Bonaparte, campaigned with his troops although he had little military experience or competence. Below: French crowds outside the Eastern Railroad terminus in Paris, applauding reservists about to travel to the front in 1870. Although the railroad was well organized, the War Ministry was not, and many troop trains left for the war zone half-empty.

of social outcasts, squeezed together in barracks two to a bed, with eight men eating from one bowl. Consequently, it was impossible to produce a real military spirit within the army; the large number of deserters and cases of self-inflicted wounds spoke for themselves. The army, as the institution it was, helped to sharpen the social tensions and the hatred of the poor for the rich. In order to avoid the militarization of the whole nation, France had produced an army of her lowest social strata, left to vegetate in barracks apart from the national life.

During the first third of the 19th century the majority of French politicians did not see in this the source of a danger potentially lethal to France. In view of the general economic upsurge, the rise of industrialization, the belief in progress and the ultimate perfectibility of man, it was thought that armies had become old-fashioned and would sooner or later outlive their usefulness. But anti-militarism and pacifism could exert their influence only for so long as France did not develop any new ambitions in the realm of foreign policy. These currents did not necessarily deny the need for an armed force, but as socialists throughout Europe were to advocate, the standing army should be replaced by a national militia, supplemented at most by a small body of professional soldiers to guard the frontiers. Various attempts were made in this direction but the National Guard was never a real national militia. It saw its task solely as the protection of the property of the bourgeoisie. The last time the National Guard played a significant part was in the civil war situation in June 1848. Thereafter the rise of Napoleon III,

beginning with a military *coup d'état*, put an end to pacifist dreams and pointed French foreign policy into new and dangerous directions.

However, Napoleon III was neither a trained soldier nor a military reformer, although even a layman could not fail to see the weaknesses of the French military establishment. One of his measures was to secure the loyalty of the army by improving its material position and its public prestige through the generous allocation of honorary posts, the granting of pensions and a general increase of pay throughout the army. The substitute system was changed so as to increase the financial intake, which was used as a fund to tempt well-trained and proven soldiers to re-enlist. This strengthened the character of the French Army as a professional army, establishing a body of *troupiers* able to fight on European soil as well as colonial battlefields. The French Army certainly improved its general image in Europe, especially in the Crimean War.

However, there was still a question as to whether it was equal to any of the other European armies. Napoleon defeated the Austrians at Solferino, but he was immediately hampered by lack of supplies. He also lacked the reserves necessary to cover his Rhine frontier against Prussian intervention, which forced him to a negotiated peace in which not all that the French desired was achieved, let alone the aims of the Italians. Indeed, for the Italians, French support had become rather costly. They had had to hand over Savoy and the Côte d'Azur, including Nice, to France.

Aware of these shortcomings as shown in the war of 1859, Napoleon tried to make up for them by calling only some of the conscripts to long-term service from 1861 onward, the others being trained for only a few months to create a viable reserve. It was a half-measure which did not achieve its objective. This was demonstrated again in 1866 when Napoleon III was not in a position to intervene effectively on Austria's behalf; Austria collapsed too quickly and a preliminary peace was speedily

signed which deprived Napoleon of any new opportunity.

The lesson was not lost on him. Napoleon entrusted Marshal Niel with the task of preparing a thorough military reform which came very close to emulating the Prussian example. However, the reform was mutilated beyond recognition in the Chamber of Deputies. Hence the Defense Law of 1868 was not only a bad compromise; in retrospect it was a disaster. The army was slightly enlarged through greater annual recruitment, and the period of service was reduced to five years. What was eliminated from the original bill was Niel's provision for the creation of an effective reserve. The parliamentarians were satisfied with the creation of a *Guard Mobile* in which all should serve who did not serve in the army and in which no substitutes were allowed. This newly created force received little military training. An organizational structure existed on paper but not in practice; the most it could be used for was guard duty.

What remained was the old traditional army, traditional, that is, since 1815, with all its weaknesses and deficiencies, especially in its administrative apparatus, its mechanism for mobilization and the completely out-dated structure of the supreme command.

After the defeat of 1870–71 it was said that military leadership was incapable, that the army had lacked order and discipline, that corruption was rife and that the officer corps showed a remarkable lack of education, while the General Staff was alleged to have been totally out of touch with the soldiers in service and the regiments of the line. There is much truth in these accusations, but they ignored the fact that the French public, and particularly the French politicians, had effectively prevented any thorough-going reform. Although the French enjoyed *la gloire*, they were unwilling to pay the price for it in military terms. There was a dichotomy between the foreign

Left: Prussian troops in occupied territory requisitioning food at pistol-point. Above: Bazaine, commander of the French Army in 1870, an unsuitable appointment imposed by ill-informed public opinion. Below: The German advance during the Franco-Prussian War.

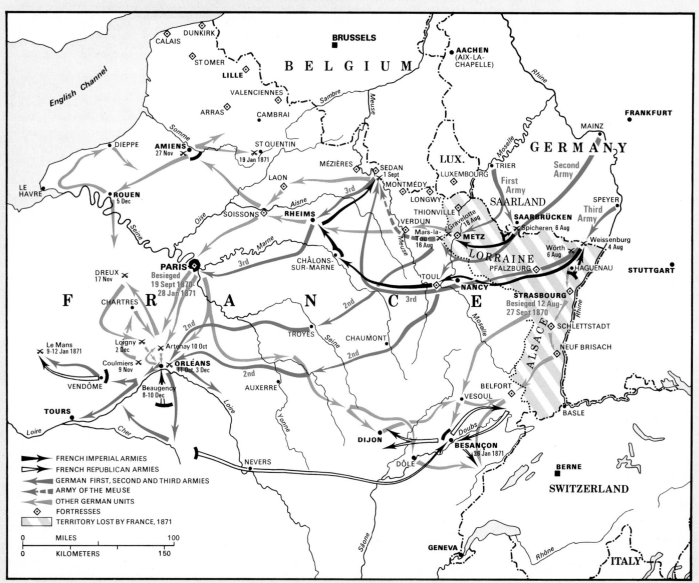

Above: French infantry in a skirmish over a railroad track in the Franco-Prussian War. The artist, portraying a touch of glory, has seen fit to renounce the use of the excellent cover provided by the railroad. Above right: French troops await the Prussians in 1870.

Below: Another combat over a railroad track; the French infantry have the Chassepot rifle. Railroads played an important role in this war, as supply and reinforcing channels and as targets for both regular troops and French guerillas.

policy aims of Napoleon III, widely supported by the French public, and the same public's unwillingness to provide the efficient instruments that would have formed the backbone for that policy. The moment of truth came in 1870. Within a period of one month all the prevailing illusions were ruthlessly destroyed. Gambetta's attempt to resurrect the *levée en masse* was only the sad and abortive epilogue to decades of mismanagement.

For France the war of 1870–71 was a watershed in its military history. The French National Assembly, which discussed a new Defense Law in 1872, was dominated by the categorical statement of the Republican General Trochu (governor of Paris in 1870–71) that the German Army was the only modern instrument of war in Europe. Like him, many others now wished to emulate the German example. The Defense Law of 1872 did away with the substitutes. The length of military service was reduced to five years, but service in the reserves ranged from 9 to 20 years. Now every Frenchman was genuinely liable to be called to arms – not only those who could not afford to pay a substitute. As in the German Army, short service commissions were introduced. But the optimism about the new military instrument was tempered by the fears engendered by the Paris Commune – that a nation in arms could become dangerous to the prosperous middle classes.

However, the new Defense Law was partly neutralized by financial considerations; some of those who should have been called to the colors were again excused in order to keep expenditures down. Of every annual age group eligible for military service (approximately 300,000 men) 110,000 were enrolled for a period of five years, a second group whose fate was decided by lottery served for six months and officer candidates who were to become reserve officers served only one year. So basically there was a division among those serving five years, one year and six months. These inequities were cause for the further development of the French military system. After 1876, when the conservative regime made way for more radical political sentiments, the idea of the nation in arms was raised again. It found support among the socialists, many of whom thought they could bring back their idea of a militia. Had this point of view prevailed, France would have, in effect, left the ranks of the Great Powers.

Although France was isolated in Europe for some years after 1871, the conclusion of the Franco-Russian military convention in 1892 and the Franco-Russian Alliance in 1894 broke that isolation. Allied with Russia, supplemented in 1904 by the Anglo-French *entente* and in 1907 by the Anglo-Russian *entente*, France attained a new feeling of security, which in the last years before 1914 led it to transform the Franco-Russian Alliance, which had had purely defensive intentions, into an offensive one.

The acts of the politicians should not be equated with the mood of the population. It is doubtful whether the new spirit ever existed that was so frequently invoked when speaking of the generation that went to war in 1914. The memories of 1870–71 had faded. French literature provided ample evidence that the people were fed up with arms and armies, and criticism of the army and the officer corps was widespread and frequent. Primary school teachers are alleged to have preached pacifism. The syndicalists called upon the soldiers to mutiny. But nothing divided French society more than the Dreyfus case. In the context of our analysis, the actual case of Captain Dreyfus is less important than its byproducts. When the case came to public attention in 1898, the French Army could inform the government, for the first time since 1871, that it was in a sufficient state of readiness to defend France's eastern frontier successfully.

True, the French Army, especially the officer corps, was not fully integrated into the republic. It was a state within a state. Rather like the *Reichswehr* of the Weimar Republic, the French Army accepted the Third Republic as the least of several evils. But it considered itself the actual receptacle of all national virtues and traditions. The army represented the historical continuity of *La France*. It kept out of politics, with the exception of the Boulangist affair, but the fact that General Boulanger had no backing was amply shown by his end. Nonetheless the army acquired allies within parliament which it could well have done without, particularly the monarchists of various brands who made themselves the self-appointed spokesmen of the army's interest – this in turn provoked opposition on the center and on the left. Whether or not it was willing, the army could not be kept out of politics. The officer corps was especially vulnerable to attack because of the alleged over-representation of the nobility there but that was the Republic's own fault: it blocked the careers of scions of the nobility except in the army and the foreign service. The case of Captain Dreyfus made public all the accumulated resentment. The call went forth that the army had to be reformed and the officer corps purged.

This crisis at the public level began and continued during a period in which France had entered dangerous waters in its foreign policy. The Fashoda Crisis of 1898 occurred at a time when the nation was divided over the Dreyfus case. French policy would have been much firmer *vis-à-vis* the British had it not been for the deep divisions at home. Under these circumstances the French had no other option but to step onto the golden bridges built for them by Lord Salisbury and withdraw from their venture. When the Rouvier government came into office the purge of the French officer corps was begun by General André. The criteria for dismissal or denial of promotion were whether an officer was a practicing Roman Catholic, whether his wife or close relatives were of the same persuasion and whether his children were educated in a convent school. Public confidence in the army was shattered and the officer corps was deeply divided. Precisely at that moment Foreign Minister Delcassé decided to pursue a forward policy in Morocco. Germany opposed it on solid legal grounds, but diplomatically the French were better prepared. Even so, at this point in 1906, when the annual class of officer cadets at St Cyr had declined from 2000 to 870, France took great risks by provoking Germany; France's only firm ally, Russia, had been neutralized by her recent defeat at the hands of Japan. If the Germans had been bent on carrying out a preventive war against France, it could have been a repetition of 1870–71. As it happened, the French were fortunate, but it was the task of subsequent governments to make good the damage inflicted on the French Army between 1898 and 1906. And an important factor in this was the realization after 1906 that France was again threatened by Germany. This caused a serious decline in the hitherto prevalent pacifist currents and the French introduced an armaments program to rival that of the Germans.

Reforms had to be carried out not only to restore public confidence in the army, but to heal the breach within the officer corps. In 1889 the five-year period of military service was reduced to three and the short service period was abolished with certain qualifications which were later nullified when a general conscription on a two-year basis was introduced in 1905. This corresponded with the German example of calling up a greater proportion of those eligible to create large reserves. Divisional or corps commands were firmly institutionalized and distributed throughout France, which facilitated the quick integration of the reserves into the existing cadres. The system of mobilization was vastly improved and the General Staff

Right: A crowded meat market during the siege of Paris. This scene, published in a British magazine, and evidently intended to shock the reader with its absence of anything apart from horsemeat and sausages of doubtful content, for some reason omits a vital indicator in the form of prices. Below: Thiers, French president from 1871. Bottom: Barracks in central Paris, 1870.

Far left: A French depiction of the Franco-Prussian War, showing French infantry in urban fighting. House-to-house fighting has been a feature of wars for centuries, becoming more destructive with the advance of weapons technology. Left: French marine infantry of the 1880s.
Below left: Horsedrawn ambulances transfer wounded to steamships on the Marne Canal during the Franco-Prussian War. Below: French colonial troops of the 1880s, armed with the Lebel tubular magazine rifle.

completely reorganized. From 1905 onward the French Army became more and more like the German in its structure and organization. There was one important difference: France could do this only at the expense of a maximum effort, since its birth rate compared unfavorably with that of Germany. Eighty percent of those eligible had to be called into active service and even that was not sufficient to produce the required number of soldiers. Against that background the French panic in 1913 is explicable; when the Germans changed their call-up arrangements, the French responded by increasing the length of military service from two to three years.

What is important to note at this point is that in France the primacy of politics was maintained at all times, however disastrous this may have been on certain occasions. Apart from Boulanger, the generals never questioned their subordination to the politicians. The legacy of Napoleon I cast its shadow over the entire 19th and early 20th century. The whole organization of the army was designed to prevent generals from playing an independent role. Before 1873 no permanent centers of command existed; in peacetime the largest formations were corps or even divisions. Every regimental commander was the direct subordinate of the Minister of War. The supreme power of decision for army and navy campaigns lay with the Superior Council for National Defense, which was chaired by the Prime Minister and comprised the Ministers of the Exterior, the Interior, Finance, War, the Navy and the Colonies. The Chief of the General Staff and of the Navy had advisory roles only. However, between 1871 and 1914 this council convened on only 17 occasions and so the opportunity to coordinate all aspects of national defense planning, including the planning of armaments was not fully exploited.

One question which posed a problem concerned the supreme command of the army. It was desirable that it should be held by one man responsible to parliament but still capable of acting militarily. Formally the President of the Republic was the Supreme Commander of the Army. He could take the initiative to convene the Superior Council for National Defense but he had only one connection with the army and that went via the Prime Minister and the Minister of War who had only political responsibility. Constitutionally, the Minister of War had the full power of command but the trouble was that in most cases he was a military administrator totally lacking in military expertise. One of the most important institutions operating under the Ministry of War was the permanent Supreme War Council which convened monthly, comprising 10 prominent generals under the chairmanship of the Minister for War. The senior general would become the commander in chief in time of war and was vice-chairman of the Council while the ordinary members were designated to become army commanders. None of these appointments carried executive authority in peacetime and in any case they were changed annually. The Chief of the General Staff was also in a weak position and was usually a comparatively junior general. A further indication of the fears that officers could develop a personal following was the rule that no general should lead an army corps for a period longer than three years.

Thus the generals were strictly subordinate to the civil power, their role at the political summit being that of technical advisors only. They were not, in a political sense, a state within a state. The drawback, of course, was the annual rotation of the Chief of the General Staff, which made for considerable discontinuity in military planning, especially in a General Staff beset with mutual animosities arising from the Dreyfus case, a division that went through the entire French officer corps. Formally, even in time of war, the Chief of the General Staff held a purely ad-

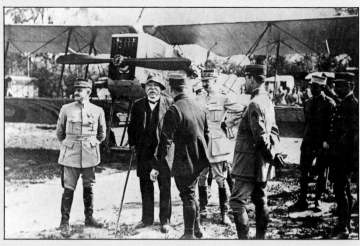

Far left: A French rail-mounted heavy gun under camouflage on the Marne. The sheer volume of artillery activity was one of the several unexpected features of World War I, and the accompanying voracious demand for shells was hard to satisfy; in the Allied countries ministers of munitions occupied a key but vulnerable office. Left: Aviation became a third arm in World War I; the French premier, Clemenceau, visits a frontline air base. The most important role of aircraft was reconnaissance, but air battles and bombing attracted most public attention.

Below: A remarkable photograph showing the last seconds of a French assault on the German line, taken on the Western Front in 1917, and showing in human terms the advantage of defense over offense.

visory position *vis-à-vis* the political leadership. He was subordinate to the Minister of War who acted as the executive organ of the Supreme Council for National Defense and to the Prime Minister who carried the political responsibility. He was also subordinate to the President of the Republic who was the Supreme Commander. Therefore, in contrast to the monarchical system as in Germany, there was never a full integration of the military leadership.

There was, of course, always the possibility that in case of war a successful military commander could gain the full support of public opinion and thus tilt the scale in favor of the military. This was a potential development continually feared by successive French governments, which tried to prevent it by frequent changes in command. They would also play one general off against the other and subject the generals to continuous and intensive control by parliament. This was bound to produce the frequent intrusion of dilettantes into military affairs.

During World War I one of the main guarantees of political predominance was the simple fact that none of the generals was ever able to achieve decisive and final results. Joffre, acclaimed as the victor of the Battle of the Marne, for a time possessed strong authority which he tried to exploit to expand his headquarters into a kind of central command operating independent of the government. He kept the ministers poorly informed, but he could only maintain this position until the end of 1914. Under Clemenceau, the French politicians took the offensive and reestablished their primacy. The Battle of the Marne, after all, had not brought the Germans to their knees. They were still deep in France. The following year showed that it was virtually unforeseeable if and when the tables could be turned against Germany. Joffre was subjected to severe and widespread criticism. Parliamentarians appeared at military headquarters and among the front-line troops to carry out their own inquiries and press their own half-baked solutions. More and more the army became involved in party politics. Politicians exercised great influence on promotions. Clemenceau in particular took personal satisfaction in taking generals down a peg or two and deflating their self-esteem.

From November 1917 Clemenceau was the strongest man in the French state, partly as a result of the many failures of the French armies to expel the Germans. He was a great manipulator of parliamentary commissions and exercised considerable influence upon public and printed opinion. Viviani's previous cabinet had failed and was toppled as a result of the abortive Dardanelles venture which Viviani had pressed upon his generals despite their opposition. Briand, who had followed him, tried his hand at the Saloniki landings. They were commanded by General Sarrail whom Joffre had earlier relieved of a command. So one commander was played off against the other. Briand also called General Galliéni to the post of Minister for War. Parliament was on the verge of entrusting him with the Supreme Command – something which Joffre just managed to prevent. But continuous military failures had begun to undermine Joffre's own position, especially the failure of the Somme offensive. Parliament clamored for his replacement, and Nivelle was appointed as his successor. But Sarrail was not subordinate to him and was responsible directly to the Prime Minister. Briand also reclaimed the right to appoint army commanders himself. When Briand fell, Ribot became his successor. He maneuvered very carefully and tried to secure all his flanks before giving General Nivelle permission to launch a series of offensives. Nivelle had first to submit his plan for a large-scale Anglo-French offensive to the prime minister. When he met with criticism he offered his resignation, but President Poincaré insisted that he stay in office. When the offensives failed, sus-

Above: French heavy artillery on the move in World War I. The heavy gun, with a range sufficient to place it in a safe position well behind the front line, and firing high-explosive shells capable of blasting great holes in earthworks, became a key weapon in trench warfare.

taining heavy losses, Nivelle was sacked and even put up before a court martial. In the meantime, large contingents of the French forces had begun to mutiny. It was up to General Pétain to restore order, which he did successfully though not without bloodshed. Pétain's position, in turn, was controlled by the appointment of General Foch as Chief of the General Staff and direct advisor to the French government. Painlevé, Minister of War during the summer of 1917, bears the credit for thus putting the two ablest French generals at the head of the French Army and also for the creation of an Interallied War Council which at

long last established effective coordination between the French and British Armies. After he had been toppled, the hour came for Clemenceau.

Clemenceau's very dynamism made him a highly popular leader who was able to get his way even in the Chamber of Deputies. He also assumed command of the Ministry of War and began to conduct the war his way. He was a frequent visitor to the front line, and branded any opposition simply as defeatism; he succeeded in revitalizing the energies of the French nation and army. Clemenceau also prevailed in his insistence that Foch be appointed Supreme Commander of the Allied Forces. And to him is due much of the credit for overcoming the crisis produced by the German offensives of March to June 1918. It was largely his will that prevented the outbreak of widespread panic when the German armies succeeded in approaching Paris again for a short time.

In August 1918, under the leadership of Foch, the allies finally managed to gain the initiative in the west. This carried with it the danger that under Foch the military power might become supreme. Foch gained decisive influence in the armistice negotiations. His struggle with Clemenceau was intense, but Clemenceau brought him to heel. When it came to the making of peace, he maintained the upper hand and the military remained firmly in the control of the politicians. The inter-war years did nothing to change that relationship, nor for that matter did the outbreak of World War II. Even in the dark days of Vichy the politicians remained in control. The primacy of politics has been maintained since 1945, despite the political troubles of the Fourth Republic and its wars in Indo-China and Algeria. Even for the Fifth Republic, led for its first 10 years by a soldier, General de Gaulle, the principle of political control has remained unchallenged.

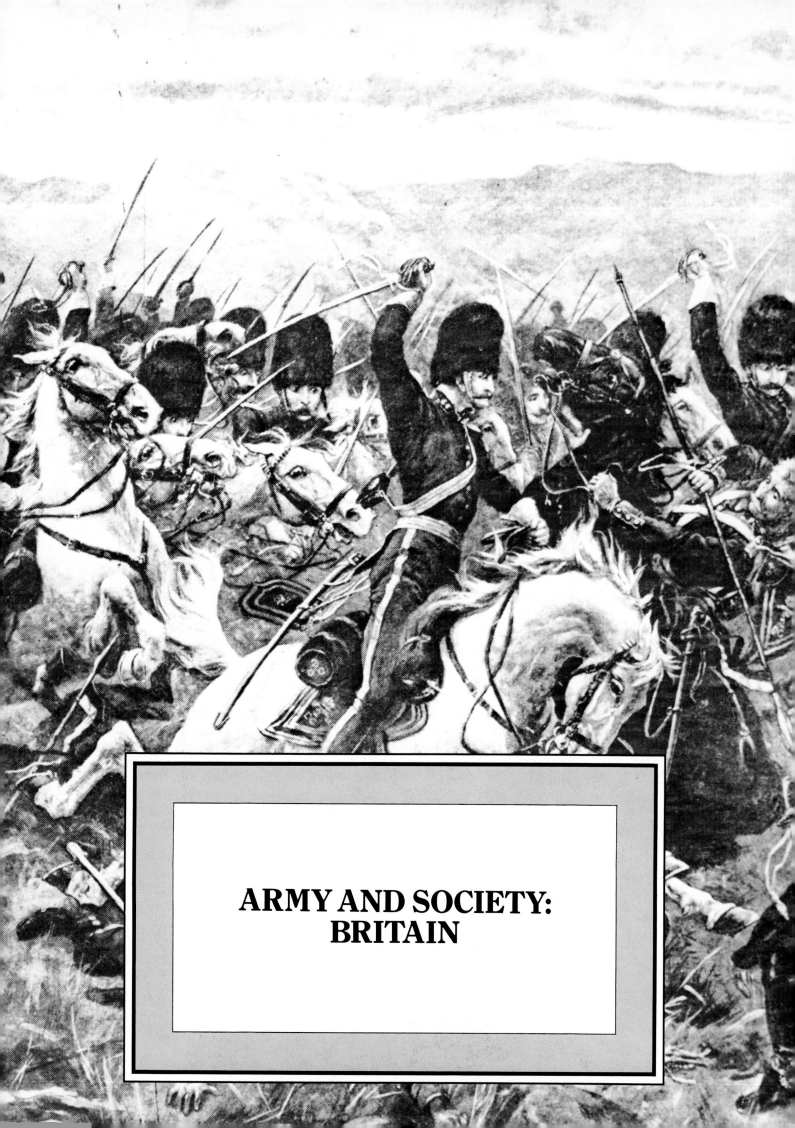

**ARMY AND SOCIETY:
BRITAIN**

Cromwell's standing army had left a lasting legacy which had weighed particularly heavily upon British public opinion. For a long time the British were deeply averse to maintaining a large standing army on British soil. Successive British governments preferred to fight their wars by paying the armies of other countries to do their fighting for them. Their own army included a large number of mercenaries. Even Wellington's army at Waterloo was made up for the most part of foreigners, Germans and Dutch-Belgian forces. Conscription for the army was out of the question. No British Parliament in the 19th century would have sanctioned it. Therefore, in the imperial context, India was particularly important to Great Britain. Not only did India pay for itself, unlike many other British colonies which were heavily subsidized by the British taxpayer, it also supplied much of the manpower for the Indian Army which could be used not only in India but also in Africa and the Middle East.

The transformation of the British Army into a modern fighting force was a very slow one, not least because the army came only a poor second to the Navy. For many, an army was the curse of the nation. They believed there was no need for Great Britain to maintain large land forces in the British Isles. The Royal Navy was sufficient to guard her interests in the world and maintain the *Pax Britannica*. Furthermore, the British governments of the early Victorian period showed little interest in army reforms, since they would be expensive. Their foreign policy was generally conciliatory and there was even a feeling that it would be wise to reduce the existing colonial commitments. In the public mind, dominated by ideas of free trade, there was little room for interest in anything military, apart from glorious memories of the past.

Nevertheless, slow and piecemeal reforms were carried out during the 19th century in two spheres, namely the increased control of Parliament over the military establishment and military reform to overcome the shortcomings that the Crimean War had made so blatantly obvious. The technological backwardness of the army had to be cured as well as the problem of replacements and supplies. But it took the Boer War to alarm the nation sufficiently to back a thorough-going overhaul.

For continental powers, and especially for Prussia, it was a source of utter amazement that since 1688 the continued existence of the British Army has depended on an annual vote by the House of Commons to grant the necessary funds. The Mutiny Acts which provided the legal framework of military discipline had also to be renewed annually. From 1721 Parliament had also voted the peacetime strength of the British Army. Thus the Army was forever unsure about its continued existence. Once the Congress of Vienna had begun, but long before it had come to any firm decisions about the future of Europe, the House of Commons drastically reduced the strength of the British Army. As a result, when Napoleon returned from Elba and Wellington prepared to encounter him, the forces available were only a shadow of the army Wellington had led prior to 1815.

Public distrust and dislike of the army turned the army itself into something of a provisional instrument. No large garrisons were built; instead barracks, old prisons and other disused public buildings were employed to house the army. The welfare of the rank and file concerned no one, and the extremely low level of the soldiers' education gave no cause for alarm. Nothing was done to improve the education of the officer corps or to create a modern general staff. Indeed, soldiers of the British Army were social outcasts even more than in France, where the situation was bad enough. The army consisted entirely of volunteers who had 'taken the King's shilling,' some of them not strictly voluntarily. Since it was a period of great economic and industrial growth,

Previous page: The well-led charge of the Heavy Brigade at Balaklava, a bold and hard-fought move against a surprise approach by Russian cavalry, was a brilliant British success which received considerably less public notice than the fiasco of the charge of the Light Brigade which followed it.
Above: William Pitt, the British statesman who organized the coalition against Napoleon. Above right: Sir John Moore, who carefully trained his infantry and with them conducted a brilliant retreat to Corunna during the Spanish Peninsula campaign. His hero's death at Corunna in 1809 was celebrated for years afterwards.
Right: The last stand of the British 44th Regiment at Gandamak during the disastrous First Afghan War.

the bulk of the soldiers were men virtually unemployable in any other position. A deep gulf divided the civilians from the soldiers. The former considered the latter roughnecks and drunkards, not without some justification. Soldiers were excluded from such public amenities as theaters and even public parks. As late as 1902, when the future Sir Henry Wilson wanted to take a marching exercise with his troops through Clacton-on-Sea, the mayor implored him to circumvent Clacton and spare the tourists the sight of soldiers. After the end of the Napoleonic Wars, Londoners complained about the number of soldiers being seen in the streets, and even in 1817 the Prime Minister raised serious objections to the building of an officers' club. The country seemed devoid of compassion for its soldiers, who were badly housed, poorly paid and underfed.

Even in times of peace the mortality rate among the soldiers exceeded that of the civilian population. They were especially prone to tuberculosis. Physical punishment was still in use, up to 300 strokes; it was abolished only in 1867. Nor did it favor the public image of the army that it was used as an instrument to enforce public order. No regular police force existed in the early 19th century and the army was often used to protect private property against 'the revolutionary actions of the

workers.' The Peterloo Massacre in which cavalry charged a demonstration, killing a number of people, is but one example. The public image of the soldier was still that of a mercenary, popular in wartime as long as he was victorious, but an outcast at home. Nothing was further from the British mind than the notion of a national army.

This was also reflected in the public's attitude to the officer corps. To be an officer in the British Army was not a treasured honor as elsewhere in Europe, but a means of providing for the younger sons of the gentry. Social origin apart, entry qualifications were very low, a private income essential and the required duties easily discharged in a few hours a day. The rank and file who served for 21 years, or virtually for a lifetime, needed no extensive training, especially when the army was fulfilling only a police function. Maneuvers were out of the question; they cost too much money. Apart from this, large troop formations did not normally exist in peacetime. The officer corps had no close contact with its men, and the ratio of officers to men was the highest in Europe.

During the 18th century, when the British aristocracy was at the apex of its power and influence, political patronage was essential to obtaining high commands in the army and a career in the army was very often combined with a seat in the House of Commons or the House of Lords. Venality was the rule; commissions were normally purchased. Good connections in Parliament and with the Secretary for War could prevent well-deserved disciplinary punishments.

In 1793 the office of Commander in Chief was created, an office of a purely military character. Its incumbent was not to be

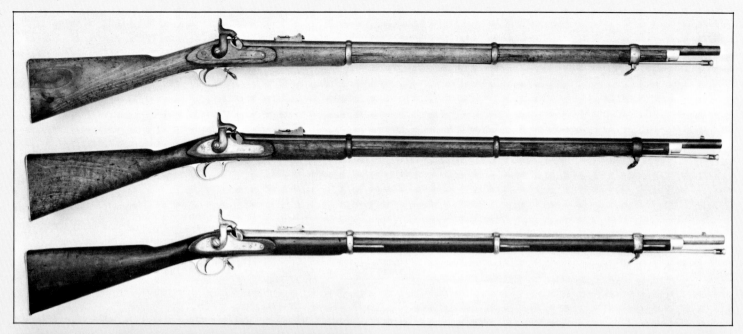

Above: The Enfield rifle (second model) of 1853. The rifling of firearm barrels, imparting spin to their projectiles, was the fundamental advance which brought accurate fire, making long-range shooting practicable and thereby necessitating great changes in battlefield tactics. Left: The percussion lock of the 1853 Enfield rifle; this too, was an advance, but the firing mechanism of rifles and pistols was still far from perfect, subject to ignition failures. Below: Kinburn, a late Crimean War engagement which is hardly remembered by the Russians or by their opponents. Above right: A general view of the Battle of the Alma, fought by the Franco-British-Turkish forces soon after they had landed in the Crimea. The Russians held a strong, elevated, position, but withdrew after some hard fighting. Below right: British horsedrawn artillery of the 1850s.

Below: The British infantry, after wading the River Alma under fire, advance in good order in the final stage of the Battle of the Alma. Explosive shells saw extensive use in this campaign, although the solid cannonball still had a role. Far left: Another view of the Battle of the Alma, the artist having contrived, it seems, to show as many different units and personalities as possible. In the center, wearing a red jacket, is the Duke of Cambridge, Queen Victoria's cousin, promoted to command a division at the age of 35. Prince Napoleon is encouraging his French infantry at the extreme right. Center left: British and Russian infantry get to grips at the Battle of Inkerman, in ruggedly mountainous terrain. Left: French chasseurs advance at Inkerman.

a member of parliament, since he was to represent the military prerogative of the Crown. The first Commander in Chief, the Duke of York, introduced stricter discipline into the army and the officer corps, and opposed with great fervor and success backstairs intrigue and influence emanating from Parliament. He also created his own personnel office staffed by proven officers and founded a training institution for officers. In 1866 royal ordinances prohibited members of the armed forces participating in party political affairs. Thus much abuse was abolished, but it was not by any means a root-and-branch reform of the armed forces. The aristocracy still occupied the best positions, since they still exercised considerable influence at court and in parliament. Although a more regular promotion system gradually took over, the purchase of commissions continued well into the 19th century, a great hindrance to many deserving officers. A final stop was put to this only in 1871; examinations for officer candidates were introduced and pensions awarded to retired officers as a right rather than an occasional reward. Formerly every regiment of the regular army had been the virtual property of an aristocratic colonel. The unit had carried his name and he hired the forces from the lump sum supplied to him by the government. Whatever he could save went into his own pocket. A more uniform system of administration was being introduced by the late 18th century, particularly after financial reforms introduced in 1782, but these were carried out only slowly, by fits and starts. Up to and including the Crimean War, the supply of uniforms was managed by the colonel. Higher tactical bodies than the battalion were permanently formed in peacetime only in the course of Haldane's army reform of 1905.

The supreme command of the armed forces was the product of a series of *ad hoc* measures, not of a clearly conceived overall plan. It was divided among numerous offices distributed over several locations in London and in the country whose cooperation left very much to be desired. On the other hand, from the parliamentary point of view, this provided security against any growing independence of the army from the political institutions of the nation.

Formally, the supreme command rested with the King who had his deputy in the Commander in Chief. The Crown defended its prerogatives in the military sphere tenaciously until the end of the 19th century. Queen Victoria especially put great store by this and even made attempts to expand it. Undoubtedly influenced by her husband, Prince Albert, she was concerned that without royal influence the genuine military experts in the army would be pushed back by the place-seekers and that dilettantes in politics, especially in parliament, would exert undue and harmful influence. There was a plan to appoint Prince Albert Commander in Chief, but it was cut short by his death.

In 1856 a cousin of the Queen, the Duke of Cambridge, was appointed to this post, which he held until 1895. However, his conservatism, allied to a very narrow intellectual horizon, was such that he proved an obstacle to the introduction of technical innovations and a new command structure, even though his authority was limited. He could award commissions and promotions, hand out medals and maintain the discipline of the forces, but he had none of the powers of a chief of the general staff, a post which did not yet exist in the British Army, nor was there a general staff as such. Even the royal command power was vague and undefined.

Parliament retained its major influence particularly in the matter of the annual army appropriations. At the beginning of the 19th century, no less than 13 other institutions competed with the Commander in Chief for authority. For all questions of armaments, from rifles to artillery, from engineers' equipment to cavalry lances, the Master-General of the Ordnance was responsible. Induction of auxiliary forces such as the militia, the yeomanry and volunteers, the deployment of the forces for police purposes and the transfer of forces from one part of the country to another was the responsibility of the Home Office. Matters of discipline and military courts were supervised by the Judge-Advocate General. All colonial forces belonged to the sphere of the Secretary for the Colonies. The feeding of the forces was in the hands of the Commissary, itself a department of the Treasury. Furthermore, there were additional offices responsible for the control of payments to the army, two Paymasters-General, a board of General Officers, an Army Medical and Hospital Office and separate commissions for the housing of troops and for recruitment.

The Commander in Chief was largely dependant on the Secretary at War in financial and administrative matters without being directly subordinate to him, but it was the Secretary for War who was directly responsible to Parliament for all operational affairs; thus in terms of influence he occupied a rather more important position than the Commander in Chief. It was Pitt the Younger who had added this office of Secretary for War, an institution that was in the future expanded into the Ministry for War and the Colonies. He was to conduct the entire military policy in peace and war, and had Cabinet rank and represented the War Office there. Until 1914 only civilians occupied this office. It soon became obvious that the Secretary for War was overburdened, mainly with colonial affairs, another factor which obstructed successful cooperation among the military authorities. The rivalry between the civilian political institutions and the military institutions remained unresolved until the end of the century.

The civilians' powers dominated, much more so than in France where military experts at least had an advisory capacity and where, with few exceptions, generals headed the War Ministry. Politically, the civilian dominance had great advantages. The British Army never slipped out of control to pursue policies separate from those of the government, but in purely military terms the civilian influence proved an obstacle to its transformation into a modern force. The Commander in Chief was really nothing more than an administrator with very limited competence. Wellington once said that he could not order a corporal and his men to march from London to Windsor and back without the approval of the civil authorities. Military plans were drawn up and marching routes for the army determined in Pall Mall and not Horse Guards Parade. In the Crimean War the Secretary for War and the Commander in Chief together exercised supreme command.

The Crimean War was the first eye-opener to the mismanagement within the British Army. In Great Britain the war enjoyed great popularity. The small opposition raised, notably by Cobden, Bright and the Peace Society, was dismissed; Cobden and Bright were even burned in effigy. Great Britain's contingent amounted to 27,000 men and *The Times* sent out its own correspondent, William Howard Russell, in itself a novelty since heretofore British newspaper had relied on reports copied from the continental press or sent to the newspapers by junior officers. Russell pitched his own tent alongside those of the British forces and sent his dispatches to London.

What he had to report was far from inspiring. Within a few days of his arrival at Gallipoli he dispatched a message to his paper to the effect that 'the management is infamous, and the contrast offered by our proceedings to the conduct of the French most painful. Could you believe it – the sick have not a bed to lie upon?' Throughout the war Russell sent messages in a

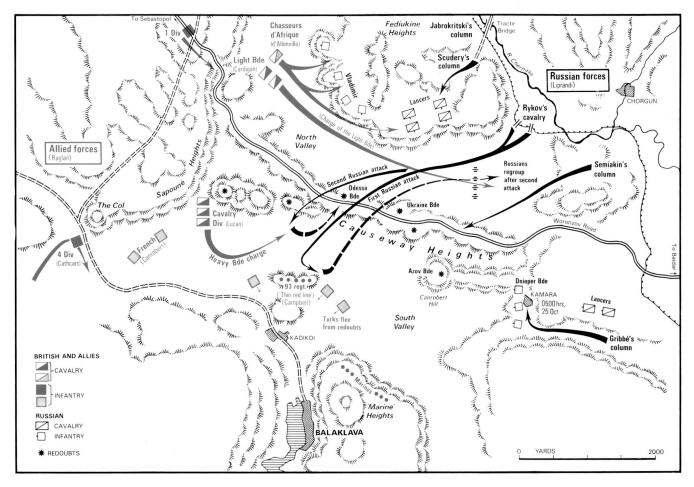

The map labels include:
To Sebastopol · 1 Div · Chasseurs d'Afrique (d'Allonville) · Light Bde (Cardigan) · Fediukine Heights · Jabrokritski's column · Tractir Bridge · Scudery's column · Vladimir · Lancers · R. Chernaya · Russian forces (Liprandi) · CHORGUN · Rykov's cavalry · North Valley · (Charge of the Light Bde) · Semiakin's column · Allied forces (Raglan) · Sapouné Heights · Second Russian attack · Odessa Bde · First Russian attack · Russians regroup after second attack · The Col · Cavalry Div (Lucan) · Ukraine Bde · Woronzov Road · To Baidar · French (Canrobert) · C a u s e w a y   H e i g h t s · 4 Div (Cathcart) · Heavy Bde charge · Azov Bde · Canrobert Hill · Dnieper Bde · KAMARA 0500 hrs. 25 Oct · Lancers · 93 regt. ('Thin red line') (Campbell) · Turks flee from redoubts · South Valley · Gribbé's column · KADIKOI · Marines · 'Marine' Heights · BALAKLAVA

BRITISH AND ALLIES · CAVALRY · INFANTRY · RUSSIAN · CAVALRY · INFANTRY · REDOUBTS · YARDS · 0 · 2000

Above: Map of the Battle of Balaklava. This, the best-known battle of the Crimean campaign, resulted when the Allies decided to capture, and then defend, Balaklava, instead of pressing on to Sevastopol without delay.

similar vein. Early in November 1854 he wrote, 'I am convinced that Lord Raglan [the British Commander in Chief in the Crimea] is utterly incompetent to lead an army through any arduous task,' and later in the month he followed up with the dispatch:

'It is now pouring rain – the skies are black as ink – the wind is howling over the staggering tents – the trenches are turned into dykes – in the tents the water is sometimes a foot deep – our men have not either warm or waterproof clothing – they are out for twelve hours at a time in the trenches – they are plunged into the inevitable miseries of a winter campaign – and not a soul seems to care for their comfort or even for their lives.'

In December The Times published a vehement leading article:

'Incompetency, lethargy, aristocratic hauteur, official indifference, favour, routine, perverseness, and stupidity reign, revel and riot in the camp before Sebastopol, in the harbour of Balaklava, in the hospitals of Scutari, and how much nearer home we do not venture to say. We say it with the extremest reluctance – no-one sees or hears anything of the Commander-in-Chief.'

The Crimean War cost the British nation more in terms of human lives and money than had the Napoleonic Wars. Army reform seemed essential by way of a Parliamentary Committee of Inquiry.

However, during the Crimean War most of the various army administration offices had been merged and reorganized under the control of the Secretary for War. He was relieved of his colonial responsibilities, so the previous diversifications had been largely eliminated or reduced. The office of the Secretary

at War was merged with the War Office, but the Secretary for War remained a civilian and a member of the Cabinet. Queen Victoria, however, was most anxious that the role and functions of the Commander in Chief should not be diminished. Indeed, his functions were expanded to the extent that he assumed actual military command and that artillery, engineers and the colonial troops came under his control. The open question was still the degree of independence with which he could carry out his command under the direct control of the crown. The Queen wanted to hold back parliamentary influence in the matter of appointment and promotion of officers, and in this she appears to have enjoyed the support of public opinion. But all bodies concerned with the reform of the British Army insisted that the Secretary for War was ultimately responsible for all military questions and that therefore he would have to exercise full control over the Commander in Chief.

To all intents and purposes it appeared that through this reorganization the relationship of the politicians and the military had found its final solution, but experience was soon to show that this was not so, that in the end it was always a problem to find a compromise solution between military needs and political requirements. Unlike France, Great Britain always pursued a peaceful policy in Europe. Only in the latter part of the century, with the onset of the New Imperialism, did a profound change affect the course of British policy and its consequences.

As it was, friction between Horse Guards and the War Office never completely ceased and after 1863, even increased. The military complained about the financial meanness of the civilians, while the civilians accused the generals of extravagance.

The most influential and effective Secretary for War in the years after the Crimean War was Edward Cardwell, who in 1870 transferred the office of the Commander in Chief from Horse Guards Parade to Pall Mall, which demonstrated clearly his subordination to the Secretary for War. He now occupied and administered a department of the War Office, although he

Below: British hussars (light cavalry) in a close engagement with Russian infantry as they overrun a Russian gun at Balaklava. Far left: The charge of the Light Brigade at Balaklava. The artist has depicted the attacking British cavalry units too close together; they would have been more widely spaced from front to rear while not filling the whole valley from flank to flank. Nevertheless the picture, unlike other artistic and poetic efforts, does suggest that the achievement of the Light Brigade in overrunning the Russian guns was not so much a result of bravery, but of the iron discipline which enabled it to maintain under intense fire its regular alignment, so important in maximizing the impact of a cavalry charge. Right: A German painting of the Light Brigade's celebrated charge.

Above left: The survivors of the charge of the Light Brigade line up for inspection after their costly exploit. Left: One more of the many pictures celebrating this event; this one gives a fine impression of the mass and momentum of a well-disciplined cavalry charge.
Above: Lord Cardigan, commander of the Light Brigade. Although a fellow-officer exclaimed 'Cardigan has as much brains as my boot,' the suicidal charge of the Light Brigade was not his fault, despite subsequent allegations.

into a position akin to an advisor of the Secretary for War which caused a wave of protest, especially since the man in that position was the Duke of Cambridge, renowned for his arch-conservatism and resistance to all military innovations. This put him particularly at odds with his more progressive and reform-minded subordinates. As far as the Secretary for War was concerned, the Duke of Cambridge made a nuisance of himself by continually using his direct access to the crown. The royal prerogative became, in a very direct way, an obstacle to further reform. The only way out was to integrate the army within the parliamentary democracy and its institutions. In 1870 a reform commission had tried to do away with the office of Commander in Chief, or at least reduce its functions and remove it altogether from the War Office. It was advocated that in its place a Chief of the General Staff should be appointed, similar to the German and French example. He, together with the civilian and military department chiefs, would form a kind of council. This plan was bitterly opposed by Queen Victoria and her supporters. The Duke of Cambridge retired in 1895, but his office continued to exist. The chiefs of the military departments could now advise the Secretary for War without interference from the Commander in Chief who was neither a responsible minister nor the sole advisor of the Secretary for War, let alone a Chief of the General Staff or even commander of the troops. All that was left to him was routine day-to-day administration. But it was still not clear who actually held the responsibility for military planning and for the condition of the army. It could not be the Secretary for War, because as a civilian he was not a military expert and he was wholly occupied with parliamentary affairs. It could not be the General Staff, because there was no such institution. Nor could it be the departmental heads who administered only specific aspects of the military.

Little wonder, therefore, that the War Office acquired the reputation of being a 'circumlocution office' whose various departments tended to work against one another rather than to cooperate. The army administration was excessively centralized, which led to a great deal of administrative work being given to officers who would have been better deployed in service with the troops. But large troop formations still did not normally exist in Great Britain. Unlike France and Germany, Great Britain was not divided into military districts, each with its own command and administrative apparatus. This underlay more serious shortcomings: the lack of training during peacetime, the absence of any organization for mobilization and the inadequate training of staff-caliber officers. In case of emergency officers and generals suitable for command and staff duties had to be collected from all parts of the country. On the whole, the British war machine was intended to do no more than protect the coasts (which, in fact, the Royal Navy did much better) or to participate in small colonial wars.

One wonders what might have happened if Great Britain had entered World War I with this kind of army and organization. Fortunately, the British Army and Parliament received a timely warning in the form of the Boer War. There could hardly have been another campaign in modern history which was as badly prepared and improvised as the British intervention in South Africa. Again, as in the Crimean War, the public supported it wholeheartedly. Kipling's poem of October 1899 reflected the sentiments of the majority of the nation as well as their somewhat ambivalent attitude to the ordinary soldier:

When you've shouted 'Rule Britannia,' when you've sung
'God save the Queen,'
When you've finished killing Kruger with your mouth
Will you kindly drop a shilling in my little tambourine
For a gentleman in khaki ordered South?

still had a direct connection to the crown. The War Office itself was reformed and its many sections structured into three main departments: one for questions of command and discipline headed by the Commander in Chief, a second responsible for finance and a third responsible for the arsenals and fortifications. Subsequently there were still other alterations in the structure of the War Office. The departmental chiefs of the last two departments were Members of Parliament, while the Commander in Chief, as a peer of the realm, had a seat in the House of Lords.

The difficulties between the departments on the one side and between the War Office and Parliament could not be eliminated. In order to deal with this problem, a new division was attempted in 1888: one side was to be a purely civilian sphere, the other a military one to whom all purely military departments and offices were responsible. This put the head of the military section

The poem was written as part of a fund-raising campaign to save soldiers' families from material hardship. It raised well over one quarter of a million pounds, appearing on tobacco tins and general bric-a-brac and was set to music by composer Sir Arthur Sullivan for rendition in music halls, drawing rooms and on bandstands.

Field Marshal Viscount Wolseley expressed his utter confidence in the supremacy of British arms. He had no doubts whatsoever about the commander of the expeditionary force, Sir Redvers Buller. Initial news from South Africa sounded favorable. A host of newspaper correspondents were sent out, but most of their reports were inaccurate because their messages were heavily censored by the army, on whose lines of communication they had to depend. The seriousness of the reverses suffered by the British Army was discovered by independent visitors to the scene of war and rarely by the correspondents. The terrible state of the military hospitals, in which a great proportion of the 16,168 deaths from wounds or disease occurred, was revealed by William Burdett-Coutts, a British Member of Parliament who toured the hospitals personally. The conditions in the concentration camps established by the British later in the war were revealed by a Quaker, Emily Hobhouse. As the quick victory did not materialize, and the war wore on, the early enthusiasm for it waned.

Gradually the consequences of the disastrous campaign could no longer be concealed; in many quarters of the world, and especially in Europe, the real strength of the British Empire was seriously questioned. In Britain immense efforts were made not only to turn the reverses in South Africa into an ultimate victory, but also to reform the entire structure of the British armed forces. Almost immediately upon the conclusion of the hostilities in South Africa, Britain, whose Navy still reigned supreme, began to try to produce an equally efficient army. The entire military structure was reformed and modernized. New equipment was introduced, major attention given to the training of officers, and provisions made for an effective reserve at all times.

Prime Minister Balfour formed a committee headed, between 1903–04, by Lord Esher, which initially referred to recommendations for reform made as far back as 1890. The reforms recommended by the Esher Commission were carried out by Orders in Council, which meant that the government's wishes were implemented by royal command without any parliamentary discussion.

The reforms put an end to the previous squabbling between the army and parliament and healed the conflict between civilian and military authority. The office of the Commander in Chief was abolished. The Secretary for War was still to be the executive organ for the royal prerogative. To a large extent the army's administration was modeled on that of the Admiralty. Under the chairmanship of the Secretary for War (a Cabinet-rank politician), a seven-man committee would decide all important questions. A Chief of the General Staff was appointed, as was a Quarter Master General, a General responsible for Ordnance and an Adjutant General. Their civilian colleagues on the committee were the parliamentary undersecretaries (junior politicians), the senior departmental civil servants and a representative of the Treasury. Military men and civilians were no longer to work separately but to cooperate in a committee with common responsibility. This was one of the features borrowed from the Admiralty. Seven military districts were formed, each having its own administration. The top-heavy centralization had been abolished.

The most important step was the creation of a General Staff. This had been recommended in 1890 but it was ignored at that

Below: A French painting of the Battle of Balaklava, showing the outnumbered Scots Greys, of the Heavy Brigade, engaged with Russian cavalry. Before the courageous fiasco of the Light Brigade's charge, the Heavy Brigade routed the Russian cavalry and, had the Light Brigade been ordered to attack then rather than later, a great and possibly decisive Allied victory would have been ensured. But the Allies, and especially the British, were encumbered by commanders who had been appointed not for their competence but because of their wealth, family, or connections. However, the aggressiveness shown by the British cavalry at Balaklava unnerved the Russians, giving the British an advantage of morale which lasted throughout the remainder of the Crimean War.

416

Top: The 'thin red line'; the 93rd Highlanders at the Battle of Balaklava. This unit, strengthened by invalids, stood firm against a strong Russian cavalry attack at an early, critical, stage of the battle. Above: Florence Nightingale, who improved the deplorable British military medical service. Right: The Allies bombard Odessa.

Above: In the Crimean War Russia was also attacked halfheartedly in the Baltic. Here the Royal Navy is using small paddlewheel ships to bombard the fortress of Bomarsund. Right: HMS *Driver*, a small and shallow-draught vessel, off the Baltic fort of Kronstadt.

time, since British politicians tended to view generals and general staffs as warmongers. Another innovation was the Committee for Imperial Defense which was chaired by the Prime Minister and included Cabinet members of his choice (usually the Secretary for War and the First Lord of the Admiralty and others) as well as a staff of officers drawn from all parts of the army and from the dominions. These, however, did not have a vote; their role was an advisory one. It was a fairly cumbersome organization but it did give a more coherent direction to military policy-making. The Prime Minister also continued to seek the advice of a cabinet committee in which military experts were included as advisors. The Boer War represents a watershed in the history of the British Army. Having started late, the British could avoid most of the problems that still affected the organization and workings of the French and German armies.

The actual reorganization of the army was begun during the Boer War, with the placement of younger and more efficient officers in important posts. A nationwide campaign to rouse the public's interest in the army and to popularize it was launched with considerable success. Not only was Great Britain called upon to carry its share, but the dominions and colonies as well. The dominions (Australia, New Zealand and Canada) re-

sponded accordingly and during World War I sent larger forces than Westminster and Whitehall had ever expected.

The general living standard of the army rank and file was vastly improved and veterans received more care than they ever had before. The Cardwell reforms had reduced the enlistment period from 21 years to 12 years, of which seven were spent in the army and five in the reserve. This provided the basis for reserve formations. Most regiments now had two active battalions, of which one was based in the British Isles training recruits while the other served in the colonies. The 'overseas' battalion could draw on the 'home' unit for replacements. National service based on short-term recruitment was not considered adequate to British requirements at that time, because a period of one or two years' service overseas was judged to be uneconomic.

What proved to be a viable source of recruitment was the Militia, an institution which had existed since the days of the Tudors. In the 18th century service in the Militia, of which each county had its own, was intended to be compulsory but the system of substitutes existed here as well. Since the middle of the 19th century the Militia had been called upon only when the

country was virtually denuded of regular troops, as during the Crimean War, for example. The Militia underwent a very elementary and superficial training. Recruits had six months' basic training under regular soldiers and thereafter had to participate in an annual exercise lasting three or four weeks. Service in the Militia was limited to six years.

Militarily, they had been of only limited value, but in course of the reforms inspired by the Boer War they attained a new status as reserves for the regular army, one of the achievements of Secretary for War R B Haldane. He foresaw that sooner or later Great Britain might well have to participate in a continental war against Germany. 'Splendid isolation' was, in Haldane's view, no longer a practical policy. Together with the Foreign Secretary, Sir Edward Grey, he backed military conversations with the French of which only the Prime Minister and some of his colleagues (but not the entire Cabinet) were informed. Haldane's objective was the creation of an effective expeditionary force which could be mobilized within a few days and shipped across the Channel. The expeditionary force was to consist of six infantry divisions and one cavalry division, all equipped and structured according to their continental

Above left: A French painting of the stand of the Highlanders against Russian cavalry at Balaklava. Above right: The harbor at Balaklava, used by the Allies as a supply port for the operations against Sebastopol, Barrack huts of the Guards are in the foreground. The British laid the first military railway here, to carry supplies from the port. Above: General Simpson, who became commander in chief after Lord Raglan died of cholera. Right: The storming of the Redan at Sebastopol; British guns and mortars at work.

counterparts. Haldane studied the German tactics for mobilization very thoroughly and then applied them to the British Army.

Having an expeditionary force was one thing, but having adequate reserves for it another. A reserve force was created in 1907, not by the introduction of universal military service, but by way of the reorganized Militia which became the Territorial Army. A typical regiment with two regular battalions would have two territorial battalions attached to it to allow wartime expansion. In some parts of the United Kingdom the Militia system had virtually disappeared, and where this had happened

Above left: The siege of Sebastopol; a captured Russian battery. The rope mantlets were to protect the gunners. Above: Artillery emplacements for the bombardment of Sebastopol. The nearest piece is a siege mortar, used for lobbing heavy projectiles. The protective earthworks are also being used to provide covered shelters. Left: An Allied gun battery at Sebastopol.

it was now re-established. The nascent Labour Party was not slow in raising the cry of 'Militarization' and 'Germanization.' Irrespective of that, by 1909 the Territorial Army comprised 270,000 men. Propaganda for the army and for volunteers for the Territorial Army in particular was promoted at all levels of British society. Schools and universities had their own cadet forces and the Boy Scouts became one of the most important organizations for youth para-military training. Field Marshal Lord Roberts headed the National Service League which advocated the introduction of conscription. Within the British General Staff this idea was seriously considered in 1912 and 1913, but dropped because it was likely to increase the existing international tensions still further and would, in any case, be strongly opposed in Parliament.

How successful these measures were in the long term is a matter of debate. The commanders of the British Expeditionary Force complained bitterly after the war that they had been sent to France with under-strength forces and insufficient equipment in arms, artillery and ammunition. They argued that Great Britain had been in no way prepared for the kind and scale of war they encountered. Then, with a very few exceptions, the generals of all belligerent armies had believed in the short war.

A slaughter of the dimensions that was to take place between 1914 and 1918 was beyond the imagination of most. Nevertheless, Haldane's reform laid a firm basis for what was ultimately to become a large national army. At conferences with the dominions between 1907 and 1911 it was laid down that the successful cooperation of the British Empire could be guaranteed only if uniforms and equipment were standardized throughout the Empire. All the officers of the dominions and colonies received British-style training. Joint plans of operation were worked out. Hence the British chief of staff had the official title Chief of the Imperial General Staff. The objective was twofold: firstly to put the dominions in a position to defend themselves without aid from the mother country, and secondly for the dominions to transfer large forces to the European theater of war. Behind these measures stood the growing 'German threat' as interpreted by Grey.

Once the war had broken out Great Britain, as compared to its allies, had one decisive advantage; Parliament tended to refrain from interfering in military affairs. Then, of course, Great Britain was not as directly threatened as France. The more the war became a *total* war, the more the whole of the nation was involved in it, the more strongly public opinion supported its own army. To this end official and semi-official propaganda was organized on a scale hitherto unknown in Europe to sustain the moral fiber of the nation and extend it to the neutral countries. Even such an eminent scholar as Lord Bryce considered it his duty to organize British propaganda in the United States and to spread the blatantly untruthful stories of the German atrocities in Belgium and France. The stories of the amputated hands and gouged-out eyes of the Belgian children disgusted the

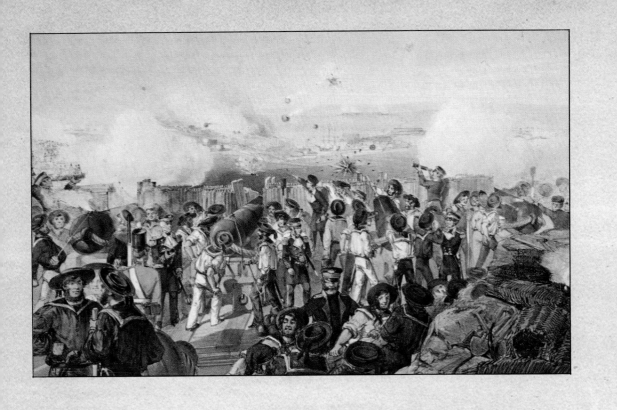

Below: Inside an Allied battery at Sebastopol. Sailors maneuver a 32-pounder into the sandbagged emplacement. Both sides used sailors for land operations in this war, often to operate guns landed from ships. The picture also shows how guns could be dismantled, so that the heavy barrel could be moved on a separate vehicle. Left: Another view of a battery in action at Sebastopol. Shellbursts in the air are another reminder of the great use made of explosive shells in this campaign. Their time fuzes were neither precise nor reliable. Right: Night action at Sebastopol.

public at home and abroad and were believed until they were
finally refuted after the war's end.

The political leadership in Westminster was never formally
questioned by the military and this remained the case because,
as in France, no British general could achieve the kind of
victories which had given Wellington not only military but
also political eminence. The British role in the war was initially
limited to holding the positions in Flanders and supporting the
French, very much the senior partners in the alliance. Only in
the colonies and in the Middle East, in East Africa and Mesopotamia, were the generals relatively free from government
control.

Even the immense energies produced by Kitchener, the first
military Secretary for War, and the efforts of first Field Marshal
French and then Haig, his successor in command of the British
forces, could do nothing to break through the German lines and
put an end to the enormous blood-letting that used up almost
all the available reserves of manpower. Only in May 1916 could
Parliament be persuaded to introduce general conscription. It
produced new manpower but no decisive change in the front
line. In the face of the lists of fatal casualties, the early enthusiasm
for war began to evaporate; like France, Great Britain became
war-weary. Lord Lansdowne – Sir Edward Grey's predecessor
as Foreign Secretary – published a 'peace letter' arguing in favor
of a negotiated peace. *The Times* of London refused to print it
but it reached the public via the press of the Labour Party.
Although parliament's political primacy was never questioned,
it was parliament and the government itself which had abandoned its responsibilities to the generals.

First French and then Haig said that the next great offensive
would bring the decisive breakthrough. Such a breakthrough
was not achieved, at least until the summer of 1918, and the
casualty list grew. Although Prime Minister Lloyd George was
rather contemptuous of his generals, he could do nothing but
leave the conduct of the war in their hands. The only other
alternative would have been to begin negotiations for the
cessation of hostilities, but that was not politically acceptable.

In any case, a British Cabinet, 30 ministers strong, would have
found it difficult to intervene in military operations. They
simply lacked the expertise to do so, with one exception: Win-

ston Churchill. As First Lord of the Admiralty (navy minister) he developed the concept of pushing into the soft underbelly of Europe by means of the Gallipoli operation. It was ingeniously conceived, but when carried out it lacked the wholehearted cooperation of the Army, Navy and French allies. It turned out to be a disaster. Churchill was made the scapegoat and had to resign.

At the beginning of the war, when Asquith was still Prime Minister, Lord Kitchener, a soldier, was appointed Secretary for War. But when the cabinet discussed the war plans, for instance, on 5 August 1914, the Chief of the Imperial General Staff was not invited to give his opinion. Instead a number of other officers were invited who did not possess all the information in the hands of the General Staff. Kitchener mobilized the nation, but he could do little to transform the cabinet into a more decisive instrument for the conduct of war. His achievement was to build up the new army and his actual aim was to produce the largest land army in Europe and thus to put Great Britain in a position to determine allied policy during and after the war.

The cabinet proved such an unwieldy instrument that by the end of 1914 Asquith had created a cabinet committee of six members, later increased to 12, which became the War Council. In 1915 it was renamed the War Committee of the Cabinet, but the General Staff remained excluded. It was not until December 1915 that the then newly-appointed Chief of the Imperial General Staff, Sir William Robertson, gained access to it in an advisory capacity and it was up to him to issue all operational orders – one sign that the politicians preferred to leave military operations in the hands of those qualified. But he remained subordinate to the Secretary for War. Robertson attempted at first to restrict the competencies of the Secretary for War to purely administrative matters, but Kitchener opposed this and proved more than a match for Robertson.

One of the byproducts of the abortive Dardanelles offensive, besides Churchill's resignation, was the fall of the Asquith Cabinet and the formation of a coalition government under Lloyd George. Lloyd George had earned his laurels as Minister for Munitions and as Secretary for War after Kitchener's death in 1916. He was a man who kept his head in times of crisis like the German offensives of the spring of 1918 but he lacked the ability to think through strategic problems and was very erratic in many respects; his own high self-esteem frequently got the better of him. Like Churchill, though with less justification, he prided himself on his strategic talents, and he devised many plans, none of which, fortunately, was ever carried out, partly

Below: Sebastopol on 8 September 1855. The Allies make their final assault on the fortifications. In this picture the French under MacMahon and Bosquet have captured the Malakoff, the key strongpoint of the defenses (marked 1 in this French painting). Meanwhile the Russians, already keen practitioners of scorched-earth tactics, have set fire to the town and have commenced an orderly evacuation across a bridge of boats. The siege lasted almost a year, and was bravely and very competently managed by the Russians, thanks largely to their skill in military engineering and to the assistance of their sailors and naval officers, whose ships had been immobilized. The last act of the retreating Russians was to place water at the side of the Allied wounded. This picture overlooks the scene from the north; the Allied assault was from the south, and the badly-led British suffered enormous casualties.

British colonial wars. Above far left: The British infantry make a bayonet charge against the Ashantis of West Africa in 1874. Above left: Lances, carbines and pistols against spears and knobkerries; the 17th Lancers pursue the Zulus at Ulundi, 1879. Far left: Carnage as the British cavalry achieve the final repulse of the Zulus at Ginghilovo in the 1879 Zulu War. Above: A celebrated battle of the Zulu War, the defense of Rorke's Drift. Queen Victoria later described the Zulu warriors as 'singularly honest' and 'merry.' Left: The British magazine *Illustrated London News* gives the Zulu War first-page coverage. This sketch of a Zulu attack on a British regiment at the Intombi River was drawn by an officer who had taken part. Those who opposed the British prime minister, Disraeli, regarded the Zulu War which he instigated as not only immoral but also shortsighted; subsequent events proved them right.

because at the last moment he feared the risk if they should miscarry. His cooperation with the sober, hard-working and systematic Robertson was uneasy, and he finally had him replaced by the politically more agile Sir Henry Wilson.

In the realm of politics Lloyd George usually managed to get his way; he was resourceful and the most powerful orator of his time. It is often asked why Great Britain never succumbed in times of dire economic trouble to another orator of equal caliber: the British fascist leader of the 1930s, Sir Oswald Mosley. The usual answer – although it ignores many other important aspects – may have a core of truth. Having once trusted a powerful orator in the person of Lloyd George, none of whose promises came true after the war, once was enough for the British: they now distrusted a splendid orator. Lloyd George had an intuitive feeling for the masses, a phenomenon of the age of mass democracy.

In the House of Commons, however, Lloyd George frequently had a deputy speak on his behalf while for his own use he created a war cabinet comprising five to seven civilian ministers temporarily freed from their other departmental duties. The generals and admirals had to submit their plans to this war

Below: An attempt to find a bright side to the humiliating British defeat by the Zulus at Isandhlwana in 1879; two dashing horsemen save the colors. It was in this engagement that the son of the exiled French emperor Louis Napoleon was killed while serving in the British army. This defeat disillusioned many Britons who hitherto had rejoiced in Disraeli's colonial excursions. Right: An incident in the Battle of Omdurman; a long line of British riflemen prepares to receive the assault of the insurgent Sudanese. A field hospital, sign of improved medical care, can also be seen.

Left: The First Boer War of 1881. With the Zulu threat removed by the British Zulu War, the Boers of the Transvaal felt strong enough to assert themselves against Britain. Their defeat of British forces at Majuba Hill weakened the conciliatory voices in the British cabinet, but Gladstone managed to negotiate an agreement with the Boers which retained a British claim to the Transvaal. This picture shows British cavalry and infantry advancing in one of the engagements of this small-scale war, the Battle of Laing's Neck. Below left: Another British last stand, this time during the punitive 1879–80 Afghanistan campaign. Below: Tribesmen of the Indian North West Frontier, long-term tormentors of the British. Then, as now, their rifles were often home-made copies. The picture dates from about 1890.

Right: Eleven men and their dog make a last stand in the Third Afghan War of 1879–80. The British press had an unjustified obsession with heroic last stands during this war; this was perhaps an echo of the disastrous Afghan War of 1842, the first of the three Afghan Wars which Britain undertook to check undue Russian influence in Afghanistan, which was thought to represent a threat to India. The British commander in the 1879–80 campaign was the future Lord Roberts, whose 10,000 men marched 320 miles in 23 days from Kabul to Kandahar. Below: A British infantryman of the 1890s, with magazine rifle and equipped for colonial service.

cabinet for approval; they served in an advisory and executive capacity. He also organized a huge staff and auxiliary offices to guide two essential sectors, the war economy and propaganda. On the domestic scene, Lloyd George's role came very close to that of a dictator. But the generals, aware of the civilian authorities' ignorance in military matters, were anything but servile to him and largely got their way as far as the conduct of operations was concerned. After General Foch had been appointed Supreme Commander of all the Allied Forces in France, the weight finally shifted to the generals until the war had been won.

The primacy of politics had finally been preserved but in what turned out to be a very perverse primacy of mass politics. The nation had been exhorted to mobilize all its physical resources; it was asked to bear a hitherto unknown loss of life. Mass democracy now asked for its price – and the price was the Versailles Treaty. The German Navy, scuttled in Scapa Flow, was no more. Her colonies had passed into the hands of the victors and for the time being German commercial competition had vanished. The formidable instrument which the German Army had once been was reduced to 100,000 men. What more could Great Britain want?

The end of the war brought the abolition of conscription. Great Britain returned to a policy in which imperial considerations were paramount, and thus the military establishment was pruned to the requirements of colonial warfare. Great Britain was determined never again to intervene with a land expeditionary force in Europe. If intervention was needed, it could be made by means of the Royal Air Force on the principle that the bomber would always get through. The appointment of Adolf Hitler did little to change this attitude at first, but finally his expansionist policies could no longer be ignored. Great Britain was committed once again on the European continent. When Churchill succeeded Chamberlain on 11 May 1940, a man of uncommon energy and military knowledge led the country through very adverse times until finally, largely through his own initiatives, the tide turned and with the aid of the Grand Alliance the German foe was smashed again. Churchill's political and military abilities were evenly balanced, and the question of the primacy of politics versus the military never seriously arose during World War II – at least as far as Great Britain was concerned.

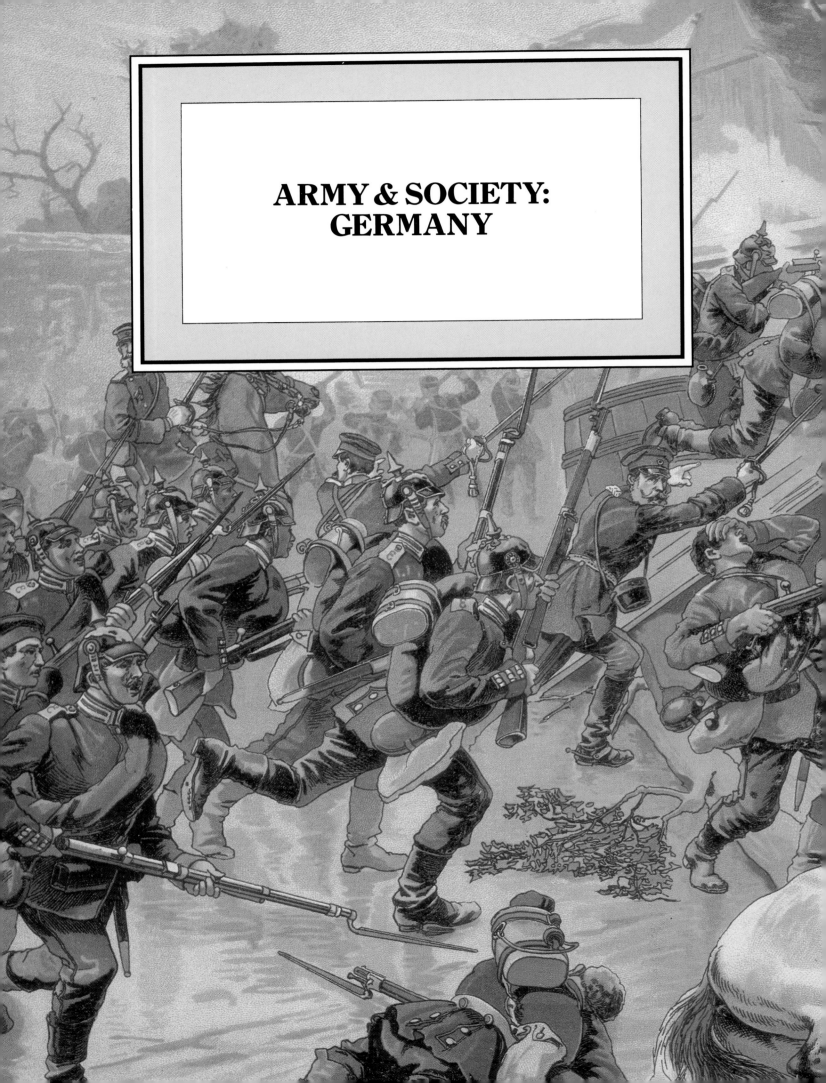

ARMY & SOCIETY: GERMANY

As we have had occasion to note before, the reforms carried out in Prussia between 1807 and 1813, particularly the military reforms, had excited the passion and opposition of many. An army which had previously been manned by the two pillars of the Prussian state, the aristocracy and the peasantry, had been opened to the middle class, precisely that part of the nation suspected by reform opponents to be most vulnerable to the ideas of the French Revolution. It had indeed become a national army. During the War of Liberation criticism abated somewhat, to be taken up with renewed vigor after 1815.

One of the institutions created was a Ministry of War, headed by the reformer General von Boyen. This body became the focal point of struggles for and against the army reforms enacted between 1807 and 1813. Conscription had been introduced for the duration of the war only. By a cabinet order of 27 May 1814 it was lifted again, causing anxiety among the reformers that a return to the *cantonal règlement* would take its place. Boyen's efforts prevented this, but he too had to pay his price, namely to sacrifice the *Landsturm*, the reserve formation for the *Landwehr*, the militia which had been created by the reformers and in which every able-bodied Prussian male had to serve. Thus before State Chancellor Prince Hardenberg's and King Friedrich Wilhelm III's departure for the Congress of Vienna, the king signed the law making conscription a permanent feature on 3 September 1814, to be supplemented a year later by new regulations governing the *Landwehr*. From then on Prussia had a relatively small regular army of approximately 136,000 men (whose members had to do three years' active service plus two years in the reserve) and a *Landwehr* of 163,000 (whose members did seven years' service) which, after receiving basic training from officers and NCOs of the regular army, met for a few weeks every year except in time of war when it was integrated into the active army. There was also a second line of *Landwehr* for purposes of territorial defense, but this did not participate in peacetime exercises.

Conscription and the *Landwehr* were institutions viewed with immense hostility by Prussian conservative reactionaries like Prince Charles of Mecklenburg and Prince Wittgenstein. The latter declared that 'Arming the nation means the organization of revolution.' Attempts were made to abolish both conscription and the *Landwehr*. The Minister of Finance, von Bülow, argued that they resulted in a financial burden which the Prussian state was unable to carry. Boyen, in reply, demonstrated that the financial burden per head of Prussia's population, considering its actual earnings and rising prices, was lower than it had been in the days of the old army, which had shown itself to be ineffective at Jena and Auerstädt. In this he found the support of the King. The issue of the *Landwehr* was more explosive. Through faults of its own, it had allowed such standards as it had possessed between 1813 and 1815 to deteriorate and now gave cause for serious complaint.

Up to the rank of captain it was commanded by its own officers, virtually elected by the men. Within each governmental district it had its own inspectors and, being a part-time army, *Landwehr* soldiers and officers were naturally deeply involved in the lives of their own communities. Only the general of the province was their direct superior officer. Boyen was emphatic in maintaining the militia traditions of the *Landwehr* because he considered it vital that it preserve its character as a people's army. Hence he insisted upon strict segregation between the regiments of the line and the *Landwehr*, which he feared would be jeopardized if the line regiments exerted a greater influence. The King, however, counseled by his generals who were especially critical of what they considered lax discipline in the *Landwehr*, wanted

greater influence for the regular army and the removal of the *Landwehr* inspectors, as well as the combination of line and *Landwehr* regiments into divisional formations. These wishes prevailed.

In 1819 the *Landwehr* was reduced in size and put under the direct command of the regiments of the line. Boyen resigned his post, as did the Chief of Staff General von Grolmann. With their departure the spirit of the officer corps of the regiments of the line began to determine the development of the Prussian Army. It was the beginning of that ministerial crisis which resulted from the reactionary policy of Friedrich Wilhelm III and culminated in the struggles of the conservative State Chancellor, Prince Hardenberg, who had originally been a reformer, and his former associates. For all practical purposes, the reform movement had come to an end. It remained a promise only half-fulfilled with a legacy of betrayal and bitter frustration that was exacerbated by the King's failure to keep his promise of 1815 to grant Prussia a constitution and a representative assembly. Though Prussia was in dire financial straits, there was no need to consult the populace about raising taxes, since a very large loan contracted from the House of Rothschild in London made Prussia independent of public sanction for increased taxation.

The King remained supreme commander of his army without any parliamentary interference. But by 1847 political and economic pressure had mounted to the point that King Friedrich Wilhelm IV found it necessary to give way by publishing a decree which called a Prussian Diet into being on 3 February 1847. It was to meet as often as called for by the requirements of the state, as when there was a need for new loans, new taxes, or an increase in existing taxation. The United Diet, as it was called, was to represent the three estates; the higher nobility such as princes were to deliberate separately as a kind of upper house, the *Herrenhaus*. However, the concessions made were too few and too late. Ultimately, in the wake of the Revolution of 1848, Friedrich Wilhelm IV had to grant a formal constitution to Prussia, but not one produced by a Prussian representative

Previous page: Prussian troops, nearing Paris, storm a street barricade to enter Le Bourget, in 1870. Above left: The Prussian army in action against Berlin revolutionaries in 1848.

Above: Infantrymen of the Prussian *landwehr*, founded 1813. Below, left and right: The 1848 revolutionaries defend their barricades.

Below: The 1st Bavarian Corps storms a railway embankment on the outskirts of Orleans, a few French infantrymen being flushed out from behind the bridge parapet. The Bavarians were Prussia's most substantial allies in the Franco-Prussian War, although other German states also made a contribution; the proclamation of a German Empire under Prussian leadership which came at the end of this war, meant that states like Bavaria would be closely tied to Berlin. Orleans is many miles from the main front of the war; in the closing stages German units ranged far to the west of Paris, so weak was the French army after the Battle of Sedan.

assembly. Instead it was drafted by the King and his advisors, although it did include many features which liberals had been demanding for decades.

General and representative elections were planned (but under the pressure of the liberals the franchise was whittled down and a three-class voting system introduced that favored the propertied class) and two chambers were to convene to discuss the final version of the constitution. The full executive powers of the Crown were retained, including its prerogative in military and foreign affairs, although these were limited by the framework of the constitution. A vital feature omitted was that the armed forces should swear loyalty to the constitution; a clause was included which stipulated that the army and civil servants swear loyalty and obedience to the King.

What had not been finally decided was whether the army was to be an instrument of the state and thus under the Minister for War and subject to parliamentary control, or whether it was the exclusive instrument of the monarchy. Discussions on this soon preoccupied the Prussian Diet, but Friedrich Wilhelm IV insisted that the constitution had given him supreme command of the army and that it was therefore removed from the diet's influence. In other words, the Minister of War was an administrator, responsible both to parliament and to the King. The immediate military advisors of the Crown did not answer to parliament at all.

The question of the status of the *Landwehr* was raised again, without, however, changing the ideas of the King and his generals. Even a man like Friedrich Engels spoke up against change: 'As long as one has a French Army on the one side, a Russian Army on the other, and has to consider the possibility of combined attack by both, one needs forces which do not have to acquire the first principles of soldiering in the face of the

enemy.' As a matter of fact, the issue of the *Landwehr* was no longer very important in itself; it served only as a point of departure for those parliamentarians who endeavored to expand parliamentary control over the entire Prussian Army. As far as the regular army was concerned, the more the *Landwehr* was allowed to deteriorate, the stronger would become the influence of the regular army, or 'the spirit of the line.'

In 1858 compulsory military service for three years was reintroduced, but it was the experience of the war in Italy in 1859 that impressed upon the military party in Prussia the need for a thorough overhaul of the entire army. This view extended to the Minister for War, Roon, and the Prince of Prussia, later the King and Kaiser Wilhelm I. The reform was nothing unique, because both the Crimean War and that of 1859 had impressed upon the staffs of the armies of Europe the need to carry out drastic reforms. Prussia's peacetime army had remained the same size between 1820 and 1859, although her population had increased during that period from 11 to 18 million. During those years, the Prussian Army inducted 40,000 recruits annually. Those who had not been drafted served in the *Landwehr*, which, in case of mobilization, was no longer an instrument with which one could seriously reckon.

One of the lessons of the Prussian mobilization of 1859 was the need to increase the cadre of the regular forces. This was done by recruiting 63,000 men annually instead of the previous 40,000. The regular army comprised all men between the ages of 20 and 26. The *Landwehr* itself was reduced to the status once occupied by the *Landsturm*, a force to guard bridges and other militarily important objectives. In this way the Prussian Army became younger and more mobile; there was no longer any need to rely on middle-aged men.

Since all this was carried out without seeking the advice,

Bottom left: Hanoverian dragoons attack a Prussian infantry square. Hanover wished to stay neutral in the Austro–Prussian War, but soon found itself fighting on the losing side, which gave Bismarck the opportunity to absorb the state into Prussia. Below: Helmuth von Moltke, commander of the Prussian army in its victories over the Danes, Austrians, and French, and subsequently the first Chief of the Great German General Staff. Below right: The Battle of Uttingen in Baden. Baden was another unwilling participant in the Austro–Prussian War, having been dragged in by Austria. Bottom: Cavalry moves by rail in 1866, and arrives faster and fresher. Moltke had noticed the military uses of railroads in the American Civil War.

counsel or approval of the Prussian Diet, differences hardened on the domestic scene. The new reformers, Generals von Manteuffel and Roon, along with Wilhelm I, acted completely independently. The army was the King's, or as Roon put it, 'The army is now our fatherland, because here the impure and fermenting elements have not yet entered.' They looked at the Prussian Army from a viewpoint that identified it with the state: the army was the state and the state the army. However, the army reforms were violently opposed by Parliament, not because Parliament saw them as unnecessary, but because it considered them and the additional revenue they required as a lever with which to subordinate the army to parliamentary control. The opposition became so vehement that Wilhelm I

seriously considered abdication. It was at this stage that Otto von Bismarck came upon the scene with his appointment as Prussian Prime Minister. Bismarck mastered the crisis, governing without the Diet and in opposition to it, and finding a dubious formula by which to appropriate monies until such time as the Crown and Parliament were 'in harmony' again. He had no great respect for generals, especially those who got themselves involved in politics, but for a time there were common interests between them. Bismarck, too, realized the need for the reforms. If Wilhelm I had resigned, the consequence would have been the extension of parliamentary control over the army, a development which Bismarck prevented. He restabilized the royal power of command over the army. In January 1863 he declared to the deputies in the Diet that the Prussian monarchy was not to be a cog within the mechanism of a parliamentary regime.

Nothing succeeds like success, and the wars of 1864 with Denmark and 1866 with Austria confirmed the efficiency of the Prussian Army. After Königgrätz, the decisive battle in 1866, most of the parliamentary opponents of Bismarck and the military party were won over and approved *post factum* the monetary appropriations which Bismarck had made without parliamentary consent between 1862 and 1866. He had avoided the extremes advocated by some of the generals, including the Chief of the Military Cabinet (head of an institution directly subordinate to the King and his advisor in military affairs) who had advocated a military coup d'état. Indeed, the King had already signed orders to this effect. But Prime Minister Bismarck usually respected the power of command vested in the King, except when it concerned decisions that entered the realm of foreign policy. Thus while the King and his generals would have been quite willing to march on to Vienna in 1866, it was

Bismarck's advice which prevailed against that of the military. The same applies to the Franco-Prussian War of 1870–71, in which he ultimately asserted the primacy of politics.

Three successful wars gave the Prusso-German Army a reputation it had never before possessed. From these successes it came about quite naturally that the Prussian Army system should be emulated throughout the states of the German Empire. This had already begun in 1867 with the creation of the North German Confederation and the alliances with the south German states. Bavaria, Württemberg and Baden took over Prussian methods of training, weapons and manuals. True, the allied states reserved rights to the extent that their Kings and princes retained supreme command over the army in peacetime, but in case of war all their armies were subordinated to the Kaiser.

Bismarck, as Prime Minister of Prussia, as Chancellor of the North German Confederation and as Chancellor of the German Empire reasserted and maintained the primacy of politics, but his concept of politics was very much his own and kept large areas of governmental activity from the Diet and the Reichstag. He was not responsible to them, but only to his King and Emperor, and his position remained unchallenged throughout the reign of Wilhelm I. Even so, he needed the cooperation of the Reichstag, which, from its establishment in 1871, had the power of the purse. This explains Bismarck's continuous endeavor to find workable parliamentary conditions that would secure him the vote on vital issues.

One factor which he had initially ignored was Germany's rapid industrialization and the rise of the Social Democratic Party which, up to the mid-1890s, adopted an explicitly revolutionary attitude never reconciled to the empire. As long as German Social Democracy was led by Ferdinand Lasalle there were few problems, but with his death in 1864 and the transfer of leadership into the hands of Wilhelm Liebknecht and August Bebel, the Marxist internationalist ideology gained dominance. (In the years before his death in 1913, Bebel even gave German naval secrets to the British.) This revolutionary attitude was bound to confront the army with serious problems.

With the induction of new recruits into the army, the monarchic legitimist conception and Socialist internationalism met head-on. The traditional officer corps had been in no way prepared to deal with such an ideological confrontation, and it set upon a collision course with the new ideology that created a

Above left: Bismarck, chief minister of Prussia from 1862, Imperial Chancellor of the new German Empire from 1871 to 1890. *Below:* Prussian-built artillery: a Krupp steel breechloader of the 1870s, designed to fire 1000lb shells. *Above far right:* The field gun, the most widely used type of artillery in Prussia's wars. *Above right:* Prussian lancers.

host of insoluble problems. In the center of the conflict between the armed forces and the new forces of democracy stood the question of the supreme command of the army and the extent of the royal powers. At the apex stood the King, followed by the Chief of the Military Cabinet and his Minister for War who alone was answerable to Parliament. Only matters within his competency were subject to parliamentary discussion. The result was a gradual reduction and erosion of the competencies of the Minister for War and an increase in the powers of the Military Cabinet and the General Staff, all of them beyond the reach of Parliament. This process had reached its full development by 1893. The Minister of War had become an administrator, not a policy maker. He had no powers of command. With that, the last segment of the reforms of 1807–1813 had been removed. The Chief of the Military Cabinet was independent of the Ministry of War and had direct access to the King and Emperor. Much the same applied to the General Staff – only Moltke was uninterested in direct access and kept on with the job at hand.

All this did not remove the conflict within the army caused by the intrusion of liberalism and social democracy. The army's main objective was to maintain a homogeneous and ideologically uniform officer corps, but as the wars of 1862, 1866 and 1870–71 had showed, the nobility was no longer numerically strong enough to command modern mass armies. Therefore access had to be provided for suitable candidates from the middle classes. This was achieved primarily via the institution of the *officer of the reserve*. Young men who had attended university or possessed university entrance qualifications could apply as candidates. They would have to apply to a particular regiment

in which the officers would subject each candidate to close scrutiny. Candidates of lowly social origin, like those whose fathers were shopkeepers, were thus excluded; so were those who held liberal or socialist opinions. In this way it was ensured that only solid conservative stock would enter the army as reserve officers. Although there was now a bridge between aristocracy and middle class, it carried only one-way traffic, and the new middle-class officers absorbed the pre-industrial feudal value system of the old officer corps.

In Prussia itself the absorption of the German middle class posed no major problems, because the divisions between aristocracy and middle class in Prussia were far less rigid than is commonly assumed. The greatest influx of new blood into the aristocratic elite had come from the middle class, whose representatives, within a few generations, were themselves part of the elite. The magnetism of the Prussian state and its nobility had been and was strong enough to attract the most talented members of the widespread middle class in Germany. Generally speaking, the pattern of the rise of Prussia's middle class was slow and steady enough to produce in it attitudes not significantly different from those that shaped the aristocratic tradition, culture and way of life. A typical pattern of social advancement began at the level of the property-holding peasant or artisan and progressed via a profession like that of teacher or clergyman to administrator or military subaltern and finally to high administrative or military office. Well-known families who followed this pattern included those of Humboldt, Scharnhorst, Gneisenau, Clausewitz, Schrötter, Schön, Yorck, Boyen, Grolmann and Steuben. Moreover, the marriage conventions were far from exclusive; the mothers of Bismarck and Bülow were of

Top: The Oldenburg Dragoons engaged with French lancers,
recognizable by their distinctive helmets, at the Battle of Mars-la-Tour in
August 1870. Above: Prussian artillery hurries down a street during the
Battle of Wörth, which the Prussians and their allies won by weight of
numbers, despite a muddled leadership. Above center: German infantry
attacks at the Battle of Gravelotte; the French, in good positions and with
their *chassepot* rifles, inflicted enormous casualties, but finally withdrew.
Above right: German artillery in action against French guns at Gravelotte.
The nearest gun seems to have been hit.

middle-class origin, as were those of Moltke and Elder and
Hindenburg. By comparison with the aristocracy of other
German territories, the figure of slightly less than 30 percent of
Prussian Junker marriage being to members of the middle class
represents an extremely high proportion.

As has been pointed out, one of the major factors making for
an integrated state was that the middle-class marriage did not
necessarily mean a permanent deviation from the Junker stock.
The spouse might adopt the Junker code and viewpoint and the
children frequently returned to the Junker fold when their turn
came to marry. The marriage traffic did not go all one way; the
scions of wealthy rising middle-class families not infrequently
married daughters of the nobility. Of the Prussian generals who
had middle-class origins on the eve of World War I, 43 percent
had married into the nobility.

The proportion of top jobs in the Prussian bureaucracy during
the 19th century held by members of the middle class amounted

to 22 percent; 34 percent of all Ministers of the Interior were members of the middle class. Between 1871 and 1918 32 percent of the Prussian diplomatic service was middle class, as was 26 percent of the Imperial German diplomatic service. In the Prussian lower house, 78 percent of the members were of middle-class origin. As a comparative analysis of the political and military leadership in Austria and Prussia between 1804 and 1918 has demonstrated, Prussia provided the middle class with greater opportunities for personal advancement while its aristocracy made a greater contribution than its Austrian counterpart in all spheres of life even outside the army and politics, especially in the arts and the sciences. Consequently, when considering the growing links between a middle class and aristocracy united in an effort to maintain the existing social and political structure, it must be borne in mind that in spite of differences past and present, the necessary conditions for this process already existed in Germany, especially in Prussia.

The increasing economic vulnerability of the landed nobility as a result of the agrarian depression between the mid-1870s and early 1890s aided the rapprochement between the two classes. Nonetheless, it was the institution of the reserve officer that was

favor of a German Army based on conscription, the Socialists in the Reichstag violently attacked this principle, advocating a militia system on the Swiss pattern in its place. As far as the officer corps was concerned, political debates were taboo. This applied also to middle-class officers. The military academies, which had previously been renowned for the broad intellectual instruction they provided for officers-to-be, had their range of courses narrowed down to strictly military subjects. What was needed was the perfect technician and not the broadly educated man. Homogeneity of the officer corps had to be achieved at all costs and it was not to be an institution marked by individualism. A broadly based humanistic syllabus could lead the army into entirely different directions and introduce a markedly different spirit.

The Military Cabinet even tried to oppose the requirement that applicants for commissions have university entrance qualifications, in which it was not fully successful. However, in Prussian cadet institutes, if a cadet did fail his matriculation examination, there always existed 'the King's grace' which would allow the candidate to be commissioned nevertheless. Increasingly, the General Inspector for Military Education

the major contributor to the process whereby that part of the German middle class that owed its rise largely to the economic and industrial transformation of the country was assimilated into a pre-industrial social order and corresponding value system.

The Reichstag, as already mentioned, possessed the power of the purse, but as far as budget appropriations were concerned, these were not made on an annual basis at first, rather for three-year periods, since it was argued that one could not confine planning for the army to a period of twelve months. In 1887 Bismarck succeeded in getting a Reichstag majority to extend this term to seven years, the so-called *Septeniat*. But from 1871 onward it was no longer possible to keep the new social and political influences out of the army. In Bismarck's view, the enemies of the Reich, the *Reichsfeinde*, were not simply knocking on the door, they were already well inside it.

Although Friedrich Engels frequently expressed himself in

raised complaints about the declining standards among officers. The War Academy became an institution specializing in military aspects of education and nothing else, and it was removed from the General Inspectorate for Military Education and subjected directly to the General Staff.

Yet all of these developments did not produce a grand strategy for an army that excluded economic, political, social and psychological thinking. In fact, the officer corps knew more than ever about railways, modern communications and improved weapons systems. The army did its best to isolate itself from new social developments though. It held at bay new currents of thought and new political factors and deliberately narrowed its horizon to figures, comparative troop strengths and mobilization plans.

However, Moltke took account of foreign policy. Having to fight a war on two fronts had been a nightmare of the General Staff since the 1860s. The question of where to achieve a quick

resolution, in the East or the West, had different answers. Any future war was, for Moltke, the affair of a highly mobile army and not of a nation fully mobilized economically. After 1871 he expressed the opinion that in any future war Germany could not expect to defeat its enemy in a quick and decisive offensive without the intervention of other European powers. Therefore the idea of a preventive war gained greater dominance in his thinking and that of his successors. Only a preventive war would provide Germany with the power of decision. And the instrument for that, the army, would have to be in expertly trained hands to effect it. War was a matter for the military and not for the politicians, a clear contradiction of Clausewitz's views. War and politics were different *métiers*. If they were to be mixed, this would be at the expense of the army. This view was, of course, reflected in the structure of the entire German Army after 1871. It led to an 'autonomy of the technocrats' with disastrous consequences during World War I.

The most important problem after 1871 was the replacement of the officer corps and the maintenance of its homogeneity. Such reforms as had been introduced in 1808 were discarded. The institution of the officers of the reserve and the criteria for selecting them have already been mentioned, but even as late as 1879 Kaiser Wilhelm I stated that as far as he was concerned, he did not place any great weight on a much-enlarged officer corps. The quality and social cohesion which the young men would have because of their family connections would represent the foundation upon which the integrity of the officer corps rested, rather than recruitment from disparate social and political elements. Many officer applicants were turned down as unsuitable on the grounds that they did not have the spirit that had to be preserved in the army at all costs. Only toward the end of Bismarck's chancellorship, when it had become obvious that it was impossible to recruit enough officers from the families of officers and civil servants, did Kaiser Wilhelm II issue a

Left: Street fighting in Bazeilles, an early phase of the Battle of Sedan. The Bavarians are in their blue uniforms. Right: An imaginative view of the Battle of Sedan, illustrating a sheet of music written in England to celebrate that battle. Below: Prussian troops take a break in a captured French town. Below right: The last shots at Sedan; the French infantry make a last stand. MacMahon's army, with Emperor Napoleon in attendance, was trapped near the French fortress of Sedan while moving to relieve besieged Metz. Explosive shells were probably the decisive factor in the French defeat; it was not the one-sided battle that some observers described. 20,000 French troops were killed, while the remaining three quarters of the army were taken prisoner, as was Napoleon. The battle marked the end of the Emperor's regime, for France was immediately proclaimed a republic by Frenchmen who were weary of their Emperor but wished to keep up the fight against the Germans.

directive according to which nobility of birth was no longer sufficient and nobility of mental attitude was equally important, thus opening the doors wide to commissions in the regular army for the middle class. The period of conscription would have to be maintained, because only over this period could the transformation of a socialist laborer into a soldier loyal to King, Emperor and Reich be ensured.

None of this could stop the rise of Social Democracy. Between the Reichstag elections of 1871 and 1890 the Social Democratic Party increased its vote from 3.2 to 19.7 percent. There was nothing the army could do about it. Gradually its recruits, who had previously come largely from the conservative peasantry, came more and more from the urban proletariat. Nor did Bismarck's anti-socialist laws, introduced in 1878, do much good either. In spite of the obstructions in their way, the Social Democrats continued to gain votes. In the army this was countered by careful political supervision down to the company

and platoon level. Mail was censored by the army authorities, the barracks were frequently searched for subversive material and blacklists of Socialist party members in the army were drawn up. Kaiser Wilhelm I recommended dispassionate treatment of all new recruits but harsh sanctions against political activists who were to be transferred to fortress battalions or to the sappers, where they would have to engage in heavy manual labor. Formations with sizable contingents of Social Democrats in their ranks should not be stationed in the vicinity of urban areas, but in isolated countryside locations. All this was without effect and the army faced the phenomenon with utter incomprehension. It seemed totally unaware of the social and economic changes which were taking place around it.

At least two factors operated in favor of the integration of Social Democracy, or some aspects of it, including the trade unions, into the Empire. One was Bismarck's social legislation, continued after his dismissal; the other was the rise of the

Left: The 1st Bavarian Corps rushes a French-held house in Bazeilles. Below left: The French surrender at Sedan; Moltke and German officers await reports from approaching horsemen. The hillside above Sedan provided a grandstand view of the battle. Not only the King of Prussia and Moltke were there, but also Bismarck, Prussian foreign office officials, British, American and Russian military observers, several princes of German states (many of whom did not relish Prussia's triumph), and the correspondent of *The Times*, watching as the German artillery slaughtered the French. Right: The King of Prussia, soon to be Emperor Wilhelm I, seen in the distance as he visits the battlefield at Sedan. Monarchs still sometimes expected to be with their fighting men.

revisionist movement starting in the mid-1890s. Bismarck's social reform legislation was without precedent in the world. It was not, as is commonly asserted, part of a stick-and-carrot policy toward Social Democracy. There is ample evidence that the alleviation of the concrete hardships suffered by the working class had concerned Bismarck for many decades, even before he became Prime Minister of Prussia, and that this concern had its roots in a specific brand of state socialism practiced in Prussia since the days of the 'soldier king,' Friedrich Wilhelm I. But it was, like all Prussian reform policy, reform from above and not from below. The best example of the extent to which Social Democracy had been integrated into the Empire by 1914 is seen in its patriotic response to the outbreak of war in that year and in the endurance and spirit of the army during more than four years of hard fighting.

Another way in which it was thought possible to counteract socialist influence was the mobilization of the masses through patriotism. From funeral associations emerged veterans' organizations which included reservists. One such group was the *Deutsche Kriegerbund* to which 241 local associations with a membership of 27,511 belonged in 1873. By 1890 this had increased to 4,728 local associations with a total membership of 404,276. In 1900 membership had reached the million mark, and this was but one of several such associations. The army viewed them as a strong defensive force against endeavors hostile to the state. It kept them under close scrutiny and ensured that retired officers and officers of the reserve played an active part in them. Commanding generals were appointed honorary chairmen. This development unfolded fully only after Bismarck had left the helm of state. But despite its benefits for the army, it sharpened divisions within the nation even further. Social and economic changes continued apace and were otherwise largely ignored by the army.

After Bismarck had retired to his estate in Friedrichsruh, there was little else for him to do but to write the occasional critical article on government policy under Wilhelm II. The young Kaiser himself proclaimed that he would adhere to the military traditions founded by Wilhelm I, which he considered his proudest legacy. To what extent the rule of Kaiser Wilhelm II

in his first decade was a personal rule is a matter of controversy. Certainly, Chancellor Caprivi's policies, especially in the economic sector, were precisely the opposite of what the Prussian conservatives expected, but as long as he enjoyed the Kaiser's support there was little they or anyone else could do about him. The Chancellor's position did not depend on the Reichstag's support but on that of the Kaiser.

One of the first measures of Wilhelm II was to combine the officers in his personal service and in his entourage into the 'Imperial Headquarters,' headed by a senior general. Wilhelm II hated new faces and he held on to the old ones as long as he could. Thus General von Plessen was the commander of the Imperial Headquarters from 1892 to 1918. He also ensured that the reports of military attachés at embassies abroad would come first to him, rather than to the Foreign Office. Caprivi still managed to contain the influence of the attachés within acceptable limits, but under his successor every form of constraint went by the board. One early issue over which Kaiser and Chancellor differed concerned the period of military service. Caprivi meant to reduce it to two years; the Kaiser, advised by his military entourage, insisted on maintaining the three-year period. In the end, the two-year period of service was introduced.

Caprivi also tried to reform certain aspects of the penal code and this included a reform of the Military Code of Punishment. While the penal reform in the civilian sector was easily implemented for the most part, that of the military sector was the subject of a tug-of-war for years, since any reform affected the role of the Kaiser as Supreme Commander. Military jurisdiction, whether applying to officers or enlisted men, had so far been carried out *in camera*. The new draft envisioned limited access for the public, a measure which also found the support of Caprivi's successor, Chancellor Prince Hohenlohe, not a Prussian but a Bavarian general and politician who had reformed Bavarian military law in a like manner. Wilhelm II, however, insisted that military jurisdiction in Prussia be carried out privately. The Kaiser was also opposed in this by the Prussian War Ministry.

The civilians endeavored to raise the whole issue to cabinet

Far left: A Prussian artillery park in 1864, at the time of the war against Denmark. The method of moving the increasingly heavy guns over longer distances involved detaching the barrels and carrying them on 4-wheel transporters formed by joining two pairs of artillery wheels by a stout beam. A derrick for lifting the barrels can be discerned in this picture. Below: Two heavy cannon serving the Prussian campaign against Denmark in 1864. The Prussians, helped by the Austrians, were quickly successful in this campaign; Denmark's provinces of Schleswig and Holstein were ceded, respectively, to Prussia and Austria. Prussia made war against Austria shortly afterwards and gained Holstein, the whole affair being regarded as a triumph for Bismarck. Left: Prince Frederick-Charles of Prussia (fourth from right) in the 1864 war.

level in order to restrain or contain the Kaiser's functions. Hohenlohe actually succeeded in persuading the Kaiser to constitute a supreme military court and to give up his power of ultimate sanction or dismissal of any judgment it made. Still the final draft of the law submitted to the Reichstag in 1897 contained provisions which seriously limited the public character of the proceedings, and in this form it was accepted by the Reichstag. However, the subsequent executive orders relating to this law emptied the Kaiser's concessions of their substance. The Kaiser, the Imperial Headquarters and the Military Cabinet had triumphed. They all held the view that the reform infringed the exclusivity of the officer corps.

Another development of this period was the *de jure* emancipation of the Military Cabinet from the Ministry for War, which had already been achieved in practice under Wilhelm I. The General Staff was also now completely free from interference from the one institution still answerable to the Reichstag. Officers of the General Staff enjoyed preferential treatment in the matter of promotion. This further increased and extended the Kaiser's power of command. Subsequent Ministers for War were content with the competencies they held. Inevitably, the increased powers of command of the Kaiser as the Supreme War Lord were at the expense of the central military administration, which was all the more serious in that the Kaiser did not have the military and political expertise required by his institutionalized military position. This lack was soon to be demonstrated in the

Left: Prussian troops skirmishing in the woods before Metz in September 1870. It was only in October that this beseiged French fortress city was surrendered. *Below:* Prussian troops bring out French wounded from the ruins of a town on the Paris outskirts, the scene of French sorties from the beleaguered capital in December 1870. *Above right:* Prussian *uhlans* (lancers) capture French guns at Loigny, a typical role for cavalry. *Right:* Lances against bayonets; Prussian *uhlans* charge French zouaves on the outskirts of Metz. Metz, on France's eastern frontier, was a key fortress.

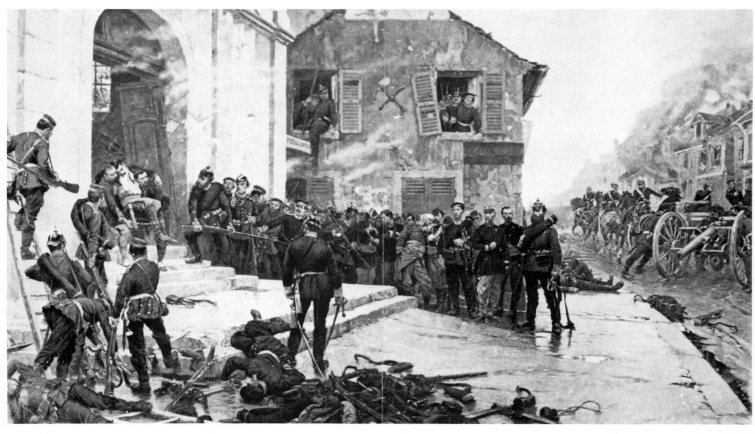

early months of World War I, which led to the Kaiser's gradual withdrawal from positions he had formerly claimed to assume the role of a mere spectator.

The gains of the Social Democrats in the elections of 1890 produced the renewed specter of the 'red danger.' While the Kaiser refused to have the anti-Socialist laws renewed on the one hand, on the other he backed increased supervision of political life within the army and preparations to be made for dealing with the Socialists in case of a national emergency. It became obligatory for military commanders to keep an eye on the Socialist organizations and leaders and agitators in their garrison area and to keep the Ministry of War fully informed about them. A Prussian law concerning the stage of siege, dating back to 1851, contained a provision by which any military commander of a district or province could, if he saw fit, proclaim a state of siege. In non-Prussian territories the Kaiser's sanction was required for this. Once a state of siege had been proclaimed, the executive power of the civil authorities was transferred to the military commander and his troops were under orders to fire if necessary. Fortunately, the occasion never arose. Troops were used to carrying out police functions during various industrial disputes, but it never came to a collision between the army and the civilians.

Within this context the War Historical Department of the General Staff produced a study in 1907 on the use of troops in cities dominated by insurgents. In cases of unrest the early proclamation of siege was recommended and a precondition for the army's success against any insurgents was that the military commander and his immediate subordinates were intimately acquainted with political developments in their area. The new guidelines also envisioned the arrest of members of the Reichstag in spite of the fact that they enjoyed parliamentary immunity. Once this became publicly known, pressure in the Reichstag became so great that this provision had to be withdrawn. But in all cases it was the duty of the police to deal first with unrest while the army should provide a backup. Only in case of extreme confrontations should the army intervene directly.

This was how the army prepared for civil war, and the measures devised were in fact applied, not in the lifetime of the Empire, but during the early phase of the Weimar Republic under a government headed by Socialists. Here again, it was not the regular army that executed government policy, but the right-wing *Freikorps* recruited by the Republic. Some generals during Wilhelm II's reign were advocates of a radical course against workers and Social Democrats. They issued a great many memoranda that went so far as to advocate a military coup, but these notes remained in the file and were never resorted to. The army as such was very careful not to allow itself to be provoked. On the whole, the military leadership recognized that a coup provided no workable alternative to the parliamentary system.

As already mentioned, the main problem besetting the German Army of this time was the shortage of officers, which reached serious proportions especially for the infantry and the artillery. The middle class had to be more strongly involved, not only in the reserves but also in the regulars. In 1865 the Prussian officer corps still had 65 percent of its members coming from the nobility, but by 1913 this proportion had declined to 30 percent. One consequence was that the nobility concentrated itself in a few regiments, notably the Guards formations, while the other regiments had a predominantly bourgeois officer corps. There is an interesting contrast between the officer corps of the army and that of the Imperial Navy, which was on the road to expansion under Admiral von Tirpitz from 1897 onward. The naval officer corps had a reputation for more open-mindedness toward the new social, economic and technical developments than the army. Indeed, Tirpitz worked to expand his navy on the basis of a broad popular consensus. He lobbied the Reichstag and mobilized mass opinion to get the necessary support. There was a touch of liberalism in the navy sadly lacking in the army. It is by no means an overstatement to say that the navy was Kaiser Wilhelm II's preferred branch of the service, yet it is a paradox that it was so much more liberal than the army. Only a very few sons of the old Prussian nobility served at sea. In 1910 48 percent of the naval officer corps came from the families of academics. And its intake of volunteers came mainly from areas of Germany outside Prussia, notably from Bavaria. By 1914 over 90 percent of the naval officer corps was qualified for university or had taken a degree.

With the appointment of increasing numbers of officers

Above left: A captured French courier is searched and interrogated by the Prussians. Above: In the Bois de Boulogne; Prussian troops take a stroll among an apparently unconcerned local population. This is 1871, when many Parisians already regard the occupying troops as safeguarding law and order; the middle classes in particular had been alarmed by the left-wing Paris Commune which had sought to fill the power vacuum left by the war. Above right: The local population studies an unconcerned member of the German occupying army. Right: A German military band plays to a sparse audience in St. Quentin's main square in 1871. Relations between the French and the occupying army were not always quite as friendly as these pictures suggest, although not as baleful as in later wars.

originating in the middle class, the educational standards of the army officer corps again increased. The concept of the elite was no longer based on noble descent but on educational standards. However, the middle-class officers continued to adopt the value system of the Prussian officer corps.

Within the corps of the non-commissioned officers there were similar developments. In the 1890s there was a serious shortage of NCOs, so financial incentives were created to encourage them to enlist for a minimum service of 12 years. Furthermore, a policy introduced by King Friedrich Wilhelm I was revived, namely that the economic status of an NCO should be secured after his retirement by taking him into the civil service. Some of the ministries raised serious complaints, arguing that the

former NCOs were not up to civil service standards and that there were not enough openings there for them. These complaints were of no avail, and in the postal administration alone the number of former NCOs increased from 8,715 in 1900 to 19,324 in 1914. It should come as no surprise, therefore, that the atmosphere in the lower echelons of the civil service was rather military even until the 1960s. Of course, the NCOs at all levels of civilian administration – Reich, Land, provincial or municipal – tended to counteract the influence of the forces of Social Democracy.

In the recruitment of the army a different pattern developed. In the case of voluntary enlistment, it was reported in 1905 that in Bavaria, for example, the greatest number of volunteers with

a Social Democratic background came from rural areas, while the smallest number came from urban areas. This reflected the decline of agriculture on the one hand and the growing prosperity that could be found in urban industries on the other. From then on, volunteers of Social Democratic background were reported to the military authorities only if they had been active 'in word and letter' on behalf of the Social Democratic Party. The state, the Empire, its constituent parts and the army in particular were no longer in a position to control or to contain the existing political and economic upheavals, but to every traditional officer's surprise, the Social Democrats proved themselves to be highly efficient soldiers.

While the Emperor and the military establishment had originally insisted on the three-year conscription period as a way of transforming the recruits into loyal subjects of Crown and country, the period was reduced to two years in 1893. We have already seen that as a result the military leadership adopted the policy of cutting the recruits off as much as possible from Social Democratic influences – be they brochures, leaflets, or any other kind of alien influence. In addition, intensive new indoctrination courses were introduced in the training of the rank and file.

Socialist publications were banned from the garrisons, but excluding all such influences from urban areas was difficult if not impossible. A further step was taken by prohibiting soldiers from visiting taverns. Then the Ministry of War found itself swamped by a wave of protests from the tavern owners which forced a compromise solution. Only on certain days of the week were the soldiers prohibited from visiting a bar. The compromise, considering the objective behind it, made no sense at all, except that the taverns' incomes no longer suffered seriously.

In the elections of 1912 the Social Democratic Party became the strongest single party in the Reichstag and in 1913 it introduced a resolution to abolish all the existing military proscriptions, which was backed by the majority of the Reichstag. Although the resolution was passed, there was nothing in the constitution which compelled the government to act in accordance with it.

Ideological indoctrination was carried out by lecture courses pointing out to the soldiers the virtues of the monarchy, its traditions and achievements. Military ceremonial played as strong a role as did regimental history. What operated here to the army's disadvantage was the essentially non-political character and education of its officer corps. The majority of officers were simply not equipped for a task which in essence amounted to political indoctrination. Some attempts to remedy this were made before World War I, but they were unavailing. Some exceptional officers who went so far as to discuss with their men the substance of the Social Democratic program incurred the disfavor of their superiors. From January 1907 onward, the discussion of social and political questions was forbidden. This was the end of the program of ideological indoctrination.

This was also accompanied by a slow, at first almost imperceptible, change in the attitude of social democracy toward the

Left: Pre-Dreadnought battleships of the German High Seas Fleet in about 1910, when all warships still burned coal. Below left: German cavalry in Warsaw, admired by young locals, in 1915. Having ejected the disliked Russians, the Germans were not yet subjected to Polish hostility. Below: A German heavy gun in action on the Western Front in spring 1918. The crew protects its eardrums in the time-honored manner; it will be decades before ear-protectors are provided as a standard item. Below right: Chief of the German General Staff, Hindenburg (left) with his Quartermaster General, Ludendorff, both looking optimistic at the time of the 1918 spring offensive. By this time they controlled German policy, both civil and military; Kaiser Wilhelm was merely a figurehead.

military action against subversive elements were seriously considered.

Two events of 1913 are worthy of notice. One was the Army Bill of that year. The General Staff had an obsession that Germany was short of the kind of manpower required to fight a war on two fronts and to carry out successfully a vast maneuver such as the Schlieffen Plan, especially in the modified form devised by Moltke the Younger, Chief of the General Staff from 1905 to 1914. The army needed to be enlarged considerably. This, in turn, would require a greater number of officers who were not immediately available. The Military Cabinet feared that the vast increase would further dilute the homogeneity and therefore the quality of the German officer corps. The fear was expressed that politically unreliable elements, if not socialists, then at least liberals, would have to be admitted. The military establishment was not prepared to risk this and preferred to settle for a smaller increase in the army than was actually required, despite the problems this would cause in the conduct of military operations.

The second noteworthy event took place in a small town in the formerly French territory of Alsace. Since 1871 Alsace had been a *Reichsland*, not a state or a province in its own right as were the other constituent parts of the Empire. It was directly administered by the Empire. But in 1911 it had been given a constitution which was in many respects an advance over the constitutions of the other German Lands, especially Prussia. Its Diet was based on a universal franchise without any property

armed forces and national defense in general. Gustav Noske, the Social Democrats' spokesmen for military affairs, became a well-received visitor in military establishments, especially those of the navy. This change was no doubt conditioned by the darkening political horizons around Germany, and was equally a result of the ascendancy of revisionist currents within the Social Democratic Party – the recognition that change could not be achieved by revolution but by evolution from within the existing system.

The change could already be seen in 1908 with the publication in London of the Kaiser's ill-fated '*Daily Telegraph* interview,' which caused a storm of protest in the Reichstag and after which the Kaiser moved more and more into the background politically and kept a strict rein on his all-too-quotable and disastrous extemporaneous remarks and pronouncements. Although the army refused to admit it, it had failed in its policy of screening off the troops from the politics of the day. It continued to lend strong support to the veterans' and reservists' organizations and partly resumed the course by which plans of

qualifications. Unlike the Prussian electoral system, Alsace did not have the three-class franchise.

Battalions of the 99th Infantry Regiment were stationed in the small town of Zabern. A young lieutenant, Günther Freiherr von Förstner, who was not even of age, instructed his recruits on 28 October 1913 that if they were ever attacked when on town leave, they should make use of their weapons. If in the course of such an action a 'Wacke' should come to grief it would not matter; indeed, he would pay the soldier concerned ten gold marks. 'Wacke' was a derogatory term for the people of Alsace. The lieutenant's statement was published in the liberal *Zaberner Anzeiger* and in the *Elsässer*, a paper of the Center Party. In fact, the use of the expression 'Wacke' had been expressly forbidden by a regimental order of 1903, but apparently Förstner used it frequently.

The story caused an uproar in Alsace. The German press was united in the demand that Förstner should be transferred to another garrison. The regimental commander, General von Reuter, could not ignore the incident, but he tried to play it down. Higher authority at XV Army Corps at Strasbourg took a similar attitude. Förstner became the joke of Zabern whenever he appeared in public, so he began to go out accompanied by a guard. More rumors emerged about what he was supposed to have said to recruits. These were denied by his superiors and three Alsatian recruits who had allegedly spread these rumors were arrested. Förstner himself was sentenced to a six-day arrest of which the public was not informed. The *Statthalter* of Alsace, Count von Wedel, also recommended to the commanding general at Strasbourg that Förstner be transferred. This too was kept from the public and the uproar in Zabern increased.

The matter was raised in the Reichstag and the Minister for War, General von Falkenhayn, gave a brief and inconclusive explanation while Chancellor Bethmann Hollweg announced that he would make a statement on the incident on 3 December 1913. Meanwhile, matters deteriorated in Zabern. The military demanded the proclamation of a state of siege but were over-ruled by the civil authorities. There was a public demonstration against which three platoons of infantry issued with live ammunition were sent. Thirty persons were allegedly arrested indiscriminately and released after a night in the cells of the garrison. Even before Bethmann Hollweg could make his statement, Förstner had created a new incident by using his saber to knock down a cobbler who was resisting arrest. In his statement to the Reichstag, Bethmann Hollweg described Förstner's behavior as unbecoming but, identifying himself with the cause of the army, emphasized that 'the king's uniform must be respected under all circumstances.' The Minister for War blamed the agitation on the press and ultimately took refuge behind the Imperial power of supreme command. Now the Reichstag was in an uproar. On 4 December 1913 the Reichstag passed a vote of no confidence in the government, carried by a vote of 293 against 54 with four abstentions.

A vote of no confidence mattered little, since the government was not dependent on the Reichstag but upon the Emperor. Nevertheless, both Förstner and his commander, Reuter, had to face a court martial which duly acquitted them, to the disgust of most of the German press. In January 1914 the Alsatian Diet unanimously condemned the incidents caused by the military. All the officers involved had to resign except the *Statthalter*, Count von Wedel. Conservative generals like von Wrochem warned of the 'terrible danger, for if the mob of all classes was seen to be victorious, the status and strength of the royal army would be damaged.'

The three Alsatian recruits who had informed the papers of the incident in the first place were sentenced to three to six weeks' arrest. Because of the incident in which he had used his saber, Förstner was sentenced to 43 days of imprisonment by the Strasbourg military tribunal. He appealed for a new trial, which subsequently acquitted him. The primacy of the military had prevailed, even in an affair which was purely local in its origins and could have been settled on the spot without much fuss if the advice of the civil authorities had been followed.

The slogan was raised that the army was in danger, and that in a country encircled by a host of enemies every sign of weakness, even in such a minor affair as this, was bound to debilitate the entire army. What those who took this line overlooked was that the assertion of the primacy of the military had showed up the fundamental weakness of the German political structure.

At a much more important level, the same was to be demonstrated during the July Crisis in 1914 which led to World War I and during the course of the war itself. Admittedly, given Germany's geographic position, the Schlieffen Plan was probably the only formula for victory, provided one had sufficient forces to carry it out. Once Russia had mobilized,

Top: German infantrymen advance on the Western Front; as was customary, their large packs have been left behind, to be brought up after the fighting. Above: On the Somme in spring 1918; advancing German troops take a rest. By this stage of the war motor transport was more in evidence, but footslogging infantry and horse transport still predominated. Right: Men of the *Freikorps* are proudly photographed at Riga, Latvia, where they were fighting the Russian Bolsheviks in 1919. The *Freikorps*, recruited largely from former soldiers embittered by Germany's defeat, was originally intended to maintain order in German cities and to oppose Polish incursions; but it soon rejected civilian authority, which it despised, and degenerated into a savage militarism exemplified by the murder of prominent pacifists.

there was no alternative but to set the plan based on railroad timetables into motion. The real failing of the German military establishment lies in the conduct of World War I, in which the politicians played only a secondary role and the Kaiser none at all. Once the Schlieffen Plan miscarried and a war of attrition began, the politicians exercised no influence whatsoever. After the Miracle of the Marne, the Allied victory that saved Paris, Moltke resigned and was replaced by Falkenhayn, who could think of very little except to try to bleed the French to the point of exhaustion. He tried to put this strategy into effect in the Battle of Verdun, but after early successes the Germans bled just as heavily.

Falkenhayn, in turn, was replaced by the Hindenburg/ Ludendorff combination and they became Germany's secret dictators, to whom Bethmann-Hollweg had to give way. All subsequent chancellors until Prince Max of Baden were no more than the marionettes of the *Oberste Heeresleitung* (OHL) – the German Supreme Command. The army introduced total mobilization and succeeded in implementing it to a considerable extent, but they had no political alternatives to offer. Even if they had, it is doubtful whether the allies would ever have considered them, especially after the US joined the war. The Allied aim was the destruction of the German Empire. Even Ludendorff recognized that Germany was at the end of its resources in August 1918, but he kept up the propaganda that victory was just around the corner. The public, destitute and starving as a result of the effectiveness of the British blockade – the victims of total warfare – held on until the news of Germany's request for an armistice. For Germans, the skies caved

in; the full parliamentarization ordered by Hindenburg and Ludendorff and carried out by Chancellor Prince Max of Baden was again a reform from above. It had come too late. Revolution broke out, the thrones toppled and what was left was the progeny of defeat – the Weimar Republic. Even that republic took well over a year to quell internal uprisings, not by means of the regular army but rather by the use of irregular troops, the *Freikorps*, without whose aid the republic would not have lasted even that one year.

The army soon found its footing again, but it had yet to find its proper position within the new state. During the days of the Empire it had been a professional elite, as well as a political and social elite, in terms of its officer corps. Such changes as growing industrialization and the impact of new technologies upon warfare had left their mark. Military requirements involved the economy and society as a whole, necessitating that technical precision, mass production and all social resources be put at the disposal of a nation at war. Whether or not the officer corps liked it, the distinctions between army and society had become increasingly blurred.

This development affected all armies, but in Germany it confronted an officer corps which was still oriented along pre-industrial lines. Furthermore, industrial and technical changes endangered the exclusivity of the officer corps all the more, since the entire society had to be involved in the conduct of total war – a society which we have seen did not possess a commonly accepted value system. The professional military expert was no longer the only man essential to the conduct of war.

The results of this development had begun to show in the 19th century within the army itself, in the division between the officers of the General Staff and the troop officers. In the navy there was a distinction between deck officers, who had general duties and could rise to command positions, and the engineer officers. All this pointed toward the disintegration of a once distinct warrior class. World War I had accelerated this problem. The death toll in the traditional officer corps was so great that commissions had to be awarded to people whom the army would never have looked at before, even to Social Democrats. New ranks emerged to make up for the deficiencies in the number of officers, such as the sergeant lieutenant or officer deputy, who led units as large as companies in the field.

After the defeat of 1918 the army continued to represent the continuity of German history, to hold on to essential elements of its historical existence. It did not at first transform itself from a social and political elite into a purely professional elite. This

Above far left: Hindenburg and Hitler in front of the Potsdam garrison church, March 1933. Hindenburg, on the basis of his military reputation, had been elected President in 1925, and he reluctantly accepted Hitler as Chancellor in January 1933, even though general elections had indicated that the Nazis' support was waning. One reason for Hitler's success was that his private army, the storm troopers, was believed capable of resisting the regular army should the latter be summoned to suppress the Nazis. Above left: Von Fritsch, army commander, and Beck, Chief of the General Staff, in 1937. Above: Armored cars parade before Hitler at the Nuremberg Nazi Party rally of 1934. Left: General von Seeckt and Hitler in conversation. Below left: Hitler with his generals; Keitel is on his right, von Leeb on his left, as all three discuss a tactical problem.

became clear only in the course of time. The army was briefly preoccupied with the revolutionary situation and its aftermath. In the course of this period, three types of men emerged in the officer corps. The first were the dyed-in-the-wool monarchists advocating a policy of restoration, but they made their bid in the Kapp-Lüttwitz Putsch in March 1920 and failed abysmally, being excluded thereafter from the new army, the Reichswehr. The second group were national revolutionaries aiming at a German socialism modeled on the socialism of the trenches, but they were too divided among themselves to present a coherent front and disintegrated as the republic found its feet, wandering off to the various paramilitary organizations on the right. The third group, under General von Seeckt, did not love the republic, but considered it the least of a number of evils. Therefore they backed it. As members of the small hundred-thousand-man army which was all the Treaty of Versailles allowed, they could shut themselves off from the rest of society very much as the French Army had done between 1871 and 1898.

In the fluctuations of day-to-day domestic politics they represented the only stable and continuing factor. In spite of all the changes that had taken place around them, they claimed to be a professional elite and cherished the belief, however unreal, that they would become a social and political elite as well. This fond hope was not dissipated until after 30 January 1933 when Hitler came to power. True, there were currents pointing to a renewal of the old attitudes and traditions of the officer corps. Between 1880 and 1913 the percentage of officers' sons joining the army declined from 30 to 28 percent. Between 1926 and 1930 it rose from 44 to 55 percent. Most of their fathers came from certain regiments, notably from the guards, and with rare exceptions they had been General Staff members. Their aim was the restoration of Germany as a great power with a minimum of risk. Using the Reichswehr offensively was not ruled out as long as the risks seemed manageable.

Under the command of Seeckt and his successors, the army remained a largely nonpolitical instrument at the service of the state. It meddled in politics only insofar as its own interests were involved. The single exception was the last head of the Reichswehr, General von Schleicher, who first tried to split the National Socialists and build a new basis not only for his position but also for the new German state. He next tried, unsuccessfully, to win trade union and Social Democratic support. However, the Nazis were not to be persuaded to part with their Führer and the trade unions refused their cooperation. The only alternative now was a military dictatorship under Schleicher which would have had to govern against the majority vote of the country.

This course of action was curtailed by President Hindenburg's appointment of Adolf Hitler as Reich Chancellor. His coalition was the only solution (a Social Democratic-Communist coalition would not have had a majority and was in any case obviated by the Communist preoccupation with fighting the 'Social Fascists') which could provide the government with a majority in the Reichstag. Thus ended the state of affairs existing since 1930, in which government was carried on by emergency decrees signed by the President – a situation which the aged Hindenburg had hated and a burden of which he was relieved by his appointment of Hitler, however reluctant. The army had nothing to do with putting Hitler into the saddle. It has been said that it did not prevent his appointment by military force, but then this accusation is raised by the very same historians who say that the German Army meddled too much in politics up to 1918. One cannot have it both ways.

In the early period, Hitler based his government on an entente – not an alliance – between the traditional elites and the NSDAP, the Nazi Party. He did not even have the opportunity to appoint his own Army Minister. Hindenburg, in order to

Left: So-called volunteers from the regular German Forces, forming the Condor Air Legion, leave for home after fighting for the victorious Nationalists in the Spanish Civil War. Below left: Hitler receives Condor Air Legion officers to hand them Spanish war decorations. Germany also sent land and sea forces to help Franco. Italy too, sent help, while Soviet forces were sent to aid the Republicans. All three countries gained valuable experience with modern weapons in this war, although the USSR wasted much of this knowledge by executing or incarcerating Soviet officers returned from Spain. Right: German tank crews attend to their vehicles, topping up fuel tanks, as they wait at a river crossing during the May 1940 *blitzkrieg* on France.

keep the army out of Hitler's reach, had appointed General von Blomberg to this post before swearing in the whole cabinet. But Blomberg, unforeseen by Hindenburg, subscribed to Hitler's theory that the new state was to be based on two pillars, the army and the NSDAP. It seemed as though the army was about to regain its position as a social and political elite. Within the army the existing differences were of a purely tactical nature. The army Commander in Chief, General von Fritsch, was essentially a conservative, insisting on the maintenance of traditional values. Only these would cement the army's autonomous position within the new state. Blomberg, and the head of his personal staff Colonel (later General and Field Marshal) von Reichenau, were not so much concerned with the maintenance of old values as they were with direct participation in the decision-making process, which in their opinion provided the only guarantee that the military elite would have a controlling voice.

On the initiative of Blomberg and Reichenau, National Socialist emblems like the swastika were introduced into the army. No such initiative was taken by Hitler or the NSDAP. Nor did Hitler demand the application of new anti-Semitic laws to the army. It was Blomberg and Reichenau who instigated this. One danger for the army arose in the form of the Nazi Party storm troopers, the SA, when the head of the SA, Ernst Röhm, demanded its inclusion in the army with the aim of creating a National Socialist army dominated by the SA. Hitler promised Blomberg that the army would be the only armed organization of the state and he kept this promise. However, Reichenau deliberately escalated the conflict between army and SA. He did not hesitate to manufacture fictitious reports about SA mobilizations which he fed to Hitler. This provocation culminated in the purge of 30 June 1934, the Blood Purge or Night of the Long Knives, in which the army provided transport and weapons to the SS to carry out the dirty business. In the course of this purge a number of old scores were also settled. General von Schleicher and his wife and General von Bredow were killed.

The army leadership refused to raise any protest about this murder of two members of its officer corps. When the President,

Field Marshal von Hindenburg, died in August 1934, and Hitler fused the offices of Reich Chancellor and President into the position of Führer, it was again solely at the initiative of the army leadership that all members of the armed forces swore loyalty to Hitler. The ties that had once existed between the army and the King and Emperor seemed to have been reestablished. However, between 1933 and 1934 the German Army had stepped onto a slippery slope which, in reality, removed it more and more from the exercise of political power. Hitler had promised Blomberg a predominant position for the army within German society, provided it stood quietly by while he carried out his internal revolution. The army did so, but very much at the expense of its own position. Some members of the army realized this, such as the Commander in Chief, General von Fritsch, who stated that Hitler had succeeded in nationalizing the working class, precisely that class to which the army had had no access in the days of the Empire and the republic. The army had conceded so much that it was no longer a political force.

The watershed of this development was reached in 1938 when Blomberg was sacked after he had married a lady of dubious repute. General von Fritsch was also dismissed on a trumped-up charge of homosexuality. The Reichswehr Ministry, which after the renunciation of the military clauses of the Treaty of Versailles had been renamed the War Ministry, disappeared. Hitler, who had also become Supreme Commander of the German Armed Forces when he merged the offices of presidency and chancellorship, now took over direct command. His instrument was the *Oberkommando der Wehrmacht* or OKW, the Supreme Command of the Armed Forces, subordinate to which were the OKH, OKL and OKM, the high commands for the army, air force and navy, respectively. General Keitel became Chief of OKW and also, at least nominally, exercised the functions of Minister for War. The coalition between the army and Hitler after 30 January 1933 did not provide the traditional military elite with a broad political base among the German people. Hitler had integrated the German nation at the expense of the old elites. For the first time in the history of the Prusso-German Army, it became a pure instrument of the state executive. The primacy of politics had been established.

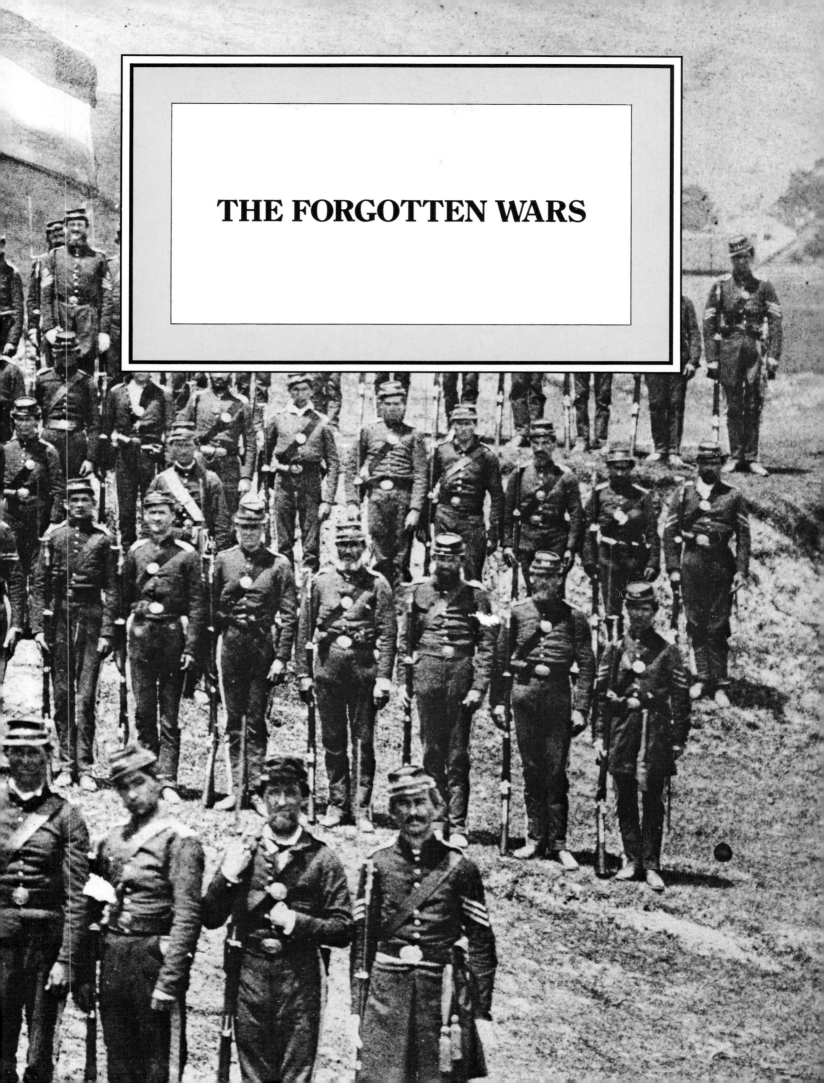

THE FORGOTTEN WARS

If one subjects the war plans of the belligerent powers of Europe on the eve of World War I to close scrutiny, the conclusion soon reached is that the image of war, the *Kriegsbild* of the various general staffs, was one based on a short war. The dogma of the battle of annihilation prevailed, the belief in the single decisive battle such as Hannibal's at Cannae. What they failed to take into account was that while Hannibal had won the Battle of Cannae, in the end, of course, he had lost the war. The only important disagreement came from Lord Kitchener, who became Great Britain's Minister of War. He believed that the war would be of rather longer duration. He was not endowed with any greater vision or knowledge than his counterparts on the European mainland, but he realized that the mobilization of Great Britain's manpower resources would take considerably longer than those of the continental countries with their conscript armies. The lessons learned by the generals of 1914 had been those of the Danish War of 1862, the Austro-Prussian War of 1866 and the Franco-Prussian War of 1870–71. More recent confirmation of the belief in a short war had apparently been provided by the Balkan Wars of 1912–13. The fact that in the 19th and 20th centuries there had been wars which seemed to contradict this traditional view was ignored. In fact, all official European observers who had been sent to America to study the American Civil War concluded that it had little relevance for war in the future and especially for war in Europe. The Boer War and the Russo-Japanese War were often similarly ignored. Each of these wars will be examined in turn.

Slavery in the southern states is often given as the reason for the war between the North and South, in spite of the fact that President Abraham Lincoln had promised not to interfere with slavery in those states where it already existed. The extension of slavery into the territories of the United States which had not yet entered the Union and were about to do so provides another reason, but this reason was devoid of practical substance because there were territories such as Kansas and Nebraska in which cotton could not be grown and slavery would have been unprofitable. Indeed, there were hardly any slaves in either of these states, but this did not dampen the ardor with which the issue was debated.

Economic differences between North and South were an additional reason. A dynamically industrializing North was confronting the stagnant agricultural system of the South, but there is no reason to assume that, on economic grounds alone, the North would not have welcomed the secession of the South as removing a political and economic burden. The insistence upon states' rights is another reason put forward, and here we have perhaps something of more substance. The question of states' rights had already preoccupied the writers of the US Constitution. Whereas Thomas Jefferson had always been concerned about a reintroduction of a monarchic system, his close friend and collaborator, James Madison, was more concerned about the protection of a minority from a dominant majority. This was precisely the situation into which the southern states were moving from the 1820s onward. Not only did their economy remain stagnant – one has only to look at the railroad system of the United States in 1860, which shows a dense network linking the northeast and the midwest while the railroad network in the South was sparse.

The acquisition of new territories, and in due course new states, affected the equilibrium between North and South which thus far had been held in balance in both Houses of Congress. Inevitably and irrevocably the South moved into the position of the permanent minority, the danger which James Madison had already described eloquently in the *Federalist Papers*. Once the equilibrium was lost, from a southern point of

Previous page: A company of the Sumter Light Guards of Georgia on parade in 1861. Left: The inauguration of the Confederates' President, Jefferson Davis (standing, to right of Senate President, who is introducing him); this is from an 1861 photograph. Below left: A Civil War recruiting poster addressed to New Yorkers. Right: The bombardment of Fort Sumter (Charleston) in 1861. Below: Robert E. Lee, the best-known Confederate general. Below right: New military technology; an observation balloon in the Civil War.

view it could be restored only by insisting on states' rights or by an altogether different conception of the Union.

Irrespective of its real importance, slavery was the great public issue. It was the ideal instrument of propaganda because as an institution it most offended man's moral sense. Yet it is hardly likely that the South would have rallied solely to the defense of its 'peculiar institution.' More than 76 percent of all Southerners were not slaveowners. Less than 10 percent of the population owned plantations with more than 50 slaves, 6 percent held up to 50 slaves and 8 percent had only one or two. Consequently, if the defense of slavery was the cause for the South entering into war with the North, over three quarters of the population did so without having any stake in slavery whatsoever.

Between 1820 and 1860 the population of the United States had increased from 9.6 to 31.3 million. Of these 31.3 million, about 22 million lived in the North and only slightly more than 9 million in the South, of whom fewer than two fifths were blacks. Industrially, the North was vastly superior. Manufacturing industries important in the production of war materials favored the North by a ratio of three and one-half to one. For every six factory workers in the North there was only one in the South. The South's economic base was its agriculture, which was about double the value of that of the North. As far as cotton was concerned, the South had an overwhelming share of world trade. The economic and communications structure had made it inevitable that the South was primarily export-oriented while the North protected its nascent industries with high tariffs. The South, for its part, largely supported free trade.

Of decisive significance for the war was the fact that the United States Navy was almost exclusively in the hands of the North, while the merchant fleet, because of the South's agricultural exports, was concentrated there where it was of little use except for blockade running.

Far left: The Siege of Vicksburg took place May–July 1863. Its fall gave Union forces control of the Mississippi Valley. The officer lower right with spyglass is Ulysses S Grant.

Right: The fall of Petersburg, 2 April 1865.

Far right: General Gouverneur Warren, Chief Engineer of the Army of the Potomac looks out from a signal post on Little Round Top hill during the Battle of Gettysburg.

Below: Confederate General Longstreet's attack on Fort Sanders on 29 November 1863 failed in part because of the wire entanglements – a portent of the use of barbed wire on the Western Front.

Left: A street in Richmond after its abandonment by the Confederates in 1865. With nearby Petersburg, Richmond occupied a key situation close to Washington and was long an objective of the Union forces. It was not until the closing stages of the war that it was taken, and its loss led directly to the Confederate surrender. Below: Map of the Civil War campaigns, demonstrating the wide extent of territory in the war zone which made the railroad a key element in this war. Right: Abraham Lincoln. Below right: Ulysses S. Grant, who after victories in the western campaign became commander of the Union armies. He is portrayed bareheaded here, in a picture designed to inspire more than instruct. Grant subsequently became US President.

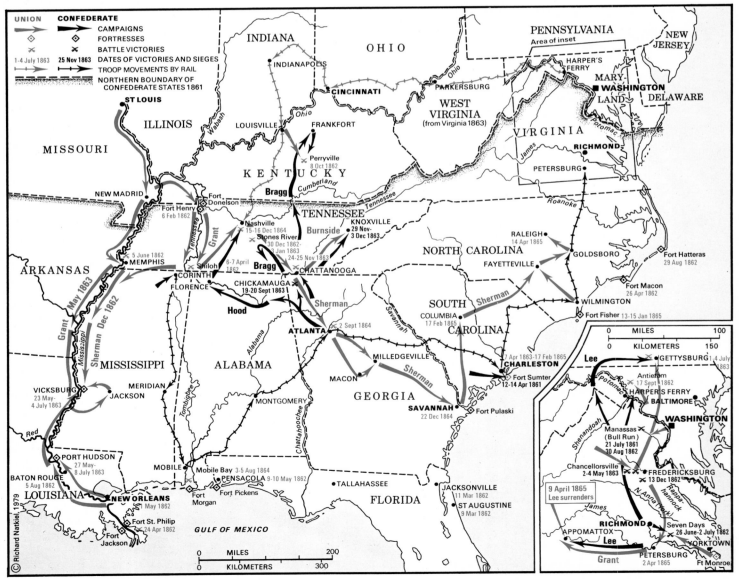

After President Lincoln's election, the South established the Confederacy under President Jefferson Davis. Ironically, both Lincoln and Davis had been born in the same border state of Kentucky. The war was formally opened by the South firing upon Fort Sumter, a step into which, according to some relatively recent studies, the South was maneuvered by President Lincoln.

Until the outbreak of war, the Army of the United States consisted of 16,000 regulars whose task, in the main, was to secure the advancing western frontier from the opposition put up by the Indians. Indeed, the settlement of the West and even the building of the transcontinental railroad was continued throughout the war. Even in peacetime there had been neither time nor opportunity to train the army to operate in large formations. Frontier Indian warfare was conducted by sizeable raiding parties but not by the large forces of all arms that were necessary in a European theater of war. In point of fact, commanding large formations effectively was one of the problems with which, at the early stages of the Civil War, American generals had the greatest difficulty.

At the outbreak of war, the Union Army was at first supplemented by volunteers from the militia who served for a period of 90 days and afterward simply left for home. Initially, they also elected their own officers. Much the same military system prevailed in the South. But dire need and experience soon necessitated a change in these methods. There were nothing like enough volunteers to cover the actual needs of the armies, especially since cases of mass desertion were frequent. Desertion was in fact a problem throughout the war. This in no way detracts from the bravery and readiness for sacrifice of most of the troops in the field. The fatal casualties of 360,000 men for the North and 258,000 men for the South speak for themselves.

It was the South that first introduced conscription in 1862. The North, as a first step, increased the period of service in the armed forces to three years and in 1863 it also introduced com-

pulsory military service for every single male. It was possible to evade conscription in return for a certain sum of money and the provision of a substitute. Also, people were hired into the army in return for a fee which was to increase with the length of service. The North did not refrain from impressing immigrants into the ranks, particularly Germans, who made up about 30 percent, and Irish, who made up 39 percent of the Union Army. Only after they had completed their military service could they become naturalized American citizens. Both conscription and impressment evoked considerable public protest, culminating in New York, where the Civil War was highly unpopular anyway, in anti-draft riots.

By European standards, the discipline of both Northern and Southern armies was very slack. Only bitter experience taught the soldiers not to throw away their equipment once it became too heavy on the march or in battle. This lack of discipline also seriously affected the civilian population, which was frequently molested by gangs of marauding soldiers. Another adverse feature, especially in the North, was that the press often undermined discipline by publishing political and strategic arguments for all soldiers to read.

Abraham Lincoln was a member of the Republican Party, while his first Commander in Chief, General McClellan, was a Democrat. Indeed, McClellan stood as a Democratic candidate for the presidency. At the time it was often suspected that Lincoln's fellow party members did not wish McClellan any great victories, in case this should affect the Republicans adversely.

For the Confederacy, once the war had broken out the primary objective was to protect its agricultural areas to ensure the continued supply of foodstuffs for the populace and the army. Then, if possible, it aimed at taking the industrialized areas of northern Pennsylvania and Maryland and at capturing Washington. In that way the Union could be hit decisively. This, at least, was the view of General Beauregard, the commander of the Confederate forces. All resources were to be mobilized and concentrated with this aim in mind, a policy that he argued would justify the temporary sacrifice of the South's harbor cities. The plan found little support among the population and President Jefferson Davis put forward an alternative war plan by which the Confederate Army was to withdraw into the interior before an invading Union army, then concentrate its forces and defeat the enemy wherever he appeared. Beaure-

Above: Confederate soldiers case their colors for the last time after Lee's surrender.
Left: The Wagon Box Fight, 2 August 1867. Men of the 9th Infantry hold off a Sioux attack. The long experience of Indian fighting did little to prepare the forces of either side for the demands of the Civil War.
Right: A Union soldier using the Beardslee telegraph. Fifteen words per minute could be transmitted on this machine.
Below right: A Union signal station in 1861. One of a number of flag signal posts established along the Potomac.

gard found little that appealed to him in this plan and viewed it as the overture to a long drawn-out campaign of attrition that was bound to reduce the South's resources to the point where it would be forced to yield to the North. This prediction proved to be correct.

It was first shown at the Battle of Bull Run in 1861. Though the Southern forces were victorious, they still failed to defeat McClellan decisively. The Confederate Army then encamped at Manassas and left the initiative to the Union Army, which became active again in March 1862. Time and again, the Confederate Army managed to win battles, but never decisively enough to exploit these victories strategically.

The Union Army, after it had failed in its early efforts to take the Confederate capital, Richmond, Virginia, adopted the policy of a war of attrition, as advocated primarily by General Ulysses S Grant. An army was to advance along the Mississippi via Memphis, Vicksburg and Port Hudson, all important military and supply bases for the Confederacy, and finally take New Orleans. In this it succeeded, New Orleans being taken by 1 May 1862, while Vicksburg capitulated in July of that year. Thus the Confederacy had been cut off from its supply bases in

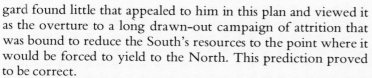

Above: 'An August Morning with Farragut' lithograph from a painting by Overerd of the Battle of Mobile Bay, 5 August 1864. Above left: The painting 'First at Vicksburg' showing the attack made by the 13th Infantry on the Confederate lines on 19 May 1863. Left: Union troops charge a Confederate barricade.

Tennessee, Louisiana and Texas.

The Union Navy blockaded the entire Atlantic coast and Southern harbors in the Gulf of Mexico. Successful blockade runners with arms and ammunition from Great Britain and France were the exception rather than the rule. For a short time the blockade was threatened by an event which was to revolutionize the whole conduct of naval warfare. The South built an ironclad warship, originally laid down as the *Merrimack*, but renamed the CSS *Virginia*. She was launched from Norfolk, Virginia and soon sank two wooden frigates of the Union Navy at the mouth of the James River. All cannon shells were repelled by the iron plates of the *Virginia*. This single vessel could have threatened the entire Union Navy blockade. It might even have been able to bombard Washington and New York. But the very next day, 9 March 1862, an 'armed chesebox on a raft' appeared. Like the *Virginia*, it was a fully armor-plated ship, but built with a very low profile. This was the Union's *Monitor*, which was armed with two guns mounted in a revolving armored turret. The two ships fought two inconclusive actions, but the Confederacy's ability to break the blockade was destroyed. From then on armored vessels were to dominate naval warfare.

In the meantime, the Union Army endeavored to take possession of the east-west communications of the South, the Cumberland and Tennessee Rivers, and the important railroad line running from Atlanta to Chattanooga to Nashville. Once this railroad link was in the Union's hands, all the other sub-sidiary lines would fall of themselves and the Union Army could advance upon Savannah, Georgia and deliver the *coup de grace* to the Army of the Confederacy. This plan was actually carried out in 1864 by General Sherman's 'March through Georgia,' which was accompanied by an orgy of destruction the like of which North America had never before experienced. In a war of attrition the civilian population was as much a strategic target as were the armies in the field. This example of ruthlessness, one of many which manifested themselves on both sides during the Civil War, showed that war was no longer the exclusive province of the professionals, but that the entire nation was seen as a legitimate object of warfare.

In Virginia, however, the Union Armies were determined to remain on the defensive in order to protect Washington, Pennsylvania and Maryland. The Battle of Gettysburg, 1–4 July 1863, effectively destroyed the offensive capacity of the Confederate Army. The tide had definitely turned; the North could move to the offensive, but it preferred to stay put and starve out the Confederates. It remained in this position until the South evacuated Richmond in March 1865. The superb defender of this sector was General Robert E Lee, but he was ultimately compelled to capitulate in April 1865 to General Ulysses S Grant at Appomattox Court House.

A war of attrition of this kind included the destruction of all foodstuffs and raw materials wherever the Union Armies found them. General Sheridan had devastated the Shenandoah Valley in 1864, as well as the entire area of Vicksburg and Port Hudson. When he was sent as an observer to the German Military Headquarters during the Franco-Prussian war of 1870–71, he expressed astonishment at the Germans' humane conduct of war. According to his views, the enemy ought to be left nothing except a handkerchief in which to shed his tears for having ever gone to war. For the Northern strategy, it was more important

Left: 'Sheridan's Ride.' Union cavalry commander Philip Sheridan led his forces through the Shenandoah Valley of Virginia in the fall of 1864 causing such destruction that 'a crow flying over it would have to bring his own rations.'
Above: An engagement between shore batteries and a river squadron. The Union victory in the Civil War was made more certain by control of the Mississippi.

to deprive the South of its depots, supply bases and railways, to seize the logistical apparatus, than to actually defeat the army in the field.

General Lee acquired military preeminence among the armies of the South because he insisted on bold and ruthless military strokes, while at the same time, once pushed onto the defensive, he conducted it with a skill that was not to be seen in Europe until the latter part of 1914. Lee displayed genius on the offensive as well as the defensive, but victory was denied him.

Grant, too, was aggressive on the offensive and certainly not inferior in spirit and boldness to Lee. He found a strategy by which a tactically inferior army could nevertheless beat an enemy by numerical and industrial superiority. This was the essentially new feature which the American Civil War displayed and which should have been a warning, especially to the German General Staff in both World Wars. Today even the best army cannot beat an enemy who is technically and industrially superior. Added to this must be the will and determination to continue the war until the opponent is totally exhausted. All of Europe ignored this important lesson, but the signs of total war were first seen in the American Civil War.

The strategy of attrition as first practiced in the Civil War has often been argued to be much the same as the strategy of attrition in previous centuries. Nothing could be further from the truth. In the 17th and 18th centuries the objective of this strategy was to force the opponent to give in by weakening his army short of his utter destruction, while husbanding one's own forces as much as possible. The purpose of Grant's strategy of attrition was to force the enemy to capitulate and accept unconditional surrender (a phrase invented in the American Civil War) and to impose his own will upon him. In this Grant succeeded to the fullest extent. He is therefore entitled to be counted among the greatest strategists of military history.

Of course one must not forget that only a protagonist who has the advantage of exterior lines can conduct a strategy of attrition as understood by Grant. It is possible to conduct it from interior lines only if there are inexhaustible supplies of the foodstuffs and raw materials necessary for the conduct of war which cannot be destroyed and if industry itself is secure from attack. This invulnerability does not exist anywhere in the world today.

Another important element in the American Civil War was that of propaganda. It was the first modern crusade, as much as America's war against Spain in 1898 was termed a crusade. To the public at large, it was a crusade for human rights and against slavery. Karl Marx was one of the first to comment upon this aspect of the Civil War, although he interpreted it as a victory for the working class against a slaveholding society. His friend and collaborator, Friedrich Engels, saw it in much the same way, but he also clearly recognized the importance of railways for the operational conduct of a war, especially in the campaigns against Tennessee and Georgia.

The second of the forgotten wars was the Boer War. At the beginning of the Boer War, the armies of the Transvaal and the Orange Free State consisted of armed farmers. It was truly a people's army, numbering about 50,000 men who had been hardened in the continuous conflicts with the natives. As hunters for their daily supplies, they had developed considerable skills as individual fighters, but they found it difficult to operate in large formations. The tactical unit was the *Kirchspiel*, or parish, led by a local man, a field cornet, who was elected every three years. In peacetime he was responsible for administration and jurisdiction. Lieutenants and corporals, also elected, supported him in his task. Several *Kirchspiele* in a district formed a commando, at whose apex stood the elected commandant who held his office in peace and war. The strength of his forces varied according to the number of *Kirchspiele* and ranged from 300 to 3000 men. Generals were selected to command the larger formations, but they had no formal rank distinctions. The discipline of this militia army was on a voluntary basis and showed serious shortcomings. Time and again, individual units simply rode home or intervened in a battle whenever it suited them.

It comes as no surprise that as a result of these conditions the British had great difficulty in assessing correctly the actual strength of their opponents. Although the government supplied rifles, other equipment was usually provided by the Boers themselves; only the poor were equipped by the *Kirchspiel*. The Boers fought as mobile infantry, with mobility being provided by their horses. In many respects they were the forerunners of the modern motorized infantry. Both of the Boer Republics had a mobile artillery and telegraph communication force, patterned on the German example. Service in this force was for three years. There were also some reservists and long-serving volunteers whose training and discipline were good. The total artillery strength available to the Boers was 87 guns served by 1200 men.

The greatest problems were encountered in the leadership of the Boer Army. There was no General Staff, not even any adjutants to aid the generals who, like most officers, habitually wore black tailcoats and top hats. Orders were issued through a war council participated in by all ranks down to corporal. Since these men were all dependent on election by their subordinates, they inevitably supported the majority view. The ultimate results of these proceedings were largely negative.

The Boer Army was nonetheless one of the greatest cavalry armies in history. It boasted a mobility that could initially compensate for its numerical inferiority. In an area about the size of western Europe, this mobility was of considerable importance. By comparison, the British Army, like all European armies since 1859, was dependent on the few existing rail lines along which most of the major engagements took place.

The Boers' standard weapon was the German Mauser rifle bolt-operated with a magazine holding five rounds of ammunition, a type of rifle which had been introduced into most armies by that time. However, lack of fire discipline often caused the Boers to waste much of their ammunition. The rifle could be fired effectively from a distance of 700 yards, but the greatest accuracy was obtained at 300 yards. The Boer War also demonstrated for the first time in history the devastating effect of machine guns, with which both British and Boers were equipped. It was in the nature of things that the British suffered most because they were usually on the attack and, like the Germans during the initial phase of the Franco-Prussian War, they often attacked at first in company columns, thus making an ideal target for the defenders, especially when they were equipped with machine guns.

Above left: A British periodical's engraving of two Boer sentinels standing guard at an outpost during the so-called First Boer War, then known as the Transvaal Rising. Top: The Gloucester Regiment charges the Boer guns at the Battle of Paardeberg Drift. This 1900 engagement resulted in surrender by the Boer General Cronje, and demonstrated that the Boers were unlikely to win set-piece battles against the growing British forces. Left: In the early stages of the Boer War, the British public was comforted by dramatized description of the sturdy defense of a few key towns as its forces retreated. This picture shows the defense of Mafeking. Above: The disreputable Jameson Raid; Jameson makes a last stand. He was later imprisoned by the British but received a baronetcy in 1911.

Below: A German painting showing the destruction of the British artillery at the Battle of Colenso in 1899. Thanks largely to the impetuosity of some subordinate officers, this became a humiliating defeat for the British, many of whose infantry fled. However, casualties were not heavy and the commander in chief, Buller, soon restored morale. Inset, far left: Colonel Baden-Powell, who conducted the successful defense of Mafeking against the Boers, became a British hero, and later founded the Boy Scout movement on the inspiration of his South African experiences. Left, inset: General Buller in 1900. Buller was blamed for the early British reverses in South Africa and was replaced; later commentators have suggested that he was not incompetent, but was a victim of poorly selected and poorly trained subordinates.

The forerunner of the modern machine gun was the French *mitrailleuse*, which had been used to deadly effect against the German cavalry in 1870–71. It had a high rate of fire, but reloading was time consuming. In 1884 an American, Hiram Maxim, patented a recoil-operated weapon, a true machine gun which could fire several hundred rounds per minute.

The British had tested the machine gun some years before the Boer War, adopting it for army use in 1889. In 1893, at the Zambezi River, 50 British soldiers had defended themselves successfully against an attack by over 5,000 natives with the aid of a single Hotchkiss machine gun. Similar successes were achieved by the British during the Afghan Campaign of 1895, a feat to be repeated in the Sudan Campaign of 1898 when the numerically inferior British forces with 20 machine guns and 38 pieces of artillery, supported by gun boats on the Nile, routed the Dervishes who left behind 12,000 dead and 16,000 wounded.

The Boer War was the first in which soldiers fought one another with these modern weapons. The conclusion drawn from all this by the European armies was that the infantry should advance in a dispersed formation as soon as defensive fire was received. But they still adhered to the principle that the first objective of an attacking infantry unit would be to gain supremacy of fire-power, which could only be achieved in closed formation, a conclusion soon to be outdated and abandoned during World War I.

The artillery force of the Boers was small, but it was highly mobile. Also, for the first time in the annals of military history, the Boers prepared alternative artillery positions into which the artillery could be moved quickly during combat. Moreover, the quality of their equipment was superior to that available to the British Army. The Boer artillery consisted mostly of 120mm Krupp guns and 155mm French Creusot guns with a range of approximately four and one-half to five miles. The reverse side of this superiority was a lack of Boer resilience when under the fire of the British artillery.

As with all militia-type forces in military history, the greatest strength of the Boer Army lay in its defense, while its attacking power left much to be desired. The Boers were past-masters in guerrilla-type tactics and in small engagements, as they had

already shown at Majuba Hill in 1886 during the first Anglo-Boer War. Creeping upon their opponents unnoticed, they opened their well-aimed fusillade to devastating effect, but because of their lack of offensive power they rarely achieved more than local tactical victories. Knowing their territory, they could exploit the terrain to the utmost. They preferred to take their positions behind the ridges or in the bushes of the veld. They used trenches extensively; later on, they had each man dig his own hole. Once they had established their defensive position, it was immensely difficult to dislodge them. When the British, in spite of the odds, did succeed, more often than not it was due to lack of discipline among the Boers. Once they believed that they could not resist a British attack, many simply left their holes without being ordered to do so. European army observers held the opinion that combat from firm entrenchments was a form of warfare which could not be transferred to Europe because of the different terrain there and the character of European armies – another fundamental error.

To the Boers' superior mobility one must add the advantages of their knowledge of the country and their ability to adapt to the prevailing climate. Unlike the British, they knew all the water holes. Their personal requirements were few and whatever supplies they needed could be carried in a train of ox-drawn carts. As the siege of Kimberley showed, this changed once the Boers were joined by their womenfolk and children, forming a large siege camp or *laager*. In February 1900 at Paardeberg the practice of families joining their men in the field presented a serious disadvantage, because although the Boer Army had achieved a clear defensive victory, it could not move on account of the many dependents. Stationary and devoid of supplies, it ultimately had to surrender. Much the same situation arose at Polar Grove shortly thereafter, but the Boers were already so demoralized by the capitulation at Paardeberg that after the first rounds of artillery fire, they ran to their carts and wagons, which contained all their belongings, and fled helter-skelter. Although the Battle of Driefontein was the last of the large engagements fought by the Boer Armies against the British, it did not put an end to the war as such. The armies of the Boers had been defeated by the British, but for another two years the guerrilla war – the 'little war,' as Clausewitz called it – was to continue.

Mounted Boer commandos interrupted the British lines of communication. The reaction of Lord Kitchener, by then commander of the British forces in South Africa, was swift and ruthless. He demonstrated that organization was more important than the tactical and operational aspects in this kind of war. First of all, he initiated what in our day we have called 'search and destroy missions.' He had the farms and villages of the Boers burned down to deprive them of their supplies. Women and children were imprisoned in concentration camps (the first use of this term) in which by mismanagement rather than deliberate mistreatment over 5000 perished. Thus deprived of their dependents, the Boers at first seemed to have regained their mobility, but when news of the starvation, disease and deaths in the concentration camps leaked out, it seriously undermined their morale.

Another measure introduced by Kitchener seriously hampered the Boers' maneuverability. He established a system of blockhouses along the rail lines which he then extended into the open country. These were secured by barbed wire and fences built several miles apart. Each blockhouse was manned by an NCO and six men. Patrols moved between the blockhouses continuously and penetrated the areas beyond. The crews in the blockhouses, on their own initiative, fortified them even more for maximum protection against artillery attack. Dogs and

Left: A drawing of 1847, when British artists were favorably disposed towards the Boers; Boer women load their menfolk's guns as the latter beat off a spear attack. Right: The reproduction in a British publication of a 1900 German illustration showing how the British in South Africa encouraged the black locals to drive white Boer women from their homes as the latter were put to the torch. British actions against the Boers were strongly criticized in continental Europe, especially in Germany; many Britons were also uneasy.

booby traps warned the occupants of any Boer approach. At first the Boers penetrated time and again, but the defense system became so closely meshed that ultimately the Boers did not venture near a railway line and were confined to smaller and more and more exactly defined areas.

The British also copied Boer tactics by creating raiding parties on horseback who chased the Boers where they found them and destroyed them. Since the Spanish rising of 1808 against Napoleon's invasion, no European troops had fought an extensive anti-partisan campaign except against ill-armed tribesmen. Partisan terror and counterterror became an established feature of the last phase of the Boer War. Europe was still to experience the renewal of this kind of warfare.

However, it was a war that the Boers could not win, any more than they could defeat any fully professional army. Although truly a people's war from the Boer point of view, they were lacking in professional leadership, had no real war plan or any other plan of operations and, above all, were short of supplies. Their only railway line, which the British cut, ran through Mozambique, and the Royal Navy also established a kind of unofficial blockade off the East African coast by which, with methods previously considered illegal, they intervened in international sea traffic, searching any ship they suspected of carrying supplies for the Boers. Among the people of the European powers, the fight of the Boers was immensely popular, but this did not produce any decisive intervention by any of their governments on the Boer side.

Although the defeat of the Boers was a foregone conclusion, the British Army encountered considerable difficulties in bringing the guerrilla war to an end. European armies were not trained for it, and even experience with the Indian Army on the Northwest Frontier with Afghanistan was of only limited value. Nevertheless, due to their superiority in numbers, equipment and efficient communications systems, the British Army prevailed while the Boers, scattered and short of ammunition and food, had to give up.

The British Army operating in the Boer Republics was about 28,000 men strong at the beginning of the war, only about half the size of the Boer armed forces. It was a professional army of volunteers, as yet too small to operate in the vast territory of South Africa. Reserves and reinforcements coming from Great Britain took three to four weeks to arrive, those coming from India two to three weeks. Initial reinforcements were recruited from volunteers in South Africa. In Great Britain, volunteers

from the yeomanry of the counties (the Militia cavalry) rushed to serve in South Africa, but the main weight of the fighting rested on the regular army. Great Britain's standing army was not yet permanently organized into divisions and corps; this was to take place only during the course of the war. Four battalions of infantry formed a brigade to which were attached formations of artillery, engineers and cavalry. The initial inferiority of British artillery was soon corrected and by the half-way point of the war proved equal, perhaps even superior, to the artillery of the Boers. Although the training of the infantry was badly dated, the British quickly adapted to the new tactic of attacking in dispersed formations.

The first uniforms adapted to the existing environment had been introduced by the British Army in India in 1857. After experience in the Sudan in 1898 it was decided to make khaki the color of the service uniforms of all British Army units although the troops in South Africa at the start of the war still had the old red and blue uniforms. This example was followed by Austria-Hungary in 1909; Germany introduced field-gray in 1910 and in the same year Russia clad its army in green uniforms. France took until 1915 to introduce the 'horizon blue' service uniforms.

In the early phase of the Boer War the British still adhered to a belief held in all European armies that it was possible to achieve fire power supremacy with infantry weapons. In time they changed these tactics and shifted their emphasis to holding down the enemy by concentrated artillery fire while the infantry attacked. However, inexperienced as they were in this, the British artillery frequently fired into its own advancing infantry. Artillery observers, to guide the fire of the artillery from a position in the front line, did not exist; this development, too, was a product of World War I.

To match the Boers, the British Army had to attain an equal standard of mobility, which was a problem. Unlike the Boers, the regular British Army was not accustomed to the prevailing temperatures, which ranged from 40 to 50 degrees Centigrade during the day to night temperatures so low as to cause snow showers. Tents were essential but difficult to transport. Considering this single problem and adding to it all the other supplies needed by an army on the march, it seems natural that the British kept as close as possible to the existing railroads. However, the British also introduced more mobile, mounted infantry units. In each battalion one company was mounted.

How the supply train was to be organized was another

Left: The winning of a Victoria Cross; Captain Towse in a heroic stance as British troops defend themselves against advancing Boers. Right: Map of the Boer War campaigns, showing campaign and supply routes. The importance of sea supply routes can be discerned. Railroads were also important in this war, and raids upon them by Boer cavalry were quite frequent, despite the armored trains which patrolled them. The British command, especially after the appointment of Kitchener as commander in chief, usually sent its troops on foot and its supplies by rail. Below: Lord Methuen is pictured rallying his broken forces at Tweebosch. This was one of the most humiliating defeats suffered by the British in the Boer War. It came when the main Boer forces faced defeat and peace seemed in prospect. The Boers had developed their 'commando' forces, fast well-disciplined horsemen who struck at times and places of their own choosing. The most successful of these was that commanded by De la Rey, and Kitchener sent mobile columns to destroy it. Lord Methuen's column was crushed by De la Rey at Tweebosch, the Boers capturing not only Methuen but his field guns as well. Only at the very end of the war did this commando force meet its heroic end, trapped by superior forces.

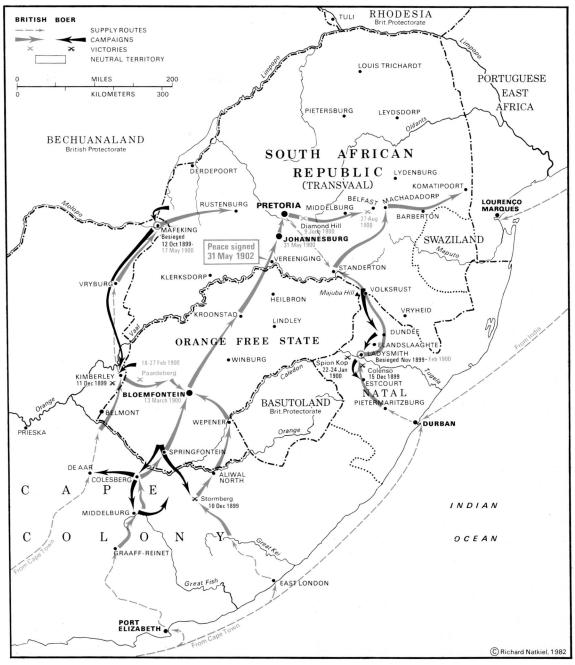

question which Kitchener solved. He had had little experience in modern warfare; as a young subaltern he had served in Egypt and later, in 1898, he made his military reputation there and in the Sudan by building up an army to beat the Mahdi. He proved a brilliant organizer and solved the supply-train problem in South Africa in two ways. First he divided it into two contingents. The first was an army train based, like the Boers', on ox-drawn carts; the second was the train for individual units in the field, in which supplies were carried by mules. The ox-drawn train had the advantage that the animals knew the country and could traverse every kind of territory, but they had the disadvantage of being able to graze only by day, and of course they were slow. Mules, on the other hand, were faster and could graze day and night. Therefore British forces on the march, once they adapted to their environment, could be on the move at any time of day and thus achieve a mobility which made them largely independent of the railroads. They became more than a match for the Boers, who could no longer rely on the vastness of their territory. Once equal or superior mobility had been achieved by the British Army, the outcome of the war became a foregone conclusion.

The third of the forgotten wars before 1914 was the Russo-Japanese war. Among the great powers of Europe the Czarist Empire was the most backward in military affairs. Nonetheless, ever since the days of Peter the Great, the Czarist Empire had wanted warm water ports, on the Black Sea with rights of access to the Mediterranean through the Dardanelles, and on the Pacific. In the 19th century this drive led to territorial expansion toward the Balkans in Europe, Persia and Afghanistan in the Near East and Sinkiang, Mongolia, the Amur Provinces and Sakhalin in the Far East. This inevitably produced a conflict of interest between Russia and the Hapsburg Empire concerning the Balkans on the one hand and between Russia and Great Britain over the Near East on the other. In the Far East Russia founded the Amur Province and in 1860 the coastal province that included the harbor of Vladivostok, a word that translates into 'Ruler of the East' and gives a clear enough indication of Russia's ambitions. In 1875 Russia handed over the Kurile Islands to Japan in return for Sakhalin. In 1896 it intervened on behalf of China against Japan, backed by both France and Germany. In return Russia received from China railroad concessions in Manchuria. Prior to this, in 1894, it had leased Port Arthur and the peninsula of Liaotung from China. Russia also used the Boxer Rising in China in 1900 as a pretext for reinforcing its military presence in Manchuria with the ultimate objective of penetrating into Korea.

Japan, whose geographic position *vis-à-vis* the Asian mainland is not entirely dissimilar to that occupied by Great Britain *vis-à-vis* the European mainland, could not, in the interest of its own military security, tolerate the establishment of a major European power dominating the disintegrating Chinese Manchu Empire. This led to the war between Russia and Japan in 1904.

In 1874 Russia had introduced conscription with a six-year period of military service, but whereas compulsory military service was backed by the whole population of the other European powers, this was not the case in Russia. Serfdom had been formally abolished in 1861, but this did not mean that in practice the Russian peasants – the vast multitude of the population – were no longer in a state of servitude. Social tensions continued and even increased. Land reforms that had been introduced proved ineffective. The peasantry had to pay the landlords for every piece of land they acquired, increasing their debts. The rising load of taxation rested mainly on the peasants. Nevertheless, the Czar, being not merely an Emperor but the head of the Orthodox Church, still retained his aura of sanctity among the peasant population. His faults and shortcomings were laid at the door of the vast bureaucracy which had spread its tentacles across the entire Empire. Russia's intelligentsia adopted a different and more revolutionary attitude. Three main currents coexisted. One comprised the Narodniks, that is, the Populists, who believed that Russia had suffered by contact with the degenerate West. They advocated strict separation from the West and the rejuvenation and modernization of Russian society from its own moral and economic strength. Then there were Nihilists and Socialists, most of them very remote from the majority of the population. It was not until later years that peasants and workers joined the revolutionary movement in large numbers. Like many representatives of the intelligentsia in Europe and the United States, most Russian intellectuals argued that patriotism was an outmoded concept and that war was a crime, or at least an anachronism. Military virtues to them were nothing but an obstacle to progress.

During the Russo-Japanese War, tendencies were apparent which, vastly enlarged and amplified, were to come to the fore during World War I: attempts by the intelligentsia to demoralize the forces, to cause unrest among the ranks, to carry out acts

Top: Manchuria in 1904. A Russian observation post awaits the Japanese. An Austrian military observer, one of many attachés sent to the Russo-Japanese War by the great powers, has his back to the camera. Above: The Russian cruiser *Varyag* sinks in the harbor at Chelmulpo (Inchon) after her hopeless battle against a Japanese squadron. Above right: Japanese battleships and cruisers were built in Britain. Here the new battleship *Hatsuse* is eased down the Tyne, her topmasts lowered to clear the rail bridges of Newcastle. Right: The Russian commander in Manchuria, Kuropatkin, greets his officers.

of sabotage were some of them. At that time this did not affect the Russian Army in any serious way. By contrast, however, the Japanese population backed its forces to the hilt.

Russia's internal condition was bound to be reflected to some degree in its army. The education of the officers was meager, to say the least. Promotion came only very slowly and not usually on the basis of merit but of social connections. There was an enormous chasm between the Guards officers serving in St Petersburg and the officers serving with the line regiments. Promotion was quicker if an officer managed to have himself transferred to one of the staffs or to the administration. The Russians also had reserve officers, but considering the low social status of the average Russian officer, there was not such a rush to become one as was the case in Germany. Hence they were in very short supply.

Below: As soon as the Japanese captured a hill overlooking Port Arthur, the Russian Pacific Squadron was doomed to succumb to artillery fire. At the left is the cruiser *Pallada*, and at the right the battleship *Pobieda* ('*Victory*'), lying on the bottom of the harbor. A sister of *Pallada* and survivor of Tsushima, *Avrora*, is preserved at Leningrad. Opposite page, top left: General Kuropatkin. Not an incompetent general, Kuropatkin was good at organization and administration, but his bureaucratic qualities did not fit him for the direction of rapidly-moving events. His strategy of a fighting retreat until his forces were overwhelmingly superior to the Japanese was basically correct, but too unpalatable for his government. Opposite page, right: The well-equipped Japanese infantryman.
This page, left: Russian artillery horses en route to the Manchurian front. In the top lefthand corner of the boxcar is the celebrated inscription '40 men or 8 horses'.

Top: A British artist's impression of the Russian garrison leaving Port Arthur as the smart Japanese troops move in. Above left: En route to his defeat at Tsushima, the Russian Admiral Rozhestvensky comes ashore at Tangiers. On leaving, his ships' anchors broke the cable connection with Europe. Above right: A Russian coastal gun at Port Arthur. Left: Japanese heavy howitzers bombarded Port Arthur, with decisive results.

To be an officer was more of a job than a calling motivated by traditions of service. The Russian General Staff and the Russian Military Academy also reflected the prevailing situation. There was a premium placed on formal training, not on individual initiative. Wargames were a rarity. In contrast to the German concept of the *Auftragstaktik*, the Russians adhered to the strict execution of orders issued by the staff, carried out to the letter right down to the last private in the army. A French military observer who inspected the Russian Army commented that it had not learned a single lesson from its past campaigns.

Russian military staffs were over-manned. Also, a great many civilian advisors were attached to them. Although the Russian Army was well-fed in normal times, the staffs lived in extreme luxury, and this caused resentment among the troops. The generally favorable condition of Russian Army supplies was largely the achievement of the Minister for War and future commander of the Russian Army in Manchuria, Kuropatkin. Though a brilliant organizer, he was, however, a mediocre general. Like every Russian general, he commanded troops who were largely illiterate. Although they hardly knew what a war was about, particularly the Russo-Japanese War, they excelled in steadfastness and stubbornness as long as their officers were with them. Once these had been killed, they soon gave up all resistance. Since the officers never had even the

vaguest outline of the situation as a whole, they were vulnerable to panic. The Czarist Empire was multi-national, and among the soldiers recruited from national minorities, morale was considerably lower than among pure Russian troops.

In the field the Russian Army was divided into corps, each with two divisions. An engineer battalion was attached to each corps. A standard infantry division included four infantry regiments, each with under 3000 combat troops, as well as cavalry detachments used for raids or for reconnaissance. By the end of August 1904 Kuropatkin had seven army corps, four divisions of Cossacks, 590 pieces of artillery, but only 16 machine guns. Artillery tactics were still influenced by the maxims of the late 18th and early 19th centuries. The Russian artillery was always stationed on the tops of hills or along ridges. They had no high-explosive shells – only shrapnel. The telegraphic system

cannot be described except by saying that it was utterly inadequate.

This was the army which met an enemy whose forces had been structured and equipped according to the most modern standards. While the Japanese Navy had been trained by the British, the army had been trained by the Germans. The only shortage of the Japanese Army was in its number of trained officers and NCOs. It was structured into armies whose size actually corresponded more closely to that of European corps. Three divisions formed an army. The infantry divisions consisted of four regiments, each with three battalions. Three squadrons of cavalry, an artillery regiment with three batteries of six guns each, an engineer battalion and a telegraph communication detachment were attached to each division.

The structure of the Japanese Army was more flexible than that of the Russian and the 224-man infantry company was a tactical unit superior to the smaller Russian formation. The Japanese placed great emphasis upon fire tactics while the Russian Army was still conducting its attack *en masse* by a bayonet charge. Moreover, each Japanese company had one heavy machine gun. The regular Japanese Army numbered 270,000 men with 870 pieces of artillery, to which must be added 530,000 men from the reserves.

In Manchuria the Russian Army had 83,000 men at first with 196 pieces of artillery. The portion of the Trans-Siberia Railroad bypassing Lake Baykal was still incomplete and initially only three trains per day could be sent with reinforcements. In the course of the war this was increased to 12 trains per day and once the Trans-Siberian Railroad around Lake Baykal had been completed in September 1904, a rate of 18 trains per day was achieved. In total the Russians transported 800,000 men, 150,000 horses and 1500 guns as well as supplies to the front during the war.

The Japanese forces had, of course, to be carried across the sea. Japanese supply vessels could not transport more than three divisions and equipment from Japan at any one time. The process of embarkation took three days, disembarkation five days. Only from the late summer of 1904 was the problem of food supplies solved when, because of a good harvest, the Japanese could live off the land.

The success of the Japanese depended on supremacy at sea. The Japanese Navy comprised 29 modern ships including six battleships and over 90 older vessels. Japanese docks were capable of repairing ships but not of undertaking new construction. The Russian Pacific Squadron consisted of 72 vessels, some of which were based at Vladivostok and some at Port Arthur.

To prevent interference with the movement of their army, the Japanese plan of war envisioned the achievement of absolute naval dominance in the Yellow Sea, to allow the land forces to aim at a final decision in Manchuria. Therefore, while Russo-Japanese negotiations were still in progress and without a declaration of war, Admiral Togo, the Japanese naval leader, was sent to attack the Russian naval units stationed in Port Arthur on 8 February 1904. The enterprise was a complete success for the Japanese and established their supremacy at sea.

Thereupon, in March 1904, the Japanese landed an army halfway up the Korean Peninsula which made its way to the Yalu River, while a second army landed northeast of Port Arthur, the bulk of which turned toward Kuropatkin's forces at Liaoyang while the rest turned toward Port Arthur, which was still held by Russian forces.

The Russian war plan envisioned holding a defensive line, backed by the Harbin-Mukden-Port Arthur railroad until sufficient reinforcements had arrived to allow a move to the offensive. However, the position of the Russian Armies

Left: The only modern Russian battleship to survive Tsushima, *Orel*, after surrender to the Japanese. The fractured barrel of one of her four 12-inch guns can be seen. A Japanese sailor stands on guard. The *Orel* was only a year old, having been built in Russia to an essentially French design. Below: Togo's flagship *Mikasa*, the only pre-Dreadnought battleship to be preserved to the present day. The inscription is in Togo's handwriting, and is his signal to his ships as they joined action at Tsushima. The Japanese officers' Nelsonian background is clear from this signal, 'The Empire's fate depends on the result of this battle . . . Let every man do his utmost duty'. At the end of the war *Mikasa* accidentally blew up in harbor, but was later salvaged. Right: Togo in his later years, when he was a national hero and something of an elder statesman too. Far right: Signed, sealed and soon to be delivered; the Treaty of Portsmouth. The Russians signed in Latin script, not Cyrillic. Because Japan, though victorious, had reached the end of her resources, the Russian negotiator Witte was able to secure an agreement which many Japanese found distasteful. A Tokyo anti-peace riot was the result.

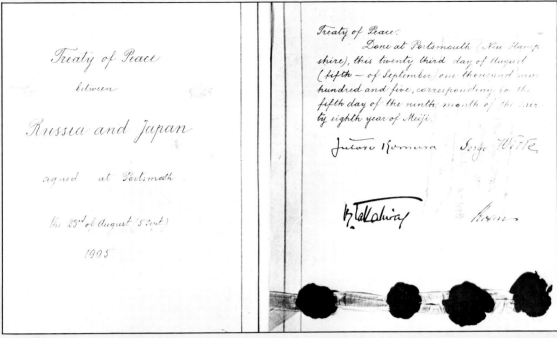

depended largely on what was happening at sea. The Japanese largely preserved their naval dominance and used it to capture harbors which would give them better access to Port Arthur. There was a temporary setback when Russian naval forces coming from Vladivostok managed to sink the vessels carrying the siege train for Port Arthur.

Russian attempts to keep open the land route to Port Arthur failed. The Japanese forces at Liaoyang linked up with the forces crossing the Yalu and forced the Russians to withdraw. Time and again the Russians counterattacked in vain. Frontal attack having failed, they tried to get around the flanks of the Japanese, but their forces were too weak to do so successfully. They continued to withdraw and to dig in. The war of movement turned into a war of fixed positions, trenches and field fortifications, very much like the one waged near Richmond in the American Civil War. For months Russian and Japanese forces confronted each other without much activity. The fact that European observers failed to draw any decisive lessons from this is shown by the report of the German General Freytag-Loringhoven, who wrote: 'A highly cultured country increases the mobility of the armies, so that the attacker does not have to halt before the fortified positions of the defenders as in East Asia, where war forms a continuous engagement of defensive fire, because in East Asia the mountains in the east and the desert in the west confine operations to a relatively small area.'

In many respects, though not in all, the siege of Port Arthur foreshadowed Verdun. The Japanese attacks were extremely costly in manpower. Fifteen thousand Japanese were killed in the process of capturing the outer ring of the fortifications. The harbor and docks were subjected to the fire of 280mm howitzers, but Port Arthur itself still held out against the Japanese onslaught. A whole network of Japanese trenches surrounded the fortress. Mortars, dynamite hand grenades and wire-cutting equipment became standard weapons and tools for the Japanese. The first artillery barrage of the type with which we have been familiar since World War I was opened upon Port Arthur without seriously denting the Russian defense. Engineers became more important than the infantry; only with their aid could the important fortifications overlooking Port Arthur be taken by December 1904. Finally, on 3 January 1905, Port Arthur capitulated.

In the north, General Kuropatkin still held his defensive line at Mukden and there the most important battle of the war raged from 23 February to 10 March 1905. In numbers, the Russians and Japanese were about equal, each side having about 300,000 men. The battle ended with a Russian withdrawal along the rail line to Harbin. Again the Russians dug in, reinforced by troops who had come via the Trans-Siberian Railway. In spite of their victories, signs of exhaustion could be seen in the Japanese Army. Operations on both sides were impeded by the thaw which put the road communications out of commission.

After the defeat of the Pacific Squadron Russian hopes rested upon regaining naval supremacy in the Yellow Sea, which was to be achieved by Russia's Baltic Fleet which made the long round-the-world trip to join the fighting. These hopes came to nought when the Japanese Navy defeated the Baltic Fleet on 27–28 May 1905, sending 30 of the 47 vessels to the bottom. To all intents and purposes, the outcome of the war had been decided, even though Russia still had large forces with which to continue the war on land. But the Czarist Empire and its army were debilitated, and mediation by President Theodore Roosevelt and the German Empire led to the conclusion of hostilities. For the first time in modern history, a European power had been defeated by an Asian army. The process of decolonization in Asia dates from that moment.

The Russo-Japanese conflict carried many lessons for the armies of all countries. It had caused a change in infantry tactics; the effective fire of modern rifles and machine guns entrenched in the first line should have put an end to the attack by company columns. Even the reserves no longer moved in compact bodies but spread out to avoid becoming an easy target for the artillery. Attacks were carried out by short rushes in dispersed formations, taking advantage of any temporary lulls in the defensive artillery fire. Companies no longer attacked as a body but in dispersed platoon formations. If losses increased seriously, the spade became the most important weapon beside the rifle, since the men would dig in. Once a firm line was established, the opposing forces fought for fire supremacy and, once this was achieved, the final attack was mounted. But as in the Boer War, the artillery was rarely used to prepare an infantry attack. Unfortunately, most of these and other lessons taught by the American Civil War, the Boer War and the Russo-Japanese War were ignored in 1914 – to be learned again only after an immense toll of life had been taken.

WORLD WAR I

It is not our task to investigate the causes of World War I. But we have to ask the question, would any of the belligerent powers have been prepared to pay the price which the preservation of peace would have involved? The answer to this must be an emphatic *No*. Russia was not prepared, for domestic as well as for foreign policy reasons, to give up its claim to dominance in the Balkans. Austria-Hungary, already showing signs of internal weakness, could not afford any further strengthening of the Serb position. Germany could not afford to be moved into a position of utter isolation – the consequence if it had forsaken its ally, nor could it view with complacency the strengthening of Russia to a point where Russia could overrun Germany (a view also held by the British Ambassador Buchanan in St Petersburg and Sir Henry Wilson, the Chief of Great Britain's Imperial General Staff). France was unable to accept the risk of isolation on the European mainland if it left its Russian ally unsupported. And Great Britain, its resources already strained, could not risk the security of its imperial position which it had obtained first through the Anglo-French entente of 1904, and later through the Anglo-Russian entente of 1907. Nor could it ignore the potential threat posed to Great Britain's sea power by the growing German battle fleet.

The lessons which the general staffs of the European armies had learned went back to 1859, 1866 and 1870–71, as well as to the Balkan Wars of 1912–13. What was totally ignored at both the tactical and operational levels was the immense fire power of modern infantry weapons, especially the machine gun. With the exception of the British Army until 1916, the armies of the European powers were mass conscript armies. The generals therefore believed in the virtue of mass, and in the infantry as the main force for bringing about a decision.

According to staff calculations, the frontage of a division in an attack should amount to little more than three miles. A German infantry regiment consisted of 12 companies and a machine-gun company which was to provide covering fire from the rear and not accompany the attacking line. Attacks were carried out initially in slightly dispersed company columns, still too tightly bunched and providing an ideal target for the defense. The cavalry was to carry out reconnaissance tasks. But Zeppelins, as well as aircraft themselves, had begun to take over that task from the cavalry. Balloons had already been used as platforms for observers directing the fire of the artillery. Trucks and tractors were already widely used for tactical movements. Telegraph communications connected the General Staff with lower-level staffs. Railroad regiments were essential for the reliable functioning of the communications network, which was still based on rail, with motor vehicles taking second place. As a rule, military forces on the advance could move only about 75 miles from their rail head. The engineers and railroad troops had to move the rail heads forward as quickly as possible. This reliance on the rail system during World War I made it impossible to carry out large pincer movements like those commonly employed in World War II, when the road network was utilized to the same extent as were the railroads. Frontal penetration was therefore limited by both space and time.

The Allies had at their disposal some 250 divisions, against which the Central Powers could bring approximately 160 divisions. The Allied supremacy was even greater at sea, the oceans being dominated by the Royal Navy. But most important, the Allies enjoyed an unquantifiable superiority in the supply of raw materials. The markets of the world were open to them – naval supremacy ensured that – while they were closed to the Central Powers. This superiority was demonstrated with a vengeance when the Allies carried out the long-range blockade of Germany, showing that fighting from the interior line with-

out sufficient raw materials and foodstuffs was hopeless against adversaries with unlimited access to all that they needed. *Ersatz* (artificial) materials including food, as developed by Germany's chemical industries, could alleviate the situation in some sectors but could not solve the problem.

The Central Powers had neither a combined supreme command nor a common and concerted war plan. There were a number of agreements made between individual members of the respective General Staffs, such as that Austria should hold the Russians at bay until the Schlieffen Plan had been carried out and the German forces could turn east. The German Eighth Army with its weak formations was to hold East Prussia. But the Schlieffen Plan was no longer the plan conceived by its originator.

Russia intended to move with four armies against the Austrians in Galicia and with two armies against East Prussia. The French planned to break through the German front in the area of Metz, but in their blue coats, red trousers and red kepis they became an ideal target for German machine guns. The British Expeditionary Force was to bolster the French left wing while the Belgian Army envisioned fighting only for the neutrality of its country.

As in most wars, unforeseen events necessitated the modification or complete alteration of the original plans. Besides tactical and strategic errors, and underestimation of the effectiveness of defensive fire power, stockpiles of ammunition, especially artillery shells and other military hardware, were consumed far more quickly than expected and the physical resources of the men actually carrying out the operations were overestimated.

Previous page: On the Western Front during the Final Allied offensive; British troops with German prisoners during the attack on the so-called Hindenburg Line near Bellicourt in September 1918. Right: A map of the European alliances on the eve of World War I. The Central Powers clearly have the advantage of internal lines of communication, but are subject to attack from several directions; the vulnerability of Russian Poland is also evident. Below: Belgian troops on the march during a sortie from Antwerp in September 1914. Below right: French infantry of 1914, occupying a shallow trench.

The Schlieffen Plan failed because, as already mentioned, Moltke the Younger, the Chief of the General Staff, had converted it into a double pincer movement, intending to launch an offensive in the north and south and thereby depleting the manpower of his right wing. The Russian forces penetrated into East Prussia much more quickly than had been expected, which required a further reduction of the German right wing in France when much of it was shipped to the east. The German armies had to swing around east of Paris, instead of west as planned by Schlieffen. The French Supreme Commander, General Joffre, recognized the German weakness and partly by commandeering all vehicles on wheels in Paris, transported all available troops and threw them against the exposed German right wing. Kluck, the commander of the German First Army, had allowed a gap to appear in his front into which British and French forces pushed. During this crisis the commander of the German Second Army, Bülow, advocated withdrawal while Kluck wanted to continue the attack. Moltke sent a staff officer to Kluck and Bülow with authority to adjudicate the dispute and he ordered a withdrawal. This was the 'Miracle of the Marne.' Moltke, beset by doubts, suffered a collapse and was replaced by General von Falkenhayn. Now the battle in the west turned into a race for the opponent's northern flank. This failed, and instead the Allied and German armies reached the Channel coast. Mobility ceased, replaced by trench warfare from the Channel to the Swiss frontier. With hindsight we can see that the outcome of the war was now decided. It became a war of attrition in which the Central Powers were burdened by disadvantages which nothing in the world could reduce.

Left: The Russian General
Samsonov, who committed suicide
after his army was shattered in the
Battle of Tannenberg, having
blundered into an encirclement
planned by Ludendorff's talented
chief of staff. The Russians' failure,
which brought to an end their
prompt invasion of East Prussia,
might have been avoided if their
cavalry, commanded by
Rennenkampf, had been more
active. But Rennenkampf and
Samsonov were on bad terms,
having come literally to blows in
the Russo-Japanese War.
Below left: Russian infantrymen
in their trenches. Their bayonet
was a fearsome four-sided blade
which, when attached to the rifle,
formed a weapon five and a half
feet long. Top right: Russian
infantry on the march to the front
in 1914; as in World War II, they
carried a rolled blanket around
their shoulders. Center right:
German infantry rests in a cornfield
during the Battle of the Marne. By
invading at harvest time, the
Germans were able to live off the
land to an unexpected extent; this
compensated for defective supply
arrangements, caused by the
advance outpacing the provision
of transport. Below: Russian
infantrymen attack through the
barbed wire entanglements of the
East Prussian front. Entanglements
covered by machine guns were a
murderous obstacle.

Left: French infantry set up barbed wire over a communication trench. A front line trench would be deeper and provided with dugouts and traverses to make defense easier. Below: Men of the 59th Field Company, Royal Engineers, prepare to leave their bivouac at Bavai on 22nd August 1914 just before the Battle of Mons.

In East Prussia General Paul von Hindenburg, pulled out of retirement, and his Chief of Staff, Erich Ludendorff, put an end to the Russian invasion of East Prussia at the Battle of Tannenberg between 26 and 30 August 1914. Two Russian armies were virtually destroyed. The Battle of Tannenberg showed the immense advantages of the principle of *Auftragstaktik*, since most commanders in the field, like General von François, had to act independently of the main headquarters. They had no more than directives and were sometimes willing to set aside these directives if the prevailing situation made it necessary. The Battle of Tannenberg was also fought over a relatively small area, whereas the German campaign in France covered a much wider area and was conducted by forces clearly under-strength for this kind of operation.

In the East the war was more mobile and, Tannenberg apart, the main actions took place largely in Galicia. There the Russians tried to inflict a serious defeat on the Austro-Hungarian forces and to open the road to Budapest and Vienna. Although the Austro-Hungarian forces were clearly inferior in numbers, the Chief of the Austro-Hungarian General Staff, Conrad von Hötzendorf, met the Russian attack offensively and achieved important victories at Krasnic and Komerov. The Russian Army was checked, and its attempt to cut Hötzendorf's lines of communication failed. But on the flank near Lvov the Russians created a situation which Hötzendorf could meet only by withdrawing part of his forces to the lower San River. Here it was a question of keeping vital lines of communication in the hands of

the Central Powers. Nonetheless, the initiative remained with the Austro-Hungarian forces. In December 1914, at the Battles of Limanova and Lapanov, the Russian threat to the important industrial region of Upper Silesia was eliminated. In the east, time and again the belligerents made attempts to encircle the enemy – attempts in most cases unsuccessful because of bad road conditions and lack of transport. The shortage of materials which afflicted the Austro-Hungarian Army was balanced by the Russian lack of flexibility in their operations. But at the level of the rank and file, the firepower of modern infantry weapons caused serious losses on both sides, especially among the regular officers and NCOs. The Austro-Hungarian Army was also much inferior to the Russian in artillery. Thus, as in the West, the Eastern fronts hardened into seemingly impenetrable lines of trenches and fortifications, from the Russian frontier in East Prussia, to Lowicz at the Bzura River, across Poland to the Carpathian Mountains.

Movement came only with the onset of spring when the Russians attempted again to make their way into the Hungarian plain but were brought to a standstill by the forces of the Hapsburg Empire. Their effectiveness was surprising, considering that it was an army of national minorities, which, with a few exceptions, kept intact until the fall of 1918.

Neither in the East nor in the West did the trench warfare produce any decision. The French mounted offensives in the Arras and Champagne areas in 1915, but failed to achieve a breakthrough. The German trench system (although it had not yet acquired any great depth) and German machine gunners brought the French attacks to a halt. The French attempt in March 1915 was followed by a German attack in April in the Ypres sector which made some territorial gains but failed to achieve its true aim, which was to break through and restore mobility to the campaign in the West. For the first time the Germans made extensive use of poison gas, which came as a surprise to the defenders, but the Germans lacked the reserves with which to exploit the initial surprise they achieved.

The problem of how to restore mobility to warfare was not tackled, as one might expect, at staff level, but in the front line and the solution was the *Stosstrupp*, the shocktroop, with which the first experiments were made in the Argonne. They were formed in groups of three and were to spearhead any attack. The leader of the party carried no rifle but had a pick and the shield of a machine gun for his protection. On each side of him was an expert handgrenade thrower loaded with shoulder-slung sacks of hand-grenades. For hand-to-hand combat they used bayonets or sharpened trench spades.

Left: The first winter of the war; German troops facing the Russians in East Prussia. Right: General Galliéni, military governor of Paris, whose advice to Joffre led to the Allied victory at the Marne in 1914 and the failure of the Schlieffen Plan.
Below: A map of the 'Battle of the Frontiers', August–September 1914.

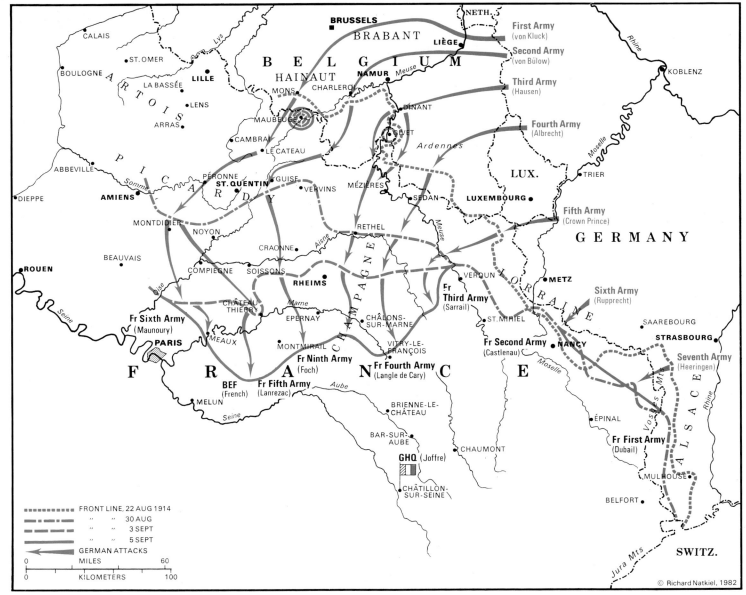

© Richard Natkiel, 1982

Below: Serbian artillery on the banks of the Danube attempts to hold off the Austrian advance. Far left: Sir John French, commander of the British Expeditionary Force in France for the first year of the war. Left: General d'Espérey, one of the best of French World War I generals.

Once the attack had been carried into the enemy's trench, one problem was how to protect the flanks, a task usually given to the artillery. But their positions were often too far in the rear to allow precisely aimed fire. At first it was believed that the shock-troops would be able to use some of their own lighter artillery, but all types tested proved too cumbersome; instead, they used the trench mortar. This added more men to the unit, while dealing with enemy fortifications required engineers as well. In this way the shocktroops became the first mixed formation.

An attack was usually launched by the small groups of expert hand-grenade throwers and engineers experienced in the handling of explosives, plus a team of wire cutters and flame throwers. They were followed by machine gunners and mortar crews to protect their flanks. Once the first trench had been reached, close combat was the rule with all the weapons available, even those of the enemy.

The principle of the *Stosstrupp*, based on a mixed formation, would have been of little use had there not been men brave enough to carry the attack forward. They would be followed by the bulk of the infantry attacking through the breaches opened by the stormtroops. Naturally, the *Stosstruppen* considered themselves a warrior elite. They had to be in top physical condition and their training was carried out with the use of live ammunition. This type of soldier has been best described in Ernst Jünger's book *Storm of Steel*.

The relationship between officers and men was rather different to that existing in the regiments of the line. It was based on comradeship, rooted in the knowledge that everyone depended upon everyone else. Ranks were considered functional, devoid of any social connotations. Stormtroop training did not include the barrack square drill, still prevalent among the troops in the rear areas. Loyalty to one another was the guiding principle.

Regular officers were extremely rare in stormtroop units. They were commanded mainly by officers of the reserve or those who had become officers only in the course of the war. For a long time the *Stosstruppen* were used mainly in raids to gather intelligence. Their great hour came in the March offensive of 1918 when shocktroop formations, attacking in platoon size, spearheaded the German attacks.

In May 1915 Italy entered the war on the side of the Allies. Besides its other war aims, Italy strove to capture the South Tyrol from the Austrians and establish a new frontier at the Brenner Pass. General Cadorna, Chief of the Italian General Staff, believed he would be able to achieve this by a push across the Isonzo River in the direction of Ljubljana, and via Toblach toward Villach. The Austro-Hungarian forces on the southern frontier were weak, but in spite of this weakness they managed to halt all the Italian attacks in the four Isonzo battles of 1915. In the western Trentino sector, the Italians cherished the belief that it was important to occupy the summits of the peaks before risking the push through the valleys. It was a fundamental error. The war on the summits and glaciers came to the same end as the fighting near the Isonzo. For many months, Italians and Austro-Hungarians fought at heights often over 10,000 feet without much gain for either side.

Below: HMS *Majestic* sinks off Gallipoli after being torpedoed by the German submarine U21. The Dardanelles operation, designed to take the pressure off Russia, is now seen to have been strategically justified but abysmally planned. However, unlike the troop losses, the sinking of several Allied battleships was not a result of muddle but an inevitable and expected price. *Majestic* was an elderly Pre-Dreadnought, as were the other sacrificed battleships; such losses were not critical although they had a depressing effect on naval morale. *Majestic* was U21's second victim, for two days earlier another Pre-Dreadnought, *Triumph*, had been sunk by the same craft.

The success of the German battlecruiser *Goeben* in evading the British in the Mediterranean and its entry into the Dardanelles was instrumental in bringing Turkey into the war on the side of the Central Powers. The Turks' task was now to close the Dardanelles to any supplies destined for Russia, a task they carried out successfully throughout the war. Winston Churchill, then First Lord of the Admiralty, successfully argued for mounting an attack to open the Dardanelles. The operation began with naval bombardments of the forts guarding the Straits. This was followed in April 1915 by the landing of Allied troops at Gallipoli. A total of 75,000 men reached the beaches. Opposing them were 80,000 Turks commanded by the German General Liman von Sanders. However, the Allies failed to take early opportunities to reach the commanding heights. Early in August they landed additional forces at Suvla Bay, but there, too, chances of success were wasted and the Turkish resistance was so ferocious that they dominated the heights overlooking the bay and contained three British and two French divisions on the beaches. Between December 1915 and January 1916 the Allies found themselves compelled to evacuate their forces and ship them back. The first great modern amphibious enterprise thus came to an end.

In 1914 Great Britain and the German Empire had the strongest battle fleets in the world. The British had 32 modern capital ships, most with the Home Fleet, soon renamed the Grand Fleet, while Germany had 17 modern vessels, 14 of an older type and four battlecruisers (plus *Goeben* in the Mediterranean). Taking into account all ships of the respective fleets, the ratio was five to two in favor of the navy of Great Britain.

The establishment of the long-distance blockade by the Royal Navy ultimately led to an attempt by the German Admiralty, after initial caution, to break it. Vice-Admiral Scheer, who took command of the German High Seas Fleet in January 1916, tried to bring about a decisive battle. The Battle of Jutland on 31 May 1916 was the only great sea battle fought in World War I. Although the Royal Navy under Admiral Jellicoe was almost twice the size of the German Navy, the battle ended in a tactical victory for the Germans. The British lost three battlecruisers, three armored cruisers and several destroyers, while the Germans lost one battlecruiser, one old battleship, four small cruisers and five torpedo boats. In terms of manpower, the British lost over 6,000, the Germans 2,500 men. In spite of its tactical success, it was not the desired strategic victory that would have achieved the lifting of the blockade.

In the Baltic the German Navy, on the whole, fulfilled its tasks, maintaining the transport of iron ore vital to Germany's war economy from Sweden to Germany and securing the flanks of the German forces advancing through the Baltic countries.

At the outbreak of war a number of German naval units operated overseas, such as the East Asia Squadron under Admiral von Spee. Spee managed to inflict a serious defeat on British naval units at Coronel, only to be blasted from the surface of the ocean by the Royal Navy at the Falkland Islands a few weeks later. A small number of individual raiders carried on cruiser warfare against British commerce, but slowly, one by one, they too disappeared from the high seas. Now the German Admiralty

placed its hopes on the U-Boats, one of which had sunk three British armored cruisers in a couple of hours one day in September 1914. On 2 November 1914 the British government had declared the entire North Sea a war zone, to which the Germans replied by opening unrestricted submarine warfare in February 1915. The U-Boat was considered by the old established naval powers to be a barbaric weapon, typical of the 'Hun.' But the German U-Boats could not afford to surface to warn passengers and crew, since most British merchantmen were soon armed and the U-Boats of that time were still so fragile that even a burst of machine-gun fire could destroy their diving tanks.

The sinking of the British liner *Lusitania* in 1915 with over one hundred Americans on board had caused a violent American protest. The Germans were alleged to have struck a medal to commemorate this event. Such a medal had indeed been struck – but in Great Britain for the purpose of propaganda. Finally, mainly as a result of pressure exerted by President Wilson, the Germans abandoned unrestricted submarine warfare in September 1915. But when the war escalated, when it became blatantly obvious that the United States supplied Great Britain and France with arms, raw materials and foodstuffs, the Germans resumed unrestricted submarine warfare in February 1917. The submarines available, however, were too few to achieve a decisive success. On the contrary, this policy caused the United

Left: A British howitzer bombards Turkish positions at Gallipoli. The rocky, hilly terrain provided good protection for the defenders; even British naval guns had little effect against the Turkish positions. Top right: A German flamethrower in use on the Western Front.
Above: French soldiers in a casemate of the Douamont fortress, one of the key strongpoints of the Verdun defenses which was captured by the Germans, then recaptured by the French.

States to enter the war in April 1917. Still, the German submarine arm posed a major danger, sinking in total over 8 million tons of shipping.

In the meantime, the war on land continued, but in spite of intensive artillery preparation, often lasting for days, once the attackers went over the top they met the deadly hail of machine-gun bullets. No weapon had been found to overcome the stalemate. Neither party could outflank the other; only a breakthrough could achieve that. In the face of this situation, the Central Powers shifted their attention to the Eastern Theater of war. In May 1915 German and Austro-Hungarian formations opened an offensive in the Gorlice-Tarnowe area. Circumstances favored the Central Powers; they could rely on an excellent rail network. After a four-hour intensive artillery preparation, the German Eleventh Army with four German and one Austro-Hungarian Corps attacked across a front of little more than 20 miles. While the artillery continued its bombardment, Germans and Austrians advanced close behind the artillery screen. The Russians were utterly surprised and unable to throw in reserves. The first major breakthrough during World War I had been achieved. But even that was not decisive, for the Germans and Austrians lacked the ability to exploit the operational freedom which they had achieved. The Austro-German lines advanced to the Bug and Dniestr, where, once again, they dug in.

Left: A German picture of the interior of the Douamont casemate. This fortress, mostly built in the 19th century, included a concrete stronghold about 200 yards long and containing numerous chambers and tunnels. There was accommodation for at least 500 defenders but, almost by oversight, there were only 60 elderly artillery reservists holding it when the Germans captured it in 1916. In October its recapture by the French was not so bloodless, but was an important step forward in the relief of Verdun, which was achieved by December; much of the German strength had been diverted to meet the Allies' Somme offensive. Below left: Another Verdun fortress, Vaux, whose defenders fought bravely against gas, flamethrowers and grenades and surrendered only when their water was exhausted. Above: French camouflage screens.

Gorlice-Tarnowe could not be compared to the battles of *matériel* raging on the Western Front. Early in 1916 the German High Command transferred its emphasis back to the West. There, from February 1916 until July of that year, General von Falkenhayn tried to cripple the French Army in the Battle of Verdun. In spite of initial German successes, French resistance was such that no victory could be gained. It was Grant's concept of the war of attrition; Falkenhayn hoped to bleed the French Army white. It was a completely abortive venture. Verdun, and for that matter most battles of World War I, reflected the inability of the generals and the politicians to find alternative solutions. The fact that these battles demonstrated heights of bravery and self-sacrifice by all the troops involved in them does not balance the failure at the military and political level.

While the Battle of Verdun still raged, the British launched their offensive at the Somme, starting with an artillery barrage that lasted seven days and nights. Then 20 British and 11 French divisions, supported by three divisions of cavalry, attacked a line held initially by only 11 German divisions on a 25-mile front. After the seven-day bombardment by 3000 guns the British did not expect any defenders to have survived. They managed in places to overrun the first trench, but the German defense, which by then was exceptionally strong, quickly threw in the reserves necessary to prevent any further penetration by the Allies. The traditional methods to which the armies of Europe had become accustomed and the technical limits of their weapons made it impossible to overcome lines of defense constructed in depth.

One weapon that provided an answer to this problem was the tank, developed by the British and first used in September 1916 on the Somme front. These tanks penetrated the German lines until they were put out of action at point-blank range by the German artillery. The new weapon helped restore mobility to warfare, but its significance in World War I must not be overestimated. At first it had a high psychological impact, but once the German Infantry had become used to the tanks, they also knew how to deal with them. Apart from that, the tanks of World War I still had too many technical shortcomings. Their range was under 20 miles and they could hardly be used for extensive raids. So the stalemate in the west remained unbroken.

The year of 1917 brought no change; the senseless slaughter continued. The Allies failed to achieve a breakthrough either in the west or on the Isonzo front. However, the Battle of Verdun had shaken the confidence of the German soldier in his leadership for the first time. Doubts began to increase, and in Germany the first voices were raised demanding an end to the bloodletting. For the French, however, Verdun for some time became the symbol of the invincibility of the French Army. But later, after the bloody failure of the Nivelle offensive in the spring of 1917, the French Army entered a period of uncertainty caused by the immense losses it had sustained and by news of the March revolution in Russia. Whole contingents of the army mutinied and court martials had to be used to restore discipline. General Pétain succeeded in overcoming the crisis and restoring confidence within the army. This crisis, which raged for a number of weeks, went unnoticed by the German leadership, but whether it could have been exploited to the benefit of the Central Powers is doubtful. In view of the overall situation at the fronts, they would have been unable to muster the reserves necessary for a vital push.

By the summer of 1917 it was clear to all that the Central Powers had not been adequately prepared for this kind of war, neither politically, militarily, nor economically. Time was working on the side of the Allies with their inexhaustible supplies of raw materials and their reserves of manpower, while the Central Powers could not so readily replace the men they had lost. Knowing this, the Allies could afford to reject any attempt at a negotiated peace.

Profound changes had taken place among the forces in the field. The belief that the infantry was the queen of battles had vanished. Defensive fire made any attack carried out without overwhelming artillery support a certain failure. Only the combined action of artillery and infantry could yield results. In defense, the artillery supported the infantry by holding down the enemy. Dugouts with various exits gave the infantry shelter and the chance to rest. The infantry needed the support of the engineers in building these positions, especially in terrain where it was difficult to establish them, such as in the Alps. The rifle line of 1914 had been transformed by 1917 into a battle zone crisscrossed with trenches, dugouts, pillboxes and bunkers. Taking the first trench in an attack was no longer decisive because reserves could be brought forward through the trench system leading far to the rear to expel the enemy from his position. Behind this network of trenches were the artillery positions, but the backbone of the entire defensive system was the system of machine-gun posts. The whole network was protected by vast barbed-wire entanglements. Such a system made it possible to survive the heaviest artillery bombardment, and every attack following it met with an energetic counterattack in which in many cases hand-to-hand fighting took place, largely with bayonets, spades and hand grenades, not over the top but within the trenches themselves. In short, the machine gun carried the main burden of the infantry fire.

The cavalry had been demoted to a minor role in the west. The last, and in terms of human lives, most costly major cavalry attack had been mounted in 1870. Cavalry was of limited use even in the plains of Russia and the Baltic countries, so it de-

Below: British battleships in action at the Battle of Jutland. The ships are of the improved Dreadnought type. The heavy tripod masts were designed to support the fire-control platforms even if one of the legs were shot away. In fact the British gunnery control system was inferior to that of the Germans, partly because an excellent British system had been rejected by the Admiralty in favor of one designed by an influential officer. Because the British lost more ships than the Germans, this battle was regarded as a defeat, although the flight of the German High Seas Fleet to its ports suggested that the defeat was only tactical, not strategic. Left: Two German submarines meet in the Mediterranean in spring 1917; by this time the U-boats were wide-ranging and a real threat to Britain's command of the sea. Right: Haig, British commander in France from 1915.

Left: A Russian howitzer crew in their firing position. Above left: The succession of battles fought in the Belgian mud around Ypres resulted in enormous casualties for very little movement. Artillery, used by attackers to disrupt the enemy's positions and by the defenders to shatter attacking formations, played a role even more massive than in previous battles. In this picture German soldiers pick their way between flooded shell craters. Above right: The first US troops disembark at St Nazaire in western France. To distribute troops and supplies the Americans operated their own trains over the French railroads. Above far right: Wounded are brought to a Russian field hospital. There were numerous volunteer nurses on the Russian front.

generated into mounted infantry, riding at great speed to the defensive line, dismounting and then doing duty like every infantry unit. Only in reconnaissance did it still play a role, less so in the west but more so in the East and the Balkans.

Among the Central Powers the artillery managed to play its role effectively on the Western front and at the Isonzo. What gave cause for serious alarm was the shortage of ammunition. The British and French adhered to the belief that they could achieve success by artillery bombardment lasting for several days, living by the rule that artillery conquers and infantry occupies. According to this rule, they calculated how much ammunition would have to be spent per square yard to destroy the enemy. The calculations looked good on paper, and there were ample stocks of ammunition, but in practice it was found time and again that many defenders had survived and sufficient machine guns were still intact to repel any attack and gain time to bring up reserves from the rear.

On the German side, artillery tactics changed. Colonel Bruchmüller, in charge of artillery at the German Army's Supreme Command, realized that the duration of artillery fire mattered less than its strength and intensity. He therefore abandoned the introductory ranging fire, beginning the concentrated artillery barrage suddenly and continuing it for several hours – a method that had proved its effectiveness in the east during 1917. Thus German artillery opened up with and maintained a high rate of fire, followed closely by the attacking infantry. This, of course, required an artillery observer to be with the advancing forces to guide and extend the range of fire. Mine throwers became more useful, as did light infantry guns.

The Western Allies based their hopes on the tank eliminating the machine-gun nests, but this required close cooperation between tanks and infantry. The Battle of Cambrai in November 1917 saw the dawning of a new age in warfare. At Cambrai, after a short artillery bombardment, hundreds of British tanks attacked and broke through the German defense system. Only when face-to-face with the artillery did they sustain serious

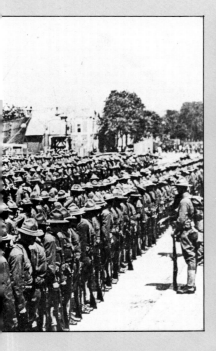

losses, and the lack of infantry reserves did not allow them to exploit the breakthrough. A few days later a German counterattack regained most of the lost territory. The tank was useful only at the tactical level; as noted earlier, it was still technically deficient for extended operations.

Like all the armies of the Central Powers, the German Army lacked the means to build tanks in adequate numbers. They suffered from an endemic shortage of raw materials. Priorities had to be placed on the production of guns, aircraft, mine throwers and U-Boats. Experience showed these priorities to be correct. What the German Army did not do was develop an effective antitank weapon which could have supported the infantry in their forward positions.

Aircraft went through rapid development during World War I. In the beginning, the aircraft of the belligerent nations were mainly unarmed and used for observation, but technical progress made such immense strides that fighter planes with machine guns mounted to fire through the propeller arc could clear the skies of observer balloons, while tactical aircraft could intervene in the ground fighting and bombers could seriously impede the enemy's supplies by destroying roads and bridges. Essentially the task of the air forces was of a tactical nature. Strategic warfare from the air was introduced by German Zeppelin raids on London. War had become more total; even the civilian population was no longer safe. But the Zeppelins proved too cumbersome and too easy a target for the enemy. Their effect, and in this sense the effect of strategic bombing, was, for the time being, short-lived.

For the staffs of all the armies, the problem of supplying forces firmly entrenched was one more of organization than of tactics. The troops had to be provided at all times with the necessities of everyday life. Among the Central Powers, suffering heavily from the blockade after mid-1916, food supply priority was given to the army at the expense of the civilian population. This seemed appropriate enough, but when soldiers came home on leave to find their families starving it was not likely to improve their morale.

Hindenburg, as Chief of the General Staff, and his General Quartermaster Ludendorff had taken over from Falkenhayn in August 1916. Falkenhayn's reputation had been destroyed by the abortive Verdun venture. Generally the people of the Central Powers acclaimed the rise of Hindenburg and Ludendorff, the victors of Tannenberg, and expected them to win the war for Germany. The Hindenburg program initiated a new policy domestically and economically. With one mighty effort it strove to mobilize all men able to carry arms and send them to the front while increasing the production of armaments. Beginning in the fall of 1916, German women entered the factories to make weapons and ammunition. There was no opposition from the trade unions who on the whole loyally supported the government. Some strikes took place, but the front-line soldier naturally showed little understanding of them.

In every country the civilian population was drawn into the vortex of war. Not only did armies fight one another – scientific research and development and industrial production vied with one another in the opposing countries. World War I was well on the way to becoming a total war. From 1916 on, Ludendorff, although nominally subordinate, was the real leader and in part practiced what he finally set down in his book *Total War*. Together with Hindenburg, he not only led the German Armies but also the country's policy. After Bethmann Hollweg's fall, subsequent chancellors received their directives from the Supreme Army Command. It amounted to a total reversal of Clausewitz's teachings. This was to reap a bitter harvest, because neither Hindenburg nor Ludendorff possessed the political training necessary to the roles they assumed. They were military specialists, nothing more. Among the Allies, Clemenceau and Lloyd George had come to the fore, with almost dictatorial powers, but they were clever enough to avoid getting mixed up in military matters. They could, however, deploy the political weapons available to them, particularly the propaganda weapon, which they wielded with a virtuosity hitherto unknown. Graphic accounts not only of mutilated Belgian children, but of the raped women and the crucified Tommy in the Belgian barn became the stock-in-trade for a gullible public ready to believe anything since the rise of sensationalist journalism at the end of the 19th century. Given the state of the public mood in the Allied countries, a negotiated peace became an impossibility. The peace resolution passed by the German Reichstag was taken by the Allies as a sign of the weakening of German moral fiber.

Allied war aims corresponded to their propaganda: Germany was to be destroyed forever as a military power. The Austro-Hungarian Empire was to be divided up, while France was to recover Alsace-Lorraine and control the left bank of the Rhine. German war aims fluctuated according to the fortunes of war,

Right: An aerial dogfight of the type that so caught popular imagination. Below: The first downing of a Zeppelin over England by a conventional fighter attack; this marked the end of the period in which Zeppelins could bomb England and return home with little risk. Below right, inset: Tsar Nicholas II, who lost his throne and his life as a consequence of the war.

but as far as Europe was concerned, the military aimed at creating large buffer zones to the west and east of Germany to make her secure from future attacks and envisioned a possible Central European Customs Federation under the aegis of the German Empire. At no time during the war, however, were these non-negotiable aims that stood in the way of making peace. Indeed, the Central Powers' war aims had never been coordinated, and in fact the political cooperation between the two powers left much to be desired. This lack of coordinated planning carried over into the military sphere: there was no joint supreme command. The Allies, for their part, appointed General Foch as supreme commander of their forces in the west only after serious reverses in early 1918.

The consequences of the lack of joint military command between the Central Powers had shown up during the Brusilov Offensive of 1916. The Austro-Hungarian front ran from Czernowicz via Jastowiec and Sapanov along the Styr to Pinsk. The forces of the Hapsburg Empire were well dug in but the front was quiet and discipline was lax. Brusilov dug trenches stretching forward toward the Austrian positions until they were about 200 paces away. The Austrian shortage of artillery prevented them from seriously interrupting these preparations. Russian artillery preparation was to be short but concentrated. When the Brusilov Offensive began on 4 June 1916 the Austro-Hungarian forces were completely surprised, and within a week the Russians captured an area 50 miles wide and 30 miles deep. By 7 July the Russians had reached the Hungarian frontier in the Carpathians. Only with the greatest difficulty could the Russian offensive be halted, and the Austrians had lost 475,000 men – among them over 226,000 prisoners. It encouraged Rumania foolishly to enter the war on the side of the Allies. The Austro-German campaign in Rumania which ensued was the only one of World War I which was characterized by mobility. Attacks, outflanking movements and pocket battles followed rapidly upon one another. By the end of the campaign the 23 Rumanian divisions had been reduced to six. A campaign such as this was only possible in a relatively confined geographic area, the superior leadership and better-trained forces of the Central Powers quite apart.

By 1917 war weariness was apparent in all the belligerent countries. The French mutinies have already been mentioned. In Great Britain, voices rose demanding an end to the slaughter, but worst was the crisis in Russia where the war weariness culminated in the Revolution of March 1917. Contrary to the expectations of the people, the Russian Provisional Government did not entertain the idea of making a separate peace with Germany. Instead it hoped to fight more efficiently than before

on the side of the Allies. The grievances about the war had first been directed against the Czarist regime, but during the course of the year they turned against the Provisional Government and thus produced the October Revolution and the victory of the Bolsheviks under Lenin. Backed by the organizer of the Red Army, Leon Trotsky, Lenin decided to end the war, cost what it might. They were sure that the revolution would spread to central and western Europe and secured their peace by the Treaty of Brest-Litovsk.

In the words of George F Kennan, the American diplomat and historian:

'The Brest-Litovsk Treaty has usually been regarded as an extremely onerous settlement – a prize example, in fact, of the ruthless brutality of the German mailed fist. I think this assertion deserves some modifications. In comparison with the settlements the western allies themselves imposed, on the basis of unconditional surrender, after two world wars, the Brest-Litovsk Treaty does not strike me as inordinately severe. No reparations were originally demanded in the treaty itself. The territories of which the Bolsheviks were deprived were ones the peoples of which had no desire for Russian rule, least of all Russian Communist rule. The Bolsheviks themselves had never at any time had authority over these territories. It was a hope rather than a reality of which they were deprived by the terms of the treaty. The settlement accepted by the Allies at the end of the Russian Civil War – the arrangement, that is, that prevailed from 1920 to 1939 – was considerably less favorable to Russia, territorially, in the Baltic-Polish region than that which the Germans imposed on Russia in 1918.'

While the war in the west was still stalemated during 1917, fluctuating in terms of territory gained or lost by a few miles either way, in Italy, Austro-Hungarian and German forces went over to the offensive in the Twelfth Isonzo Battle, also known as the Battle of Caparetto. Seven German and five Austro-Hungarian divisions commanded by General von Bülow attacked in the last days of October 1917, broke out from the Tolmino area southwesterly and took the Italians on the Isonzo from the flank and the rear. It made the position of the Second and Third Italian Armies untenable. Circumventing the Monte-Nero massif, the forces of the Central Powers moved toward Saga, then Stolrücken and the valley of the Natisone. The Italian withdrawal quickly turned into a rout which did not stop even at the River Tagliamento. Only at the Piave River, which was deep, did the Italians stop, and there with the aid of British, French and their own reserves, they managed to establish a defensive line. Numerical weakness now forced the Central Powers to abandon any out-flanking movement, but the success was still considerable. The Italians had lost all the territorial gains of the last two years, as well as 40,000 dead,

Above left: German infantry assembled in their trenches, presumably waiting for the signal to begin an attack, or to proceed to the main trenches. The depth of this trench and the absence of firing positions suggests that it is a communications trench, used for providing a covered approach to the main trenches, or sometimes to assemble men for an action. Above: The German offensive of spring 1918; British prisoners of war under German escort pass eastwards through a French town. The German drive, Ludendorff's last throw, was initially directed against the British-held sector of the Western Front. Thanks partly to shorter but very intensive preliminary bombardment, and partly to the undermanned and unrepaired situation of the British line, the German offensive gained considerable ground in the first days. As the situation worsened Haig called for French reinforcements, but the latter were small. The appointment of Foch as supreme commander then brought better coordination. Right: A map of this campaign.

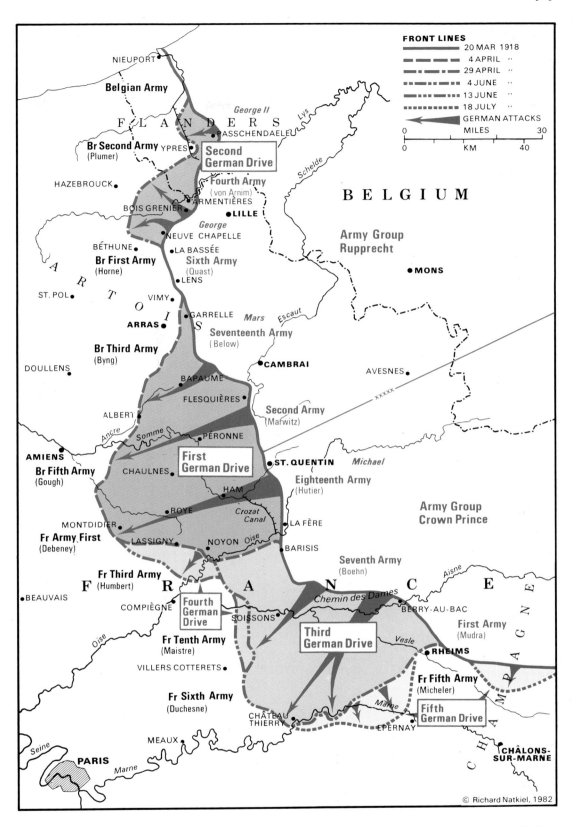

265,000 prisoners, 3000 guns and much other war materiel.

The method of attack as originally devised by Colonel Bruchmüller, which had proven its value in the east and in Italy, was to be applied by Hindenburg and Ludendorff in the offensives of March–July 1918. In all cases a breakthrough was achieved, but none of them could be exploited decisively. Fighting on foot, the army could not sustain the impetus of the original attack. The German Army in the west was short of men and had no genuinely motorized infantry, which alone would have given the German forces operational liberty. Initially, the German offensives caused trouble. Paris was in danger once again, but it did not affect Foch's belief in ultimate victory. Since 1917 fresh

American troops had been arriving in France, first divided up over the various Allied contingents and ultimately formed into an American Expeditionary Force under the command of General Pershing. The production of tanks, aircraft, guns and trucks outdistanced anything the Central Powers could produce.

In July 1918, under General Foch, the Allies moved into the counteroffensive which culminated in the 'Black Day,' 8 August 1918, for the German Army. The tide had finally turned. The German Army withdrew beyond the Siegfried Line and by 14 August 1918 the German military leaders had to admit to themselves that the continuation of war to German victory was an impossibility.

Above left: A North Atlantic convoy, consisting mainly of American vessels. The convoy system was to be the best defense against the German U-boat campaign. Although in itself it did not guarantee an increase in the number of submarines sunk, it made it harder for the U-boat to find worthwhile and attainable targets; in other words, it reduced the monthly tonnage of Allied shipping sunk by submarine action. Despite the dangerously high losses being incurred by Britain, the Admiralty was for long reluctant to introduce convoys; although the role of the prime minister, Lloyd George, has been exaggerated, it was his pressure which caused the admirals to change their minds. The ships in this picture carry 'dazzle paint' an effective device for breaking up the form of a ship, as viewed from a submarine. Left: A painting of the Battle of Soissons, an engagement in the third German drive of 1918. French tanks were important in turning back the Germans here; tank support can be seen in the background. Above: An American machine gun post in France.

In September 1918, when the Central Powers' ally, Bulgaria, collapsed and asked for an immediate peace, Austria-Hungary was directly threatened and Ludendorff demanded an immediate armistice from the German politicians on the basis of Wilson's Fourteen Points, which the American President had proclaimed the previous spring. Thus the primacy of politics was restored. Upon the orders of the German High Command, full parliamentarization was introduced in Germany and the three-class franchise in Prussia abolished. However, when the German Navy planned one last sortie against the British at the risk of its own utter annihilation, the crews of the German High Seas Fleet mutinied. The torch of revolution had been lit and spread rapidly throughout Germany and Austria. On 9 November revolution broke out in Berlin, and on 11 November the Germans signed the armistice at Compiègne. World War I had ended; the Kaiser and all the German monarchs and princes had abdicated. But the blockade of Germany was not lifted and the peace that followed laid the groundwork of yet another war.

Strategically, World War I had demonstrated that continental powers can be contained by powers enjoying naval supremacy. The Central Powers had become a fortress under siege, militarily and economically inferior to the Allied powers. This was underlined once the United States had joined the war. But even while still neutral, it could supply the Allies with all the essentials. Allied naval supremacy ensured that the Central Powers would be cut off from their traditional sources of raw materials and foodstuffs. The unrestricted German submarine warfare was waged with too few resources and, above all, came too late. For the Allies, it was only a question of starving out the fortress of the Central Powers.

It has been argued that before the United States entered the war, the Central Powers enjoyed the advantage of operating from interior lines. This is misleading. The British Empire and the French Colonial Empire could tap resources closed to the Central Powers; whatever was lacking was already being provided by the United States between 1914 and 1917. Even before the United States entered the war, the Central Powers did not have economic self-sufficiency, the necessary condition for successful conduct of a war on interior lines. At a different level, it was a serious disadvantage that the Central Powers did not possess a joint political and military policy or command.

At the operational level it was shown that modern infantry weapons were so devastating that a breakthrough was virtually impossible or involved losses no army could afford. If an attack succeeded, the farther the distance between the attacker and his point of departure, the slower his movement, so his effectiveness was reduced. Mobility was what was required, and it did not yet exist. What emerged for all to see clearly was the primacy of defense, although this had already been foreshadowed in the 'Forgotten Wars.' The defender was closer to his supply bases, and as long as he still had reserves of manpower, foodstuffs, arms and ammunition, he could bring the offensive to a halt. Even in such an area as France, it had become impossible to carry out large encirclements because of the lack of mobility. No attacking force could afford to move more than about 80 miles from its rail heads. Only the Twelfth Isonzo Battle and the Battle of Cambrai pointed toward new forms of attack, but both fell short of their aims due to lack of the reserves that could have been thrown into battle by means of motorized transport.

Some of the lessons that had been learned were expressed in the armistice conditions and the political demands of peace treaties. Naval supremacy had to be ensured. Therefore, the disposition of the German High Seas Fleet, interned in Scapa Flow, was a potential difficulty solved only when the German crews scuttled their ships. More important was the prohibition denying submarines to Germany. The armies of the defeated powers were reduced to a minimum size which restricted their role virtually to that of a police force. Furthermore, no reserves of any size could be built up. The Allies gave their support wholly to the successor states of the Hapsburg Empire, thus ensuring the Balkanization of Eastern Central Europe and the disruption of what had once been a viable unified economy. No doubt these demands were justified from the point of view of military expediency, but politically they were unwise, as the history of the next two decades was to demonstrate.

The lessons of World War I entered the manuals of the post-war armies. Opinion was unanimous on the point that the infantry alone would no longer decide the outcome of a war. Attacks *en masse* were discarded. Instead, attacks were to be carried out by units widely dispersed. The firepower of infantry weapons forced the soldiers to make the most of the ground they were covering, and they had to dig in. Infantry weapons were developed with a power to penetrate steel.

There was a great difference of opinion about how to deploy tanks and other armored vehicles. Both the French and British General Staffs adhered to the belief that the tank was primarily an infantry support weapon. Their thinking was still dominated by extensive field fortifications, trench systems and barbed wire. Only three people in Great Britain realized the full potential of armor, and they were Major General J F C Fuller, Captain B H Liddell Hart and General Sir Percy Hobart. General de Gaulle is usually added to this list. While he was certainly a 'tank enthusiast' in the 30s, ideas about independently operating armor are fully developed in his works only in their first English translation published in 1943. Fuller, Liddell Hart and Hobart recognized the true dimensions of the armored warfare of the future, but they were not taken seriously by their compatriots. Fuller dismissed the value of the horse in modern warfare and thus violated one of the sacred cows of the traditional British officer corps. In 1927, however, his pressure brought the intro-

Top: A US rail-mounted gun in action against German positions. This is a 14-inch piece, of naval origin, with an effective range of about 20 miles. Above: The German retreat of November 1918; a scene at a town on the Dutch-Belgian frontier. The variety of transport in use can be noted; the horse is still dominant and no motor vehicles are in sight, although good use is being made of steam tractors, pulling road-trains. Top right: American troops are welcomed in the Ardennes, relieved after four years of German occupation. Above right: Australian infantry in trenches near Bois de Crépy at the beginning of the 1918 Allied offensive.

duction of a mechanized brigade on a trial basis. In point of fact, it was an infantry brigade equipped with a few tanks. Fuller wanted to resign.

However, his vision was not without its faults. According to him, the time for mass conscript armies was past. The future, according to Fuller, would be determined by small, excellently equipped mechanized armies supported by a strong air force, which would push deep into the enemy's territory with lightning speed. Armor would replace infantry. Specialized tanks would have to take over the various tasks of the infantry, artillery and cavalry.

Liddell Hart was more correct in his assessment. He developed the theory of the 'Strategy of the Indirect Approach.' The attack was to be carried out at the enemy's weakest point and where least expected. Simultaneous attacks elsewhere would divert the enemy's attention from the point of impact of the main attack. Liddell Hart had learned the lessons of the German stormtroops. These attacks were then to be followed by armored formations whose function was to penetrate in depth, cut the enemy's supply routes, encircle him and annihilate his forces. The future land army should consist of mechanized infantry, armor and a tactical air force.

Far left: US infantrymen stroll into a captured settlement in their sector of the Western Front. Although inexperience led to many unnecessary American casualties, the arrival of US forces tipped the balance against the Germans, whose last throw, the offensive of spring 1918, was designed to grasp victory before the Americans were ready in full strength. Left: General John J. Pershing, commander in chief of the American Expeditionary Force. Pershing was a general of extensive active service. After graduating from West Point, he served against Spain in Cuba and the Philippines, became a brigadier general in 1906, and 10 years later commanded the US force which invaded Mexico in search of anti-American activists. As US commander in France, he opposed the 1918 Armistice because, having a brand-new army, he felt confident that the Germans could be forced to a complete surrender. Below: Allied infantry in pursuit. Right: US Marines capture a machine gun.

But the role of the air force was conceived differently by the Italian General Douhet, another important theorist, who advocated the strategic role of air forces whose task it would be, through intensive bombardment of the enemy's hinterland, to devastate his cities and thus demoralize him with much the same effect achieved by the British blockade of the Central Powers. At the outbreak of World War II, Great Britain was well on its way to creating a strategic air force – the Wellington bomber, introduced in the RAF in 1938, had a range that extended from the British east coast to Munich and back, as compared to the German Heinkel 111 which could not even cover the whole of Great Britain from its bases in France, Belgium and Holland.

Most of the European states maintained conscription as the basis for their recruitment. Only Great Britain had abandoned it at the end of World War I and returned to the concept of the small professional army. Conscription was only revived in Britain in 1939. Of course Germany's army was kept at 100,000 men until 1935, but under General von Seeckt as chief of the *Heeresleitung* the first steps were being taken to transform it into a cadre army readily expandable if and when the time came. Limited cooperation with the Red Army allowed the Reichswehr to train panzer drivers and aircraft pilots, while cooperation with Sweden and Spain ensured a limited opportunity for training submarine crews.

WORLD WAR II

In the 1920s Europe experienced a serious erosion of the democratic process. Of the newly established democracies that existed when the Versailles Treaty came into force in 1920, all but one had disappeared 10 years later. All that remained was the multi-national state of Czechoslovakia, a democracy characterized by the Czech historian Boris Czelovsky as a democracy in which a lot of talking was done, but in which the Czechs ensured that they would always have the last word.

Previous pages: German refugees move west to escape the advancing Russians in 1945. Right: A German *Stuka* dive-bomber. Dive-bombing was less inaccurate than conventional bombing, and the *Stuka* destroyed many targets, including several British warships. Top: A German tank crew in France. The padded berets were for protection against concussion when moving over rough ground; other tank corps adopted similar measures. Below: German infantry takes a rest under cover during the 1940 campaign in France. Below right: A German Mark IV tank in France in 1940. Tanks like this, although of recent construction, were soon to become obsolete, being superseded by new designs with, among other improvements, longer guns.

The five years following the coming to power of Adolf Hitler on 30 January 1933 saw a considerable change in the map of Europe. Why should the Western powers have acquiesced to Germany's departure from the League of Nations at the end of 1933, to renunciation of the military clauses of the Versailles Treaty in 1935, the reoccupation of the demilitarized Rhineland zone of Germany in 1936, the *Anschluss* of Austria and the annexation of the Sudetenland in 1938? Any answer is bound to be complex. For brevity's sake, we can quote the British historian, the late Professor E H Carr:

'The mass of political opinion in Great Britain and Germany (and in most other countries) agreed for many years that a criterion of justice and injustice could properly be applied to the Versailles Treaty; and there was a surprisingly considerable, though far from complete, consensus of opinion about the parts of it which were just and unjust respectively. Unfortunately, Germany was almost wholly deficient for fifteen years after the war in that power which is a necessary motive force in political change; and this deficiency prevented effect being given, except on a minor scale, to the widespread consensus of opinion that parts of the Versailles Treaty ought to be modified. By the time Germany regained her power, she had become – not without reason – almost wholly disillusioned about the role of morality in international politics. There was not, even as late as 1936, any reasonable prospect of obtaining major modifications of the Versailles Treaty by peaceful negotiation unsupported by the ultimatum or the *fait accompli*. Even though she continued to base her claims on grounds of justice, Germany expressed them more and more in terms of naked force; and this reacted on the opinion of the *status quo* countries, which became more and more inclined to forget earlier admissions of the injustices of the Versailles Treaty and to consider the issue as exclusively one of power. There is no doubt that the easy acquiescence of the *status quo* powers in such actions as the denunciations of the military clauses, the reoccupation of the Rhineland or the annexation of Austria was due, not wholly to the fact that it was the line of least resistance, but in part also to a consensus of opinion that these changes were in themselves reasonable and just. Yet they were greeted in each case by official censures and remonstrances which inevitably created the impression that the remonstrating powers acquiesced merely because they were unable or unwilling to make the effort to resist. In March 1939, the British Prime Minister Neville Chamberlain admitted that in all the modifications of the Treaty down to and including the Munich Agreement there was "something to be said for the necessity of a change in the existing situation." If, in 1935 and 1936, this "something" had been clearly and decisively said, to the exclusion of scoldings and protests, by the official spokesmen of the *status quo* powers, it might not yet have been too late to bring further changes within the framework of peaceful negotiation. The tragedy by which successive removals of long-recognized injustices of the Versailles Treaty became a cause not of reconciliation, but of further estrangement, between Germany and the Versailles Powers, and destroyed instead of increasing the limited stock of common feeling which had formerly existed, is one for which the sole responsibility cannot be laid at Germany's door.

'The negotiations which led up to the Munich Agreement of 29 September 1938 were the nearest approach in recent years to the settlement of a major international issue by a procedure of peaceful change. The element of power was present. The element of morality was also present in the form of the common recognition by the Powers, who effectively decided the issue, of a criterion applicable to the dispute: the principle of national self-determination. The injustice of the incorporation into Czechoslovakia of three-and-one-quarter million protesting Germans had been attacked in the past by many British critics, including the Labour Party and Mr Lloyd George. Nor had the promises made by M. Benes [the Czech leader] at the Peace Conference regarding their treatment been fully carried out. The change in itself was one which corresponded both to a change in the European equilibrium of forces and to accepted canons of international morality.'

This, in a nutshell, sums up the background and the motives of the policy of appeasement toward Hitler and his regime pursued by the Western Powers. Obviously, Hitler could not pursue an active foreign policy without expanding his army. Officially it began in 1935, but with considerable difficulty, since there were serious shortages of officers and NCOs to command the new forces. Reserves were initially in short supply and consisted mainly of soldiers who had served in World War I. Equally difficult was rearmament, which was hampered by a shortage of raw materials that were obtainable on the international market but had to be paid for in gold, of which Germany was in very short supply. Rearmament was carried out to the accompaniment of a huge wave of propaganda. German economic recovery was not achieved by rearmament but by a policy of guns *and* butter, and Hitler's public statements on German rearmament were based largely on bluff and inflated figures. Nor was it in any way a coordinated policy of rearmament. The three branches of the services, Army, Navy and Air Force, competed with one another for the available raw materials. Each service developed armament plans which, if combined in 1939, would have required the establishment of fuel reserves in excess of the world's total oil production at that time.

Rearmament could not be carried out in depth. The only advantages possessed by the German armed forces were many excellently trained regular officers and NCOs and a concept of warfare which General Guderian had borrowed almost exclusively from Fuller and Liddell Hart. But Guderian had a very difficult stand *vis-à-vis* his Commander in Chief, General von Fritsch, who hated anything to do with engines and motors. Hitler, however, fully realized the potential of this new system of warfare and backed Guderian.

The rebuilding of the Luftwaffe concentrated on fighters and tactical aircraft. Until 1936, General Wever had advocated a strategic air force with four-engine strategic bombers – a policy that was ignored after he died in that year. It was difficult enough to provide the existing force with adequate fuel, let alone four-engine bombers.

The navy, like the other services with their extravagant plans, had not by 1939 even achieved the levels granted to her by the Versailles Treaty, much less built up the U-Boat force conceded by the Anglo-German Naval Treaty of 1935. At the outbreak of war only 25 U-Boats fit for Atlantic service were operational, as compared to the 75 which Germany was allowed to build under the Anglo-German agreement.

If one compares all the forces on the eve of war in 1939, there were a total of 2.9 million German soldiers confronting 4.07 million Polish, French and British forces. But the German troops were better trained for the type of war that would ensue. This ensured their superiority for the first two years of the war. In the west, German armor and that of the Western Allies was about evenly balanced in numbers, though German tanks had inferior guns and armor compared with some of their French and British counterparts. The margin in favor of the Allies was frittered away by deploying armor as infantry support weapons instead of freely and independently operating formations.

On the German side, the command structure was a source of serious weakness, with Hitler as Supreme Commander in Chief and under him the *Oberkommando der Wehrmacht* (OKW), the *Oberkommando des Heeres* (OKH), the *Oberkommando der Luftwaffe* (OKL) and the *Oberkommando der Marine* (OKM). The deficiencies of this setup were not realized until 1941, but until that time the supreme commands of Germany's opponents were not much better.

Concerning raw materials, Germany was as badly off as during World War I; only the Russo-German Non-Aggression Pact of 23 August 1939 alleviated the situation. Financial resources were equally inadequate. In 1939–40 Germany spent 63.5 thousand million marks while its official receipts amounted to only 61 thousand million marks. Germany's only chance was to conduct a short and limited war.

The campaign in Poland was just that. Poland had mobilized and concentrated its major forces in an offensive forward position in which they became an easy victim of the German attacking forces – 53 divisions in all, including all six panzer divisions. Only 30 low-grade divisions protected Germany's western frontier. Within the first three days of the campaign, from 1 to 3 September 1939, the Luftwaffe destroyed the Polish Air Force virtually on the ground. The German Army was divided into Army Groups North and South, each supported by panzer corps employed as operationally independent units. The panzers used were primarily the Mark I armed with two machine guns and the Mark II with a 20mm gun. The Mark III

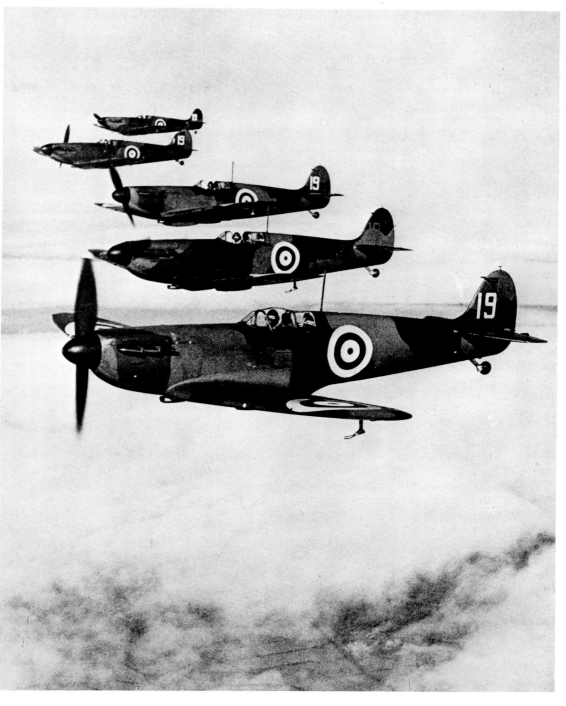

Above: After Dunkirk; the British Army's motor transport abandoned on the dunes. By no means all of the vehicles have been wrecked by their former users; ex-British Army motor trucks were to play a notable role in Germany's invasion of the Soviet Union a year later. Left: General de Gaulle, leader of the Free French, at work in Algiers. It was here that he gained recognition for his Liberation Committee by the Allies, enabling it to become the French Provisional Government. Right: A flight of five Spitfires. These aircraft won British supremacy in the Battle of Britain and, in successive improved versions, continued to serve the Royal Air Force in a first-line capacity throughout the war.

and Mark IV, with greater speed and heavier guns, were not yet available in large numbers. But coming from the south and the north, they cut the Polish forces into ribbons. When on 17 September 1939 Russia invaded the eastern part of Poland, conceded to her in the Russo-German Friendship Treaty, the war in Poland was at an end for all practical purposes. Only isolated pockets of the Polish Army still offered resistance. Warsaw also held out and was defended by the die hard Polish military leadership. German aircraft circled the city several times, dropping leaflets demanding surrender or the evacuation of the civilian population. No heed was paid to these warnings, and Warsaw was subjected to an intensive aerial bombardment, after which it finally surrendered.

Germany acquired the former territory of East Prussia and the Province of Posen, Russia the territories east of the Curzon Line. The rest of Poland was organized as the General Government which Hitler held on to until August 1940 as a bargaining tool in negotiations out of which a Polish satellite state could emerge. He abandoned this plan only in August 1940. Having

ended the campaign, he thought of making peace, but Allied hopes still rested on their knowledge of a military and civilian resistance movement inside Germany, with which they had been regularly in touch since 1937 and which assured the Allies that it would replace Hitler. However, nothing came of this fond hope. With no peace in sight, Hitler decided to attack in the west but the weather conditions in October and November 1939 proved unsuitable for such an undertaking.

Germany's supplies of foodstuffs and raw materials were now adequate; the Russians provided what the British Navy blockaded. This brought Germany into an ever-increasing dependence on Russia, which, as the following year would show, was potentially dangerous. Apart from Russian supplies, Germany's oil came mostly from Rumania and its iron ore from Sweden. After the outbreak of the Russo-Finnish War on 30 November 1939, the Allies believed that they would be able to use this conflict as a pretext to aid the Finns with the actual objective of cutting Germany off from its iron ore supplies from Sweden and its nickel supplies from Petsamo.

As signs of Allied intervention in Scandinavia increased, Hitler decided upon a preemptive strike there with the code-name *Weserübung*. On 9 April 1940 the operation was launched, involving almost all the existing units of the German Navy. Denmark was occupied almost peacefully. There had, in fact, been previous feelers between the two governments. It was hoped that Norway could be occupied in much the same way. While Oslo was occupied peacefully, German bands already playing in Oslo's public squares on the first day, in the north Norwegian resistance began to build. In the Narvik region it was supported by British and French forces. Here the situation first became critical for the German forces, and only German supremacy in the air ensured that the mountain forces could hold on until events in France compelled the British and French to withdraw from Norway.

On the Western Front, on the eve of 10 May 1940, 137 German divisions confronted a roughly similar number of Allied divisions. In addition there were now 10 German panzer divisions, though the Allies had 3124 tanks as against 2580 for the Germans. However, as already stated, the Allied tanks were mainly deployed as infantry support weapons. In contrast, the German panzer formations could operate independently, break through in depth and encircle the Allied forces. As far as the air forces were concerned, 2979 planes of the Luftwaffe confronted 2513 Allied planes, but most of the French Air Force was hopelessly outdated. Only the RAF had aircraft on a par with those of the Germans. But such Allied air power as existed was also frittered away piecemeal, while the Luftwaffe was organized into *Luftflotten*, air fleets, to support the various sectors of the German advance.

When the initial planning for the campaign in the west had begun, all the OKH could offer to Hitler was a revamped version of the Schlieffen Plan in which the 'right hook' was to hit Holland as well as Belgium. Colonel (later Field Marshal) von

Manstein, chief of staff at one of the German army groups, offered an alternative solution in line with the strategy of the indirect approach – to place the main weight of the attack where the Allies expected it least. He advocated attacking through the Ardennes with panzer formations, pushing toward Sedan, crossing the Meuse and then moving on to the English Channel. This movement would cut off any British and French troops who advanced to help the Dutch and Belgians. These forces would also be confronted by the German forces advancing from their bases on the lower Rhine. Manstein's plan was at first dismissed by the General Staff, but Hitler's adjutant, Colonel Schmundt, drew the Führer's attention to it. Hitler convened a staff meeting to which Manstein was invited, and he was given the opportunity to state his case. Hitler was immediately convinced by Manstein's plan and adopted it.

In the plan, Army Group C was to hold the upper Rhine opposite the Maginot Line, while it was Army Group A's task to cut through the Ardennes with five panzer and three motorized divisions, push into the rear of the Allied forces to the north of them and continue to Abbeville. Army Group B was to invade Belgium and Holland, closing the pincers behind the Allies with Army Group A.

Thus the campaign in the west began in the early hours of 10 May 1940. The Dutch were the first to surrender, followed by Belgium by the end of May, while the British Expeditionary Force was finally contained in the Dunkirk area. It is not the place to enter into the controversy about Hitler's decision not to have his armored forces attack and annihilate the British. No doubt the German armor required rest and refitting after the race to the coast, especially as the German Army expected strong resistance from the remaining French forces at the Somme. In spite of intensive bombardment by the Luftwaffe, the bulk of the BEF and a French contingent managed to escape across the Channel, minus their heavy equipment.

Below: A German anti-tank gun in action. Until the development of specialized armor-piercing rockets, the gun was often the main defense against tanks, and was not always effective against thick armor. Far left: Soviet tanks bogged down in marshland and captured by the Germans. Huge expanses of western Russia are marshland, and in two wars have constituted a natural defense; but, as this picture shows, they could embarrass the Russians, too. Left inset: German paratroops (recognizable by their special helmets, with unbroken rim) take it easy in 1941. These airborne troops played a distinguished, probably decisive, role in the capture of Crete, the last foothold of the British troops who had been sent to help Greece.

The Italians, afraid of getting no share in the spoils of victory, entered the war at this point, but their advance was soon halted by the French. Now the time had come for the Germans to turn south, break through the Weygand Line and cut across France to the Spanish frontier in the south; to take Paris and to take the Maginot Line from the rear. The attack on the Maginot Line was coordinated with Army Group C which attacked across the Upper Rhine. France was defeated.

On 25 June 1940, France under Marshal Pétain accepted the German armistice conditions. The Germans occupied all of northern France, including Paris, and all coastal areas from Holland to the Spanish border. Alsace-Lorraine was occupied and a closed frontier introduced from the Atlantic to the Swiss border. Beyond that was the unoccupied part of France where Marshal Pétain established his government in the spa town of Vichy. The Germans had won another campaign, but not the war. From May until August 1940 Hitler remained optimistic, expecting a British peace offer at any time. He demobilized more than 10 divisions and ordered a halt to all weapon development that could not be completed by the end of 1940. In Germany the public mood was most enthusiastic, though at the back of many minds was the question of how the war should now continue.

Hitler introduced orders for the invasion of Great Britain, but unlike his previous military planning, he was rather half-hearted about this enterprise. Some of his entourage claimed that, in fact, he was totally uninterested in it. The precondition for any landing was the establishment of German dominance of the British air space. Göring promised that, but within two months it became apparent that the strength of the Luftwaffe was not up to this task. The bomber formations, so valuable as tactical weapons, showed their shortcomings when used in a strategic role. German losses could not be replaced by increased aircraft production, for in Germany on the whole a peacetime economy still prevailed. Women were not drafted into armaments factories, as in Great Britain, and the entire industry worked on the basis of a single shift per day. This raises an important question. Why did Hitler fail, until it was too late, to put the German economy on a total war footing, or for that matter, why did he not put the whole of Germany's industrial effort behind rearmament before 1939. The answer lies in the trauma of 1918 when the German domestic front collapsed, thus allowing the allies a free hand in formulating the Versailles Peace Treaty. Throughout 1919 the German government was concerned with internal disorders and would have been unable to fight even a purely defensive war until a more acceptable peace was forthcoming. That trauma lies very much at the core of Hitler's domestic policy in peace and war time. On the one hand were the concentration camps, initially established for the internment of active political dissidents, while on the other hand there was a consumer boom, maintained to a great degree also when war broke out. Hitler wanted to ensure the best possible conditions at home in order to prevent any internal upheaval. Hence productive capacities were not fully utilized. Albert Speer, who became Minister of Armaments in 1942, reversed this policy and by 1944, with no greater productive capacity than existed in 1941, German arms output was quadrupled. By that time it was too late. Allied advances on the ground and effects of the strategic bombing campaign meant that there was little fuel to power the tanks and aircraft which were now available. Hitler also gave orders early in the war that the development of new weapons was to be stopped. This also had serious consequences. What was to be the first operational jet fighter of World War II was already on the drawing board and its first engines were being tested. Willy Messerschmitt carried

Above: A British 6-pounder antitank gun comes under artillery fire in the Desert in 1942. The open spaces and clear air of North Africa added to the potential of both tanks and antitank weapons. The Germans were particularly skilled in drawing the British armored forces into attacking prepared antitank positions. The British were handicapped at first by being equipped with the rather ineffective 2-pounder gun but the 6-pounder and the later 17-pounder were far better. Right: Map of the initial stages of the German advance into the Soviet Union showing the three main axes of advance.

on the development on a small scale because he was under-financed. Tank development was cut back, which was a serious error, as shown by the events of 1941.

The invasion of Norway had been the German Navy's greatest hour, but the losses sustained, particularly to destroyers, were never fully made up during the war. Two battleships, the *Bismarck* and the *Tirpitz*, were not yet completed. The existing battlecruisers *Scharnhorst* and *Gneisenau* were prone to mechanical failures. So the main weight of the war at sea rested on the German U-Boats, which during 1940 were dogged by faulty torpedoes, insufficient numbers and the low output of U-Boat manufacturing shipyards.

Two problems preoccupied Hitler throughout 1940 – how either to end the war with Great Britain or bring her to her knees. Obviously, Britain was not willing to make peace, and the attempt to bring her to her knees by air had led to defeat in the Battle of Britain. The other problem arose out of the situation in the east where in June Russia had annexed Estonia, Latvia and Lithuania. Admittedly, these countries had been included in Russia's sphere of interest in the Russo-German Nonaggression Pact, but their occupation and annexation was another matter, especially since the uneasy peace prevailing between the Soviet Union and Finland since March 1940 seemed fragile and likely to rupture at any time.

In the face of this development, it was not Hitler but the Chief of the Army General Staff, General Halder, who issued the first orders to make a preliminary study for the invasion of Russia. Hitler himself, for the time being, kept his options open. Unable to cripple Great Britain, he set about trying to forge a continental league against her. His attempts to draw Spain and Vichy France into it failed, because for them the precondition of joining such a league would have been the prior defeat of Great Britain. As far as Russia was concerned, a new political settlement was the precondition.

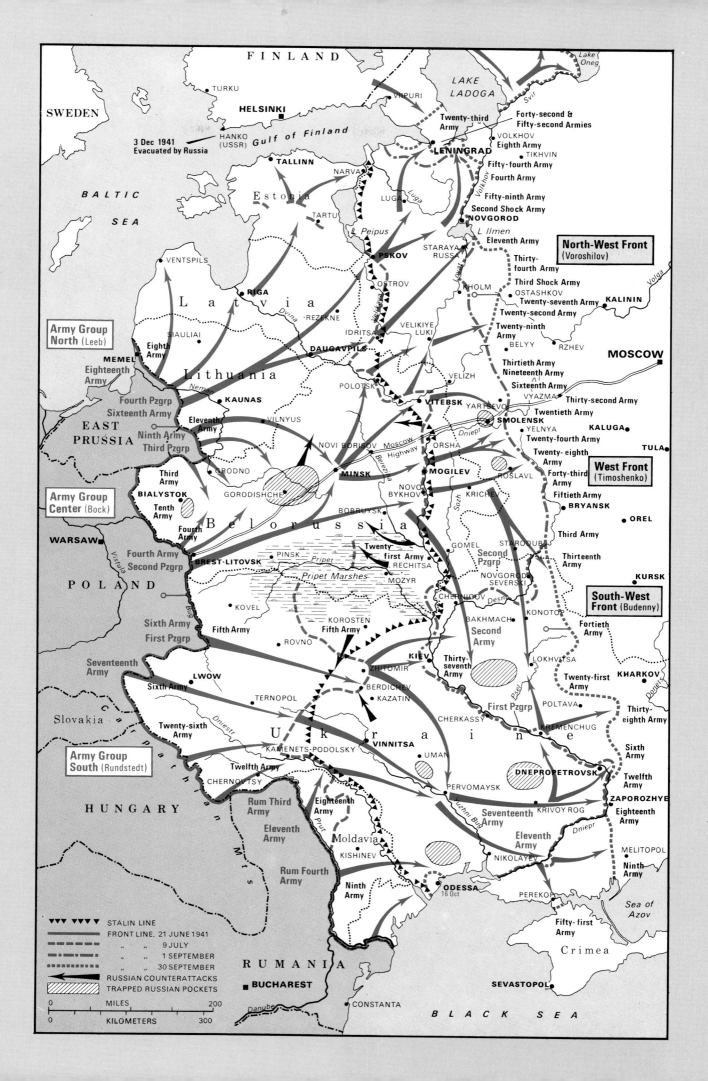

Below: The US cruiser *Savannah* at Algiers in July 1943. North Africa had been the objective of a big Allied combined operation in 1942, Operation Torch. Algiers then became one of the ports used for supporting the invasion of Sicily and in the summer of 1943 was the object of a U-boat campaign against Allied shipping in its waters. In this picture two 'Liberty' ships can be seen burning. Above: Fighters on the deck of a US escort carrier during Operation Torch. Escort carriers, small aircraft carriers converted from merchant ship or cruiser hulls, were one of the most successful innovations of the war, enabling fighter and air reconnaissance cover to be abundantly provided for convoys at sea. Above right: General George Marshall, a great American general who later won a Nobel Peace Prize for his post-war Marshall Plan. Above far right: US paratroopers in North Africa.

Left: Soviet tanks on the outskirts of Stalingrad. The steppes of southern Russia were regarded by both sides as perfect tank country, and the world's greatest tank battles were fought there. In these the Germans were usually out-numbered, but this was not the only reason for the Soviet successes in the latter part of the war. Below: Soviet infantry in street fighting. Although obviously a carefully posed photograph, it is not at all unrealistic. Stubborn street fighting was a frequent role of the Red Army, and the techniques, for example, enabled Stalingrad to be held until reinforcements could be assembled. In the foreground is one of the celebrated Degtyarev light machine guns.

Russia was also increasingly exercising its influence in the Balkans. Bessarabia had also been included in Russia's sphere of influence, and it was occupied in the summer of 1941. Now Russia also claimed the Dobruja from Rumania, which Hitler opposed because it would have brought the Russians too near the oilfields of Ploesti on which Germany depended so heavily. True, the manufacture of synthetic fuel in Germany had begun before the war, but it proved inordinately expensive and the output did not match the requirements. Further Russian offensive steps included the occupation of vital islands in the mouth of the Danube, which established Russian control of this entrance to the Black Sea.

Hitler believed that there was still a possibility of a political settlement with Russia, and to this end Molotov was invited to Berlin on 12 November 1940. Hitler's and Ribbentrop's attempts to divert the Soviet Union away from southeastern and northeastern Europe toward Persia and Asia failed. When Hitler asked how Molotov envisioned the solution to the Finnish problem, Molotov blandly replied that the solution would be similar to that carried out in the Baltic countries. Ribbentrop produced a draft treaty for Russia's adherence to the Tripartite Pact (which had been signed between Germany, Japan and Italy the previous summer) which Molotov took with him when he returned to Moscow. Stalin's reply contained conditions that seriously affected German interests in southeastern and northeastern Europe. Hitler did not bother to reply. Now the planning for 'Operation Barbarossa,' the invasion of Russia, went ahead.

Germany's ally Italy, meanwhile, had precipitated the very action which Hitler had meant to avoid at all costs. Late in October 1940 Italian forces from Albania had attacked Greece, and although they were quickly stopped by the Greeks, the danger that the Balkans would be set aflame became a reality. Germany was compelled to assist its ally because the Italian action provided the British, who had just chased the Italians out of Cyrenaica in North Africa, with the possibility of landing in Greece to lend support to the Greek forces. The offshoot of this was Germany's 'Operation Marita,' the German invasion of Greece via Bulgaria. Furthermore, it was necessary to send support to Italy's forces in North Africa, and Rommel arrived with a small force during the middle of February 1941. In addition, Yugoslavia, which under Prince Regent Paul had joined the Axis Powers, was rent asunder by a popular revolution against the government. As a result, an invasion of Yugoslavia was launched simultaneously with Operation Marita which began on 6 April 1941.

Many of the armored and motorized formations of the German armies intended for Barbarossa had to be detached and transferred to the Balkans. The German operation against Yugoslavia and Greece was successfully concluded by 23 April 1941. Once again, armor and motorized formations and air supremacy had been decisive. However, as far as Yugoslavia was concerned, the operations had been conducted along the main arteries of communications, ignoring the barely accessible mountainous territory – the very area in which Tito's Partisan movement was to develop. The success also obscured difficulties due to the absence of a joint combined command of the German-Italian forces, even though the British were expelled from Greece, as they were shortly afterward from Crete in May 1941, by German airborne forces.

Rommel, in the meantime, achieved unexpected successes in Africa. Even when driven back, he was always resourceful enough to turn the operations to his own advantage again. He was dependent on supplies reaching him across the sea, but the British generally had naval supremacy in the Mediterranean. The Italian naval forces, though strong, avoided major engagements as much as possible. With Gibraltar, Malta and Alexandria in British possession, the British position remained intact, although twice, in 1941 and 1942, Rommel knocked at the gates of Egypt. In many respects, the warfare in the desert reintroduced many devices already in use during World War I. Extensive barbed wire entanglements and the mining of substantial areas were used by both sides. At El Alamein, hopelessly outmanned and outgunned by Montgomery's Eighth Army, Rommel had to give way, though Montgomery failed to achieve his objective of destroying the German Afrika Korps. Defensive line after defensive line had to be overcome until the Germans had been pushed back to Tunisia.

In the meantime, in November 1942 Allied forces had landed in Morocco and Algeria under the command of General Dwight D Eisenhower. Pushing east, despite several reverses inflicted by Rommel, the Americans and British contained the remaining Axis forces in a bridgehead around Tunis where some 250,000 German and Italian soldiers capitulated in May 1943. After the disastrous reconnaissance in force carried out by largely Canadian forces on the French coast at Dieppe in August 1942, the landings in Algeria and Morocco were the first successful major Allied amphibious operation in the war. The subsequent landing in Sicily and the invasion of Italy once again established a two-front war for Germany.

The Americans had acquired much experience in amphibious operations from 1942 onward in the Far East, where Japan had entered the war on the side of the Axis in December 1941. The period 1941–43 also contained the height of the German submarine offensive – the Battle of the Atlantic. However, by increasing aerial surveillance of the Atlantic convoy routes, and by the introduction of highly sensitive radar equipment, the Allies were in a position to decide that battle in their favor. From May 1943 the U-Boats were fighting a losing action. As in World War I, American resources of raw materials and weapons had reached Great Britain after changes were made in US neutrality laws in November 1939, and from 1941 the Soviet Union also received ever-larger shipments.

Beginning in 1941, the German Army increased the number of its motorized infantry divisions and doubled the number of panzer divisions, but in the latter case by halving the number of tanks per division, which reduced their combat value. Divisions were no longer deployed in regiments and battalions but in the form of battle groups of regiment or battalion size, equipped with half-track vehicles, self-propelled artillery and assault tanks. As its strength declined, the Luftwaffe could intervene less in land battles and the self-propelled artillery became all the more important. But all this depended on adequate supplies of spare parts and fuel, two items which were in short supply on the Eastern Front.

Two important new weapons for defense against tanks were also introduced into the German infantry's armory from 1943 onward. The *Panzerfaust* was a recoilless antitank projectile fired from a light, easily manufactured metal tube. The *Panzerschreck* was virtually a direct copy of the American bazooka rocket launcher (first used in North Africa) and was operated by two men. These three weapons and their British counterpart, the PIAT, could be used only at close range – usually 100 yards or less – which required considerable nerve in those using them.

In postwar literature the German Army is often described only in terms of tanks and motorized units. This is entirely invalid. Horse and cart and sheer hard foot-slogging were often the rule. Motorization was far from standardized. True, there were a number of standardized army vehicles, but the bulk were requisitioned in Germany and the occupied countries. The only thing they had in common was their camouflage. Standardization to the extent carried out by the Western Allies and the Russians did not exist.

The US and British armies were fully motorized and mechanized. When the draft was introduced in the United States the army was faced with an apparently insoluble problem. Its regular officer corps was well trained but small, too small to train an army of millions. The solution was to use the regular officers to prepare detailed training programs which were distributed to all recruitment camps. There, people who had previously occupied managerial positions in industry were commissioned and given the task, with the aid of these manuals, of training the conscript army. Every officer had his 'Master-Lesson' according to which recruits were to be trained. The short-term disadvantage of this system was that the officers who actually took these fresh forces into combat had had little or no previous contact with them, which initially led to inferior performance. But as the lessons were learned the hard way on the battlefield, this drawback was soon eliminated. Neither American nor British forces during World War II fully adopted the German concept of *Auftragstaktik*; only after the war was it adopted in the US Army. However, the British and Americans had an efficiently functioning integrated command structure that was totally lacking between Germany and her allies.

When the German Army launched Operation Barbarossa on 22 June 1941 the army leadership's picture of the enemy forces and his military and economic capacity was vague, or even nonexistent. What did exist was a vast underestimation of the Soviet potential. The German attack, contrary to current opinion, did not come as a surprise to the Soviet Union. The Red Army had almost completed the forward assembly of its forces, the first wave of which consisted of some 130 divisions, the second wave of 80 divisions and the third wave of 33 divisions and five brigades. Added to this were the forces that could be transferred west after the conclusion of the Russo-Japanese Pact in April 1941 – mainly elite Siberian units. By the middle of October the number of divisions in the Red Army had increased to 240. To some extent the Russian divisions were still in the

process of re-equipment. However, the entire southern wing was already equipped, to the shock and surprise of the German Army, with the new and formidable T-34 tank. In the central and northern areas this process was still under way. The Russians could recruit 1.2 million men per year, the Germans only 430,000. In other words, if Germany failed to achieve victory in 1941 it would find itself faced by ever-increasing Russian manpower, while the German reserves would dwindle. The Russians had over 20,000 tanks in service, but these included many of outdated types. In 1941 alone the British and Americans supplied the Russians with more tanks than the whole German Army possessed.

The German attack forced the Russians onto the defensive at first. The Soviet artillery was not as experienced as it would be 12 months later. Instead of supporting its infantry by concentrated fire, it tended to fire over the entire width of a battlefield. Nor had the Red Army organized its defense in depth; its antitank screens were rarely deeper than 3 miles compared to 15 miles in 1943. However, the Russian tank guns were vastly superior to anything the Germans had. The 3.7cm gun was still used in most German tanks, whereas the Russians already had 76.2mm weapons.

The attacking German forces found an enemy who fought with a tenacity and bravery never before encountered by the Germans, but in the initial phase the German leadership proved more flexible and superior in communications. Even the powerful T-34 did not normally carry a radio set. The German aim was to defeat Russia in a single *Blitzkrieg* campaign. The OKH centered its hopes on the capture of Moscow. But the OKW and Hitler failed to clarify the actual objectives. The army was still dominated by the concept of the battle of annihilation, in its mistaken interpretation of Clausewitz. Hitler gradually came around to the view that economically it was more important for Germany to capture the Baltic countries and the Ukraine, with their immense agricultural and industrial resources. He believed that only the possession of these reserves would make it possible for Germany to sustain a war of attrition. Only at a slightly later stage was Hitler prepared to make the decisive thrust toward Moscow. As allies, Germany had the Finns, the Rumanians and two Italian divisions, as well as Slovak and Hungarian contingents.

At the propaganda level, the campaign was proclaimed to be a 'Crusade against Bolshevism' which had to be carried out with all the ruthlessness attendant on a war of religion, including the

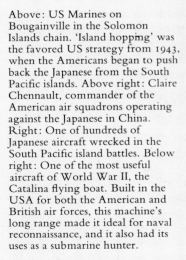

Above: US Marines on Bougainville in the Solomon Islands chain. 'Island hopping' was the favored US strategy from 1943, when the Americans began to push back the Japanese from the South Pacific islands. Above right: Claire Chennault, commander of the American air squadrons operating against the Japanese in China. Right: One of hundreds of Japanese aircraft wrecked in the South Pacific island battles. Below right: One of the most useful aircraft of World War II, the Catalina flying boat. Built in the USA for both the American and British air forces, this machine's long range made it ideal for naval reconnaissance, and it also had its uses as a submarine hunter.

Above: On a visit to the Eastern Front in 1941, Mussolini accompanied by Hitler inspects Italian troops in the Ukraine.
Below left: Speer, Hitler's minister responsible for arms production,

immediate execution of all captured Russian Commissars. The attacking German armies advanced over the entire front without producing a desirable *Schwerpunkt*. Their ranks included volunteers from Spain, France, Belgium, Flanders, the Netherlands, Denmark and Croatia. Until 1943 the Luftwaffe retained supremacy in the air, a supremacy which it lost in the summer of that year, but which was still in effect over specific areas such as the Baltic and the Black Sea. The Russian Navy, on the whole, remained in a passive role in both these areas.

The German Army Group South was assigned to penetrate in the direction of Kiev and to destroy the enemy in the western Ukraine. For the first time in World War II, the German Army with its armor failed to break through and obtain the necessary operational freedom. But then Army Group South had encountered the best-equipped segments of the Red Army. They had come across the T-34 for the first time.

Army Group Center operating in Belorussia was to reach Smolensk as quickly as possible, destroying the Russian forces north and south of Minsk on the way. Then it was to detach some of its armored formations and transfer them to Army Group North to support it in its operation to capture the Baltic countries and Leningrad. Army Group Center achieved its goal, but several weeks behind schedule due to the fierce resistance of the Russians plus some supply problems. The pocket battles of Bialystok and Minsk were its major engagements, but in spite of capturing huge numbers of prisoners and quantities of equipment, at no time were the German pincers strong enough to prevent sizeable Russian contingents from escaping their encirclement and forming new defenses.

Army Group North was to destroy the Red Army in the Baltic countries, capture the various ports and ultimately take Leningrad. It made headway without, however, being able to destroy any significant number of Russian forces.

The Russian leadership replied to the German invasion with a policy of scorched earth and the formation of partisan units to operate in the rear of the German Army. Early in July the Germans launched their attack in the south upon Uman, and the following month the battle for Smolensk was fought and won. In the north, the original Russo-Finnish border had been recaptured. But then the northern operations came to a halt. The terrain, largely swamps, was unsuitable for armored warfare and Hitler decided to lay siege to Leningrad instead of capturing it in a bitter house-to-house battle. Army Group North had also failed to interrupt the important rail link to Murmansk. In the northern sector, therefore, both armies dug in, and remained in much the same positions until 1944.

At this point Hitler decided to rest the armored formations for urgent repairs and then to move southward into the Ukraine and capture the oilfields of the Caucasus. But the dream of defeating the bulk of the Russian forces was over. After seven Russian armies had been defeated at Kiev in September, Hitler changed his mind again and ordered the attack upon Moscow. Early in October Army Group South attacked both the Donets Basin and the Crimea, while Army Group Center, en route to Moscow, achieved a brilliant victory at Vyazma and Bryansk. Although Stalin remained in Moscow, the government offices were transferred to Kubishev. General Zhukov was appointed to lead the defense of Moscow.

Just as the preparations for the attack on Moscow were completed, the weather changed for the worse. Incessant rainfall made the land virtually impassable for the German vehicles. Then, late in November 1941, freezing temperatures set in, ranging between minus 20 and minus 40 degrees Centigrade. The German troops were not equipped with winter uniforms, though these were stocked in the areas to the rear. Weapons failed, and the oil in the tanks and other vehicles froze. Only 25 percent of the necessary daily supply trains could be run. Still, after overcoming many difficulties, 'Operation Typhoon,' the attack on Moscow, was launched, the vanguards penetrating as far as Moscow's suburbs. There, on 6 December 1941, they came face to face with the Russian counteroffensive launched by Zhukov.

The German front seemed on the point of collapse when Hitler intervened and dismissed Brauchitsh, the Commander in Chief of the Army, and a number of other generals. Hitler himself assumed direct control of the conduct of operations in the East. Hitler's order to hold fast prevented a retreat from becoming a rout. The front stabilized itself again. At Demyansk and Kholm, two sizeable contingents of the German Army were encircled by the Russians and cut off. They were supplied by the Luftwaffe and managed to hold out until relieved by German counterattacks in the spring of 1942, an experience which undoubtedly influenced Hitler's decision later in 1942 to hold Stalingrad.

The Battle for Moscow was decisive, because from that moment on the German Army in the East could no longer take the offensive over the whole length of the front. Its overall offensive capacity had been broken and the turning point of the war had come. The German defeat at Stalingrad served only to confirm this. For Germany, the war on two fronts had become reality. From 22 June 1941 until 31 December 1941 the German Army in the east had lost 1,073,066 men, 276,540 of them killed. This exceeded by far the available reserves. The Russians now began to apply *Blitzkrieg* tactics. The Soviet artillery increased in firepower, armor operated independently in depth and infantry attacked in narrow sectors.

inspects a captured Soviet T34 tank. It was thanks to Speer's energy that German industry was belatedly mobilized for a long and expensive war. He lived long enough to enjoy some years of freedom after release from post-war imprisonment as a war criminal, and his penitent memoirs are a rich source of information.
Below: Soviet partisans in action.

Below: An Allied convoy at sea. An escort carrier can be discerned in the background. In the foreground is an anti-aircraft gun platform of a US warship. Unlike World War 1, the convoy system was adopted right from the beginning of hostilities by all belligerents, with the partial exception of the Japanese. Bottom left: A U-boat at sea. For much of the war U-boats made their attacks on convoys while on the surface, several submarines forming a 'wolf pack' and relying for surprise on their low profile and poor visibility or darkness. However, improved radar enabled convoys to cope with these tactics in the later years of the war. Bottom right: Von Manstein and his staff. General (later Field Marshal) von Manstein was possibly the most competent of Hitler's generals.

The German policies in all the occupied territories were such as to drive the population into the arms of the emerging partisan movements. This was especially the case in the Soviet Union. However, in areas entirely under military administration, the Germans could depend upon a considerable amount of collaboration, to the extent that some Russians even joined the German Army. By the end of 1941, unknown to Hitler, over 1 million Russians were serving as auxiliaries within the German forces, but much of the existing good will was destroyed when, in 1942, a policy of compulsory labor in Germany was introduced and males and females in eastern and western Europe were deported to Germany. So far as its labor force was concerned, Germany still lived in a virtual peacetime economy. Total war had come, but those directly affected by it should preferably be foreign workers and not German women, whose British and Russian counterparts worked around the clock in their war industries.

By 1942 German strength was no longer sufficient to maintain offensive actions over a 2000-mile front. But Army Group South captured the Crimea and Sevastopol. Then began the attack which was to carry the German Army to the summit of Mount Elbrus in the Caucasus, to Maykop and to Stalingrad. The oilfields found at Maykop had been destroyed, and they could not be used by the Germans.

The German lines of communication had not only become overextended but extremely undermanned as well. The advance upon Stalingrad exposed the entire German flank in the south. Neither rail nor trucks could solve the supply problems of the Sixth German Army under Paulus at Stalingrad. The city was to be taken by a pincer movement, but the Germans, once in the city, had to engage in fierce house-to-house fighting. What Hitler had feared in the case of Leningrad became reality in Stalingrad. In the course of August Hitler also became aware of the vulnerable points at which the Sixth Army could be cut off by the Russians. Orders were issued to the Chief of the General Staff, Halder, to build up a 'corset' consisting of antitank guns deployed in depth behind the Rumanian and Italian units holding the exposed sectors. The transfer of a panzer division from France to this sector of the front was also ordered. Halder did nothing and precisely at the point which Hitler had predicted, on 19 November 1942, Russian armored corps broke through the lines and closed the circle around the Sixth Army. Hitler, who meanwhile had parted company with Halder and appointed General Zeitzler Chief of the General Staff, was in two minds about what to do. To hold or to break out? Göring's promise that the Luftwaffe would supply Stalingrad resulted in the decision to hold on to the city at any price. However, the Luftwaffe was quite incapable of meeting the supply demands of over 300,000 men. Of the defenders of Stalingrad, 100,000 were killed in action. Ninety thousand became prisoners of war, of whom 6000 survived the ordeal – including the commanding generals, Field Marshal Paulus and General von Seydlitz-Kurtzbach. In December 1942 Manstein had led a relief operation and came as close as 30 miles from the city. He waited for the garrison to break out, but Hitler forbade them to do so. On 2 February the rest of the Stalingrad garrison capitulated.

Hitler took the responsibility for the disaster upon himself, and in recent years his decision has been vindicated by none other than General Chuikov, the Soviet commander of the Stalingrad defense, who argued that the siege of Stalingrad tied up so many Russian forces as to make it impossible to bring about the total collapse of the German Army Group South. As it happened, Manstein managed to build up a new defensive line and the Russian advance farther west was prevented for the better part of another year.

Before the fall of Stalingrad, the Casablanca Conference between Roosevelt and Churchill had resulted in three major conclusions. The first was to demand 'Unconditional Surrender' from Germany and her allies, and the second was to put an end to the threat of the German submarines. Thirdly, they placed priority on strategic bombing in order to undermine Germany's morale and industrial production. What had been achieved by the blockade in World War I was to be achieved by bombing from the air in World War II.

In fact, the principle of area bombing of German cities had already been approved by Churchill upon assuming the premiership in May 1940. He had advocated it in 1917. We have it on the authority of the then Principal Assistant Secretary in the Air Ministry, J M Spaight: 'We began to bomb objectives on the German mainland before the Germans began to bomb objectives on the British mainland. That is an historical fact which has been publicly admitted. Yet because we were doubtful about the psychological effect of propagandistic distortion of the truth that it was we who started the strategic offensive, we have shrunk

from giving our great decision of May 1940 the publicity which it deserved. That surely was a mistake. It was a splendid decision. It was as heroic, as self-sacrificing, as Russia's decision to adopt her policy of "scorched earth." '

The strategic air offensive against Germany started in May 1940, though with bomber forces of an insignificant size compared with the armadas of the air that appeared over Germany beginning late in 1942. But even in 1940 public opinion samples collected by members of SS Security Service, the SD, express time and again the concern of the people in the Ruhr about being bombed and machine gunned.

The Allied air offensive could not break the resistance of the German civilian population any more than the German bombing had affected British morale in 1940. Industries were dispersed, but Germany was still far from conducting a total war. Goebbels was its propagandist, but could not make much headway in practice, even after he had been appointed Plenipotentiary for Total War after 20 July 1944. However, largely because of the efforts of Albert Speer, Armaments Minister from February 1942, German output of arms and weapons in 1944 was many times that achieved in 1940.

The last large-scale offensive mounted by Germany in the east was the Battle of Kursk which began on 5 July 1943.

Top: General Zeitzler, appointed Chief of the Army General Staff in 1942, as successor to the more experienced Halder, whose good advice became increasingly irksome to Hitler. Above: Soviet tanks in the 1944 advance through Byelorussia. They are of the T34 type, which by that year was the standard Red Army tank. First introduced in 1941, this medium tank won the reputation of being the best all-round tank of World War II. In 1941 it proved clearly superior to German tanks, but had not been built in sufficient numbers to affect the campaign of that year. Right: A map of the operations around Kursk in summer 1943; the Germans fail to capture the Soviet salient and are then counterattacked.

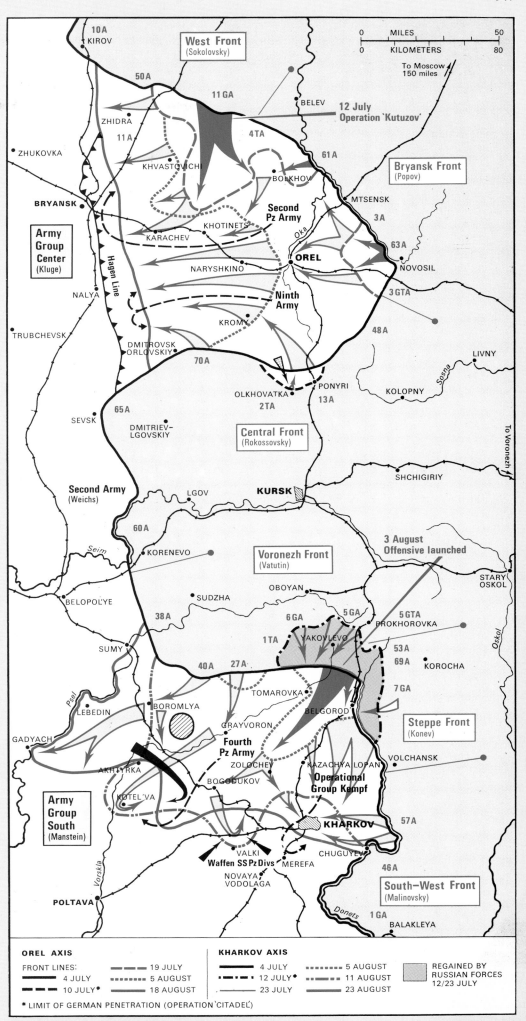

Below: British aircrews join their Stirling bombers at an airfield in England. The Stirling was the RAF's first four-engined bomber and for a time was the workhorse of the bomber offensive against Germany. But it was soon superseded by the Lancaster and Halifax; it was not an easy aircraft to pilot, and its bomb bays could not accommodate the very large bombs which soon became standard weapons. Left: General Eisenhower and his colleagues. Right: The US Air Force in Britain. The pilot is sitting in a P-51 fighter. This, the Mustang, was the best US fighter of World War II, although originally designed for the RAF by North American Aviation. Far right: The observer at his post in a US bomber; bomb-aiming was his major function.

However, the Russians had detailed advance knowledge via an espionage group, the so-called Red Orchestra, and made their preparations accordingly. The offensive bogged down in the deep network of Russian defenses and had to be broken off. The initiative had come to rest firmly in Soviet hands. The time had come to make peace, but who could make peace with Hitler? In an ideological war as total as was World War II, this was no longer possible. The agony was to go on for another two years, until the German armies had been thrown back to Berlin.

Shortly after the Kursk Offensive had begun, Mussolini was toppled from power on 19 July 1943 and the Italian government taken over by Marshal Badoglio. The Allies had already landed in Sicily, and the campaign in Italy which followed was marked by hard defensive battles of which Monte Cassino serves as but one example. A decisive Allied breakthrough was not achieved until April 1944, and the Allies' entry into Rome occurred only two days before the D-Day invasion of the coast of northern France. Right up to the capitulation in May 1945, the Germans, though being steadily pushed back, maintained their foothold on the Italian peninsula. Mussolini had been rescued by a German commando raid, but he no longer played a role of any political significance.

Operation Overlord began in the early hours of 6 June 1944. Now it was no longer the Luftwaffe which dominated the skies but the Allied air forces, and under their protection the Normandy beachhead was consolidated, though it was nearly two months before General Patton could break out into the open country. Coinciding as all this did with the Russian offensive of June 1944, those German officers who formed a resistance to Hitler believed that the last possible moment had come in which to act. A bomb planted by a Colonel Stauffenberg exploded in Hitler's conference room, but Hitler survived with a few minor injuries. From that moment on, he was utterly convinced that Providence had selected him to lead Germany to final victory. There was not a chance. The Russians crossed the East Prussian frontier, and although they were thrown back for a time, Russia proper was liberated and the Russian armies stood at the gates of Warsaw. After Patton's breakout in the west the German Army disintegrated until it came to a standstill again at the frontiers of the Reich.

Hitler's last hope was the Ardennes Offensive launched on 16 December 1944. But Antwerp, his objective, was out of reach of the German armies. Once the weather changed and clear skies allowed the Allied air forces to intervene, the German forces were quickly thrown back to their points of departure. In March 1945 the British and Americans crossed the Rhine, and in spite of using the last German reserves, children and old men, there was no escape from defeat. After Hitler's suicide on 30 April 1945, shortly before Berlin fell to the Russians, Grand Admiral Dönitz became his successor. Under his guidance, the German forces in north-western Germany surrendered to Montgomery and on 7 May General Jodl, on Dönitz's behalf, signed the instrument of unconditional surrender of the German Army in the presence of General Eisenhower at Reims, a procedure repeated by Field Marshal Keitel before Soviet representatives in Berlin the following day.

During the last few years of the war, the techniques used had changed considerably. Although capable of conducting the war Blitzkrieg-style, on the whole the Soviet forces preferred a battle of attrition, to which they resorted time and again. In contrast to the German plan at Verdun, they also aimed at the conquest of considerable slices of territory. When forming up for battle, the Russians deployed what they called a 'long-range battle group' consisting primarily of armored units as their leading formation. Accompanied by motorized rifle formations, they had to take and hold important geographical points. Objectives and directions were described in minute detail by the Soviet High Command and were to be adhered to to the letter. This deprived the army of the flexibility which they might have had otherwise and provided the Germans at a local level with repeated opportunities to launch effective counterattacks. The bulk of the Russian infantry, with its supporting armor, was to keep as close as possible to the long-range battle group, which in effect slowed down the armor and reduced the speed of the attack. Moreover, although the Soviets had held air supremacy since the summer of 1943, battles were marked less by cooperation between armor and air force (as had been the case in Poland and the west in 1939 and 1940) than by the cooperation between armor and artillery. This led to a Russian concentration of artillery which had never been seen before. During his offensive of 1918, Ludendorff had concentrated 100 pieces of artillery per $\frac{3}{4}$ mile of frontage, but the Russian offensive operations, on the average, concentrated over 500 guns on the same size sector. Their firepower was immensely increased by their rocket artillery, the 'Stalin Organs.' The Germans, too,

question. Instead, defense with mobile forces was conducted in depth in the form of battle zones, a development which pointed to the future of defensive warfare.

The defenders had the task of stopping an enemy attack in the depth of the battle zone and gaining time for further evacuation. Behind the immediate front line was a system of small strongholds consisting mainly of two-man bunkers which was to wear down the attack. Concentrated enemy artillery fire thus often hit areas of no importance. Broad belts of minefields were to play a key role in slowing down the advance of enemy armor and/or pointing it in the direction desired by the defender. It was of primary importance to recognize the beginning of an enemy attack. Once this was done, the bulk of the forces moved to the rear of the battle zone, the artillery moved into their prepared positions and the armored reserves waited for the moment to intervene. Much depended also on expert camouflage, a lesson which the Germans learned from the Russians, who are past masters of this art to the present day. What had above all to be hidden from the enemy's eyes was the point of concentration of the defensive armor. This new type of defense proved its value.

Mainly *Volksgrenadier* divisions were used for the defense of

Above far left: Otto Skorzeny, leader of the SS airborne detachment that snatched Mussolini from his Italian captors after the fall of his Fascist regime. Above left: General Rommel, shortly before his enforced suicide, inspects German troops manning defenses on the northern French coast. The self-propelled gun has French-built chassis. Left: Generals Patton, Bradley and Montgomery in France, summer 1944. Right: Allied troop-carrying gliders, their life-cycle accomplished, await disposal in Normandy.

had rocket artillery, the *Nebelwerfer*, but not in the necessary numbers, and only a very few were self-propelled, as they were mounted on half tracks. The same was true of American rocket launchers, of which only relatively few had been mounted on the turrets of Sherman tanks. But the principle of using the rocket or rocket-powered weapons was firmly established during World War II, ranging from the bazooka to the rocket-propelled Me 163 fighter and the rockets of the V1 and V2 types.

During the last few years of the war air forces were dominant. In the course of the breakthrough operation from the Normandy beachhead at Avranches, the Allies used 1500 four-engine bombers, 500 twin-engine bombers and 500 fighter bombers which concentrated their attacks on a German defensive area measuring 4.8 miles by 1.5 miles. This amounted to an increase in firepower which surpassed anything known during World War I.

Although 1944 witnessed the highest output of German arms, including armor and vehicles, there were neither adequate fuel reserves nor a transport system sufficiently intact to carry them to the forces in the field. This necessitated a new type of defense – but not from fixed and firmly held positions as during World War I. For that type of defense, the German manpower reserves no longer sufficed. Defense on a wide front was out of the

these battle zones, each of which was about one-third experienced infantry men, the rest being hastily trained recruits. These divisions had no effective offensive power, but their equipment was superior to that which the German Army had had in 1939. They were more than adequately supplied with light machine guns and the newly introduced fully automatic assault rifles and *Panzerfausts*. What they lacked were antitank guns, but forces thus equipped could be quickly assembled to form a concentrated defense against attacking armor.

At the operational level, the German Army conducted its battles on the defensive most expertly, especially under Field Marshal von Manstein and General Model, as long as resources were available and Hitler did not intervene with one of his 'hold at any price' directives. Defense was carried out in 'wandering pockets' cut off by the Russians until they had succeeded in breaking through the Russian lines from the rear and rejoining the main front. When this was no longer possible, linear defense was reintroduced by Hitler, but the lines were so thinly manned that it was a relatively easy matter to break through them. Mobile defense, however, had shown its value and once again pointed to a new confirmation of the primacy of defense.

The most important German infantry weapon issued during the final phase of World War II was the *Sturmgewehr 43*, the

fully automatic assault rifle already mentioned. Although its range was shorter than that of a light machine gun, its firepower was considerably greater. The rocket-propelled antitank missiles already mentioned gave the infantry added protection against enemy armor. Among German battle tanks the tendency was toward heavier and heavier vehicles. Possibly the best was the Mark V Panther, which mounted a 75mm long-barreled gun and weighed just over 40 tons. The Tiger, mounting an 88mm gun, initially weighed 58 tons (in its final radically-different Tiger II version, 70 tons) while still powered by the same engines as the Panther. Its fire was accurate and deadly. With the exception of the Soviet Joseph Stalin Mark III, there was no Allied tank which could match it in this respect, but firepower was not matched by great mobility; this was its chief disadvantage. While the Mark IIs and IIIs in 1940 had no difficulty in using the roads through the Ardennes, during the Ardennes Offensive of 1944 the very weight of the new German armor transformed the road system into a quagmire, which made it impossible for the supply columns to follow.

The Luftwaffe, from early 1944 on, was equipped with the first operational jet fighter, the Me 262. Much has been made of the delay in the deployment of this plane being caused by Hitler's demand to transform it into a fast bomber. That decision was not as nonsensical as it seems at first glance. Air combat at speeds approaching Mach 1 requires different training and different

Above left: A US battleship
bombards land targets with its
16-inch guns. In the Pacific war
gun engagements between battleships were rare but the effectiveness
of naval artillery against coastal
objectives provided an important
role for both old and new US
battleships. Left: 'Big Three'
meetings between Roosevelt,
Churchill and Stalin (here shown
with their foreign ministers
standing behind them) took place
at Teheran and Yalta, and also at
Potsdam with different American
and British participants. Right: For
defense against low-flying aircraft,
external machine guns were fitted
to several tank designs. Above,
inset: Rocket launching arrays, of
which the Soviet *Katyusha* was the
first to see widespread service, were
also developed for the US Army,
as shown here.'

tactics but low-level bombing runs, compared with combat in the air, are relatively simple. Special training proved to be time-consuming. Nor were the existing jet engines completely free from defects. More German jet fighter pilots died because of engine failure or generally inadequate handling of the aircraft than by being shot down by the Allies. Added to the Me 262 was the Me 163 aircraft which was rocket-propelled. This type was used mainly for the defense of the Leuna synthetic fuel installations at Magdeburg. Its unprecedented rate of climb and speed allowed it to penetrate far above the bomber formations, then glide down upon them and open fire with rockets and cannon from a distance out of range of the aircraft gunners.

Other German jet aircraft which came into operation in 1944–45 were the Arado 234 *Blitz* bomber and the *Volksjager* He 162. However, the ultimate weapon of World War II, fortunately for Germany, came too late to be used over Europe: the atomic bomb, first used at Hiroshima and Nagasaki.

To sum up, the image of war, the *Kriegsbild*, had profoundly changed by 1944 from what it had been in 1940. During the first few years of the war, armor supported by tactical aircraft could make a breakthrough and achieve operational freedom. Later in the war defensive positions were built in increasing depth and in stages, providing the manpower to keep them functional was still available. What in World War I had been

Top left: A German *Volkssturmer* does his gallant best with a *Panzerfaust* one-man missile launcher, in May 1945, the month of Germany's surrender. Above left: General Bor-Komorowski surrenders to the SS general in Warsaw, after the final defeat of the insurgents, in November 1944. The captured Poles, members of the Home Army, were treated as regular prisoners of war by the Germans; Bor-Komorowski was imprisoned at Colditz, but finally settled in Britain. Above: The main street of Bastogne, in the Ardennes, in January 1945. Taken at the height of the Ardennes campaign, this picture illustrates the high degree of motorization in the US Army. Above right: An obvious publicity photograph of a US three-man combat team.

the role of the barbed wire entanglements was, in World War II, largely taken over by extensive mine fields.

In 1944 infantry in an attacking role had weapons with a much greater rate of fire than had been the case in 1940. Nonetheless, support from armor, especially self-propelled assault guns, provided the backbone for any infantry counterattack as well as for its defense. The task of the attacker was first to destroy the enemy antitank positions, as well as the armor held in reserve in the rear, before attacking armored wedges could begin to smash their way through the defensive system. The intensity of firepower had a higher priority than mobility, a reversal of the position held in 1940. The air force supplemented the fire of the artillery while the mechanized infantry followed close on the heels of the armored formations. Tactical fighter bombers held down the enemy's artillery and, wherever possible, attacked its reserve armor. Other air force formations attacked roads, bridges and intersections to prevent supplies from reaching the enemy. The United States Army Air Force, and to a lesser degree the RAF, attacked vital centers of communications in the enemy's hinterland where American precision bombing succeeded in almost destroying Germany's synthetic fuel production.

The Red Army was still highly dependent on railroads and horse-drawn carts for its supplies, which meant that the Russians were forced to pause after every offensive, giving the Germans the chance to reorganize their disrupted defense. The American and British Armies, however, were supplied largely by trucks to the extent that their advancing forces could move as far as 360 miles from their base. Transport aircraft and fuel pipelines made them partially independent of the railroads, and this model has determined the pattern of warfare ever since.

Left: A US aircraft carrier with escorting destroyer in the Pacific theater of operations. The naval war in the Pacific was essentially a war between the seaborne aircraft of the US and Japan, whose outcome was decided by the superior productive strength of the US, which guaranteed a numerical preponderance both of aircraft carriers and of aircraft. Below left: The first Soviet tanks enter Berlin. Above: 'Enola Gay', the bomber entrusted with the dropping of the first atomic bomb, during training in New Mexico. The aircraft flew the mission from a Pacific island base, to which the bomb had been delivered earlier by a US cruiser.
Below: A bomb-damaged Japanese drydock at the time of surrender, crammed with midget submarines.

Psychological warfare played a major role in the war. At first the initiative seemed to be in the hands of the dictatorships. The Soviet Union, as well as National Socialist Germany, were one-party states. A *Politruk*, a political commissar, was attached to every unit in the Red Army right down to the company level. The Germans sought to emulate this from 1943 on by the introduction of the *Nationalsozialistischer Fuerhrungsoffizier*, the National Socialist Leadership Officer. At first Allied propaganda about German atrocities was relatively ineffective because much the same propaganda had been used during World War I and afterward had been shown to be blatant lies. Therefore, the perpetration of genuine atrocities had not been completely believed even in high official quarters. The real stories, such as the 'Final Solution of the Jewish Problem,' were revealed in their full gruesome details only after the war. They were products of an ideological warfare, and only wars of religion, which essentially belong to the realm of ideological warfare, have ever been conducted with anything approaching equal ferocity and bestiality.

The real victors of World War II were the United States of America and the Soviet Union. The Great Powers of Western and Central Europe have disappeared, insofar as their greatness depends on their ability to impose their will upon any of their neighbors. But the military consequences of World War II are still shaping and influencing not only Europe, but the entire globe.

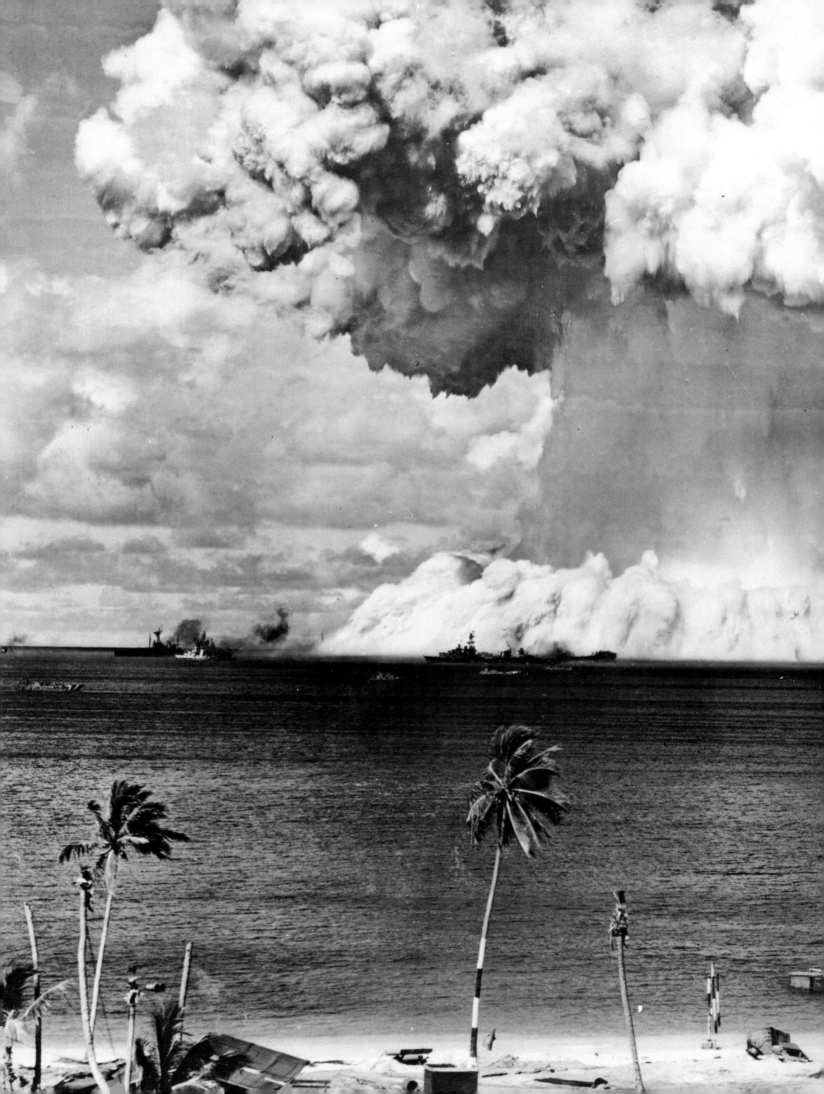

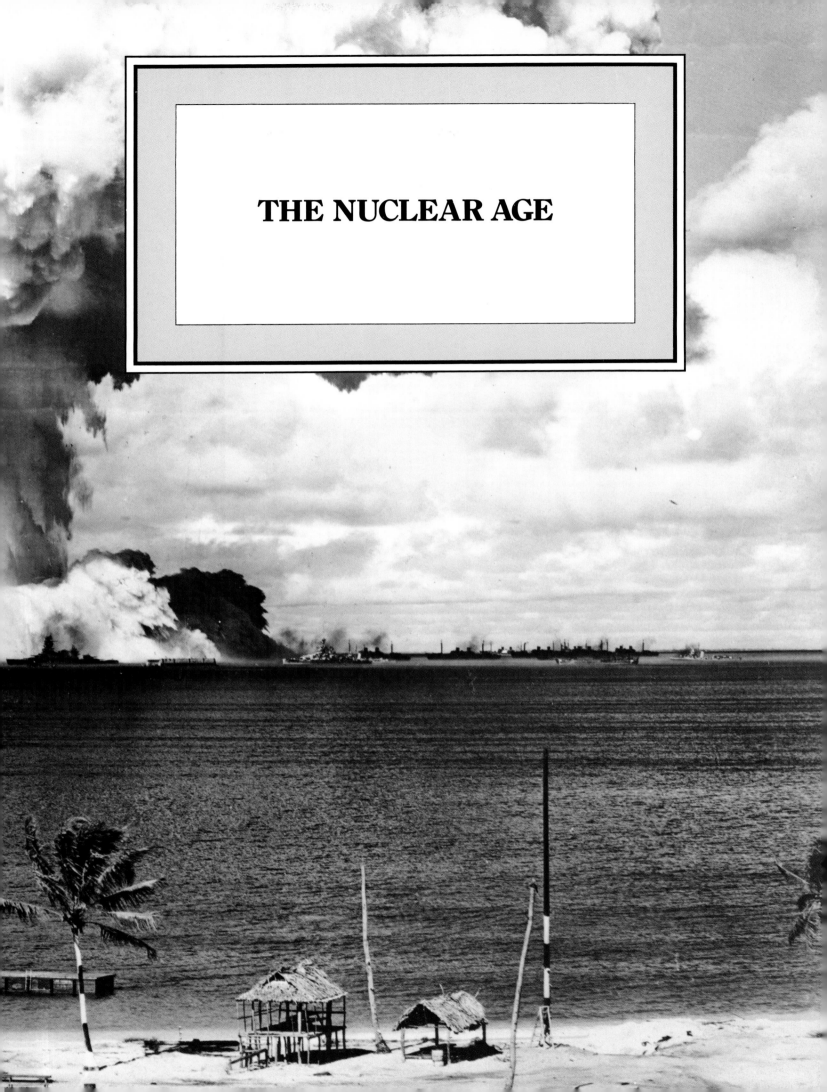

THE NUCLEAR AGE

In this final chapter, it will be our task to examine the emergence of the *primacy of the defense* from an historical perspective and then to look at the role it plays at present and consider the lessons NATO and the Warsaw Pact countries have learned from the past.

The primary problem in the conduct of conventional warfare in Central and Western Europe in the past resulted, other factors apart, from the nature and the character of defense in a given geographic area. Throughout the latter part of the 19th century and the first half of the 20th century, the geography of these areas has become more and more complicated and is at this very moment going through changes in its urban structure. It is still in a process of transformation such that a future battlefield in Western and Central Europe will bear little resemblance to that which existed at the end of World War II.

Apart from this, the definition of the concept of conventional warfare provides some difficulties, because it is not only a question now of whether or not it includes tactical nuclear weapons, but also of whether conventional warfare includes guerrilla warfare. This problem can be left open for a time while we turn to warfare in the past and look first of all at the basic change in the role of defense. From the historical perspective of the last 160 years, one major change is clear – a much smaller number of troops is needed to defend a given line and hold it successfully. Wellington's army at Waterloo had approximately 20,000 men per mile of defense line. In the American Civil War this ratio decreased to 12,000 men per mile, and during the last two years of the Civil War the forces of the Confederacy repelled attacks successfully with 5000 men per mile, even though these attacks were doubled in strength. The army of General Lee defended, for over nine months, a long line between Richmond and Petersburg, yielding only when its strength had declined to 1500 men per mile.

The Franco-Prussian War seemed to contradict this development, but superior strategy and greater tactical maneuverability resulted in the defeat of the French forces before they were able to organize an effective defense within a large framework. Nevertheless, the bloody and successful defense against the German attack at Gravelotte shows the potential power of the defense in isolated local actions.

If we turn to the Boer War we find a further decline in the defensive strength necessary to hold a given line. The Boers, with forces ranging between 600 and 800 men per mile, successfully repelled attacks carried out by the flower of the British professional army. Near Magersfontein the Boers held a front of around six miles with only 5000 men, and at Colenso a front of over seven miles with 4500 men. During the Russo-Japanese War, in the Battle of Mukden the Russians defended with 7450 men per mile a front that stretched over 40 miles, until the Japanese succeeded, by threatening the Russian flank, in driving them from their positions.

After the Battle of the Marne in World War I there was a defensive line of roughly 450 miles from the Channel coast to the Swiss border. In 1915, when the German armies on this front were on the defensive, they held it with roughly 90 divisions – there was one division approximately every five miles, or 3480 men per mile. This, however, requires qualification because the Vosges Mountains were at the southern end of the front, approximately 100 miles long and considered by both sides as unsuitable for major attacks. There the strength of the defense was lower than elsewhere on the Western Front. This circumstance enlarges the defense figure on the main sectors to almost 6000 men per mile. Since, however, these figures include strategic reserves, logistical personnel and so forth, this means that the effective defensive strength amounted to one division

per $5\frac{1}{2}$–6 miles, which brings us back to the actual ratio which ranged between 4475 men and 3000 men per mile of front including local reserves. This line of defense stopped the major autumn offensive of the Allies, an offensive which in individual sectors was carried out with a superiority of five to one.

In the face of the growing superiority of the Allies, particularly in medium and heavy artillery, the German Army leadership changed its defensive tactics; it grouped its divisions in depth rather than in width. In practice this meant that now only one-third of the combat strength of a division held the first line while the rest stood in reserve. The Allied artillery bombardment, which usually preceded every attack, in effect hit a defense line which was either not manned at all or manned very thinly. Attacks could be absorbed immediately and repelled by counterattacks from depth, preferably at the weakest points of the Allied attack.

Previous page: An underwater detonation, one of the series of atomic weapon tests staged by the US government at Bikini Atoll in 1946. The ships, anchored at varying ranges from the device, include several well-known survivors from both the US and hostile navies of World War II. Below: An air view of a Bikini test. The circular line is the rapidly advancing shock wave, and this is followed by a dust storm.

The problem for both sides was how to get out of a war which had become stuck in the mud of the trenches – in other words, to return to mobility. The British found their answer in the development of tanks, but it would be wrong to name the tank as the weapon which, in a military context, was the decisive instrument in World War I. As already mentioned, its operational radius was relatively small, roughly 20 miles, and its technical defects were many. Large numbers of tanks were put out of action before they could become really effective. The German Army had its own answer for bringing about greater mobility in warfare, the shock troops. They realized that mass infantry attacks would lead only to mass butchery, and therefore they changed their offensive tactics by dividing them into two stages. The first stage was to consist of a wave of shock troops deployed against key points of the Allied defense. A shock troop could range in strength from platoon to company size – from about 30 men to 120 – comprised of expert marksmen, hand grenade throwers, machine-gun units, trench mortars, flame throwers and engineers who were to penetrate the first line of defense and largely clear out the first trenches before the second wave, the bulk of the division, would follow. Ludendorff supported this development enthusiastically and gave the shock troops a key role in the March Offensive of 1918.

It was precisely this offensive, in which the British confronted a German superiority of three to one, which demonstrated the

real value of the defense, because the bulk of the German attacking units could move forward only relatively slowly. The German attack finally failed to exploit the initial breakthrough. In other words, the German forces could not maintain in depth the original impetus of their attack; the farther they went, the weaker this impetus became until the attack was halted. The attackers, once again, were compelled onto the defensive.

In the late summer and autumn of 1918, when the Allied Forces obtained a superiority of three to one over the German Forces, it allowed them to develop multiple leverages, thanks to which the German defensive line could gradually be pushed back. However, Field Marshal Haig, as well as Winston Churchill, estimated the remaining German fighting capacity as high enough to be able to continue the war for another year.

Neither tanks nor shock troops were the real solution to the problems of trench warfare. They represented partial solutions, but together, as mobile armored units and mechanized infantry, they became the answer. This development changed the strategy and tactics of land warfare and could be applied in the attack as well as in defense.

Again, one could take the German successes of World War II in Poland and in France as examples contradicting the idea of the primacy of the defense. However, the defeat of Poland, other factors apart, was caused in large part by the deployment of the Polish forces in forward positions which lacked the depth necessary for defense. The Poles became quick victims of an enemy who used the new concept of the *Blitzkrieg*, which combined the mechanized speed of the armored units and the tactical support of aircraft.

As we have seen, this concept was first developed by Major General Fuller and Captain Liddell Hart. But the prophet is never recognized in his own country. Also, in Germany, General Beck, the Chief of the General Staff of the Army until 1938 and the Commander in Chief of the Army, General von Fritsch, were rather reluctant to support these ideas as expounded in their country by Guderian. But in the end, Guderian was successful. On 10 May 1940 the strength of the German and Allied units was evenly balanced, with roughly 140 divisions on each side, while the Allies had more – and in many respects, more powerful – tanks. One element in which the German armor was superior to that of the Allies was speed. But much more important was the fact that the Allied tank forces played a role subordinate to the infantry and did not represent an integrated, independently operating unit that could penetrate in depth or be deployed as a kind of fire brigade at critical points on the front.

The Allies, especially the French, were not only the victims of the *Blitzkrieg* concept, they were also the victims of their ignorance of how to deploy the available materials and the mechanized forces so as to adapt them to the requirements of a new kind of warfare. They had six armored divisions available, with two more in reserve, as well as a considerable number of motorized divisions, compared with 10 German armored divisions and 7 motorized divisions, all deployed near the Ardennes sector. The German breakthrough was carried out by only a small number of the German divisions before the mass of their forces entered the fray. The ordinary infantry divisions were still marching on foot and using horses and carts for transport.

The French had mobility; they possessed the means for a flexible defense without realizing it. Among the reasons which Fuller enumerates for the German success, and which also illustrates the essence of the *Blitzkrieg* concept, is the strategy of annihilation, because under favorable conditions the advantages of this strategy outweigh those of attrition. As deployed by the Germans, this strategy was unwittingly favored by the French because of their belief in solid fronts – the so-called Maginot complex – but also because the French did not realize that this idea had been overtaken by rapid armor operations supported by a tactical air force. This deprived the French forces of any initiative and handed it over to the enemy.

There were also the tactics of speed which the strategy of annihilation requires for consistent maintenance of the impetus of the attack. The German forces were not only organized so that they could maintain this impetus, but they also included engineers and building troops. In fact, the entire logistical apparatus was structured in such a way that it could be present at any point where it was required, whether this meant refitting tanks, overcoming fortifications, securing the road network, rebuilding bridges, regulating the traffic or the supply of fuel and ammunition at all times. The German Stuka dive bombers paralyzed the French rail network, but where possible they avoided the destruction of roads and bridges upon which the German advance was to be carried out.

This new kind of warfare required the integration and co-operation of all service branches in order to maximize the effective power, the power at the point of contact, which, during the western campaign, was between 100 and 200 miles away from the point of departure of the attack. The German Air Force had been built up almost exclusively for a tactical role. The speed of the attack required the concentration at the point of contact and in this context the German dive bomber was, in the last analysis, nothing other than a flying field howitzer. In this function, integrated with the panzer units, it doubled the impact of the latter.

There are other factors which played a role, such as the demoralization of the French staffs by the superior German strategy and tactics and that psychologically imponderable will to victory which many British and German observers of the time found lacking in the French Army.

Therefore, we come to the conclusion that France fell because she did not recognize the antidote to the concept of the *Blitzkrieg*, and this antidote brings us back to the rise of the defensive over the offensive, a remedy which the Soviet forces used, at first reluctantly and then increasingly, toward the end of 1941 and 1942, until they had successfully regained a position in which they could return to an offensive strategy.

The campaign in North Africa provides further examples of successful defensive actions, including those in April and May 1941 when the 9th Australian Division held Tobruk against Rommel's German and Italian forces. The Australians defended a badly built position roughly 30 miles in circumference with a strength of 800 men per mile against two German armored divisions and three Italian divisions. About a year later, at Alam Halfa and El Alamein, the defensive showed its great potential

Right: Berliners celebrate the arrival of the first truckload of oranges after the lifting of the Berlin Blockade. Below: Douglas Skymasters, 4-engined transport aircraft which were a mainstay of the Berlin airlift, await their next flight. The German failure to air-supply Stalingrad in 1942 probably encouraged Stalin to undertake the Berlin Blockade, which failed because of the number and size of transport aircraft available to the US and Britain. Below right: A time-exposure photograph tracing the navigation and signal lights of supply aircraft circling a Berlin airfield.

once again. In both cases there were no open flanks, and at Alam Halfa in September 1942 Montgomery repelled Rommel's attack with a plan that had actually been drawn up largely by his predecessor, Auchinleck, and carried out with roughly the same force as that available to the defender. At El Alamein in October the Afrika Korps tried to hold a defensive line of 40 miles with a strength of roughly one division per eight miles of front. Montgomery opened his attack at El Alamein with a superiority in combat troops of three to one (or eight to one if the Italian forces are excluded) as well as a six-to-one superiority in the number of tanks over the Germans. In spite of this overwhelming power of attack, the intention of which was to wage a battle of annihilation, the British achieved their breakthrough only after 13 days of hard fighting. British tank losses were three times greater than those of the defenders. However, one must

not forget that in this battle the German tank units were already very weak and in the course of this engagement were almost annihilated. The British operational aim, to destroy the Afrika Korps, was not achieved. The Germans made their retreat and in the course of the following seven months were in a position to inflict serious losses upon the British Eighth Army and the British and American forces in Algeria and Tunisia.

In Normandy in 1944 there was a similar situation. Although the Allies enjoyed almost total superiority in the air, it took virtually two months for them to succeed in breaking out from the Normandy beachhead. At that time the Allies had a superiority of five to one over the German defense. As an example, on 30th July 1944 an unsuccessful attempt was made by the British Second Army to achieve a breakthrough at Caumont, coordinated with the American attempt to break through at Avranches to the west of the bridgehead. This 'Operation Bluecoat' faced a German front about 10 miles wide. The German forces were low-grade divisions, but nevertheless they held. Local breakthroughs were achieved only in the western part of the sector, and these were eliminated by German reserves three days later. The British Official History comments upon this episode with the words, 'It is a measure of the German soldier's fighting quality that notwithstanding these disadvantages he continued to offer effective opposition and to make skilful use of country that is in itself an obstacle to rapid movement.'

The German strength in Normandy amounted to roughly one German division per eight miles of front on a front which totalled almost 80 miles. It must also be borne in mind that most of these divisions were understrength and in France for refitting. When Patton succeeded in breaking through at Avranches eight weeks after the Normandy landing, the German reserves were so reduced that they could no longer threaten the Allied flanks and Patton broke out into territory ideally suited for large-scale armored operations in depth. The German reserves were so thin, and the area in which to outflank them so large, that the Allied armies could press forward for a time almost unhindered. This was all the easier since the bulk of the German infantry divisions were still not motorized, in contrast to those of the Americans and the British. Nevertheless, near the frontier of Germany, they held once again with forces of highly various quality, and a counteroffensive was waged which, although it failed, yet provided examples of holding frontal sectors with fewer men than had been thought feasible a few years earlier.

On the Eastern Front, as we have seen, the German attack had first splintered the Soviet armies and the German armored units penetrated into the depths of Russia. Russia's most important allies, the geography and climate of the country, gave the Red Army an amount of time much beyond that which France had in 1940 – the time necessary to reform as well as rethink, to adapt to the *Blitzkrieg* concept strategically and tactically. In the history of World War II Stalingrad is described, almost without exception, as a turning point in the east. But the turning point had already been reached in the winter of 1941 during the attack on Moscow. After the unsuccessful attempt to conquer Moscow, the German forces were no longer in a position to mount an offensive over the entire front in the East. Signs of exhaustion in the German offensive power increased month by month, and Stalingrad was nothing more than the dramatic confirmation of this development. After Moscow, and even more so after Stalingrad, the Russians, with new and growing reserves, could turn to the offensive. However, they faced an enemy who immediately adopted the concept of the flexible defense – a defense which might have been even more flexible had Hitler allowed it. In some instances the Germans defended successfully against a superiority of seven to one.

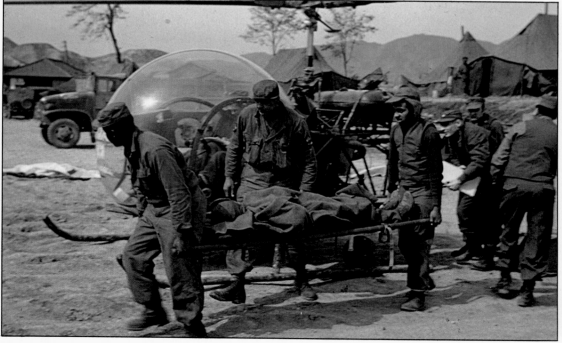

Left: The war in Korea; US medium artillery in action. The USA and her allies had a preponderance both of artillery and of ammunition supplies, but this advantage could be decisive only in rarely occurring tactical circumstances, set-piece battles in which the enemy did not have overwhelming manpower. Below: MacArthur and Truman meet during the Korean War. The General advocated all-out war against China and the President disagreed. This classic conflict between civil and military authority ended with the dismissal of MacArthur. Below center: MacArthur surveys his master-stroke, the landing at Inchon. This combined operation threatened to cut off the advancing North Koreans and forced them into a retreat which continued almost up to the Chinese frontier, at which point China intervened to turn the tide and, indirectly, bring MacArthur's military career to an end. Below, center right: US infantry in Korea clean their rifles and check ammunition belts. Bottom left: A wounded US soldier evacuated by helicopter. Bottom center: US tanks await orders in Korea. Bottom, right: United Nations infantry moves along a highway in Korea. The two files and extended order of march suggest that this is an area subject to enemy ambush.

Left: The East Berlin riots of 1953, following the death of Stalin; interested crowds at the boundary of the US sector watch the burning of a propaganda kiosk in the Russian sector. Below: An East Berlin demonstrator clambers on to a Soviet tank, encouraged by his friends. Right: Ho Chi Minh, inspiration and organizer of the revolutionary movement in Vietnam. Far right: The Vietnam People's Army received much of its supply by bicycle, a form of transport highly resistant to air attack. Below right: The Soviet AK 7.62mm assault rifle. Although superseded in the Red Army by the improved AKM, this weapon is still used by armies which have been equipped with Soviet help.

Three conclusions emerge from all of this. First, in an age of mass armies combined with a development of arms and weapons and weapon systems which can almost be described as revolutionary, the effectiveness of the individual soldier has increased to an extent that one is almost tempted to speak of the primacy of the defensive over the offensive. Second, the *Blitzkrieg* strategy proved its value in World War II, at a time when the necessary technological and organizational preconditions for its application did exist. Third, although the *Blitzkrieg* concept achieved success, its preconditions could also be applied in the defensive, which had thereby gained a new dimension – that of flexibility. And so we come to the question: To what extent have the tactics and techniques of World War II been adopted and adapted by the forces of the Warsaw Pact countries and by those of NATO, even in a modified form?

In trying to answer this question, one thing becomes immediately apparent – the position of the Soviet Union today is not dissimilar to that of the Third Reich of 1939, in whose military thinking it was important to remember that the economic position of Germany and its poverty of essential raw materials for armaments did not allow a long war. The concept of the *Blitzkrieg* was not only a product of the military technological development, it was also a product of economic conditions. By comparison with the economic structure of the NATO powers – although they too have their weak points, for instance, in oil resources – the Warsaw Pact powers are still underdeveloped. In the long run, they are not yet in a position to mobilize those economic resources which NATO can mobilize in the short term.

The economically weaker side cannot attack the stronger side and expect to be victorious, except, of course, when maximizing and concentrating all its resources of men and material with the aim of defeating the enemy in one mighty blow before the enemy can unfold its full economic resources. Warsaw Pact military maneuvers over a number of years have shown that the Soviet leadership has adopted the maxim that the decisive battle must be fought within the first 48 hours. In short, the Soviet military leadership has adopted the *Blitzkrieg* concept, and only this concept explains why the Russian and East German Army units are deployed as they are. It explains why in recent years

there has been extensive new road and rail construction in certain areas, and why an air base has been built near Parchim within 35 miles of the West German border capable of dealing with large transport aircraft. The maneuvers which preceded the building of the Parchim Air Base had demonstrated that Soviet and East German armored units could not reach their operational bases in the necessary record time. Prior to the construction of the Parchim Air Base the second strategic wave from Russia had to disembark in Berlin and Dresden.

Two factors, therefore, determine Soviet planning: first, the fuller development of a superior military system based on the German panzer division of World War II, and second, the development of a system of mobilization which allows overwhelming the enemy before he is in a position to gather his forces. It is the aim of Soviet strategy to prevent full expansion of the military potential of NATO by quick offensive action with an irresistible force. While a mass attack by tanks spearheaded any offensive movement until a few years ago, present Warsaw Pact maneuvers demonstrate that the Warsaw Pact powers have not ignored recent advances in antitank defense technology. Now the tank formations are widely spread out, with self-propelled artillery and antiaircraft units interspersed among them, so that the artillery within the tank units can

effectively clear the line of attack by concentrated fire and thus pave the way for the armored units. This scheme could also include the use of tactical atomic weapons. Consequently, the *Blitzkrieg* strategy can be applied to our atomic age without any real difficulty.

All in all, one can say that the Soviets have succeeded since 1946 in keeping the superior strategic power of the US in check while simultaneously extending and consolidating their control over their satellite states and building up an atomic arsenal equal to that of the US. At the same time the Soviet Union has modernized its conventional forces and those of its satellites and turned to the third dimension of warfare: the fleet. Today, in spite of its lack of large aircraft carriers, the Russian Navy represents a considerable threat to NATO's rather weak northern and southern flanks. Particularly in the organization of its land forces, the Soviet Union has achieved the maximum of effective combat strength in its divisions, especially through a logistical reorganization which increased the combat strength of the division. The logistical personnel of a Soviet division comprise roughly 25 percent of its strength, as compared to 50 percent per division of the NATO unit.

In spite of the smaller number of soldiers per Soviet division, its combat power can be estimated as equal to or even greater than that of a NATO division. This increased effectiveness has been achieved by centralizing the logistical apparatus and by integrating many of the training units into the organizational structure. The net result is that units at all levels, as compared to those of NATO, are smaller but at no sacrifice of effective combat strength; moreover, cadre divisions have been retained on an active basis. If one divided the total strength of the forces by the number of divisions, it would be seen that within the American Army there are 60,000 men per division, in the Russian 11,000, or, if one considers the American forces stationed in the German Federal Republic, it means 41,000 as compared to 21,500 in units of the Warsaw Pact.

The Soviet variation on the *Blitzkrieg* concept envisions a massive, but narrow, breakthrough of a defensive front which is lacking in depth. This means that they look for a decision on the battlefield before large-scale replacements of men and material become necessary. Compared with this, NATO, with its highly complicated logistical apparatus, is at a serious disadvantage. Quite apart from the costs involved, the oversized logistical units of NATO really obstruct the mobility of the combat units. *Blitzkrieg* divisions require relatively little logistic support and also need relatively little indirect fire support except during the breakthrough. After that has been achieved, it is expected that logistical and artillery support will be needed to a small extent in a theater of war in which the enemy forces have presumably been split asunder. To supply each division in an operation of this kind with its own logistical apparatus is therefore unnecessary.

An armed force built up with the aim of overwhelming the enemy quickly and effectively does not require a complicated infrastructure. The centralization of the logistical apparatus of an army on the offensive under the command of higher staffs has the advantage that the support necessary can be directed to any division where it is required, according to the prevailing situation. And since losses among the logistical personnel are naturally fewer than among combat troops, there is also a reserve of combat troops among the logistical troops.

The land *Blitzkrieg* is supported in the air, a dimension in which the NATO forces have so far seemed to enjoy a high degree of superiority. However, in central Europe, particularly over the North German Plain, the prevailing weather conditions are such that they can neutralize the use of the air force. The technology involved in building all-weather aircraft is very complex, but it is being developed and the trinational Tornado may prove to be a satisfactory answer.

The concept of a successful *Blitzkrieg* also presupposes an efficient command structure, which is naturally much easier to create in a national army than in a complicated alliance-and-pact system. Even among the best of allies, as in the case of the British and the Americans in World War II, personality problems and other factors can reach a pitch that obstructs operations rather than assisting them. From this perspective, of course, the Warsaw Pact powers carry a much heavier burden, and the Russians experienced the consequences of this when they occupied Czechoslovakia in August 1968. The result was a thorough reform in the command structure of the Warsaw Pact.

Until 1969 the chain of command ran from the Headquarters of the Warsaw Pact powers to the respective national ministries

of defense which, as the example of Rumania or Czechoslovakia between January and August 1968 demonstrated, were not always willing to comply with Soviet wishes. Having learned from this experience, the Soviets realigned the entire command structure. Since 1969 the most important forces have been directly subject to Warsaw Pact Headquarters, that is, to Russian command. The Russians also supply the liaison staff between headquarters and the respective national contingents of the Warsaw Pact forces. The role of the national ministries of defense has been virtually reduced to training and supervising logistical functions. This process of restructuring is the military consequence of the Brezhnev doctrine, according to which any internal threat in a socialist brother country is a matter to be dealt with by all nations in the Warsaw Pact. In practice this means that should another situation arise similar to that of the spring and summer of 1968, the Kremlin is no longer in a position that forces it to ask its allies for support. In 1968 the Rumanians refused, while the Hungarians reacted only after considerable delays. The Kremlin now has the freedom to act when it sees fit. Among other things, the Kremlin also retains for itself the right to intervene in Germany's western half, a right derived

Post-war Soviet weapons. Far left: SA4 ground-to air missiles on their launchers. Left: T55 medium tank. This successor to the wartime T34 appeared in the 1960s and is used by the Warsaw Pact forces. Above: BTR-50P armored personnel carrier accompanied by scout cars. Below left: Mi-24 assault helicopter. Below: The nuclear-powered guided missile cruiser *Kirov*, the most formidable ship in the growing Soviet fleet.

from the Potsdam agreements of 1945. This means that the restructuring is not limited only to the internal affairs of the Warsaw Pact countries – Germany, Austria and Yugoslavia could be potential victims.

General Steinhoff, a retired former NATO commander, listed the most important criteria for a successful defense of Europe, namely a common military concept, standardized weapon systems, joint arms development, joint technological development, common logistical apparatus and common training methods. If one measures the Warsaw Pact powers and those of NATO by these criteria, obviously the Warsaw Pact powers are much more advanced.

At the risk of overgeneralizing, one can say that while the Soviet Union has adopted the *Blitzkrieg* concept of World War II, NATO adopted the concept of flexible defense after the doctrine of massive retaliation (1950s and early 1960s) had proved to be politically as well as militarily unusable. But there appear to be different opinions as to what flexible defense means exactly, and some influential experts, including General Fourquet, actually reject the value of conventional defense in principle. General Fourquet's objections were based on the

excessive expenses necessitated by conventional armaments. From his point of view, conventional forces should only be strong enough to recognize and test the intentions of the enemy. Once these are recognized as predicting a major attack, the nuclear threshold has been crossed and the use of atomic weapons becomes necessary. Fourquet understood that the conventional forces' sizes, which had first been laid down in the Lisbon Conference in 1952 and obliged NATO to keep 50 divisions in arms, were an attempt to match the Soviet and Warsaw Pact forces numerically. This, in fact, does not seem to be necessary, because today it would amount to almost doubling the size of existing NATO forces. The problems are: how can the available and potential strength be converted into actual combat strength, what kind of combat strength is required, which tactical doctrine and organizational form results from it and to what extent technological developments compensate for fewer troops. In other words, can NATO, with its present strength, organization and weapon systems, repel an attack from the east?

One objection to a stronger conventional defense points out that by increasing conventional forces, the atomic deterrent is weakened as an operative factor, since it is a sign that the West is not prepared to use its atomic weapons as quickly as possible. According to this assessment, the atomic threshold has to be kept as low as possible in order to prevent an attack – this is a return to the doctrine of massive retaliation. This argument is popular with French military leaders who, before they left NATO, had objected to any reduction in the US military presence in Europe, while at the same time they objected to any enlargement of the general conventional forces because of the costs involved.

Another argument against conventional warfare in Europe points to the extent of the destruction that would ensue. This argument directly contradicts the prevailing conviction in NATO staffs that a war in Central Europe will necessarily be a short one. This conviction has been confirmed so far by all maneuvers of the Warsaw Pact countries. The picture of an extensive long-term strategic air offensive belongs to the past. Wastage of bombers and fighters at rates comparable to those occurring in World War II is simply no longer possible. The technical development of the aircraft into highly complicated integrated arms attack and defense systems has reached a point which not even the economic capacity of NATO as well as that of the Eastern Bloc countries could cope with in terms of the losses and replacement figures of World War II.

General Gallois' main objection to the strengthening of the conventional forces of the NATO armies is based on the assumption that strong conventional forces and atomic warfare are mutually exclusive. Nuclear weapons are bound to triumph over conventional ones. In his view, with the system of conventional defense based upon a concentration of men and material, firepower stands in a direct relationship to troop concentration. That, in turn, requires a complicated logistical system to deal with the masses of men and material. Therefore, in a conventional war, a long time is needed to mobilize all military and economic reserves fully. This argument, again, is really based on World War II thinking and ignores the fact that the defensive tactics of mechanized units and the application of tactical nuclear weapons do not mutually exclude one another.

There is also the objection to strong conventional forces based upon the assumption that the Soviet Union in a European conflict will fight from the outset on a nuclear basis; thus strong conventional armaments amount to a waste of money and effort. There is Marshal Sokolovsky's maxim that every war in Central Europe will inevitably escalate into a nuclear war, since the conventional NATO forces are too weak to check the forces of the Eastern Bloc countries so that NATO will be forced to use its atomic arsenal. Yet this argument underlines the importance of strong conventional forces in order to heighten the atomic threshold once again.

Apart from that, all these arguments against strong conventional forces are based on a false understanding of their function. Conventional forces were once the means by which the sovereign state defended itself. This is only the case in very limited instances today, and it does not apply to Europe at all. NATO's present conventional forces are a means of crisis management, designed to meet a smaller danger effectively before it can transform itself into the danger of atomic warfare. An atomic power without strong conventional forces occupies an immensely weaker position than the power which possesses them. Lacking the strength which could reduce the risk of a conventional war escalating into an atomic one, weaker conventional forces actually help increase the instability that can give rise to a situation in which one is forced to use atomic weapons.

We have mentioned before that NATO has adopted the concept of flexible defense within the framework of what is called the flexible response, consisting of the triad of conventional forces, tactical atomic forces and strategic nuclear weapons. The only question is whether this triad does exist – whether or not the definition of conventional warfare does already imply tactical atomic weapons. Among the Warsaw Pact forces there are many indicators that the use of tactical atomic weapons are automatically included in the *Blitzkrieg* concept and this is also believed to be the case within NATO plans for land warfare. For economic reasons, but also for strategic and tactical reasons, the concept of flexible defense has been given some credibility by giving NATO units greater mobility, as, for instance, recent structural reforms of the Federal German Army demonstrate. Since these reforms are still in their infancy, we will have to see what effects they have. However, there is cause for concern, because the reforms imply reduced forces in actual readiness. If one confronts an enemy who operates on the basis of the *Blitzkrieg* concept, who is determined to enforce a decision within the first 48 hours, then the amount of time it takes cadre units to achieve their full strength is irrelevant; it does not matter with what speed the main power of the western alliance, the USA, can bring its reinforcements, as in the Reforger exercises, from their home bases in North America to the bases in Western Germany. What counts in this situation is the number of effective combat units available at the critical moment and the locations at which they are available.

Much has been written about these problems in the last few years, among them the book by General Close, *Europe Without Defense*, and General Hackett's *The Third World War*. Hackett's book is really based on a presumption that cannot be taken for granted, namely, that at D-Day or Day X or whatever we may call it, NATO will be fully equipped with all its forces available, that American forces can be brought from the USA to Europe without any serious interruption and so on. By comparison, General Close is rather more skeptical, basing his arguments on the situation as it is now and not as it might be. Taking into account the time necessary to transport Belgian and Dutch forces into the theater of operations, and for the Federal German Army, the British Army of the Rhine and the Fifth and Seventh United States Armies in Western Germany to mobilize, it is clear that the result on Day X would be a series of highly complicated movements in all directions before units could reach their operational areas. The main weight of the defense within the first 36–48 hours would lie on the shoulders of the NATO air forces, who must prevent a breakthrough from the east.

At the present moment, and probably for some years to come, effective use of the NATO air forces will be dependent on weather conditions. However, if we look at the Soviet Air Force, we see that until the end of the 1960s its main emphasis lay on the development of a tactical air force to defend Soviet airspace. But with the recent introduction of the MiG-25 and the SU-24, there is a change of emphasis toward neutralizing Western airpower as well as increasing offensive capacity, a capacity which not only complements the offensive capability of the land forces, but in fact increases them. NATO dominance of the airspace of Central Europe is now far from assured.

Even assuming its practicality the when and where of flexible defense is also open to question. In answer to the question *where*, one ordinarily sees the short formula – forward defense – a formula which does not answer this question but actually circumvents it. One must understand the demarcation line between east and west in Central Europe. That this is often misunderstood is demonstrated by the fact that the kill zones of the tactical atomic weapons of the Seventh American Army all lie within West German territory. This is supported by the observations of the former Deputy Supreme Commander of the American Forces in Europe, General Collins. According to his argument, tactical atomic warfare will occur first in Western Germany; only later will it extend into Eastern Germany and other Soviet satellites. From that one can conclude only that NATO's conventional defense is no longer in a position to absorb an attack carried out on the *Blitzkrieg* concept.

Defense in depth to the Pentagon means defending the whole of Western Germany and part of western Holland. In spite of the signs of erosion appearing in the units of several NATO allies, this does not mean – at least not yet – that NATO does not have the conventional strength to absorb such an attack; what it does mean is that its forces are located in the wrong places and cannot be at hand immediately to deal with such an attack successfully. The reason for this unfortunate situation is a legacy of the former zones of occupation of Germany and of the early phase of West German rearmament, when NATO still planned to stop any attack west not east of the Rhine. This would have meant that the West German forces would have to withdraw to their own western border in order to reconquer their own national territory at a later time.

Forward defense, therefore, still belongs to those formulae with which one tries to cover up the existing discrepancy between that which is necessary and that which, for whatever reasons, one is prepared to do for defense. The instruments of defense do exist, but in the wrong places. Add to these contradictions the complication referred to by the American defense expert, Paul Bracken of the Hudson Institute, which is likely to modify both the *Blitzkrieg* concept and that of flexible defense as well. All existing scenarios of a war in Central Europe take as their point of departure the conduct of a battle in the North German Plain where, according to the old *Blitzkrieg* concept, the aggressor would circumvent densely populated areas. This precondition is in the process of fundamental change by virtue of changes in the urban structure of this area. Urban development has extended to the point where the suburbs of various towns virtually merge with one another, connected by a road network on which the enemy could move forward under the protection of tall buildings.

A typical NATO brigade is deployed to cover an area 15 miles square containing approximately 85 villages. Villages and woods make up 60 percent of West Germany. This makes it more difficult for the aggressor to circumvent towns and villages. But he can turn their existence to his own advantage by what Bracken calls 'urban hugging' tactics, thereby making

Above right: A captured US
bomber pilot is presented to the
world through a press conference
staged in Hanoi. B-52 bombers were
occasionally brought down over
North Vietnam, although for the
most part their bombing missions
in the Vietnam war were carried
out with impunity. However, even
with modern target finding
techniques, heavy bombers were
not suited to this kind of war;
advanced technique and sheer
weight of munitions expended did
not prove to be war-winners.
Above far right: A US infantryman
in Vietnam. High temperatures and
vigilance is well conveyed in this
picture, which does not, however,
fully explain why this war was so
unpalatable for the ordinary US
soldier. Added to climatic and other
physical discomforts, and
knowledge that a determined
enemy might be lurking anywhere,
was the feeling that local friends by
day might be enemies at night, that
unnecessary cruelties were being
inflicted on innocents, and that the
war lacked strong moral incentives.
Center right: Firefighting crews at
work on the deck of a US Navy
aircraft carrier after an accident during
operations off the coast of Vietnam.
Below: A US type M48 tank bogged
down while accompanying supply-
carrying personnel carriers, in
Vietnam.

Left: An American B-52 bomber emptying its bomb bays over Vietnam. Below left: US helicopters over Vietnam. The picture well illustrates the kind of terrain over which the war was fought, and which was well suited to guerilla warfare: paddyfields, copses, and densely-wooded hills. Right: A CH-54 helicopter delivers a field gun to US forces in Vietnam. Even more than the Korean War, the Vietnam campaign emphasized the role of helicopters. Below right: Assault rifle held high, a US infantryman fords a watercourse in Vietnam. Bottom right: A file of US infantrymen ford one of Vietnam's seemingly innumerable watercourses.

Top left : An Israeli A-4 Skyhawk fighter bomber, one of the many aircraft supplied to the IDF by the United States. Far left: Ariel 'Arik' Sharon led his forces over the Suez Canal to cut off Ismailia during the 1973 Yom Kippur War. He subsequently became Minister of Defense in Menachim Begin's government, but was forced to resign after the refugee camp massacres which took place in Beirut after the Israeli invasion of Lebanon in 1983. Near left: Moshe Dayan was the architect of Israel's victory in the 1967 Six-Day War. He also became Minister of Defense after leaving the IDF. Above: An American built F-16 fighter of the IDF. Above right: Two Kfir C2 fighters. These aircraft are built in Israel and are a home-built

derivative of the French Mirage V
using General Electric J79 engines.
Below left: An Israeli-modified
Centurion tank moves through the
Sinai Peninsula during the Yom
Kippur War of 1973. In spite of the
early Egyptian successes Israel
managed to recover from a surprise
attack and force the Arabs back.
Below center: A Reshef-class fast
patrol boat of the IDF. Below right:

US Marines enter Beirut as a peace-
keeping force in 1958. In 1983 they
were again called upon to fulfill
this role in the aftermath of the
Lebanese Civil War and the Syrian
and Israeli invasions.

576

Below: Crew and Royal Marines relax on the flight deck of HMS *Hermes* on their journey south to the Falkland Islands in Spring 1982. Below center: A Wessex helicopter lands Marines on East Falkland. It is armed with Milan anti-tank rockets.

Bottom: The Atlantic Conveyor with Sea Harriers and Chinook helicopters on deck. This vessel was later destroyed by Argentinian Exocet missiles fired from Super Entendards.

Above center: Sea Harriers in the below-deck hangar of the carrier HMS *Invincible* on her way to the Falkland Islands. Superior British training and equipment enabled the Task Force to defeat the Argentinian troops occupying the Islands despite heroic efforts by the Argentinian Air Force. Above right: British paratroopers leap ashore at dawn on East Falkland. The landings were accomplished with remarkably light casualties, considering the inherent risk involved in amphibious operations. Center right: A Sea Harrier on the deck of a Royal Navy assault ship. These V/STOL aircraft proved their worth during the Falklands campaign, shooting down more than 30 Argentinian planes. Below: HMS *Hermes* makes a triumphant return to Britain after the Argentinian surrender.

Left: A modern ground attack and interceptor aircraft, the SAAB *Viggen*. Designed and built in Sweden from the 1960s, this carries air-to-surface or air-to-air missiles and can operate from 500-metre runways. Below: Belgian F.16 fighters, whose long, slim radar noses illustrate the electronic nature of modern warfare, in which instant information about the enemy is so crucial. Left, inset: A military communications satellite undergoing final checks. Bottom, inset: A US ballistic missile submarine, showing its launching tubes open; much of the strategic significance of such vessels lies in the ability to launch missiles underwater.

himself less vulnerable to the use of nuclear weapons. At the beginning of the 1980s the urban Rhine/Ruhr complex has almost merged with the Dutch area, a stretch of about 190 miles reaching from Bonn in the south to the Hook of Holland. From a strategic point of view, this development would make it impossible to repeat the pincer movements of the past, due to the concentration of buildings which does not allow the assembly and unfolding of mass forces. More important, however, is the fact that this development is also noticeable in an east-west direction, parallel to that of a Soviet attack, which could facilitate the urban hugging tactics already mentioned. We must also take into account the reforestation in this area which amounts to 0.8 percent annually, and the extension of the road network by 1 percent per year. This trend increases the tendency for armies to stick to well-built roads – a fact confirmed in recent Eastern Bloc maneuvers which featured very strong armored cars as a prominent factor.

However, in a 1975 report by the American Secretary of Defense to Congress on the nuclear forces in Europe, no reference was made to the significance of this growing urbanization.

Perhaps this is understandable, because who will take seriously a doctrine of deterrence that requires the firing of several thousand nuclear weapons upon one of the densest urbanized areas in the world? It also seems that the time for panzer battles conducted over ranges of several thousand yards is a thing of the past. In fact, even the new generation of guided missiles is almost useless in street fighting in urban areas, compared with such older antitank weapons as the bazooka or the German *Panzerfaust*. There is no NATO antiarmor weapon that can actually be fired in a closed room without injuring the soldier who fires it. This includes the otherwise excellent Milan missile. Rockets guided by wires, such as the American TOW rocket, are not stable in flight when fired at the close range demanded by any conflict within an urban area. On the other hand, this development seems to favor a kind of super Maginot Line for defensive purposes. Whether it is worthwhile to develop this possibility further is another question, but in any case, the training of the soldiers would have to place much greater emphasis on urban fighting. Appropriate new weapons are needed, and consideration of the Maginot concept requires the beginning of planning to evacuate the civilian population. No such plans exist at this juncture.

Under whatever aspect one looks at the problem of a defense of Western Europe, one confronts the apocalypse. Even such alternatives as those proposed by Carl Friedrich von Weizäcker and Horst Alhfeldt are not real alternatives but only a new variation of the Bonin concept. General von Bonin, in the early 1960s, suggested the elimination of any offensive features in the Federal German forces by doing away with strong battle tanks and replacing them with much cheaper self-propelled antitank guns, placed and disposed in depth according to the model of Soviet defense in the Battle of Kursk. Adherents of this strategy suggest a new variation which they call Techno-commandos. Armed with antiarmor weapons, the commandos are supposed to be deployed in depth with the object of halting the Eastern armored nations. They lack any offensive capacity but have the alleged advantage of lower cost. However, even assuming that an attack could be halted by this means, the possibility arises that the enemy will attempt the breakthrough with all available weapons. The most important question is, can the Soviet Union afford to fail in even a limited attack on Central Europe? To take such a risk, the Soviet leaders would have to be fairly convinced that it would succeed, with all the consequences which that would imply for us all, because a failure would completely alter the relationship between the Soviets and their satellites and might well bring fundamental political changes in the Soviet Union itself. This risk would appear to add to the security of the West, but we must remember that this would not be the first time that a state tried to solve its internal problems by external warfare. The temptation to this can be especially strong if the potential aggressor has reason to believe that the enemy is badly prepared to resist and has a weak or divided leadership.

Although the political situation was much more relaxed in the 1970s, the military argument that this should not be confused with a permanent change should be borne in mind. Politics, especially in systems where power is concentrated in the hands of a few, can move suddenly and unexpectedly in new directions, and the primary question for the soldier is how he can adapt the instruments of defense at hand to the changing conditions so as to guarantee security at any time. Whether the primacy of politics in Clausewitz's sense will be maintained, not only in Europe but in the numerous trouble spots throughout the world, is a question not even the superpowers can answer with confidence. Their means of control are limited; the possibilities for irrational action are limitless.

INDEX

Page numbers in *italics* refer to illustrations

Picture Credits

Pictures: 155 right, 229, 231 bottom, 232 bottom, 262 bottom, 370 top, 378, 389 below, 391 below, 393 all, 394 above right and below, 395, 400-1, 403 below, 416, 419 below, 424, 428-9 all five, 430, 431, 432-3 all five, 442 above, 444-5 all four, 455 above right, 468 below, 478, 479 below, 483 below, 484, 485, 488 inset left, 504-5, 508-9, 516-7, 516 inset
Novosti Press Agency: 318-9, 329 both, 333, 486 above, 487 below, 488-9, 488 inset left, 489 inset, 493 right, 499 top and bottom, 515, 556 below
Osterrshisde Nationalbibliothek, Vienna: 132 top
Patrimonic National, Madrid: 137
Historical Society of Pennsylvania: 291
Petit Palais, Paris: 6
Photo Bulloz, Paris: 90 top, 130, 134, 302 bottom, 306-7

Photo Giraudon: 57 bottom, 112, 115 bottom, 154 bottom, 186-7, 191 top, 243, 259 top, 192-3, 296, 307 top, 339 top, 362-3
Pierpont Morgan Library: 54 top
Public Record Office, London: 46 right
SAAB: 578 top
Scala: 124
Schloss Charlottenburg: 323 bottom left
Smithsonian Institution: 290 top
Rolf Steinberg: 152 both, 159 bottom, 208 top, 212-3, 215, 216 top, 217 top, 224-5, 228 bottom, 231 top, 238 bottom, 239, 244 bottom, 248 top, 250 both top, 264, 334, 337 top left, 345
Svenska Portrattarkivet: 154 top, 155 top left, 156 center, 157, 159 top left
Master and Fellows of Trinity College, Cambridge: 38, 39
Uffizi Museum, Florence: 124

Ullstein Bilderdienst: 153, 159 top right, 160 both, 162, 163 bottom right, 166, 167, 211 bottom left, 217 right, 219, 228 top, 240-1, 244 top, 248 left, 254 top left, 256 both, 257, 260 bottom, 263 top, 265 top, 332 bottom left, 335 bottom, 340 top right, 344 left and top right, 346 bottom three, 376 below, 377 top, 384 above left, 436-7, 437 below right and left, 438-9 all three, 440, 441 above right and below, 448 above, 453 above, 454, 455 below, 462 above and below, 562-3 all three, 566 both
USAF: 541 top and bottom, 548, 558-9, 560-1, 571 top left, 572
US Army: 284, 288 bottom, 289 both, 536 inset right, 537, 550 below, 552, 554, 554-5, 564-5 all seven, 571 bottom, 572-3, 573 top and center
USIS: 514-5
US Marines: 540-1, 571 top right, 573 bottom, 380

US Navy: 1, 474, 536 inset left, 536-7, 552-3, 556 above, 568, 568-9, 571 center, 578
Victoria and Albert Museum, London: 48, 191 bottom, 192 bottom, 236 right, 272 top right, 320 bottom, 324 bottom, 335 top, 349 top and bottom right, 364 top, 365 top, 369, 373, 376 top right, 384, 402
Viking Ship Museum, Oslo: 25
Wallace Collection: 155 bottom left, 163 bottom left, 204, 208 bottom two, 236 top, 253 bottom
Yale University Art Gallery 2-3
Peter Young: 165 bottom, 303, 313 all, 320 top, 337 bottom, 347, 350 bottom, 354 top, 357 top right

The Publishers have tried to acknowledge all copyright material where this has been possible. Nevertheless apologies are made for any errors or omissions.